NAPOLEON

Also by Adam Zamoyski

Chopin: A Biography

The Battle for the Marchlands

Paderewski

The Polish Way

The Last King of Poland

The Forgotten Few: The Polish Air Force in the Second World War

Holy Madness: Romantics, Patriots and Revolutionaries, 1776–1871

1812: Napoleon's Fatal March on Moscow

Rites of Peace: The Fall of Napoleon and the Congress of Vienna

Warsaw 1920: Lenin's Failed Conquest of Europe

Poland: A History

Chopin: Prince of the Romantics

Phantom Terror: The Threat of Revolution and the
Repression of Liberty 1789–1848

NAPOLEON

A LIFE

Adam Zamoyski

BASIC BOOKS
New York

Basic Books
Hachette Book Group
1290 Avenue of the Americas, New York, NY 10104
www.basicbooks.com
Printed in the United States of America
First Edition: October 2018
First published in Great Britain by William Collins in 2018

Published by Basic Books, an imprint of Perseus Books, LLC, a subsidiary of
Hachette Book Group, Inc. The Basic Books name and logo is a trademark of the
Hachette Book Group.

The Hachette Speakers Bureau provides a wide range of authors for speaking events.
To find out more, go to www.hachettespeakersbureau.com or call (866) 376-6591.

The publisher is not responsible for websites (or their content) that are not
owned by the publisher.

Print book interior design by Six Red Marbles Inc.

Library of Congress Cataloging-in-Publication Data

Names: Zamoyski, Adam, author.
Title: Napoleon: a life / Adam Zamoyski.
Description: First edition. | New York: Basic Books, 2018. | Includes bibliographical
references and index.
Identifiers: LCCN 2018015891| ISBN 9780465055937 (hardcover) |
ISBN 9781541644557 (ebook)
Subjects: LCSH: Napoleon I, Emperor of the French, 1769–1821. | France—Kings and
rulers—Biography. | France. Armâee—History—Napoleonic Wars, 1800–1815. |
Napoleonic Wars, 1800–1815.
Classification: LCC DC203 .Z36 2018 | DDC 94405092 [B]—dc23
LC record available at https://lccn.loc.gov/2018015891

ISBNs: 978-0-465-05593-7 (hardcover), 978-1-5416-4455-7 (ebook)

LSC-C

10 9 8 7 6 5 4 3 2 1

In memory

of

GILLON AITKEN

Contents

CONTENTS

Maps

GABRIELE
BUONAPARTE

LUCIANO
1711–91

SEBASTIANO
d. 1760

MARIA-
ANNA
1767–67

JOSEPH
1768–1844
m.
JULIE
CLARY
1771–1845
(issue)

JOSÉPHINE   m.   **NAPOLEONE**   m.   MARIE-
DE   1796   1769–1821   1809   LOUISE
BEAUHARNAIS   HABSBURG
1763–1814   1791–1847

MARIA-
ANNA
1771–71

EUGÈNE
DE
BEAUHARNAIS
1781–1824

HORTENSE*   m.   LOUIS
DE   1802   1778–1846
BEAUHARNAIS
1788–1837

NAPOLÉON
1811–32

NAPOLÉON
CHARLES
1802–1807

NAPOLÉON-LOUIS
1804–31

LOUIS-NAPOLÉON
1808–73
EMPEROR OF THE FRENCH

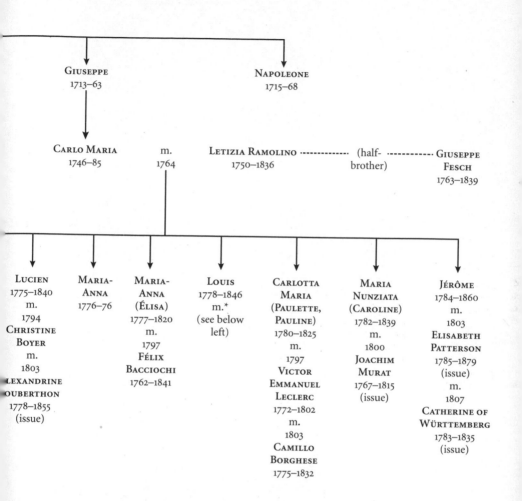

GIUSEPPE
1713–63

NAPOLEONE
1715–68

CARLO MARIA   m.   LETIZIA RAMOLINO ·············· (half- ··········· GIUSEPPE
1746–85   1764   1750–1836   brother)   FESCH
                                                                                     1763–1839

LUCIEN   MARIA-   MARIA-   LOUIS   CARLOTTA   MARIA   JÉRÔME
1775–1840   ANNA   ANNA   1778–1846   MARIA   NUNZIATA   1784–1860
m.   1776–76   (ÉLISA)   m.*   (PAULETTE,   (CAROLINE)   m.
1794   1777–1820   (see below   PAULINE)   1782–1839   1803
CHRISTINE   m.   left)   1780–1825   m.   ELISABETH
BOYER   1797   m.   1800   PATTERSON
m.   FÉLIX   1797   JOACHIM   1785–1879
1803   BACCIOCHI   VICTOR   MURAT   (issue)
LEXANDRINE   1762–1841   EMMANUEL   1767–1815   m.
OUBERTHON   LECLERC   (issue)   1807
1778–1855   1772–1802   CATHERINE OF
(issue)   m.   WÜRTTEMBERG
                                                               1803   1783–1835
                                                               CAMILLO   (issue)
                                                               BORGHESE
                                                               1775–1832

THE
BUONAPARTE
FAMILY

Preface

A POLISH HOME, English schools, and holidays with French cousins exposed me from an early age to violently conflicting visions of Napoleon—as godlike genius, Romantic avatar, evil monster, or just nasty little dictator. In this crossfire of fantasy and prejudice I developed an empathy with each of these views without being able to agree with any of them.

Napoleon was a man, and while I understand how others have done, I can see nothing superhuman about him. Although he did exhibit some extraordinary qualities, he was in many ways a very ordinary man. I find it difficult to credit genius to someone who, for all his many triumphs, presided over the worst (and entirely self-inflicted) disaster in military history and single-handedly destroyed the great enterprise he and others had toiled so hard to construct. He was undoubtedly a brilliant tactician, as one would expect of a clever operator from a small-town background. But he was no strategist, as his miserable end attests.

Nor was Napoleon an evil monster. He could be as selfish and violent as the next man, but there is no evidence of him wishing to inflict suffering gratuitously. His motives were on the whole praiseworthy, and his ambition no greater than that of contemporaries such as Alexander I of Russia, Wellington, Nelson, Metternich, Blücher, Bernadotte, and many more. What made his ambition so exceptional was the scope it was accorded by circumstance.

On hearing the news of his death, the Austrian dramatist Franz Grillparzer wrote a poem on the subject. He had been a student in

Vienna when Napoleon bombarded the city in 1809, so he had no reason to like him, but in the poem he admits that while he cannot love him, he cannot bring himself to hate him; according to Grillparzer, Napoleon was but the visible symptom of the sickness of the times, and as such bore the blame for the sins of all. There is much truth in this view.[1]

In the half-century before Napoleon came to power, a titanic struggle for dominion saw the British acquire Canada, large swathes of India, and a string of colonies and aspire to lay down the law at sea; Austria grab provinces in Italy and Poland; Prussia increase in size by two-thirds; and Russia push her frontier 600 kilometres into Europe and occupy large areas of Central Asia, Siberia, and Alaska, laying claims as far afield as California. Yet George III, Maria Theresa, Frederick William II, and Catherine II are not generally accused of being megalomaniac monsters and compulsive warmongers.

Napoleon is frequently condemned for his invasion of Egypt, while the British occupation which followed, designed to guarantee colonial monopoly over India, is not. He is regularly blamed for re-establishing slavery in Martinique, while Britain applied it in its colonies for a further thirty years, and every other colonial power for several decades after that. His use of police surveillance and censorship is also regularly reproved, even though every other state in Europe emulated him, with varying degrees of discretion or hypocrisy.

The tone was set by the victors of 1815, who arrogated the role of defenders of a supposedly righteous social order against evil, and writing on Napoleon has been bedevilled ever since by a moral dimension, which has entailed an imperative to slander or glorify. Beginning with Stendhal, who claimed he could only write of Napoleon in religious terms, and no doubt inspired by Goethe, who saw his life as 'that of a demi-god', French and other European historians have struggled to keep the numinous out of their work, and even today it is tinged by a sense of awe. Until very recently, Anglo-Saxon historians have shown reluctance to allow an understanding of the spirit of the times to help them see Napoleon as anything other than an alien monster. Rival national mythologies have added layers of prejudice which many find hard to overcome.[2]

Napoleon was in every sense the product of his times; he was in many ways the embodiment of his epoch. If one wishes to gain an understanding of him and what he was about, one has to place him in context. This requires ruthless jettisoning of received opinion and nationalist prejudice and dispassionate examination of what the seismic conditions of his times threatened and offered.

In the 1790s Napoleon entered a world at war, and one in which the very basis of human society was being questioned. It was a struggle for supremacy and survival in which every state on the Continent acted out of self-interest, breaking treaties and betraying allies shamelessly. Monarchs, statesmen, and commanders on all sides displayed similar levels of fearful aggression, greed, callousness, and brutality. To ascribe to any of the states involved a morally superior role is ahistorical humbug, and to condemn the lust for power is to deny human nature and political necessity.

For Aristotle power was, along with wealth and friendship, one of the essential components of individual happiness. For Hobbes, the urge to acquire it was not only innate but beneficent, as it led men to dominate and therefore organise communities, and no social organisation of any form could exist without the power of one or more individuals to order others.

Napoleon did not start the war that broke out in 1792 when he was a mere lieutenant and continued, with one brief interruption, until 1814. Which side was responsible for the outbreak and for the continuing hostilities is fruitlessly debatable, since responsibility cannot be laid squarely on one side or the other. The fighting cost lives, for which responsibility is often heaped on Napoleon, which is absurd, as all the belligerents must share the blame. And he was not as profligate with the lives of his own soldiers as some.

French losses in the seven years of revolutionary government (1792–99) are estimated at four to five hundred thousand; those during the fifteen years of Napoleon's rule are estimated at just under twice as high, at eight to nine hundred thousand. Given that these figures include not only dead, wounded, and sick but also those reported as missing, whose numbers went up dramatically as his ventures took the armies further afield, it is clear that battle losses were lower under Napoleon than during the revolutionary period—despite the increasing use of heavy artillery and the greater size of the armies. The majority of those classed as missing were deserters who either drifted back home or settled in other countries. This is not to diminish the suffering or the trauma of the war, but to put it in perspective.[3]

MY AIM IN THIS BOOK is not to justify or condemn, but to piece together the life of the man born Napoleone Buonaparte, and to examine how he became 'Napoleon' and achieved what he did, and how it came about that he undid it.

In order to do so I have concentrated on verifiable primary sources, treating with caution the memoirs of those such as Bourrienne, Fouché, Barras, and others who wrote principally to justify themselves or to tailor their own image, and have avoided using as evidence those of the duchesse d'Abrantès, which were written years after the events by her lover, the novelist Balzac. I also ignore the various anecdotes regarding Napoleon's birth and childhood, believing that it is immaterial as well as unprovable that he cried or not when he was born, that he liked playing with swords and drums as a child, had a childhood crush on some little girl, or that a comet was sighted at his birth and death. There are quite enough solid facts to deal with.

I have devoted more space in relative terms to Napoleon's formative years than to his time in power, as I believe they hold the key to understanding his extraordinary trajectory. As I consider the military aspects only insofar as they produced an effect, on him and his career or the international situation, the reader will find my coverage very uneven. I give prominence to the first Italian campaign because it demonstrates the ways in which Napoleon was superior to his enemies and colleagues, and because it turned him into an exceptional being, in both his own eyes and those of others. Subsequent battles are of interest primarily for the use he made of them, while the Russian campaign is seminal to his decline and reveals the confusion in his mind which led to his political suicide. To those who would like to learn more about the battles, I would recommend Andrew

Roberts's masterful *Napoleon the Great.* The battle maps in the text are similarly spare and do not pretend to accuracy; they are designed to illustrate the essence of the action.

The subject is so vast that anyone attempting a life of Napoleon must necessarily rely on the work of many who have trawled through archives and on published sources. I feel hugely indebted to all those involved in the Fondation Napoléon's new edition of Napoleon's correspondence. I also owe a great deal to the work done over the past two decades by French historians in debunking the myths that have gained the status of truth and excising the carbuncles that have overgrown the verifiable facts during the past two centuries. Thierry Lentz and Jean Tulard stand out in this respect, but Pierre Branda, Jean Defranceschi, Patrice Gueniffey, Annie Jourdan, Aurélien Lignereux, and Michel Vergé-Franceschi have also helped to blow away cobwebs and enlighten. Among Anglo-Saxon historians, Philip Dwyer has my gratitude for his brilliant work on Napoleon as propagandist, and Munro Price for his invaluable archival research on the last phase of his reign. The work of Michael Broers and Steven Englund is also noteworthy.

I owe a debt of thanks to Olivier Varlan for bibliographic guidance, and particularly for having let me see Caulaincourt's manuscript on the Prussian and Russian campaigns of 1806–07; to Vincenz Hoppe for seeking out sources in Germany; to Hubert Czyżewski for assisting me in unearthing obscure sources in Polish libraries; to Laetitia Oppenheim for doing the same for me in France; to Carlo De Luca for alerting me to the existence of the diary of Giuseppe Mallardi; and to Angelika von Hase for helping me with German sources. I also owe thanks to Shervie Price for reading the typescript, and to the incomparable Robert Lacey for his sensitive editing.

Although at times I felt like cursing him, I would like to thank Detlef Felken for his implicit faith in suggesting I write this book, and Clare Alexander and Arabella Pike for their support. Finally, I must thank my wife, Emma, for putting up with me and encouraging me throughout what has been a challenging task.

Adam Zamoyski

A Reluctant Messiah

A T NOON ON 10 December 1797 a thunderous discharge
from a battery of guns echoed across Paris, opening yet another of the many grandiose festivals for which the French
Revolution was so notable.

Although the day was cold and grey, crowds had been gathering around the Luxembourg Palace, the seat of the Executive Directory which governed France, and according to the Prussian diplomat
Daniel von Sandoz-Rollin, 'never had the cheering sounded more
enthusiastic'. People lined the streets leading up to the palace in the
hope of catching a glimpse of the hero of the day. But his reticence
defeated them. At around ten o'clock that morning he had left his
modest house on the rue Chantereine with one of the Directors who
had come to fetch him in a cab. As it trundled through the streets,
followed by several officers on horseback, he sat well back, seeming
in the words of one English witness 'to shrink from those acclamations which were then the voluntary offering of the heart'.[1]

They were indeed heartfelt. The people of France were tired after eight years of revolution and political struggle marked by violent
lurches to the right or the left. They were sick of the war which had
lasted for more than five years and which the Directory seemed unable to end. The man they were cheering, a twenty-eight-year-old
general by the name of Bonaparte, had won a string of victories in
Italy against France's principal enemy, Austria, and forced her emperor to come to terms. The relief felt at the prospect of peace and

the political stability it was hoped would ensue was accompanied by a subliminal sense of deliverance.

The Revolution which began in 1789 had unleashed boundless hopes of a new era in human affairs. These had been whipped up and manipulated by successive political leaders in a self-perpetuating power struggle, and people longed for someone who could put an end to it. They had read the bulletins recounting this general's deeds and his proclamations to the people of Italy, which contrasted sharply with the utterances of those ruling France. Many believed, or just hoped, that the longed-for man had come. The sense of exaltation engendered by the Revolution had been kept alive by overblown festivals, and this one was, according to one witness, as '*magnifique*' as any.[2]

The great court of the Luxembourg Palace had been transformed for the occasion. A dais had been erected opposite the entrance, on which stood the indispensable 'altar of the fatherland' surmounted by three statues, representing Liberty, Equality, and Peace. These were flanked by panoplies of enemy standards captured during the recent campaign, beneath which were placed seats for the five members of the Directory, one for its secretary-general, and more below them for the ministers. Beneath were places for the diplomatic corps, and to either side stretched a great amphitheatre for the members of the two legislative chambers and for the 1,200-strong choir of the conservatoire. The courtyard was decked with tricolour flags and covered by an awning, turning it into a monumental tent.[3]

As the last echoes of the gun salute died away, the Directors emerged from a chamber in the depths of the palace, dressed in their '*grand costume*'. Designed by the painter Jacques-Louis David, this consisted of a blue velvet tunic heavily embroidered with gold thread and girded with a gold-tasselled white silk sash, white breeches and stockings, and shoes with blue bows. It was given a supposedly classical look by a voluminous red cloak with a white lace collar, a 'Roman' sword on a richly embroidered baldric, and a black felt hat adorned by a blue-white-red tricolour of three ostrich feathers.

The Directors took their place at the end of a cortège led by the commissioners of police, followed by magistrates, civil servants, the judiciary, teachers, members of the Institute of Arts and Sciences, officers, officials, the diplomatic representatives of foreign powers, and the ministers of the Directory. It was preceded by a band playing 'the airs beloved of the French Republic'.[4]

The cortège snaked its way through the corridors of the palace and out into the courtyard, the various bodies taking their appointed seats. The members of the legislative chambers had already taken theirs. They wore costumes similar to that of the Directors, the 'Roman' look in their case sitting uneasily with their four-cornered caps, which were David's homage to the heroes of the Polish revolution of 1794.

Having taken their seats, the Directors despatched an official to usher in the principal actors of the day's festivities. The airs beloved of the French Republic had been superseded by a symphony performed by the orchestra of the Conservatoire, but this was rudely interrupted by shouts of '*Vive Bonaparte!*', '*Vive la Nation!*', '*Vive le libérateur de l'Italie!*', and '*Vive le pacificateur du continent!*' as a group of men entered the courtyard.

First came the ministers of war and foreign relations in their black ceremonial costumes. They were followed by a diminutive, gaunt figure in uniform, his lank hair dressed in the already unfashionable 'dog's ears' flopping on either side of his face. His gauche movements 'charmed every heart', according to one onlooker. He was accompanied by three aides-de-camp, 'all taller than him, but almost bowed by the respect they showed him'. There was a religious silence as the group entered the courtyard. Everyone present stood and removed their hats. Then the cheering broke out again. 'The present elite of France applauded the victorious general, for he was the hope of everyone: republicans, royalists, all saw their present and future salvation in the support of his powerful arm.' The dazzling military victories and diplomatic triumph he had achieved contrasted so strikingly with his puny stature, dishevelled appearance, and unassuming manner that it was difficult not to believe he was inspired and guided by some higher power. The philosopher Wilhelm von Humboldt was so impressed when he saw him, he thought he was contemplating an ideal of modern humanity.[5]

When the group reached the foot of the altar of the fatherland, the orchestra and choir of the Conservatoire struck up a 'Hymn to

Liberty' composed by François-Joseph Gossec to the tune of the Catholic Eucharistic hymn *O Salutaris Hostia*, and the crowd joined in an emotionally charged rendition of what the official account of the proceedings described as 'this religious couplet'. The Directors and assembled dignitaries took their seats, with the exception of the general himself. 'I saw him decline placing himself in the chair of state which had been prepared for him, and seem as if he wished to escape from the general bursts of applause,' recalled the English lady, who was full of admiration for the 'modesty in his demeanour'. He had in fact requested that the ceremony be cancelled when he heard what was in store. But there was no escape.[6]

The Republic's minister for foreign relations, Charles-Maurice de Talleyrand, limped forward in his orthopaedic shoe, his ceremonial sword and the plumes in his hat performing curious motions as he went. The President of the Directory had chosen him rather than the minister of war to present the reluctant hero. 'It is not the general, it is the peacemaker, and above all the citizen that you must single out to praise here,' he had written to Talleyrand. 'My colleagues are terrified, not without reason, of military glory.' This was true.[7]

'No government has ever been so universally despised,' an informant in France had written to his masters in Vienna only a couple of weeks before, assuring them that the first general with the courage to raise the standard of revolt would have half of the nation behind him. Many in Paris, at both ends of the political spectrum, were expecting General Bonaparte to make such a move, and in the words of one observer, 'everyone seemed to be watching each other'. According to another, there were many present who would happily have strangled him.[8]

The forty-three-year-old ex-aristocrat and former bishop Talleyrand knew all this. He was used to shrouding his feelings with an impassive countenance, but his upturned nose and thin lips, curling up on the left-hand side in a way suggesting wry amusement, were well fitted to the speech he now delivered.

'Citizen Directors,' he began, 'I have the honour to present to the executive Directory citizen Bonaparte, who comes bearing the ratification of the treaty of peace concluded with the emperor.' While reminding those present that the peace was only the crowning glory of 'innumerable marvels' on the battlefield, he reassured the shrinking general that he would not dwell on his military achievements, leaving that to posterity, secure in the knowledge that the hero himself viewed them not as his own, but as those of France and the Revolution. 'Thus, all Frenchmen have been victorious through Bonaparte; thus his glory is the property of all; thus there is no republican who cannot claim his part of it.' The general's extraordinary talents, which Talleyrand briefly ran through, were, he admitted, innate to him, but they were also in large measure the fruit of his 'insatiable love of the fatherland and of humanity'. But it was his modesty, the fact that he seemed to 'apologise for his own glory', his extraordinary taste for simplicity, worthy of the heroes of classical antiquity, his love of the abstract sciences, his literary passion for 'that sublime *Ossian*' and 'his profound contempt for show, luxury, ostentation, those paltry ambitions of common souls' that were so striking, indeed alarming: 'Oh! far from fearing what some would call his ambition, I feel that we will one day have to beg him to give up the comforts of his studious retreat.' The general's countless civic virtues were almost a burden to him: 'All France will be free: it may be that he will never be, that is his destiny.'[9]

When the minister had concluded, the victim of destiny presented the ratified copy of the peace treaty to the Directors, and then addressed the assembly 'with a kind of feigned nonchalance, as though he were trying to intimate that he little liked the regime under which he was called to serve', in the words of one observer. According to another, he spoke 'like a man who knows his worth'.[10]

In a few clipped sentences, delivered in an atrocious foreign accent, he attributed his victories to the French nation, which through the Revolution had abolished eighteen centuries of bigotry and tyranny, established representative government, and roused the other two great nations of Europe, the Germans and Italians, enabling them to embrace the 'spirit of liberty'. He concluded, somewhat bluntly, that the whole of Europe would be truly free and at peace 'when the happiness of the French people will be based on the best organic laws'.[11]

The response of the Directory to this equivocal statement was delivered by its president, Paul François Barras, a forty-two-year-old minor nobleman from Provence with a fine figure and what one contemporary described as the swagger of a fencing-master. He began with the usual flowery glorification of 'the sublime revolution of the French nation' before moving on to vaporous praise of the 'peacemaker of the continent', whom he likened to Socrates and hailed as the liberator of the people of Italy. General Bonaparte had rivalled Caesar, but unlike other victorious generals, he was a man of peace: 'at the first word of a proposal of peace, you halted your triumphant progress, you laid down the sword with which the fatherland had armed you, and preferred to take up the olive branch of peace!' Bonaparte was living proof 'that one can give up the pursuit of victory without relinquishing greatness'.[12]

The address meandered off into a diatribe against those 'vile Carthaginians' (the British) who were the last obstacle standing in the way of a general peace which the new Rome (France) was striving to bestow on the Continent. Barras concluded by exhorting the general, 'the liberator to whom outraged humanity calls out with plaintive appeals', to lead an army across the Channel, whose waters would be proud to carry him and his men: 'As soon as the tricolour standard is unfurled on its bloodied shores, a unanimous cry of benediction will greet your presence; and, seeing the dawn of approaching happiness, that generous nation will hail you as liberators who come not to fight and enslave it, but to put an end to its sufferings.'[13]

Barras then stepped forward with extended arms and in the name of the French nation embraced the general in a 'fraternal accolade'. The other Directors did likewise, followed by the ministers and other dignitaries, after which the general was allowed to step down from the altar of the fatherland and take his seat. The choir intoned a hymn to peace written for the occasion by the revolutionary bard Marie-Joseph Chénier, set to music by Étienne Méhul.

The minister for war, General Barthélémy Scherer, a forty-nine-year-old veteran of several campaigns, then presented to the Directory two of Bonaparte's aides bearing a huge white standard on which the triumphs of the Army of Italy were embroidered in gold thread. These included the capture of 150,000 prisoners, 170 flags, and over a thousand pieces of artillery, as well as some fifty ships; the conclusion of a number of armistices and treaties with various Italian states; the liberation of the people of most of northern Italy; and the acquisition for France of masterpieces by Michelangelo, Guercino, Titian, Veronese, Correggio, Caracci, Raphael, and da Vinci and other works of art. Scherer praised the soldiers of the Army of Italy and particularly their commander, who had 'married the audacity of Achilles to the wisdom of Nestor'.[14]

The guns thundered as Barras received the standard from the hands of the two officers, and in another interminable address, he returned to his anti-British theme. 'May the palace of St. James crumble! The Fatherland wishes it, humanity demands it, vengeance commands it.' After the two warriors had received the 'fraternal accolade' of the Directors and ministers, the ceremony closed with a rendition of the rousing revolutionary war hymn *Le Chant du Départ*, following which the Directors exited as they had come, and Bonaparte left, cheered by the multitude gathered outside, greatly relieved that it was all over.[15]

For all his apparent nonchalance, he had been treading warily throughout. The Directory had not welcomed the coming of peace. The war had paid for its armies and bolstered its finances, while the victories had deflected criticism of its domestic shortcomings. More important, war kept the army occupied and ambitious generals away from Paris. This peace had been made by Bonaparte in total disregard of the Directory's instructions, and it was no secret that the Directors had been furious when they were presented with the draft treaty. A few days after receiving it, they had nominated Bonaparte commander of the Army of England, not because they believed in the possibility of a successful invasion, but because they wanted him away from Paris and committed to a venture which would surely undermine his reputation. Their principal preoccupation now was to get him away from Paris, where he was a natural focus for their enemies.[16]

The day's event had been a politically charged performance in which, as Bonaparte's secretary put it, 'everyone acted out as best they could this scene from a sentimental comedy'. But it was a dangerous one; according to one well-informed observer, 'it was one of those occasions when one imprudent word, one gesture out of place can decide the future of a great man'. As Sandoz-Rollin pointed out, Paris could easily have become the general's 'tomb'.[17]

The hero of the day was well aware of this. The ceremony was followed by illuminations 'worthy of the majesty of the people' and a banquet given in his honour by the minister of the interior, in the course of which no fewer than twelve toasts were raised, each followed by a three-gun salute and an appropriate burst of song from the choir of the Conservatoire. Closely guarded by his aides, the general did not touch a morsel of food or drink a thing, for fear of being poisoned.[18]

It was not only the Directors who wished him ill. The royalists who longed for a return of Bourbon rule hated him as a ruthless defender of the Republic. The extreme revolutionaries, the Jacobins who had been ousted from power, feared he might be scheming to restore the monarchy. They denounced the treaty he had signed as 'an abominable betrayal' of the Republic's values and referred to him as a 'little Caesar' about to stage a coup and seize power.[19]

Such thoughts were not far from the general's mind. But he hid them as he assessed the possibilities, playing to perfection the part of a latter-day Cincinnatus. He refused the offer of the Directory to place a guard of honour outside his door, he avoided public events and kept a low profile, wearing civilian dress when he went out. 'His behaviour continues to upset all the extravagant calculations and perfidious adulation of certain people,' reported the *Journal des hommes libres* approvingly. Sandoz-Rollin assured his masters in Berlin that there was nothing which might lead one to suspect Bonaparte of meaning to take power. 'The health of this general is weak, his chest is in a very poor state,' he wrote, 'his taste for literature and philosophy and his need of rest as well as to silence the envious will lead him to live a quiet life among friends. . . .'[20]

One man was not fooled. For all his cynicism, Talleyrand was impressed, and sensed power. 'What a man this Bonaparte,' he had written to a friend a few weeks before. 'He has not finished his twenty-eighth year: and he is crowned with all the glories. Those of war and those of peace, those of moderation, those of generosity. He has everything.'[21]

2

Insular Dreams

THE MAN WHO had everything was born into a family of little consequence in one of the poorest places in Europe, the island of Corsica. It was also one of the most idiosyncratic, having never been an independent political unit and yet never been fully a province or colony of another state. It had always been a world of its own.

In the late Middle Ages, the Republic of Genoa established bases at the anchorages of Bastia on the northeastern coast and Ajaccio in the southwest to protect its shipping lanes and deny their use to others. It garrisoned these with soldiers, mostly impoverished nobles from the Italian mainland, and gradually extended its rule inland. But the mountainous interior held little economic interest, and although they penetrated it in order to put down insurgencies and exact what contributions they could, the Genoese found it impossible to control its feral denizens and largely left it alone, not even bothering to map it.

The indigenous population preserved its traditional ways, subsisting on a diet of chestnuts (from which even the local bread was made), cheese, onions, fruit, and the occasional piece of goat or pork, washed down with local wine. They dressed in homespun brown cloth and spoke their own Italian patois. They were in constant conflict over issues such as grazing rights with the inhabitants of the port towns. These considered themselves superior and married amongst themselves or found spouses on the Italian mainland, yet with time they could not help being absorbed by the interior and its ways.

It was a pre-feudal society. The majority owned at least a scrap of land, and while a few families aspired to nobility, the differentials of wealth were narrow. Even the poorest families had a sense of pride, of their dignity and of the worth of their 'house'. It was also a fundamentally pagan society, with Christianity spread thinly, if tenaciously, over a stew of ancient myths and atavisms. A profound belief in destiny overrode the Christian vision of salvation.

As there was hardly any coinage in circulation, most of the necessities of life were bartered. The result was a complicated web of favours granted and expected; rights established or revindicated; agreements, often unspoken; and a plethora of litigation. Any violent move could provoke a *vendetta* from which it was almost impossible to escape, as nothing could be kept secret for long in such a restricted space. Shortage of land meant that ownership was divided and subdivided, traded and encumbered with complicated clauses governing rights of reversal. It was also the principal motive for marriage. And so it was for General Bonaparte's father, Carlo Maria Buonaparte.

When his son came to power, genealogists, sycophants, and fortune-hunters set about tracing his ancestry and came up with various pedigrees, linking him to Roman emperors, Guelf kings, and even the Man in the Iron Mask. The only indisputable facts concerning his ancestry are that he was descended from a Gabriele Buonaparte who in the sixteenth century owned the grandest mansion in Ajaccio, consisting of two rooms and a kitchen over a shop and a store room, and a small garden with a mulberry tree.

Where Gabriele came from remains uncertain. The most convincing filiation is to minor gentry of the same name from the little town of Sarzana on the borders of Tuscany and Liguria, some of whom took service with the Genoese and were sent to Corsica. Recent DNA tests have shown that the Corsican Buonaparte belonged to the population group E, which is found mainly in North Africa, Sicily, and particularly the Levant. This does not rule out a Ligurian connection, since people from those areas washed up over the ages on the coasts of Italy as well as those of Corsica.[1]

Gabriele's son Geronimo had been notable enough to be sent as Ajaccio's deputy to Genoa in 1572 and acquired, by marriage, a house in Ajaccio as well as a lease on some low-lying ground outside the town known as the Salines. His descendants also married well, within the circle of Ajaccio notables, but the need to provide dowries for daughters split up the family's property, and Sebastiano Buonaparte, born in 1683, was reduced to marrying a girl from the upland village of Bocognano, apparently for the two small plots of land in the hills and the ninety sheep she brought him in her dowry. She bore him five children: one girl, Paola Maria, and four boys: Giuseppe Maria, Napoleone, Sebastiano, and Luciano.

The family home had been partitioned by dowries, and the seven of them were crammed into the forty square metres that remained theirs. The building was so dilapidated that a military billeting commission classified it as unfit for any but lower ranks. Thus, although they were still considered among the *anziani*, the elders or notables of Ajaccio, the family's lifestyle was anything but noble. A smallholding provided vegetables and their vineyards wine for their own needs and some extra to sell or exchange for oil and flour, while their flocks produced occasional meat for their own consumption and a little income.

Luciano was the most intelligent of the brood and joined the priesthood. He bought out other family members and installed an indoor staircase in the house. His nephew, Giuseppe's son Carlo Maria, born in 1746, also set about rebuilding the family fortunes, and it is his social ambitions that were to have such a profound effect on European history.[2]

History had begun to take an interest in Corsica. The corrupt inefficiency of Genoese rule had sparked a rebellion on the island in 1729. It was put down by troops, but simmered on in the interior. In 1735 three 'Generals of the Corsican nation' convoked an assembly, the *consulta*, at Corte in the uplands and proclaimed independence, attracting the sympathies of many across Europe. One of the dominant themes in the literature of the Enlightenment was that of the noble savage, and Corsica seemed to fit the ideal of a society unspoilt by the supposedly corrupted Christian culture of Europe. In 1736 a German baron, Theodor von Neuhoff, landed in Corsica with weapons and aid for the rebels. He proclaimed himself King of the

Berlin PRUS

Brussels

AUSTRIAN NETHERLANDS

HOLY

SAXONY

ROMAN

Paris

Prague

EMPIRE

Basel

AUSTRI

Autun   Auxonne

Brienne   SWISS
Geneva   CONFEDERATION

Bordeaux

Lyon

Bayonne

Valence

Turin   Milan   Venice   Trieste

Avignon   Genoa

Montpellier   Aix-en-
              Provence   Nice   Oneglia

Marseille   Pisa
Toulon   Livorno   Florence   Ancona

Golfe Juan

Barcelona   Calvi Bastia *Elba*
                         Corte   Orezza   Rome
                         Ajaccio *Corsica*   *Adriatic S*

                              Maddalena

                         Sardinia   Naples

                         Cagliari

Algiers   Palermo

Tunis   *Sicily*

                                      Malta

                        M e d i t e r r a n e

EUROPE
1792

Revolutionary France

Corsicans and set about developing the island according to current ideals. Genoa called on France for military assistance, the rebels were obliged to flee, and Theodor settled in London, where he died, a declared bankrupt, in 1756. His vision did not die with him.[3]

In 1755 Pasquale Paoli, the son of one of the three 'Generals of the Corsican nation', had returned from exile in Naples and proclaimed a Corsican Republic. Born in 1725, Paoli had been eleven years old when Theodor expounded to him his vision for the island, and it had haunted him throughout his exile. Styling himself General of the Nation, over the next thirteen years he worked at building an ideal modern state endowed with a constitution, institutions, and a university. His charisma ensured him the love of the majority of the Corsicans, who served him devotedly, referring to him as their *Babbo*, their father. He gained the admiration of enlightened European opinion, with Voltaire and Rousseau in the lead. The British traveller James Boswell visited him in 1765 and wrote up his experiences in what turned into a best-seller, further enhancing his reputation.[4]

While Paoli ruled the Corsican nation from the Lilliputian hilltown of Corte at the heart of the island, coastal towns remained in the hands of the Genoese, who had twice called in French military assistance to maintain their grip. The French at first confined themselves to holding the port cities and surrounding areas, but it was unlikely that France would countenance the existence of a utopian republic on its doorstep for long, and wise Corsicans hedged their bets.

On 2 June 1764, a year after the death of his father, the eighteen-year-old Carlo Buonaparte married Letizia Ramolino, who was just under fifteen years of age. She was by all accounts a beauty, but that was not the motive for the match, which had been arranged by Carlo's uncle Luciano. The Ramolino family, descended from a Lombard nobleman who had come to Corsica a couple of hundred years earlier, were of higher social standing than the Buonaparte. They were also better connected and richer. Letizia's dowry, which consisted of a house in Ajaccio and some rooms in another, a vineyard, and about a dozen hectares of land, enhanced Carlo's position. The marriage did not take place in church since the essence of any Corsican marital union was property, the principal element was the contract, and it was customary to sign this in the house of one of the parties, after which the newly-weds might or might not have their marriage blessed by a priest.[5]

Soon after their wedding, the couple moved to Corte, where Carlo's uncle Napoleone had already joined Pasquale Paoli. Their first child was stillborn; their second, a daughter born in 1767, died in infancy. On 7 January 1768 they had a son, baptised Joseph Nabullion. Carlo enrolled at the university and eventually published a dissertation on natural rights which reveals a degree of education.[6]

Paoli resided in a massive structure made of the same dark-grey rock as all the other houses and the paving of the streets in Corte. He imported furniture and textiles from Italy in order to create within this grim building a few rooms in which a head of government could receive. Good-looking and amiable, the young Joseph quickly won his friendship. Letizia was by Corte standards a sophisticated and well-dressed lady, and her beauty and strong personality meant that along with her sister Geltruda Paravicini she was a welcome member of Paoli's entourage.

Paoli admitted to Boswell that he placed great trust in Providence. That, and the praise being directed at him from various parts of Europe, had lulled him into a state of complacency. He believed that the British, who had taken an interest in supporting the Corsican cause before, and were now in thrall to Boswell's *An Account of Corsica*, would come to his aid if he were threatened. By the same token, France could not countenance the possibility of the strategically important island falling into the hands of a hostile power. Still smarting from overseas losses to Britain during the recently ended Seven Years' War, French wounded pride would welcome the balsam of a colonial gain. Genoa had given up on Corsica and owed France a great deal of money. By the Treaty of Versailles of May 1768 it ceded the island to France, pending the repayment of the overdue debt. French troops moved out of their coastal bases to impose the authority of King Louis XV.[7]

Paoli issued a call to arms, but his was a lost cause, though the men of the uplands put up a stiff resistance, inflicting heavy casualties on the French. Carlo was at Paoli's side during the decisive engagement at Ponte-Novo on 8 May 1769 but did not take part in the fighting; Paoli hovered some three kilometres away as his men were routed by a superior French force under the comte de Vaux. Paoli fled over the mountains to Porto Vecchio, whence two British frigates took him and a handful of supporters off to exile in England.[8]

Carlo Buonaparte was not among them. Family legend has it that Paoli insisted he stay behind in Corsica, but it is more likely that Carlo made the decision himself. The island had never entirely submitted to any regime, and among its inhabitants family came a long way before loyalty to any cause. While Carlo and his uncle Napoleone had served Paoli, his other uncle Luciano had remained in French-held Ajaccio, where he had sworn fealty to the King of France, as had most of the notables of the coastal cities. Unperturbed by the cause of independence, Letizia was writing to her grandfather Giuseppe Maria Pietrasanta in French-held Bastia asking him to send her bales of Lyon silk and new dresses fit for a noblewoman.[9]

'I was a good patriot and a Paolist in my heart as long as the national government lasted,' Carlo wrote. 'But this government has ceased to exist. We have become French. *Eviva il Re e suo governo.*' Having submitted to Vaux, he went back to Ajaccio. On the way home over the mountains, Carlo almost lost his wife and the child she was carrying in her womb when her mule stumbled in the torrent of the river Liamone.[10]

The child was born on the night of 15 August 1769, and named after his great-uncle Napoleone, who had died two years before. The name did not figure in the liturgical calendar as belonging to a saint, but it was not unknown in Genoa and Corsica, where it was sometimes spelt Nabullione or even Lapullione, and had been given to several members of the family in the past. He would not be christened until the following July, by which time his father had repositioned himself with considerable skill.[11]

Since the legal profession was the key to obtaining civic office under any government, Carlo set off for Pisa to obtain the necessary qualifications. 'One can have no idea of the facility with which the title of doctor is granted here,' wrote a contemporary French traveller of the university of Pisa. 'Everyone in the locality is one, even the inn-keepers and post-masters.' Carlo presented a hastily written thesis for which he obtained a doctorate, and within six weeks he was back in Ajaccio, where he found no shortage of work.[12]

With a population of 3,907, according to the French census of 1770, Ajaccio was the second largest city in Corsica, but it was in essence a sleepy, smelly village. When Balzac visited it more than half a century later he was stunned by the 'unbelievable indolence' pervading the place, with the menfolk wandering about all day smoking. It consisted of a minuscule citadel stuck out on the promontory shielding the port, and behind it a walled town not more than 250 metres across in any direction, clustered around three radiating streets intersected by another three narrower ones, with an attractive promenade and square between the two named the Olmo after a large elm that grew on it. Within the walls there was a cathedral whose roof fell in in 1771 and would not be repaired for twenty years, and which was unusable in summer due to the stink emanating from the dead buried under its floor. There was also a Jesuit college and a governor's residence, tucked into an assortment of mean-looking townhouses ranged along narrow streets bordered by small shops whose trade spilled out onto them. The smell of fish drifting over from the harbour mingled with that of the hides put out to dry by the butchers cutting up carcases in the street and the stench from the moat of the citadel. Outside the city walls stood a convent, a hospital, a military barracks, and a seminary, and, along the road leading up to the town from the north, an agglomeration of dwellings known as the Borgo, where the poorer inhabitants lived.[13]

The city was dominated by families such as the Ponte, Pozzo di Borgo, Bacciochi, and the Peraldi, and an oligarchy of notaries, lawyers, and clerics with 'noble' connections such as the Buonaparte. This society was supplemented by the magistrates, judge, officers, and other officials of the French administration. The houses within the city walls were mostly divided by multiple ownership like the Buonaparte home, and, since all their inhabitants were related to each other by blood or marriage, the whole area was a familial congeries connected by tangled ties. Ajaccio's lawyers, Carlo among them, thrived on the squabbles generated by the resulting disputes over restricted space and scant resources. Carlo himself would be engaged for many years in a legal battle over some used wine-making equipment and a few leaky barrels. In one case, he pleaded for a client over one kerchief. There was plenty of work, but it was not remunerative enough or commensurate with Carlo's ambitions. On the basis of his doctorate, in 1771 he obtained a minor post at the court of Ajaccio, but he was aiming higher.[14]

He had wasted no time in seeking the favour of the French military governor of the southwest of the island, the comte de Narbonne. On being fobbed off, he offered his services to Narbonne's superior in Bastia. Charles Louis, comte de Marbeuf, needed a party of supporters among the notables of Ajaccio, and the Buonaparte were ideally placed to provide it. Their collaboration developed so well that Carlo felt bold enough to invite Marbeuf to stand godparent at the christening of his son Napoleone on 21 July 1771, and Marbeuf agreed. In the event, Marbeuf was prevented from attending, so he sent a Genoese patrician and later royal lieutenant at Ajaccio, Lorenzo Giubega, to act as proxy. Marbeuf did come to Ajaccio less than a month later for the festivities of the feast of the Assumption and the little Napoleone's second birthday on 15 August. He was so struck by the beauty of the child's mother that he insisted she take his arm on the afternoon *passegiata* up and down the Olmo, and after walking her home he stayed there until one in the morning. Carlo's ambitions soared.[15]

France was interested in Corsica both for its strategic importance and for its economic potential. It was accorded the status of a semi-autonomous province within the kingdom, and the French authorities set about organising it. A survey revealed to them the idiosyncratic nature of Corsican society, with its broad base of land tenure and plethora of hunting, gathering, and fishing rights and obligations. These would hinder rationalisation, while the egalitarianism that had so enchanted Boswell and Rousseau impeded not only progress but the establishment of a hierarchy necessary for successful political control. One of the first actions of the new French regime was to correct this by recognising as noble the most prominent families. In large measure thanks to the usefulness of Carlo and the charms of his wife, the Buonaparte were included. 'Ajaccio is struck with astonishment and filled with jealousy by the news,' Carlo wrote to his wife's grandfather.[16]

The connection with Marbeuf was invaluable. In 1772 Carlo was elected to represent Ajaccio in the newly established Assembly of Corsican Estates only because Marbeuf intervened to have his successful rival's election annulled. The governor's direct intercession also helped resolve a lengthy court battle between the Buonaparte and their Ornano cousins over a dowry that included a significant part of the house in which they lived. By way of a series of buy-outs, swaps, and court cases, Carlo would extend his possession over the years against a backdrop of running battles between the various members of the family involving the use of the staircase and other areas where interests clashed. These occasionally flared into violence, and inevitably ended up in court, where the knowledge that Carlo had the backing of Marbeuf counted.[17]

The rise of Carlo's fortunes and the governor's interest in Letizia aroused jealousy and gave rise to gossip. Marbeuf, a widower, did have an official mistress in Bastia, a Madame Varese, but whatever charms she may have possessed, at fifty she was past her prime, while Letizia was still young. It is difficult to see any reason other than an amorous one for him to spend time with an uneducated woman forty years his junior, and he gave every sign of being besotted by Letizia. There is no evidence that the relationship was sexual, but it was widely believed that it was, and that her next child, Louis, born in 1778, was his.[18]

Letizia would bear a total of thirteen children, of whom three died young and two in childbirth. The first surviving child was Joseph, born in 1768, the next Napoleone, born in 1769. As his mother was unable to feed him, he was provided with a wet-nurse, Camilla Carbon Ilari, who grew so fond of him that she neglected her own son. Napoleone and his elder brother, christened Joseph but known as Giuseppe, were also spoiled by their father and their grandmother Saveria Paravicini, known in the family as Minanna. But they were kept under strict control by Letizia. Strong, brave, and characterful, Letizia was endowed with common sense. Unlike the rest of her family, she was pious and hardly went out other than to church. She was also a strict disciplinarian, administering slaps to all her children, and once giving Napoleone a thrashing which he remembered to the end of his life. She exerted a strong influence on him, and he would later say that he owed everything to her.[19]

There is no evidence that Napoleone ever attended school, although according to his mother he did go to lessons at a girls' school. He was probably taught to read at home by a local priest, the Abbé Recco—presumably in Latin rather than the local patois they all spoke. His great-uncle Luciano, effective head of the family, must have found other teachers, as Napoleone from an early age showed an almost obsessive interest in and remarkable aptitude for mathematics.[20]

His seems to have been a happy childhood, much of it spent in the street playing with various cousins, while the summers were passed up in the hills at Bocognano. The family grew, with the birth of a boy, Luciano, in 1775, and a girl, the fourth to be christened Maria-Anna and the first to survive, in 1777. While most of the anecdotes collected by early biographers can be dismissed as 'remembered' under the suggestive influence of the boy's later trajectory, one thing can be retained. His mother admiringly reminisced that of all her children Napoleone had been 'the most intrepid'. In fact, he seems to have been aggressive and quarrelsome, leading to frequent fights with his elder brother.[21]

There was violence all around him, since much of the population continued in its lawless ways, and in order to stamp out the remaining resistance and the inherent banditry, the French applied the harshest measures. Mobile columns scoured the countryside burning down the houses and crops and slaughtering the flocks of suspected rebels, breaking them on the wheel and hanging the corpses on public highways as a warning. The five-year-old boy could not have avoided seeing them.

Whatever his feelings, Carlo had tied his family's fortunes to the French regime and its representative in Corsica. Being thought a cuckold was a small price to pay for the benefits brought by Marbeuf's favour, which he drew on at every upward step. While Luciano saved every penny and literally slept on his moneybags, Carlo spent lavishly, dressing well in order to keep up appearances when he attended the assembly in Bastia or other official functions. Having gained recognition of his status as a Corsican nobleman, he was determined to propel himself into the French nobility, as only that opened the door to careers in the kingdom. It had been decided that his elder son, Joseph, would go into the Church and Napoleone into the army. Marbeuf's nephew was the bishop of Autun, in eastern France, and Joseph was easily secured a place at the city's seminary, with the position of a sub-deacon and a stipend lined up for him.

Placing Napoleone would be more difficult. In 1776 Carlo applied for a place at one of the royal military academies, but the boy would require a royal bursary to pay for his studies. These were awarded to sons of officers and indigent nobles, so Carlo had to prove his noble credentials and provide evidence of his lack of means. The recognition of nobility he had gained in 1771 was based on proofs dating back only 200 years, which was not sufficient. In 1777 Carlo was chosen as one of the deputies to represent the nobility of Corsica at the court of Louis XVI, but he would not be presented to the king unless he could provide proofs of more ancient lineage.

When he had gone to Pisa to obtain his doctorate, Carlo had obtained from the city's archbishop a document attesting that his birth entitled him to the status of a 'noble patrician of Tuscany'. He now returned to Tuscany and located a canon by the name of Filipo Buonaparte, who provided him with documents purportedly relating him to his own family, which could trace noble status back to the fourteenth century. Armed with these, Carlo hoped to be able to gain recognition in France, and with it the right to a bursary for Napoleone.[22]

On 12 December 1778 Carlo left Ajaccio, accompanied by Letizia and their sons Joseph and Napoleone. The party also included two other young men. One was Letizia's half-brother Giuseppe Fesch. When her father had died soon after Letizia's birth her mother had remarried a Swiss naval officer in Genoese service and produced a son. Giuseppe Fesch had been awarded a bursary to study for the priesthood at the seminary of Aix-en-Provence. The other young man was Abbé Varese, a cousin of Letizia who, like Joseph, had been granted the post of sub-deacon at the cathedral of Autun. They travelled by cart and mule via Bocognano to Corte, where a carriage sent by Marbeuf waited to conduct Letizia in greater comfort on the rest of their journey to Bastia. From there, Carlo and the four boys sailed for Marseille while Letizia moved into Marbeuf's residence.[23]

They reached Autun on 30 December, having left Fesch at Aix on the way. On 1 January 1779 Joseph and Napoleone entered the college of Autun, the first to prepare for the priesthood, the second in order to learn French. Napoleone would spend three months and twenty days at the college, whose thirty boarders were taught by priests of the Oratorian order. During that time he would learn French well enough to carry on a conversation and to write a simple essay, but he did not, then or ever, learn the language well, and his grammar and use of words remained poor. His handwriting never developed beyond an ugly scrawl.[24]

Carlo travelled on to Paris, where he learned that Napoleone had been deemed eligible for a bursary, subject to the submission of the necessary proofs of nobility. He duly presented these, before joining the other Corsican deputies to be presented to the king at Versailles. On 9 March the three Corsicans were admitted into the royal presence, bowed low and handed their petition to the monarch, who handed it to an attendant minister and graciously watched them leave his presence, stepping backward and bowing repeatedly. They were then presented to the queen, the dauphin, and various dignitaries, after which they were driven around the park in a carriage and rowed up and down the grand canal before being allowed to depart.[25]

On 28 March the minister of war, the prince de Montbarrey, officially informed Carlo that his son had been admitted with a royal bursary to the military academy of Brienne. As he could not leave Versailles, Carlo asked the father of another boy due to be transferred from Autun to Brienne to take Napoleone there. On 21 April, after an emotional farewell to Joseph, the nine-year-old Napoleone set off on his military career.[26]

3

Boy Soldier

N APOLEONE ARRIVED AT the military academy of Brienne on 15 May 1779, three months short of his tenth birthday. The regulation kit each boy brought with him consisted of three pairs of bedsheets; a set of dining silver and a silver goblet, engraved with his family arms or initials; a dozen napkins; a blue coat with white metal buttons bearing the arms of the academy; two pairs of black serge breeches; twelve shirts, twelve kerchiefs, twelve white collars, six cotton caps, two dressing gowns, a hair-powder pouch, and a hair ribbon. The powder and ribbon would be redundant for the first three years, as up to the age of twelve the boys wore their hair close-cropped.[1]

The academy occupied an inelegant sprawl of buildings in the small town of 400 people, dominated by the château of the Loménie de Brienne family (to whom Marbeuf had recommended the boy). It had some 110 pupils, about fifty of them beneficiaries of royal bursaries like Napoleone. It was an austere institution, run by friars of the Order of Minims, founded in the fifteenth century by St Francis de Paola in Calabria and dedicated to abstention and frugality, so the atmosphere was Spartan. The boys attended mass every morning and discipline was strict, although there was no corporal punishment. At night they were locked in cells furnished with a straw-filled mattress, blanket, ewer, and basin. In order to teach them to do without servants, they had to look after themselves and their kit. There were no holidays, and they were only allowed home in exceptional circumstances.[2]

Following the defeats in the Seven Years' War, thought to have been partly due to the dilettantism of the officers, French military thinking focused on ways of producing an officer class inured to hardship and inspired by a sense of duty. Institutions such as Brienne were not meant to provide military training; the curriculum, taught by the friars supplemented by lay teachers, included the study of Suetonius, Tacitus, Quintillian, Cicero, Horace, and Virgil, and, most importantly Plutarch, whose lives of the heroes of antiquity were meant to serve as role models for the aspiring soldiers. The works of Corneille, Racine, Boileau, Bossuet, Fénelon, and other French classics were to awaken in them the instincts of chivalry, honour, duty, and sacrifice, as well as teaching them elocution and rhetoric. The curriculum also included German, history, geography, mathematics, physics, drawing, dancing, fencing, and music.[3]

His new environment must have presented a challenge for the young Napoleone at many levels. He was by all accounts a puny child, showing signs of a delicate constitution. He had an olive complexion, which along with his poor French and atrocious accent marked him out as a foreigner. Corsica was seen in France at the time as a land of treacherous brigands. His outlandish first name, pronounced in the French way with the last syllable accented, ended with a sound like 'nez', leading to jibes based on the nose. Having a bursary singled him out as the son of a poor family, while his noble status was open to question, or at least mockery, from those of a higher social standing. The patronage of Marbeuf, and occasional visits to the château on Sundays, fed rumours about his mother's morals and his own paternity. All this laid him open to teasing and bullying, which must have aggravated the homesickness he would have felt on entering this alien world and the cold, sunless climate of northeastern France. But in boarding schools where boys are cut off from home, those with character or certain gifts easily impose themselves and can achieve a status they do not have in the outside world. And Napoleone did not lack character.[4]

Apart from Charles-Étienne de Gudin, who became a fine general, and Étienne-Marie Champion de Nansouty, later a distinguished cavalry commander, few of Napoleone's contemporaries at Brienne made much of their lives. Later, some could not resist laying a claim to fame by recording memories, true or invented, of their days together. Childhood reminiscences are unreliable at the best of times, and in this case should be treated with the greatest caution. Typical is the story of a snowball fight that probably took place in the winter of 1783, which assumed epic proportions in various memoirs, with Napoleone organising his colleagues into armies, building elaborate fortifications out of snow, and staging assaults which supposedly revealed his tactical talents and leadership qualities.[5]

The concurrent image of an alienated youth drawn by such memoirists and developed by romantically minded biographers should likewise be taken with a pinch of salt. Napoleone was capable of standing up to his schoolmates, displaying a 'ferocity' and even 'fury' born of contempt when provoked, but he did not seek their friendship. 'I do not recollect, that he ever showed the slightest partiality in favour of any of his comrades; gloomy and fierce to excess, almost always by himself,' recalled one of the few fellow pupils whose accounts can be trusted, 'averse likewise to all that is called children's plays and amusements, he never was seen to share in the noisy mirth of his school-fellows....'[6]

He did have friends. One was Louis Antoine Fauvelet de Bourrienne, whose family origins in trade may have made him less arrogant than the others. Jean-Baptiste Le Lieur de Ville sur Arce, four years older than Napoleone, recalled being drawn to him by the 'originality' of his character, his 'somewhat strange' manner, and his intelligence, and the two became close. Another friend was Pierre François Laugier de Bellecour, whom Napoleon liked in spite of his frivolity. There were others with whom he was on good terms, and he also had some friends among the friars and the teachers.[7]

What did set Napoleone apart from his peers was his application and his intellectual curiosity. With a library at his disposal for the first time in his life, he read voraciously. The cadets were assigned small allotments of land to cultivate, and Napoleone fenced his off and planted it so as to provide himself with a place of solitude in which he could read. 'Reserved in his temper, and wholly occupied by his own pursuits, Buonaparte courted that solitude which seemed to constitute his delight,' recorded the librarian.[8]

With Napoleone at Brienne and Joseph at Autun, Carlo with a seat in the Corsican Estates, and the appointment in 1779 of his uncle Luciano as archdeacon of Ajaccio cathedral, the senior clerical post in the city, the standing of the family seemed assured. But Carlo's social ambitions bred requirements which imposed new struggles on him and anxieties on his family. By a complicated transaction in 1779 he managed to gain sole title to most of the lease granted to his ancestor Geronimo in 1584 on the Salines, twenty-three hectares of land outside Ajaccio. Originally a salt-marsh, it had been partly drained and turned into a cherry orchard, but had reverted to an unhealthy swamp. Carlo applied for a subsidy from the French government to drain the land on grounds of public health and turn it into a nursery for mulberry trees, which, it was hoped, would be planted all over the island and provide raw silk for the French textile industry. Thanks to Marbeuf's support, the subsidy was granted in June 1782.[9]

The next objective required more tortuous negotiations, in which his patron's assistance would be even more necessary. Almost a century earlier, a great-aunt of Carlo had married an Odone, and in her dowry brought him a property which was to revert to the Buonaparte if the progeny of the union were to die out. But instead of returning the property, the last of the Odone bequeathed it to the Jesuits. When the Jesuits were expelled from France in 1764, the property devolved to the state. Carlo intended to prove that the Odone bequest was illegal and laid claim to Les Milleli, another former Jesuit property, as compensation.[10]

The matter required a trip to Paris and Versailles, and in September 1782 Carlo set off, taking Letizia with him for a cure at the spa of Bourbonne-les-Bains before going on to Paris. At some stage during this trip she visited Napoleone at Brienne and recorded being struck by how wasted and sickly he looked.[11]

Carlo marked his social ascent by restoring the Buonaparte home in Ajaccio, putting in marble fireplaces and mirrors, lining his bedroom with crimson silk, draping the windows with muslin curtains, and installing a library. Behind the scenes, things looked different, according to inventories of the family possessions, which list every pot and pan in the kitchen, buckets, iron pokers, pewter plates (three large and twenty-nine small), knives, forks, and spoons. The path to grandeur was not without its difficult moments. A row over possession of the part of the house occupied by Carlo's cousin Maria Giustina and her Pozzo di Borgo husband, which Carlo escalated by trying to deny them the use of the only staircase, climaxed in Maria Giustina emptying her chamberpot over Carlo's best silk suit, airing on the terrace below, which entailed yet another court case.[12]

The intimacy with Marbeuf would soon be at an end. He had married a young lady of his own class and lost interest in his Corsican protégés. This came at a bad moment. The mulberry nursery was not going well, and the costs soon outstripped the amount of the subsidy. Another trip to Paris would be required, for family reasons too. Carlo had succeeded in getting his third son, now referred to as Lucien, admitted to Autun, where he joined Joseph. And he had achieved a social triumph in having his eldest daughter, Maria-Anna, accepted into the Maison Royale de Saint-Cyr, founded a hundred years before by Louis XIV's mistress Madame de Maintenon for the daughters of indigent nobility, which provided not only a free education but also a dowry when they left. In June 1784 he set off for Paris with her. He needed to get more money out of the government for the Salines project, to press his suit over the Odone inheritance and the Milleli compensation, and to lobby for the nine-year-old Lucien to be granted a bursary at Brienne, where he was now due to join Napoleone. After stopping off at Autun to pick up Lucien, Carlo's appearance at Brienne, dressed in a cerise coat with puce breeches and silk stockings, with silver buckles on his shoes and his hair curled, caused Napoleone embarrassment. 'My father was a good man,' he later reminisced, but added that he was 'a little too fond of the ridiculous gentility of the times'.[13]

Carlo's plans were beginning to come unstuck. Joseph had come to the conclusion that he was not made for the priesthood and announced that he too would like to pursue a military career, as an artillery officer. Carlo was dismayed and pointed out that Joseph was neither hardy in health nor courageous. With Marbeuf's backing he would easily obtain a good position and end up a bishop, which would be of advantage to the whole family, while, as Napoleone explained, he could at best make a passable garrison officer, being entirely unsuited for the artillery on account of his lack of application and his 'weakness of character'.[14]

These comments were made in the first extant letter written by Napoleone, to his half-uncle Joseph Fesch in June 1784. He was still only fourteen, but while his spelling and grammar are atrocious, he adopts an authoritative tone, particularly with relation to his elder brother, whom he discusses as a parent might a wayward teenager. Of his younger sibling Lucien he remarks that 'he shows a good disposition and good will' and 'should make a good fellow'. Lucien claimed that on his arrival at Brienne Napoleone received him 'without the slightest show of tenderness' and that 'there was nothing amiable in his manner, either towards me or towards the other comrades of his age who did not like him', but these reminiscences, written down much later by an embittered Lucien, are unreliable.[15]

Napoleone had originally intended to go into the navy. The voyages of exploration of Admiral Louis-Antoine de Bougainville and the creditable part played by the French navy against the British during the War of American Independence had raised its profile and made it fashionable. The navy offered a better chance of action in peacetime, and with it better prospects for promotion. It held greater appeal than garrison service in some gloomy northern town. In the navy consideration rested on talent, and social origins counted for little. Napoleone was good at mathematics and geography, and he was small and agile, all vital assets. But in 1783 higher powers decided that he should go into the army. Carlo's interventions in Paris proved fruitless and he was destined for the artillery—which came as a relief to Letizia, as the navy involved the danger of death by drowning as well as by enemy action. The artillery had also gained in prestige due to recent technical advances, and as it was an arm in which favour could not trump ability and mathematics was a prerequisite, Napoleone would also have an advantage. On 22 September 1784 he was interviewed by the inspector Raymond de Monts and selected for the École Militaire in Paris.[16]

The fifteen-year-old Napoleone and four other cadets set off, under the care of one of the friars, on 17 October, travelling by heavy mail coach to Nogent-sur-Seine, where they changed to a *coche d'eau*, a barge with a superstructure for passengers and goods, drawn by four Percheron horses along a tow-path. Two days later they disembarked on the left bank of the Seine opposite the Ile de la Cité and walked through what was then known as the *'pays latin'* to their new school. On the way they stopped at a bookshop to buy books, and at the church of Saint-Germain-des-Prés to say a prayer.[17]

The École Militaire, founded in 1751, had been reformed in the 1770s by the war minister Claude Louis de Saint-Germain. The 200 cadets wore military uniform of blue coat with yellow collar and red facings, red waistcoat, and breeches. They were housed in a grand stone building which still stands at the end of the Champ de Mars, with a spacious courtyard in which they performed drills and played ball games. They slept in a dormitory with wooden partitions, each compartment containing an iron bedstead with curtains and minimal built-in furniture for their clothes, ewer and basin, and a chamberpot.[18]

The day began with mass at six o'clock, followed by eight hours of instruction, except on Thursdays, Sundays, and feast days, when the only obligations were four hours of reading and letter-writing, and sometimes target practice. Although the school was run by laymen, the routine included grace before and after breakfast, dinner, and supper, prayers in chapel before bedtime, vespers and catechism as well as mass on Sundays, and confession once a month. The cadets were not allowed out and were punished by detention on bread and water.

The curriculum included Latin, French, German, mathematics, geography, history, moral studies, law, fortification, drawing, fencing, handling of weapons, letter-writing, and dancing (those destined for the navy and the artillery were too busy with technical subjects to attend these). The accent was on developing character and a military ethos: the cadets would be taught soldiering when they joined their regiments.[19]

Napoleone did not take to the establishment, which he found too grand. The food was good and plentiful, and the cadets were waited on by servants, which he found inappropriate. He thought the austerity of Brienne more in keeping with the military life as he imagined it. Although the director, the Chevalier de Valfort, had risen from the ranks, the presence of fee-paying young men not destined for a career in the army lent the place an aristocratic atmosphere Napoleone did not like. At Brienne, the fee-paying cadets had been provincial gentry. Here they were of a higher social and economic standing, and they made the others feel it. Napoleone was teased for his origins, and the allusions to his being Marbeuf's bastard resurfaced. But he should have felt in good company, given that one of his brother cadets, Władysław Jabłonowski, a Pole of mixed race referred to as '*le petit noir*', was supposedly the son of King Louis XV.[20]

In a letter to his father of September 1784, four and a half years after arriving at Brienne, the fifteen-year-old Napoleone had asked him to send a copy of Boswell's book and any other historical works on Corsica he could find. He had left his homeland at the age of nine, at which time he can have known little of its history or circumstances. His reading at Brienne would have exposed him to the current intellectual and emotional trends, which included the cult of the *patrie*, the motherland which demanded to be served and died for. Paoli's Corsican project chimed with this, and his fate appealed to the growing fashion for glorifying victimhood and lost causes. During his last years at Brienne, Napoleone went through a phase of what he called '*grande sensibilité*', and he embraced this one, casting himself as a Corsican patriot and an ardent worshipper of Paoli. The motivation may have been partly the need for a modern hero to emulate. The study of Plutarch had inspired a cult of heroes in late-eighteenth-century France, which was in matters of taste entering the age of neoclassicism. Alexander the Great, Caesar, Brutus, Cicero, and others were the lodestars of Napoleone's generation. A little wishful thinking could cast Paoli in the same mould. Napoleone's newfound emotional association with Corsica may also have had something to do with his sense of social inferiority, with a desire to claim for himself a status distinct from and morally superior to that of his fellow cadets with their noble pretensions, that of the persecuted patriot. It was certainly some kind of attempt to capture the moral high ground.

But it sat uneasily with his family's having hitched its fortunes to the French monarchy, let alone his aim of making a career in the service of the King of France. The ambiguities of his situation, both national and social, were inescapable, and made no less real by his father's increasingly desperate efforts to position his family.[21]

Carlo was not well. He had taken Joseph away from Autun and back to Corsica, hoping the boy would take a law degree and assume the responsibilities of head of the family. But Joseph persisted in his desire to become an artillery officer. After undergoing a short cure and assisting at the birth of his youngest son, Jérôme, at the end of 1784 Carlo left the island with Joseph, meaning to take him to Brienne and then go on to Paris to petition for a bursary on his behalf, as well as press his own case for the award of the Milleli estate. The sea crossing was so rough they were nearly shipwrecked, and by the time they made land, at Saint-Tropez, Carlo was in a bad way. They travelled to Aix, where they met up with Joseph Fesch and decided to consult doctors at the medical school of Montpellier. There they found a close friend of Letizia from Corsica, now married to a tax official by the name of Permon, who helped Joseph and Fesch look after the thirty-nine-year-old Carlo. But he was sinking fast, and the doctors could do nothing for him. The end came on 24 February 1785: the post-mortem suggests either stomach cancer or a perforated ulcer as the cause of death.[22]

Napoleone had never known his father well. Carlo was away for long spells during his childhood and they only saw each other once in France, when Carlo came to drop off Lucien at Brienne (and possibly when Letizia visited him). That short visit had not made a favourable impression on the boy, and frequent allusions to his paternity made him wonder whether Carlo really was his father. When, as was customary in such circumstances at the École Militaire, his confessor came to console him, Napoleone brushed him off, saying he had enough strength of character to cope with his loss without spiritual consolation. 'There would be no point in expressing to you how much I have been affected by the misfortune which has befallen us,' he wrote to his great-uncle Luciano. 'We have lost in him a father, and God knows what a father, with his tenderness and his attachement.' The letter dwells on the cruelty of Carlo's having had to die away from his home and his family and ends by dutifully imploring Luciano to take the place of the father he has lost.[23]

His father's death might have come as something of a liberation in one sense: the socially embarrassing and pushy Carlo, with his limited aspirations, fitted ill with Plutarch's heroes who filled the boy's imagination, and his obsequious attachment to France even less with the idealised vision of Paoli's struggle for the liberation of the Corsican nation which had become central to his view of himself. In Napoleone's imagination, Paoli was now not only a modern-day Plutarchian hero, a role model to be emulated, but also a spiritual father figure.

His obsession with Paoli was mocked by his fellow cadets, as a surviving caricature attests. But his pose as a representative of the heroic nation wronged by France was psychologically convenient for confronting the superior airs of his aristocratic comrades: he could parry their arrogance with self-righteous contempt. Such sparring should not be made too much of, and he only seems to have had one real hate in the school, a cadet by the name of Le Picard de Phélippeaux.[24]

Napoleone's friend Laugier de Bellecour had come to the École Militaire from Brienne with him. Le Lieur de Ville sur Arce had left to join his regiment just before Napoleone arrived, but before leaving he had asked his friend Alexandre des Mazis to look out for him, warning him that he was prickly and difficult. Their first meeting bore this out, but the two soon became close. Napoleone found in him 'someone who understood him, liked him, and to whom he could without constraint uncover his thoughts', in the words of des Mazis.[25]

Napoleone hated drill, and his mind would drift, with the result that his was always the last musket to be shouldered or lowered, despite des Mazis nudging him, incurring a sharp 'Monsieur de Buonaparte, wake up!' from the drill-master, at whom on one occasion Napoleone threw his musket in a rage. As a result he was made to perform his drill under the supervision of des Mazis. He loved fencing, but was a dangerous sparring partner. He was aggressive and, if touched, would go for his adversary with such fury that he laid himself open to further touches, which made him all the angrier. He often broke his foil, and sometimes the fencing-master would have to separate the combatants.[26]

The two boys shared an interest in mathematics, and des Mazis admired the way his friend relished the challenge of a mathematical problem. 'He would not give up until he had overcome every difficulty,' he recalled. They were taught by Le Paute d'Agelet, a mathematician and astronomer who had circumnavigated the globe with Bougainville, and who enthralled them with his accounts, reviving Napoleone's naval aspirations. In 1785 he was preparing to set off on a voyage of discovery with the explorer Jean François de La Pérouse, and along with several others Napoleone applied to accompany the expedition. Only one was chosen, and it was not him. The voyage ended in disaster in the South Pacific, and nobody survived.[27]

Napoleone showed a great curiosity about geography and history, as well as mathematics, and read widely in both. Although he loved literature, he seemed to have little interest in improving his French, and the exasperated French teacher eventually told him not to bother attending his classes. He also showed what one teacher described as 'an invincible repugnance' for learning German. But he was generally popular with the teachers, who were impressed by 'the persistence with which he argued his points'.[28]

He struck teachers and cadets alike as serious-minded and was described by one of them as 'preferring study to every kind of amusement', interested in literature and ideas, 'uncommunicative, fond of solitude, capricious, arrogant, extremely self-centred', 'having high self-esteem' and a good deal of ambition. Much of the time he appeared to be in a world of his own, pacing up and down, lost in thought, sometimes gesticulating or laughing to himself.[29]

According to des Mazis, 'he groaned at the frivolity of the other pupils', and disapproved of their 'depravities', going so far as to say the school authorities should do more to 'preserve them from corruption'. This was not driven by religious feelings: he had taken his first Holy Communion at Brienne and was confirmed at the École Militaire, and while he went through the motions, never rebelling against the obligation to hear mass every day, he showed no religious zeal. It probably had more to do with his own awkwardness, which made him dismiss sex as something silly and embarrassing. He later admitted that puberty had made him 'morose'. This was exacerbated by the behaviour of his friend Laugier de Bellecour, who had found some like-minded young gentlemen at the École Militaire and flaunted his homosexuality. Napoleone admonished him on the subject and declared that they could not remain friends unless Laugier reformed, as he could not countenance such immoral behaviour. When Laugier teased him for a prig he lost his temper and attacked him physically. Napoleone later expressed regret and often spoke of his former friend 'with sincere affection'. But a prig he remained.[30]

In September 1785 he sat the exam to be admitted into the artillery and passed forty-second out of fifty-eight candidates. All the others had spent two or in some cases four years longer than him preparing for it, so it was not a bad showing. He was posted second lieutenant to the prestigious regiment of La Fère, stationed at Valence. He quickly put together his new uniform, which consisted of a blue coat with red facings and lining, blue waistcoat, red piping, and one epaulette. He was so proud of it that he could not resist showing it off to the Permons and other Corsicans in Paris, as he was now allowed out of the school building.[31]

Des Mazis had been posted to the same regiment, and on 30 October 1785 the two left Paris together. They took a coach as far as Chalon-sur-Saône, where they transferred to the *coche d'eau* for the rest of the journey to Lyon, and continued by post-boat down the Rhône to Valence. It was the first time the sixteen-year-old Napoleone had been unsupervised, and at one point he exclaimed, 'At last, I am free!' and ran around gesticulating wildly.[32]

4

Freedom

VALENCE WAS A medieval town of tortuous muddy streets dominated by a citadel built to guard the valley of the Rhône and surrounded by fortifications designed by the celebrated engineer Vauban. It had a population of some 5,000, a significant portion of which was accounted for by its fourteen convents, abbeys, and priories. Napoleone arrived on 3 November 1785 and took lodgings above a café belonging to Claudine-Marie Bou, a merry and cultivated forty-year-old spinster who washed his linen and looked after his needs. He messed with his fellow officers at the Auberge des Trois Pigeons nearby.[1]

Second Lieutenant Napolionne de Buonaparte, as he was listed, was placed in command of a company of bombardiers manning mortars and howitzers. He had never handled a piece of ordnance before, and now acquainted himself with the practical aspects of gunnery during frequent exercises on a training ground outside the town. He also had to familiarise himself with the works of the founders of modern French artillery, Generals Gribeauval and Guibert, take more advanced courses in mathematics, trigonometry, and geography, and learn how to draw maps and plans.

The regiment of La Fère was one of the most professional in the French army. Its officers were a close-knit family with none of the snobbishness Napoleone had encountered up till now. His messmates included des Mazis and another friend from Brienne, Belly de Bussy, who had joined the regiment a little earlier, and two new ones who were to have distinguished careers, Jean-Ambroise de

Lariboisière and Jean-Joseph Sorbier. Napoleone's company commander was a kindly man who befriended him and invited him to stay at his country house.[2]

The officers of the regiment were welcomed by the local gentry, and Napoleone took dancing lessons to enable him to participate in social gatherings (he remained a graceless dancer). He was befriended by two English ladies who lived nearby and was a frequent guest at the château of a Madame du Colombier a dozen kilometres outside the town. He flirted with her daughter Caroline, whom he would describe as an '*amie de coeur*'. 'Nothing could have been more innocent,' he recalled: they would arrange secret meetings during which 'our greatest delight was to eat cherries together'. He was not yet seventeen and had spent the past eight years cloistered in all-male institutions, so his first emotional stirrings were confused. There is some evidence that he had tender relations with another young woman, a Miss Louberie de Saint-Germain, but these probably did not amount to much either. 'He was of a moral purity very rare among young men,' recalled des Mazis, adding that Napoleone could not conceive how anyone could allow themselves to be dominated by feelings for a woman.[3]

Napoleone was able to nourish his mind as well as his heart, as he was a welcome guest at the house of Monsegnieur de Tardivon, abbot of the abbey of Saint-Ruf, to whom Bishop Marbeuf had given him a letter of introduction. Tardivon, a friend of the renowned anti-colonialist author Abbé Raynal, was the leading light in the intellectual life of Valence, and the gatherings at his lodgings gave Napoleone an opportunity to broaden his views and for the first time in his life take part in intellectual discussion. He caught the spirit of the times and began to question received wisdom and reappraise the world around him; according to one of his brother officers he became insufferably voluble. There was a bookshop which doubled as a reading room opposite his lodgings, to which he took out a subscription, which gave him access to books he could not afford to buy. He read fast, occasionally misunderstanding texts, and erratically: of Voltaire's works he read some of the least influential, little of Diderot's, and less of Montesquieu's, and only those passages of Raynal which related to Corsica. Given his emotional and sexual immaturity, it is not surprising that he was horrified by Sade, but adored the straightforward sentimentality of Roussseau's *La Nouvelle Héloïse* and Bernardin de Saint-Pierre's *Paul et Virginie*.[4]

Like most educated young men of ambition at the time, Napoleone began to fancy himself as a man of letters. With France at peace, literature provided a welcome distraction as well as an opportunity to shine, as another artillery officer, Choderlos de Laclos, had shown with his publication four years earlier of *Les Liaisons dangereuses*. For Napoleone it was a way of formulating his views, and more importantly a conduit for his feelings about his island home and his own identity. His first surviving essay, written in April 1786, is a brief sketch of the history of Corsica.

Barely ten days later he produced a short essay on suicide, a stilted piece full of self-pity and self-dramatisation. 'Always alone while surrounded by people', he prefers to come home and indulge his melancholy. He wonders whether he should not end his life, as he can see no useful purpose for himself in this world. 'Since I must die one day, would it not be as well to kill myself?' he asks rhetorically. What does come through the verbiage is unhappiness at having recently suffered 'misfortunes' as a result of which life holds no pleasure for him, and a sense of disgust at the mediocrity and corruption of people, which has led him to despise the society in which he is obliged to live. Whether this was a response to some amorous rejection or social snub, or just an outburst of teenage angst, one can only speculate. It is not the expression of a deeper malaise. Less than a week later, on 9 May, he wrote an impassioned defence of Rousseau against the Swiss pastor Antoine Jacques Roustan's criticism of him. Rousseau's works exerted a profound influence on Napoleone's emotional development, and although he would later change his mind and deride Rousseau's sentimentality, he would never shake it off entirely.[5]

With Carlo gone, Napoleone had become the family's man in France, and it now fell to him to obtain places in various institutions for his siblings and petition on behalf of the family's interests. These were not looking good. The Salines had been only partly drained during Carlo's lifetime, and as only a fraction of the intended mulberry trees had been planted, the government had decided to stop throwing good money after bad. However, the Buonaparte had won their case for compensation for the Odone legacy in the form of Les Milleli. It was a fine property with a small house and olive groves above Ajaccio. But Napoleone's great-uncle Luciano was ill and incapacitated, and Joseph was proving incapable in practical matters. Aged seventeen, Napoleone was obliged to take over the management of the family's affairs. He applied for leave, and on 15 September 1786 was back in Ajaccio. His mother and Joseph were on the quayside to greet him, but the place was unfamiliar. He was seeing Corsica after an absence of seven years and nine months. He had left as a child, and returned a young man. He met for the first time four younger siblings: Louis aged eight, Maria Paolina six, Maria Nunziata three, and Geronimo only two. He even found it difficult speaking to them, as he had not used his Corsican Italian while he was away.[6]

Luciano had resigned his post as archdeacon, which was taken by Napoleone's half-uncle Joseph Fesch, but he had some money, which lent him weight in family affairs, and it was with Fesch and Joseph that he took charge of them. Napoleone applied for an extension of his leave and busied himself with the harvest, the family properties, and other practical matters.

During that time he got to know his family, not only his mother, whom he had seen just once briefly since he was nine, but also his siblings and the extended network of cousins, uncles, and aunts. He revisited his wet-nurse and others who had looked after him when he was little and spent much time with the ailing Luciano, whom he revered. He developed a relationship with his brother Joseph, who recalled with fondness their long walks along the coast, breathing in the scent of myrtle and orange blossom, sometimes returning home only after dark.

Napoleone explored the island and tried to acquaint himself with its people and their lore, of which he had only dim childhood memories. He was taken aback by primitive aspects of Corsican life that had not struck him when he was a child, but convinced himself that his fellow islanders were noble savages whose vices were the consequence of the barbarous French occupation. He had brought with him a trunk full of books, which no doubt sustained him and provided the moral and emotional arguments which would enable him to construct an appropriate vision of Corsica.[7]

He spent almost a year on the island and did not leave until 12 September 1787. He did not rejoin his regiment, but set off instead for Paris, where he hoped to obtain payment of the 3,000 livres of the subsidy still due for the Salines. It was a considerable sum, roughly equal to three years of his pay as a lieutenant. When he reached the capital he called on ministers and people of influence, probably including Loménie de Brienne, now minister of finances. He also went to great lengths to obtain a place at the seminary in Aix for his brother Lucien. An impecunious outsider in a city in which the aristocracy's wealth and privilege were on display, the provincial subaltern's social inhibitions could only have been aggravated by the need to beg for favour.[8]

When not petitioning ministers, he was reading, taking notes, and writing draughts of essays which display a critical attitude to the political system. In one, he argued that while Alexander the Great, Charlemagne, Machiavelli, and others were undoubtedly great men, they were driven by the desire to win acclaim, which made Leonidas, who had set out to lay down his life for his country unconditionally at the battle of Thermopylae, superior to them, a typically Romantic value judgement showing the influence of Rousseau and a tendency to reject the practical. It sat uneasily with his own instincts, if his brother Joseph is to be believed. He recalled that during one of their walks on Corsica Napoleone had told him he wished he could perform some great and noble act which would be recognised by posterity, and that he could, after his death, witness a representation of it 'and see what a poet such as the great Corneille would make me feel, think and say'. Such transference of the desire for recognition, normal in any teenager, suggests a disinclination or perhaps inability to engage with the world around him. A combination of awkwardness and disdain certainly marked his attitude to sex.[9]

On the evening of 21 November he went to see a play, and on leaving the theatre strolled through the Palais-Royal, the Paris residence of the Orléans branch of the royal family. It had extensive gardens at the back, flanked by arcades with shops, cafés, and small premises in which whores plied their trade. The higher-class ones sat at their windows beckoning to the passers-by, the next degree down would sit in the cafés, and the cheapest would loiter under the colonnade or along the avenues of the garden.[10]

The following morning, Napoleone sat down and described what happened next as though he were writing up a scientific experiment. 'My soul, agitated by the vigorous sentiments natural to it, made me bear the cold with indifference,' he wrote, 'but when my imagination cooled, I began to feel the rigours of the season and made for the arcades.' There a young girl caught his eye. She was obviously a prostitute but did not have the brazen manner of the others, and returned his look with modesty. 'Her timidity encouraged me and I addressed her…I who more than anyone else felt the horror of her kind, and had always felt myself sullied by a mere look from one….' In his account, he makes it clear that he was looking for someone 'who would be useful for the observations I wished to make'. He admits that previous attempts to pick up a prostitute had not been 'crowned with success', which might appear odd, as a young officer would not normally have difficulty carrying out such a transaction in the Palais-Royal. His record of their conversation goes some way to explain why: he began by asking how she came to her present condition, which was neither tactful nor to the point, and after more such banter on a freezing November night, it was she who suggested they go back to his lodgings, only to be asked what for. 'Well, we could warm ourselves and you could satisfy your fancy,' she answered. The clinical account does not mention whether the experience had been pleasurable or not.[11]

On 1 December, having obtained a six-month extension of his leave, Napoleone set off for Corsica once more. His efforts in Paris had come to nothing, which only contributed to his disenchantment with a state of affairs that seemed to exclude him as well as his native land, whose subjugation he was beginning to take personally. His vision of a noble nation oppressed by a wicked and corrupt France fitted well with a feeling that he and his family were being thwarted, or at least disrespected, by the regime in Paris.

He spent the next four and a half months in Corsica, and it was not until 14 June 1788 that he rejoined his regiment, now stationed at Auxonne, after an absence of twenty-one months. This was not unusual, as in peacetime officers were allowed to absent themselves for long periods.

Auxonne was a fortified town on the river Saône with an artillery school under the sixty-six-year-old lieutenant general baron Jean-Pierre du Teil, a clever and innovative commander who worked his men hard by setting them challenges that upset their routines. Du Teil took an immediate liking to Napoleone. He set him the task of designing and constructing earthworks, which involved calculations of firepower, resistance, and ballistics, followed by ten days of physical work, with Napoleone marshalling 200 men with picks and shovels. 'This extraordinary mark of favour earned me the ill-feeling of the captains who claimed it was insulting to them that a mere lieutenant be charged with such an important task and that if there were more than 50 men involved one of their rank should be in command,' he wrote to Joseph Fesch on 29 August. He nevertheless pacified them and even gained their friendship; considering him an intellectual, they tasked him with drawing up the *Calotte*, a regimental code of conduct. He rose to the challenge and produced a document that was both reasoned and idealistic, very much in the spirit of Rousseau, which could have been the constitution for a popular dictatorship.[12]

From his essays and notes it is clear that he was already a republican, having, like Rousseau, come to the conclusion that existing systems of government were absurd and that kings had no right to rule. In the introduction to what was to be a dissertation on royal authority, he argued that this was entirely 'usurped', since sovereignty resided in the people, adding that 'there are very few kings who have not deserved to be dethroned'. He also adopted Rousseau's thesis that religion was destructive, since it was in competition with the state as it held out the promise of happiness in another world, when it was for the state to provide people with the means to achieve it in this.[13]

He continued to read, annotating and commenting as he went, on subjects as varied as ancient and modern history, geography, the fiscal systems of different states, the role of artillery and ballistics,

Greek philosophy, Arab culture, biology, natural history, the possibility of digging a canal through the isthmus of Suez, and many more. That summer he read Richardson's *Clarissa* and Goethe's *Sorrows of Young Werther*, and himself wrote *Le Comte d'Essex*, a gothick novella about an imagined conspiracy against Charles I featuring ghosts, blood, and daggers, and *Le Masque Prophète*, a short piece set in the Arab world which is a kind of parable about dictatorship. The plots are melodramatic, the prose bristles with adjectives and metaphors, not to mention spelling mistakes, the characterisation is nonexistent.[14]

Auxonne lay in a marshy, misty part of the Burgundian plain, and Napoleone believed it was the insalubrious exhalations from the stagnant moat beyond the ramparts which brought him down with a fever that autumn, but it may in part have been a consequence of his lifestyle. He was economising on food in order to be able to send money home to his mother. He lived in barracks, in a small room with a bed, a table, six straw-seated chairs, and one armchair. He messed with the other officers, but although his lodgings were free, he was still only on the pay of second lieutenant, so he had to be careful. But there was also a manic element to his life at this time. 'I have no other resource here but work,' he wrote to his great-uncle Luciano in March 1789. 'I only get dressed once a week, I sleep very little since my illness. It is incredible. I go to bed at ten o'clock and get up at four in the morning. I only take one meal and dine at three; it suits my health very well.' He would keep the shutters closed to help his concentration. He did in fact go out, for, as he proudly explained in the same letter, 'I have gained quite a distinguished reputation in this little town with my speeches on various occasions.'[15]

The French monarchy was virtually bankrupt, and as a last resort to raise money the king called the Estates General. As this body, representing the clergy, the nobility, and the non-noble 'third estate', had not been summoned for nearly two centuries, this opened up a Pandora's box of questions about the nature of the government. All over the country people of every station aired their views and propounded solutions to the political crisis. This was accompanied by popular unrest, and on 1 April Napoleone was sent to the town of

Seurre with 100 men to suppress riots. The rebellious spirit inspired bad behaviour, and one day he was sent to the monastery of Citeaux to quell a mutiny by the monks. Over dinner a grateful abbot served him 'delicious wine' from the Clos Vougeot in the monastery cellar, which the monks had tried to raid. In a letter to Letizia, he described the sumptuous Easter dinner he was given by a local nobleman. 'But I would rather have been eating ravioli or lasagne in Ajaccio,' he concluded.[16]

He was in high spirits. His health had recovered, the weather was glorious, and he bathed in the Saône (once he got a cramp and nearly drowned). 'My friend, if my heart were susceptible to love, what a favourable moment this would be: fêted everywhere, treated with a respect that you could not imagine,' he wrote to Joseph, boasting, 'The prettiest women are delighted with our company.'[17]

Like most of his generation, he was in a state of excitement about political events. 'This year heralds some beginnings which will be very welcome to all right-thinking people,' he wrote to his proxy godfather Giubega from Auxonne in June, 'and after so many centuries of feudal barbarism and political slavery, it is wonderful to see the word Liberty inflame hearts which seemed corrupted by luxury, weakness and the arts.' But this raised questions closer to home. 'While France is being reborn, what will become of us, unfortunate Corsicans?' he asked. The moment seemed ripe for him to strike a blow for his island nation by publishing a history of Corsica, but he felt he needed the support or at least approval of Paoli, so he wrote to him in his London exile.[18]

'I was born as the fatherland was perishing,' he wrote. 'My eyes opened to the odious sight of 30,000 French who had been vomited onto our shores drowning the throne of liberty in rivers of blood. The screams of the dying, the moans of the oppressed, tears of despair surrounded my cradle from the moment of my birth.' There is some doubt as to the authenticity of this letter, as the original has never been found and there is no trace of a response from Paoli. But it would have been an odd one to forge, given Napoleone's later career, and the melodramatic style is in tune with his contemporary writings, most notably his *Nouvelle Corse*. This is a confused rant against the French, represented as irredeemably cruel and corrupt, with a plot derived from *Robinson Crusoe* and *Paul et Virginie*, so lurid and violent as to be incoherent, couched in a pornography of gore, rape, and mutilation, punctuated by flights of sentimentality.[19]

The history he had been planning for the past few years was finally taking shape in the form of *Lettres sur la Corse*, an emotional account of events up to the beginning of the eighteenth century which anthropomorphises the Corsican 'nation' in the fashion of the day. When the first two letters were finished he sent them to his former French teacher at Brienne, the Abbé Dupuy, asking him to edit them. As well as rewriting whole passages, Dupuy delivered a withering verdict, suggesting in the politest terms that he cut out all the 'metaphysical' content.[20]

On 15 July, Napoleone was in the process of writing to his great-uncle Luciano when two brother officers came into the room with the news they had just received from Paris about a riot having got out of hand and the mob having stormed the Bastille. Whatever his feelings about the monarchy, he was alarmed at the disorders. Four days later, riots broke out in Auxonne, and in a letter to Joseph he expressed contempt for the 'populace' and the 'assortment of brigands from outside who had come to pillage' the customs house and the tax gatherer's office. Nor was he impressed by the attitude of his own men, who showed reluctance to quell the riot. On the night of 21 July he acted as the general's aide, marshalling troops against the rioters. While he claims to have brought matters under control with a forty-five-minute harangue (which sounds unlikely given his oratorical skills), he makes no bones about his frustration at not being allowed to fire on the mob, a profound distaste for which shines through his account.[21]

He was nevertheless excited by the developments. 'All over France blood has flowed,' he wrote to Joseph on 8 August, 'but almost everywhere it was the impure blood of the enemies of Liberty and the Nation.' His commander had put him in charge of a group of officers with the brief of studying the possibilities of firing bombs from siege pieces, and he wrote up its report diligently, but his thoughts were elsewhere. He had applied for long leave, meaning to go to Corsica and play a part in whatever might take place there. Both his feelings and his ambition drew him there: the ideal of the island nation he had nourished over the past few years beckoned, as did the fact that there he could play a more prominent part than in France.[22]

On 16 August his regiment mutinied. The soldiers confronted their officers demanding they hand over the regimental chest, which they were obliged to do. The soldiers then got drunk and tried to fraternise with the officers, forcing them to drink with them. Napoleone's thoughts are not recorded, but there can be little doubt as to what they were. When, a few days later, the regiment went on parade to swear a new oath, to the Nation, the King, and the Law, he was probably thinking of another nation. His request for leave had been granted, and in the first days of September he left Auxonne for Corsica.[23]

5

Corsica

NAPOLEONE REACHED AJACCIO at the end of September 1789. Apart from Maria-Anna, who was still at Saint-Cyr, the whole family was there. Joseph had a judicial post in the city, but Lucien, who had abandoned a military career because of poor eyesight and then given a clerical one a try, was idling, along with Louis. Their prospects in France had faded and they were reduced to Corsica once more. Napoleone intended to play a part in the island's affairs, but the political scene was not quite as he had imagined.

There had been riots in the coastal cities in the wake of events in France, but there was no impetus for revolution, since none of the grievances which motivated it in France resonated in Corsica, where feudal privilege and class differences were not major issues. Here, the conflict was between the separatists and those who had thrown in their lot with France, and between rival clans. In the early summer of 1789 a Corsican assembly had sent four deputies to the Estates General at Versailles: Matteo Buttafocco representing the nobility, the Abbé Peretti the clergy, and the lawyer Cristoforo Saliceti and Captain Pietro Paulo Colonna Cesari the third estate. The only thing uniting them was resentment of the French administration. Even the French loyalists Buttafocco and Peretti wanted the island administered by its inhabitants, meaning their own sort. The representatives of the third estate, Saliceti and Cesari, belonged to a faction describing themselves as 'patriots', some of whom wanted greater autonomy or even independence, others integration into France.

The Estates General had transformed itself into a National Assembly, and this would decide Corsica's future. On 17 June 1789 Saliceti and Cesari appealed to it demanding that Corsica be governed by a committee of locals and the formation of a native civic guard on the model of those which had sprung up all over France. Meanwhile, a rash of opportunistic disturbances covered the island as latent gripes were voiced and scores settled. On 14 August the assembly which had chosen the deputies to the Estates General set up a revolutionary municipal authority in Bastia. The following day the festivities of the Assumption of the Virgin in Ajaccio resulted in the formation of a 'patriotic committee' there, with Joseph as secretary (since he was the only one of them who could read and write French). Napoleone assumed that the next step would be the formation of a civic guard, and with another young enthusiast, Carlo Andrea Pozzo di Borgo, went about distributing tricolour cockades to be worn as a mark of solidarity with the Revolution in France and encouraging people to form a citizens' militia.

On 17 October the National Assembly, which had by then transferred from Versailles to Paris, decided against allowing Corsica its own assembly and civic guard, on grounds of cost. Napoleone composed a letter of protest, signed by all the revolutionary activists in Ajaccio. He continued to agitate, and on 30 November his appeal demanding for Corsica the same rights enjoyed by the rest of France was read out to the National Assembly in Paris. It was backed by Saliceti and supported by the revolutionary tribune Mirabeau, and in one of those moments of wild enthusiasm characteristic of the early days of the Revolution, Corsica was integrated into the French nation and all those who had fought against the French were amnestied. Paoli was invited to leave London and come to Paris, where he would be welcomed as a hero before travelling on to Corsica. There were celebrations with the *Te Deum* sung in the island's churches, and Napoleone hung a banner on the façade of the Buonaparte house bearing the inscription '*Vive la Nation! Vive Paoli! Vive Mirabeau!*'[1]

The words encapsulated a confusion as to which 'nation' Napoleone now associated with. 'This young officer was brought up at the École Militaire, his sister is at Saint-Cyr, his mother has been showered with benefactions by the government,' the French commander in Ajaccio wrote to the minister of war in Paris, adding that he should be with his regiment instead of stirring up trouble in Corsica. But Napoleone was not recalled, and the question of his allegiance would be complicated further with the arrival on the island of Paoli.[2]

The Babbo was preceded by various of his followers returning from exile whose sufferings in the cause endowed them with a sense of self-righteousness that led them to call into question the loyalty of those who, like the Buonaparte, had accommodated themselves to French rule. This made it incumbent on the Buonaparte brothers to demonstrate their devotion to the Corsican cause. They took down a portrait of Marbeuf which hung in their drawing room and hid it, but it was not clear where they stood.[3]

As Napoleone was writing his violently anti-French history of Corsica at the time, one must assume he still considered himself a Corsican patriot rather than a Frenchman. But given the uncertainties of the situation, he had to hedge his bets and remember that he had a career in the French army. His immediate priority was to secure position and influence. In February 1790 the two brothers agitated for the election of their friend Jean Jérôme Levie as mayor of Ajaccio, and of Joseph to the municipal council (which entailed archdeacon Fesch falsifying his birth certificate to make him of eligible age).[4]

The next step was to get Joseph elected to the general assembly which was to meet at Orezza to set up an administration for the island. Joseph was successful, and Napoleone accompanied him as they set off on horseback on 12 April, but on arrival they found themselves looked on askance by many of Paoli's faithful. Napoleone expressed anti-French feelings and wrote an appeal demanding that all Frenchmen be expelled from the island. He befriended Filippo Buonarotti, a revolutionary and supporter of Paoli from Tuscany, and Filippo Masseria, Paoli's right-hand man who had been sent ahead from London (and was a British agent). He also wrote to his commanding officer asking for an extension of leave, citing health reasons.[5]

None of this did much to enhance his credibility with Paoli's henchmen at Corte, but it did affect his standing in Ajaccio, and when the two brothers returned they faced the enmity of the more conservative inhabitants. In the first days of May, while strolling on the Olmo they were attacked by a gang led by a local priest, but were saved by the appearance of a bandit of their acquaintance. They managed to mobilise their suporters in the Borgo, and on 25 June all French officials were expelled from Ajaccio.[6]

Joseph was one of those selected to meet Paoli on his way from Paris and accompany him back to his native island, where they landed on 14 July 1790. Napoleone and others from Ajaccio met him at Bastia on 4 August, and the two brothers joined some 500 supporters who rode with him on his triumphal progress to Corte.[7]

The General of the Corsican Nation was sixty-five and marked by twenty-one years of exile in London, during which he had grown to appreciate the merits of monarchy. Although it was the Revolution that gave him back his homeland, he was no revolutionary. On 8 September he opened a congress at Orezza which he packed with his family and supporters. Over the next three weeks this reorganised the administration of the island, giving him unlimited executive power, overall command of the National Guard, and a considerable income. This was out of tune with what was being done in Paris, and many of the measures taken were against the law, given that Corsica was now a department of France.

Napoleone was not put off by such high-handed methods. Thanks to Paoli's favour, Joseph had obtained a seat in the congress and the presidency of the district of Ajaccio. And although he did not benefit personally, Napoleone supported Paoli, accusing anyone who showed less than full commitment of being 'bad citizens', and suggesting to Carlo Andrea Pozzo di Borgo the physical removal of three officials whose zeal he found wanting. 'The means are violent, possibly illegal, but indispensable,' he insisted. He considered that Paoli was still placing too much trust in democracy and felt he should be more ruthless.[8]

Napoleone's leave was running out, so at the end of October he sailed for France. His ship was twice driven back by gales, and it was not until the end of January 1791 that he would finally make it off the island. In the meantime, he remained politically active. On 6 January, along with Joseph, Lucien, and Joseph Fesch he took part in the opening session of the Globbo Patriotico, the Patriotic Club of

49

Ajaccio, affiliated to the extreme revolutionary Jacobin Club of Paris. Napoleone attended regularly, making frequent speeches. He was at his most fervent when it came to denouncing Buttafocco and Peretti, who had been agitating in Paris against Paoli. Napoleone wrote a pamphlet titled *Lettre à Buttafoco* in which he denounced the deputy as a traitor and blamed him for all the blood spilt by the French in Corsica. He read the letter out in the club, where it was enthusiastically received, with a vote that a hundred copies be printed.[9]

When Napoleone did eventually sail for France, he took with him his younger brother Louis. The boy was twelve years old and unlikely to obtain an education if he were left in Ajaccio, and as there was no money to send him to a proper school, Napoleone decided to take this in hand himself.

On 12 February he was back with his regiment at Auxonne. He took two small rooms in the town, one for himself and one for Louis. 'He is studying hard, learning to read and write French, and I am teaching him mathematics and geography,' Napoleone wrote to Joseph on 24 April. 'He will be a fine fellow. All the ladies here are in love with him. He has adopted a slightly French manner, correct and elegant; he goes into society, greets people with grace, makes the usual small talk with the gravity and dignity of a man of thirty. I have no doubt that he will be the best fellow of the four of us.' He did not mention that young Louis sometimes required a thrashing to encourage him.[10]

On their journey from the south coast Napoleone had rejoiced in the revolutionary ardour he witnessed everywhere. Passing through Valence he attended a session of the local revolutionary club, and on 8 February in a letter to Joseph Fesch he assured him that the whole country was behind the Revolution, and that the only royalists he had met were women. 'It is not surprising,' he quipped. 'Liberty is a woman more beautiful who eclipses them.' This reflection seems to have prompted him to scribble some thoughts for an essay on the subject of love, which, he maintained, was an entirely superfluous emotion.[11]

He was welcomed at Auxonne by his friend des Mazis and his commanding officer du Teil, but many of his brother officers gave him a chilly reception when he began to voice his opinions. In its first stages, the Revolution had been welcomed by most educated

Frenchmen, and certainly by young officers in provincial regiments, who resented the aristocracy's monopoly over higher ranks. The abolition of noble rank itself in June 1790 removed all barriers to advancement, but it was not well received by all, and subsequent developments turned many against the way the Revolution was going. Napoleone's revolutionary enthusiasm grated on them, and his obsession with Corsica would not have won him much sympathy.

He was busy seeing to the printing of his *Lettre à Buttafocco*, of which he sent copies to the National Assembly in Paris and to Paoli in Corsica. He was hoping to complete and publish his history of Corsica and wrote to Paoli requesting access to his archive. Paoli was dismissive, describing the pamphlet as a pointless gesture, and not only failed to comply with Napoleone's request for access to his papers but let off the parting shot that history should not be written by young people, making it clear he considered him immature.[12]

In the process of reorganising the army, the National Assembly replaced the names of artillery regiments with numbers, and that of La Fère now became the First. Napoleone was transferred to the Fourth, formerly the regiment of Grenoble, now based at Valence, in which he was posted first lieutenant. He left Auxonne on 14 June and reached Valence two days later, moving into the same rooms he had occupied before and messing at the same inn. Madame du Colombier and her daughter had left the area, but many of the friends he had made during his previous sojourn were still there. Mademoiselle de Lauberbie de Saint-Germain, with whom he had flirted before, had in the meantime married Jean-Pierre Bachasson de Montalivet, an intelligent man whom Napoleone befriended.

Having settled in, Napoleone composed *Dialogue sur l'amour*, a Platonic discourse addressed to des Mazis, who was wont to fall in love and then extol the condition's joys and sufferings to Napoleone. In it he admitted to having been in love himself, but argued that what was at bottom a simple sensation had been garlanded with too many 'metaphysical definitions'. 'I believe it to be harmful to society, to the individual happiness of mankind, and I believe that love does more harm than good,' he argued, 'and that it would be a blessing if some protective divinity were to rid us of it and deliver the world from it.' It seemed absurd to him that men, 'this sex which is master of the world through its strength, its industry, its mind and other faculties, should find its supreme felicity in languishing in the chains of a weak passion and under the sway of a being more feeble than itself in mind and body.' He might have jettisoned the sentimentality of *La Nouvelle Héloïse*, but Napoleone was still a child of Rousseau in believing that man's first duty is to society and the state.[13]

The nature of the French state was being transformed, testing allegiances and polarising society. A few days after his arrival, news reached Valence of the king's attempt to flee the country and arrest at Varennes near the border with the Austrian Netherlands on the night of 21 June 1791. Back in October 1789 Louis XVI had been obliged by a mob of women to leave Versailles and move to Paris. He and his family effectively became prisoners in the royal palace of the Tuileries, and the increasing hostility of the Paris mob precipitated a decision to flee. This was seen as a betrayal, since his intention had been to join the anti-revolutionary forces gathering against France at Koblenz in Germany under his younger brother, the comte d'Artois.

Napoleone had joined the Club des Amis de la Constitution, of which he soon became secretary, at whose meetings he made republican speeches. On 14 July, as his regiment paraded to celebrate the second anniversary of the fall of the Bastille, the officers and men swore a new oath of loyalty, to the National Assembly. A *Te Deum* was sung and at a banquet that evening Lieutenant Buonaparte was among those raising republican toasts. Not wishing to perjure themselves by taking an oath which overrode that pledging loyalty to the king, many of his brother officers resigned their commissions, and some would cross the frontier to join the royalist forces. Napoleone felt no such scruples. In his cherished narrative of a Corsica violated by the French, the monarch was the incarnation of the archenemy, and since he had begun to develop a more positive attitude to France, the king drew the residue of his negative feelings.

Having to support both himself and Louis, Napoleone was short of money, and it was partly the prize of 1,200 francs (more than his annual pay) that induced him to enter a competition announced by the Académie of Lyon for an essay on the theme of 'Which truths and which sentiments it is most necessary to inculcate in people in order to ensure their happiness'. In the event, neither he nor any of the other fifteen applicants won the prize, as the jury found their efforts wanting. One of its members described Napoleone's essay as a wild dream, and another commented, 'It may be the work of a man of some sensibility, but it is too poorly ordered, too disparate, too rambling and too badly written to hold the attention.' It is indeed pompous, florid, full of cultural references and recherché words (he had made a list of them before starting), but it is nevertheless a fascinating document.[14]

It bristles with contradictions as Napoleone's libertarian instincts jostle with an authoritarian urge to order things for the best. He prefaces it with some verses by Pope to the effect that man is born to enjoy life and be happy, and opens with the sentence: 'At his birth, man acquires the right to that portion of the fruits of the earth which are necessary to his existence.' He rages against those such as profiteers who stand in the way of this, and against authority in general. He stipulates that everyone should have their portion of land and the full protection of the law, and that people should be allowed to say and write what they like. Yet the law should direct people according to the rules of reason and logic, and protect them from 'bad' and 'perverted' ideas, which should not be permitted to circulate in word or in print. Intriguingly, he identifies ambition as the principal scourge of mankind, above all 'the ambition which overthrows states and private fortunes, which feeds on blood and crime; the ambition which inspired Charles V, Philip II, Louis XIV', which he sees as an 'unruly passion, a violent and unthinking delirium', since 'Ambition is never satisfied, even at the pinnacle of greatness.' Although he rejects Rousseau's premise of man's natural goodness in favour of a more cynical view of human nature, he indulges the noble savage myth and holds up Paoli as a paragon of virtue who had revived the spirit of Athens and Sparta.[15]

Having managed to obtain leave once more, Napoleone was back in Ajaccio by the beginning of October 1791. He canvassed for Joseph, who was seeking election to represent Corsica at the Legislative Assembly which was to meet in Paris (the National Assembly had dissolved itself). But Paoli placed his favoured candidates, and Joseph was rewarded with no more than a local post at Corte. Paoli showed ambivalence with regard to the Buonaparte clan, and particularly to Napoleone, who wore a French uniform and was beginning to behave more like a French Jacobin than a Corsican patriot.[16]

Although Paoli had sworn loyalty to the French nation before the National Assembly in Paris on 22 April 1790, he had regarded the French as the enemy for so long that it was difficult for him to trust them. As well as being a monarchist, he was a devout Catholic and a friend of the clergy, who had backed him and sheltered his partisans. The Revolution's disestablishment of the Church and persecution of the clergy was as offensive to him as to most Corsicans.

Only a couple of weeks after Napoleone's arrival, on 16 October, his great-uncle Luciano died. Hardly had he breathed his last than his nephews and nieces groped under his mattress and then ransacked the room in search of the money they assumed he had squirrelled away. It turned out there was little left, as Luciano had been obliged to dig into his savings to pay Carlo's debts. But Joseph managed to persuade the administration (of which he was a member) to reimburse the money Carlo had invested in the Salines over the years. The funds were invested in a number of properties confiscated from the Church, the royal domain, and the nobility which were being sold off as *biens nationaux*, 'national assets'. It seems that in order to scotch rumours of malversation, the Buonaparte brothers put about the story that they had found a fortune under Luciano's mattress.[17]

While Joseph grafted at Corte, Napoleone obtained a command in the National Guard of Ajaccio, which relieved him from having to report back to his regular unit. But a new law stipulated that officers below the rank of lieutenant colonel must leave the National Guard and rejoin their units. Determined to remain in Corsica, he decided to try for that rank. He would have to dispute it with two formidable candidates. One was Mateo Pozzo di Borgo, a member of the most powerful clan in Ajaccio and brother of Carlo Andrea, Paoli's trusted collaborator and currently a deputy to the Legislative Assembly in Paris. The other, Giovanni Peraldi, an infantry captain, was equally well connected, and his brother Marius was the other Corsican deputy in Paris.

Napoleone spent most of February 1792 at Corte, ostensibly as guide and amanuensis to the visiting philosopher Constantin de

Volney, but in fact probably trying to obtain Paoli's favour. His behaviour was not calculated to engage it: he was hyperactive, attending political gatherings and holding discussions with people in the street, voicing extreme views and calling for action. He did not cut a convincing figure. Although he was now twenty-two he looked much younger, and people made jokes about his small stature. According to one source, when he challenged Peraldi to a duel, the other did not bother to turn up.[18]

As the elections to the colonelcies of the Ajaccio battalions approached, Napoleone was back at home canvassing. All comers were welcomed into the Buonaparte home to dine. Mattresses were laid out on the floor for supporters from the interior, who would be useful in swaying the national guards, most of whom were also from the country, and it was they who would elect the officers. The opposition also canvassed, but they had not taken into account the determination of the Buonaparte.

The election, set for 1 April, was to be presided over by three commissioners, who arrived in Ajaccio two days before. One, Grimaldi, was lodged with the Buonaparte; another, Quenza, stayed with Letizia's Ramolino family; but the third, Murati, had accepted the hospitality of the Peraldi. On the eve of the election Napoleone sent one of his henchmen from Bocognano, a patriotic bandit who had fought with Paoli against the French, to the Peraldi house with his gang of cut-throats. They burst in while the household were at dinner and kidnapped the commissioner, bundling him off to the Buonaparte house, where his protests were countered by Napoleone with the assurance that he only wished to preserve his independence of judgement from the influence of the Peraldi.[19]

In the morning, the 500 or so national guards gathered to elect their officers. Pozzo di Borgo and Peraldi were shouted down, and in a travesty of procedure Giovanni Battista Quenza was elected commanding officer, with Napoleone as lieutenant colonel and second in command. The celebrations in the Buonaparte home that evening were accompanied by a military band.

The following day Colonel Maillard, commander of the French garrison of Ajaccio, inspected Napoleone's volunteers, but the presence of the two forces in the town made for tension. Just as tense were relations between the generally conservative citizens, who saw in the French regulars a guarantee of stability, and the volunteers, most of them wild men from the hills. On the afternoon of 8 April a quarrel developed between some girls playing skittles on the Olmo, and as on-lookers and passers-by took sides, insults began to fly which had nothing to do with the original dispute. Shots were fired and Napoleone went out to restore order, but more people spilled out into the streets in a confused outburst of animosities. After one of his officers had been killed, Napoleone was obliged to retire to the safety of the former seminary, where his men were stationed. Quenza and he agreed that the insurgency justified retaliation, and they began shooting at any of the townsfolk who came within range. The fighting gradually turned into a chaotic brawl with guns as private scores were settled. Napoleone tried to exploit the crisis by requesting permission from Maillard to take refuge with his men in the citadel, which aroused the Frenchman's suspicion, and the following day Maillard ordered the volunteers to withdraw from Ajaccio. Napoleone insisted they remain, and again attempted to gain admittance to the citadel—he even tried to subvert the soldiers by denouncing their colonel as an '*aristo*'.

Hearing of the disturbances, the authorities in Corte despatched commissioners to find out what was going on. Napoleone set off to meet them in order to tell the facts his way and wrote up a version justifying himself. After a cursory examination of the circumstances, the commissioners had a number of citizens arrested and ordered Napoleone and his volunteers to leave Ajaccio. He duly led them off on 16 April, and intended to go to Corte himself to explain, but he could not expect a welcome there. Paoli's verdict on the events at Ajaccio was that one could expect nothing less when 'inexperienced little boys are placed in command of the national guards'. He had had enough of the Buonaparte. 'The General returned here yesterday evening, he is badly disposed towards me; I saw him this morning, we had an argument, and all is over,' Joseph wrote to his brother, urging him to go to Paris as soon as he could to justify himself before the government.[20]

6

France or Corsica

NAPOLEONE HAD MUCH explaining to do when he reached Paris two weeks later, at the end of May 1792. More than one damning report of his activities in Ajaccio had reached the capital, and he had been denounced in the Legislative Assembly by the Corsican deputies Carlo Maria Pozzo di Borgo and Marius Peraldi, no friends of the Buonaparte since the National Guard elections in which their brothers had been trounced. Peraldi had made up his mind that the family had 'never, under whatever regime, had any merit other than spying, treachery, vice, impudence and prostitution'. Pozzo di Borgo was more amenable, and Napoleone managed to placate him.[1]

Napoleone also needed to placate the War Ministry, since he had overstayed his leave and could be classed as a deserter. Fortunately for him, war had broken out against Austria barely a month before, and since the emigration of thousands of officers had left a shortage, the ministry was not about to deprive the army of a trained officer on account of a squabble between small-town Corsicans. Colonel Maillard's denunciation was passed to the Ministry of Justice, and although this had received similar unfavourable reports from other quarters, the matter rested there.[2]

The day after his arrival in Paris, on 29 May, Napoleone unexpectedly met an old friend from Brienne, Fauvelet de Bourrienne. Bourrienne had not pursued a military career but had joined the diplomatic service, which took him to Vienna and Warsaw, and he was now at a loose end. The two young men teamed up, sharing what little money they had and thinking up ways of making some more. Napoleone also found friendship at the home of his mother's childhood friend Panoria Permon, a beautiful woman of doubtful virtue who presided over what appears to have been something of a gaming house in which she received Corsicans and others.[3]

On 16 June he visited his sister Maria-Anna at Saint-Cyr. 'She is tall, well-formed, has learned to sew, read, write, dress her hair, dance and also a few words of history,' he reported to Joseph Fesch, but he was worried that she had lost touch with her roots and become 'an aristocrat', and feared that if she had known he was a supporter of the Revolution she would never have agreed to see him. But his own attitude to the Revolution was about to be tested.[4]

A couple of days later, on 20 June, he met up with Bourrienne for lunch at a restaurant in the rue Saint-Honoré. On coming out they saw a crowd of several thousand men and women armed with pikes, axes, swords, guns, and sticks making for the Tuileries. They followed and took up position on the terrace of the Tuileries gardens, from which they watched as the mob surged up to the palace, broke down the doors, overpowered the National Guards on duty, and swept inside. Napoleone could not hide his indignation, and when he saw the king submitting to don a red cap of liberty and appear at the window to drink the health of the people, he exploded. 'Che coglione!' he reportedly exclaimed, disgusted that nobody had prevented the rabble from storming the palace, and declared that if he had been the king things would have turned out differently. He kept returning to the subject, making pessimistic prognoses for the future. 'When one sees all this close up one has to admit that the people are hardly worth the trouble we take to win their favour,' he wrote to Lucien two weeks later, adding that the scenes he had witnessed made their scrape in Ajaccio look like child's play.[5]

A week later, on 10 July, he was reintegrated into the artillery with the rank of captain and awarded six months' back-pay. Although he was ordered to rejoin his regiment, he was in two minds as to what course to take. He had put the finishing touches to his *Lettres sur la Corse*, which was now ready for the printer, but as he admitted to Joseph, the political context was unfavourable. He was beginning to think that his future might lie in France and advised Joseph to get himself elected to the Legislative Assembly in Paris, as Corsica was becoming peripheral. At the same time, he urged him to encourage Lucien to remain close to Paoli. 'It is more likely than ever that this will all end in our gaining independence,' he wrote, suggesting they keep their options open.[6]

Lucien failed to get taken on as a secretary to Paoli. He was seventeen, exalted and rebellious. His spirit was, as he put it himself in a letter to Joseph, gripped by boundless 'enthusiasm'; he had looked inside himself and was 'developing' his character in a 'strongly pronounced way'. His soul had been set on fire by reading the immensely fashionable Edward Young's poem *Night Thoughts on Life, Death and Immortality*, and he had been inspired to discover his identity through writing. He was composing a poem about Brutus, and his pen flew over the paper 'with astonishing velocity'. 'I correct little; I do not like rules which restrain genius and I do not observe any,' he wrote. He had also embraced the most radical revolutionary ideals. He assured Joseph that he 'felt the courage to kill tyrants' and would rather die with a dagger in his hand than in a bed surrounded by priestly 'farce'.[7]

Warned by his younger brother Louis that Lucien was about to take a step that 'might well compromise the general interest of the family', Napoleone wrote to him more than once, trying to restrain him. Lucien was having none of it. He resented Napoleone's dominant influence, accusing him of having fallen for the courtly attractions of Paris, and expressed his resentment at being told what to do in an impassioned letter to Joseph on 24 June, couched in the obligatory revolutionary idiom. 'He seems to me to be well suited to being a tyrant and I think that he would be one if he were a king, and that his name would be one of horror for posterity and for the sensitive patriot,' he wrote, casting himself as a 'pure' revolutionary and Napoleone as one who had sold out. 'I believe him capable of being a turncoat....'[8]

Napoleone was in fact switching allegiance. He had nourished a vision of himself as the champion of a noble persecuted nation and its heroic leader Paoli, demonising France, on which he heaped responsibility for every ill. But over the past couple of years he had acquainted himself with that downtrodden nation and found it was less innocent than in his dreams. Its heroic leader turned out to be just as unprincipled and tyrannical as any other ruler—and had failed to accord Napoleone the recognition he felt to be his due. Meanwhile, the demonic France had been reborn as the torchbearer for everything he had come to believe in. Viewed from Paris, Corsica was beginning to look small and mean. On 7 August Napoleone wrote to Joseph that he had made up his mind to remain in France. In its present financial condition, the family would benefit from his rejoining his regiment: at least one member would be drawing a salary. There was a war on, and sooner or later he would get the chance to gain promotion. But only three days later something occurred which changed his mind.[9]

On 10 August he was roused at his lodgings on the rue du Mail near the Place des Victoires by the sound of the tocsin. Hearing that the Tuileries Palace was being stormed, he set off for the place du Carrousel, where Bourrienne's brother had a furniture shop, from where he would be able to see what was going on. 'Before I reached the Carrousel I encountered in the rue des Petits-Champs a group of hideous men bearing a head on the end of a pike,' he reminisced many years later. 'Seeing me passably well dressed and looking like a gentleman, they accosted me and made me shout *Vive la Nation!*, which I readily did, as one can imagine.'[10]

A mob numbering some 20,000 armed with guns, pikes, axes, knives, and even spits had attacked the Tuileries, which were defended by 900 men of the Swiss Guards and a hundred or so courtiers and nobles. The king and his family fled to the protection of the Legislative Assembly, but the defenders of the palace were butchered. When it was over, Napoleone ventured into the palace gardens, where people were finishing off the wounded and mutilating their bodies in obscene ways. 'Never since has any of my battlefields struck me by the number of dead bodies as did the mass of the Swiss, maybe on account of the constricted space or perhaps because it was the first time I had seen anything like it,' he recalled. 'I saw even quite well dressed women commit the most extreme indecencies on the bodies of the Swiss guards.' Napoleone was terrified as well as horrified and never shed his fear of the mob.[11]

He was not going to remain in Paris to watch the slide into anarchy, and he could not afford to leave his sister in an institution that identified her as a noblewoman. On 31 August he went to Saint-Cyr to collect Maria-Anna and brought her to Paris. On 2 September mobs began breaking into prisons and slaughtering the inmates in reaction to a declaration by the Duke of Brunswick, commander of the allied army marching into France to restore the monarchy, in which he vowed to deal severely with the population of the French capital if the king or any of his family were harmed. The massacre of aristocrats, priests, and others detained for one reason or another went on for five days, and it was only on 9 September that Napoleone and his sister were able to leave Paris. They stopped at Marseille just long enough to collect his pay arrears, and on 10 October, by which time the monarchy had been abolished and France declared a republic, the two siblings embarked at Toulon, reaching Ajaccio five days later. Napoleone promptly set off for Corte, hoping to restore the Buonaparte clan to favour.

Paoli may have been a dictator, but his attempts to set up an efficient executive had failed. The culture of the island had been profoundly affected by French rule: the influx of specie upended a system in which the majority of the population had never previously held a coin, while the creation of a salaried administration launched a rush for official posts which opened up new fields for conflict between rival clans and tempting prospects for corruption. Most of those in office were more concerned with score-settling, nepotism, and profiteering than running the country. It was they who would acquire the *biens nationaux* being sold off: these made up 12 percent of the land surface of the island, but only 500 out of a population of 150,000 were able to benefit. This altered the previously egalitarian pattern of land ownership, while newly introduced regulations impinged on unwritten age-old grazing and gathering rights, leading to disputes and banditry on a scale no government could control.[12]

Paoli was not well and was unable to exercise the same authority as in the past. His relationship with France was strained, and he could not but be wary of those who identified with that country or with the Revolution. He viewed the Buonaparte brothers with mistrust. He had dismissed Joseph, whom he regarded as too ambitious for his merits, and had refused to take on the hot-headed Lucien as secretary. When Napoleone appeared in Corte hoping for a senior command, Paoli brushed him off with vague promises and sent him back to Ajaccio to await orders in connection with an impending invasion of Sardinia.

The idea had been mooted in Paris more than a year before. The island was only a few hours' sailing from Corsica. It was rich in grain and cattle, which the French government needed to feed its armies, and it was assumed that its people needed liberating. Its ruling dynasty, the house of Savoy, also reigned over Piedmont and Savoy and had joined the coalition against France.

The invasion was to be carried out by a combined force of French regulars, volunteers from Marseille, and Corsican National Guards. At the end of October, a few days after Napoleone's return from Corte, the French naval squadron carrying the regulars and a detachment of volunteers dropped anchor off Ajaccio. Its commander, Rear-Admiral Laurent Truguet, was received by the principal families of the town, who entertained him with dinners and dances. The forty-year-old sailor was a frequent guest at the Buonaparte house, having taken a fancy to the sixteen-year-old Maria-Anna. Accompanying him on his flagship was Charles Huguet de Sémonville, on his way to take up the post of ambassador in Constantinople. He too was courted by the Buonaparte family, and he agreed to take Lucien along as his secretary. According to Lucien, Napoleone contemplated going east too, to take service with the British in India, calculating that his professional credentials would provide the chance for a command that would give him the opportunity of achieving great things. In the meantime, he nearly met his end on the streets of Ajaccio.[13]

When allowed off their ships, the French troops roamed the city picking fights. On 15 December a force of volunteers from Marseille sailed in. It was made up of the dregs of the city's port, and three days later they teamed up with some of the regulars and began lynching people they accused of being 'aristos', including members of the Corsican National Guard, mutilating their bodies and parading them around town before dumping them in the harbour. Order was restored with some difficulty, but in January 1793 a further contingent of volunteers sailed in and Napoleone was only saved from being lynched by some of his guardsmen.

On 18 February, to the relief of the people of Ajaccio, the expedition sailed. Napoleone was in command of a small artillery section under his colleague Quenza. The expedition had been divided into two forces, the larger of which, composed of French regulars, was to attack Cagliari, the capital of Sardinia, while the smaller, made up mostly of Corsican volunteers, took the island of Maddalena off the island's north coast. This force, commanded by Colonna Cesari, consisted of the corvette *La Fauvette* and a number of troop transports. Unfavourable winds pushed the flotilla back, and it was only four days later that it sailed, landing on Maddalena on 23 February. The Sardinian garrison took refuge in the small town of Maddalena. Napoleone set up a battery which began bombarding the place into submission, and after two days it was on the point of surrendering. But the crew of *La Fauvette* decided to sail home, and Cesari was obliged to order immediate withdrawal, with instructions to jettison guns and other heavy equipment. Napoleone and Quenza had to scramble back to the boats, whose crews had been seized by panic. The flotilla was back in Corsica by 28 February.

Napoleone wasted no time in covering his own back. He wrote up a detailed account of the events for Paoli; another, critical of Cesari and by extension Paoli, for the minister of war in Paris; and signed another jointly with the other officers who had taken part, in which he defended Cesari. It was not as easy to defend himself from more direct threats, and he was on the point of being lynched as an 'aristo' by sailors from *La Fauvette* when a group of his own men delivered him.[14]

In Paris, Saliceti had been putting it about that Paoli was no longer fit to rule and that his clan was embezzling on a gigantic scale. The Convention, which had replaced the National Assembly, decided to investigate and designated three commissioners with Saliceti at their head to travel to Corsica. Their official brief was to see to the defence of the island against a potential attack by the Royal Navy, as the international situation had become critical. King Louis XVI had been guillotined on 21 January, which shocked public opinion across Europe and broadened support for the coalition of Austria, Prussia, Spain, and Sardinia already fighting France. On 1 February France declared war on Britain and the Netherlands. Paoli's monarchist and Anglophile sympathies were no secret in Paris. The Convention ordered the four battalions of Corsican National Guards to be disbanded and replaced by French regulars, and it placed all the forces on the island under the command of a French general.

On 14 March, Lucien, who had accompanied Sémonville back to Toulon when he was recalled, made a speech in the local Société Patriotique denouncing Paoli. He may have been put up to it by some of Paoli's enemies gathered in Toulon, and he would later claim that he did not really know what he was saying. Nevertheless, on 2 April his speech was read out to the Convention in Paris, which only the day before had received news that the commander of the French army facing the Austrians, General Dumouriez, had defected to the enemy. Seeing treason everywhere, it issued a decree outlawing Paoli and ordering his arrest.[15]

Saliceti and the other two commissioners were still riding at anchor in the Golfe Juan awaiting favourable winds when they heard the news and wrote to Paris asking for the decree to be suspended while they investigated. It was not until the beginning of April that they reached Bastia, where they were joined by Joseph Buonaparte. Given the intricate web of alliances, enmities, and motivations spread over the island, and that almost everyone involved later destroyed and doctored documents, falsified evidence, and spun colourful tales, it is impossible to be certain what the commissioners intended. Saliceti probably hoped to maintain Paoli but replace those around him with his own clan and associates, in which category he may have included the Buonaparte.[16]

On 18 April news of the Convention's decree outlawing Paoli reached the island. Paoli tried to calm tempers and sent two delegates to the Convention to justify himself, but Corsican patriots were in uproar, demanding war with France. Napoleone was in Ajaccio, where he wrote a defence of Paoli, which he personally posted on walls around town with a demand for the Convention's decree to be rescinded. He also attempted to persuade his fellow citizens to affirm their loyalty to the French Republic, in the hope of avoiding a break with France. But most of the notables of Ajaccio had turned against the Buonaparte clan, and he was warned of a plan to assassinate him. He thought of joining Saliceti in Bastia, but changed his mind, and on 2 May set off for Corte to see Paoli. By then news of Lucien's Toulon speech had reached the island. Worse, a letter from Lucien to his brother boasting that he had provoked the Convention's decree against Paoli had been intercepted and sent to Corte.[17]

On his way, Napoleone met a kinsman who warned him that if he went to Corte he would never get out alive. He turned back and reached Bocognano on the evening of 5 May. But he was by no means out of danger, as Marius Peraldi, brother of his erstwhile rival for the Ajaccio colonelcy, was hot on his heels meaning to arrest him and take him to Corte. The various accounts of what happened next read like an adventure story, with Napoleone arrested, locked up under guard, freed at night by cunning subterfuge, pursued, caught, held with a gun to his temple in a stand-off, and finally spirited away while rival gangs of bandits settled scores. What is certain is that he was arrested in Bocognano, that he was freed by a cousin, briefly held again, and eventually taken to a kinsman shepherd's hut outside Ajaccio.[18]

Napoleone could not show himself openly, so he slipped into the poor suburb, the Borgo, where he was popular, and that night went to the house of his friend Levie, former mayor of Ajaccio, in which his partisans had gathered. There they cowered, sleeping on the floor, their guns at the ready, for two days, while a boat was prepared to take Napoleone away at night. On the evening of his intended escape the house was surrounded by gendarmes. Levie told his guests to hide and invited the chief of the gendarmes in. As they talked, both noticed that some of the sleeping mats had not been hidden. The gendarme, fearing for his life, pretended to see nothing, and the two men continued to drink and talk while Napoleone was smuggled out of the back of the house and down to the beach, where a boat was waiting. By 10 May he was safe in Bastia.[19]

On the night of 23 May, Letizia was woken by a knock on the door; a cousin had come to warn her that Paoli's partisans were on their way to seize everyone in the house. He had brought a handful of armed relatives to escort them to safety. Letizia left her two youngest children, Maria Nunziata and Geronimo, in safe hands and took Louis, Maria-Anna, Maria Paolina, and Fesch with her. They crept out of town and made for the hills. A few hours later the Buonaparte home was sacked.

Meanwhile, Napoleone had persuaded Saliceti and the other commissioners at Bastia that it would be easy to recover control of Ajaccio with a show of force. Four hundred French regulars were assembled and set sail in two ships, with Napoleone, Joseph, and the three commissioners on board. The attempt to take the city failed, but Letizia and her children, Joseph Fesch, and various French loyalists were evacuated.[20]

By 3 June Napoleone and his family were in Calvi, one of only three ports still held by the French. The rest of the island was under Paoli's sway. On 27 May a thousand-strong assembly in Corte had issued a proclamation condemning the Buonaparte. 'Born in despotism, nourished and brought up at the expense of a lustful pasha who ruled the island, the three brothers turned themselves with ardent enthusiasm into the zealous collaborators and the perfidious agents of Saliceti,' it ran. 'As punishment, the Assembly abandons them to their private remorse and to public opinion which has already condemned them to eternal execration and infamy.'[21]

Whether the French could hang on at Calvi for much longer was open to doubt, and the Buonaparte could no longer hope to play a part in Corsican affairs. On 11 June Letizia, her half-brother Fesch, and her brood sailed for France. It was not a good time to be going there.

7

The Jacobin

ON 2 JUNE 1793, eleven days before the Buonaparte family reached the mainland, the Revolution had entered a new phase. The extremist Jacobin faction in the Convention, known as Montagnards or *La Montagne* because they sat on the highest seats in the amphitheatre, had expelled the more moderate Girondins. France was plunged into what was effectively civil war. In Toulon, where the Buonaparte landed, the Jacobins were laying down the law through terror and intimidation, arresting nobles, dragging wealthy citizens out of their houses, and stringing them up from lampposts or bludgeoning them to death in the streets.

The Buonaparte family were not immediately threatened: they were unknown and destitute, and Lucien was prominent in the local Jacobin club. But the city was in ferment, crowds could be volatile, and the Buonaparte were, after all, *ci-devant* nobles. In such a climate nobody was safe. They moved to the village of La Valette outside the city. Having settled Letizia and his siblings there, Joseph made contact with Saliceti, who had also fled Corsica. He had publicly distanced himself from the Buonaparte, declaring, 'Neither of these little intriguers will ever count among my friends,' but he was not a man to burn bridges. He too needed associates, and with his backing Lucien was given an administrative post as quartermaster in nearby Saint-Maximin, and Joseph Fesch, who had shed his ecclesiastical garb, a similar post at Chauvet. Joseph himself accompanied Saliceti to Paris, where he lobbied the Convention to provide funds for the sustenance of exiled Corsican 'patriots' such as the Buonaparte who had suffered in the cause of the Revolution. His efforts were rewarded, and Letizia obtained her dole. Joseph then looked around for career opportunities and secured the lucrative position of commissary to the army.[1]

Napoleone had gone to Nice, where the greater part of his regiment was stationed as part of the Army of Italy. Given the dearth of officers, he was welcomed back and given 3,000 francs in back pay. It so happened that the commander of the artillery of the Army of Italy was Jean du Teil, younger brother of Napoleone's old friend and commander at Auxonne. He gave Napoleone the task of inspecting the coastal batteries between Nice and Marseille, as Admiral Hood's fleet was looking for an opportunity to land troops. At the beginning of July he was ordered to Avignon where he was to organise the convoy of ordnance and powder destined for Nice. He had not gone halfway when he found himself entering a war zone.[2]

The events of 2 June in Paris had provoked violent reactions and an anti-Jacobin backlash around the country. Ten provinces defied the Convention, a royalist rising had taken over the Vendée in the west, and in the south Marseille, Toulon, and the valley of the Rhône were in open revolt. The *fédérés*, as the rebels were called, overran the region, including Avignon, stopping Napoleone in his tracks. An army under General Carteaux was marching south to defeat them, and by the end of July the *fédérés* had been expelled from the former Papal fief. Napoleone was present but probably played no part in the fighting.[3]

There is little firm evidence about his movements over the following weeks, but he probably spent them carrying out his orders of convoying powder and shot from Avignon to Nice, possibly delayed by a bout of fever at Avignon. If so, it may have given him the time to reflect on his position. France had become a dangerous place for young men like him, and he needed to assert his political stance. He did this by writing *Le Souper de Beaucaire*, a polemic in the form of a dialogue which may or may not have taken place over dinner shared by a group of people at an inn at Beaucaire, on Napoleone's route from Avignon to Nice.[4]

It is a political diatribe against the *fédérés*, in which the narrator, an officer, discusses the political situation with a group of citizens of

Marseille, Nîmes, and Montpellier who had come to the fair at Beaucaire, and argues in support of the Convention in Paris. He admits that the Girondins are good republicans and that the Montagnards might not be perfect, but asserts that the former showed weakness and the latter strength, and their authority should therefore be acknowledged: the successful faction has right on its side. He takes the opportunity to denounce Paoli, who only feigned loyalty to the French Republic 'in order to gain time to deceive the people, to crush the true friends of liberty, to lead his compatriots into his ambitious and criminal projects'.

It was a political manifesto, calculated to establish Napoleone's revolutionary credentials and position himself politically in a way that would shield him from the kind of accusations that had sent many an officer to the guillotine. It also aimed to represent the Buonaparte clan as the victims of the counter-revolutionary Paoli. Patriots such as they had welcomed Paoli believing him to be a good republican, and only gradually became aware of his 'fatal ambition' and his perfidy.[5]

The piece is couched in the flowery hyperbole so beloved of revolutionary France (and every totalitarian regime since), but there are few traces of the idealism that still haunted Napoleone's recent writings, and it represents an emotional as well as an ideological coming of age. Reality had not lived up to his adolescent dreams of a Corsica reborn under Paoli, and his disappointment and sense of rejection had turned into anger, and even bitterness. He renounced Corsica; henceforth he would angrily reprove anyone who called him a Corsican and declare that he was and always had been French, since the island had already been incorporated into the kingdom when he was born. He was not bothered by the apparent inconsistencies or what might be seen as his betrayal of the Corsican and Paolist cause: it was Paoli who had betrayed him, and Corsica had let him down. In addition, he had smelt weakness in Paoli, and he had come to see that as a failing.

The riots he had witnessed over the past three years had dispelled any faith he might have had in the inherent goodness of human nature. The disgust and fear he had felt outside the Tuileries on 10 August the previous year had convinced him that the lower orders must be contained. The small-town struggles for power in Corsica had taught him that subterfuge, cheating, treachery, and brute force were the only effective means of achieving a goal in politics. He had participated in several elections in which rules had been disregarded and results falsified, and he had taken part in two coups. As an officer on full pay he had tried to subvert troops from under the authority of a brother officer. He still saw himself as a soldier, but the Revolution had politicised the army, and in politics the rules of chivalry did not apply. The winning side was the one to be on. The dreamy romanticism of his youth had been confronted with the seamy side of human affairs, and at the age of twenty-four he had emerged a cynical realist ready to make his way in the increasingly dangerous world in which he was obliged to live.

On his way from Avignon to Nice in mid-September, Napoleone passed through Le Beausset, where Saliceti and the *représentant en mission* of the Convention Thomas Gasparin were staying, and he naturally called on his compatriot. 'Chance served us well,' Saliceti wrote of the encounter: they were in urgent need of a capable and politically reliable artillery officer.[6]

As well as being torn by internal dissent and civil war, France was now under attack from the combined forces of Austria, Prussia, Britain, Spain, the Dutch Republic, Sardinia, Naples, and several other small Italian states, on five fronts. By the late summer of 1793 the Prussians had pushed back the French on the Rhine, the Austrians had taken the French fortress of Valenciennes, Spanish forces had crossed the Pyrenees and were moving on Perpignan, the Sardinians were invading from the east, and the British had laid siege to Dunkirk. The minister of war, Lazare Carnot, had ordered a *levée en masse* to defend the motherland, but things were not looking good.

Marseille had been retaken from the *fédérés* by the forces of the Convention on 25 August, but Toulon was still holding out, and retaking that was not going to be easy. Horrified by the bloody reprisals visited upon the inhabitants of Marseille, the *fédérés* and royalists in Toulon had opened the port to Admiral Hood's Anglo-Spanish fleet, which had landed troops and occupied the city in the name of Louis XVII, now languishing in a revolutionary gaol. Toulon, the home of France's Mediterranean fleet, was a natural harbour, with a large inner roadstead sheltered by land and an even larger outer one protected by a long promontory. The city was defended on the landward side by a string of forts and from the sea by batteries that could cover both the inner and outer roads. These defences were now held by nearly 20,000 British, Neapolitan, Spanish, and Sardinian regulars, guarding not only the city but the roads in which Hood's fleet was anchored. General Carteaux was not the man to dislodge them. A painter by trade who owed his command to political connections, he had 4,000 men plucked from the Army of the Alps and from among defeated *fédérés* who sought safety in his ranks.

On 7 September Carteaux began operations, taking the village of Ollioules but in the process losing the commander of his artillery, Lieutenant Colonel Dommartin, a former colleague of Napoleone at the École Militaire, who was gravely wounded. A replacement was required. Saliceti had mixed feelings about Napoleone, but after reading *Le Souper de Beaucaire* he had no doubts as to his political reliability, and even decided to publish it at government expense. And, as he put it, 'At least he's one of us.' He nominated Captain Buonaparte to the vacant command and sent him off to join Carteaux outside Toulon.[7]

What he found on arrival was not encouraging. The besieging army's headquarters at Ollioules were a nest of political intrigue and infighting between Carteaux and General Jean La Poype, who had joined him with 3,000 men from the Army of Italy. Anyone could see that Toulon was all but impregnable and that only bombardment could yield results, but as Buonaparte quickly realised, Carteaux had no idea how to lay siege to a city. He insisted that he would capture it '*à l'arme blanche*', that is to say with sword and bayonet, and ignored Buonaparte's advice.[8]

If Toulon was impregnable on the landward side, it could not hold out unless it was resupplied by sea, and no ship could approach the harbour if the heights commanding the roads were not secured. Buonaparte was not the first to see that capturing these was the key to taking the city—it was obvious from a glance at the map, as even the governing Committee of Public Safety in Paris had pointed out. But while most of those at headquarters saw the area of La Seyne on the inner roads as the place from which to threaten the allied

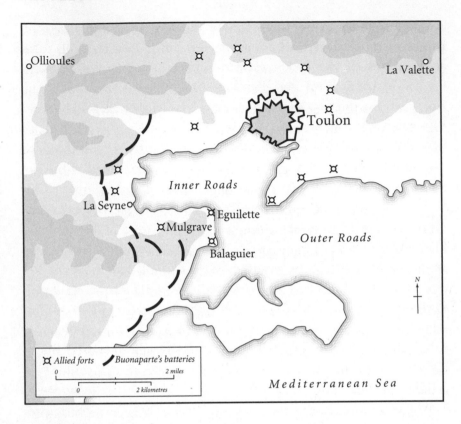

Ollioules

La Valette

Toulon

Inner Roads

La Seyne

Eguilette

Mulgrave

Balaguier

Outer Roads

N

⊠ *Allied forts*   ⟋ *Buonaparte's batteries*

0   2 miles

0   2 kilometres

Mediterranean Sea

fleet, Buonaparte believed that it was the two forts of Balaguier and l'Éguillette on the promontory of Le Caire, commanding access to the outer roads, that were crucial. They were held by allied troops, and it would take artillery to dislodge them. But all Buonaparte found on arrival were two twenty-four-pounders, two sixteen-pounders, and two mortars. It was not much to be going on with, but enough to enable him to chase an allied force and a frigate away from the La Seyne area and set up a battery there which he named, to stress his loyalty, *La Montagne*.[9]

Over the next weeks, Buonaparte built up his artillery park. Not bothering to seek authorisation, he scoured the surrounding area, visiting every military post as far afield as Lyon, Grenoble, and Antibes and stripping them of everything that might come in useful—cannon, gun carriages, powder and shot, tools and scrap metal, horses and carts, along with any men who had ever handled ordnance. He set up a foundry to produce cannonballs, forges to supply iron fittings for gun carriages and limbers, and ovens to heat the balls to set ships on fire. He also picked men from the ranks to train as gunners.

The first attack on Fort Éguillette on 22 September was a failure. Carteaux did not share Buonaparte's conviction about the fort's importance and deployed too few men, while the British quickly brought up reinforcements. They realised the French had identified the military significance of the promontory, and reinforced the position with a new battery which they named Fort Mulgrave. They added two earthworks on its flanks, covering the approaches to forts Éguillette and Balaguier. Buonaparte complained to Saliceti and Gasparin that his hopes of a quick victory had been scuppered; now he would have to take Fort Mulgrave before he could get at the key positions, and that would take time. He carried on building up his batteries and stores of shot and powder, ignoring orders from Carteaux, who complained but could do nothing as Buonaparte had the ear of the representatives of the government. Saliceti passed Buonaparte's criticisms of Carteaux to his colleagues in Marseille, Paul Barras, Stanislas Fréron, and Jean-François Ricord, who wrote to Paris recommending that Carteaux be replaced and Buonaparte promoted. On 18 October he received his nomination as *chef de bataillon*, equivalent to the rank of major, and five days later Carteaux was removed from his command.

Buonaparte had become adept at disregarding his superiors and bypassing their instructions without giving offence, employing flattery where necessary. He also knew when to force the issue and to intimidate in order to have his way. Saliceti was now permanently at headquarters in Ollioules and backed him up. Napoleone nevertheless had to tread carefully, as the waves of terror rippling out from Paris led people to denounce others for treason as a means of avoiding being denounced themselves, and with many officers defecting to the enemy, the nobleman Buonaparte was not beyond suspicion. He nevertheless did stick his neck out to protect his former superior in the regiment of La Fère, Jean-Jacques Gassendi, who had been arrested, by insisting he needed him to organise an artillery arsenal in Marseille.[10]

Carteaux's command had been given to the hardly more martial General François Doppet, a physician who dabbled in literature, and had only won high rank by finding himself in the right place at the right time. But on 15 November his nerve failed during an attack on Fort Mulgrave: he gave the order to retreat when he saw the English making a sortie, only to have a furious Buonaparte, his face bathed in blood from a light wound, gallop up and call him a *jean foutre* (the closest English approximation would be 'fucking idiot'). Doppet took it well. He was aware of his limitations and realised that *chef de bataillon* Buonaparte knew his business.[11]

Buonaparte's orders and notes during these weeks are succinct and precise, and while their tone is commanding, he takes the trouble to explain why compliance with his demands is essential. In war, as in any other critical situation, people quickly rally to the person who gives the impression of knowing what they are about, and Buonaparte's self-confidence was magnetic. He showed bravery and steadiness under fire, and did not spare himself, which set him apart from many of the political appointments milling around at headquarters. 'This young officer,' wrote General Doppet, 'combined a rare bravery and the most indefatigable activity with his many talents. Every time I went out on my rounds, I always found him at his post; if he needed a moment's rest, he took it on the ground, wrapped in his cloak; he was never away from his batteries.'[12]

Through effort and resourcefulness, Buonaparte had built up an artillery park of nearly a hundred guns and set up a dozen batteries, provided the necessary powder and shot, and trained the soldiers to man them. For his chief of staff he had picked the apparently vain and frivolous Jean-Baptiste Muiron, who had trained as an artillery officer and quickly became an enthusiastic aide. In the twenty-six-year-old Félix Chauvet he identified a brilliant commissary who earned and returned his affection as well as serving him efficiently. During an attack on one of the batteries, Buonaparte had noticed the engaging bravery under fire of a young grenadier in the battalion of the Côte d'Or named Andoche Junot. When he saw that the man also had beautiful handwriting he appropriated him as an aide, only to discover that he had trained for the artillery in the school at

Châlons. A couple of weeks later, another young man joined Buonaparte's entourage. He was the handsome nineteen-year-old Auguste Marmont, a cousin of Le Lieur de Ville sur Arce, who had trained for the artillery at Châlons with Junot.[13]

On 16 November a new commander arrived to take over from Doppet. He was General Jacques Dugommier, a fifty-five-year-old professional soldier, a veteran of the Seven Years' War and the American War of Independence who knew how to call the troops to order. He had brought General du Teil and a couple of artillery officers with him, but quickly realised that Buonaparte had the situation in hand, and he did little more than endorse his decisions. 'I can find no words to describe the merits of Buonaparte,' he wrote to the minister of war. 'Much technical knowledge, as much intelligence and too much bravery is only a faint sketch of the qualities of this uncommon officer.'[14]

On 25 November Dugommier held a council of war, attended by Saliceti and, in place of Gasparin, who had died, a newly arrived *représentant*, Augustin Robespierre, younger brother of one of the leading lights of the Committee of Public Safety. They considered Dugommier's plan, then that drawn up in Paris by Carnot. Both involved multiple attacks. Buonaparte argued that this would disperse their forces, and put forward his own plan, which consisted of a couple of feint attacks and a massive assault on forts Mulgrave, Éguillette, and Balaguier, whose capture he was confident would precipitate a rapid evacuation of Hood's fleet and the fall of the city. The plan was accepted and preparations put in hand.[15]

On 30 November the British commander in Toulon, General O'Hara, made a sortie and succeeded in capturing a battery and spiking its guns before moving on Ollioules. Dugommier and Saliceti managed to rally the fleeing republican forces and lead up reinforcements. They retook the battery, a battalion led by Louis-Gabriel Suchet taking O'Hara prisoner in the process, and Buonaparte unspiked the guns and opened up on the fleeing allies. He had been in the thick of the fighting and earned a mention in Dugommier's despatch to Paris.[16]

The day's fighting had nevertheless demonstrated the lack of mettle and experience of the French troops. The worsening weather combined with food shortages to sap morale. Despairing of their ability to take Toulon, Barras and Fréron considered raising the siege and taking winter quarters. Saliceti pressed Dugommier to attack, but the general hesitated, as a failed assault might cost him his head. As it was, they were being accused in Paris of lack of zeal and of living in luxury.[17]

Dugommier resolved to act on Buonaparte's plan, and the batteries facing Fort Mulgrave began bombarding it on 14 December. The British batteries responded vigorously, and Buonaparte was thrown to the ground by the wind of a passing shot. The attack, by a force of 7,000 men in three columns, began at 1 a.m. on 17 December. A storm had broken and Dugommier hesitated, but Buonaparte pointed out that the conditions might actually prove favourable, and the impatience of Saliceti carried the day. The French infantry went into action in pouring rain, the darkness lit up by flashes of lightning, the sound of the guns drowned out by peals of thunder. Two of the advancing columns strayed from their prescribed route and lost cohesion as many of the soldiers fell back or fled. Other units reached Fort Mulgrave and began escalading its defences. The fighting was fierce—the attack on the fort would cost the French over a thousand casualties—but Muiron eventually forced his way into the fort, closely followed by Dugommier and Buonaparte, who had his horse shot under him at the beginning of the attack and was wounded in the leg by an English corporal's lance as he stormed the ramparts.

As soon as he had taken possession of the fort, Buonaparte turned its guns on those of forts Éguillette and Balaguier and ordered Marmont to start bombarding them. The British mounted a counterattack, but it was repulsed and they were forced to evacuate the two remaining forts. By then it was light, and Buonaparte began firing incendiary shells and red-hot cannonballs at the nearest British ships, blowing up two. He told anyone who would listen that the battle was over and Toulon was theirs, but Dugommier, Robespierre, Saliceti, and others were sceptical, believing the town would only fall after a few more days' fighting. They were wrong—the explosions of the two ships were a signal the allies could not ignore, and that morning they decided to evacuate; they began moving men out while the ships struggled in a strong wind to pull out of range of the French guns.

The evacuation proceeded through that day and the next, with the allies towing away nine French warships and blowing up a further twelve, setting fire to ships' stores and the arsenal, and taking on board thousands of French royalists. Anyone who could get hold of a boat was rowing out to the allied ships, and some even tried swimming. They were under constant fire from batteries newly set up by Buonaparte on the promontory and the heights above the city. That night the burning ships lit up the scene, revealing what Buonaparte described as 'a sublime but heart-rending sight'.[18]

The French entered the city on the morning of 19 December, looting, raping, and lynching anyone they pleased to label as an enemy of the Revolution. On the quayside people were throwing themselves into the water to reach the departing British ships. Those who did not drown were subjected to the fury of the republican soldiery. Over two decades later, Buonaparte recalled the revulsion he had felt at the sight, and according to some sources he managed to save a number of lives.[19]

Barras, Saliceti, Ricord, Robespierre, and Fréron carried out a purge of the population of Toulon. 'The national vengeance has been unfurled,' they proclaimed, listing those categories which had been 'exterminated'. Barras suggested it would be simpler if they removed all those who were proven 'patriots', that is to say revolutionaries, and killed all the rest. The population of the city, which would be renamed Port-de-la-Montagne, fell from 30,000 to 7,000.[20]

On 22 December 1793 Buonaparte was promoted to the rank of brigadier general. He was only twenty-four years old, but this did not make him an exception. Over 6,000 officers of all arms had emigrated since 1791, and another 10,000 would have done so by the summer of 1794. Generals and higher-ranking officers were guillotined by the hundred as suspected traitors. In consequence, the Republic had been obliged to nominate no fewer than 962 new generals between 1791 and 1793. But in the case of Buonaparte, the promotion was merited, and he knew it.[21]

'I told you we would be brilliantly successful, and, you see, I keep my word,' he wrote banteringly from Ollioules to the deputy minister of war in Paris on 24 December, using the familiar '*tu*' form, no doubt to stress his revolutionary attitude. He had already noted that in the current climate the story that was told first was the one that stuck in the mind, and he informed the minister that thanks to his action, the British had been prevented from burning any of the French ships or naval stores, which was a blatant lie.[22]

He had proved not only that he was a capable and resourceful officer but also that he was a leader of men. He had won the admiration of all the real soldiers present, starting with Dugommier. More than that, he had revealed a charisma that many of his young comrades found hard to resist.[23]

'He was small in stature, but well proportioned, thin and puny in appearance but taut and strong,' noted Claude Victor (another who had distinguished himself at Toulon and had also been made a general), noting that 'his features had an unusual nobility' and his eyes seemed to send out shafts of fire. His gravity and sense of purpose impressed those around him. 'There was mystery in the man,' Victor felt.[24]

Buonaparte was exhausted. Three months of intense activity, poor diet, frequent nights spent sleeping on the ground wrapped only in his cloak, and that during the winter months, must have placed a heavy strain on his constitution. He had a deep flesh wound and had also caught scabies, which was then endemic in the army. That may be why, at a moment when he could have obtained a posting to one of the armies actively engaged against the enemy, he was content to accept that of inspector of the coastal defences along the stretch between Toulon and Marseille. Another reason may have been a desire to lie low. He had seen how easily people could lose their commands, and he had probably made a number of enemies.[25]

It may just have been that he wished to be close to his family, which had moved further away from Toulon, first to Beausset, then Brignoles and finally Marseille, where he joined them on 2 January 1794. His general's pay of 12,000 livres plus expenses would have been welcome, as the cost of living had risen dramatically in the course of 1793. The family had lived through lean times, with Letizia taking in washing, and the daughters, as gossip had it, resorting to prostitution. The youngest, Maria Paolina, now Paulette, who had grown into a rare beauty, had been caught stealing figs from a neighbour's garden.[26]

8

Adolescent Loves

BUONAPARTE SPENT THE first weeks of 1794 travelling up and down the coast inspecting the defences and issuing quantities of crisp instructions. These go into minute detail on the exact quantities of powder and shot required, which spare parts should be assembled, and even the manner in which horses should be harnessed for specific tasks.

At the beginning of February he was appointed to command the artillery of the Army of Italy, operating against the forces of the King of Sardinia. They had invaded southern France in 1792 but were driven back, following which Savoy and Nice had been incorporated into the French Republic, but they still held the Alpine passes, from which they threatened to recover the lost provinces. The port of Oneglia, a Sardinian enclave in the territory of the neutral Republic of Genoa and the chief link between the king's island and mainland provinces, was also considered a threat, since it resupplied British warships and harboured corsairs who preyed on French shipping.

Buonaparte's new salary allowed him to install his family in the comfortable if modest Château-Sallé outside Antibes, not far from his headquarters in Nice. Joseph, whose job as commissary had awakened an interest in trade and speculation, was currently in Nice too, exploring business opportunities. Lucien was at Saint-Maximin, where as head of its Jacobin club he had changed the town's name to 'Marathon', in homage as much to the 'martyr of the Revolution' Jean-Paul Marat, who had been assassinated in his bath by the

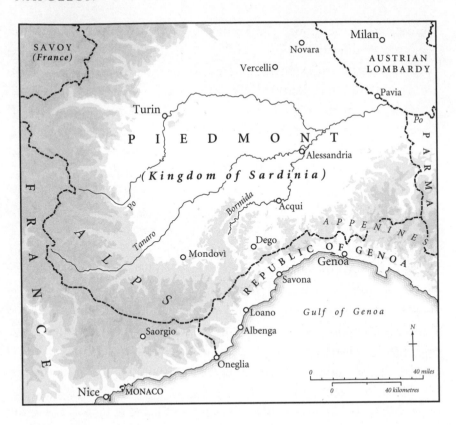

royalist Charlotte Corday, as to the heroic ancient Greek defenders of their homeland. He had also changed his own name, to 'Brutus', and had married Christine Boyer, the sister of the keeper of the inn at which he lodged.[1]

The commander of the Army of Italy was General Pierre Dumerbion, a sixty-year-old professional. He was supervised by the political commissioners Saliceti, Augustin Robespierre, and Ricord, who commissioned Buonaparte to prepare a campaign plan. As the Sardinian positions in the mountains were almost unassailable, he suggested ignoring them and striking at their bases: their left wing on the lower ground nearer the sea was vulnerable, and if the French could break through there, they would be able to sweep into the enemy rear. His plan was accepted, and operations began on 7 April, spearheaded by General André Masséna, who captured Oneglia two days later, and by the end of the month the French were in Saorgio, strategic gateway into Piedmont.

Buonaparte's role consisted of ensuring the artillery was in position and adequately supplied. To assist him he had selected two old comrades from the regiment of La Fère, Nicolas-Marie Songis and Gassendi, his new companions Marmont and Muiron, and as aides de camp Junot and his own younger brother Louis. By 1 May he was back in Nice, drawing up further plans which would have taken the French into the plain of Mondovi, but the operations were halted by the war minister Lazare Carnot, who was against involving French forces any deeper in Italy. The Midi was still politically unstable, and there might be unrest if the army moved off. Carnot also needed all available troops to roll back the Spanish invasion.

Buonaparte composed a memorandum for the Committee of Public Safety giving a strategic overview of France's military position. He argued that invading Spain would yield no tangible benefits, while invading Piedmont would result in the overthrow of a throne that would always be inimical to the French Republic. More important, it would make it possible to defeat Austria, which would only make peace if Vienna were threatened by a two-pronged attack, through Germany in the north and Italy in the south. Austria, he argued, was the cornerstone of the coalition against France, and if it were knocked out that would fall apart.[2]

Robespierre suggested that Buonaparte accompany him to Paris. The two men had grown close over the past four months, drawn together by the zeal with which they approached their respective tasks and by the shared conviction of the need for strong central authority. Under the dominant influence of Robespierre's elder brother Maximilien, the Committee of Public Safety in Paris was exercising just such authority, through a reign of Terror which sent thousands to the guillotine. But Robespierre's grip on power was weakening, and Augustin's suggestion that Buonaparte come to Paris might have had something to do with that: he allegedly suggested placing him in command of the Paris National Guard.[3]

Buonaparte briefly considered the proposal, and according to Lucien discussed it with his brothers before deciding against it. To

Ricord he admitted a reluctance to get involved in revolutionary politics, and his instinct was to stay at his post with the army. Whether the fact that he was also having an affair with Ricord's wife, Marguerite, had any bearing on his decision is unclear.[4]

At the beginning of July he was sent by Saliceti to Genoa to assess the intentions of the city's government, which was neutral but under pressure from the anti-French coalition, and to inspect its defences for future reference. He left on 11 July, accompanied by Junot, Marmont, and Louis, as well as Ricord, but was back at Nice by the end of the month. Yet he was too busy to attend the wedding of his brother Joseph on 1 August.[5]

Joseph's bride, Marie-Julie Clary, was twenty-two years old, not pretty, but pious, honest, generous, dutiful, family-minded, intelligent, and rich. She came from a family of Marseille merchants with extensive interests in the ports of the eastern Mediterranean, and she brought him a considerable dowry. With this under his belt, Joseph's bearing changed, and he now assumed a gravitas he felt appropriate as head of the family.[6]

Buonaparte was still at headquarters when, on 4 August, news reached him of the coup in Paris which had toppled Robespierre on 27 July—9 Thermidor in the revolutionary calendar. He was deeply affected by the misfortune of his friend, who was guillotined along with his brother the following day. And he did not have to wait long to be arrested himself.[7]

As soon as he heard of the fall of Robespierre, Saliceti wrote to the Committee of Public Safety accusing Augustin Robespierre, Ricord, and 'their man' Buonaparte of having sabotaged the operations of the Army of Italy and conspired against the Republic with the allies and with Genoa, whose authorities had bribed Buonaparte with 'a million' (the currency was not specified). He ordered the arrest of Buonaparte and the seizure of his papers prior to his being sent to Paris to answer charges of treason.[8]

It is not clear whether Buonaparte was actually put in gaol or merely under house arrest. Junot managed to pass a note to him offering to arrange his escape, but Buonaparte refused. 'I recognise your friendship in your proposal, my dear Junot; and you well know that which I have vowed you and on which you know you may count,' he wrote back. But he was confident his innocence would be recognised and urged Junot to do nothing, as this could only compromise him. Innocence was no guarantor of safety under revolutionary conditions, but Buonaparte was lucky. Saliceti's accusation had been no more than a reflex of self-preservation, and as soon as he felt he was in the clear he sent another letter to Paris stating that examination of the general's papers had yielded no evidence of treason, and, bearing in mind his usefulness for the Army of Italy, he and his colleagues had ordered his provisional release. Nobody apart from Junot seems to have taken the charges against Buonaparte seriously. His landlord, Joseph Laurenti, with whose daughter Buonaparte was carrying on a flirtation, had stood bail, and as a result he spent most of the eleven days of his detention in his own lodgings.[9]

Meanwhile, the Austrians had sent an army to reinforce the Sardinian forces, and General Dumerbion felt he had to do something. 'My child,' he wrote to Buonaparte, 'draw me up a campaign plan as only you know how.' On 26 August the child handed him one, and on 5 September he was at Oneglia to implement it. The French forces advanced on the point at which the two enemy armies met, aiming to split them apart. On 21 September Buonaparte witnessed his first pitched battle, an attack on Dego in which General Masséna distinguished himself. But further operations were called off by Carnot in Paris, and Buonaparte was left with nothing to do. This should have been welcome to him.[10]

Shortly after his release from arrest he had gone to Marseille to see Joseph, who was enjoying his newfound wealth and having himself addressed by the title of count by his in-laws. On meeting the family, Buonaparte had been struck by Marie-Julie's much prettier younger sister, Bernardine Eugénie Désirée, and declared himself to be in love. Désirée, or Eugénie as he would call her, was sixteen or seventeen, modest and innocent, with just enough education for a deferential companion and obedient wife. 'A stranger to tender passions', Buonaparte wrote to her on 10 September, he had succumbed to 'the pleasure' of her company. 'The charms of your person, of your character, imperceptibly conquered the heart of your love.' His letters to her are stilted, rushes of passionate prose alternating with suggestions that she buy a piano and take a good teacher, as 'music is the soul of love, the sweetness of life, the consolation of sorrows and the companion of innocence'. They lack conviction, which is not surprising.[11]

A new envoy from the Convention, Louis Turreau, had arrived at headquarters in Loano. As he had only just married, he brought his twenty-three-year-old wife with him, but it turned out to be not much of a honeymoon, as she took a fancy to Buonaparte and wasted no time in having an affair with him. 'I was very young then, happy and proud of my success,' he later recalled and admitted that his exhilaration had led him to act irresponsibly: he had taken her on an excursion to see the front line, and to impress her he ordered a battery to open fire on an enemy position. The ensuing cannonade had cost the lives of several men. He later reproached himself bitterly for his childish action.[12]

Operations on the Italian front had come to a standstill, and at the beginning of November the Committee of Public Safety switched its priority to Corsica. The British had responded to Paoli's appeal by occupying the island as a colony, with George III as monarch, Sir Gilbert Elliot as viceroy, and Pozzo di Borgo as chief administrator. Paoli was bundled off to a second exile in London. As General Dumerbion had paid generous tribute to Buonaparte's talents, he was given the task of preparing the artillery of the expeditionary force intended to recapture the island.[13]

He spent most of the last month of 1794 and the first two of 1795 in Toulon where it was assembling. The city was scarred by the siege and subject to riots by mobs seeking 'aristos' to lynch. One day a captured Spanish ship with some émigré French noble families aboard was brought into harbour, and a mob gathered in expectation. The city authorities tried to protect the émigrés, only to be accused of being royalist stooges and threatened with lynching. Buonaparte managed to calm the crowd, which contained some gunners who had served under him at the siege, and then smuggle the émigrés out of town in his artillery caissons.[14]

The Corsican expedition sailed from Toulon on 11 March, but soon ran into an Anglo-Neapolitan fleet, and after a brief encounter in which it lost two ships, sailed back into port. Disheartened by the prospect of inaction, Buonaparte asked to be transferred to the Army of the Rhine. His request remained without response, and he spent the next weeks mainly in Marseille, where on 21 April he became engaged to Désirée.[15]

He had been seeing her intermittently over the past months and corresponding with her regularly. Most of his letters are couched in the tone of a schoolmaster, as he tells her which books to read and which not, frets about whether her music teacher is good enough, arranges for a publisher in Paris to send her the latest tunes, reminds her to sing her scales regularly, going into tedious detail about the effects of striking a wrong note. He was a great music lover, with a passion for the Italian composers of the day, and enjoyed lecturing those French ones he found wanting, sometimes entering into arguments of a technical nature with them.[16]

The engagement had probably been precipitated by the fact that at the end of March he had received a transfer to the Army of the West, operating against insurgents in the Vendée region of western France. The order to take up this posting reached him on 7 May, and to his chagrin he learned that he had been struck off the list of artillery generals, as their quota had been exceeded and he was the youngest, so he was relegated to what he regarded as the inferior status of infantry general.

The following day he set off for Paris, accompanied by his brother Louis, to whose education he was continuing to attend, drilling him mercilessly with mathematical tests even as they travelled up the valley of the Rhône and through Burgundy. He also took with him his devoted Junot and Marmont, who had come to hero-worship him. 'I found him so superior to everything I had encountered in my life, his intimate conversation was so deep and so captivating, his mind was so full of future promise,' wrote Marmont, 'that I could not bear the idea of his impending departure.' When Buonaparte suggested he accompany him he did not hesitate, even though he had no authorisation to do so.[17]

Marmont insisted they break their journey at Châtillon-sur-Seine, where his parents lived. His mother found Buonaparte taciturn to the point of being impossible to communicate with and took the 'little general' off to visit her friends, the Chastenay family who lived nearby. 'On this first visit, in order to pass the time I was asked to play the piano,' recalled the daughter of the house, Victorine. 'The general seemed to appreciate it but his compliments were curt. I was then asked to sing, so I sang one in Italian which I had just learnt the music for. I asked him if I was pronouncing right, to which he just said no.'[18]

The following day the Chastenays dined at the Marmonts', and afterward Victorine asked Buonaparte about Corsica. He unwound, and in the course of the conversation, which lasted a full four hours, he spoke of his love for the epic poems supposedly written by the thirteenth-century Gaelic poet Ossian and Bernardin de Saint-Pierre's novel *Paul et Virginie*. He spoke earnestly about politics, about happiness and self-fulfilment. On the third day he helped her make a posy of cornflowers and they played games, flirting and dancing. She was dismayed when, the day after that, he continued his journey.[19]

On reaching Paris in the last days of May, Buonaparte called on François Aubry, Carnot's successor at the War Ministry, but any hopes of reversing the decision striking him off the list of artillery generals were quickly dispelled. Aubry, a former artillery officer embittered by career disappointments, was not to be swayed. Buonaparte began to look around for someone who might help him.

One of the most prominent among those known as the *'jeunesse dorée'*, a faction persecuting the fallen Jacobins, was Stanislas Fréron, who was in love with Buonaparte's fifteen-year-old sister, Paulette, whom he had met in Marseille and whom he wished to marry. Buonaparte was not averse to the match if it could help his own cause.[20]

A potentially more useful acquaintance was Paul Barras, who had also been at Toulon. His chequered past included fighting the British in India, voting for the death of Louis XVI in the Convention, a minor role in the downfall of Robespierre, and the defeat of a royalist attempt to overthrow the Republic. A spell as commissary to the army had provided the opportunities for graft which enabled him to acquire considerable wealth, with which he indulged his love of luxury and women. He had turned his Jacobin coat inside out, surrounding himself with a court of roués and courtesans, and would have welcomed another ex-Jacobin with a realist's ability to change his tune, but Barras trusted nobody. There had been Jacobin riots a few days before Buonaparte's arrival, and the political situation remained unstable, with people representing every shade of revolution and counter-revolution manoeuvring in a kaleidoscopic succession of alliances and realignments. Barras would see no point in helping Buonaparte until he needed him. But he did take him under his wing to keep in reserve.

On 13 June Buonaparte received his posting to the Army of the West under General Lazare Hoche, operating against royalist rebels in the Vendée. He had no intention of going and obtained sick leave until 31 August, which gave him time to consider his options.

The fall of Robespierre had put an end to the Terror, and the resulting release from fear produced an eruption of hedonism. Buonaparte was astonished at the extent to which the people of Paris threw themselves into a life of pleasure. 'To dance, to go to the theatre, to parties out in the country and to pay court to women, who are here the most beautiful in the world, is the main occupation and the most important thing,' he wrote to Joseph. 'People look back on the Terror as on a bad dream.'[21]

Antoine Lavalette, a contemporary of Buonaparte, was horrified at what had happened to his native city, where 'the dissolution of society had plumbed new depths'. He noted disapprovingly that 'it was the newly rich who sought to set the tone, combining all the errors of a bad upbringing with all the ridicule of an inborn absence of dignity'. He was shocked at the 'barely believable level of licentiousness' on display, at the 'lovely, well-bred women of high birth' who 'wore flesh-coloured pantaloons and buskins on their feet, barely covered by dresses of transparent gauze, with their breasts uncovered and their arms naked to the shoulder'. As another explained, 'The aim of these ladies and the *ne plus ultra* of their art was to show as much nudity as possible without being naked'. Some moistened their dresses with oil to make them cling to the body.[22]

There were balls to which only relatives of those who had been guillotined were invited, in some cases held in prisons where the September massacres had taken place, at which the guests wore a red ribbon round their necks in a gesture somewhere between gallows humour and exorcism. Buonaparte may have been shocked, but he showed understanding of people's need to compensate for the sufferings and the anxieties of the past—and he was a good deal less censorious than Lavalette when it came to the *nouveaux riches*.[23]

A disastrous economic situation and a financial crisis provoked by the vertiginous fall in value of the paper currency, the *assignats*, coupled with the emigration or execution of nobles, entailing the confiscation of their property, meant that there were a large number of properties on the market. People who had grown rich during the Revolution were desperate to park their depreciating cash in solid assets, creating a febrile market in which there was money to be made. On leaving Châtillon for Paris, Buonaparte had made a detour to view a country house at Ragny in Burgundy. 'The château itself consists of a new residence or pavilion in the modern style,' he wrote to Joseph on 22 May, going on to list its merits and pointing out that if the turrets which gave it 'an aristocratic look' were demolished it could be marketed as a splendid residence, with its 'superb' dining room four times the size of their old one in Ajaccio.[24]

The pursuit of pleasure had spawned a taste for luxuries of every kind, and some were scarce in Paris. Three days after reaching the capital Buonaparte took time off from promoting his career to research the price of sugar, soap, and coffee. As it was far higher than in Marseille, he instructed Joseph to buy up a stock there and ship it to Paris. Ragny had been sold, he informed his brother a few weeks later, but there were plenty of other investment opportunities.[25]

At the beginning of July he reported that he had put in hand the sale of the coffee Joseph had sent and urged him to buy up in Genoa, where the Clary family had moved, silk stockings, shawls, and Florentine and English taffeta (which would have to be imported into France through Leipzig, since Britain and France were at war), all of which were at a premium in Paris. He had succeeded in finding a sales outlet in Paris for Joseph Fesch, who had set himself up in the porcelain trade in Basel in Switzerland. He even urged Joseph to investigate the price of pasta in Italy, as the food shortages in Paris might make it worthwhile to import that. He had located a promising property in the valley of Montmorency and was looking for others. He wanted Joseph to finance these speculations, but he also identified ways of buying on credit and selling at a profit before having to realise the purchase. If only Joseph had followed his first suggestion, he complained, they would have made a million. Buonaparte could see people making fortunes all around him and was exasperated by Joseph's lack of interest.[26]

Naturally lazy, Joseph had no wish to hazard his easily acquired fortune in property speculation. He had followed the Clary family to neutral Genoa, where they had managed to take most of their money with them and from where they carried on their Levantine trade. Joseph was living well, and supporting his mother and sisters at Château-Sallé. Yet he badgered Buonaparte to use his influence to obtain for him a post as French consul in some trading city in Italy or the Levant, where he would be able to benefit from the salary and use his position to further his commercial activities. 'We have lived so many years so closely bound together that our hearts have become entwined,' Buonaparte wrote back, promising to try. 'You know better than anyone how profoundly mine is entirely devoted to you.'[27]

He had managed to place Louis in the officers' school at Châlons, which was costing him a considerable share of his half-pay, and was exploring the possibilities of getting the youngest, Geronimo, into school in Paris. He had used his connections to free Lucien—'Brutus' had got himself arrested for his Jacobin connections. He found Lucien tiresome, impudent, and irresponsible, 'a born intriguer', but he was family.[28]

In the culture to which Buonaparte had been brought up, the family operated as a clan, providing a security which he was missing in Paris. Although he was now twenty-five years old, and had been through a great deal over the past few years, he was still in many ways a child, with his displays of aggressive defensiveness and of emotion clothed in cynicism. Yet he was now having to deal with a complex set of challenges and sensations and was emotionally torn between two different worlds. The one associated with Désirée held strong appeal.

Joseph's was a perfect match. The Buonaparte and the Clary were grounded in the culture of the Mediterranean, with its mainstay of the family. Both families were bent on financial and social advancement, but were essentially middle-class in outlook. Their aspirations to noble status were driven by material rather than ideological motives and had nothing in common with the supposedly chivalric impulses of the *noblesse*. Nor were they bound by its prejudices.[29]

It is unlikely that Buonaparte's feelings for Désirée were profound. Yet he did kindle strong feelings in her. Her surviving letters and drafts exude all the passion and sentimentality one would expect of a lovelorn teenager. When he left for Paris in May she spelled out her desolation, assuring him that every instant they were apart pierced her soul. 'The thought of you is with me always, and will follow me to my grave,' she wrote shortly after his departure, her only consolation the knowledge that he would always be faithful. She hoped he would not find the Parisian beauties too alluring and reassured herself that 'our hearts are much too closely united for it ever to be possible for them to separate'.[30]

Shortly after his arrival in Paris, Buonaparte wrote saying that although he had met some 'pretty and very charming women' at Châtillon, none could compare with his 'sweet and kind Eugénie'. He wrote two days later, sending her some songs, and again three days after that, with more sheet music, chiding her for not writing more often. On 14 June, on hearing that she had moved to Genoa with her brother and sisters, he wrote a long and barely coherent letter reproaching her for letting him down.[31]

He had made her promise that she would wait for him in Marseille, and her leaving made it impossible for them to see each other. A French citizen who went abroad was liable to be labelled an émigré and proscribed. For a serving officer to do so was tantamount to treason. Her going to Genoa suggested that her family were opposed to their marriage, and he saw it as a betrayal on her part. In an emotional letter of 14 June, Buonaparte assumes that their liaison is over while expressing the conviction that she will always love him. Feigning noble abnegation, he expresses the hope that she will find one worthier than himself. In a welter of self-deprecation he describes himself as a being cursed with 'a fiery imagination, a cool head, a strange heart and an inclination to melancholy', who is 'surrounded by the savagery and immorality of men', believes himself to be 'the opposite of other men' and despises life. Yet he insists that he can only find happiness in her love, and begs her to find a way for them to be reunited. 'There is nothing I will not undertake for my adorable Eugénie,' he affirms. 'But if fate is against us think only of yourself and of your own Happiness: it is more precious than mine.' Perhaps significantly, that was the day he resolved not to join the Army of the West and extended his sick leave.[32]

He wrote again ten days later, complaining of her silence and assuring her that although Paris was brimming with pleasures of every kind he could think only of his Eugénie and consoled himself with looking at her portrait, promising to send her his own. The same day in a letter to Joseph he wrote that 'if the business with Eugénie is not concluded and if you do not send me any funds with which to operate, then I will accept the post of infantry general and go the Army of the Rhine to seek my death'. He intimated that the engagement was broken off and suggested that as she would not want the portrait he had sent, Joseph should keep it for himself. She continued to cover notebooks with his name and initials, but there is little doubt her family wanted no more to do with him, and he too now had other things on his mind.[33]

'So there we were the three of us in Paris,' recalled Marmont. 'Bonaparte without a job, me without any formal permission, and Junot attached as aide de camp to a general whom they did not want to employ [...] passing our time at the Palais-Royal and at the theatres, having very little money and no future.' Money does not in fact appear to have been a major problem; Buonaparte may have been on half-pay, but that did represent a regular income, and Junot, who came from a comfortably-off family, received subsidies from his father. Their future was indeed uncertain; Buonaparte's military career had stalled and his political connections were not influential enough to restart it.[34]

Barras had opened a new world to Buonaparte by introducing him to those who set the tone in Paris. Chief among them was the great beauty, the daughter of a Spanish banker, Thérèse de Cabarrus, known as '*Notre Dame de Thermidor*' because the revolutionary Jean-Lambert Tallien had fallen in love with her, freed her from prison and then helped bring down Robespierre and end the Terror in order to save his own as well as her neck. Other social lionesses included Juliette Récamier, Aimée de Coigny, Julie Talma, and Rose de Beauharnais, as well as the more intellectually prized Germaine de Staël and older, more experienced ladies such as Mesdames de Montansier and Château-Renaud. They were seductive, sophisticated and assertive women who did as they pleased, and Buonaparte's references in letters to Désirée and to Joseph leave no doubt that he was fascinated and excited by them.

He cut a poor figure with his small stature, lean and sallow features, hungry look and worn clothes, and he had no idea of how to present himself, enter a room, greet people, or respond. His manner was farouche, a mixture of shyness and aggression that baffled people. While it could be appealing to the provincial girls he had encountered up till now, it grew disagreeable when he became defensive. He was particularly awkward with sophisticated women and gave the impression of not caring what they thought of him. He was out of his depth, not so much socially as in terms of simple human communication: he showed a curious lack of empathy which meant that he did not know what to say to people, and therefore either said nothing or something inappropriate.

His gracelessness, unkempt appearance, and poor French, delivered in staccato phrases, did not help. Laure Permon, in whose parents' house he and Junot found a second home, thought him ugly and dirty. Bourienne's wife found him cold and sombre, and little short of savage. He could sit through a comedy with them and remain impassive while the whole house laughed, and then laugh raucously at odd moments. She remembered him telling a tasteless joke about one of his men having his testicles shot off at Toulon, and laughing uproariously while all around sat horrified. Yet there was something about his manner that some found unaccountably attractive.[35]

The sophistication of the liberated ladies both attracted and repelled him. They made Désirée seem provincial and uninteresting on the one hand, yet pure and sublime on the other. But the ardent love of a virginal teenager would not stand up to the sensual draw of the more sophisticated older woman, particularly in a young man who was still a child craving a mother figure. It seems he made a pass at Thérèse Tallien, who rebuffed him but apparently retained a fondness for him, as he was welcome in her salon, and she even used her contacts to obtain some cloth for him to have a new uniform run up.

He appears to have been more successful with other women, perhaps including Letizia's childhood friend Panoria Permon.[36]

He was feeling sorry for himself. On 5 August he wrote to the Committee for Public Safety complaining that his merits and devotion to the Republic had not been recognised. A few days later he admitted to Joseph that he was 'very little attached to life', and suggested he might as well throw himself under a passing carriage. Those are not the only things he said and wrote which suggest that he did on occasion contemplate suicide.[37]

With little else to do, he spent whole days at the Bibliothèque Nationale, established in 1792 with the amalgamation of the old royal library and the noble and ecclesiastical libraries seized during the Revolution. He was not only reading, as he always did when he had time on his hands. He was also writing.

The fruit was a novella titled *Clisson et Eugénie*, no doubt in homage to one of his favourite novels, Bernardin de Saint-Pierre's *Paul et Virginie*. Its hero, Clisson, feels the call to arms from earliest childhood, excited by the sight of a helmet, a sabre, or a drum. At the age when others read fairy tales, he studies the lives of great men; while others chase girls he applies himself to the art of war. He grows up to be an inspired young soldier who 'marked every step with brilliant actions', and quickly attains the highest rank. 'His victories followed one after the other and his name was known to the nation as that of one of its dearest defenders.' But he is the victim of 'wickedness and envy', having to endure the 'calumnies' of his peers. 'They called his loftiness of spirit' pride and reproached him for his 'firmness'. Disenchanted, feeling out of place in social gatherings, he flees society, wandering remote forests and abandoning himself to 'the desires and palpitations of his heart' on moonlit nights, brimming with melancholy and self-pity. He meets Eugénie, who is 'like the song of the nightingale or a passage of Paisiello [his favourite composer], which pleases merely sensitive souls, but whose melody transports and arouses passions only in those which can feel it keenly'. They fall in love, settle down and start a family, but after a few years he hears the call of duty from the endangered motherland and resolves to gird his loins once more. 'His name was the signal for victory', and his triumphs 'surpassed the hopes of the nation and the army'. He sends one of his aides, his best friend, to console Eugénie in his absence, which he does only too well. When Clisson discovers that they have fallen in love he writes her a letter full of generosity and tenderness, and charges into battle and his death.[38]

The work requires little comment. It is a psychoanalyst's feast with its display of emotional immaturity, dreams of glory, and sense of superiority combined with a desperate awareness of inferiority in some areas, with aggression coupled to a curiously mawkish sensibility, and total self-obsession.

On 17 August, having received orders to take up his posting with the Army of the West, Buonaparte called on Aubry's successor at the Ministry of War, Doulcet de Pontécoulant. The new head of military affairs was struck by the way the frail, sickly-looking man came to life as he spoke, his eyes sparkling with fire as he uttered the words 'army', 'battle', and 'victory'. He appointed him to the Cabinet Historique et Topographique, a general staff consisting of twenty officers. Buonaparte applied himself with his usual single-mindedness, producing plans and memoranda on every aspect of the military situation, often staying up until 3 a.m. 'When I work on a plan of campaign, I cannot rest until I have finished, until I have worked through all my ideas,' he later explained. 'I am like a woman in labour.' He presented Pontécoulant with a plan for the conquest of northern Italy which when it was sent to the commander of the Army of Italy was rejected as the figment of a madman who should be sent to an asylum.[39]

The work did not distract him from more prosaic matters; he was looking at properties within easy reach of Paris and had located one with 'a very fine house' whose drawing rooms, dining room, kitchen, pantry, bedrooms, garden, orchard, kitchen garden, fields, pastures, and woods he listed for his brother's benefit. 'In any case, I shall buy it, because it seems to me that it cannot fail to be a good deal,' he concluded. His confidence in being able to find the necessary funds may have had something to do with a revival of his marriage plans.[40]

'I have friends, much esteem, balls, parties, but far from my sweet Eugénie I can have only some pleasure, some enjoyment, but no happiness,' he wrote to Désirée at the end of August, urging her to join him, adding, 'time flies, the seasons follow each other and old age advances'. To Joseph he wrote that he wanted to 'conclude the business of Eugénie', as it was interfering with his plans; he felt it was time he married, and there was no lack of willing women in Paris. 'It is for her to sort things out, since she spoiled everything by her journey [to Genoa]. If she really wants it, everything can be easily arranged.'[41]

'You well know, my friend, that I live only for the pleasure I can give my own family, happy only in their Happiness,' he wrote to Joseph. 'If my hopes are assisted by that success which never fails me in my enterprises, I will be able to be of use to all of you, make you happy and fulfil your desires. . . .' He was trying to obtain Joseph a consulate in Italy and had managed to land Fesch a job provisioning the Army of the Rhine. He was sending Louis 300 francs a month: 'He's a good sort, and, also, just like me, he has warmth, wit, health, talent, attention to detail, all of it.' He was pleased with the way the family was doing and full of hope for the future. 'I could not be better situated or have a more pleasant and satisfactory position here,' he assured Joseph on 8 September. 'The future should be held in contempt by a man who has courage.' In between various proposals for speculating on property he returned to 'the business of Eugénie', which he insisted must be resolved. 'If these people do not wish to conclude the matter of Eugénie, so much the worse for her, since she is stupid enough to listen to them,' he wrote a couple of weeks later, making out that he would have done her family an honour by marrying her. He had better things to do than wait on them, and he crossed 'Eugénie' out of the title of his novella.[42]

He got wind of a project to send officers to Constantinople to modernise the Sultan's artillery and applied to lead it. As he explained to his brother, he would be in command of an important mission, he would probably be able to get him the post of consul, and they would make a deal of money. On 15 September 1795 he was confirmed in command of a military mission to the Porte. He selected Songis, Marmont, Junot, and Muiron to accompany him on what promised to be the adventure of a lifetime. Yet a different adventure would change his plans.[43]

9

General Vendémiaire

W HAT REALLY HAPPENED on 5 October 1795 remains a mystery. The events of that day, 13 Vendémiaire in the revolutionary calendar, were rich in consequences, not so much for the continuing course of the Revolution as for the future of one man—General Buonaparte. Yet it is his role in the events that is the most elusive.

While he was absorbed by his contradictory feelings for Désirée, his financial speculations, his military career, and his dreams of oriental riches, a new political crisis had been brewing. The men who had taken power after the fall of Robespierre had provided neither strong government and stability nor any principles which could unite the nation. They reflected all the vices and uncertainties of a society that had lost its way. Jacobins lurked in the wings, and the more extreme such as 'Gracchus' Babeuf were plotting the ultimate revolution. At the opposite end of the scale, royalists mustered for a restoration of the monarchy.

On 8 June the ten-year-old son of Louis XVI died in the Temple prison in Paris. His uncle, the late king's younger brother, issued a proclamation from Verona, where he had taken refuge, assuming the succession as Louis XVIII. Less than three weeks later the Royal Navy landed 4,000 émigrés in Brittany to support royalist insurgents. General Hoche, commanding the army in which Buonaparte should have been serving, forced them back to the Quiberon peninsula, where they and another 2,000 men landed by the British were defeated on 21 July. The following day peace was signed between France and

Spain, whose invasion force had been driven back as far as Bilbao. The Republic appeared to be secure. But royalist feeling remained strong, and discontent with the existing government simmered on.

There was a degree of consensus that the country needed a new constitution. The first, passed in September 1791, had turned France into a constitutional monarchy. It had been superseded, along with the monarchy, by a republican one in June 1793, Year I in the revolutionary calendar. But this had been quickly suspended in the state of national emergency provoked by the threat of invasion. A new one, the Constitution of Year III, was adopted on 22 August 1795. It replaced the Convention with a Council of the Five Hundred and a Council of Elders of half that number, both elected by suffrage based on property ownership. The governing Committee of Public Safety was to be superseded by an Executive Directory of five elected by the chambers through a complex procedure. 'The government will soon be formed,' Buonaparte wrote to Joseph on 12 September. 'A serene future is dawning for France.' He could not have been more wrong.[1]

Those who sat in the Convention had no intention of relinquishing power. Realising that in free elections royalists would capture a majority in both new chambers, they passed a law stipulating that two-thirds of the seats, 500 out of 750, would go to members of the existing Convention. This provoked an insurrection in Normandy and agitation in Paris. Royalists were dominant in several of the sections, the neighbourhood assemblies of the capital, and by the first days of October the city was in a state of ferment.

On the evening of 3 October Buonaparte received a note from Barras, still a member of the Committee of Public Safety, asking him to call at his house in Chaillot at ten the following morning. Barras needed 'men of execution' to deal with what he called 'the royalist terrorists' mustering their forces. It is not known what was agreed at their meeting, but Buonaparte seems to have remained noncommittal, and Barras also contacted two former Jacobin generals who had been set aside after the fall of Robespierre: Carteaux and Guillaume Brune.[2]

Insurrection was in the air, and by the time Buonaparte returned from Chaillot one of the sections, Le Pelletier, was mobilising its national guard. He nevertheless went to the theatre. By the time he came out, at about seven or eight in the evening, the situation had grown critical. The Le Pelletier section was in open revolt, turning its narrow streets into an impregnable fortress. General Jaques Menou and representatives of the Convention had set out with troops to confront the rebels, but seeing the impossibility of dislodging them without heavy casualties and realising that they would soon be trapped, they negotiated a truce and retreated. The Le Pelletier section declared itself to be the rightful authority, and called on other sections to join it.

Menou, a former officer of the royal army, was accused of treason and placed under arrest, and the search was on for someone to replace him. Writing more than twenty years later, Buonaparte asserts that he went to the Convention and found the deputies in a state of panic. The names of various generals were put forward, including his. Hidden among the spectators, he was able to slip out to consider his position. He relates that it took him half an hour to decide whether to take up the challenge: he did not like the existing authorities, but if the royalists were to get the upper hand and bring back the Bourbons, everything that had been achieved since 1789 (and his own future) would be in jeopardy. He maintains that he then offered his services to the Committee of Public Safety, on condition he was given absolute authority, without having to take instructions from its representatives as was usual.[3]

Barras tells a different story. 'There is nothing simpler than replacing Menou,' he claims to have told the Committee. 'I have the man you need; a little Corsican officer who will not be so squeamish.' In Buonaparte's version, Barras assumed nominal command of the Convention's forces, which dispensed with the requirement of government representatives, and he, as second in command, took effective control of operations.[4]

Either way, neither of them slept that night. Sometime after one o'clock on the morning of 5 October, Buonaparte ordered a young *chef d'escadron* of the 21st Mounted Chasseurs, Joachim Murat, to ride over to the plain of the Sablons and secure forty cannon stored there before the rebels could get hold of them. At first light, as the drumrolls summoning the national guards of the various sections re-sounded across the city, Buonaparte was positioning the guns at stra-tegic points around the seat of the government at the Tuileries, such as the Pont Neuf in the east, the rue Saint-Honoré to the north, and what is now the Place de la Concorde in the west.

The government troops, numbering just over 5,000 men, sup-ported by 1,500 'patriots' ready to defend the Republic against the royalists, and several hundred deputies armed with muskets, faced probably about four times their number of national guards converg-ing from all sides. There followed a lengthy stand-off. A heavy down-pour dampened the ardour of the insurgents, and it was not until around four o'clock in the afternoon that the first shots were fired. The batteries were positioned in such a way that the insurgents could not deploy and bring their superior numbers to bear, and the canister shot they fired precluded any attempt to rush them. It was all over within two hours, and while gunfire was heard at various points in the city during the night, all remaining rebel forces were mopped up the following day. Reports of casualties vary from around 400 to over a thousand.[5]

Buonaparte's version, which became official history and then leg-end as the 'whiff of grapeshot' which demonstrated his ruthless sense of purpose, has him in charge, directing everything, generously wait-ing for the insurgents to fire first, using only enough of the canister shot to show that he meant business, and firing blanks thereafter. The truth of this is hard to ascertain. 'The enemy came to attack us at the Tuileries,' he wrote to Joseph. 'We killed a lot of them. They killed 30 of our men and wounded 60. We disarmed the sections and everything is quiet.' Later he claimed that casualties were no higher than 200 dead and wounded on each side.[6]

Long after he had been shunted aside by the 'little Corsican of-ficer', an embittered Barras would describe the events differently. It was he who had planned everything, he who had ordered the guns brought from the Sablons, he who had instructed Brune to fire canis-ter shot over the heads of the oncoming rebels. 'On the 13 Vendémi-aire Bonaparte played no role other than that of my aide de camp,' he summed up. In his official report delivered to the Convention on 10 October, he praised Brune and others and did not mention Buonaparte. When Barras had finished, Fréron, still hoping to marry Paulette, rose to speak and reminded him of Buonaparte's contribution, which Barras reluctantly acknowledged. His report is not the only one to omit Buonaparte. While one account does record that he had a horse killed under him, it states that it was General Verdier who positioned the guns. There must nevertheless have been something remarkable about Buonaparte's conduct on that day.[7]

The events had shown that with well-led troops on its side, a government could put an end to the mob rule that had plagued the Revolution. High prices and food shortages meant that Paris remained vulnerable to riots, and in the following days Barras increased the military presence in the city. He recommended Buonaparte for the post of his second in command, and as he himself was about to take up that of a member of the Executive Directory, he would have to give up the command, which meant that his second would be in charge of the most powerful force in the land. It seems unlikely that he would have placed it in any but the most capable hands. There was no further mention of Constantinople, and Buonaparte was now being referred to as 'General Vendémiaire', which suggests that his role had been decisive.

On 16 October Buonaparte was promoted to divisional general, and ten days later he was confirmed as commander of the Army of the Interior. He had been effective military governor of Paris since 6 October and had immediately set about pacifying the city, reforming the National Guard, and confiscating privately held arms, discharging officers with royalist leanings and closing down the Jacobin Club, and taking in hand the police of the capital. Not confining himself to his headquarters in the Place Vendôme, he rode about the city, escorted by a retinue of staff officers and a growing number of aides, including his brother Louis, for whom he had obtained the rank of lieutenant, Junot, Marmont, and Murat, whose dash in the early hours of 5 October had impressed him. 'He never went anywhere without his moustachioed officers with their long sabres,' recalled Barras. 'He would mount his tall palfrey, wearing a huge hat with its tricolour plumes and its turned-up rims, his boots turned down, and a dangling sabre larger than its wearer.' Junot and Murat had been promoted by Buonaparte and wore with panache the distinctions of a rank they did not officially hold, while Murat embellished his uniform with various outlandish accoutrements.[8]

Buonaparte himself had grown into his role. Gone was the awkward gait. 'He already had extraordinary aplomb, a grand manner quite new to me,' remembered Marmont. He would go to the theatre, making a dramatic entrance with his entourage of swaggering young bloods, their spurs and sabres clinking as they went. He was developing a taste for the theatrical and was learning a new part. During a food riot in one of the poorer *quartiers* as he rode through it one day with his glittering cavalcade, he confronted a huge woman who accused his like of growing fat on their salaries by asking her which of them was the fatter, which provoked mirth and defused the situation.[9]

While he had not gained weight, he was certainly growing fat in the sense the woman meant. Barras, himself one of the great embezzlers of history, had seen to it that Buonaparte was well provided for. How, we do not know. Although he was drawing a salary of 4,000 francs a month, the value of the *assignats* in which it was paid had fallen dramatically: by 23 October it had dropped to 3 percent of its nominal value, and specie was extremely scarce. With a pound of sugar costing 100 francs and a bushel of potatoes 200, his salary would not have gone far. He did get a daily allowance for food and other essentials and fodder for his horses. But that does not explain how he was able to provide his mother with financial assistance adding up to more than his annual salary, send Joseph 400,000 francs, and badger Bourrienne to find him a property to buy.[10]

Further, he was not short of influence. He now wrote to Letizia that Paulette must not marry Fréron, who no longer counted politically. He was in the process of arranging a consulate in Italy for Joseph and in the meantime obtained for him letters of marque licensing two corsairs to operate out of Genoa and prey on British shipping. He found Lucien a job as commissary to the Army of the North, and Fesch one as a secretary, pending a better job overseeing the Paris hospitals. Nor did he forget more distant relatives. 'The family wants for nothing,' he declared to Joseph with satisfaction in a letter of 18 December. 'I have sent them all money, *assignats*, clothing, etc....'[11]

Barras relates that he was arranging to set Buonaparte up by marrying him off to Madame de Montansier, an older lady who owned several theatres in Paris, a sure source of income at the time. Thoughts of Désirée would not stand in the way: in a letter to his sister-in-law Marcelle Clary, Buonaparte mentions every member of the family but her. In a letter of 9 December he bids Joseph to give her his regards, but for the first time refers to her as Désirée, not Eugénie. He does ask for news of her in one written ten days later, but without the impatience that accompanied previous requests. Buonaparte did not, however, marry Madame de Montansier.[12]

Shortly after he had ordered all privately owned arms to be confiscated, a fourteen-year-old boy called at his headquarters, begging that he might be allowed to keep the sword which had belonged to his father, a general guillotined under the Terror. Moved by the boy's request, Buonaparte agreed. The following day, the story goes, the grateful mother called. Or he may have called on her, bringing the document permitting the family to keep the sword. Or, as Buonaparte would have us believe, he sent along one of his aides, who reported back that she was a beautiful widow. Or the whole story may be a fable woven round some incident to do with the sword. It is unlikely that Buonaparte had never met the widow in question, since she was a close friend of the ladies whose salons he had been frequenting for months and, being the mistress of Barras, was often at his side. One thing is certain—that General Buonaparte fell madly, almost obesssively in love with her.[13]

Marie-Josèphe-Rose de Beauharnais was born into the parvenu and scandal-ridden family of Tascher, who owned La Pagerie, a plantation in the French island colony of Martinique. She was brought to France and married off at an early age to an undistinguished nobleman, Alexandre de Beauharnais, who paraded under the assumed title of vicomte. He was jealous and abusive as well as unfaithful and repudiated her after having sired two children. During the Revolution he had briefly presided over the National Assembly and then been put in command of the Army of the Rhine. An inept soldier, he had allowed the fortress of Mainz to fall to the enemy in 1793 out of fecklessness, but was accused of treason and executed the following year. His wife, known in childhood as Yéyette and later as Josephine, was incarcerated in the same prison, Les Carmes, where, while he was conducting an affair with the widow of an executed general, she was doing the same with General Lazare Hoche, also a prisoner.

Prisons were hotbeds of sexual activity during the Terror, and Les Carmes, whose walls were still smeared with the blood of the 115 priests massacred there in September 1792, was no exception. The usual instinct in the presence of impending death was in this case reinforced by the hope of getting pregnant, which would spare a woman the guillotine. As a result, the multiple-occupancy chambers throbbed to the sound of couplings, often with the warders themselves, in scenes of fear and degradation which left their mark on those like Josephine who were fortunate enough to survive.

On her release from prison following the fall of Robespierre, Josephine made the most of the friendships forged there with, amongst others, Thérèse Tallien. She resumed her affair with General Hoche and was prominent in the exuberant new society, the salons, and the extravagant macabre entertainments of the capital. Sometime in the early summer of 1795 she became the mistress of Barras, but by the beginning of the autumn he was ready to move on and began looking around for a husband who might provide for her. She had no money and was living from day to day on the generosity of lovers, currently that of Barras, who had rented a small house for her off the rue Chantereine.

Josephine was thirty-two and, as Barras put it, 'growing precociously decrepit'. She had never been a beauty, and with her freshness wilting, she had to resort to what he called 'the most refined, the most perfected artistry ever practised by the courtesans of ancient Greece or Paris in the exercise of their profession'. She knew how to overcome every disadvantage, concealing her rotten teeth by keeping her mouth shut when she smiled, which many found irresistible. She possessed an almost legendary charm, grace, and a languor of movement which people associated with her creole origins, lending her a certain spice in their imagination. She was both dignified, with elegant manners and bearing, and girlishly light-hearted, displaying a devil-may-care attitude to practicalities. And there is little doubt that she was an accomplished lover. But she had no position to fall back on when these assets failed, and marriage was the only practical way of securing her future.[14]

According to Barras she had set her cap at Hoche, but he was married, and had allegedly commented that 'one could take a whore as a mistress for a time, but not as a legitimate wife'. It seems that Barras then suggested she marry Buonaparte. She was not taken with the idea, allegedly saying that of all the men she might bring herself to love, this 'puss in boots' was the last, and objecting that he came from 'a family of beggars', even though he was by then showering her with presents. Barras encouraged the match, partly in order to establish her on a respectable footing, perhaps also to tighten his grip on the useful young general, who was growing alarmingly independent.[15]

Buonaparte had begun to do as he pleased, appointing and cashiering officers, reorganising units, and extending his brief beyond military matters. He called on the Directors almost daily, not so much advising them as telling them what to do, and castigating them for their incompetence. When they reproved him for acting in an arbitrary manner, he reputedly countered by saying it was impossible to get anything done if one were to stick to the law, and he usually managed to get them to see things his way. Getting Buonaparte settled might make life easier for the Directors. Barras advised him that 'a married man finds his place in society', and that marriage gave a man 'more substance and greater resilience against his enemies'. Most people thought he was merely trying to park an unwanted mistress, and the Marquis de Sade would publish that version, thinly veiled, in his *Zoloé et ses deux acolytes*.[16]

Buonaparte was not as fussy as Hoche. He allegedly told Barras that he did not like the idea of seducing a virgin and preferred to find *'l'amour tout fait que l'amour a faire'*, in other words the ground well prepared. Whether those really were his words or not, there is a ring of truth about what they expressed; such cynical bluster is characteristic of the sexually insecure.[17]

The first extant letter from Buonaparte to Josephine is undated, but it was written at seven in the morning, probably in the second half of December 1795, and almost certainly after their first night of love. 'I have woken full of you,' he wrote. 'The picture of you and the memory of yesterday's intoxicating evening have left no rest to my senses. Sweet and incomparable Josephine, what a strange effect you have had on my heart!' He goes on to say that he cannot stop thinking about her and what she is doing, and cannot wait to see her again, in three hours' time. 'Meanwhile, *mio dolce amor*, a million kisses from me; but do not give me any, as your kisses set my blood on fire.'[18]

The incomparable courtesan had clearly given him his first plea-surable amorous experience. 'It was, it seems, his first love, and he experienced it with all the intensity of his nature,' noted Marmont. He also noted something else. 'What is incredible, and yet absolutely true, is that Bonaparte's vanity was flattered,' he wrote, explaining that for all his republican talk, the young general was beguiled by the social grace of the old nobility, and that in the company of the for-mer pseudo-vicomtesse de Beauharnais he felt as though he had been accepted into its charmed circle; he was not Carlo Buonaparte's son for nothing. Josephine fed Buonaparte's social aspirations with talk of her estates in Martinique, cleverly disguising her penury and hint-ing at great wealth. She had taste and flair and had managed to create a sense of elegance in the little house on the rue Chanteriene with the few sticks of furniture and meagre ornaments she possessed, and de-spite the chipped assorted china and unmatched flatware her dinners exuded refined aristocratic ease. The house itself, designed for the philosopher Condorcet by Claude Nicolas Ledoux, was an intimate retreat, reached by a narrow walled lane, a refuge from the political turmoil of the capital. Buonaparte felt well there not just on account of his love for Josephine. He quickly captivated her two children, the fourteen-year-old Eugène and the twelve-year-old Hortense. They had begun by resenting his intrusion, but gave in when he started telling them ghost stories and playing with them. Still something of a child himself, he had found a home in Paris.[19]

Josephine was unsure about this third child. 'They want me to marry, my dear friend!' she wrote to a confidante. 'All my friends urge me to, my aunt almost orders it and my children beg me to! "Do you love him?" you will ask.—Well...no. "So you find him unappealing?"—No, but I find myself in a state of tepidity which I find unpleasant....' She goes on to say that she feels she should feel greater ardour: 'I admire the general's courage, the extent of his knowledge in all things, of which he speaks equally well, the agility of his mind, which allows him to seize the thoughts of others almost before they have expressed them; but I am fearful, I confess, of the control he seems to wish to exert over everything around him. His piercing look has something about it quite mysterious which impresses even the directors: you can judge for yourself how it intimidates a woman!'

What seems to have bothered her most was his ardour. His various sexual encounters to date had evidently left him cold, and what he experienced with Josephine had opened up a gamut of new sensations and unlocked feelings he had either never known, or had repressed with all the vehemence with which he had lambasted his friend des Mazis at Valence. 'Above all,' continues Josephine, 'that which should please me, the strength of a passion of which he speaks with a force which does not permit any doubt as to its sincerity is precisely that which holds back the consent which I am often ready to give. Having passed my first youth, can I hope to preserve this violent love which, in the general's case, resembles an access of madness?' She also found it faintly ridiculous to be the object of adoration of a younger man. She was astonished at his 'absurd self-confidence', while admitting that at moments she believed him capable of anything. Her friends encouraged her, and Barras reassured her that he would soon be sending the young general off to war to cool his ardour.[20]

By then the coalition against France was in poor shape: Tuscany, Prussia, Holland, and Spain had dropped out and made peace. Only Austria, Britain, and Sardinia were actively pursuing the war. On 31 December an armistice was signed with Austria, but it was expected that hostilities would resume in the spring, and Buonaparte had pronounced ideas on how they should be conducted. Although he was now in command of Paris and the interior, he could not help meddling in overall strategy, to the annoyance of most of the Directors.

Buonaparte's plan for a two-pronged attack on Vienna, to be delivered through Germany by the Army of the Rhine under General Jean-Victor Moreau and through the Tyrol by the Army of Italy, had been sent to the relevant commanders in September 1795. It had been ridiculed by General Kellermann, who had succeeded Dumerbion at the Army of Italy, but was implemented by General Scherer, who had replaced him in command. He carried out the first stage successfully, but then, instead of moving on as prescribed, came to a standstill, pleading insufficient strength and the low morale of his troops. In January 1796 Buonaparte produced an amended version of the plan, but this too met with a critical reception, and one of the commissioners attached to the Army of Italy protested at orders being sent by 'project-mongers' 'gnawed by ambition and greedy for posts above their abilities', 'madmen' in Paris who knew nothing of the realities of the situation on the ground yet thought they could 'seize the moon with their teeth'. Scherer tendered his resignation.[21]

The Directory sent Saliceti to Nice to investigate. He reported that not only was the Army of Italy lacking in all the necessities, it was suffering from low morale, due largely to Scherer's poor leadership. At the suggestion of Barras, the head of the Directory, Carnot, appointed Buonaparte to succeed him. Carnot regarded the Italian theatre of operations as secondary and supposed that this 'little captain', as he referred to him, would be up to the limited task. The appointment nevertheless raised eyebrows, as Buonaparte had never commanded a unit, let alone an army in the field, and had never been in a real battle. There were plenty of experienced generals to choose from who, as some observed, were not treacherous Corsicans.[22]

Buonaparte set to his new task with his characteristic sense of purpose. He bought all the maps and books on Italy he could find and shut himself up for a week in his office reading, lying on his stomach on maps spread on the floor and tracing possible routes and lines of advance. On the afternoon of 8 March he met Josephine at the offices of her notary Raguideau to draw up their marriage contract and sign a *séparation de biens*, a prenuptial agreement, after which they parted and spent the night apart (Barras claims she spent it with him). Buonaparte almost certainly worked through the night, and did not emerge from his offices until that night of 9 March, when he remembered, two hours late, an important appointment.[23]

At ten o'clock he drove across a Paris thickly carpeted in snow, accompanied by his aide Jean Le Marois, to the offices of the *deuxième municipalité* of Paris, housed in the former residence of an émigré marquis, situated in the rue d'Antin. Josephine had been waiting for him there for two hours, along with Barras, Jean-Lambert Tallien, now a member of the legislative chamber, and her lawyer Étienne Calmelet, who were to witness their marriage. The man who was to marry them, the *officier de l'état civil* Carles Leclercq, had grown tired of waiting and gone home to bed, leaving a minor functionary to act in his stead.

The resulting marriage was invalid. The functionary in question had no authority to marry anyone, Buonaparte's witness Le Marois was under the required age of twenty-one, and the documents provided by both parties were spurious: pleading the impossibility of providing a birth certificate due to the British blockade of Martinique, Josephine produced a document drawn up by her notary attesting that she had been born on the island in 1767, four years after her real date of birth, while Buonaparte, using the same argument, produced a similar one giving his date of birth as 5 February 1768 (the day Corsica became French).[24]

After the ceremony, without so much as a celebratory drink, the participants went home singly, except for the newlyweds. But their wedding night was not a success, as Josephine's pet pug, Fortuné, would not let Buonaparte get into her bed and bit him in the calf when he tried. The next day he accompanied her to Madame Campan's school at Saint-Germain-en-Laye to visit Hortense. That night he may have had access to his spouse, but by the following evening he was on his way south, travelling by night in the company of Junot and the commissary Félix Chauvet. Wisely, he had opted to have his own men running the supply services, and he trusted Chauvet, who was an old friend of the family from Marseille and had served him at Toulon. After much begging he had also persuaded Jean-Pierre Collot, an efficient victualler, to come with him.[25]

They went by way of Marseille, where Buonaparte had a serious matter to attend to. He had not asked his mother for permission to marry, a mark of disrespect and a sin against Corsican family lore, nor had he informed any of his siblings of the forthcoming event— with good reason. He knew that Josephine did not conform to their idea of a desirable wife or a useful addition to the family. She came from an alien milieu, and not only did she not bring any money with her, her interests and those of her children were bound to conflict with those of the Buonaparte. He had himself berated Lucien for his marriage to the lowly Christine Boyer, and more recently had ruled out allowing Paulette to marry the waning Fréron. Lucien, who knew Josephine and disliked her, would no doubt have enjoyed alerting Letizia to his brother's *mésalliance*. On reaching Marseille, Buonaparte apprised Letizia of his marriage and delivered a fittingly deferential letter from Josephine. She took some persuasion and consulted Joseph before grudgingly responding with a letter whose text Buonaparte had prepared in advance.[26]

He did not call on Désirée, now back in Marseille, but she heard his news and wrote him a suitably heartbroken and melodramatic letter: 'You have made me miserable for the rest of my life, and yet I still have the heart to forgive you. My life is a horrible torture for me since I can no longer devote it to you. . . . You, Married! I cannot accustom myself to the idea, it is killing me, I cannot survive it.' She ended by assuring him that she would never marry another.[27]

Her letter might have moved the 'Clisson' of a few months earlier, but now Buonaparte had thoughts only for Josephine. 'Every instant takes me further away from you, my adorable love, and with every instant I find less and less strength with which to bear being away from you,' he wrote as he sped south two days after leaving her in Paris. 'You are the constant object of all my thoughts,' he assured her, wishing he could be back reading 'our wonderful Ossian' together. It is the first extant document he signed 'Bonaparte'.[28]

10

Italy

WHEN HE REACHED the headquarters of the Army of Italy at Nice on 26 March 1796, the twenty-six-year-old Bonaparte faced one of the greatest challenges of his life. He had never held independent command of so much as a platoon in the field, yet he was now commander-in-chief of an army, staffed with men older and more experienced than him, with sound reputations. Such was André Masséna, eleven years his senior, a big, tall man with expansive gestures and an ironic, malicious smile, the son of a petty grocer from Nice who had been orphaned early and run away to sea, then joined the royal army in which he rose as high as a plebeian could, before, after a spell as a smuggler, fighting his way to general's rank in the army of the Republic. He was a force of nature, uneducated, ostentatiously brave, determined and effective in battle, displaying tactical flair—and a piratical lust for treasure. Another was Charles-Pierre Augereau, twelve years older than Bonaparte, the son of a servant and a Parisian fruit-seller who had a long career behind him as a mercenary in the Neapolitan and Prussian armies before rising in that of the Republic by his conspicuous bravery. He too was a tall, martial figure, with a big nose, the blustering demeanour of a bully, and the subversive attitude of a proletarian revolutionary. Foul-mouthed and violent, this child of the streets was popular with his men. The only thing the third corps commander shared with the others was a massive physique. Jean-Mathieu Sérurier was an educated fifty-three-year-old minor nobleman and veteran of the royal army who had seen action in the Seven Years' War, a conscientious, steady, brave, and efficient general.

Unlike regular armies, in which a man's rank is taken as a mark of his worth, in the armies of the Republic officers and men learned to trust and esteem only those with a reputation bestowed by those who served under them and spread by word of mouth. Masséna had come across Bonaparte at the siege of Toulon, but was unaware of his contribution to the fall of the town, and to him and the other officers in the Army of Italy, its new commander was an unknown quantity. But they did know he had taken part in the events of Vendémiaire and that he was a political appointment, a 'Parisian general' and an 'intriguer' with no substance, in the words of another who had come across him at Toulon, *chef de bataillon* Louis-Gabriel Suchet. They had been expecting the worst, but when they actually saw the man they despaired. In their eyes his diminutive stature, pathetic appearance, awkward manner, and rasping voice ruled him out as an effective leader of men.[1]

Bonaparte immediately assumed a tone which brooked no argument. 'I have taken command of the Army of Italy,' he wrote to Masséna less than forty-eight hours after his arrival. 'Nominating me, the executive Directory hopes that I may be of use in leading it towards the brilliant destiny which awaits it. Europe contemplates it with awe, and France expects from it all the triumphs of a campaign.' At the same time he flattered the commanders, officers, and men, raising their hopes of action, glory, and rewards, while Junot and Marmont spread their own admiration and love of the new commander. With a dose of wishful thinking, four days after his arrival he assured Josephine that 'my soldiers display a confidence in me impossible to describe'.[2]

The troops were in poor shape. To have any idea of the conditions, one has to forget all the paintings of finely uniformed officers leading ranks of men with immaculate white facings and bright-red epaulettes on their well-cut blue coats, with blue, white, and red plumes in their hats. Few of the men had boots, and many had no trousers. Some had no uniform jackets. They made themselves footwear out of woven straw and in the absence of hats wore knotted handkerchiefs on their heads. Most of them looked more like scarecrows than soldiers.[3]

They had scant equipment and were expected to find themselves shelter for the night as best they could when on operations, as there were no tents. Disease and infections dramatically reduced the number of effectives. The companies contracted to supply them pocketed most of the money they received from the government. Even in cantonment around Nice the troops were poorly fed, with meat once every four days, beans once in three, and bowls of rice flavoured with lard the rest of the time. In the autumn they had been able to supplement their diet by gathering chestnuts, but the winter had robbed them of this resource. They could not buy food, as they were paid irregularly, and then only in worthless *assignats*. Some of the senior officers who received cash contributions from the local administration to pay the men did not pass it on. The men had been stuck in the same place for months with nothing to do, and morale was low. Desertion was rife and acts of insubordination frequent. Disaffection had reignited anti-government and even royalist feeling among the older men, and shouts of '*Vive le Roi*' were not infrequent. One demi-brigade mutinied shortly before Bonaparte's arrival, one soon after.[4]

Bonaparte realised extreme measures were needed, and with Saliceti as the Directory's commissioner, he was in a position to take them. He had a couple of officers court-martialled to set an example. He sent Chauvet to Genoa to raise a loan and purchase supplies and wrote to the local authorities demanding food and forage, threatening to send the men out to loot and rape if these were not provided. With a mixture of threat and flattery he managed to get the contractors to disgorge victuals and the local administration to make up for some of the arrears in pay. He gave instructions that the men must have fresh or salt meat every day.[5]

He had selected as his chief of staff a man of experience, his senior in rank and age, whom he had met only recently. The forty-two-year-old Alexandre Berthier had trained as a military engineer and cartographer before receiving his baptism of fire as a captain in the American War of Independence. With his steady temperament, extraordinary memory, unmatched attention to detail, precise mode of expression, and legible handwriting, Berthier was the perfect man for the job. He could grasp in a second some hastily-rapped-out order and give it coherent form, while his team ensured it was passed on to the appropriate quarter with a professionalism hitherto unknown in the army of the Republic. Bonaparte supervised and inspected, noting deficiencies and passing them on to Berthier, demanding immediate action. He was so confident that within two days of his arrival he reported to Carnot that 'I have been very well received by the army, which shows a confidence in me for which I am deeply grateful.' Quite how much confidence the army felt is questionable.[6]

François Vigo-Roussillon, a sergeant in the 32nd Demi-Brigade under Masséna, was astonished when his neighbour whispered that the diminutive figure who had just ridden up to their ranks was the new commander-in-chief. 'His appearance, his dress, his bearing did not appeal to us,' he recalled; '...small, slight, very pale, with great black eyes and hollow cheeks, with long hair falling from his brow to his shoulders in two dog's ears, as they were then known. He wore a blue uniform coat and over that a nut-brown overcoat. He was mounted on a large bony sorrel horse with a docked tail.' He was followed by a single servant 'on a rather sad looking mule' borrowed from the supply train. The new general introduced himself to the assembled troops with a speech in which he held out the prospect of glory and the possibility of rich plunder if they managed to defeat the enemy and break into Italy. His address produced little effect, and one officer recalled that afterward the men made fun of his hairstyle and mimicked his accent.[7]

The troops were an amalgam of former royal soldiers, volunteers, and conscripts. Most of the younger men came from the poorer mountainous regions of southern France. They were physically hardened and used to rigorous marches. The make-up of the officer corps was overwhelmingly plebeian (the percentage of nobles had fallen from 80 to 5 between 1789 and 1793), which contributed a sense of fraternity between officers and men, enhanced by the universal penury, as officers and even most of the generals could not afford a horse (the artillery was drawn by mules). The most disciplined units were those which had just been transferred from Spain, where they had fought a victorious campaign.[8]

The infantry divisions each had between three and five demi-brigades, the basic fighting unit at the time. The heavy demi-brigades were supposed to number 3,000 men and the light ones 1,500. Masséna commanded two divisions, Augereau and Sérurier one each. The cavalry, which numbered less than 5,000 men and was of poor quality and short of horses, was led by General Henri Stengel, a fifty-two-year-old German who had been in French service from the age of sixteen. The overall strength of the French Army of Italy was, on paper, 60,000 men, but most historians agree that the real figure was no more than about 47,000. Some put it as low as 35,000.[9]

Facing them in the Alpine passes were 18,000 men of the Sardinian army, well-trained, hardy Savoyard mountain men under the command of the Austrian field marshal baron de Colli. Beside them stood 35,000 Austrians under the seventy-one-year-old Field Marshal de Beaulieu, a Belgian by birth. His troops were disciplined, well-trained, steady, and motivated, but they were used to set-piece battles and methodical manoeuvres, which would disadvantage them in the tight valleys and boulder-strewn terrain on which they were to fight.

Bonaparte's orders were to stage a diversion that would tie down the maximum number of Austrian forces in Italy while the two stronger French armies poised on the Rhine defeated the main Austrian army in Germany and marched on Vienna. But he did not think like a soldier content merely to carry out the task he had been set. He believed that as long as the Habsburgs remained dominant in Italy they would present a threat to France and that the centuries-old rivalry between the two states for hegemony over the peninsula should be resolved. He had studied the various Franco-Austrian wars over Italy, most recently Marshal Maillebois's campaigns of 1745–46. He had pored over maps of the area over the past two years, becoming familiar with the lie of the land and making mental notes of which passes were practicable by artillery, where rivers could be forded, and which were the possible lines of advance and retreat not only for his own army but for the enemy as well. He meant to wipe out the threat to France by expelling the Austrians from Italy.

One weapon in this struggle would be the nascent Italian national movement, which identified the Austrians as oppressors. Many of the nationalists were living in exile in Nice, and Bonaparte held meetings with them. He did not think much of those he met, and had a poor opinion of Italians in general, but he decided to take 150 of them, led by Filippo Buonarotti, along with him. On 31 March he issued a proclamation to the people of Piedmont announcing that the French nation would shortly liberate them.[10]

The following day his divisions were on the move. On 4 April he set up headquarters at Albenga, where he heard of the death of his friend Chauvet in Genoa. Collot was shocked by the apparent indifference with which Bonaparte received the news, merely instructing him to take over. Here and on similar occasions he made a show of calm, even brash self-control, hiding the emotional turmoil that comes through in his letters, particularly to Josephine. 'Not a day has passed without my writing to you, not a night has passed without me pressing you in my arms, I have not drunk a cup of tea without cursing the desire for glory and the ambition which keep me far from the soul of my life,' he had written from Nice, complaining that her letters were scarce and cold, and that in contrast to his soldiers, only she withheld her trust and remained 'the joy and the torment' of his life.[11]

To her he poured out his despair at the news of Chauvet's death. 'What is the future? What is the past? What are we?' he questioned, wondering at the purpose of life, and 'what magical fluid shrouds us and conceals all that we should most want to know?' But this was no time to brood, and he must think only of the army. Two days later he wrote to her in a more passionate vein, telling of his burning desire for her and sending her a kiss on a point of her body 'lower than the heart, much, much lower'.[12]

On 9 April Bonaparte transferred to Savona as his three corps took up their positions, with Masséna on the right, Augereau in the centre, and Sérurier to their left. But it was the Austrians who struck first. Beaulieu had misinterpreted a French reconnaissance along the coast as the vanguard of an attack on Genoa, and, assuming that the whole French army would be following, decided to drive in its flank through Montenotte and Monte Legino. His attack on what he

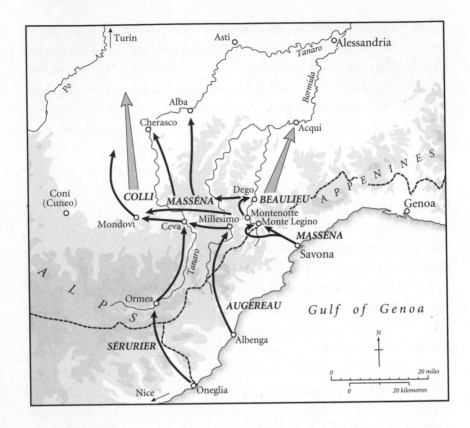

assumed to be the French flank ran head-on into the units at Monte Legino preparing to attack.[13]

Bonaparte had intended to strike at the gap where the Alps ended and the Appenines began, which was the juncture between the Sardinians and their Austrian allies. While Sérurier pinned down the Sardinians frontally and Augereau turned their flank at Millesimo, Masséna was to move into the gap between the two armies. Bonaparte calculated that if he inserted a wedge between the two and prised them apart, strategic imperatives would force the Sardinians to fall back in a northerly direction toward their base at Turin and the Austrians to retreat eastward toward theirs at Milan. He would then be able to defeat them separately. His studies had convinced him that it was superior numbers that won battles and that the art of war could be reduced to the one principle of bringing greater forces to bear at a given point.[14]

As they sheltered from the torrential rain that night, planning to renew their attack the next morning, the Austrians at Monte Legino were unaware that, quickly appraising the situation, Bonaparte had ordered Masséna to veer right and make a forced march through the night to Montenotte in their rear. 'Everything suggests that today and tomorrow will go down in history,' Berthier wrote to Masséna with his latest orders.[15]

The following morning, as the Austrian commander was about to push home his attack, the dispersing mist revealed Masséna's divisions deploying on his flank and rear. Coming under simultaneous attack from two sides, he ordered a retreat which quickly turned into a rout. It had been little more than a skirmish, with Austrian losses in dead, wounded, and prisoners around 2,700 and the French no more than a hundred, but Bonaparte accorded it the status of a full-scale battle. In his self-aggrandising report to the Directory, he claimed that the main Austrian force commanded by Beaulieu himself was involved, that it had lost up to 4,000 men and 'several' flags (in fact only one was captured), and blew the event up to epic proportions. His order of the day to the troops echoed this, praising them for their glorious exploit. It was the first brushstroke of what was to be a masterpiece of mendacity.[16]

Beaulieu had in fact spent the day several kilometres away, sitting badly bruised by a roadside while his escort struggled to repair the carriage that had pitched him to the ground. He had realised his mistake too late and had lost valuable time, which Bonaparte was not going to let him regain. He urged Augereau, most of whose men were still marching without boots, and many without muskets, to hasten his attack on Millesimo, and Masséna to strike further into the Austrian rear at Dego. Once Augereau had accomplished his task, he was to swing left and begin to roll up the extremity of the Sardinian line.

Bonaparte needed to keep up the momentum so that neither of his opponents had time to regroup and strike back; if they did, he would be caught between two fires. He therefore reacted violently to any apparent hitch. After Augereau had sent the Sardinians reeling at Millesimo, one force of about 1,000 men under General Provera had ensconced themselves in an old fortress at Cosseria. Knowing them to have no more supplies or water than those they carried, Augereau meant to leave a few hundred men to pin them down and take their inevitable surrender while he went after the retreating main body of Sardinians. But Bonaparte insisted he storm Cosseria. In the ensuing assault the French suffered heavy losses from the Sardinians sniping from the battlements. Provera offered to capitulate, but Bonaparte tried to bully him into unconditional surrender, threatening to take no prisoners, and ordered Augereau to attack once more. This attack proved as futile as the first. Provera duly surrendered the next morning, having lost no more than 150 men, while Bonaparte's impatience had cost the French at least 600 and possibly as many as 1,000 casualties. He did have the good grace to admit his mistake and express regret.[17]

To Augereau's right, Masséna attacked the citadel of Dego, where over the next two days some of the most serious fighting took place, with the citadel changing hands several times. After the final assault, which he directed himself, Bonaparte promoted a young *chef de bataillon* named Lannes whose dash had caught his attention.

On 16 April Bonaparte learned that Beaulieu was retreating to Acqui on the road to Milan; his plan had worked. He ordered Masséna to move northward against the Sardinians. Colli's dwindling force was falling back in order to defend Turin. It fought doggedly, inflicting heavy losses on the French, but on 21 April, after a brief defence it had to abandon its base and stores at Mondovi. That evening the King of Sardinia, Victor Amadeus, summoned a special council in Turin. As Beaulieu had signalled that he was not able to come to his aid, further resistance seemed pointless; on the morning of 23 April Colli requested an armistice.

Bonaparte replied that he lacked the necessary powers and continued his advance. When pressed by the desperate Sardinians to agree to a ceasefire, he replied that he would be putting himself at risk if he did so without guarantees and could only sign one if they handed over the fortresses of Coni, Tortona, and Alessandria. In order to prevent Beaulieu from attempting to succour his Sardinian allies, he moved quickly on Cherasco and Alba, where he encouraged Piedmontese revolutionaries to establish a 'Republic', as a signal to the king that he could overthrow him if he wished. He applied further pressure by raising his demands to include the cession of Savoy and Nice to France and the supply of his army with all its needs. These he delivered as an ultimatum on 27 April.[18]

The two men sent to conclude the negotiations and sign the armistice, the old Piedmontese general La Tour and Colli's chief of staff, Colonel Costa de Beauregard, found Bonaparte late on the night of 27 April in a barely guarded house in Cherasco. He was haughty and firm, threatening to launch further attacks every time they suggested softening his terms. At one o'clock in the morning he informed them that his troops were under orders to begin the advance on Turin at two. But having bullied them into signing the armistice he offered them a snack of broth, cold meats, hardtack, and some pastries made by the local nuns, during which he became talkative. Although Beauregard was impressed by the brilliance and wide-ranging interests Bonaparte displayed, he found him cold, proud, bitter, and lacking in any grace or amenity. He also noted that he was very tired and his eyes were red. As they parted he said to Bonaparte, 'General, how sad that one cannot like you as much as one cannot help admiring and esteeming you!'[19]

Bonaparte had weightier concerns than the affection of his enemies. He had exceeded his brief and his duty as a soldier. He was single-handedly deciding French foreign policy, presenting the Directory with a *fait accompli*. He was, it is true, acting in concert with commissioner Saliceti, who was with him during the negotiations, but he was still at risk of being recalled in disgrace. As he had meant to act independently all along, he had anticipated this eventuality and been shoring up his position.

His treatment of the troops under his command had been designed from the start not only to make them more effective as fighting men but also to turn them into *his* men. He had achieved the first aim by giving them victory: nothing acts on the soldier's self-esteem like success. It was clear to them that this success was largely due to Bonaparte's talents, yet he made them feel it was all down to them. He had developed a gift for talking to the men as equals. His extraordinary memory allowed him to remember their names, their

units, where they came from, their ages, histories, and above all their
military exploits. He would come up to a man and ask about some
personal problem or congratulate him on a past feat like an old comrade. He was not shy of reprimanding officers in front of the troops,
to show that he was their friend.

He had refrained from being too strict with them at first, allowing
these men who had been starved of food, comforts, and action for
so long to indulge their basic instincts. They preyed on the country
they went through, and by the time he had reached Cherasco he had
to admit to being frightened by the 'horrors' they were committing.
'The soldier who lacks bread is driven to excesses of violence which
make one blush for humanity,' he reported on 24 April. By then
they had had a chance to fill their bellies and pull boots and items of
clothing they lacked from Austrian and Sardinian dead or prisoners.
Once he had halted his advance and managed to capture Sardinian
stores, Bonaparte was able to begin reining them in. 'The pillage is
growing less widespread,' he reported to the Directory on 26 April.
'The primal thirst of an army lacking everything is being quenched.'
He had three men shot and six others condemned to hard labour,
then shot a few more for looting a church. 'It costs me much sadness
and I have passed some difficult moments,' he admitted.[20]

While he tightened discipline, he took care to flatter the soldiers'
self-esteem, making throwaway statements such as 'With 20,000
men like that one could conquer Europe!' He described their feats
of arms in superlative terms in his proclamations. In that of 26 April
he listed the engagements they had taken part in as if they were great
battles, gave inflated figures of enemy dead and wounded, guns and
standards captured, and told them they were heroic conquerors and
liberators who would one day look back with pride on the glorious
epic they had shared in. He encouraged the sense that they were
making history with references to Hannibal as they came over the
Alpine passes.[21]

A mixture of growing self-confidence and the urge to earn
praise fed their eagerness to live up to his expectations of them. 'I
can hardly express to what degree of intoxication and pride such resounding, repeated and rapid triumphs transported our army, and

what a noble emulation inspired all ranks,' noted Collot. 'They vied with each other to be the first to reach a redoubt, to be the first to storm a battery, the first across a river, to show the most devotion and audacity.'[22]

Bonaparte's despatches to the Directory were no less hyperbolic. He wrote dramatic descriptions of every engagement, exaggerating the obstacles and the efforts with which they had been overcome, playing fast and loose with facts and figures, and singling out individual acts of courage in melodramatic images of republican heroism. At the same time, he stressed his lack of equipment and berated his masters in Paris for failing to send him guns and trained artillery officers and engineers. To Carnot he expressed his 'despair, I could almost say my rage' at not having the tools with which to do the job he had been set.[23]

Desperate to reap the fruits of success, the Directory proclaimed the victories of French arms loudly and published extracts from the despatches. The name of Bonaparte was soon familiar throughout the country, and was becoming subliminally associated with heroism, genius, and victory. On 25 April Bonaparte sent Joseph and Junot to Paris with the twenty-one enemy standards captured so far, knowing that their progress through France and their arrival in Paris would make an impression. 'It would be difficult to convey the enthusiasm of the population,' Joseph confirmed. After signing the armistice of Cherasco, Bonaparte sent Murat with the document and more standards. Whatever their feelings about him and his doings, the Directory were happy to bask in the reflected glory and could only hail him as a national hero.[24]

Murat was burdened with another mission—to persuade Josephine to come to Italy. From the moment he left Paris, Bonaparte had not stopped thinking about her and longing for her to join him, and nothing could banish her from his thoughts. He could not understand why she did not write more often, why her letters were often lukewarm, and why she had not made haste to join him. He wrote to her every day, sometimes more than once, even after exhausting marches and hard-fought engagements. He had thoughts for nobody else. After Dego he was brought a beautiful young woman taken prisoner along with an Austrian officer, but he passed up the chance of having her and allowed her to go on her way.[25]

When he sent Joseph to Paris he entrusted him with a letter for Josephine, whom he had yet to meet. She was sure to like him, he wrote. 'Nature has endowed him with a gentle, even and thoroughly good character; he is full of good qualities,' he assured her. He wanted her to come out to Italy with the returning Junot. 'You must come with him, do you understand?' he wrote, urging her to seek inspiration and strength by reading Ossian. 'Take wing, come, come!' He had also written to Barras, asking him to press her to come. From Cherasco the day following the armistice he assured her that no woman was ever 'loved with more devotion, fire and tenderness', and that his love grew with every day that passed. He could not understand how she had come to mean so much to him. He had a carriage, silver, and china for her, so all she needed was to bring a chambermaid and a cook.[26]

Josephine had no intention of leaving Paris, with its parties and theatres and the many friends she loved. And she had recently taken up with Hippolyte Charles, a dashing hussar officer, a good lover, and a jovial companion who kept her entertained. Bonaparte had begun to suspect something of the sort, but his mind was taken up with more pressing matters.

Lodi

BEAULIEU WAS BY no means beaten, and given the chance to rally he would be in a position to crush the French. Bonaparte's forces had been whittled down by fighting and forced marches, and although he had received reinforcements, his army's cohesion and morale were still frail. According to his own assessment, the French soldier's outstanding quality was the ability to march quickly in pursuit of a retreating enemy, building up as he went a determination and an impetus which gave him the edge. But this was lost when he came under attack from seasoned regulars.[1]

He ordered Sérurier to feign crossing the Po at Valenza in order to prompt Beaulieu to defend that stretch of the river. He himself led a small body of troops in a forced march covering sixty-four kilometres in thirty-six hours along the right bank of the river to Piacenza. There, deep in the Austrian rear, he crossed the river on 9 May 1796, hoping to cut off Beaulieu's line of retreat. 'The second campaign has begun,' he wrote to Carnot that evening. 'Beaulieu is disconcerted; he calculates poorly and constantly falls into the traps set for him.' But the Austrian commander had realised what was happening and hastily fell back across the next line of defence, the river Adda. Bonaparte pursued him but failed to catch up, reaching the little town of Lodi as the Austrian rearguard was crossing the river. He only just managed to bring up a couple of guns and open fire to prevent them from destroying the bridge.[2]

No sensible general would have considered trying to cross this 200-metre-long wooden bridge, no more than ten metres wide, at the other end of which the Austrians had placed cannon which could rake it with fire. But Bonaparte was not a sensible general, and his men were buoyed by success. Without waiting for the rest of his force to arrive, he drew up the troops at his disposal, made a rousing speech, and ordered them to storm the bridge. They surged forward, only to be mown down by canister shot, but others followed, led by Berthier, Masséna, and Lannes, who showed total disregard for danger. Having got halfway across, some of the men climbed down the piles onto a sandbank from which they waded across to the opposite bank, where they engaged the Austrian defenders from the flank. After two more attempts the French managed to charge across the bridge and dislodge the Austrians, who fell back leaving 153 dead, 182 wounded, and 1,701 prisoners. French losses totalled less than 500, possibly as little as 350.[3]

'*Pero non fu gran cosa,*' Bonaparte commented that evening at dinner in the residence of the Bishop of Lodi. But he was determined that to the outside world it should be a *grandissima cosa*. 'The battle of Lodi, my dear Director, gives the whole of Lombardy to the Republic,' he wrote to Carnot that evening, announcing that he was about to pursue and finally defeat Beaulieu. His description of the capture of the bridge was predictably florid, and he claimed for this 'battle' a significance which it would acquire only thanks to his efforts. Saliceti followed up with an account that was outright poetic. These would be broadcast to the public in France and would soon be supplemented by images. Bonaparte asked the French minister in Genoa, Guillaume Faipoult, to commission an engraving of the glorious feat, the result of which was an image of himself, standard in hand, leading his men across the bridge under a hail of shot. He made sure that from now on every feat of arms was immortalised by an icon.[4]

He needed to enhance his authority by any means available. While at Lodi he had received two letters from Paris, one welcome, one less so. The first was from Murat, informing him that Josephine had only delayed coming out to join him in Italy because she was pregnant and feared travelling. It was not true, but she could think of no other excuse to avoid leaving Paris. Bonaparte was pleased by the news that he was to become a father, and while he was concerned for her health, he felt that her supposed condition would guarantee her fidelity.[5]

Earlier that day he had received less welcome news. The Directory felt he had accomplished his prescribed aim of creating a diversion to assist the two French armies operating in Germany, and now sent him new instructions. They ordered the remainder of the Army of the Alps into Italy and planned to divide the French forces on the peninsula into a northern one under the sixty-five-year-old professional soldier and acclaimed victor of the invading Prussians at Valmy in 1792, General Kellermann, and a southern under Bonaparte, which was to march on Rome and overthrow 'the last of the popes'.

This did not suit him at all, as he was set on his cherished enterprise of the subversion of Italy. On 1 May he had written to Faipoult in Genoa asking for material on the topography, resources, constitutional arrangements, and economic potential of every state on the peninsula. During his march to Piacenza he had crossed territory belonging to the neutral duchy of Parma. He had made a feint as though he were about to attack its capital, which prompted the duke to despatch envoys to ask for his neutrality to be respected—which it was, in return for a huge bribe in silver, corn, oats and other victuals, 1,600 horses, twenty works of art, and an undertaking to maintain hospitals for the French wounded. 'These little princes need to be managed,' Bonaparte commented in his report to the Directory, ignoring the fact that it was not his business to manage anybody beside his soldiers. 'The war in Italy at this moment is half military and half diplomatic', he explained, instructing his superiors in Paris on the positions they should take in negotiating a treaty with the King of Sardinia.[6]

He sent off three letters protesting against the plan to split the command—an official one to the Directory, one to Carnot, and one to Barras—all three couched in a mixture of petulance and disingenuousness. 'If I have lost the trust I enjoyed at the beginning of the campaign, I entreat you to let me know,' he wrote to Barras. 'In that case I would ask to be allowed to resign. As well as certain talents, nature has endowed me with a strong character, and I cannot be of any use here unless I have your entire confidence. If the intention is to make me play a secondary role, to oblige me to flap about under the orders of commissioners, to be subjected *in my operations* to a German whose *principles* I esteem no more than his manner, then I will leave the field to him.' That, as the Directors well knew and Saliceti reminded them, would not have gone down well with the public, which had just received news of the epic feat of Lodi. To drive home his usefulness, Bonaparte sent a number of messages over the next few days, announcing the despatch of 2 million francs in gold from here, a fortune in jewellery and ingots from there, not to mention a hundred 'fine horses, the finest that could be found' for the Directors' own carriages.[7]

'It is only after Lodi that it struck me that I might become a major actor on our political scene,' he would later tell his secretary. 'It was then that the first spark of a higher ambition was ignited in me.' He was sitting, lost in thought, by the fireside in the corner of a room on the evening of 7 May when it dawned on him that he was better qualified than the government he was serving. In writing up the fluke result of his actions at Lodi as a grand feat of arms he seems to have convinced himself that he possessed, or was possessed by, some kind of superior force. This is not entirely surprising, given that over the past four weeks success had followed success in an almost miraculous progression. Writing home to his father, Marmont could not contain his wonder. The less-than-admiring Costa de Beauregard reflected that 'Bonaparte makes one think of those heroes who would cleave mountains with a flourish of their sword,' a kind of magician who could do anything. A few days after Lodi, Bonaparte told Marmont that Fortune had singled him out and become his mistress. Such grandiloquent, emotionally charged phrases might sound like so much hot air, but they did express genuine thoughts and aspirations.[8]

The eighteenth century had seen the gradual replacement of the Christian view of life as a preparation for the next world with one which envisaged ways of attaining fulfilment in this. The French Revolution was born largely from the desire to reorder the world in this sense. The rejection of Christianity had suggested a return to the world of ancient Greece and Rome, which seemed more in tune with the republican ideals of the day. This was expressed in and nourished by the neo-classical movement in the arts. The legislative bodies of the French Republic dressed in togas, prominent figures assumed names taken from antiquity such as Brutus and Gracchus, and political discourse was peppered with classical references. The break with the civilisation of Christian Europe was symbolised by the adoption of a new calendar and the metric system with which to measure time and space in the new world the legislative bodies of the French Republic had created. It was Man, not God, who was central to the new value system, and his collective identity, the Nation or 'patrie', became the object of worship. Henri Beyle, to become famous as the novelist Stendhal, was thirteen when Bonaparte took command of

the Army of Italy and recalled that for his generation 'our only religion was [...] *to be of service to the patrie*'.[9]

The Revolution generated a cult of self-sacrifice for the cause
whose 'martyrs' were represented in paintings by David and others
in much the same manner as Christian saints had been. Where the
crusaders of old sought Christian salvation, the soldiers of the French
Republic believed their exertions would be crowned by a human version of immortality, loosely expressed in the word '*gloire*'.

'The eldest of our generals had barely reached the age of thirty,'
recalled Bonaparte's contemporary Lavalette, serving in the Army of
the Rhine. 'All of them aspired only to glory, and in their eyes it
was only real if it involved danger.' Marmont had a signet ring made
which 'expressed all the wishes with which my young heart was filled:
it featured three interlaced crowns, one of ivy, one of laurel and one
of myrtle, with this motto: *I hope to deserve them*' (ivy was the symbol
of eternity, laurel of fame, and myrtle of manhood and love).[10]

'Of all the passions which affect the human heart, there is none
which is more forceful than the love of *la gloire*,' wrote Germaine de
Staël in her book *De l'Influence des passions sur le bonheur des individus
et des nations*, published that very year of 1796. She did not belittle the
part played in this by ambition or vanity, but saw the pursuit of *gloire*
as a force in itself. 'It is, without doubt, an intoxicating sensation to
fill the universe with one's name, to go so far beyond the bounds of
one's being that it becomes possible to delude oneself as to the limits
and extent of one's life, and to believe that one possesses some of the
metaphysical attributes of infinity.' She pointed out that in this psychological climate, anyone who could achieve *gloire* and offer to others
the chance of a share in it would excite in them the spirit of emulation
to such a degree that they would exert themselves to the very limit and
beyond, creating a seemingly superhuman surge of energy.[11]

Brought up reading Plutarch's lives of the heroes, Bonaparte and
his peers yearned to emulate them. They were also profoundly affected by the Romantic sensibility expressed in the works of Rousseau, Goethe, and Macpherson. The conflation of the urge to the
heroic with that for emotional transcendence developed in many a

subliminal belief that they were living a legend and conquering the impossible, like not just the heroes but also the gods of antiquity.

It was in the guise of a conquering hero that, on 15 May, Bonaparte made a triumphal entry into Milan, the capital of Lombardy, mounted on a white horse, preceded by a column of Austrian prisoners and followed at a respectful distance by his staff and then his troops. He passed under a Roman triumphal arch and another made of foliage and flowers, greeted with enthusiasm by Italian Jacobins and nationalists who had been awaiting him, in the words of one of them, 'as the Israelites awaited the Messiah', hailing him as their deliverer from Austrian rule and, they hoped, the godfather of an independent Italian state. Those less politically aroused also turned out in force to get a look at this man whose deeds were assuming legendary proportions in the public imagination. As it was a Sunday and the feast of the Pentecost they were dressed up, presenting a curious contrast with the conquerors of the mighty Austrian army.[12]

'Our uniforms, worn out by long spells of mountain warfare, had been replaced by anything the soldiers could lay their hands on,' recalled Sergeant Vigo-Roussillon. 'In place of our long-rotted cartridge-cases we had belts made of goatskin in which we carried our cartridges. Our heads were covered with bonnets made of sheep, cat or rabbit fur. A fox-fur bonnet with the tail hanging down the back was a prized possession.' They wore breeches or trousers of every colour, fancy, even embroidered waistcoats, and a variety of footwear.[13]

Two comrades-in-arms, a major and a lieutenant, shared three shirts, one pair of brown trousers, one uniform coat, and one overcoat, which was worn by the one not wearing the trousers that day. One young officer brushed up as best he could when invited to dinner by the marchesa in whose residence he was billeted, but nevertheless padded into the dining room on bare feet.[14]

Bonaparte had gone straight to the archbishop's residence, where he slept for a couple of hours and had a bath before attending a banquet in his honour. He then moved into the Serbelloni Palace, which had been placed at his disposal. He was also offered the beautiful *prima donna* of La Scala, Giuseppina Grassini, but could think only of Josephine, so Berthier stepped in. Bonaparte was not going to waste time in Milan.

On 20 May he issued a proclamation to his 'brothers in arms': 'Soldiers! You rushed like a torrent from the heights of the Apennines, you defeated, dispersed, scattered all that opposed your progress. Delivered from Austrian tyranny, Piedmont gave in to its natural sentiments of peace and friendship with France. Milan is yours, and the republican standard flies over the whole of Lombardy. The dukes of Parma and Modena owe their continued political existence only thanks to your generosity. The army which threatened you with such arrogance can no longer find a bulwark strong enough to shield it from your courage.' He could see they were already tired of inactivity, and burning to achieve greater glory: 'Well, let us go forward!' he continued. 'We still have forced marches to make, enemies to subdue, laurels to pick, wrongs to avenge.' While they must be ready to defend the Republic, they must also fly to the aid of sister nations: 'You will have the immortal glory of changing the face of the most beautiful part of Europe. The French nation, free, respected throughout the world, will give Europe a glorious peace which will redeem all the sacrifices it has made over the past six years. You will then return to your homes, and your fellow-citizens will say as they point you out: "He was in the Army of Italy!"'[15]

More to the point, he decreed that whereas they had hitherto been paid in paper money, which few, particularly in foreign lands, would accept, henceforth they would receive half of their pay in specie. The move was probably dictated in part by the need to stem the looting, but it also created a new bond of gratitude and loyalty between him and his men. The Directory was appalled by this act of independence, which diverted some of the cash being sucked out of Italy, on which it was coming to depend, into the pockets of the troops. But there was nothing it could do. Bonaparte was the only one of the army commanders helping to finance it; he was winning battles and riding high in public opinion. He was beyond the Directors' control, and whether they liked it or not, their fate was closely tied to his popularity. On 29 May a fête of thanksgiving and victory would be held in Paris at which the captured banners were paraded, a contingent of wounded were honoured with oak leaves, sprigs of laurel, and palm fronds, symbolising valour, glory, and martyrdom, and a 'Song of Victory', while Junot presented Josephine, now hailed as '*Notre Dame des Victoires*', to garner acclaim for her husband and Carnot praised his 'invincible phalanxes', whose deeds would astonish future generations.[16]

On 17 May Bonaparte wrote to the Directors disingenuously asking for instructions on how to deal with the local patriots. He knew they were thinking of giving Lombardy either to the King of Sardinia, in order to secure his alliance, or to Austria as a bargaining chip in the forthcoming peace negotiations. But he had his own vision. 'Nature drew the limits of France at the Alps, but it also drew those of the Empire at the Tyrol,' he pointed out. He had already promised liberty to the people of Lombardy and sanctioned a national guard, whose colours were to be the tricolour of the French Republic with the blue replaced by green. He began reorganising the former Austrian province along French lines, aided by Italian patriots from various parts of the peninsula who saw this as the cornerstone of an independent Italy. He was by now consciously implementing his own ideas. 'I'm doing what I want,' he told a surprised Italian patriot.[17]

'I believe in the French Republic, and in Bonaparte her son,' ran a *Credo* composed by some Italian nationalists; but others cursed him. The depredations of the French, both by officials and by soldiers on the rampage, caused hardship to ordinary people, and all those opposed to the French intrusion, be they fearful upholders of the old regime or Catholics horrified at the godlessness of the invaders, gave vent to their grievances. Riots broke out in various places. Bonaparte reacted with energy and in some cases brutality, most notably at Binasco, where the locals had massacred French soldiers. 'Having killed a hundred people, we burned down the village, a terrible but efficacious example,' he wrote to Berthier afterward. At Pavia, which had risen against the French, he let his troops loose on the town for a couple of hours. He admitted that 'although necessary, this spectacle was none the less horrible, and I was painfully affected by it'. The measures did prove efficacious, and he was soon able to report that the province was quiet. He enrolled young men coming forward to serve in what they believed to be the cause of Italy into a Lombard armed force which could maintain order.[18]

The improved supply situation did not stop the looting; it merely refocused it, as officers and men began to think of enriching themselves rather than just helping themselves to what they needed. The example was set by Masséna, who exacted protection money from towns he passed through, and it was widely followed. Bonaparte turned a blind eye, and even encouraged his subordinates to enrich themselves while ostentatiously declining to accept bribes offered him by the authorities of cities such as Lucca and Modena in order to distinguish himself from other generals by his moral stance.[19]

At the same time, Saliceti was bleeding the country dry in the service of the French Republic, as well as his own. At Lodi he raided the cathedral treasury and the Monte de Pietà, the charity which served as pawnbroker, removing five cases of silver plate and a number of ingots, and requisitioned the city's cash funds. In Milan he helped himself to the contents of the banks, the city chest, and the Monte de Pietà, although this time he returned to poor debtors their paltry treasures. He repeated the pattern in every city. 'You are creating a hundred times more currency with your bayonets than we can with all our imaginable financial laws,' one of the Directors acknowledged.[20]

It was not only cash and disposable valuables that were taken. Seeing the French Republic as the second Rome, its rulers believed the greatest works of art and science, libraries and archives, mechanical and scientific instruments, and any collections that could serve progress should be brought together in Paris. A commission consisting of the mathematician Gaspard Monge, the chemist Claude Berthollet, the botanists André Thouin and La Billardière, as well as a number of artists, was on its way with orders to select the objects worthy of being included in the libraries and museums of the capital. (It is worth noting that a protest against this was signed by the painters David, Hubert Robert, Moreau le Jeune, Girodet, the architects Percier and Fontaine, and many others.[21])

Bonaparte had never accepted the secondary role of staging a diversion in Italy while Moreau carried out the main operations in

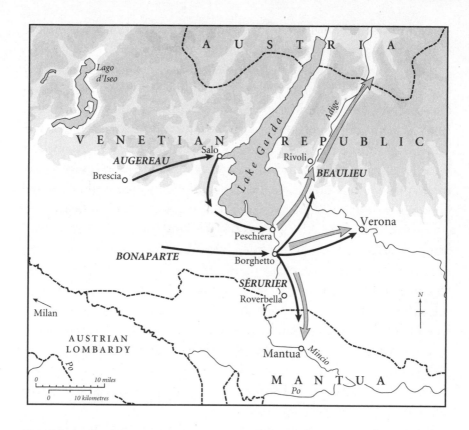

Germany and was determined to reverse this by striking first. Assuming that Moreau must have crossed the Rhine, he was eager to press on. Beaulieu had fallen back behind the river Mincio, his right wing resting at Peschiera on the southern shore of Lake Garda and his left on Mantua. Moving briskly, Bonaparte pierced his line at Borghetto and then turned north to roll it up. Disorientated Austrian units raced north in order to avoid being cut off, but some were overtaken by the French advance. At Valeggio, where he had just sat down to a light lunch with Masséna and Murat, Bonaparte was surprised by an isolated enemy unit and only had time to pull on one boot before making a dash for safety over a wall. By dawn the following day he was pursuing the Austrians falling back on Peschiera and Verona, which he reached on 3 June. He was overwhelmed by the beauty of the city. 'I have just seen the amphitheatre,' he reported to the Directory. 'These remains left by the people of Rome are truly worthy of it.

I could not help feeling a sense of humiliation when I thought of the tawdriness of our Champ de Mars.'[22]

Beaulieu had made his escape northward along the eastern side of Lake Garda, pursued by French cavalry, while part of his army took refuge in the fortress of Mantua, where it was bottled up by Sérurier. Bonaparte was now in control of the whole former Austrian province of Lombardy, and he set about securing it. Without consulting with the Directory, he signed an armistice with the kingdom of Naples, which thereby retired from the anti-French coalition, and received a Spanish diplomat sent by the Pope to negotiate peace with the Holy See.

He raced back to Milan expecting to find Josephine waiting for him. Instead he found instructions from the Directory ordering him to march on Rome, which he could not easily disobey. He set off, reaching Bologna on 19 June, where he was met by the Pope's envoy offering a bribe of 5 million francs to ward off a French invasion. Bonaparte demanded 40 million, as well as the treasure of the shrine of Loretto and a hundred works of art. On 23 June the Pope's emissaries agreed, and signed an armistice. Bonaparte then crossed the Apennines and made for Livorno to secure the port against a possible landing by the British.

From there he made a trip to San Miniato to visit Canon Filippo Buonaparte, the last surviving member of the Tuscan branch of what might at one stage have been the same family as his own. He then marched on to Florence, where he went to the opera on the evening of 30 June and the following day lunched with the Grand Duke of Tuscany, brother of the Emperor Francis II with whom he was at war. By 4 July he was back at Roverbella, where he had established his headquarters.

He was worn out physically and mentally, and racked by anxiety alternating with jealousy over Josephine, whom he showered with increasingly despairing letters which reveal his changing moods. The brevity and lack of feeling of her infrequent letters inspired reproach and jealousy, followed by fears that she might be ill and self-reproach for having questioned her feelings. He pestered Joseph for news of her. On 18 May from Milan he wrote a letter full of joyful anticipation of what he thought was her imminent arrival, describing the beauties of Italy and the happy times ahead as they listened to divine music while watching her belly grow (he was still under the impression that she was pregnant). Five days later, worried by the lack of news from her, he wrote of how he had left a ball given for him at which he looked in vain among the many beauties for any who came close to her. 'I could see only you, think only of you, and the thought made everything else unbearable, so, half an hour after arriving I went home to bed full of sadness.' Thinking she would arrive on 13 June, he prepared her lodgings, but then discovered she had not left Paris yet. 'I had opened my soul to joy, and it has filled with suffering,' he wrote. He awaited the couriers with impatience, either to find that there was no letter from her, or if there was that it lacked the passion he craved. He concluded that her feelings for him had only been a 'mild caprice' which he had misunderstood, that while he had given himself to her entirely and lived only for her, she had merely toyed with him, and that she wanted a different kind of man. '*Farewell*, Josephine, stay in Paris, do not write to me any more, and at least respect my retreat,' he wrote despairingly. 'A thousand daggers are tearing my heart asunder, do not plunge them any deeper. Farewell, my happiness, my life, everything that existed for me on earth!!!'[23]

Having heard no more from her, three days later he wrote that there was nothing left for him but to die: 'All the serpents of the furies are in my heart, and already I am half dead,' he wrote, still faintly hoping she might be on her way. 'I hate Paris, women and love...' he protested. 'Farewell, my Josephine, to think of you made me happy, but everything has changed entirely,' he went on, saying that he would never stop loving her. He had spent the night rereading all her letters and wallowing in self-pity. The same day he wrote to Barras: 'I am in despair as my wife won't come, she has some lover holding her back in Paris, I curse all women but heartily embrace my good friends.' Writing three days later from Tortona, he apologised to Josephine for expressing himself with such feeling, but explained that he had been 'drowning in sorrow'. He had just received a letter from Murat informing him that she was unwell, and although he assured him that it was only a slight indisposition, Bonaparte flew into a panic that she might die. 'If you die, I will also die, of despair, of devastation,' he wrote, asking her to intercede with Barras to obtain leave for him to return to Paris. He no longer cared for glory or the service of the motherland, and could not think of victory while she was ill. This long letter was followed the next day by another, even longer and more tortured, in which he blamed himself for having accused her of inconstancy. 'My life is a continuous nightmare,' he complained. 'I am suffocated by a deadly presentiment. I no longer live; I have lost more than life, more than Happiness, more than tranquillity; I am almost without hope.' He longed to be able to come to Paris. 'I am nothing without you,' he went on. 'I can hardly imagine how I existed before I knew you.'[24]

Josephine found his letters, and the teenage frenzy they expressed, ridiculous and embarrassing. She amused her friends by reading them out, and after sharing one particularly self-dramatising passage in which he referred to Othello, she exclaimed, 'He *is* funny, Bonaparte!' But, no doubt fed up with continual enquiries as to her health and afraid that Bonaparte might indeed turn up in Paris, where he was not wanted, Barras persuaded her to go. According to some accounts he bundled her into the carriage himself, along with her dog, her maid, Hippolyte Charles, and Junot. She was followed by several men of business to whom she owed money and to whom she promised to obtain lucrative contracts supplying the army.[25]

Their journey was a regal progress, every city along the way wishing to honour the wife of the national hero. At Lyon she went to a special performance of Gluck's *Iphigénie en Aulide*. At Turin, where she found Marmont waiting to escort her on her onward journey, she was treated like visiting royalty by the king. Her entry into Milan on 13 July was triumphal. She was settled in the magnificent Serbelloni Palace with its pink marble columns and showered with honours by the city authorities. Bonaparte was in such transports of joy to see her that, as she informed Thérèse Tallien, she thought he would go mad. He could not keep his hands off her and seemed unaware of the presence of Hippolyte Charles, whose role almost everyone else had guessed.[26]

Two days after her arrival, on 15 July, Bonaparte had to rejoin his troops besieging Mantua, which was sheltering some 12,000 Austrians. Josephine remained in Milan, where she was bored, despite the receptions and entertainments laid on for her, particularly when Lieutenant Charles could no longer delay taking up his duties at the side of General Leclerc in Verona.

Bonaparte, who still suspected nothing, was in ecstasy. 'What nights, my love, were those I spent in your arms!' he wrote. 'In my memory I ceaselessly relive everything we did, your kisses, your tears, your sweet jealousy, and the charms of the incomparable Josephine keep stoking an ardent and burning flame in my heart and in my senses. [...] A few days ago I thought I loved you, but, since seeing you I feel that I love you a thousand times more.'[27]

That night he hoped to storm Mantua with a surprise attack from the lake, but the waters unexpectedly went down and the attempt failed. He was already planning another trick that might deliver him the fortress, but this did not prevent him from thinking of Josephine. The next evening he was walking by the lake by 'silvery moonlight' in the village outside Mantua where Virgil was born, 'not one hour without thinking of my Josephine'. He was by now aware of the gossip about Lieutenant Charles and had stumbled on evidence when he opened letters to Josephine from Barras and Thérèse Tallien. He playfully cursed her while professing his faith in her fidelity and her love for him. 'Far from you, the nights are long, dull and sad, close to you one wishes it could always be night,' he wrote, inviting her to join him at Brescia.[28]

She arrived on 26 July, meaning to go on to Verona to see Lieutenant Charles under the pretext of sightseeing, but soon after she set off she ran into enemy troops. Bonaparte sent Junot with a squadron of dragoons to escort her back; on the way they came under fire, and she had to leave her carriage and take cover in a ditch. He resolved to send her out of the war zone on a trip to Tuscany. At Parma she met Joseph Fesch, who was busily putting together an art collection by requisitioning anything that caught his eye. In Florence she was received by the grand duke. Bored by Florence, she went back to Brescia and, Bonaparte being absent, summoned Lieutenant Charles to share his quarters with her.

Bonaparte was desperate to take Mantua, whose garrison remained a threat, making vigorous sorties which prevented him from securing the area. Although he had concluded treaties with Naples, the Papacy, and various smaller states of the peninsula, treaties were regularly broken, and a landing by British or Russian troops in Naples or elsewhere remained a possibility. If one were to take place when his back was turned, these states might be tempted to throw their considerable forces into the fray against him. And by the end of July it was clear that Austria was about to make a concerted effort to relieve Mantua and reconquer Lombardy.

Victory and Legend

BEAULIEU HAD BEEN replaced by the no less aged Field Marshal Dagobert von Würmser. He divided his army into three columns which moved out in July 1796. One, consisting of 18,000 men under General Quasdanovitch, marched down the western side of Lake Garda, aiming to take Brescia and cut Bonaparte off from Milan. Another, of 5,000 men under General Meszaros, came down the valley of the Brenta further east in order to distract the French, while Würmser himself with 24,000 marched down the eastern side of Lake Garda aiming for Verona, where it was planned that the three forces were to come together to defeat the French and relieve Mantua.[1]

Bonaparte, who had just under 40,000 men in total, would be overwhelmed unless he defeated the Austrian columns separately. He took a bold decision, ordering Sérurier to abandon the siege of Mantua and pulling all his forces out of Würmser's path. Although this would allow the Austrian to relieve Mantua and add its garrison to his force, it gave Bonaparte the opportunity to concentrate enough men to rout Quasdanovitch, which he did at Lonato on 3 August, before turning about to face Würmser with a slight numerical superiority, at Castiglione on 5 August. In a classic manoeuvre, he encouraged Würmser to turn his right flank, then launched a powerful attack on his exposed centre which cut the Austrian army in two, forcing it into a disorderly retreat back to whence it had come. 'There you have another campaign finished in five days,' Bonaparte rounded off his report to the Directory, in which he grossly exaggerated the enemy's losses.[2]

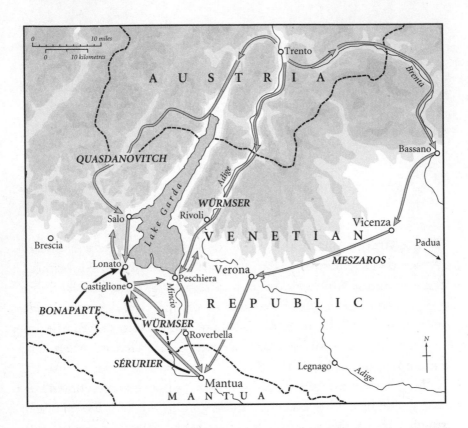

It had been a brilliant feat of arms, with Bonaparte exploiting his central position to great effect. It had also demonstrated the qualities specific to the French army which gave it such an edge over its enemies. The Austrian army operated like a machine, observing tested routines such as only marching for six hours in twenty-four. The French followed no rules. The poor or nonexistent supply system obliged them to operate in self-contained divisions or smaller units that the land they moved through could support, which encouraged greater independence and flexibility, particularly when it came to timing and distance.

Over those five days, Bonaparte had ridden more than one horse to death as he darted about. Marmont had spent twenty-four hours in the saddle, followed by another fifteen after only three hours' rest. Augereau's division had covered eighty kilometres in thirty-six hours, in the August heat. Masséna noted that two-thirds of his men had no coats, waistcoats, shirts, or breeches, and marched barefoot. When they complained of the lack of provisions, Bonaparte told them the only ones available were in the enemy camp.[3]

The French army was made up of individuals with minds of their own. Bonaparte's new aide, Józef Sułkowski, noted their agility and 'astonishing vigour' and was struck by the fact that the French soldier would surrender when cornered on his own, but never in the company of his fellows, and would 'go out to his death rather than face shame'. In some units, shirkers and cowards were hauled before 'juries' of elder comrades who would condemn them to being beaten on their bottoms and despised until they had redeemed themselves with acts of valour.[4]

'The French soldier has an impulsive courage and a feeling of honour which make him capable of the greatest things,' believed Bonaparte. 'He judges the talent and the courage of his officers. He discusses the plan of campaign and all the military manoeuvres. He is capable of anything if he approves of the operations and esteems his leaders,' and would march and fight on an empty stomach if he believed it would bring victory.[5]

Many observers of the campaign of 1796 commented on the almost festive spirit in which these men appeared to banter with death, singing on the march and laughing as they went into battle. 'We were all very young,' recalled Marmont, and 'devoured by love of glory'. Their ambition was 'noble and pure', and they felt 'a confidence without limit in [their] destiny', along with a contagious spirit of adventure. 'It was during this campaign that moral exaltation played the greatest part,' reminisced an old grenadier.[6]

Exceptional leadership also played a part. At Lonato, Bonaparte led the 32nd Demi-Brigade into withering enemy fire. After the battle he presented it with a new standard, embroidered with the words: 'Battle of Lonato: I was confident, the brave 32nd was there!' 'It is astonishing what power one can exert over men with words,' he later commented about the incident. He also knew when to be harsh. After Castiglione he demoted General Valette in front of his men for having abandoned his positions too soon and allowed his unit to retreat in disorder. He hailed another demi-brigade, the 18th, as it took up positions before battle with the words: 'Valorous 18th, I know you: the enemy won't hold in front of you!' At Castiglione, Augereau had excelled himself leading troops into the melée. 'That day was the finest in the life of that general,' Bonaparte later commented. Masséna too had electrified his men with his blustering courage.[7]

The cost of these heroics had been heavy. By the end of the campaign, almost as many men were in hospitals as in the ranks. Some of the older officers were burnt out, and Bonaparte himself was exhausted. Yet there was no time for rest. Würmser had fallen back to where he could be resupplied and would soon be in a position to attack again. Bonaparte's only hope lay in forestalling him. 'We are on campaign, my adorable love,' he wrote to Josephine on 3 September, having set off up the valley of the Adige. 'I am never far from you. Only at your side is there Happiness and life.' The next day, at Roveredo, he defeated an Austrian force under Davidovitch barring his way and pressed on, forcing Davidovitch to fall back beyond Trento.

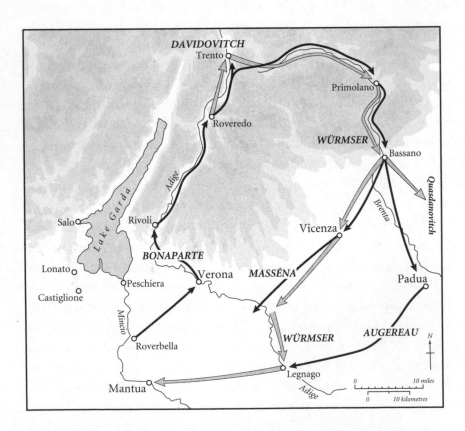

Würmser instructed him to hold on there while he himself marched down the Brenta valley into Bonaparte's rear, meaning to take him between two fires.[8]

Bonaparte guessed Würmser's intentions. He left around 10,000 men under General Vaubois to keep Davidovitch bottled up, and with the rest of his force set off behind Würmser, who was now marching down the Brenta hoping to penetrate into the rear of the French, without realising that they were on his tail. On 7 September Augereau caught up with and routed Würmser's rearguard at Primolano, capturing his supply train, then forged on, hardly pausing for rest. Bonaparte spent that night under the stars, 'dying of hunger and lassitude', having eaten nothing but a small piece of hard-tack offered him by a soldier. He did not get much sleep, as by two in the morning he was on the move again. Würmser was unable to deploy his forces as they marched down the valley, and the French were able to defeat his divisions singly at Bassano, taking 5,000 prisoners, thirty-five pieces of artillery, and most of his baggage. Quasdanovitch veered east with part of the army and made for Trieste, while Würmser with the main body made a dash for Mantua, which he entered on 15 September with no more than 17,000 men. This brought the number of Austrians bottled up in the fortress to over 25,000, including some fine cavalry, whose horses would only serve to feed them. It had been a strategic disaster. Marmont was sent to Paris with the flags taken in those two weeks, to spread the fame of the Army of Italy and its commander.[9]

Not for a moment during those frantic days did Bonaparte forget his 'adorable Josephine', to whom he complained from Verona on 17 September that 'I write to you very often my love, and you very seldom,' announcing that he would be with her soon. 'One of these nights your door will open with a jealous crash and I will be in your bed,' he warned. 'A thousand kisses, all over, all over.' Two days later he was back in Milan, where they would spend the best part of a month.[10]

Quite how happy that month was is open to question. In a letter to Thérèse Tallien on 6 September Josephine admitted to being 'very bored'. 'I have the most loving husband it is possible to encounter,' she wrote. 'I cannot wish for anything. My wishes are his. He spends his days adoring me as though I were a goddess...' She was evidently sexually tired of him; he complained that she made him feel as though they were a middle-aged couple in 'the winter of life'. But he had little time to brood over it.[11]

His recent triumphs had resolved nothing: there was still a large enemy force in Mantua which he reckoned could hold out for months, and while Lombardy was relatively quiet, there were stirrings in other parts of the peninsula. The King of Sardinia had disbanded his Piedmontese regiments, with the consequence that bands of former soldiers were threatening the French supply lines. 'Rome is arming and encouraging fanaticism among the people,' Bonaparte wrote to the Directory, 'a coalition is building up against us on all sides, they are only waiting for the moment to act, and their action will be successful if the army of the Emperor is reinforced.' He suggested that given the circumstances he should be allowed to make policy decisions. 'You cannot attribute this to personal ambition,' he assured them. 'I have been honoured too much already and my health is so damaged that I feel I ought to request someone to replace me. I can no longer mount a horse. All I have left is courage, and that is not enough for a posting such as this.'[12]

The Austrians would try harder than ever to relieve Mantua, now that it contained such a large force. And they were in a better position to achieve their goal, since the two French armies operating in Germany had been beaten and had retreated across the Rhine, releasing more Austrian troops from that theatre. Bonaparte wrote to Würmser suggesting an honourable capitulation on humanitarian grounds: Mantua was surrounded by water and marshland, and large numbers on both sides were suffering from fever. Würmser refused and sat tight, knowing help was on its way (it was only by chance that General Dumas, commanding the siege, discovered that Würmser was being delivered messages in capsules hidden in their rectums by men disguised as civilians). By the end of October there was a fresh imperial army in position under a new commander, Field Marshal Baron Josef Alvinczy.[13]

All Bonaparte could muster against it were some 35,000 men, exhausted after eight months of almost continuous campaigning in extreme conditions. He had received reinforcements, but these only just made up for the 17,000 who had been killed, those invalided out, those in hospitals, and the deserters. The troops were also of increasingly dubious quality, as a result of a process of negative selection. 'The soldiers are no longer the same,' wrote Bonaparte's brother Louis. 'There is no more energy, no more fire in them... The bravest are all dead, those that remain can be easily counted.' According to some estimates, only 18 percent of the original complement were still in the ranks, and the proportion was probably lower among officers. 'The Army of Italy, reduced to a handful of men, is exhausted,' reported Bonaparte. 'The heroes of Lodi, of Milesimo, of Castiglione and Bassano have died for their motherland or lie in hospital'.[14]

His dazzling successes had won him not only adulation but also a host of jealous rivals and enemies. Chief among these were the various civilians—commissioners, administrators, and suppliers—in the wake of the army, whom he had been preventing from enriching themselves, and who were sending slanderous reports back to Paris, warning that he was intending to make himself King of Italy. A military setback at this point might prove fatal to him.

His forces were dispersed in bodies of about 5,000, with one around his headquarters at Verona, one at Brescia in the west and one at Bassano in the east, one besieging Mantua, another in reserve at Legnago, and a smaller one in a forward position to the north at Trento. They were placed in such a manner that they could easily concentrate, but this time it was going to be more difficult to deal with the enemy piecemeal. The Austrians were on the move by the beginning of November 1796: Davidovitch pushed back Vaubois from Trento while Alvinczy, with the main force of some 29,000, marched down the Brenta and on 6 November forced Masséna's division out of Bassano. Bonaparte rushed to Rivoli to arrest the retreat of Vaubois, which he did in inimitable style. He called out two units which had shown lack of mettle and announced that their standards would be inscribed with the words 'These no longer belong to the Army of Italy!' Many of the men wept, and, as he had anticipated, they would redeem themselves with acts of surpassing bravery a couple of days later.[15]

But Alvinczy was by now threatening the French centre at Verona. Bonaparte attempted to hold him off at Caldiero, but the already dispirited troops were subjected to a violent storm. Drenching rain was succeeded by volleys of hail. 'This storm blew straight into their faces, the heavy rain hiding the enemy who was pounding them with artillery, while the wind blew away even their fuses and their bare feet slithered in the clay soil, lending them no support,' in the words of Sułkowski. They trudged back in mournful silence.[16]

Bonaparte was down to around 17,000 men facing Alvinczy's 23,000, and he was strategically blocked, with Verona at his back. 'We may be on the eve of losing Italy,' he warned the Directory. He decided to take a chance. Leaving a small force in position before Verona, on the night of 14 November he crossed the Adige under cover of darkness and marched east along its right bank, recrossed it at Ronco and, leaving Masséna to cover his own left flank and distract Alvinczy, made a dash for Arcole, where he meant to cross the river Alpone and move into Alvinczy's rear at Villanova. This would have cut the Austrians' line of communications and forced them to retreat into his arms. They were caught in a funnel between the mountains and the river Adige and had no other exit—and the different corps of a retreating army can be taken on and defeated individually, in this case as they tried to cross the Alpone at Villanova.[17]

Everything went smoothly until the French spearhead came in sight of the small town of Arcole on the opposite bank of the Alpone across a thirty-metre-long straight wooden bridge resting on stone piles. It was defended by two battalions of Croat infantry numbering around 2,000 men with several field-guns positioned so as to sweep not only the bridge but the access to it on a dyke raised above the marshy floodplain.[18]

Bonaparte was in a hurry. He ordered General Verdier to storm the bridge, but his men came under withering fire before they got anywhere near it. He despatched a force to cross the river further south and threaten the defenders' flank, but persisted in trying to cross the bridge. News had reached him that Alvinczy had perceived the threat to his rear and abandoned Verona. Masséna could distract him for a time, but if the Austrians crossed the Alpone at Villanova before Bonaparte could do so at Arcole, his plan would have failed and the French position would be critical once more.

Augereau and then Lannes attempted to lead the troops to the bridge, without success. Then Bonaparte dismounted and seized a

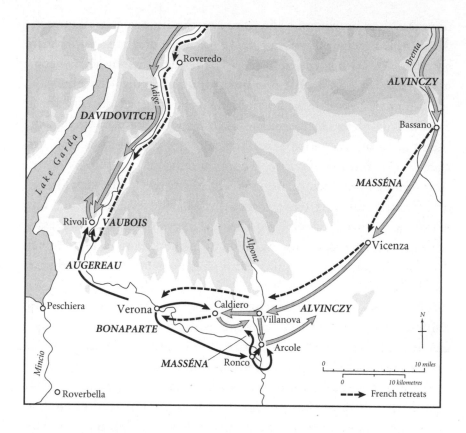

flag. He challenged the men to show they were still the heroes of Lodi, but they would not follow him, even when he moved forward, accompanied by his aides and a small group of soldiers. Having covered a short distance and still a couple of hundred metres from the bridge, they were met by a volley which killed several around Bonaparte, including his aide Muiron. They rushed for cover, knocking Bonaparte off the dyke and into a drainage ditch where he landed up to his neck in water. He was eventually dragged out of it, but there could no longer be any question of taking the bridge.[19]

That evening, 15 November, he withdrew and recrossed the Adige. Although his initial plan had failed, he had nevertheless positioned himself in such a way that he now paralysed Alvinczy: if the Austrian moved west, Bonaparte could strike in his rear, and if he moved east he had to abandon hope of linking up with Davidovitch to achieve his objective of relieving Mantua. On the night of 16 November Bonaparte learned that Vaubois had been overwhelmed by Davidovitch, which opened the possibility of the two Austrian armies joining forces. The only way of preventing this was to threaten Alvinczy's rear. Bonaparte had a bridge built over the Alpone downstream of Arcole and ordered Augereau to cross it while Masséna moved against Arcole, and despatched another force along the Adige to cross it further east to threaten Alvinczy's communications. The ploy worked, and Alvinczy fell back on Villanova. This allowed Bonaparte to detach troops and send them to head off Davidovitch and force him back up to Trento. Alvinczy, who had moved west again to assist Davidovitch, now gave up and retired up the Brenta valley. He had lost many men and had failed in his purpose to liberate Würmser from Mantua.

The two-week campaign had been a messy, close-run business with no set-piece battle to present to the French public as grand spectacle. It was therefore necessary to fabricate one. In his despatch to the Directory, Bonaparte announced that the battle of Arcole had decided the fate of Italy. He grossly exaggerated Austrian losses while diminishing his own and presented an account of derring-do to flatter French national pride. The captured flags were borne to Paris by Le Marois, who at the public ceremony in which they were handed over made a speech portraying Bonaparte tracing the path to victory, flag in hand, conveying the notion that he had stormed the bridge. In no time a print appeared in Paris depicting Bonaparte and Augereau leading the troops across it on horseback, each clutching a banner, succeeded by another showing Bonaparte on foot, brandishing the flag and encouraging his troops to follow him.[20]

For centuries kings and commanders had had their deeds immortalised in painting out of a mixture of vanity and political assertiveness. The Revolution had created a thirst for information among the illiterate which was satisfied by crude allegorical depiction, and this led to an explosion of semi-sacral illustration in praise of the nation, its leaders, and its martyrs. Generals were depicted in heroic poses, and there were engravings of commanders such as Hoche and Moreau in circulation before any image of Bonaparte.[21]

But he took propaganda to new levels. His mendacious despatches to the Directory, excerpts from which were printed and even plastered on walls for the public to read, were dramatic and exciting. The hyperbolic language of the Revolution in which they were couched created a subliminal sense of the supernatural, of the miraculous, of an adventure being enacted by men who appeared as superhuman as the heroes of the *Iliad*. Poets, playwrights, and hacks of every sort saw in this excellent raw material for their own craft, and their works added to the concert of myth-making verbiage. This was accompanied by an iconography to suit, and between the moment he took command of the Army of Italy in 1796 and the end of 1798, no fewer than thirty-seven different prints of Bonaparte appeared on the market, some commissioned, some spontaneous, some based on actual representations of him, others giving him entirely imagined features, but all representing him as a hero.[22]

The propaganda surrounding Arcole saved Bonaparte's position, but it could do little to assuage the pain inflicted by Josephine. 'At last, my adorable Josephine, I am coming back to myself, death no longer stares me in the face,' he had written with understandable relief the day after the fiasco of Arcole. Back in Verona two days later, he wrote her a tender note just before going to bed, reproving her as usual for not writing. 'Don't you know that without you, without your heart, without your love there can be no happiness of life for your husband,' he wrote, going on to say how he longed to touch her shoulder, hold her firm breast and to plunge into her 'little black forest'. 'To live in Josephine is to live in Elysium. To kiss her, on the mouth, the eyes, the shoulder, the breast, all over, all over!' Two days after that, having heard nothing, he wrote in teasing vein: 'I don't love you at all any more, on the contrary I hate you.' He asked her what occupied her days so fully to prevent her from writing. 'Who can it be, this wonderful and new love who absorbs all your time, tyrannises your days and prevents you from caring for your husband? Take care, Josephine, one of these nights your door will be forced and I will be in your bed. You know! The little dagger of Othello!' He then reverts to a more loving tone and looks forward to being in her arms again and planting a kiss on her 'little rascal'.[23]

He reached Milan panting with love on 27 November, only to find that she had gone to Genoa (with Lieutenant Charles). His disappointment and bitterness are given full expression in a note dashed off to her that evening and a letter the following day. 'Farewell, adorable woman, farewell, my Josephine,' he ended. General Henry-Jacques Clarke, who arrived from Paris the next day, found Bonaparte 'haggard, thin, all skin and bone, his eyes sparkling feverishly'.[24]

Clarke had been sent by the Directory with the ostensible mission of opening negotiations with the Austrians, but in fact to spy and report on the commander of the Army of Italy. He was pleasantly surprised when Bonaparte agreed that negotiations with Austria were in order. Bonaparte knew that having driven back the French in Germany, Austria was about to launch an all-out offensive in Italy and would not be inclined to negotiate. But he had to gain Clarke's support, so he set out to charm him. In little over a week, Clarke was assuring the Directory, 'There is nobody here who does not regard him as a man of genius....' He praised the general's judgement, his authority, and his efficiency. 'I believe him to be committed to the Republic, and without any ambition other than that of conserving the glory which he has acquired for himself,' he followed this up.[25]

Clarke's support was an important asset in Bonaparte's long-running battle with the other arm of the Directory's control—its commissioners. Their brief had varied with unfolding events: lured by the cash and spoils he sent back, the Directory charged them with political and financial control of the occupied territories, but with the discovery earlier that year that General Pichegru commanding the Army of the Rhine and Moselle had been plotting with the enemy, their brief had been extended to surveillance of the military. They rode about in civilian dress with tricolour sashes and plumes that gave them the aspect of high-ranking commanders, often overruling officers.

In Saliceti, Bonaparte had at his side a man who for all his venality and opportunism was someone he could work with. The other commissioner, Pierre-Anselme Garrau, an unprepossessing hunchback with a virulently Jacobin background, was a thorn in his side. Soon after the conclusion of the armistice at Cherasco, Bonaparte had received instructions from the Directory that diplomatic negotiations were the preserve of the commissioners, not the army commander. He had by then concluded an armistice with the kingdom of Naples and was negotiating with envoys of the Pope.[26]

He left these negotiations to the two commissioners, who allowed themselves to be drawn into labyrinthine discussions which withered fruitless after three months. Worse, Garrau had inadvertently revealed Bonaparte's plan to surprise and capture British ships in Livorno, allowing them to get away. Bonaparte had for some time been informing the Directory of the commissioners' incompetence and reporting the venality and scandalous behaviour of the civil functionaries operating in Italy. In July, after Saliceti was transferred to supervise the French reoccupation of Corsica, Bonaparte set about destroying Garrau. He forbade him to give orders to soldiers while bombarding him with demands for supplies and blaming him for every shortage. Bonaparte appointed his own officers to rule the occupied territories and began eliminating the 'shameless scoundrels', as he termed the officials following in the wake of the army, replacing them with equally venal ones who owed everything to him. Such usurpation of the Directory's authority could end badly for Bonaparte, and the matter had reached a climax in November, at the time of the Arcole campaign. He needed to watch his back.[27]

In October, he ordered the arrest in Livorno of a Corsican by the name of Panattieri, the man Paoli had sent to search the Buonaparte house in Ajaccio in 1793 and bring all the papers he could find to Corte. At Bonaparte's request, all the papers in Panattieri's possession were seized. Meanwhile Joseph, who had gone to Corsica as soon as the British had evacuated it in order to secure the remains of the Buonaparte estate and see what could be added to it as a result of the flight of the pro-British Corsicans, scoured archives in Ajaccio and Corte. It was the first step in what was to be a methodical editing of the Buonaparte brothers' activities on the island.[28]

In the context, the arrival of Clarke proved fortuitous: his glowing reports of Bonaparte's ability and devotion to the Republic persuaded the Directors that it was best to retreat. On 6 December 1796, they abolished the role of comissioners altogether.

Meanwhile, Josephine had returned to Milan and a semblance of harmony was restored. She gave a ball on 10 December at which the couple presided in regal manner. Although he had a low opinion of Italians, considering them to be lazy and effeminate, morally defective and politically immature, Bonaparte went along with the wishes of the Milanese intellectual elites for an independent Italian republic. Pre-empting any hopes the Directory might still entertain of using Lombardy as a bargaining counter, on 27 December he announced the creation of the Cispadane Republic (covering the nearside of the river Po, *Padus* in Latin). It was given an armed force made up of Poles forcibly enlisted by the Austrians who had either deserted or been taken prisoner, under the command of General Jan Henryk Dąbrowski.

At the beginning of January 1797 the Austrians were on the move once more, Alvinczy marching down the valley of the Adige while two other corps swept down the valley of the Brenta to relieve Mantua. Leaving only a small force to parry these, Bonaparte collected all the troops he could muster and on the night of 13 January made a rapid march up to Rivoli, where Joubert was attempting to stem Alvinczy's advance. He arrived at two o'clock in the morning and quickly took in the situation. Alvinczy had split his force into six columns, and Bonaparte set about them separately, defeating one after the other. By late afternoon Alvinczy was in full retreat. This was turned into a rout by the intervention of Murat on his flank, and the Austrians fled, leaving behind nearly 3,500 dead and wounded and 8,000 prisoners, representing 43 percent of Alvinczy's total effectives.

This obviated the need for pursuit, which was as well, since late that afternoon Bonaparte received news that one of the Austrian prongs to the south, under General Provera, had broken through and was close to Mantua. He ordered Masséna to gather up his exhausted troops and dashed south. On 16 January, while Colonel Victor contained a sortie from Mantua by Würmser, Bonaparte directed Augereau's division against Provera at La Favorita outside the city, forcing him to surrender. It was an extraordinary result: in the space of less than four days he had depleted the Austrian forces by more than half. In the space of the week the French had taken 23,000 prisoners, sixty guns, and twenty-four flags. With all hope of relief dissipated, Würmser would surrender Mantua and its garrison of 30,000 men, half of them too sick

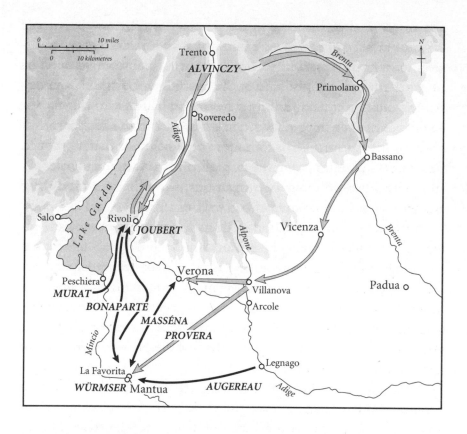

to walk, on 2 February, giving Bonaparte another twenty standards to send back to Paris. The victory had been achieved through extraordinary exertion—Masséna's corps had fought at Verona on 13 January, at Rivoli the following day and outside Mantua two days later, covering nintey-odd kilometres in the process.

Bonaparte did not need to wait for the surrender of Mantua to know how complete his triumph was, and on 17 January he wrote to the Directors announcing that in the space of 'three or four days' he had destroyed his fifth imperial army. 'I've beaten the enemy,' he wrote to Josephine that evening. 'I am dead tired. I beg you to leave immediately for Verona. I need you, because I think I am going to be very ill. A thousand kisses. I am in bed.'[29]

She did come, but there could be no question of a long rest. Austria would not admit defeat and was mobilising a new force. It was also negotiating with the Vatican and the kingdom of Naples, which had a sizable army. The Directory had long before ordered Bonaparte to overthrow the papacy, which it regarded as the source of all obscurantism in the world and the avowed enemy of the French Republic. Bonaparte felt no animus against the Church and treated the clergy in the lands he occupied with respect, if only out of calculation. But he despised Pius VI, whom he regarded as a treacherous opportunist ready to stir against him every time the Austrians looked as though they might be winning. He was also short of cash, both for his army and to send back to France to placate his political masters, and there was no shortage of that to be found in Rome.

With 8,000 men, some of them Italian auxiliaries, he entered Bologna, where on 1 February he declared war on the Pope. He defeated a contingent of papal troops at Imola and took possession of Ancona. He had a cold and was depressed by the farcical nature of 'this nasty little war', as he wrote to Josephine on 10 February. Confronted by badly led mercenaries and displays of religious fanaticism, at Faenza he rounded up all the monks and priests of the place to lecture them about true Christian values.[30]

The Pope sent a delegation to negotiate, but the honey-voiced prelates who had been so successful with Garrau were no match for a bullying Bonaparte. By the Treaty of Tolentino, signed on 19 February, Pius ceded the former papal fiefs in France, Avignon and the Comtat Venaisin, the Legations of Bologna, Ferrara and Romagna, along with Ancona. He also agreed to close his ports to British ships, and undertook to pay 30 million francs and deliver a number of works of art and manuscripts.

Five days later Bonaparte was back in Bologna with Josephine, who accompanied him to Mantua, where he prepared for the next campaign. The Directory had accepted that only he was capable of beating the Austrians decisively and reversed its policy of treating the Italian theatre as a diversion. It transferred two strong divisions from the northern theatre, under generals Delmas and Bernadotte, reinforcing Bonaparte significantly: he could field 60,000 men while leaving 20,000 guarding his rear. This made him undertake what was under any circumstances a daring enterprise—a march on Vienna.

Three Austrian forces stood in his way, one under Davidovitch at Trento, another blocking the valley of the Brenta, and the main force concentrated along the river Tagliamento. They were under the overall command of Archduke Charles of Austria, a capable general two years younger than Bonaparte who had defeated the French in Germany. His presence was helping to restore the morale of the Austrian troops, and Bonaparte decided not to give him time. On 10 March he went into action, forcing Davidovitch up the valley of the Adige towards Brixen while Masséna advanced up the Brenta and Bonaparte took on the archduke himself on the Tagliamento. He breached his defences and forced him to fall back on Gratz (Gorizia) and Laybach (Lubljana). By then two of the passes were in French hands, and the archduke had to beat a hasty retreat if he were to avoid being cut off as Bonaparte reached Klagenfurt, on 30 March.

He was now poised to advance on Vienna, but if he did so, the Austrian armies in Germany could sweep into his rear. Behind him lay the whole of Italy guarded by a mere 20,000 men. Anti-French feeling simmered throughout the peninsula, with Naples, Venice, the papacy, Parma, and Modena only waiting for a chance to strike. His army had advanced so far that it was running out of supplies, and the rocky region in which it now found itself would not sustain it for long. He therefore had to conclude peace urgently.

The one thing that would convince Austria to give in was a French advance across the Rhine by Moreau and Hoche, who had taken over from Pichegru, and Bonaparte sent request after request to the Directory urging it to order one. But he had learned to rely only on his own resources. On 31 March he offered Archduke Charles an armistice, but pressed on swiftly, reaching Leoben and taking the Semmering pass, less than a hundred kilometres from Vienna. There was panic in the Austrian capital, with people packing their valuables and leaving for places of safety. But with no support from Moreau and Hoche, Bonaparte could not afford to go any further. On 18 April preliminaries of peace were signed at Leoben.

Bonaparte had no right to negotiate a peace, let alone one which redrew the map as drastically as this one. The terms were that Austria

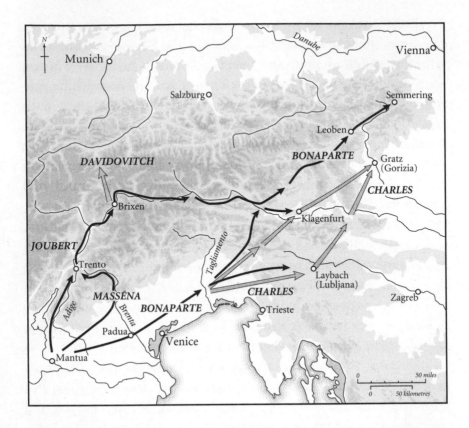

ceded Belgium to France, gave up its claim to Lombardy and recognised the Cispadane Republic. In return, Austria was to receive part of the territory of the Republic of Venice.

Venice had remained neutral throughout the conflict, but French and Austrian armies had operated on its territory, using cities such as Verona and Bassano as military bases. Their depredations had provoked reprisals against French soldiers, and on 7 April Bonaparte had sent Junot to Venice with an insulting ultimatum to its government to stop them. When the Venetian authorities sent envoys to Bonaparte he lambasted them and declared that he would act like Attila if they did not submit. On 17 April there was a riot in Verona, almost certainly provoked on his orders, in the course of which some French soldiers were killed. He responded by making fresh demands of the Venetian government, insisting it reform its constitution along French lines. Provocations on either side ratcheted up the conflict, and a

French vessel was fired on from one of the Venetian forts. On 1 May Bonaparte declared war on Venice and sent in troops. A puppet government was set up and instructed to settle with Austria the cession of territory, for which Venice was to be compensated with the former papal province of the Legations. Meanwhile, the plunder of the city's treasures began and the horses of St Mark's were removed to Paris.[31]

Such treatment of a neutral sovereign state was nothing new for Austria, which had joined in the partitions of Poland and had long been eying Venetian territory, with its access to the sea. But for the French Republic, the liberator of oppressed peoples, to act in such a way was shocking, and when they heard of it the members of the Directory were incensed. Clarke, who reached Leoben two days after the signature, was aghast. But Bonaparte had already sent Masséna to Paris with the document and an accompanying letter in which he listed the advantages for France of the agreement, which he termed 'a monument to the glory of the French Republic'. He went on to state that if the Directory did not accept the terms of the peace, he would be content to resign his post and pursue a civilian career with the same determination and single-mindedness as he had his military one—a clear threat that he would go into politics. There was nothing the Directory could do: news of the signature of peace had been greeted ecstatically throughout France, with celebrations in some towns lasting three days.[32]

13

Master of Italy

B Y THE BEGINNING of May 1797 Bonaparte was back in Milan. In the space of twelve months he had won a succession of battles, taken 160,000 prisoners and 1,100 pieces of artillery, and well over 150 standards, as well as some fifty warships, and forced the emperor to make peace after five years of war. A rest was in order, and finding the summer heat oppressive, he had installed himself at Mombello, a stately villa a short distance from the city. Set on a rise which gave it fine views, of snow-capped Alpine peaks to the north and the Lombard plain to the south, it was a perfect place for him to recover from his travails. But it soon turned into what visitors described as 'a glittering court' to which many gravitated.[1]

Pontécoulant, who had last seen Bonaparte at the War Ministry in 1795 pleading to be given back his rank, could not believe the change that had come over him. His previously hunched figure had assumed a commanding poise, and his features now put Pontécoulant in mind of classical cameos. 'It was difficult not to feel an involuntary emotion on approaching him,' he wrote. 'His height, below the average, rarely equalled that of his interlocutors, yet his movements, his bearing, the decisive tone of his voice, all seemed to proclaim that he was born to command others and to impose on them the ascendancy of his will.' Pontéccoulant noted that he was polite and cordial to newcomers, speaking to each of the things which interested them. 'There was no pride in his behaviour, only the aplomb of a man who knows his worth and has found his place,' according to the playwright Antoine-Vincent Arnault, another who had arrived from Paris.[2]

As he exerted authority over the whole of northern Italy, either directly or by proxy, Bonaparte was constantly receiving representatives of the civil authorities and the administration seeking guidance or approval. And as the political system on the peninsula remained fluid, a stream of diplomats trickled through Mombello, from the emperor of Austria, the kings of Sardinia and Naples, the Pope, the republics of Genoa and Lucca, the dukes of Parma and Tuscany, from civic corporations and other bodies, even from Swiss cantons and minor German states. Couriers came and went. So did individuals seeking redress, protection, or favour. In order to accommodate the numbers, a large tent was erected beside the villa to extend the drawing room.

An etiquette gradually established itself, distancing Bonaparte from his comrades-in-arms, who were made to feel they could no longer use the familiar '*tu*' when addressing him. In French military custom, a commander kept table for all his officers when on active service, and until now Bonaparte had sat down with his comrades to eat whatever and wherever they could. At Mombello, he dined in public with Josephine as French monarchs had done, to the accompaniment of music and watched by his court, only occasionally inviting one or other of his staff to join them. In the evenings, the company was entertained with music, and La Grassini would drive out from Milan to sing for the conqueror. 'He did not appear in the least embarrassed or put out by these excessive marks of honour, and received them as though he had been used to them all his life,' commented the French diplomat André François Miot de Melito.[3]

The painter Antoine Gros, who had been travelling in Italy, came to Mombello and started work on a portrait. Bonaparte would not sit still, so Josephine made him sit on her knee, and by playfully holding his head and caressing him she managed to immobilise him long enough for Gros to sketch the face. He would later work these sketches into the memorable painting of Bonaparte on the bridge of Arcole.[4]

Josephine reigned over this court with a relaxed grace that impressed visitors: she seemed born to the station of regal consort. The ladies of Milan who called were charmed by her easy and friendly manner. 'Never has a woman combined more kindness with more natural grace and done more good with more pleasure than her,' in the words of Miot de Melito. She was nevertheless bored and pined for Paris. Her relationship with Bonaparte seems to have been passing through a good phase, as she informed Barras. 'My husband has promised not to leave me any more,' she wrote, '...you helped to marry us, and you made his happiness and mine. I could not love him more than I do.' To Bonaparte's delight, the cook's dog killed Josephine's pug Fortuné, who could no longer prevent him taking what one observer called 'conjugal liberties' with her in public, but the spontaneous and unaffected nature of his caresses disarmed even the most prudish.[5]

Josephine was less happy at having to put up with her husband's family. Letizia arrived on 1 June, bringing Maria-Nunziata, now styling herself Caroline; little Geronimo; and Maria-Anna, who had taken to calling herself Élisa and brought her fiancé, the Corsican Félix Bacciochi. She needed a dowry, which only her brother could provide, and though he disliked Bacciochi, Bonaparte had to give in to the entreaties of his mother, who approved of the marriage, as the man came from a prominent family of Ajaccio. Joseph had also turned up, followed by Joseph Fesch, who brought Paulette and Josephine's son, Eugène, from Paris.

It was not a happy family gathering. Letizia, who now met Josephine for the first time, saw no reason to change her views on the subject of what she considered her son's disastrous marriage. The rest of the family concurred. For her part, Josephine was unimpressed by her in-laws. She had already met Lucien, whom she detested, and Louis, who did not like her and who since falling ill in February had turned into a hypochondriac prone to fits of depression. She found Joseph amiable enough, as he kept up a diplomatic show of friendliness toward her. It was her sisters-in-law who horrified Josephine. She appears to have believed the gossip that they had all slept with Bonaparte, and Paulette's behaviour did little to gainsay it. She was stunningly beautiful, but her demeanour combined the pranks of a schoolgirl with the morals of a harlot. One moment she would be pulling faces and sticking out her tongue, mimicking and joshing distinguished personages, the next she would be fornicating behind a curtain with whichever young officer came to hand. Bonaparte resolved to put a stop to it by marrying her off to one of his most able officers, Victor-Émmanuel Leclerc, who was in love with her and could be counted on to keep her occupied. They were married on 14 June along with Élisa and Bacciochi. Soon after, Letizia departed for Ajaccio with the Bacciochis, and a little later Joseph left for Rome to take up the job of French ambassador to the Holy See which Bonaparte had obtained for him.[6]

To distract Josephine, Bonaparte arranged excursions to the lakes of Garda, Maggiore and Como, to Monza and Isola Bella. But he was himself not in holiday mood. More than one witness noted that he looked not only exhausted but also sad and often dejected, that on occasion his look was filled with melancholy and reflection, that he was sometimes sombre.[7]

He had experienced a great deal over the past year and had learned much about himself and others, about war, politics, and human affairs in general. Most of it, including the deceptions of Josephine, had lowered his opinion of human nature. He had debased his own standards and made compromises, in his relationship with his wife, his political calculations, and his financial dealings. By the beginning of 1797 he was systematically siphoning off a considerable proportion of the resources being sucked out of Italy, and following the last campaign he had taken most, at least a million francs, of the wealth uncovered by his commissary Collot at the mercury mines of Idrija in Slovenia.[8]

In conversation with the agronomist André Thouin at Mombello one day, he said that once peace had been signed he would retire to the country and become a justice of the peace. There is no reason to doubt the sincerity of such sentiments, but they were no more than idle thoughts: in the uncertain state France was in, no government of whatever persuasion could tolerate the existence of a man of his capacities and following as an uncommitted private individual. In August, one of the army victuallers who had known him at Valence wrote to a friend that he could see 'no end for him other than the throne or the scaffold'.[9]

Partly through his ambition and partly by force of circumstance, Bonaparte had become a figure famous throughout Europe. Between the spring of 1796, when he took command of the Army of Italy, and the end of 1797, no fewer than seventy-two pamphlets would have been published about him. People in the most distant parts of the Continent were either inspired or disgusted by him. Some feared him like the devil, others pinned their most ardent hopes on him. He was the source of fascination for young people of all classes and nations. But in France itself, he had become a political figure. Since the army had become an indispensable tool of government, any popular general was, whether he liked it or not, a player in the power struggle which was going on over the future governance of France. Having proved his competence during the Vendémiaire rising, he was now both feared and needed by the Directory, and by every political faction in Paris.[10]

For a man not shy of saying what he thought of others, Bonaparte was surprisingly sensitive to criticism. He had recently come under attack from the right-wing press in Paris, which portrayed him as a Caesar only waiting to cross the Rubicon, as a Jacobin and a fiendish 'exterminating angel'. He decided to respond in kind. On 19 July the first issue appeared in Milan of the *Courrier de l'armée d'Italie*, a paper ostensibly meant to keep the army informed, but whose primary aim was to work on public opinion in France, where it was disseminated. Other commanders had published papers to keep their troops informed, but this one was different. The main feature of the first number was a description of the parade held in Milan on the anniversary of the fall of the Bastille on 14 July. It abounded in touching vignettes, mostly apocryphal. 'As the army marched past, a corporal of the ninth demi-brigade approached the commander-in-chief and said to him: "General, you have saved France. We, your children who share in the glory of belonging to this invincible army will make a rampart of their bodies around you. Save the Republic; may the hundred thousand soldiers who make up this army close ranks in defence of liberty." '[11]

While Bonaparte made it clear that he and his army stood firm in support of the Republic, the *Courrier* subtly distanced him from the Directory, which, by contrast with the pure republicanism of the Army of Italy and its commander, was made to appear weak and corrupt. A second journal, which came out once a *décade* (ten days—the revolutionary week) under the editorship of the moderate constitutionalist royalist Michel Regnaud de Saint-Jean-d'Angély, printed articles 'correcting' 'false' impressions of Bonaparte held in Paris and building up the image of him as a miracle-performing hero.

This positioning had a great deal to do with recent events in France, where the April elections had returned a majority of right-wing deputies to the two chambers, setting these in conflict with the Directory. Barras resolved to cow them by force and summoned General Hoche from the Army of the Sambre-et-Meuse under pretence of giving him the job of minister of war. On 16 July, as his troops crossed the sixty-kilometre exclusion zone supposed to keep the military away from the institutions of government, the chambers denounced the action and the attempted coup was blocked. Barras and his fellow Directors then concentrated on winning over those troops legally stationed within the zone, but they needed a popular general to lead them. Bonaparte wrote to the Directory on 15 July that the Army of Italy was alarmed at news of a slide to the right in Paris and hoped they would take energetic steps in defence of the Republic, assuring them of its support. He had cause for anxiety.[12]

When they invaded Venetian territory in May, his troops had arrested a royalist agent, the comte d'Antraigues, and from him and the papers found on him, Bonaparte discovered that Generals Pichegru and Moreau were involved in a plot to overthrow the Directory and bring back the Bourbons, a plot which specifically involved killing him. This explained why the Austrians were dragging their feet over concluding peace.[13]

The preliminaries signed at Leoben were just that, and a treaty still needed to be negotiated. The Austrian foreign minister Baron Thugut sent the Neapolitan ambassador in Vienna, Marchese Gallo, to negotiate this on his behalf, and when he met Bonaparte in Milan in May they agreed to conclude rapidly. But Thugut was in no hurry. At the last moment Bonaparte had insisted that France be allowed to keep all her conquests on the left bank of the Rhine, which meant that the territory's rulers would have to be compensated. Since their lands had formed part of the Holy Roman Empire, the emperor would need to sanction this and make whatever compensations were necessary. It was also hoped that some of Austria's allies in the anti-French coalition would be persuaded to accede to the settlement, which would be finalised at a congress to be convoked at Rastatt at the beginning of July. The possibility of a restoration of the Bourbon monarchy radically altered the situation; Louis XVIII would be only too happy to recover France reduced to her old frontiers and let northern Italy revert to Austria. When all this dawned on Bonaparte, he was outraged.[14]

Both sides prepared for a resumption of hostilities. Austria took possession of the Venetian territory promised to it, while Bonaparte took over Venice itself and reorganised the area under his control. He had turned the lands taken from Venice into a Transpadane Republic, but then incorporated that with the Cispadane into one, to be known as the Cisalpine Republic. His aim was to deny the whole of northern Italy to Austria and create a political unit that could stand on its own but remain under French control. He hoped to introduce an administration which would allow it to raise and pay for enough troops to defend both itself and French interests. It was not a new idea, as Dumouriez had done much the same in the Austrian Netherlands and Hoche on the Rhine. The policy made sense to the generals operating in the respective areas, if not to the Directory. It was also partly inspired by the *mission civilisatrice* the Revolution was supposed to be carrying out as it liberated sister nations from feudal 'slavery'. Bonaparte had the establishment of the Cisalpine Republic immortalised in a print showing himself before the tomb of Virgil, with the French people represented by a Herculean figure tearing the chains off a female figure representing Italy.

The reality did not live up to the ideal. Aside from a small number of Italian nationalists and Jacobins, the population had greeted the French incursion with varying degrees of hostility, which was greatly increased by the depredations of the troops and civilian administrators. Bonaparte had been careful not to upset local sensibilities by spreading revolutionary ideas, had refrained from toppling any throne (except that of Modena) or abolishing the privileges of the nobility, and had shown respect for the Church and the Pope (the

Directors raged about his use of the terms 'Holy Father' and 'His Holiness' when writing and referring to him). Yet the majority of Italians remained sceptical and uncommitted. There were moments when Bonaparte despaired of the enterprise, and he was beginning to be distracted by other thoughts.

In April, the former French minister in Constantinople, Raymond Verninac, turned up at Leoben on his way back to France. He was concerned at the treatment of French citizens and interests in Egypt by the Mameluke beys who ruled it as a semi-autonomous province on behalf of the Ottoman Porte. For the past two years he had been receiving alarming reports from the French consul in Cairo, Charles Magallon, who since 1790 had been pressing for France to intervene militarily and, if necessary, take Egypt over as a colony.[15]

The Levant had been a French sphere of interest since the Crusades, when a French dynasty was established in Jerusalem, and later France had entertained close diplomatic and commercial ties with the Ottoman Porte. The two powers were united in opposition to Austria and Russia, both of which threatened Ottoman interests in the Balkans. Toulon and Marseille had grown up on trade with the Levant, which attracted colonies of French merchants. An Ottoman province since 1517, Egypt was ruled by a pasha nominated by the Porte assisted by Mameluke soldiers of Albanian and Circassian origin. The pasha had lost control, the beys did as they pleased, and the population suffered from their maladministration, corruption, and cruelty. In the course of the eighteenth century many came to believe that Egypt was crying out for stable administration and development.

The loss of Canada and other colonies to the British in the 1760s prompted the French to look east. Featuring prominently in the art and literature of the eighteenth century, in the course of which France developed relations with Persia, the region seemed to offer great promise. The decline of the Ottoman Empire was a source of concern for France: if it were to fall apart, Austria and Russia would be the beneficiaries. A French base in Egypt would permit France to deny them that and Syria at least. It would also enable her to safeguard her interests in India, where she had a number of partisans among the Indian princes, chief among them Tipu Sahib of Mysore, who in October 1797 would make the last of several appeals for military assistance. A French force from Suez landing in Bombay at the heart of Mahratta territory would at the very least divert British forces.

As France lost further colonies to Britain in the West Indies in the 1790s, the case for acting in Egypt grew stronger. Magallon pointed out that the Nile delta provided the conditions to grow all the goods formerly derived from the Caribbean—cotton, rice, sugar, coffee, and so on—while others could be obtained from neighbouring Arabia and Persia. When the British seized the Cape of Good Hope, cutting off the sea route to India, the appeal of obtaining a port on the Red Sea grew stronger, as did that of piercing the Isthmus of Suez with a canal. The idea of turning the Mediterranean into a French sea was a logical one, and with Spain onside and Corsica in French hands once more, it appeared practicable.[16]

When he occupied the port of Ancona earlier in the year, Bonaparte noted its strategic value and that of the Ionian islands across the Adriatic. They had been part of the Republic of Venice, and as soon as he was able to, he despatched a force to occupy them. He made overtures to the Ottoman rulers of Albania, assuring them of France's good intentions and respect for their faith, and also to the Maniotes of the Peloponnese. Contemplation of those shores triggered a host of cultural references: Athens, Sparta, Homer, and Alexander the Great litter his correspondence at the time.

Another strategic imperative for control of the eastern Mediterranean was Malta, and Bonaparte began gathering information on the state of its defences and the morale of its masters, the Knights of the Order of St John. He pressed the Directory to investigate the possibility of having a Spaniard elected Grand Master, which, Spain being France's ally, would bring the island into France's orbit.[17]

General Louis Desaix, who turned up at Mombello in late July, was intrigued to find Bonaparte poring over maps of Egypt and Syria. A year older than him, looking, according to Lavalette, 'like a savage from the Orinoco dressed in French clothes', Desaix had much in common with Bonaparte, always wearing a plain, poorly fitting blue coat with no marks of rank, ill at ease in society and paying little attention to women. He caught Bonaparte's enthusiasm, and they discussed the details of an invasion of Egypt sailing out of Venice with a corps of 10,000 French and 8,000 Polish troops.[18]

In his report to the Directory on 16 August Bonaparte warned that Austria was arming and would soon be in a position to field formidable forces for the reconquest of Italy and argued that France must seek alternatives. 'The islands of Corfu, Zante and Cephalonia are of greater interest to us than the whole of Italy taken together,' he went on. 'I believe that if we were forced to choose, it would be better to restitute Italy to the emperor and to keep the four islands, which are a source of riches and prosperity for our commerce. The empire of the Turks is crumbling by the day; the possession of these isles will put us in the position to support it for as long as that will be possible, or to take our share of it. It will not be long before we feel that, in order to really destroy England, we have to take Egypt.'[19]

Unbeknown to him, the Directory had a few weeks before received a memorandum from its foreign minister, Talleyrand, in which he put the case for seeking replacements in Africa and Egypt for the colonies lost to the British in the western hemisphere, and followed this up with three more documents developing the putative advantages, suggesting Egypt as a suitable place to begin.

The Directors had other things on their mind: they needed a general who could help them intimidate the chambers, and they approached Bonaparte. While he shared their alarm at the counter-revolutionary tide in Paris and urged them to act, he was wary of getting involved. He therefore sent them Augereau, a stalwart republican who was sure to be able to carry the troops with him. The manoeuvre had also rid him of a man he did not like or trust, and who was inconveniently popular among the rank and file.[20]

In the course of the past year, Bonaparte had become aware of the perils threatening him, and he created a unit of bodyguards, the Guides, to act as an escort. But he needed to make sure that the Army of Italy was also entirely his. He bought the loyalty of the other generals with a mixture of encomiums, promotions, mentions in despatches to the Directory and his Bulletins, and cash hand-outs. On the cessation of hostilities with the signature of the preliminaries of

Leoben, the army was just over 80,000 strong, but a large proportion was made up of recent reinforcements, men who had seen little or no service under his command. He refrained from promoting more recent arrivals and filled the higher ranks of every unit with men who had proved themselves under him, even if it meant giving them precedence over senior officers. On 14 July he celebrated the anniversary of the fall of the Bastille with a parade at which he honoured men and units, followed by a banquet for all those who had distinguished themselves in battle. On 28 August he presented a hundred sabres of honour, ten to cavalrymen, ninety to grenadiers, whom he was already singling out as a kind of elite, his Praetorians.[21]

'What I have done so far is nothing,' he said to Miot di Melito and the Italian statesman Francesco Melzi d'Eril as they strolled in the gardens of Mombello one summer day. 'I am only at the beginning of the career I must pursue. Do you think it is to enhance the position of the lawyers of the Directory, the Carnots, the Barras, that I have been winning victories in Italy? And do you think it is in order to establish a republic? What nonsense! A republic of thirty million people! With our manners and our vices! It is an impossibility! It is a dream with which the French are in love, but it will pass like so many others. They want glory, they want their vanity to be satisfied, but liberty? They don't understand it at all. [...] The nation needs a glorious leader and not theories of government, phrases and speeches by ideologues which Frenchmen don't understand. [...] I do not wish to leave Italy until I can go and play in France a role similar to that I am playing here, and the time has not yet come: the pear is not yet ripe.'[22]

For all his cynicism, Bonaparte was still a child of the eighteenth-century Enlightenment, a believer in human progress, to be achieved through the better organisation of society. 'A France with *honest and strong government*, that is what I want,' he told Pontécoulant. He had long ago come to the conclusion that this could only be achieved by dictatorial means. While dining with his staff at Ancona in February, he had astonished them by affirming that the only decent government since the beginning of the Revolution had been that of Robespierre. Strong central authority, he explained, was necessary in order to carry the Revolution to its logical conclusion; to create new institutions based on solid rational foundations, ensure the rule of law, stabilise the currency by abolishing paper money and introducing a functional system of tax collection, re-establish the Church as a moral base for society, regenerate its morals and make France great once more. He concluded by saying that Robespierre had only failed because he lacked the experience and strength of 'a military commander'.[23]

The Directory had once again demonstrated the truth of this. Having placed Augereau in command of the troops in the Paris region, on 4 September (18 Fructidor) it felt strong enough to invalidate the April elections, expelling 154 deputies and thereby recovering its majority. Sixty-five were sent to the penal colony of Guyana. Bonaparte had sent his aide de camp Antoine de Lavalette to observe and report back on events. Once the coup had been accomplished, he was therefore able to gauge public reactions and act accordingly. As these had been generally unfavourable, he distanced himself from the actions of the Directory. 'Your silence is very curious, general,' wrote Barras, prompting Bonaparte to issue a proclamation expressing his satisfaction at the defeat of 'the enemies of the fatherland'. In private, he condemned the coup and particularly the deportations to Guyana. Barras remained suspicious and sent his secretary Bottot to Italy to ascertain what was going on.[24]

Bonaparte had acquired a new ally in Talleyrand, who had written him a flattering letter seeking his friendship. He responded with an appropriately cordial one full of praise for the minister's distinguished record, which he, Bonaparte, would certainly reward were he to be in a position to do so. 'You ask for my friendship, and you have it along with my esteem,' he wrote. 'In return, I ask for your counsels, which I will value, I assure you.' He went on to say that the Revolution had destroyed too much and built nothing, so 'everything remained to be done', and the only question was who would be the one to 'close the Revolution'. Subsequent correspondence confirmed that it was not only their views on Egypt that coincided.[25]

With the possibility of a Bourbon restoration dismissed by the Fructidor coup, there was no longer any reason for Austria to delay making peace. Britain too was inclined to end the hostilities, and peace talks had been going on at Lille since July between Lord Malmesbury and Charles-Louis Letourneur. But they were undermined by the Directory, which saw them as part of an Anglo–royalist plot. Bonaparte was highly critical of the missed opportunity, arguing that the British could have been allowed to keep the Cape in exchange for agreeing to a French colonisation of Egypt.[26]

It was not until the end of August that the Austrian chancellor Thugut sent a senior diplomat, the monstrously fat forty-four-year-old Count Ludvig Cobenzl, to direct the negotiations along with Gallo. They took up residence at Udine while Bonaparte installed himself a short distance away at Passariano, a grand country residence set in beautiful parkland belonging to Ludovico Manin, the last Doge of Venice. They skirmished ferociously but dined together, either at Udine or Passariano.

While Thugut was now eager to proceed so as to secure Venice for Austria as quickly as possible, the Direcory felt strong and belligerent. Following the unexpected death of General Hoche on 19 September it appointed Augereau commander of the Army of Germany in his place, which suggested the possibility of a fresh offensive against Austria in that theatre. This was unwelcome news to Bonaparte, as it raised the possibility of Augereau stealing a march on him, or at least dimming his glory with a victory. Equally unwelcome were the despatches which arrived from Paris on 25 September informing him that the Directory was sending someone to conduct the negotiations in his stead.

He responded with one of his tantrums. 'I am ill and I need rest,' he wrote to Barras the same day, asking him for a discharge, adding that he wanted to settle outside Paris and enjoy at least a couple of years of peace. He wrote to the Directory in the same vein. 'No power on earth could make me continue to serve after this horrible mark of ingratitude by the Government, which I had been very far from expecting,' he complained. 'My health is considerably impaired, it urgently demands rest and tranquillity. The state of my soul is also such that it needs to reimmerse itself in the mass of my fellow citizens. I have for too long had great power placed in my hands.'

The idea of Bonaparte immersing himself in the mass of his fellow citizens was too frightening for the Directory to contemplate.[27]

The negotiations continued, Cobenzl trying to intimidate Bonaparte with courtly mundanity, only to be met with bullying and feigned rages. The Austrian diplomat was unused to such tactics, and through Gallo he persuaded Josephine to exert a calming influence (for which she would be rewarded by the emperor). But Bonaparte was not to be controlled as he steered his own course; he was under strict orders from the Directory not to cede any part of Venice to Austria, and while he had no intention of following these, he used them to pressure Cobenzl over other things, as by then Austria was set on having the territory. At the same time, he did not want to push the Austrian too hard, as he feared a possible resumption of hostilities, for which his army was unprepared, and he reserved his belligerence for the peace talks.[28]

These were eventually concluded, and the treaty was to be signed on 11 October, but at the last moment Bonaparte insisted a guarantee be inserted that France would obtain the left bank of the Rhine. Co- benzl demurred. Bonaparte, who had spent two sleepless nights, was in an agitated state and fortified himself with numerous glasses of punch as he read out his proposed draft of the treaty. When Cobenzl attempted to explain the impossibility of his acceding to the new terms, Bonaparte got up from the table clearly drunk, put on his hat, and stormed out of the room, vomiting barrack-room imprecations. By his own account, he smashed Cobenzl's favourite coffee set before walking out, pursued by a vainly emollient Gallo.[29]

Bourrienne records that two days later he awoke to see snow on the mountaintops and informed Bonaparte of it as he roused him. With winter on its way, a French threat to Vienna through the passes was dissolving fast, and Bonaparte realised he had to conclude speed- ily. The treaty was signed on the night of 17–18 October and named after a place equidistant from the two in which the negotiations had been conducted, the village of Campoformido, mis-spelt by a French secretary as Campo Formio. Bonaparte had gained most of what he wanted. He was in high spirits, and at dinner he entertained the Aus- trians by telling them his favourite ghost stories.[30]

'My services have earned me the approbation of the Government and the nation,' he wrote to the Directory. 'I have received many marks of its esteem. It now remains for me only to step back into the crowd, take up the plough of Cincinnatus and set an example of respect for the magistrates and aversion for military rule, which has destroyed so many republics and undermined several States.'[31]

On 5 November he received his nomination as commander of a projected Army of England and also as plenipotentiary at the congress due to convene at Rastatt to settle questions arising from France's acquisition of the left bank of the Rhine. On the morning of

17 November he left Milan with Eugène de Beauharnais. Travelling fast and through the night he was at Mantua the next day, where he paused only to review the troops stationed there, hold a ceremony in honour of the deceased Hoche and attend the theatre, before rushing on, to reach Turin at two on the morning of 19 November. He paused there long enough to have a talk with Miot di Melito, in the course of which he again expressed his conviction that 'those Parisian lawyers who have been put in the Directory understand nothing about government'. 'As for me, my dear Miot, I tell you that I cannot obey; I have tasted command and I would not be able to give it up. I have made up my mind: if I cannot be master, I will leave France. . . .'[32]

At three that afternoon he left Turin, and two days later he was in Geneva. People came out to catch sight of him as he passed through, not just to see the victorious hero whose reputation was spreading over the Continent, but to cheer the man who had brought peace after so many years of war. '*Vive Bonaparte, vive le pacificateur!*' they shouted. According to Bourrienne, Bonaparte was furious when one of their former colleagues from Brienne now living in Switzerland came to see him and addressed him with the familiar '*tu*'.[33]

He was even angrier when, after rushing on through Berne, Basel, and Huningue and reaching Augereau's headquarters at Offenburg, he was informed that the commander of the Army of Germany was busy getting dressed and could not see him. He hurried on to Rastatt, which he drove into on 26 November in a magnificent coach drawn like a sovereign's by eight horses, with an escort of thirty hussars, before installing himself in the Margrave of Baden's residence.[34]

He impressed the representatives of the Imperial Diet not just by his grand manner but by his familiarity with the Golden Bull of 1356, the constitution of the Holy Roman Empire, and the Treaty of Westphalia. On 29 November he met the prime minister of Baden and exchanged the ratified copies of the Treaty of Campo Formio. On the same day he received a despatch from the Directory summoning him to Paris.[35]

14

Eastern Promise

ONAPARTE ARRIVED IN Paris at five o'clock on the dark winter evening of 5 December in an ordinary mail coach, dressed in civilian clothes, a broad-brimmed hat hiding his face, accompanied by generals Berthier and Championnet, also out of uniform. He went home to the house on the rue Chantereine, which was empty since he had left Josephine behind in his rapid journey through Rastatt to Paris. Before going to bed he dashed off a note to Madame Campan asking her to send Hortense to come and join him and made an appointment to meet Talleyrand the following morning.

He arrived at the Ministry of Foreign Relations at eleven o'clock. Waiting in Talleyrand's anteroom were two eminent people desirous of meeting him: the old admiral and circumnavigator Bougainville and the celebrated writer and bluestocking baroness Germaine de Staël, whom he barely acknowledged in his haste to get down to business with the minister. It was their first meeting, and Talleyrand was enchanted, noting that 'twenty battles won sit so well with youth, a fine look, pallor and a kind of exhaustion'. After an hour's confabulation they set off to meet the five Directors, whom they found assembled in Barras's quarters at the Luxembourg Palace. Bonaparte was greeted warmly by Barras himself and one other Director, the hideously ugly Louis-Marie Lareveillère-Lépaux, a dreamer more interested in horticulture and his pet project of a new religion, Theophilanthropy, than in the minutiae of government. The more practical and dominant Jean-François Reubell was amicable, but the

Napoleon's mother Letizia Bonaparte in 1800, by Jean-Baptiste Greuze. She
brought him up strictly, and he would later say that he owed her everything.

Two sketches of Bonaparte
by Jacques-Louis David.

General Bonaparte drawn from
life by Giuseppe Longhi during
the Italian campaign of 1796.

Founding myth: General Bonaparte leading his troops accross the Bridge of Arcole, by
Antoine-Jean Gros. Napoleon never got anywhere near the bridge, and his attempt to
do so ended ignominiously with his being pulled out of a muddy drainage ditch.

This portrait of Bonaparte by Francesco Cossia was commissioned in 1797 by his English admirer Maria Cosway. Cossia found his model so nervous and restless that he gave up and refused to accept any money for it – yet the unfinished work captures some of the energy and immaturity of the tortured twenty-seven-year-old general.

Josephine Bonaparte in 1797, by Andrea Appiani. Feted and covered in looted jewels by her adoring husband, she cheated on him shamelessly throughout his epic campaign.

Auguste Marmont, by Georges
Rouget, was the first of a series
of exalted young men who
hero-worshipped Napoleon and
attached themselves to him.

Andoche Junot, sketched ten
years later by Jacques-Louis
David, was plucked out of the
ranks by Major Buonaparte at
Toulon in 1794 and became an
inseparable and adoring friend.

The swashbuckling cavalryman Joachim Murat rendered vital service in the events of 13 Vendémiaire which launched Napoleon's political career, would marry his youngest sister and become a central (if untrustworthy) figure in his entourage.

Josephine's son Eugène de Beauharnais, depicted here by Antoine-Jean Gros as Napoleon's aide-de-camp, fulfilled the role of a surrogate son.

Napoleon's younger sister Pauline, by Jean Jacques Thérésa de Lusse,
was his favourite, however much he might disapprove of her promiscuity,
and she remained the most faithful to him.

remaining two, Lazare Carnot and Charles Louis Letourneur, were hostile. They were incensed by the Treaty of Campo Formio and its destruction of the Venetian Republic. While they were powerless to do anything about it, given the popularity of Bonaparte and the universal joy at the coming of peace, they had shown their feelings by giving him command of the Army of England and delegating him to the congress of Rastatt—both designed to keep him away from Paris.[1]

After his meeting Bonaparte stayed to dine with Barras and then went home. As news of his return spread, people wondered what his next move would be. He was still commander of the Army of Italy, he had been placed in command of that of England, and as president of the French delegation to the congress of Rastatt he had overall command of French troops in Germany. A number of units were making their way across France to the Channel coast, passing within reach of Paris. Bonaparte was therefore in a position to stage a military coup, and many expected him to act. There would be little resistance, as the great hope of the royalists, General Pichegru, had been sent to Guyana and the leader of the extreme left, Gracchus Babeuf, guillotined. But as the Republic was not under threat, he had no credible motive.[2]

He was to return to Rastatt in a little over a week, and in the meantime he kept the door of his house firmly shut, instructing his servant to admit nobody and even to refuse to accept calling cards. To his intense irritation, the Directors had decided to hold a ceremony in his honour on 10 December, and he could not wriggle out of it. But afterward he went to ground once more, and at dinner the following day, to which he had invited a handful of distinguished intellectuals, he talked metaphysics to the philosophically minded Abbé Sieyès, poetry to the poet Chénier, and geometry to the mathematician Laplace.[3]

He only ventured out in civilian dress, his face hidden by a hat, and when he went to the theatre he sat at the back of his box. While the Directory was wary of him, he was afraid lest it feel threatened enough to resort to extreme measures. He could not avoid going to a banquet for eight hundred guests held in his honour by the two chambers on 24 December in the great gallery of the Louvre, hung with the paintings he had sent back from Italy, but he ate nothing. When dining out he partook only of dishes he had seen others taste, and otherwise confined himself to tamper-proof boiled eggs.[4]

On 25 December the Institute of Arts and Sciences elected him a member. He was genuinely thrilled. 'The real conquests, the only ones which come with no regrets, are those one makes over ignorance,' he wrote in this letter of acceptance. 'The most honourable occupation, and that most useful to all nations, is to contribute to the extension of human thought,' he went on, declaring that the real greatness of the French Republic should lie there. The following day he took his seat, between his friends Monge and Berthollet. He would attend over a dozen of the Institute's meetings over the next three months, acquiring a pool of admirers among the intellectual elite of France. He would spend hours with scientists, acting the eager pupil or astounding them by his knowledge, flattering them with his deferential interest, declaring that war, which might be necessary at times, was a lowly trade that could not aspire to the level of an art or a science such as theirs. Although his friendship with Monge, twice his age, Berthollet, and some of the others was heartfelt, his courting of the intellectuals was calculated. The same went for the artistic establishment. Astonishingly for someone as impatient as him, he spent no less than three hours sitting for the painter Jacques Louis David. 'Oh, my friends, what a head he has! It is pure, it is magnificent, it has the beauty of antiquity!' David exclaimed afterward. 'In all, my friends, this is a man to whom in those days altars would have been raised, yes, my friends, yes, my dear friends! Bonaparte is my hero!'[5]

His membership of the Institute also allowed him to sidestep a thorny issue when the Directory insisted he attend the ceremony held annually on 21 January celebrating the execution of Louis XVI. He tried to exempt himself by arguing that he did not hold any public position, protesting that the supposed celebration was inappropriate given that it commemorated a national disaster, that no government, only a faction would ever celebrate the death of a man, and that it brought no credit to the Republic or ease its relations with the other states of Europe, most of which were monarchies. The Directors were adamant, fearing that his absence would be interpreted as a sign of defiance and give heart to royalists. He eventually agreed to attend in the ranks and uniform of the Institute, thereby underlining that his attendance was purely official and did not reflect his views

He was careful to maintain good relations with the Directors, and Lareveillère-Lépaux was delighted by his modesty, his simplicity of dress, his apparent domesticity and his declared interest in Theophilanthropy. Consistently self-effacing, Bonaparte was all things to all men—the Prussian minister was flattered when he sang the praises of Frederick the Great, dismissing his own victories as the result of 'good luck and some hard work'.[6]

As commander of the Army of England, Bonaparte was supposed to invade it. He saw France as the new Rome and Britain as Carthage, and his vanity would have been caressed by the success of a play titled *Scipion l'Africain* in which audiences picked out parallels between him and Scipio. Another, on the fall of Carthage, made even more obvious allusions to the heroics he was about to embark on. But it is doubtful that he ever considered the possibility seriously.[7]

A week after his return to Paris, on 13 December, he issued his first orders relative to the invasion, and over the next days had a number of meetings with the minister of the navy. The French navy had been irredeemably damaged by the Revolution; crews had mutinied and discipline could not be restored for ideological reasons. By 1792 all but two out of nine admirals and three out of eighteen rear-admirals had left, along with three-quarters of the captains. Training replacements was impossible, as most of the ships were confined to port by the British blockade, and after the loss of so many at Toulon, the French navy was not up to carrying out an operation of the sort envisaged.

It is doubtful that Bonaparte felt any desire to invade England. He nurtured an admiration for the British, condemned the Directory's failure to make peace the previous summer, and reproached Barras for the belligerence of his speech at the ceremony of 10 December. He conferred with Wolfe Tone and other Irish revolutionaries but was unimpressed. If he had intended to carry through the plan he would have applied himself to the task with his usual determination, spending his nights poring over maps and inspecting embarkation ports, identifying landing places and organising the invasion force. He did none of these and did not present the Directory with a plan for over a month, while in the past he had produced them in a matter of days. It is doubtful that the Directors themselves believed in the possibility of a successful invasion.[8]

The arrival of Josephine on 30 December put an end to Bonaparte's low-profile life. On the same day, the rue Chantereine was renamed rue de la Victoire, and that evening they went to the theatre. Four days later they attended a party given in their honour by Talleyrand, a grand affair for some two hundred guests, widely commented on for its lavish scale and ancien-régime elegance. The rooms were decorated with trees and foliage, with backdrops presenting views of a military camp. The ladies wore scanty 'Greek' dresses, and while Josephine stood out, Bonaparte was self-effacing in civilian dress and did not stay long. He was annoyed when Madame de Staël engaged him in conversation. He would later claim she tried to seduce him, but on this occasion he was plain rude. When she asked him what kind of woman he respected most, no doubt hoping for a flattering response, he replied curtly that he esteemed only those who bore many children, before turning to talk to the Ottoman ambassador Ali Effendi.[9]

His opinion of women would not have been enhanced by the behaviour of Josephine. On his departure for Rastatt he had left her in Milan, from where she was to travel directly to Paris. She prolonged her journey in order to spin out her amours with Lieutenant Charles, who was travelling with her. Once she reached Paris, she dismissed her maid Louise, who had displeased her by having a fling with Junot on their way out to Italy. Louise took her revenge by spilling the beans to Bonaparte about Hippolyte Charles. He angrily reproached his wayward wife, but she managed to placate him.[10]

By mid-January 1798 it had become clear that Bonaparte's presence was not after all required at Rastatt, which left him with no excuse to delay an invasion of England he had no intention of embarking on. He had gradually worked his way into the confidence of the Directors, whom he saw regularly, and contemplated joining them, but being less than forty years old he did not qualify.[11]

He was being urged by many to stage a coup against them, but felt the time was not ripe and remained uncertain as to the depth or durability of his popularity. There were rumours of plots to poison him, and he was aware that he had enemies at both extremities of the political spectrum. It was time he returned to his real trade and took command of an army—in the midst of which he would be safe.[12]

Since England was such an unpromising objective, the only viable alternative was the invasion of Egypt, which Talleyrand was advocating. On 25 January news reached Paris of the death of the French ambassador in Constantinople. While the implications were being discussed by the Directors, Bonaparte set to work with Talleyrand on a fresh report which the minister delivered to them the following day. It repeated the old arguments, adding that the Porte had effectively lost control of Egypt and would not mind France administering the colony provided it remained its nominal sovereign: the corrupt and backward Mameluke administration would simply be replaced by a French one, and the Porte might actually benefit from such an arrangement. French diplomats in the area were of one voice that Mameluke rule was unpopular with the Egyptians themselves, who longed for deliverance. Talleyrand proposed to go to Constantinople himself to arrange matters.[13]

The Directors were divided in their opinions and ostensibly still favoured an invasion of England. On 23 February, after visiting Etaples, Ambletuese, Boulogne, Calais, Dunkirk, Nieuport, Ostend, Ghent, and Antwerp, Bonaparte reported that an invasion was impracticable. The following day he discussed his findings with the Directors and declared that he would not take on the job, offering to resign his commission. Reubell, who hated him, handed him a pen. The gesture was a dig at his vanity, but no more—the Directory did not want a disgruntled war hero hanging about Paris, and they needed to find him an assignment. On 5 March they sanctioned the plan to invade Egypt.[14]

Financing the expedition was not a problem. The weak and largely conservatively ruled confederation of Swiss cantons provided a base for British secret agents and miltary access to the borders not only of France but of her Cisalpine 'sister republic', which had long bothered the Directory. Bonaparte had already sliced off the Valtelline and added it to the Cisalpine Republic, thereby gaining control of the Simplon Pass. The Directory encouraged Jacobins bent on revolution in various parts of the country, and French troops marched in to support them in overthrowing the most conservative of all the cantonal governments, that of Berne, whose treasure, as well as its two emblematic bears, were sent to Paris at the beginning of March.

Bonaparte set to work planning the expedition. The new Army of the Orient would be composed mostly of men from the Army of Italy. They would embark at Toulon, Marseille, Ajaccio, Genoa, and Civitavecchia. The respective fleets were to assemble off Malta, which was to be captured for France as the first step in denying the Royal Navy bases in the Mediterranean. The next step would be to land in Egypt, overthrow the Mamelukes and organise the country. A naval base was to be created at Suez which would connect with the French colony of Île de France (Mauritius), whose strategic position in the Indian Ocean could be exploited for trade and military purposes. As soon as it was practicable, the Isthmus of Suez was to be pierced with a canal. The plan could only work if the British navy stayed out of the Mediterranean, so it was kept a secret and preparations for the invasion of England proceeded.

Bonaparte was thinking of more than conquest. While they were both in Italy, Monge had drawn his attention to the disparity between how much was known about Greco-Roman civilisation and how little about the Egyptian, and when they discussed the possibility of an invasion he had suggested that a commission of experts should accompany it to study the pyramids and other remains. Bonaparte agreed, and his boundless interests suggested something more. He had a vision of extending the fruits of the Enlightenment to backward lands; the regeneration of what he referred to as the cradle of civilisation by the new metropolis that was France. The venture was to be beneficial to mankind, a voyage of discovery as well as one of illumination. He therefore decided to take with him the most eminent figures in the arts and sciences, as well as engineers and technicians who would develop the country. With the greatest secrecy, he began approaching them without telling them where they would be going.

Some, like the painter David, refused. The composer Méhul also backed out, as did the poet Ducis and the renowned baritone François Lays, whom Bonaparte had imagined singing Ossianic odes at the head of the troops on the march. He had the greatest difficulty in persuading Monge, who felt too old and was currently still in Italy; Bonaparte personally visited Madame Monge, pressing her to use her influence on her husband.[15]

He bade Bourrienne put together a travelling library, arranged in the following categories: 1. Sciences & Arts, 2. Geography & Travels, 3. History, 4. Poetry, 5. Novels, and 6. Political Sciences (which contained the Old and New Testaments, the Koran, and the Vedanta). Pride of place in the poetry section went to Ossian; Rousseau's *La Nouvelle Héloïse* and Goethe's *The Sorrows of Young Werther* were among the novels. He also had 2,000 bottles of good Burgundy sent to Toulon. To keep the soldiers happy, he wanted to take along a troupe of actors from the Comédie-Française. He also, it seems, had 'a leather helmet richly embroidered with gold' run up which made him look 'like an actor in an opera'.[16]

As there was a risk of the fleet being intercepted by the British, Josephine would not be sailing with him. He would send a frigate to fetch her once he had landed and pacified Egypt. Their marriage had gone through yet another trauma in mid-March when a delighted Joseph presented his brother with evidence that his wife was shamelessly carrying on her affair with Lieutenant Charles under his very nose, meeting him regularly in the afternoon at the house of a supplier to the military in the Faubourg Saint-Honoré. A natural liar, Josephine denied everything and challenged Bonaparte to divorce her. To Charles, she wrote in torrid terms of her love for him and her hatred for all the Bonapartes. 'Hippolyte, I will kill myself,' she wrote on 17 March. 'Yes, I must end [a life] which will be a burden to me if it cannot be devoted to you. [...] Oh, they can torment me as much as they like, but they will never part me from my Hippolyte: my last breath will be for him. [...] Adieu, my Hippolyte, a thousand kisses as ardent as my heart, and as loving.' As usual, she managed to placate Bonaparte, to whom she seems to have grown sincerely attached. He bought the house in the rue de la Victoire, inserting a clause giving her life tenure in the event of his death. He also agreed to her plan of buying a house outside Paris, at La Malmaison.[17]

On 17 April he ordered Admiral Brueys, who was to command the fleet, to prepare to sail within ten days. There is some evidence that he made one last proposal to the Directors to share power with them, pointing out that if the war with Austria were to resume they would need a strong man. On 22 April, which was supposed to be his last night in Paris, he went to a performance of *Macbeth*. But the next day news arrived of a diplomatic incident provoked by France's ambassador to Austria, General Bernadotte, which momentarily threatened to provoke a fresh war, and it was not until 27 April that the Directory felt it safe to order him to proceed to Toulon.[18]

He went to Saint-Germain with Josephine and Lavalette to visit her niece Émilie, whom Bonaparte had ordered Lavalette to marry, and to take her and Hortense for a picnic in the woods. The following day, 30 April, he attended a session of the Institute and then called on the Directors, who pressed him to leave as soon as possible. Others were still urging him to stay and overthrow the government. 'Bonaparte must either get away or destroy the Directory or be crushed by it,' Colonel Morand of the 85th Demi-Brigade wrote to his parents, revealing that even in Civitavecchia where he was stationed the political situation was no secret.[19]

Bonaparte left Paris incognito at three o'clock in the morning of 4 May, in a mail coach with a passport made out in a false name, accompanied only by Josephine, Eugène de Beauharnais, and Bourrienne. They travelled to Lyon, where they embarked on a boat which took them down the Rhône as far as Aix, and from there went by carriage to Toulon, which they reached in the early hours of 9 May. He took a parade of the 18th, and then the 32nd and 75th Demi-Brigades, all old soldiers of his Army of Italy. 'We greeted him with enthusiastic cheering lasting more than a quarter of an hour,' recalled one officer. Bonaparte then walked through the ranks talking to officers and men and ended with a speech comparing them to the Roman legions which conquered Carthage. He reminded them that only two years before he had found them covered in rags, had led them to glory and provided for their every need. He asked them to trust him now and assured them that they would return with the money to buy enough land for a farm (six *arpents*, or about five acres).[20]

The enthusiasm was great, and even the hesitant Monge came to life. 'I am transformed into an Argonaut!' he wrote to Bonaparte, comparing him with Jason but pointing out that instead of going after some worthless fleece, he would be carrying the torch of reason to a land where no light had penetrated for centuries.[21]

Monge was one of the few in on the secret. The rest were kept in darkness and speculated wildly as to whether their destination was England, Ireland, Portugal, Brazil, Sardinia, Malta, Sicily, Gibraltar, the Crimea, or even India. Bonaparte announced to the 75th Demi-Brigade that they were 'one of the wings of the Army of England', which was about to cross the seas and conquer the new Carthage. He assured them that great destinies awaited them, that the eyes of Europe were on them, and that although they would have to overcome great dangers and hardships they would bring lasting benefits to their motherland. 'The genius of liberty, which has made of the Republic the arbiter of Europe from her very birth, wishes that she should be that of the seas and of the most distant lands,' he concluded. Similar exhortations were echoed all over the country. 'Alexander subdued Asia, the Romans conquered the world,' thundered the leading article in *L'Ami des Lois*. 'Do more, make the whole world happy and free, you can, you must...'[22]

On 13 May the ships in the roads were bedecked with flags and fired gun salutes as Bonaparte went aboard the flagship, the 120-gun *l'Orient*, one of the largest ships afloat and one of the few French vessels of recent construction. He had asked Admiral Brueys to prepare a cabin for him, bearing in mind that he would be spending much time in it feeling seasick. Brueys did not stint, and according to the chief uniform supervisor who went to take a look, 'everything was arranged in the most useful and agreeable manner, with the greatest refinement and good taste'; Bonaparte's '*salon de compagnie*' struck him as 'marvellous' and 'fit to accommodate a sovereign'.[23]

At seven on the morning of 19 May the huge fleet weighed anchor. Five days later it was off Corsica, where it was joined by a flotilla carrying a contingent of troops from Ajaccio, and then sailed down the coast of Sardinia. The soldiers were kept busy with drills and taught to climb rigging and man the naval guns, while military bands played rousing marches and revolutionary hymns. In the evenings, they had less martial music: the band of the Guides was up to playing whole symphonies. Once he had recovered from the first bouts of seasickness, Bonaparte took a keen interest in all things nautical, and in the evenings after dinner either listened to music or held court with his entourage of generals and savants. They took turns to read aloud, the works of Montaigne and Rousseau among others. Junot would fall asleep, and snored so loudly that he was excused. Bonaparte had Arnault read the *Odyssey* to him aloud, but after a time declared that Homer and the Greeks in general were not heroic enough compared with Ossian. He produced a luxury edition bound in vellum of the fake bard's poems which he kept by his bedside and began declaiming them to the assembled company. Arnault noted that he read very badly, but Bonaparte was entranced by his own rendition and declared that next to Ossian, Homer was nothing but an old driveller.[24]

Bonaparte did most of the talking, and while he made observations which were original and interesting, he was prolix in sweeping generalisations, holding for instance that the only subject worthy of tragedy in the theatre was politics, and that introducing love into a tragedy was merely to reduce it to comedy. How seriously he meant his perorations to be taken is debatable. On one occasion he began to rant against women in public life. 'Women are at the heart of all intrigues; they should be kept in their family circles and the salons of government should be closed to them,' he pronounced. 'They should be forbidden to appear in public otherwise than in a black dress and veil, in a *mezzaro* like in Genoa and Venice.' He digressed wildly, skipping from one subject to another. One moment he was discussing Hannibal's military talents, the next he was indulging in flights of fancy. 'If I were master of France,' he declared one evening, 'I would like to make Paris not only the most beautiful city that ever existed but the most beautiful one that could ever exist. I would like to bring together in it all that was most admired in Athens and Rome, in Babylon and Memphis; vast open spaces embellished with monuments and statues, fountains at every crossroads to purify the air and wash the streets, with channels running between the trees of the boulevards surrounding the capital; monuments required for public utility, such as bridges, theatres, museums, whose architecture would be as magnificent as was compatible with their function.' All the skill and resources were there. All that was needed was 'an intelligence to guide them' and 'a government which loved glory'.[25]

On 9 June the contingents from Genoa and Civitavecchia joined the main fleet off the south of Sicily, from where it sailed for Malta, the first object of the expedition. The island was the stronghold of the last of the great crusading orders, the Knights of St John, and its fortress at Valetta one of the most formidable in Europe. But the Order was in terminal decline and unloved by the population, its Grand Master Ferdinand von Hompesch weak and unpopular, its knights demoralised and the French ones mostly favourable to France. This was common knowledge, and several powers, including Britain, Russia, Spain, and Naples, had been eyeing the strategic harbour with intent.

Bonaparte sent the Grand Master a message requesting to be allowed to take on water. When he received the reply that only four ships would be allowed into the harbour at a time, he took this as a hostile move and sent troops ashore. The forces of the Order put up a token resistance and fell back. Bonaparte sent the mineralogist Déodat Dolomieu, an erstwhile member of the Order, armed with a mixture of threats and bribes. It did not take long to come to an arrangement, and by 10 June Valetta had surrendered. Hompesch was promised a pension and a principality in Germany, his knights more modest compensation, and the French ones the possibility of moving back home or taking service in the French army. Bonaparte promptly put in hand the transformation of the administration of the island to bring the new colony into line with its metropolis. Titles of nobility were abolished, religious orders dissolved, the judiciary reformed on the French model, and non-criminal prisoners were freed, as were the mostly Muslim galley slaves. A new French-style schooling system was set up, with the brightest in every year to be sent to Paris for their education (he even designed a uniform for them). The forms Bonaparte introduced were similar to those he had imposed in the Cisalpine Republic and clearly indicated how he would like to see France itself reorganised. The Catholic Church was left in place, and the Jewish and Muslim faiths were granted equal standing. The treasury and assets of the Order were confiscated, along with those of the Church, which was stripped of everything not essential to its rites—reliquiaries were melted down while chalices were left.[26]

On 19 June the fleet sailed on, leaving behind a small garrison under General Vaubois. It now consisted of over 330 vessels, 'an immense city floating majestically on the sea', in the words of one passenger. It was loaded with around 38,000 soldiers and civilian passengers, over a thousand horses and nearly two hundred field guns, as well as seven hundred freed Egyptian galley-slaves. It covered an area of ten square kilometres, presenting a huge target. 'The possibility of an encounter with the British was on everyone's mind,' recalled an infantry officer.[27]

The Admiralty in London had been alerted by its spies to the preparations being made at Toulon and elsewhere, but the reports varied considerably as to their purpose, some speculating about an invasion of England, others about the West Indies, India, and Egypt. The Admiralty despatched a fleet under Admiral Horatio Nelson to the Mediterranean to blockade Toulon and destroy the French fleet if it put to sea. Nelson had arrived off Toulon on time, but damage from a sudden storm had obliged him to sail away for repairs and miss the French force's departure. He was now making a dash for Egypt in pursuit of it. He overtook it without spotting it and, on reaching Alexandria and not finding it there, doubled back, assuming it was making for England after all.

The French fleet arrived off Alexandria on 1 July, two days after Nelson had left. Bonaparte had intended to land enough men to secure the port there and sail on to Rosetta or Damietta, from where he could march along the Nile to Cairo, which he must seize quickly if he were to succeed. But when the French consul Magallon came aboard with news that Nelson had called there two days earlier, he realised the English would soon be back, so he decided to go ashore without delay. Disregarding the advice of Brueys, he ordered immediate disembarkation in the bay of Marabout to the west of Alexandria, even though night was falling and the sea was rough.

The operation was carried out in small boats under sail which took only fifteen minutes to make it to shore, but a good deal longer to get back to the ships to take on more men. The horses swam ashore, held on leading reins by men in the boats. A number of men were drowned as some of the boats foundered on shoals, crashed into each other, or capsized, and others lost their equipment. Bonaparte was ashore by one o'clock in the morning of 2 July and had a short sleep on the beach while his men continued to disembark. By two o'clock he was able to begin the march on Alexandria.

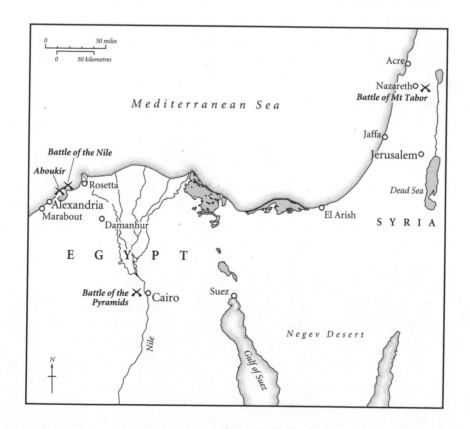

The previous day he had written to the pasha of Cairo, the Porte's governor, assuring him that he came as a friend. He also wrote to the French consul in Constantinople instructing him to explain to the sultan that he was only there to punish the Mamelukes, who had been persecuting French merchants, and to defend the country on his behalf against the British. He was expecting Talleyrand to reach Constantinople soon and smooth any feathers that might have been ruffled. He was in for a surprise.[28]

By the time they reached Alexandria its ramparts were bristling with troops and civilians who put up an unexpectedly fierce defence, those who had no weapons showering them with stones. They did not give up even when the walls were scaled, with the consequence that many of the inhabitants were put to the sword by the enraged attackers. They had never come across such 'fanatical' resistance. Combined with the sense of having entered a different world, it affected their view of the enemy, and of the civilian population. In Italy or on the Rhine, there had been no hatred between the soldiers on either side, and even less of the civilian population, which just wanted to be left alone. Here it was different. How different, they would soon find out.[29]

15

Egypt

BONAPARTE WAS DETERMINED to reach Cairo as quickly as possible and chose the most direct route. This turned out to be a mistake. The desert they found themselves marching through, so different from the cultivated landscape of Italy, had an immediate depressive effect on the troops. They were ill-prepared for the temperature and had not been issued with water bottles. The first cistern they came to was filled with stones, and wherever they did come across water it was so brackish even the horses refused to drink it. 'We marched during the day under a sky and over sand that were equally scorching, without any shelter or water with which to slake our thirst,' wrote Eugène de Beauharnais. The blazing sun and the glare of the sand brought on blindness in some, while others thought they were going mad when they experienced mirages, for which no-body had prepared them. The cold desert nights brought little relief, as their paltry supplies ran out on the first day and the roving Mam-eluke horsemen prevented them from going in search of food and kept them awake.[1]

Some died of heat stroke, others of exhaustion, many committed suicide. One soldier cut his throat in front of Bonaparte, shouting, 'This is your work!' It was unlike any war they had known. Those who failed to keep up with the marching columns were surrounded by groups of horsemen ready to pick them off, or worse. Bonaparte had delivered an address to his men, warning them that 'the peoples we shall be visiting treat women differently from us, but, in every country, he who rapes is a monster', but neither he nor any of his men had reckoned with another local custom.²

He had managed to ransom some men taken by Mamelukes shortly after they disembarked, and these recounted how some of their comrades had been decapitated while they themselves had been beaten and sodomised by their captors. The news was unsettling as it spread through the ranks. Even once they had occupied the town, lone soldiers walking in the streets of Rosetta would be set upon and 'compelled to undergo this shocking outrage', as one wrote to his wife in France. In a letter to his brother Joseph, Louis Bonaparte reported that Rousseau had got it horribly wrong in believing primitive man was born inherently noble and was only spoiled by civilisation.³

Buggery was the least of the perils awaiting those who fell into enemy hands. The Bedouin, Mamelukes, and insurgent fellaheen regularly tortured and murdered prisoners. To make matters worse, there was a crossover between civilians and combatants, since many of the inhabitants were warriors when the need arose. There were few things more disturbing to regular European soldiers than the possibility that any 'civilian' might suddenly turn into a fighter.⁴

After three days they reached Damanhur, where they found water, and pressed on toward Rahmaniya, where they were cheered by the sight of the Nile. The men leapt into the water and guzzled on watermelons, but morale did not improve much and discipline had all but disintegrated, and the troops took their exasperation out on the villages they passed through. Bonaparte's grandiloquent exhortations assuring them that their efforts would be of immense value for the 'civilisation and commerce of the world' and that 'Destiny is on our side!' sounded hollow. On 12 July he had the army parade before him and promised they would soon be on their way back to France, and then on to attack England. Three days later he was informed that one of his divisions was on the brink of mutiny. 'Courage on the battlefield is not sufficient to make a good soldier,' he admonished the men, 'he must also have the courage to bear fatigues and privations.' Some did rise to his challenge and, as one infantry officer put it, 'wished to live up to the Romans', but they were in the minority, and most blamed Bonaparte for his lack of foresight.⁵

'The lives of many brave men who died of thirst, committed suicide or were assassinated during those terrible marches and the cruel sufferings of the army could have been spared,' noted Sergeant Vigo-Roussillon. 'All that was needed was for every soldier to have been supplied with a small can in which to carry water. The commanding general, who knew which country he was going to lead us into, is responsible for this carelessness.' They had been issued with some stale tack, and not enough of that. At Wardan on 17 July Bonaparte wandered among the troops listening to their complaints and promised them that in a few more days they would find meat and drink in Cairo, but they remained sceptical and morose. Some treated him with outright insolence.[6]

His generals were hardly more respectful, with Berthier, Lannes, and even the stalwart Davout complaining bitterly, and General Dumas (the father of the novelist) so critical that Bonaparte accused him of inciting mutiny and threatened to have him shot. Murat was more cheerful. Although he had been shot through the jaw at the taking of Alexandria, the ball, which penetrated below one ear and exited below the other, did not disfigure him. His abundant dark locks would soon hide the scars, and he wrote home triumphantly telling a friend to inform the beauties of Paris that 'Murat, though perhaps not as handsome will be no less brave in love'. He was the exception, and despondency spread through the army, particularly among the officers, who could not accommodate the supposedly heroic nature of their enterprise with the squalor of the reality.[7]

The first encounter with a force of Mamelukes occurred at Chebreis on 13 July. It was no more than a skirmish, with horsemen galloping up to fire their carbines and pistols, seeking an opportunity to slash their way into the French ranks. They did not represent any real threat, but they were no less alarming for that. The onward march was executed in squares, with artillery at each corner, but although it was effective, it required huge effort. 'Every irregularity of the terrain lengthens or presses them in, the artillery hinders them, the wagons clutter them,' noted Sułkowski. 'As soon as the soldiers are tired, they fall behind or press together, bump into each other, and a terrible amount of dust concentrated in a confined space in which no air can circulate blinds and suffocates them.' One such march lasted eighteen hours without a break.[8]

At the end of that, on 21 July, they came up against the main Mameluke army, led by Murad Bey, one of the two rulers of Egypt. Cairo was visible in the distance, and on the other bank of the Nile, the pyramids of Giza. This prompted Bonaparte to exhort his men with a stirring line about forty centuries of history gazing down on them from the top of the pyramids. What impressed the troops more than some nonsense about antiquity which few of them would have understood was the magnificent spectacle that unfurled before their eyes as the Mameluke cavalry galloped up. 'The splendour of their attire and their arms reflected the rays of the sun at us and dazzled our sight,' recalled Captain Moiret. The French were fascinated by their horsemanship and military skill, which, even though it was of another age and bound to fail when confronted by volleys of musketry, was extremely effective when the Mamelukes did manage to cut their way in among the enemy and slice off arms and heads with their scimitars. The outcome was never in doubt. The French held their squares and overpowered the Ottoman foot-soldiers, many of whom were killed or drowned in the Nile trying to escape. The Mamelukes left the ground strewn with corpses, abandoned forty guns and their camp, with its baggage, horses, and camels. After the battle this turned into a market as soldiers traded booty.[9]

The next day, 22 July, a delegation from Cairo surrendered the city, and two days later Bonaparte made his triumphal entry. He took up residence in the house of a Mameluke bey, in which he occupied the first floor and accommodated his staff below. It had a garden with trees and pools in which he strolled while giving orders to his staff and administrators. He was delighted by what he had seen of Egypt and was convinced that given some organisation and sensible development it would flourish. 'The Republic could not wish for a colony within easier reach with such rich soil,' he wrote to the Directory that evening. 'The climate is very healthy, because the nights are fresh.' But at this moment of triumph he endured a heavy personal blow.[10]

When he parted from Josephine at Toulon their relationship was as tender as ever. Bonaparte wrote frequently, saying he would bring her to Egypt as soon as it was safe, and she fully intended to go. In the meantime, she went to the spa at Plombières, from where she wrote to Barras asking for news of her husband. 'I am so sad to be parted from him that I am overcome by a melancholy which I cannot vanquish,' she wrote. 'I am therefore hastening my prescribed cure so that I may quickly be able to go and join Bonaparte, whom I love very much despite his little faults.' She was planning to travel in the company of Marmont's wife, but at the beginning of July a balcony that she and others were standing on collapsed under her and she was so badly hurt that there could be no question of going soon.[11]

'I have much, much domestic sorrow, for the veil has been lifted entirely,' Bonaparte wrote to Joseph the day after his entry into Cairo. Every time he had been told of Josephine's infidelities she had managed to lie her way out of it and make him feel unworthy for having believed what she dismissed as spiteful gossip, but on the evening of his entry into Cairo, Junot, Berthier, and his aide Thomas Jullien presented him with incontrovertible evidence. He poured out his grief and indignation to his stepson Eugène. He confessed to Joseph that he wanted to return to France and shut himself away from people, and asked him to find him a house somewhere deep in the country. 'I am fed up with humankind,' he wrote. 'I need solitude and isolation; greatness has damaged me; all feeling has dried up. Glory already lacks lustre at the age of twenty-nine; I am all used up. There is nothing left for me to do but become a complete egoist!'[12]

He had little time for introspection. Murad Bey might have been defeated, but his colleague Ibrahim was hovering in the vicinity with another force. Bonaparte marched out of Cairo on 9 August. He only managed to catch up with Ibrahim's rearguard, which he defeated in a protracted cavalry battle at Salayeh, but having obliged the Mamelukes to retire into the desert, he turned back towards Cairo. On his way, on 14 August, he received news that altered everything.

At 2:45 p.m. on 1 August one of Nelson's ships, HMS *Zealous*, had spotted Admiral Brueys's squadron at anchor in Aboukir Bay, and by dawn the next day it had ceased to exist. Only two ships of the line and two frigates managed to get away. The rest were sunk or captured, and the *Orient* blown up, with Brueys on board. Bonaparte took the news calmly. He declared that they had to face up to the new state of affairs and show themselves to be 'as great as the figures of antiquity' and began contemplating the implications of not being able to return to France any time soon.[13]

He lost no time in laying the blame on Brueys, whom he had instructed to take his ships into the harbour of Alexandria or else sail to Corfu. Brueys had decided against the former, fearing his ships might get stuck in the shallow entrance to the harbour, and he had delayed until he was sure Bonaparte did not need to be evacuated. The aide bearing Bonaparte's definite order to leave the bay of Aboukir never reached him, as he was killed on the way, but he would have arrived too late. Brueys's lack of resolution was partly the consequence of a general demoralisation in his squadron and his lack of faith in his crews and the state of his ships. He had disposed them unwisely, allowing the British to sail between him and the land, which meant that he received broadsides from both sides, so responsibility for the disaster must rest with him. Having taken the precaution of distancing himself from it, Bonaparte did write his widow a moving letter praising him as a hero.[14]

Bonaparte was determined that the enterprise should bear fruit despite the naval disaster. His first priority was the health of his troops. He established four hospitals in Cairo, and one each in Alexandria, Rosetta, and Damietta. He imposed quarantine on all the ports under French control and introduced measures covering the rapid burial of the dead, street cleaning, and rubbish collection. He ordered his chief physician, Dr René Desgenettes, to study the causes of the dysentery and ophthalmia that had attacked the troops. He gave orders for them to be issued with loose-fitting uniforms more suited to the climate—blue cotton jackets with no facings or tails and a sheepskin cap with a woollen bobble of different colours to distinguish the units from each other.[15]

He ordered the man in charge of uniforms, François Bernoyer, to design a new one for the medical staff, suggesting the colour brown so blood would not show. Bernoyer was also given the task of designing the uniform for a new corps of camel-mounted Guides. The upshot was the normal French military hat with its front turned down to form a sunshade, surmounted by red ostrich feathers, a green 'Greek-style' waistcoat with 'Hungarian' gold embroidery, a 'Turkish' belt, crimson trousers 'à la mamelouk', 'Roman-style' slippers, scarlet 'Polish-style' coat trimmed with gold, and a green cloak. Bonaparte was delighted with the design and surprised Bernoyer by showing it. 'When one does something for him he does not usually show the slightest approbation, let alone pleasure,' Bernoyer explained. 'In that, he reminds one of the attitude of children, who always seem to want more.'[16]

Bonaparte put in place a new administration, began minting money, brought in a system of taxation based on wealth, introduced street lighting, and put in hand a land registry. The benefits of European civilisation bestowed upon the new colony included the introduction of windmills to replace hand querns, new crops, and the production of everything, from gunpowder to cloth, that the army would need now that it was cut off from France.

On 22 August he created the Institute in Cairo, and the savants were put to work on the most pressing and practical tasks. 'Some are working out ways of making beer without hops, others with a simple method for the purification of Nile water, others busy themselves with the building of ovens, others still with framing legislation for the country, building wind-powered machines for moving water, etc., etc.,' the zoologist Geoffroy de Saint-Hilaire wrote to his father. Other subjects investigated were the sexual organs of crocodiles, the date palm, magic, dancing, the true colour of the sea, prostitution, the ostrich, sand, and the formation of dunes. One group, mainly archaeologists and artists, were sent off with General Desaix, who marched up the Nile on 25 August in pursuit of Murad Bey. His orders were to defeat him and chart the course of the Nile as far south as he could. He was to occupy Thebes, which the archaeologists were to explore, and the port of Koseir on the Red Sea, and to set up a network of forts along the Nile. Wherever the French went, everything, from ancient ruins to geographical and physical phenomena, was to be recorded and studied.[17]

Bonaparte was living out a dream. From his earliest years he had shown a passionate interest in progress as he, and his generation, saw it. He had also shown a remarkable proclivity for organisation. He was now effective ruler of a huge, backward country with a self-imposed mission to civilise it and could give rein to his most basic instinct of imposing order. 'I was never again as free as in Egypt,' he would later reflect. He did not mean to apply Western forms indiscriminately, but dreamed of a fusion, believing he would be able to organise the country and civilise its inhabitants without offending their sensibilities. He had, primarily from his reading of Voltaire's play, formed a view of the Prophet Muhammad as a kind of wise tyrant and thought he could understand how his followers responded to authority. He dreamed, as he would later put it, of writing a new Koran.[18]

The organs of administration he established were on traditional forms of *ulemas* and *diwans*. Officials were under French supervision, often through the agency of local Copts, and were made to wear tricolour cockades and sashes of office, but allowed to administer in traditional ways. He believed he would be able to introduce European forms and practices gradually once he had gained their confidence. They referred to him as 'Sultan Kebir', which flattered him and gave him the impression that they were responsive. He made grand gestures to win their approval, such as publicly liberating the Muslim galley-slaves he had found in Malta and promising to assist the caravan taking pilgrims on the *Haj*. On 18 August he presided over the annual ceremony of the opening of the dykes. Surrounded by sheikhs, he distributed coins to the people as the water was released into the canals that would irrigate the surrounding countryside. On 23 August, the feast of the Prophet, he paid his respects to the Divan of Cairo, and in the evening attended a banquet, at which all the French made great show of respect for the Islamic faith, although afterward they laughed at the charade. He did not; he was convinced he had captivated the locals.[19]

On 22 September, the anniversary of the founding of the French Republic, Bonaparte staged celebrations meant to underline his loyalty to the French state, boost the morale of his troops, and impress the locals. An amphitheatre was created with two columns at its centre representing the Republic, a triumphal arch commemorating the victory at the battle of the Pyramids, an obelisk dedicated to the fallen, and so on. A turban featured alongside the red Phrygian bonnet of liberty. All the troops in Cairo were present, drawn up in parade order, and listened as Bonaparte recalled their glorious deeds over the past five years and assured them that a fine destiny awaited them: they would be immortalised in death or on their return home as heroes. He ended with the cry 'Vive la République!', which normally elicited a hearty cheer, but on this occasion hardly a mutter came out of the serried ranks. They were in no mood to celebrate. 'The army showed only indifference for this feast,' recalled Captain Pelleport. 'It was suffering from *spleen* that day, which it often did after the loss of the squadron.' The parade was followed by a banquet which the local dignitaries and the soldiers appeared to enjoy more than the official proceedings. Sporting events and horse races were held, and the day ended with fireworks and illuminations.[20]

At the news of the destruction of the fleet there had been much cursing of Bonaparte, who was accused of adventurism and ambition. Some of his generals made defiant statements, but the pointlessness of such talk, and the lack of any prospect of returning to France soon, concentrated minds on making the best of the situation. Cairo would have to make do for Paris. Many found themselves fine houses with gardens and enjoyed the exotic comfort they provided.

The city contained a number of European residents, mostly traders of one sort or another, and they were quick to spot the opportunities offered by the influx of homesick Frenchmen. They opened shops, coffee houses, Turkish baths, and other amenities. Officers and men trotted about the city on donkeys, lounged in the cafés delighting in the hookahs and coffee, and went on excursions, particularly to see the pyramids and other ancient monuments. French ingenuity was stretched to provide comforts of every kind. Balls were held and a theatre built, in which, owing to the lack of women willing to act, young men had to take the female roles.[21]

Yet none of this could cure the underlying homesickness. 'Whatever efforts are made to provide for the wellbeing of the troops, to keep up the spirit of emulation among the officers, memories of France torment most of them and the officers much more than the

men, and the generals and staff officers much more than the officers of the line,' noted Lieutenant-Colonel Théviotte. 'People only
address each other to exchange regrets at having left France and to
express the desire to return. The deprivation of women is that which
is felt most keenly.'[22]

On arrival, most of the senior officers had taken over the wives of
prominent Mamelukes along with their houses, but having satisfied
their lust they found them wanting and passed them down the ranks.
The men were mostly horrified by the local women, mainly because
respectable ones were locked away by their families, and the only
ones they saw were either old, ugly, or prostitutes. A market developed, and a black woman could be bought for 500 francs, 800 if she
were a virgin, while Caucasian women cost several thousand. Eugène
de Beauharnais bought himself a beautiful black woman, and so presumably did Junot, since he sired a boy whom he called Othello and
brought back to France. Despite Bonaparte's ban, possibly as many
as three hundred of his men had smuggled their wives or mistresses
onto the ships disguised as soldiers, and given the scarcity of European women, these now had the pick of the higher ranks.[23]

Bonaparte had some local girls brought to him, but although he
later praised their grace and beauty, he rejected them as too fat if
not downright repellent. He dallied briefly with the sixteen-year-old
daughter of a sheikh, but was more at home with French women. It
was rumoured that he had an affair with the wife of General Verdier,
who had accompanied her husband in the uniform of an aide de camp.

At the ball which followed the celebration of the birth of the Republic, Bonaparte spotted 'a little woman some twenty years old,
charming, plump, vivacious', and took an immediate shine to her. She
was Marguerite-Pauline Bellisle, a dressmaker's assistant from Carcas-
sonne, locally known as Bellilotte. She had just married a Lieutenant
Fourès when his regiment was assigned to the Egyptian expedition,
and she decided to follow him. The day after the ball, Bonaparte ordered Junot to invite her and her husband to lunch, and by a subterfuge she was lured into a separate room alone with Bonaparte. She
resisted him, and went on doing so stoically despite his showering
her with gifts and letters, but finally gave in and they became lovers.

Bonaparte was by all accounts besotted by her, and they spent every available moment together, she often riding out with him dressed in uniform. She wore a miniature of him around her neck and he a locket of her hair around his.

Fourès was promoted and sent to Paris with despatches to the Directory, but his ship was taken by the British, and as he had fallen ill they released him on parole and he was back in Alexandria in April 1799. Bonaparte, who was considering marrying Bellilotte but waiting to see whether she would give him a son, asked for Fourès's assent to a divorce, which he was only too eager to give. He was sent away again, just in case. So was the mineralogist Louis Cordier, who had apparently caught Bellilotte's roving eye.[24]

To reinforce his authority, Bonaparte founded a paper, *Le Courrier de l'Égypte*, which built up his image, and to advertise what he was doing as a triumph of European Enlightenment over backwardness, he started another, *La Décade égyptienne*. He attended sessions of the Institute, discussed religion and local custom with imams, and visited the pyramids and other remains. He went to Suez to look for the ruins of the original canal, which he was excited to discover. He was also fascinated to find the Wells of Moses and other places associated with the scriptures, even crossing the Red Sea at low tide and nearly being trapped when it came in.

'Everything is going perfectly here,' he assured the Directory on 8 September. 'The country has been subdued and is beginning to get used to us.' He went on to list the advantages of France's new colony and expressed the view that its possession should facilitate reaching a satisfactory peace with Britain. He argued that they should move the whole French navy into the Mediterranean, which would not only improve communications but also force the British to bear the strain and expense of maintaining battle squadrons far from home and friendly bases, which would in the end force them to the negotiating table. He was preparing to build a naval base at Suez to open up communications with French colonies in the Indian Ocean.[25]

On 21 October a revolt broke out in Cairo. It was quickly put down, but it cost a number of lives, including that of one of Bonaparte's favourite aides, Sułkowski. It had been started by young students from one of the mosques, and only spread to other disaffected groups when the rumour got about that Bonaparte had been killed. The reasons behind the discontent included annoyance over taxes, street-cleaning regulations, and the land registry which obliged the inhabitants to list their properties. It had not been a grassroots upheaval, and numerous locals had sheltered Frenchmen from the insurgents.

The next day, Bonaparte received the sheikhs and imams and announced that he forgave the city and would not exact any retribution. He delivered a theatrical address, stating that God had instructed him to show mercy and urging them to inform those who had raised a hand against him that they would find refuge neither in this world nor the next. 'Could there be on Earth any man so blind as not to see that it is destiny itself which directs my actions?' he asked rhetorically, before going on to represent himself as a kind of messiah who had been foretold in the Koran, one who knew how to read in their hearts, a superior being against whom all human efforts were vain. He kept on making pronouncements and gestures intended to demonstrate his openness to what he saw as the spirit of the Orient, even though his ultimate intention was to turn Egypt into a French colony.[26]

A child of the Enlightenment, Bonaparte held a set of assumptions and prejudices which he took to be universal. Having moved away from Rousseau's belief in his inherent goodness, he had moved on to the view that man is a rational creature guided by self-interest yet susceptible to being inspired by ideals. He therefore took it as self-evident that when shown the benefits of French administration and technological progress, the inhabitants of Egypt would embrace them. He had liberated them from the cruel incompetence of the Mameluke beys, he had cleaned up and lit the streets of Cairo, he was bringing them civilisation. He had taken the trouble to acquaint himself with their religion and had made a rational assessment of it which was not entirely superficial. He thought the absence of the kind of hierarchy and ritual which characterised the Catholic Church would make Muslims more open to reason. What he failed to grasp was that Islam represented a mentality as much as a faith, and that was fundamentally at odds with Christian and secular Western values, along with their underlying assumption of superiority. He deluded himself that he was gaining acceptance because many styled him with Arab titles and kissed his hand. But however charming they may have shown themselves on occasion, they were at best not interested and regarded him as an alien intruder. Ironically, many of the measures he took would serve as a model for Mehmet Ali when he took over Egypt in 1805, but a Muslim could do what a Frenchman could not.

It took Bonaparte some time to appreciate that people obeyed only out of fear, and that showing mercy or consideration were seen as signs of weakness. He began beheading transgressors as an example, taking hostages, or razing villages whose inhabitants had attacked his men. This did not achieve the desired results, as the locals saw it not as just punishment but as unwarranted aggression, and only waited for chances of retaliation. It was only then that he understood reason and logic had no purchase and began showing he meant business by shooting and beheading suspects almost at random. The locals responded in kind, cutting off the arms, legs, noses, ears, or genitalia of prisoners, usually after sodomising them, or beheading, flaying, or burying them alive. Outside Cairo and the other towns, the French occupation remained frail.

This was the more alarming as the second assumption on which the viability of the Egyptian venture had been predicated now crumbled. The first had been that Egypt was within reach of France and therefore easier to protect and exploit than more distant colonies, but the destruction of the fleet in Aboukir Bay had made it as vulnerable as the Carribean ones it had been meant to replace. The second assumption had been that the Ottoman Porte would remain neutral. Yet having packed Bonaparte off on his pet venture, Talleyrand had failed to carry out his part in the plan. Bonaparte had written to him from Cairo, telling him he could inform the Sultan that the Islamic faith and mosques were being protected, pilgrims to Mecca were being assisted, that he had personally attended the feast of the Prophet, and that Turkish shipping and interests were being respected. Yet not only did Talleyrand not go to Constantinople, he had entirely omitted to approach the Porte, which was astonished to discover that a French army had invaded its dominion.

News of Nelson's victory emboldened the Sultan to declare war on France. British supremacy in the Mediterranean prompted the kingdom of Naples to do likewise. Russia, which had long been eyeing the Ionian islands as a potential naval base, buried its hatchet with the Porte and signed an anti-French alliance with it on 23 December and with Britain on 29 January. Two Ottoman forces gathered to expel the French from Egypt. One was to march from Syria under the command of Djezzar Pasha of Acre, the other was to go by sea and land at Aboukir.

Bonaparte had two options: either to wait for the attack in the hope that Djezzar's force would be weakened by a march across the Sinai desert and the other could be prevented from landing, or to attack and defeat one force before the other could be deployed. If he were to defeat Djezzar and take Acre, he would at the same time deny the British squadron blockading Egypt one of its bases, thus opening up the possibility of communication with France. The fall of Acre might also frighten the Porte into making peace.

He therefore left Desaix in Upper Egypt to contain Murad Bey and Marmont at Alexandria to defend the coast and marched out himself on 10 February 1799. It was just this kind of snap decision that had enabled him to triumph over successive Austrian armies in Italy, and a victorious outcome would open up all sorts of possibilities. He was, as he would later confess, carried away by the dreams they gave rise to.

16

Plague

A LL WE COULD see in this new project was another chance of glory as well as incalculable hardships,' recorded Captain Moiret, adding that the moment his men had been told they were to march out to Syria the grumbling ceased; they set off in high spirits on 6 February 1799.[1]

Bonaparte assumed that after a quick march his advance guard would capture the presumably well-stocked fortress of El Arish, and he did not take sufficient supplies with him. As the troops marched over the Sinai, hugging the Mediterranean coast, they ran out of victuals and were reduced to drinking brackish water and eating seaweed, which gave them dysentery. 'We ate dogs, donkeys and camels,' Bonaparte admitted to Desaix. It was not just the troops who were grumbling by the time he joined his vanguard at El Arish on the evening of 17 February. His generals too were fed up, and his theatrical rhetoric only irritated them. General Kléber, an experienced soldier who had served in the Austrian army before the Revolution, was difficult to ignore with his Homeric stature, booming imperious voice, and tendency to use it to say what he thought. 'Never a proper plan, everything goes by leaps and bounds, every day rules the action of that day,' he declared of Bonaparte's method. Yet even he had to admit that this 'extraordinary man' possessed something which set him apart and lent him an authority he could not dispute. 'It is to dare, and to keep daring, and he carries that art to the limits of temerity.' That capacity was to be tested severely over the next weeks.[2]

Desperate to move on but fearful of leaving possibly mutinous generals behind to continue the siege, Bonaparte offered the garrison of El Arish generous terms, and it capitulated on 20 February. The men were allowed to leave with their arms and baggage under oath that they would not bear arms against France for twelve months. The chief surgeon of the Army of the Orient, Dr Jean-Dominique Larrey, disinfected the fort against the plague, which had broken out in the area, and established a hospital before they set off for Gaza.[3]

They were now marching through fertile country, but under drenching rain that turned the tracks to seas of mud. Entering Gaza after a brief skirmish, Bonaparte made a pompous speech informing the inhabitants that he was bringing them liberty. He addressed the griefs of his own men with an order of the day full of references to the Philistines and the Crusaders. To some soldiers who complained of lack of food he said that the Roman legionaries had eaten their leather equipment but kept going.[4]

On 3 March they reached the pretty town of Jaffa. The officer sent under a white flag to summon its defenders to surrender was beheaded and his body thrown into the sea. This enraged the troops, who after three days of siege stormed the defences and entered the town. While the soldiers who had been defending it withdrew to a citadel, the French unleashed their rage on the mainly Christian population in an orgy of looting, rape, and murder. 'One would require very dark colours in order to paint the hideous scenes which took place,' recorded one officer. Worse was to follow.[5]

Two of Bonaparte's aides, his stepson, Eugène, and Captain Croisier, had persuaded the soldiers holed up in the citadel to surrender by assuring them their lives would be spared. When he saw them filing out, Bonaparte flew into a rage with his stepson, asking him what he was supposed to do with them, given that he could neither feed them nor spare men to escort them back to Egypt. As they were mostly the same men who had been released on parole at El Arish, after deliberating for some time with his senior officers he concluded that they all deserved to be shot. When Berthier pleaded for their lives, Bonaparte told him to go and join a monastery. Over the next couple of days some 1,500 to 2,000 men (accounts vary) were led out onto the beach and shot, bayoneted, or drowned. According to one officer, 'the heart of the French soldier heaved with horror', but it had not done so during the sack of the town, after which the camp had turned into a bazaar where loot, including women, was traded.[6]

Bonaparte's decision to execute the prisoners was seized on by the British and has been made much of by his detractors ever since, but cities which resisted generally suffered the consequences, and British troops behaved no better during the concurrent war in India against the Mahrattas, or later in the Peninsular War; the Spanish and British treatment of those who surrendered at Bailén would be a good deal less humane. The morality of the time was far removed from present-day standards, and it was accepted that a general had to put his own men first.[7]

They may have expressed reservations, but the nerve required to act decisively earned Bonaparte the respect of his officers and men. Visiting the town, he inspected the hospital and impressed his entourage by walking among the plague victims, talking to and touching them. To set an example to reluctant orderlies, he allegedly approached one patient, 'pressed the bubo and forced out the pus'. Whether he actually did this or not, the story circulated among the troops, enhancing his standing.[8]

Image was important, and Bonaparte could not be accused of underestimating its power. 'You should know that all the efforts of humans are powerless against me, as everything that I undertake must come to pass,' he announced in a proclamation to the inhabitants of the area. 'Those who declare they are my friends prosper. Those who declare themselves my enemies perish.' In another, to the inhabitants of Jerusalem, he warned that 'I am as terrible as the fire of heaven to my enemies, clement and merciful to the people and to those who wish to be my friends.' Some of his entourage were growing anxious over what appeared to be an increasingly delusional sense of his role and expressed fears that he was being carried away by belief in his 'fate' and his 'destiny'. He may by this stage have been bolstering himself psychologically in a situation which was growing increasingly perilous.[9]

The army marched on to Acre, which it reached on 19 March. The city was the seat of the Ottoman governor of Syria, Djezzar Pasha

(Ahmad Pasha al-Jazzar), a Bosnian by origin, known colloquially as 'the butcher' (in 1790 he had drowned all the women of his harem and honoured his favourite by personally eviscerating her). Bonaparte sent him an offer of accommodation, stating that there was no reason for them to be enemies. The Pasha's response was to massacre the Christian population of the city.[10]

Bonaparte's siege artillery, which had been sent by sea, had been intercepted by the British, and many agreed with Kléber, who said bluntly that it would be impossible to take a place defended by European methods with Turkish ones. Bonaparte ignored them, and the first assault, on 28 March, nearly succeeded. Two days later the defenders made a sortie, which was successfully repulsed. On 1 April Bonaparte made a second attempt to storm the defences, in which he was nearly killed by an exploding shell, and this was followed by another sortie, which was also repulsed.[11]

Meanwhile Ottoman forces were gathering to relieve Acre, with some 7,000 warriors from Nablus and 40,000 under the Pasha of Damascus moving south. Bonaparte sent Murat with 500 infantry and 200 cavalry out to confront him, while Junot covered his flank at Nazareth with a smaller force. Junot was himself assailed by superior forces and Bonaparte sent Kléber to assist him, but they both found themselves facing more than ten times their own number at the foot of Mount Tabor. They sent urgent messages to Bonaparte and held off the Turks for a full day before being relieved on 16 April by Bonaparte, who had made a night march of forty kilometres.

The following day he visited Nazareth, where he attended mass and stood godfather to a soldier who wished to be baptised. Two days later he was back at Acre planning another assault. This, and the next one, failed just as the first two had done. Without siege artillery the only way to breach the walls was to dig tunnels and trenches in order to place mines underneath them, a painstaking and dangerous business at the best of times. It was made no easier as, being low on powder and shot, the French artillery could not supply adequate covering fire, while the British naval squadron under Commodore Sydney Smith was not only resupplying the defenders but also bombarding the French trenchworks.[12]

Most of Bonaparte's generals were by now clamouring for him to give up and return to Cairo. He was regularly hissed and booed by the troops, but he insisted on trying yet again to take the fortress. There was undoubtedly an element of personal pique involved: this was his first setback, and he could not accept it, the more so as the man directing Sydney Smith's guns was Le Picard de Phélippaux, a hated classmate from Brienne who had emigrated and fought against the Republic. A weightier motive for Bonaparte's determination to take Acre was that the Druze and the Shiite Muslims who made up the population of the region were keen to rise up against their Ottoman overlords; if Bonaparte could crush Djezzar, he would be able to raise the whole region, march on Damascus and Aleppo, and force the Porte to switch sides, thus denying all facilities in the eastern Mediterranean to the British and confirming France's possession of Egypt. But the prospect was dim: news had begun to trickle through that in Europe the coalition against France had gone over to the offensive.[13]

Following the failure of a final assault on 10 May, Bonaparte accepted the inevitable. He sent a report to the Directory announcing that he had destroyed Acre, which, he assured them, was not worth holding on to as it was a ruin full of plague victims. As usual, he diminished his losses. He despatched another declaration to the Divan in Cairo which made even more outrageous claims—that Djezzar was wounded, that he had sunk Turkish ships, and so on. Before striking camp, he praised his troops in an address which suggested that although they had been about to capture Acre they were needed more urgently elsewhere, and promised them more glory ahead.[14]

The march back to Cairo took twenty-five days, and they were among the worst many of the soldiers would remember. They trudged in temperatures in the forties Celsius, with no shoes to protect their feet from the scorching sand, and at night the rags to which their uniforms had been reduced could not protect them from the cold of the desert night. They only found food and water sporadically. Many of them were wounded and some sick; those who could not walk were carried on improvised stretchers.[15]

Before striking camp outside Acre, Bonaparte had suggested to Dr Desgenettes that those suffering from the plague and those so badly wounded that they could not be moved should be given fatal doses of laudanum, assuming that if they were left behind they would fall victim to the barbarous practices of the enemy. Desgenettes replied that his duty lay in preserving, not ending, lives. Bonaparte then approached the pharmacist Boyer and ordered him to prepare the potions. There is no certainty as to what followed, at Acre and at Jaffa and Tentura, where there were also several hundred sick and wounded. The available evidence is wildly discrepant, all of it written down after the events. The British press, conflating Acre and Jaffa, painted a black picture of the evil French general poisoning hundreds of his men. Defenders of Bonaparte's reputation either dismissed the story entirely or brought the number down to a handful of the dying. A careful reading of the evidence suggests that a potion was administered by Boyer on Bonaparte's orders to about twenty-five men, some of whom vomited and survived.[16]

Before leaving Jaffa, Bonaparte ordered all carriages and carts, and horses not pulling field guns, including his own, to be used for the evacuation of the sick and wounded. He gave detailed instructions as to the separation of the sick from the wounded and how they were to be transported. When his groom suggested he keep at least one horse for himself, Bonaparte struck him with his riding crop in fury. He showed his exasperation and dealt out harsh reprimands. He had vented his anger on the 69th Demi-Brigade when it fell back during one of the assaults on Acre, accusing the men of cowardice and having nothing between their legs, and suggested he would put them in skirts instead of breeches when they got home. In the interim he made them march with their muskets butt-end up.[17]

The march from Jaffa to Cairo was the worst part of the retreat, and despite Bonaparte's orders the sick and wounded were dumped by those whose horses had been requisitioned to transport them, and left to die or be decapitated by preying Bedouin. At the same time there were acts of self-sacrifice, and some did slow down to help the walking wounded keep up with the columns.[18]

The Syrian campaign had been an unmitigated disaster. Bonaparte had lost at least 3,000 men, and by some estimates as much as one-third of the force he had set out with had been put out of action.

Even those who had never criticised a decision of his expressed the opinion that he should not have embarked on the campaign. At the same time, the episode had demonstrated one thing—that Bonaparte, a man of twenty-nine in charge of an undisciplined army in many cases little better than a rabble, led by unruly generals many of whom resented or even hated him, with no superior authority to support him, was able, in the face of defeat, plague, adverse conditions, and lack of supplies, to pull that force together and maintain authority over it. The Syrian campaign had tested his mettle and shown that he was up to the challenge.[19]

Ever aware of the power of appearances, he prepared his return to Cairo carefully. His uniform officer was put to work, replacements were despatched from every available store, and the remnants of the Syrian expedition were kitted out with the greatest possible panache. Bonaparte entered Cairo at their head through a victory arch with bands playing, marching over streets strewn with palm fronds. Having crossed the city from end to end, the columns made their way around it and marched through once again, an operation lasting for five hours designed to confuse anyone who might have been trying to count how many men he had lost.[20]

Back in Cairo, Bonaparte carried on as though nothing had changed and continued to send optimistic reports to the Directory (many of which never got through, as they were intercepted by the Royal Navy). On 19 June he not only expounded on the advantages of Egypt as a colony for France but also devoted much ink to criticising the way the French navy was organised. He was building a couple of corvettes at Suez and was shocked when a French vessel was blown up by a single shot from a British ship as a result of negligence. The French navy would never be of any use, he argued, while the practices brought in during the Revolution survived and until the captain was given absolute authority.[21]

He was confident that he could make up his losses in men by the purchase of a couple of thousand black slaves who could be incorporated into his units. He nevertheless pressed the Directory to send more men, and particularly arms. From his despatches and correspondence it is clear that he found the challenge of running his own fief exhilarating. He had begun to treat the army as his legion, distributing sabres of honour not in the name of the Republic, but his own. He courted the natives, prefacing every statement with the words: 'There is no other god than God, and Mahomet is his Prophet!'[22]

He also attended meetings of the Institute, which had been carrying on its work throughout this time, but at a session on 4 July he ran into trouble when he blamed the lack of success in Syria on the plague and the inability of the physicians to find a cure. He argued that by treating it as a contagious disease, they had undermined morale, and that for the general good it would be better to declare it to be non-contagious. Desgenettes insisted that scientific integrity demanded the truth be told. Bonaparte denounced him and his kind as fastidious theorists, to which the doctor responded by accusing him of despotic leadership and lack of foresight and laying the blame for all the carnage and death during the Syrian campaign at his door.[23]

On 15 July at the pyramids, where he was encamped, Bonaparte received news that a Turkish fleet had appeared off Aboukir. He quickly gathered a force of some 10,000 men and marched north. The Turks disembarked between 10,000 and 15,000 men and entrenched on the narrow peninsula with the fortress of Aboukir at their back.

On 24 July Bonaparte pitched his tents about seven kilometres from Aboukir. It would not have taken him long to assess what had to be done once he had seen the Turkish positions. Yet that night when everyone else was asleep, Michel Rigo, a young painter who had been allowed to bed down in the same tent as Bonaparte and his staff, saw the general get up in the middle of the night and go over to a table on which maps were spread. He observed him pore over them, measuring distances with a compass, pace up and down, return to the table to study the maps again, belabouring the table with a small knife, and then step into the opening of the tent and stare for a long time into the distance.[24]

At dawn two divisions, under Lannes and Destaing, attacked the enemy line, while Murat's cavalry broke through at its extremity and swept into its rear. The Turks had nowhere to retreat to, and most ran into the sea in an effort to reach their ships. Those that did not drown were taken prisoner. Within the space of an hour some 3,000 had been put out of action. Bonaparte then attacked the fortress. The initial assault was repulsed and the defenders rushed out to decapitate the wounded, whereupon the French surged forward and drove the entire Turkish army into the sea. The final toll was 10,000–12,000 Ottoman dead, mostly drowned, to 250 French dead and about a thousand wounded. 'It is one of the finest battles I have seen,' Bonaparte wrote to General Dugua.[25]

He had been at the forefront, directing the troops under a hail of bullets which killed several around him. When one of his aides was struck by a cannonball, 'then, the whole of this army which only yesterday was insulting him during its long and painful march, and seemed for some time to have drifted away from him, uttered a cry of horror', recalled one sergeant. 'Everyone trembled for the life of this man who had become so precious to us, while, only a few moments earlier, he had been universally cursed.' The sergeant's feelings that day were by no means isolated. 'The army had to believe, like him, in fate,' wrote another soldier, 'for it seemed as though he had it written on his forehead that cannonballs and grapeshot must respect his person.' Even the obstreporous Kléber was impressed. After the battle he embraced Bonaparte, with the words, 'General, you are as great as the world!'[26]

The great man spent the next ten days at Alexandria before returning to Cairo. He had much to ponder. The victory of Aboukir ensured that the Ottomans would not be menacing Egypt in a hurry, so he was safe to continue organising his colony. But developments in Europe raised alarming questions. Although he had been cut off from France since the destruction of the fleet, he was kept informed, by small French naval vessels which got through and by neutral shipping, which brought news and even despatches. The British ships of Sydney Smith's squadron blockading the Egyptian coast also regularly communicated with the French on shore, passing them copies of English newspapers.

French gains in Italy had been almost wiped out, and the situation on the Rhine was precarious. It looked as though the coalition might succeed in invading France and toppling the Republic.

Bonaparte could hold Egypt and await better days, but if there were to be a Bourbon restoration in France, his future would be bleak. The Republic was in peril, and it must be saved, both because he genuinely believed in it, albeit better governed, and because he had committed to it to such an extent that he would never have a future under any other system.

He had never meant to spend long in Egypt and had been considering a return to France for some months. There is evidence to suggest that he colluded with Sydney Smith to make this possible, the Englishman seeing in it a chance to get him out of the way, which he supposed would make the French left behind more likely to capitulate. Either way, Bonaparte had already made arrangements for a couple of frigates and two smaller craft to be made ready.[27]

He was back in Cairo on 11 August. Two days later he attended the feast of the Prophet, giving every appearance of intending to continue governing the colony. On being informed that Sydney Smith's squadron had sailed for Cyprus to take on supplies, he and those he had selected to go with him made their final preparations. Officially, he was going to sail down the Nile on a tour of inspection. On the evening of 17 August he called on Bellilotte to say goodbye. He had meant to take her with him, but changed his plans and she was to follow (when she did, she was captured by the British and did not return to France until after Bonaparte had taken power; he never saw her again, but would find her a husband and buy her a château).[28]

He sailed down the Nile to Menouf, where he took a parade of the 32nd Demi-Brigade. 'Don't look so sad,' he said to them. 'Before long we will all be drinking wine in France.' Sergeant Vigo-Rousillon thought he looked preoccupied and anxious, while Lannes, Murat, and others in his suite were beaming. The next day he was off, supposedly to inspect various French positions, and on 22 August he turned off his planned route and made for the coast at a point to the west of Alexandria.[29]

Two frigates, the *Muiron* and the *Carrère*, rode at anchor a small distance from the shore, along with two xebecs (small three-masted vessels), the *Revanche* and the *Fortune*. At midnight Bonaparte and his party embarked, jostling each other regardless of rank to pile into the longboats in their anxiety not to be left behind.[30]

The four vessels, under the command of Rear-Admiral Honoré Ganteaume, weighed anchor in the early hours. On Bonaparte's orders they hugged the coast, sometimes sailing only at night. He was terrified of being captured by the British and preferred the option of putting ashore anywhere and taking his chances. 'Suppose I were taken by the English,' he said to Monge. 'I would be locked up in a hulk and in the eyes of France I would be nothing but a common deserter, a general who had left his post without authorisation.' He had charges laid in the hold and made Monge promise to blow up the ship if it were boarded by the British.[31]

The winds did not favour them so close inshore, and it took a full month to pass Malta, where they would veer north and make a dash for France. The company included Berthier, Bonaparte's aides Marmont and Lavalette, Lannes, Murat, Bonaparte's secretary Bourrienne, and several of the savants, including Monge, Berthollet, and the art expert Vivant Denon. Bonaparte's entourage also included a nineteen-year-old Mameluke named Roustam Raza, taken into slavery in the Caucasus as a boy of seven and presented to Bonaparte as a gift by Sheikh El-Bekri.

Although he railed at the incompetence and corruption of the Directory, Bonaparte did not discuss any political plans he may have been nurturing, and according to Vivant Denon he behaved like a passenger on a cruise, discussing scientific topics, playing cards (cheating shamelessly), and bantering with his friends. He avoided chess, at which he was surprisingly bad. In the evenings he entertained his companions with ghost stories, 'a genre of story-telling in which he was highly skilled', according to Lavalette.[32]

The longueurs of the crossing induced in Bonaparte reflection on the past as well as the future, and one evening in conversation with Monge he broached the subject of his paternity. He referred to the gossip surrounding the relationship between his mother and Marbeuf, saying that he would like to know for certain who his father was. The dates suggested it was indeed Carlo Maria Buonaparte, but he wondered where, in that case, he had got his military inclination and talents from. The uncertainty intrigued more than it nagged him, and he appeared even to derive a slight sense of superiority from it, as it placed him outside the common run.[33]

As they sailed north, past Lampedusa, Pantellaria and the west of Sicily, the danger from hostile ships became greater. Bonaparte ordered Ganteaume to hug the west coast of Sardinia, as he believed that in the worst case he could go ashore there and get away. They were low on water and had to put in to Ajaccio on 30 September to tank up.

Bonaparte went ashore and revisited his home. Letizia had used the indemnity obtained from the French government as a good Republican patriot whose property had been sacked to enlarge and redecorate the family home to unprecedented grandeur. His sister Élisa's husband, Bacciochi, was now commander of the citadel and a personage in the town. Joseph and Fesch had been buying land around Ajaccio, and Bonaparte could take his companions to stay at Les Milleli in comfort.[34]

Before leaving Corsica on the evening of 6 October he bought a longboat and hired a dozen strong oarsmen, to enable him to make a run for the coast in the event of an encounter with the Royal Navy. They did spot several British ships as they neared the French coast on the evening of 8 October, and Bonaparte ordered a change of course. They spent the night in a state of anxiety, fearing that they might have been spotted, but in the late morning of 9 October they sailed into the bay of Saint Raphael unhindered.

As soon as news got about that it was the commander of the Army of the Orient who had arrived, the cannon of the local fort fired a salute and people climbed into boats to row out to greet him, ignoring the rules on quarantine which required all ships arriving from foreign lands to lay up for forty days before anyone could land or come aboard. Since the rules had been broken, Bonaparte went ashore and, extricating himself from the enthusiastic attentions of the locals, by six that evening he was on the road to Paris.

17

The Saviour

ERE IS OUR liberator; the heavens have sent him!' people
greeted Bonaparte when he came ashore. Others hailed him
as their 'saviour', and some wanted to make him king. At
Aix, which he reached the following day, crowds gathered outside
his hotel and the municipal authorities called on him as though he
were a dignitary on official business. Along the road peasants cheered
and even carried torches beside his coach at night to safeguard him
from the brigands with whom the region was infested—which did
not prevent his baggage being stolen by what his Mameluke Roustam termed 'French Arabs'.[1]

At his next stop, Avignon, 'word suddenly got around with extraordinary speed that General Bonaparte had arrived from Egypt
and would be entering the city in a few hours', recorded the young
artillery lieutenant Jean-François Boulart.

> In a flash the whole city was in motion, the troops stood to and marched
> out beyond the city walls on the road along which the hero of Italy
> and Egypt would come. The crowd was immense. At the sight of the
> great man the enthusiasm reached its peak, the air resounded with ac-
> clamations and with shouts of *Vive Bonaparte!* and that crowd and those
> shouts accompanied him all the way to the hotel in which he stopped.
> It was an electrifying spectacle. As soon as he reached it, he received the
> authorities and the officers; it was the first time I saw this prodigious
> being. I contemplated him with a sort of voracity, I was in a state of
> ecstasy. [...] From that moment, we looked on him as being called to

save France from the crisis into which the pitiful government of the Directory and the reverses suffered by our armies had precipitated it.

Boulart had no doubt that Fate had brought Bonaparte back.[2]

Similar scenes greeted him at Valence, where his erstwhile landlady came to see him and received the present of a cashmere shawl. When he reached Lyon on 13 October he provoked enthusiasm which turned into a civic festival, with illuminations and fireworks, and a play glorifying his deeds was staged. Enthusiastic crowds obliged him to show himself on the balcony of his hotel time after time. Again, the city dignitaries and prominent citizens called on him to pay their respects as they might to a king on his progress, and the pattern was repeated at every stop.[3]

The news of his advent preceded him in Paris, eliciting the same reactions. 'It is difficult to give an idea of the universal enthusiasm produced by his return,' recalled Amable de Barante, then a student at the École Polytechnique. 'Without knowing what he would want to do, without attempting to foresee what would happen, everyone, of every class, had the conviction that he would not tarry to put an end to the agony in which France was expiring.... People embraced in the street, people rushed to meet him, people longed to see him.' The nineteen-year-old poet Pierre-Jean de Béranger was in a reading room when he heard the news, and he and his fellows leapt to their feet as one man with shouts of joy. Workers in the cafés of the Faubourg Saint-Antoine hailed the return of 'our father, our saviour, Bonaparte', while according to a popular verse heard in the streets of the capital, 'The gods, who are friends of this hero, have brought him to our shores.'[4]

Accounts of these events bristle with the words 'fortune', 'providence', and 'destiny', and in many Bonaparte is described and greeted as a 'saviour'. 'Nations cannot escape their destiny,' wrote Mathieu Molé, who, fearing another lurch to the left, was preparing to emigrate when he heard the news of Bonaparte's return. He could not repress a feeling that the French nation was being guided by instinct to submit to the man Providence had intended.[5]

Years of often bloody political upheaval and intermittent war, punctuated by economic crises and accompanied by fiscal chaos, had obscured the benefits of the Revolution and left the nation deeply dissatisfied. The Directory had introduced a modicum of stability and did achieve some positive results, but it was mired in corruption and had a propensity for war. While Bonaparte was in Egypt, it had responded to the new coalition stacking up against France by invading Holland, Switzerland, and Naples, setting up new republics which would involve France in further conflict, and by that summer of 1799 its armies were in retreat.

Governments are rarely judged in rational terms, and their popularity is subject to a variety of emotional responses. The Directory, along with the two representative chambers which appointed it, figured in the public imagination as a collection of ineffectual lawyers in togas bandying slogans while pursuing their own interests, venal as well as political. It was despised by the majority across the political spectrum as a pseudo-revolutionary oligarchy, 'a provisional tyranny' too weak to guarantee stability and rule effectively, too corrupt to engage the support of society. Yet nothing could be done to reform it, as the constitution could not be altered before nine years had elapsed.[6]

The situation cried out for a radical solution. 'The state of our country was such that the entire French nation was prepared to give itself to whoever could save them at the same time from the foreign menace and the tyranny of their own government,' according to the royalist Louis d'Andigné. Recent experience had shown that, in the words of one young man, 'nothing could be undertaken or accomplished except by a general and with military force'. That was also the view of the man currently preparing a coup to overthrow the Directory (of which he was a member) and change the constitution, the former priest Émmanuel-Joseph Sieyès. He made no bones about the fact that in order to do so he needed 'a sabre'. But he failed to appreciate that people no longer wanted some politician such as him supported by a general, they wanted the general himself. As another nineteen-year-old put it: 'The time had come for a dictatorship, and everything pointed to the dictator.'[7]

There were other generals on hand, such as Bernadotte, Moreau, Augereau, and Jourdan. Bonaparte himself would later say that if it had not been him it would have been another. That is certainly true up to a point, but that 'other' would have served his purpose and been sooner or later hung out to dry. French society was thirsting for something more. The intellectual, moral, and emotional conditioning of the past half-century had given rise to new beliefs and mythologies, and to illusory expectations of life and therefore of politics, which had themselves entered a new sphere with the Revolution. The subliminal emotions and expectations traditionally focused on the person of the monarch as the anointed representative of God on earth could, up to a point, be redirected onto abstract concepts such as the Nation and the Republic, which were anthropomorphised in art and ritual for the purpose. But they did not easily settle on a group of officials, however epically they were decked out in their togas and plumed hats. Those emotions and expectations required a cynosure more numinous, a figure sanctioned by some substitute for God, by Fate, Providence, Fortune, or whatever other euphemism the theologically challenged intellectuals of the time preferred.

Philosophers had, over the centuries, addressed the question of what differentiated some men from the herd, either by seeking a physical explanation or a celestial inspiration of some sort. In the eighteenth century it became customary to label outstanding individuals as 'men of genius'—Shakespeare, Descartes, and Newton were among those thus branded. And while the idea of equality among men eroded respect for traditional aristocracy, a new aristocracy of genius emerged to replace it—the figure of the 'genius' sometimes even replaced the king on decks of cards. The concurrent withdrawal of God and the saints from the public imagination made room for the genius as a kind of lay saint, even a kind of god. For the Swiss philosopher Johann Caspar Lavater, a man who could achieve exceptional things was 'a being of a higher kind', a 'counterpart of the divine', a 'human god'. According to the philosopher Immanuel Kant, genius was something inexplicable bestowed on men by nature. It was not even necessary to be dead to be labelled one. Benjamin Franklin, who had managed to tame the celestial fury of lightning, was widely acclaimed as a saint, and a cult developed around him that included the worship of relics. Rousseau was often referred to as 'divine', and during the French Revolution the former church of Sainte-Geneviève was turned into a Pantheon, a sacred space in which he, Voltaire, and others were laid to rest and venerated as saints. The armed struggle in defence of the Revolution had raised military valour to the highest status among virtues. The Paris veterans' hospice the Invalides was renamed the Temple of Mars.[8]

Bonaparte's gift for self-promotion had over the past four years fashioned the image of him as someone out of the ordinary, courageous, wise, modest, but also decisive and above all successful. In excess of 500 distinct images had been produced to cover his exploits during the Italian campaign which represented him not just as a hero but also as the embodiment and symbol of the army, which in the revolutionary imagination was equated with the nation itself. The Egyptian episode had added new dimensions. In the absence of hard facts due to the difficulties of communication, journalists gave free rein to their fantasy, with the result that the public was regaled with visionary depictions of victory and dominion. Prints showed Bonaparte bestowing the benefits of French culture on exotic-looking natives, representing him as a man of peace and an administrator creating a new colony for France, and one even depicting him being greeted in India by Tippu Sahib.[9]

Over this hovered a more subtle suggestion that his triumphs, which were described by himself as well as others as 'prodigious', 'fabulous', even 'miraculous', were the consequence of his being beloved of the gods, or Providence, Fortune, or Fate. This explained his seeming invulnerability to bullets and plague alike. The impression conveyed was by no means restricted to revolution-weary France: Shelley, Byron, Beethoven, Coleridge, Blake, Goethe, and countless other intellectuals all over Europe saw in Bonaparte a superhuman element which excited their imagination, if only for a time. Young people all over the Continent and even across the Atlantic, including aristocrats firmly wedded to monarchist principles, felt the appeal and in various degrees sought to emulate his example. It is not difficult to see why a despondent society such as France in the autumn of 1799 saw in him a longed-for messiah.

Nor were subliminal factors the only ones at play. The fulsome report of his victory at Aboukir (which conveniently overshadowed the naval disaster in the bay of the same name) had reached Paris after a tortuous journey only a few days before Bonaparte's arrival in France. As it happened, the fortunes of war had turned: General Brune had seen off the British and Russian forces in the Netherlands, and Masséna had defeated the Russians in Switzerland. But it was news of Aboukir that gave people the impression that France was victorious once more, and when five days later it became known in Paris that its victor had come to save the Republic, it produced what the old revolutionary Antoine-Claire Thibaudeau described as 'an electric commotion'. He was at the theatre when it was announced, in mid-performance, and while the actors resumed after the cheering had died down, the audience paid them no heed, arguing over the possible implications: 'every face and every conversation reflected only the hope of salvation and the presentiment of happiness'.[10]

Josephine heard the news of his landing on 13 October, while dining at the Luxembourg Palace with the president of the Directory, Louis-Jérôme Gohier, an admirer of hers hostile to Bonaparte. She had not received her son's letter from Cairo warning her of Bonaparte's fury at having been told the full extent of her infidelities, as it had been intercepted by the Royal Navy (and published, to general amusement, in the London press). She did know that his brothers were out to discredit her, so she was determined to get to him before they did. She set off at once with her daughter, Hortense, of whom Bonaparte was particularly fond, meaning to meet up with him along the way. Unfortunately for her, he had decided against taking the main road.

By the time he reached Lyon, he had all the evidence he needed regarding his popularity. Not wishing to enter Paris with the same *éclat* as the other cities along his way lest it annoy the Directors, and wishing to give himself time to take stock, he had taken a route through Nevers and Montargis. He reached the capital at six o'clock on the morning of 16 October, and was able to go without being spotted straight to the rue de la Victoire, where he no doubt meant to confront Josephine and tell her of his intention to divorce her.

He found the house empty, except for his mother, who, although she had recently shown some consideration for Josephine, would not have tried to dissuade him. As nobody else knew of his presence in town, Bonaparte had most of the day to brood on the faithlessness of his wife—and indeed on the debts she would have run up, for the house had been redecorated in neo-classical style with Egyptian motifs. The tented bedroom was designed to represent the rigours of campaigning, with what resembled a camp bed and drums as seats. The furniture, in supposedly Roman style, was by the foremost Parisian *ébéniste*, Georges Jacob, and the rooms were adorned with antiquities Josephine had picked up in or been sent from Italy.

In the afternoon he received a visit from the Directory's executive officer and effective head of police for the department of the Seine, Pierre-François Réal, who had got wind of his arrival. He found the general angry and depressed, railing at the inconstancy of women and comparing his homecoming to that of the returning heroes of the Trojan war. Réal, who was close to Barras and Josephine, did what he could to calm Bonaparte, warning him that a divorce would do his image no good and might make him look ridiculous.[11]

Bonaparte knew the Directory would be less than enthusiastic about his return. He had deserted an army in the field and broken the law on quarantine, a serious offence. He did not know that, faced with the threat of war closer to home, they had in fact sent a despatch on 26 May ordering him to return to France with his army, as this had never reached him. They had subsequently repeated these orders, though how he was to transport an army without a fleet they did not say. From Aix, where he had intercepted this second order, he wrote of his concern for the Republic and declared his readiness to serve it in any way he could.[12]

That evening he went to the Luxembourg to see Gohier, who received him moderately well, from which Bonaparte could deduce that while his desertion of the army had given the Directors a golden opportunity to court-martial and discredit him (which some of them did consider), they felt powerless in the face of public opinion. This gave him confidence when he confronted them as a body the following morning.

His appearance expressed an attitude they had not been prepared for: he wore an olive-green civilian frock-coat and a broad-brimmed hat, and, attached by silk straps, an Oriental scimitar. The Directors received him in open session, and when he arrived he found members of the public and officers present. Among the sentries he recognised veterans of his Italian campaign and shook their hands, bringing tears to their eyes. He addressed the Directors 'like a man who had come rather to demand an explanation of their conduct rather than to justify his own', according to one witness. He assured them that he would never draw his sword except in defence of the Republic and deflected their questions about the army in Egypt by asking his own about the state of France. Gohier embraced him, as was customary, admitting that the accolade 'was neither given nor received very fraternally'.[13]

Later that day he had an interview with his brother Lucien. Lucien had until now had little time for Bonaparte, whom he did not know well or rate highly. He was intelligent, energetic, and unscrupulous in pursuit of his own aims, though liable to take unbending moral stands when it suited him. He was a natural politician and a good orator. Having been elected, like Joseph, to the Assembly of the Five Hundred, he was now angling to be chosen as its president. Whatever they thought of their brother and he of them, they were family, and their Corsican upbringing would not let them forget that.

Joseph's political skills were not on a par with Lucien's. He had enriched himself, acquiring a residence in Paris and an estate at Mortefontaine, and fancied himself as a literary figure, publishing a fatuous novel and surrounding himself with writers. In the interests of enlisting the support of a prominent former Jacobin, he had arranged the marriage of his sister-in-law Désirée to General Bernadotte. Bonaparte's brother-in-law General Leclerc had also set himself up, with a residence in town and a château in the country, and had sent Paulette, now styling herself Pauline, to Madame Campan's school to learn to read and write, not to mention some manners. Of the whole family, only Louis, who had returned from Egypt earlier, had failed to find a place for himself and worried about how Bonaparte was faring there.[14]

Both Joseph and Lucien wanted Bonaparte to divorce Josephine, and for a couple of days it looked as though they would succeed. According to Barras, Bonaparte called on him in despair and announced that he intended to divorce her. Barras claims to have put him off, saying he would make himself ridiculous, that only lower-class people were offended by their spouses' faithlessness, and that she might yet prove useful to him. Collot records giving him similar advice. 'No! I have made up my mind; she will never set foot in my house again,' Bonaparte retorted. 'I don't care what people will say.' Collot observed that his anger betrayed the strength of his feelings for her and that he would soon give way. 'Me forgive her? Never!... You know me well!... If I were not firmly resolved, *I would tear out my heart and throw it on the fire.*'[15]

Having realised her error, Josephine had turned round and raced back to Paris, arriving at the rue de la Victoire on 18 October. Bonaparte shut himself away and refused to admit her, but she would not go away, weeping and professing her love, begging his forgiveness. She deployed Hortense and Eugène to plead her cause, and after a few hours he opened the door and let her in. However much he had been wounded in his self-esteem by her behaviour, he was still in love with her, and he needed her. She could give him the solace and the domestic warmth he craved; she was a clever, resourceful woman whose advice he had come to value; and she provided the social confidence he was keenly aware of lacking. At a more practical level, Josephine knew a great many people and had access to circles Bonaparte needed to cultivate. Finally, he had to accept that as various people had pointed out, a public domestic row and a divorce would not serve the image of the man who had come to save France.[16]

He moved cautiously, keeping to his pose of the self-effacing warrior at rest. He dressed in civilian clothes, rarely went out, avoided public appearances and assemblies, and refused to receive official delegations, civic or military. He visited wounded veterans at the Invalides and spent time with his friends at the Institute. At one session, he gave a lecture on the Suez Canal.

Yet all the while he was sounding out people across the political spectrum. After his first meeting with the Directory, he called on the minister of justice Jean-Jacques Cambacérès, who confirmed that the political class was exasperated with the state of affairs and that there was widespread desire for change. But there was considerable divergence of expectation as to what kind of change, and what Bonaparte needed to ascertain was which faction was the strongest.[17]

The house in the rue de la Victoire was the scene of constant comings and goings. Among the first to call was Talleyrand, who had been dismissed from the Ministry of Foreign Relations and hungered for power. He was followed by Pierre-Louis Roederer, editor of the *Journal de Paris*, whose endorsement would be crucial. Bonaparte's firm supporter Regnaud de Saint Jean d'Angély was on hand to furnish the necessary propaganda. Other callers included Talleyrand's friend Hugues Maret, a minor diplomat who now became Bonaparte's secretary. On 21 October Talleyrand and Roederer brought Admiral Eustache Bruix, with whom they had dined, judging him a potential ally. Others hovered on the sidelines. One such was the police minister Joseph Fouché, a self-effacing man whose cadaverous features sat well with his past as a violent Jacobin, which had earned him the sobriquet of 'butcher of Lyon'. He had long since enlisted the collaboration of the debt-ridden Josephine by providing her with financial and other assistance.[18]

On 22 October Bonaparte dined with Gohier and met General Moreau for the first time. The meeting was written up by Roederer in his paper the following day, giving the public the impression that the two generals were on good terms. This was important, since Moreau was universally popular. He had been approached to save France by the Director Sieyès, who was planning a coup to overthrow the government of which he was a member. When his preferred 'sabre', General Joubert, had been killed at the battle of Novi that summer, Sieyès had cast around for another, and fixed on Moreau. He had invited him to the Luxembourg to discuss this on the evening of 13 October, and the general entered his office shortly after the Director had heard the news of Bonaparte's return. When he was told of it, Moreau reportedly interrupted Sieyès with the words, 'He's your man; he will carry out your coup d'état far better than I.' That did not mean he had given up his own ambitions.[19]

Sieyès had been colluding with Lucien Bonaparte over the past months, but recruiting his brother was not going to be as easy as might appear. Bonaparte did not like Sieyès, considering him a self-important pedant. Sieyès was not popular, and many suspected him of having monarchist leanings; he was hated by the surviving Jacobins. Talleyrand and Roederer believed Bonaparte should ally himself with the other Director who might be prepared to act, Barras. Réal was of the same mind, knowing that Barras would wish to assume a leading role in any event. But Bonaparte remained non-committal.

It had become clear that he was the object of a great deal of wishful thinking. Those who favoured a restoration of the monarchy saw him as the man who could bring it about. The Jacobins were hoping he might be the man to restore the Republic in its more radical guise. Liberal republicans, loosely referred to as 'Ideologues', saw him as the strong man who could bring stability and preserve them from both Jacobins and royalists. If he could keep them all thinking that he was their man, he would not arouse the enmity of any party. He had correctly assessed that what offended public opinion was the sense that politics had been taken over by factions which had only their own interests at heart. If he was to engage wider support he must show himself to have nothing to do with any of them. He therefore remained aloof while Talleyrand, Roederer, and others prepared the ground.

Sieyès was offended that Bonaparte had not approached him, while Bonaparte felt Sieyès should make the first step. At one point in this stand-off Bonaparte lost his temper in front of a number of witnesses, shouting that it was to him people should come, because it was he who was 'the glory of the nation'. He nevertheless did call on Sieyès and his fellow Director Roger Ducos on 23 October. Things got off to a sticky start. Bonaparte was offended by the lack of ceremony with which he was received on his arrival at the Luxembourg: the detachment on guard had not saluted him with the appropriate drum-roll, he had been made to wait, and they had not opened both wings of the doors for him. Yet when they got down to business, the three of them agreed that France was not being properly governed and that something had to be done. The two Directors returned his visit the next day, but that meeting too did not go beyond the exchange of pious wishes.[20]

Fouché, supported by Josephine, was still advocating an alliance with Barras, but although Bonaparte felt comfortable with him and appreciated his intelligence, Barras was hated by the Jacobins and his reputation was tarnished in the eyes of public opinion, which associated him with the worst excesses of the Directory.

Joseph wanted to bring Bernadotte and Bonaparte together—no easy thing, given not only the ideological differences between them but the lack of mutual esteem or sympathy. On hearing of Bonaparte's return from Egypt, Bernadotte had publicly called for his court-martial. It did not help that he had married Désirée. Joseph organised a party at Mortefontaine to which he invited Lucien, Talleyrand, Roederer, Regnaud, and others in order to create an ambience in which the two generals could make their peace. As Bonaparte and Josephine had to share their carriage with Bernadotte and Désirée, whom he had not seen since Marseille, the four-hour drive would hardly have been merry. Discussions between the two generals over the next two days yielded nothing, with Bernadotte hiding behind his Jacobin principles. Although it was evident he would not be able to enlist the support of the Jacobins, Bonaparte could see that with leaders as indecisive as Bernadotte they were unlikely to prove a serious obstacle.[21]

On the morning of 30 October he went out for a ride with Regnaud, and on the way back his horse stumbled over some rocks in the park, throwing Bonaparte, who lost consciousness. It took several hours to bring him round, but that evening he was back in Paris, dining with Barras, who was still trying to enlist his support. There was something about Barras's behaviour on this occasion that produced a violent reaction in Bonaparte, who made up his mind to have nothing more to do with his former protector. The next morning Barras called, seemingly in apologetic mood, and he returned the following day, 1 November, declaring that he was prepared to back him. But Bonaparte brushed him off, saying that he was not contemplating taking action as he was too tired and ill after his Egyptian exertions and would be good for nothing for at least three months. That evening he met Sieyès at Lucien's lodgings.

Sieyès frankly declared that he meant to take power in order to introduce a new constitution and needed a general to provide backing and keep the populace at bay. Bonaparte made a show of democratic convictions, stating that he would never support anything that had not been 'freely discussed and approved by a properly conducted universal vote'. Sieyès had no option but to accept Bonaparte's terms, although he was probably beginning to see that he himself would be sidelined. 'I wish to march with General Bonaparte,' he told Joseph, 'because, of all the military men he is the most civilian.'[22]

Bonaparte was now approached by General Jourdan, who had been delegated by a group of Jacobins to propose that if he were to join them in overthrowing the government they would make him head of the executive power, provided it was a strictly republican one. He made a show of gratitude and pretended to give the proposal his consideration.[23]

It was by now common knowledge in Paris that something was afoot, and people speculated openly as to what was about to happen, but there was no sign of alarm on the part of the authorities. The Directors were in the dark, as Fouché kept his police reports bland. At the same time, each of them was either planning something himself, like Sieyès and Roger Ducos, contemplating joining in, like Barras, or had at least been sounded out, like Gohier and his colleague Moulin. But their lack of unity precluded them from taking any action. With so many people looking over their shoulders in what remained a fluid situation in which nobody trusted anyone else, danger lurked everywhere. It was not so much the wish to be on the winning side as the fear of finding themselves on the losing one that made people dangerous.[24]

Bonaparte called on Talleyrand late one night to discuss the action to be taken. At one point they heard a carriage and a troop of horses trotting down the street come to a halt outside the door. There was a sound of voices and some commotion. Fearing they were about to be arrested, Talleyrand blew out the candles and crept to the window. It turned out that a carriage carrying the evening's takings of one of the more popular gaming houses of Paris, which always had an escort of cavalry, had suffered a broken wheel. Talleyrand and Bonaparte laughed, but their fear was not groundless, and tension mounted in the capital. One evening Bonaparte sought relief by listening with Fouché to a recital of the Odes of Ossian set to music.[25]

On 6 November the two chambers hosted a banquet for 750 in honour of Bonaparte and Moreau in the Temple of Victory, formerly the church of Saint-Sulpice. The building was decked out with tapestries and captured standards, and trestle tables had been set up in the shape of a horseshoe, but it was cold, with the autumn damp filling the vast unheated church. When Bonaparte arrived accompanied by his staff, the crowd outside cheered '*Vive Bonaparte! La paix! La paix!*' He duly drank the toasts proposed, from a bottle he had brought himself along with a loaf of bread, the only food he touched. He had also taken the precaution of surrounding himself with a ring of faithful aides. 'I have never seen a more silent assembly with less trust and gaiety among the company,' noted Lavalette. A newspaper report observed that the only conversation was made by musical instruments. Bonaparte left while most of the guests were only halfway through their dinner.[26]

Later that evening he had a long talk with Sieyès about a course of action. They both wished to stick as closely as possible to legality and to avoid the need for military intervention, other than to keep the peace and prevent a possible assault on the assemblies by a mob called out by the Jacobins. The plan was straightforward: a majority if not all of the Directors would resign, creating a vacuum of power which would force the two assemblies to step in, declare that the government had ceased to exist, and sanction the introduction of a new constitution. Sieyès felt the task of drafting it should go to him—he had been writing the ideal constitution in his head for years. But Bonaparte insisted it be drafted by a committee nominated by the two assemblies and then approved by national plebiscite. This committee, which would also fulfil the role of a provisional government, was to consist of three 'consuls': Sieyès, Bonaparte, and Roger Ducos.

To ensure that everything went smoothly and to eliminate any possibility of the Tuileries being invaded by a Jacobin mob, it was decided to use the constitutional clause which allowed the two assemblies to transfer from Paris to a place of safety in case of danger. As the presidents of both, Lucien Bonaparte and Louis Lemercier, and the two men in charge of the administration, the inspectors of the assemblies, were in on the plot, there should be no problem in arranging this. The date was provisionally set for 7 November, but Bonaparte would insist on putting it back by two days.

He wanted to make a last attempt to neutralise the Jacobins, and on 7 November he had lunch with General Jourdan at the rue de la Victoire. Jourdan, a principled republican, was probably the only man who could have roused the left to action. After lunch they walked in the garden and Jourdan proposed that Bonaparte join him in a Jacobin coup. Bonaparte told him his faction was too weak but reassured him about his own republican convictions, and as they parted Jourdan intimated that he would not oppose him. That evening, Bonaparte attended a dinner given by Bernadotte, after which he once more attempted to engage his support, but Bernadotte appears to have thought that he was in a strong position, and that if he kept aloof he would hold the trump card at the decisive moment.[27]

The next day was devoted to final preparations and the composition of announcements and declarations to be posted on walls and published in the press immediately after the event. There was also the question of securing the necessary funds, and last-minute talks with bankers and men of business bore fruit. That evening there was a final confabulation at which the details of the next day's action were finalised.

Captain Horace Sébastiani, a fellow Corsican devoted to Bonaparte, was ordered to deploy his dragoons early the next morning before the Tuileries, seat of the two assemblies. Murat was to rally two other cavalry regiments. Bonaparte had notified those officers who had come to pay their respects and whom he had declined to receive on his return from Egypt that he would now be pleased to see them, but that due to pressing circumstances he could only do so at six on the morning of 9 November. They were invited individually, and until they reached his house in the rue de la Victoire in the early-morning dark they would be under the impression that they were to have a private interview with the hero of Italy and Egypt. He had instructed those already in on the plot to convene there at the same time, so when they arrived they would find themselves in a crowd of over fifty high-ranking officers.

Bonaparte went to bed at two in the morning. At the Tuileries the two inspectors of the chambers, Mathieu-Augustin Cornet and Jean-François Baraillon, sat up all night writing out summonses to members of the Council of Elders to come to an emergency meeting at seven o'clock in the morning. They were watched over by the Guard of the Assemblies, whose non-commissioned officers would deliver the messages at six, but only to those members of the assembly deemed reliable. Those who might cause trouble would be left to sleep.

18

Fog

AS THE BLEARY-EYED representatives of the people made their way down still-dark streets on the morning of 9 November (18 Brumaire, the month of mist in the revolutionary calendar), Sébastiani's dragoons and Murat's chasseurs were taking up positions around the Tuileries, and the National Guard stood to on the Champs Élysées. Once the members of the Council of Elders had donned their togas and taken their seats, they were informed by Cornet that there was a sinister plot by infamous brigands to bring down the government. The assemblies were in grave danger, he declared, and they must make immediate arrangements to transfer to a place of safety, suggesting the former royal palace of Saint-Cloud outside Paris. In order to safeguard the move and protect them they must, he went on, call on the hero of Egypt, General Bonaparte, who was devoted to the defence of the Republic.

A few of the deputies raised questions of substance and others of order, but with only the most favourable 150 of the 250 members present, these were easily brushed aside by the president, Lemercier, and a decree whose text had been prepared beforehand was duly passed. It stipulated that on the following day the assemblies would remove to Saint-Cloud, where they would resume their legislative function under the protection of General Bonaparte, who was invested for the purpose with command of all the troops in the Paris region. It was borne by the two inspectors to the rue de la Victoire.

There, Bonaparte had been busy, calling officers into his study one at a time to assure himself of their support or to discuss details of the day's operations. Those who had accepted his invitation as a purely social call were effectively trapped. On seeing the gathering, one reportedly told his coachman to drive away but was prevented by Bonaparte, who almost pulled him out of his carriage. Once there, they found it difficult to leave, and the more notables they saw at Bonaparte's side the more likely they were to go along.[1]

Bonaparte was annoyed at Bernadotte's failure to show. A greater disappointment was that Gohier, whom Josephine had disingenuously invited to take breakfast with her that morning, also failed to turn up. But Moreau came, as did General Lefèbvre, military governor of Paris, whom Bonaparte charmed by presenting him with the sabre he had used at the battle of the Pyramids. The old Alsatian was so moved that he vowed 'to throw those lawyer buggers into the river'.[2]

When the copy of the decree of the Elders arrived, Bonaparte emerged from his study and, after reading it out, called on those present to assist him in saving the Republic. Then, mounting a magnificent black Andalusian lent him for the occasion by Admiral Bruix, he set off for the Tuileries, escorted by cavalry and a suite of generals and senior officers in brilliant uniforms, cheered along the way by ignorant yet admiring onlookers. At about ten o'clock he entered the chamber of the Council of Elders, flanked by Berthier and a handful of other generals, and gave a rehearsed speech, praising them for their wisdom in entrusting the safety of the Republic to him, and swore to uphold it.[3]

Lemercier accepted his oath and confirmed him in command of the guard of the assemblies (Bonaparte surreptitiously added the Directors' guard), which he now went out to inspect. These were not his soldiers, and he could not take their loyalty for granted. An unexpected opportunity presented itself in the person of Bottot, the secretary of Barras, who had been sent out to see what was going on. Bonaparte collared him, drew him toward the ranks of troops, and delivered a rousing address, cribbed from a newspaper report he had recently read. 'What have you done with this France which I left in such a brilliant state?' he harangued the unfortunate Bottot. 'I left you peace, and I find war! I left you victories and have found defeat!

I left the millions of Italy and I now find only extortionate laws and misery everywhere!' he thundered, accusing, in the person of the hapless Bottot, the entire French political class of having squandered the sacrifices made by the 'hundred thousand' brave men, his 'companions in glory' who had laid down their lives in defence of the Republic. He accused them of factionalism and said it was time to entrust the Republic to the brave soldiers who could be counted on to defend it selflessly. The men were his to command.[4]

Bonaparte mounted his black horse, which he was having some difficulty in mastering, and made the rounds of the units that had mustered in the city, exciting their enthusiasm for they knew not what with dramatic statements empty of substance. He looked heroic, his reputation spoke to every soldier, and his suite of generals and senior officers, which had now swelled to 150, lent him unquestionable authority.[5]

Meanwhile, Sieyès had turned up at the Tuileries, on horseback to give himself added allure (he had taken riding lessons a couple of days before). He was accompanied by Ducos, and they were soon joined by their colleagues Moulin and Gohier. All four Directors endorsed the decree of the Elders for the removal of the assemblies to Saint-Cloud. But when Sieyès suggested that Gohier and Moulin resign their office as he and Ducos had done, they refused and set off for the seat of government in the Luxembourg to compose a letter of protest. This would be of no consequence, since the building was hermetically sealed by troops under Moreau. The Council of the Five Hundred, which had in the meantime convened in its usual seat, the Palais-Bourbon on the left bank of the Seine, was equally powerless. Outraged Jacobin deputies had to accept the decree passed by the Elders as constitutional, and Lucien closed the session, instructing them to reconvene on the morrow at Saint-Cloud.

In order to bring about the key event, the dissolution of the Directory, it was essential that a majority of its members resign, and since both Gohier and Moulin had refused, it was now imperative to get Barras to do so. He had been alerted that something was afoot but decided to keep out of the way by prolonging his morning toilette, taking twice as long as usual to shave and bathe while he sent

Bottot out on reconnaissance. As he waited hopefully for an offer of some kind from Bonaparte, the Luxembourg emptied, first of its guards, then of its servants. Power gradually dissipated around him. At about midday he received a visit from Talleyrand and Admiral Bruix, who produced the draft of a letter of resignation for him. He realised that he was finished. Obediently he wrote out the prepared text, which protested his 'passion for liberty', which alone had made him accept a part in the government. 'The glory which accompanies the return of the illustrious warrior for whom I had the honour of opening the road to glory' had at last allowed him to give up this unwanted task and return with joy to the ranks of ordinary citizens. Talleyrand had brought a purse with 2 million francs, intended as a reward, but there is some doubt as to whether he did not keep it for himself. Outside, a troop of cavalry was ready to escort the former Director to his country residence.[6]

By all accounts Paris remained peaceful throughout the day, and that evening the theatres were as full as ever. The more politically ambitious, or vulnerable, began calling on Bonaparte at the Tuileries to make their act of obeisance just in case. The principals of the coup lingered at the palace that night to discuss plans for the following day, which was to see the decisive act, but they inexplicably failed to agree to a concrete plan of action. Sieyès was prolix in abstractions, Ducos said nothing. The only specific suggestion made by Sieyès was that they should have forty of the most obviously hostile representatives arrested. Bonaparte rejected this proposal, declaring that he stood above such methods, confident that his prestige would carry the day. When they parted, the stage had been set but there was no script for what was to be played out on it. As he drove home through the pouring rain, Bonaparte declared himself satisfied with the way things had gone. He nevertheless laid a pair of loaded pistols by his bedside before retiring for the night.[7]

Although he had seemingly neutralised Jourdan, Bonaparte could not be sure the Jacobins would remain passive. He had been using Saliceti, now a member of the Five Hundred, as a go-between to calm their fears about his intentions. Saliceti had warned the Jacobins to stay away that morning, assuring them that it was only thanks to Bonaparte that Sieyès had not had them arrested. But while Bonaparte and his associates confabulated at the Tuileries, Bernadotte had been trying to persuade the Jacobins to use their influence in the assemblies to have himself appointed to command alongside Bonaparte.[8]

Bonaparte was up at four o'clock on 10 November and drove to Saint-Cloud with Bourrienne, escorted by a clutch of aides and a troop of cavalry. He was aware that if he did not carry off the coup he would end up on the scaffold, but he trusted in his luck. He could certainly not trust in many of his associates. As soon as the principal actors had left Paris, Fouché, who was not entirely confident the coup would succeed, set up an efficient chain of communication with Saint-Cloud and prepared to arrest the conspirators if they were to fail.[9]

On arrival at Saint-Cloud, where the two assemblies were to take their seats at midday, Bonaparte found preparations being made to provide them with accommodation in the seventeenth-century palace. The Elders were to convene in the impressive Gallery of Apollo, decorated with frescoes by Mignard, which had been cleaned up and furnished with a few tapestries and rows of unmatched chairs hastily taken from the royal furniture store. The Five Hundred were to meet in the orangery, a long building overlooking the garden with tall windows reaching almost to the floor on one side. As it was too long, a partition was being erected halfway along, and its discoloured, shabby walls were being hung with tapestries, while carpenters laboured to build a rostrum and stepped seating. The building, which had stood empty for ten years, only occasionally hosting a public ball or other festivity, was cold and damp.

Bonaparte took over one of the palace's drawing rooms as his headquarters. Talleyrand had rented a house nearby in which he, Roederer, and others waited, ready to climb into a waiting carriage if things went wrong. Sieyès too had taken the precaution of parking his carriage in a discreet place nearby in case he had to make a quick getaway. It was said that some of the conspirators were carrying large sums in ready money for the same reason. Bonaparte himself seems to have had an attack of nerves shortly after his arrival and flew into a rage with an officer for no reason.[10]

There was good reason to be nervous. As they waited for the chambers to be made ready, the deputies of the two assemblies, most of whom had been excluded from the previous day's session, strolled about discussing the situation, joined by Parisians who had driven out to see what was going on. In the course of these discussions those hostile to any change grew firmer in their resistance, while supporters of the coup began to have second thoughts. Bonaparte had a total of about 6,000 troops at hand, some sitting around their stacked weapons in the courtyard giving evil looks to the deputies, those hated 'lawyers' and 'chatterboxes', others deployed in the grounds and the surrounding streets. He was determined to achieve his end constitutionally, so had no wish to use them, but their presence raised the hackles of many of the deputies, who muttered darkly about the threat of a military coup and bandied epithets such as 'Caesar' and 'Cromwell'.

It was not until well after one o'clock that the Five Hundred were able to take their seats, in a flapping of scarlet Roman togas and plumed Polish caps. Lucien and his supporters were to persuade their assembly to nominate a commission to investigate the dangers threatening the Republic. But things got off to a bad start. Sensing what was afoot, the Jacobins among them began denouncing the incipient dictatorship, declaring that they would defend the constitution to the death. It was the kind of emotive language that swayed the majority in assemblies of the period, and a vote was carried to have every deputy renew their oath to it. That would take all day.

The Elders had already filed into the Gallery of Apollo in their blue togas, preceded by a band playing the *Marseillaise*. They were to take notice of the resignation of the three Directors, declare the government thereby dissolved, and appoint three consuls to prepare a new constitution. But the session had hardly opened when some of the deputies began questioning the legality of the previous day's proceedings. One of the conspirators cleverly observed that the Elders could not debate anything until the Five Hundred had properly constituted themselves—which they had not, as they were still busy renewing their oaths. A letter was then read out from the secretary of the Directory to the effect that the government had ceased to exist. By half past three the entire legislative body of the French Republic had tied itself in a knot, and with every moment that passed the Jacobins' influence grew in the Five Hundred, while Bonaparte's supporters in the Elders, many of them moderates, grew increasingly uneasy.

In the damp room, hardly warmed by a smoking fire, where Bonaparte, his brother Joseph, Sieyès, and the other leaders sat, 'people looked at each other but did not speak', according to one of those present. 'It was as if they did not dare to ask and feared to reply.' People began making excuses and slipping away. Bonaparte tried to hide his nerves by giving unnecessary orders and moving troops about. Every so often Lavalette would come and report on what was going on in the chambers.[11]

Outside, more and more people began to drift in from Paris. Jourdan and Augereau had also turned up, alert to the possibility of exploiting the situation for themselves. Augereau advised Bonaparte to abandon his plan. 'The wine has been drawn, it must be drunk,' Bonaparte replied. He sensed that if he were to remain inactive much longer his position would become untenable. Just before four o'clock he announced that he wished to speak to the Elders and, followed by a number of aides, entered their chamber. Their session had by then been suspended, but they gathered to hear what he had to say.[12]

Bonaparte was not a good speaker, often having difficulty in finding the right words. He was flustered and did not have a specific case to put, only a series of slogans which had proved sufficient up until now. 'Allow me to speak to you with the frankness of a soldier,' he began. He had, he told them, been minding his own business in Paris when they had called on him to defend the Republic. He had flown to their aid, and now he was being denounced as a Caesar and a Cromwell, a dictator. He urged them to act quickly, as there was no government and liberty was in peril. He was there to carry out their will. 'Let us save liberty, let us save equality!' he pleaded. At that point he was interrupted by the shout, 'And what about the constitution?' After a stunned silence, Bonaparte pointed out that they themselves and the Directory they had named had violated the constitution on at least three occasions, which was not tactful, and did not lend conviction to his main theme, to which he returned, plaintively assuring them that he was only there to uphold their authority and did not nourish any personal ambitions, and exhorting them to emulate Brutus should he ever betray their trust. His friends tried to restrain him, but many of the members of the assembly had been angered, and now began asking awkward questions. He carried on, growing more and more aggressive in tone and grasping at any words and phrases that came to mind, conjuring up visions of 'volcanoes', of 'silent conspiracies', and at one point defiantly warning them: 'Remember that I march accompanied by the god of victory and the god of war!' He ranted on incoherently until Bourrienne dragged him away by his coat-tails.[13]

Astonishingly, Bonaparte felt he had galvanised his partisans among the Elders and despatched Bourrienne to Paris to inform Josephine that all was going well. He also sent a message to a worried Talleyrand to the same effect. It is tempting to wonder whether the concussion he had suffered falling from his horse at Mortefontaine just over a week earlier might not have had something to do with his erratic behaviour and lack of judgement that day. It was with astonishing confidence that he now strode forth to confront the Five Hundred. He knew he would be facing a hostile chamber and was expecting trouble, so he took a few trusted grenadiers along as well as his aides.[14]

Hardly had he entered the orangery than shouts of 'Down with the tyrant!', 'Down with the dictator!', and 'Outlaw!' greeted him as the assembly rose to its feet in outrage at this military incursion. He was instantly assaulted by a multitude of deputies pressing in on him, shouting, shaking him by his lapels and pushing so hard that he momentarily lost consciousness. He was rescued by Murat, Lefèbvre, and others, who kept the enraged deputies back with their fists, and by the grenadiers he had brought with him. The scuffle grew fierce, and a number of the members of the public in the spectators' gallery fled through the windows. Bonaparte was eventually carried out, pale, struggling for breath, his head lolling to one side, barely conscious, pursued by cries of 'Outlaw! Outlaw!', which in the course of the Revolution had come to signify a condemnation to death. With his brother out of the way, Lucien did his best to calm tempers and to deflect a vote declaring him an outlaw, which would have put in question the allegiance of the troops. The assembly then got bogged down in discussion of what they should do next.[15]

Bonaparte had returned to his centre of operations. He seemed completely undone, making strange statements and at one point addressing Sieyès as 'General'. He soon recovered himself, but for the rest of the day his words and actions remained disjointed and not entirely coherent. Those who were still with him had come to the conclusion that their purpose could no longer be achieved by constitutional means and that it was time to resort to force. Murat and Leclerc were keen, but Bonaparte felt he needed an excuse and attempted to obtain some kind of authority from the Elders to brandish against the Five Hundred.[16]

On hearing an erroneous report that he had been voted an outlaw by the Five Hundred, he drew his sword and, leaning out of the window, shouted, 'To arms!' The cry, taken up and repeated, flew through the ranks and the waiting troops mounted up and stood to. Bonaparte came out of the palace followed by his suite and asked for his horse. The fiery beast lent by Bruix had been frightened by the shouting, with the result that when he mounted it began rearing and bucking. After some less than heroic tussles with it, he rode up to the bewildered grenadiers of the legislative guard, who failed to show much interest. It was not until he reached the troops of the line and Sébastiani's dragoons outside the courtyard that he elicited the desired enthusiasm. Riding up and down on his unruly mount he struck a heroic pose, venting his fury at the way he had been treated by the Five Hundred, telling the troops that he had gone to them offering to save the Republic but had been attacked by these traitors, paid agents of Britain, who had brandished daggers and tried to murder him. His agitation had brought out a severe rash on his face, and while considering his next move he had scratched so hard that he had drawn blood, which now seemed to confirm the story of daggers raised against him—the rumour that he had been wounded flew through the ranks, the crowd, and eventually all the way to Paris. Murat and Leclerc embellished the story and Sérurier, commanding the troops further out, told them, 'The Elders are behind Bonaparte, but the Five Hundred tried to assassinate him'.[17]

Some members of the Five Hundred had been trying to rally the legislative guard, which was wavering. If Augereau or Jourdan had stepped forward then and taken command of it, they could have defeated the coup. But they merely hung about waiting for an opportunity for themselves. As five o'clock approached and a misty November dusk settled, the fate of the country hung in the balance. Yet most of its political class dithered and watched each other, waiting to see what would happen next rather than acting out of conviction.

In the Five Hundred, Lucien had done what he could to calm things down, but the shouting match continued, so in the end he made a histrionic gesture, taking off his toga and cap, untying his gold-fringed sash and laying them down as a sign that liberty had been silenced and he could no longer preside over the proceedings. At the same time he sent one of the assembly's inspectors with a message for his brother to act immediately. This gave Bonaparte his excuse.

He ordered a captain to take ten grenadiers with him and rescue the president of the Five Hundred. The captain carried out his task, bringing out a dishevelled and haggard Lucien. He was greeted with acclamations. He asked for a horse, which an obliging dragoon provided, and then rode through the ranks beside his brother, telling the troops that the majority of the Five Hundred had been terrorised by a handful of dagger-wielding fanatics in British pay into defying the Council of Elders and declaring its defender and emissary General Bonaparte an outlaw. As president of the Five Hundred, he assured the troops that these deputies had put themselves outside the law by their behaviour, and he ordered them to deliver the well-meaning majority from the clutches of these monsters who 'are no longer the representatives of the people, but the representatives of the dagger'. He then took a sword from an officer and, putting the point to his brother's breast, solemnly swore that he would kill him if he were ever to raise a finger against the liberty of the French people.[18]

The legislative guard appeared convinced. They could hear the enthusiasm of the troops of the line behind them, and as the traditional drum-roll that sounded the attack thundered around the palace, Murat formed up a column of grenadiers and led them with bayonets fixed into the building. As the sound of the drum beating the charge crashed into the orangery, some of the Five Hundred climbed onto their benches and began swearing to defend the Republic and the constitution, while others followed the spectators out of the conveniently low windows. Pandemonium broke out as the troops entered the orangery. Murat marched toward the president's podium and declared in a loud voice that the Five Hundred was dissolved and then, turning to the soldiers: 'Chuck this lot out of here!' The grenadiers did not use unnecessary force, only manhandling a few of the more recalcitrant in order to carry them off the premises, and within a few minutes the now darkened building had been cleared.[19]

With their colleagues of the Five Hundred fleeing or skulking in the grounds, the Elders were jerked into life by Lucien, who appeared in their chamber, denounced a member of the Five Hundred who had come to complain, and with tears in his eyes related a version of events worthy of Rousseau. In order to demonstrate that all was well, the assembly then dealt with a couple of matters which had been on the order of the day.

Lucien turned his mind to wrapping up the business legally, which required a vote by the Five Hundred. He had with him those deputies who had been behind the coup, but he needed more. It was by then quite dark, and soldiers were sent out into the park and the surrounding streets, taverns, and hostelries in search of any members of the Five Hundred who had not yet made their escape. Even coaches returning to Paris were searched for the reluctant and often terrified representatives of the people. The number thus assembled varies according to different accounts, from thirty to a hundred, but it was certainly far below the required quorum of 200.[20]

They were brought back to the orangery, where among the overturned benches and chairs, by the light of a few candles, Lucien guided them through the formalities of denouncing and excluding the sixty-two of their colleagues who had supposedly tried to 'terrorise' them, followed by a vote of thanks to Bonaparte and the soldiers who had delivered them. They proceeded to constitute a commission which in turn nominated as the executive power three provisional consuls: Sieyès, Ducos, and Bonaparte. At around four o'clock in the morning, by the light of guttering candles they solemnly swore fidelity 'to the sovereignty of the people, to the one and indivisible French Republic, to equality, liberty and to representative government'. The Five Hundred also nominated an interim legislative commission and decreed the recess of the two legislative assemblies until 20 February 1800.[21]

This was then communicated to the Elders, who took an inordinate amount of time nominating a commission to consider the facts and report on them, holding a symbolic debate and then voting on it. The two assemblies then issued a joint declaration to the effect that they had saved liberty and the Republic.[22]

A bulletin composed by Fouché had already been read out in all the Paris theatres, informing the audiences that during the session of the two chambers Bonaparte had nearly perished from an assassination attempt, but had been saved by 'the spirit of the Republic', the *génie de la République*, and was on his way back to the capital. Printed notices composed earlier by Roederer were going up all over the city, giving a similar version of events and hailing Bonaparte as the saviour of France. In his own description of the events of the day, twenty daggers had been raised above his head to strike him dead. A grenadier whose uniform had been torn in the scuffle would be turned into a hero who had shielded the general with his body.[23]

Back at Saint-Cloud, to which many of those who had decided to distance themselves earlier that day had by now returned, followed by others drawn by the lure of a rising power, Bonaparte read out a proclamation in the grand style. 'On my return to Paris I found division in every branch of government, and consensus only on the fact that the Constitution was half-dead and could not protect liberty. Each of the factions came to me in turn, confided their plans, unveiled their secrets and asked for my support; I refused to be the man of any faction,' he declared, basing the legitimacy of his assumed power on the totality of the nation. He went on to say that conservative and liberal ideas could now take their place alongside other principles.[24]

He had understood that the prime concern of most of the nation was the desire for peace. 'It is peace that we have just conquered,' he announced. 'That is what must be announced in all the theatres, published in all the papers, and repeated in prose, verse and even in songs.' The troops marching back to their barracks sang '*Ça ira*', the most bloodcurdling of all the revolutionary ditties, but the Jacobin deputies were fleeing the capital or in hiding—Fouché's police were already on their trail. Like the events of the day, it was all rather confused, but one thing was certain—the Revolution was over.[25]

Bonaparte drove back to Paris at five o'clock in the morning with Bourrienne, Lucien, General Gardanne, and Sieyès, who were dropped off one by one before the carriage reached the rue de la Victoire. According to Bourrienne they were all tired and pensive. When they were alone, Bonaparte allegedly broke the silence to admit to having said a great many stupid things in the course of the day. 'I prefer talking to soldiers than to lawyers,' he said. 'Those buggers intimidated me.'[26]

When he got home Josephine was still awake, and he sat on the bed for hours reflecting on the day's events. She told him that his mother and Paulette had rushed over in a state of great agitation: they had been at the theatre, where the performance was interrupted and the author of the play came on stage to announce that Bonaparte had survived an assassination attempt and saved France.[27]

19

The Consul

THE NEXT DAY, 11 November 1799, was a *décadi*, a republican Sunday. The weather was mild and it was raining. At ten o'clock, citizen consul Bonaparte left home in civilian dress and was driven through empty streets to the Luxembourg in a carriage escorted by six dragoons. He went directly to Sieyès's apartment, where the two of them discussed the situation for over an hour. Shortly before twelve they were joined by Ducos, and all three crossed the courtyard to the council chamber in the main building, where some of the principal supporters of the coup had gathered.

Bonaparte tried to strike a solemn note as he thanked them for their support, but the effect was, according to Roederer, 'painful': he struggled to find the right words, committing a number of malaproposims, and his turn of phrase was abrupt, as though he were giving commands on a battlefield. They were going to need more than fine phrases. They had toppled the Directory and declared themselves the rulers of France, but that was about as far as it went. The notices that had been plastered on the walls of Paris proudly announced the beginning of a new order, but that remained so much wishful thinking. For all the talk of Bonaparte the Saviour, cynics assumed that five Directors had been replaced by three consuls who would govern with much the same levels of honesty and competence. Bonaparte was determined to prove them wrong.[1]

The first thing that needed to be settled was who would preside over the three-man consulate. Sieyès had assumed it would be him, but he was to be disappointed. According to one version of events,

Ducos turned to Bonaparte and said, 'It is quite unnecessary to vote on the presidency; it is yours by right.' Another has Bonaparte simply taking the president's chair. On doing so he declared modestly that they should each preside for a day in rotation, but that never happened.[2]

Thus constituted, the consuls, or rather Bonaparte, proceeded to nominate the new government. He replaced the left-leaning minister for war with his trusty Berthier, left Cambacérès at the Ministry of Justice, and in a gesture to the ideologues nominated as minister of the interior the mathematician and astronomer Pierre-Simon Laplace (his examiner on graduation from the École Militaire in 1785). He left the current incumbents at the ministries of police, the navy, and foreign relations (though he would slip Talleyrand into that ten days later), and allowed Sieyès to nominate his candidate, Martin Gaudin, minister of finance. 'He was an honest and thorough administrator who knew how to make himself liked by his subordinates, proceeding gradually but with purpose,' Bonaparte would later write of him, a quality he did not appreciate at the time. 'Come on, take the oath, we're in a hurry,' he chivvied the astonished Gaudin. For reasons that would become apparent later, probably Bonaparte's most significant appointment was that of the thirty-six-year-old Hugues Maret as secretary to the consuls.[3]

'Gentlemen, you have a master,' Sieyès is reported to have said to the others after Bonaparte left the room. '[Bonaparte] wants to do everything, knows how to do everything, and can do everything. In the deplorable position in which we find ourselves, we had better submit rather than excite divisions which would lead to certain defeat.' He had been completely outmanoeuvred. Bonaparte had long ago concluded that effective government required a dictator. He had been borne to power by a disparate assemblage of people who consequently believed they should have a say in shaping the future. He was prepared to include them, declaring that he was willing to work with all honest patriots. But he made it clear that he would not favour any of the factions, since he now belonged to 'the faction of the nation'. The nation, he believed, wanted strong government. The posters proclaiming the establishment of the 'new order' made it clear that this regime would not be like the others. 'The old government was oppressive because it was weak; the one which succeeds it has set itself the duty of being strong in order to fulfil that of being just,' they proclaimed. 'It appeals for support to all friends of the Republic and of liberty, to all Frenchmen.'4

As far as hard power went, the consuls could count on most of the military in Paris, but not on units stationed around the country, on the Rhine, and in Italy, which would probably follow the lead of their immediate commanders, many of whom were not devotees of Bonaparte and had their own views, political or otherwise. The new regime would have to tread carefully and to be all things to all men in order to disarm opposition, which chimed with Bonaparte's wish to ground his rule on national reconciliation. But he made a false move at the outset.

At their next meeting the consuls took the decision to proscribe what they deemed to be the most dangerous Jacobins, thirty-seven of whom were to be sent to the penal colony of Cayenne and a further twenty-two to be placed under police surveillance on the Île de Ré. The news aroused widespread disapproval and fears that there would be a new wave of score-settling. Cambacérès and Roederer rushed to the Luxembourg and argued vehemently against the measure, which was reversed. It is unclear who suggested it in the first place, as all those involved shifted the blame onto others. Bonaparte did his best to appear as the one who had been for clemency all along and wrote conciliatory letters to some of those on the list. On 24 December he would proclaim an amnesty for many who had been proscribed following previous coups.5

Many royalists saw Bonaparte as a potential French equivalent of General George Monck, who had enabled the restoration of the Stuarts to the English throne in 1660. Bonaparte thought such a restoration neither desirable nor viable. But he did not wish to provoke its supporters; they kept a civil war simmering in the west of France, where royalist and Catholic sentiment was fanned by émigrés based in England. He began by negotiating a ceasefire with the insurgents, on 23 November, and implemented a policy of firmness with regard to the intransigent and leniency to those prepared to lay down their arms. He aimed to weaken the religious resistance to the Republic by permitting churches to re-open and allowing people to worship on Sundays and feast days, and followed this up by releasing imprisoned priests and honouring the remains of the late Pope, who had died at Valence that summer.

A concurrent policy was to drain the pool of support for the monarchist cause. One of his first acts as consul, on 13 November, was to repeal the so-called Law of Hostages, which allowed the authorities to imprison the relatives of émigrés and active royalists. Having abrogated the law, he went to the notorious Temple and other prisons, and personally released the hostages held there. 'An unjust law deprived you of liberty, and my first duty is to return it to you,' he told them.[6]

The previous day, 12 November, he had gone to the Institute to flatter its members, and after releasing the noble prisoners he called on the octogenarian naturalist Louis Daubenton, who was gravely ill. It was no empty gesture. While the threat from Jacobins and royalists was evident, it was the Ideologues, moderate republicans and constitutional monarchists of the centre ground, whose support was crucial; it was they who would draw up the new constitution.

Bonaparte had moved from the rue de la Victoire to the seat of power. He established himself in a set of rooms on the ground floor of the Petit Luxembourg, while Josephine made herself at home on the floor above, in the apartment vacated by Gohier. The two were connected by an internal staircase leading from his study to her apartment and on to private quarters of his own on the floor above that. He rose early and worked, sometimes with Bourrienne, until about ten o'clock, when he would take a light lunch, after which he was joined by aides and ministers to work on specific subjects. He dined at five, after which he would go up to Josephine's apartment, where he met and conferred with other ministers and members of his family in a less formal atmosphere. Establishing himself as the driving force in the Consulate had only been a first step; the next required much informal positioning.[7]

Following the coup, each of the two chambers had delegated a commission of twenty-five members to work on a new constitution, which would be proposed by the Five Hundred and vetted by the Elders once they had reconvened. Its nature would determine whether there had been any purpose to the coup; only if it created a strong executive could political stability be achieved and the work of rebuilding France begin.

Since Sieyès considered himself an authority in this sphere, many looked to him. He set to work with alacrity and soon came up with a project based on universal male suffrage in which the democratic element was, as Bonaparte put it, 'entirely metaphysical': six million voters would elect 600,000, who would in turn choose 60,000, who would select 6,000 'notables', whose votes would determine the composition of two legislative chambers. These would be supervised by a 'collège de conservateurs' and presided over by a 'Grand Elector' who would reside in the palace of Versailles and fulfil largely ceremonial functions, assisted by two consuls.[8]

According to Fouché, after Sieyès had read out his draft on 1 December, Bonaparte burst out laughing, dismissing it as metaphysical twaddle. He pointed out that the Grand Elector would be no more than the idle king of caricature. 'Do you know anyone vile enough to enjoy playing such a farcical role?' he asked, whereupon Sieyès, who had presumably devised it as a political padded cell for Bonaparte himself, accused him of wanting to rule as a sovereign. In a state of dudgeon, he threatened to withdraw from the whole business. Although he had a considerable following, Sieyès had no way of mustering it. On the morning after the coup, the leading Ideologue Benjamin Constant had told him that he had made a mistake in assenting to the adjournment of the two assemblies for three months, as it deprived him of a forum in which to oppose Bonaparte.[9]

At their meeting the following day, Sieyès delivered a lecture on the principles of democracy in support of his project, and Bonaparte made a show of submission; he decided not to oppose it, and to concentrate instead on the status and powers of the executive. He suggested that five delegates from each of the commissions meet in the presence of the consuls to give it final form, and they duly convened in his rooms on the evening of 4 December. He kept them there until the early hours of the following morning, going through each article, stripping it of unnecessary verbiage and dictating the lean précis to Pierre-Claude Daunou, who had been designated as secretary. The exercise was repeated relentlessly over the next days. Bonaparte found 'those long nights of lengthy discussions during which one had to hear out so much nonsense' utterly exhausting. These men were all significantly older than him. They represented a wealth of knowledge and experience, and watching them grapple with the task taught him that brilliant minds could be remarkably cloudy when it came to converting concepts into comprehensible prose and practical form.[10]

Although he did manage to slip in a visit to the opera on 9 December, he devoted most of his time to the task, holding meetings on consecutive evenings until he judged it had been accomplished, on 10 December, seven days after the first session. There were still elements to be added, but he feared the process might drag on if it were not wrapped up, so on the evening of 13 December he persuaded all fifty members of the two commissions to sign the project as it stood.

It was a brilliant fraud. It guaranteed universal male suffrage, with every citizen aged over twenty-one having the right to vote. But there were to be no elections as such: they would meet in their commune and choose a tenth of their number. These would convene at the level of the department and repeat the process, designating a tenth of their number, who would then select a tenth of theirs as notables at the national level. These notables would provide a pool from which communal and departmental authorities and members of the four new assemblies were picked—by nomination in the first instance and rotating co-option thereafter.

Only the executive had the right to propose new laws, which were to be formulated by the Council of State (*Conseil d'État*), a body of thirty to forty experts. The proposed legislation would be submitted for evaluation to the Tribunate (*Tribunat*), a body of one hundred nominated for five years, a fifth of whom would be replaced annually. It would then be passed to the Legislative Body (*Corps législatif*), consisting of 300 members also renewed by a fifth each year, which would listen to the spokesmen for the executive and the Tribunate, and then pass or reject the law. The members of the Tribunate and the Legislative Body were to be nominated by the Senate, composed of eighty men aged over forty who were the ultimate guardians of the law, sitting in closed sessions and making up their number by co-opting new members.

This roughly conformed to Sieyès's project, but his idea of a Grand Elector was replaced by an executive consisting of three con-suls nominated by the Senate for terms of ten years. The first consul's prerogatives included the power to initiate laws; nominate members of the Council of State, ministers, state functionaries, and judges (ex-cept for justices of the peace, who were locally elected); declare war; and sign peace. The other two consuls had a purely consultative func-tion. They did not, like the Directory, constitute a Consulate: they were Consuls of the Republic. And since the Senate had not yet con-stituted itself, the first three were to be chosen by the two commis-sions that had just endorsed the new constitution, on 13 December.

A ten-litre measuring jar was placed on the table in lieu of an urn, and the fifty members of the two commissions duly wrote out their choices on slips of paper, folded and dropped them in. Before they could be counted, Bonaparte, who had been nonchalantly leaning on the mantelpiece warming his legs before the fire, strode over and snatched the urn. Turning to Sieyès, he addressed him solemnly as though on behalf of the whole assembly, saying that they should ac-knowledge his outstanding merits and contribution by allowing him to nominate the three consuls. Sieyès knew he had been sidelined and was rapidly losing the will to stand up to the energetic young man. He duly nominated Bonaparte as first consul and acquiesced in his choice of Cambacérès as second, and as third the sixty-year-old former ancien-régime functionary Charles-François Lebrun. As Bonaparte emptied the contents of the urn onto the fire, it was re-corded that he and the others had been nominated 'by unanimous acclamation'. The coup d'état of Brumaire was complete.[11]

The 'Constitution of Year VIII' was proclaimed two days later, on 15 December 1799. In Paris, the garrison was under arms as mu-nicipal officers read out the text in the streets and public places. The new constitution came into being ten days after that and was en-dorsed by a national plebiscite, the results of which would be an-nounced on 7 February 1800: by over three million votes to 1,562.

It has been generally assumed that the figures were rigged, but only recent research has revealed to what extent. Lucien, who had by then replaced Laplace at the Ministry of the Interior, made his functionaries in the departments 'round up' the figures, giving another 900,000 'yes' votes, and simply added on a further 550,000 in the name of the army, which had not been consulted, adding nearly one and a half million votes in total. In reality, only 20 percent of the electorate voiced their approval, but that was not much less than in other plebiscites held at various points during the Revolution.[12]

The publication of the constitution was accompanied by a proclamation composed by Sieyès which affirmed that it was based on 'the real principles of representative government, on the sacred rights of property, equality and liberty', and ended with the words: 'Citizens, the Revolution is affirmed in the principles which initiated it. It is accomplished!'[13]

Nothing could have been further from the truth. The ninety-five articles of the constitution did not include anything about liberty, equality, or fraternity and made no mention of the Rights of Man. The constitution gave absolute authority to one man and provided no channels of opposition that he could not block with a stroke of the pen. It was highly prescriptive, Article 88 stipulating, for instance, that the National Institute must work for the perfection of the arts and sciences. Sieyès, who was nominated president of the Senate, summed up its underlying principle with his comment, 'Authority comes from above; trust from below.' It established absolutist rule decked out in the spirit of the age.[14]

It would be wrong to see in the constitution purely the product of Bonaparte's lust for power. Sieyès and other idealists who had launched the Revolution had seen with their own eyes where unbridled democracy could lead, and all but a very few of those who had witnessed the events of the 1790s longed to close the Pandora's box they had opened. The new constitution promised to do just that. 'Here we have democracy purged of all its inconvenience,' noted the physiologist, philosopher, and revolutionary Pierre Cabanis, a member of the Five Hundred, adding that 'the ignorant classes no longer exert any influence'.[15]

On 22 December Bonaparte convened in his private apartment at the Luxembourg the twenty-nine men he had chosen to make up the Council of State. Two days later, after he, Sieyès, and Ducos had resigned their office as provisional consuls, he held a meeting at eight in the evening with his two new colleagues, his ministers, and the Council, at which he formally took office as first consul. Aged thirty years and four months, he dictated a proclamation to the French nation pledging 'To make the Republic dear to its citizens, respectable to foreigners, formidable to enemies.' The task ahead was immense, but he could count on the assistance of some of the greatest brains and most talented administrators, jurists, economists, and statesmen of the day.[16]

The second consul, Cambacérès, was a highly intelligent forty-six-year-old lawyer from Montpellier. He had played an active part in the Revolution, working on successive projects for a new civil code of laws worthy of the times. He had been in the Convention that condemned Louis XVI, but voted for a suspended sentence. His political activities had not interfered with his flourishing legal practice, which made him a wealthy man. An urbane homosexual, he was a fastidious dresser, with cascades of lace at his throat and cuffs, who wore his hair studiously curled. He was also a gourmet, boasting the finest table in Paris, at which guests were served by liveried servants. His judgement was sound, his manner subtle, and, thanks to his position as a senior Freemason, his contacts widespread. He valued Bonaparte for what he had done and could do for France and would serve him well; he was not blind to his faults and would prevent him making many a mistake.

The third consul, Lebrun, was thirty years older than Bonaparte, a minor noble from Normandy who had been secretary to René de Maupeou, the chancellor of France under the ancien régime who had fought to reinforce the authority of the crown. A man of literary tastes, he had translated the works of Homer and Tasso and written poetry of his own. He had sat in the Convention as a moderate royalist, miraculously escaping the guillotine under the Terror, and was a deputy under the Directory. Bonaparte had been wary of Lebrun on account of his monarchist connections, and before making up his mind insisted on being shown his literary works. Though retiring by nature, Lebrun was a clever man with a firm grasp of economics, convinced

of the necessity of strong executive power and opposed to unruly parliamentary structures. In this he reflected his senior colleague's views:
Bonaparte was determined to work through people and bodies he
could direct and control, not 'chattering chambers' which wasted time
and impeded the efficient functioning of the state.[17]

His prime instrument for the reconstruction of the French polity
was the Council of State, initially composed of twenty-nine people chosen by himself, grouped in five sections (Legislation, Interior Affairs,
Finances, War, and Naval), all of them with high levels of expertise in
their fields and well versed in the issues of the day. They represented a
spectrum of social origins, ideology and political affiliation. It was the
powerhouse in which the wishes of the first consul took shape.

Bonaparte worked them hard, as he did himself, almost frantically
determined as he was to get as much done as quickly as possible. 'At
that time, the work of a councillor of state was as painful as it was extensive,' recalled one of them. 'Everything needed to be reorganised, and
we would meet every day, either as a whole council or in our sections;
almost every evening we would have a session with the First Consul, in
which we would discuss and deliberate from ten o'clock until four or
five in the morning.' According to Bourrienne, the first consul would
give vent to his elation after work well done by singing—horribly flat.[18]

In order to cut out needless discussion, the eight ministers who
made up Bonaparte's executive did not operate as a cabinet—he sent
for them when he needed them, as a general might his officers. He
communicated with them through the secretary of state, Maret, who
acted as a kind of civil chief-of-staff. 'I am a man you can say anything to,' he instructed Maret when he took up the job, and Maret
claims he did in those days often argue with Bonaparte. A lawyer under the ancien régime and a diplomat during the Revolution, Maret
was regarded by some as an obsequious nonentity, but he had the
requisite skills for this task, marshalling the eight ministers to do his
master's will. They had to regularly submit written reports of their
activities and be prepared to be summoned into Bonaparte's presence
to answer questions about them. Like his generals, they soon learned
to have the facts at their fingertips, as he might suddenly ask how
many barges with grain were moored on the Seine or how much had

been expended on a given project and would not accept an approximate answer.[19]

That did not mean they were subservient cyphers. Laplace, who had been overwhelmed by the task facing him at the Ministry of the Interior, had been replaced by Lucien. Cambacérès had been succeeded at the Ministry of Justice by André-Joseph Abrial, a distinguished lawyer and an efficient administrator. The minister of finance, Gaudin, had worked in the treasury under Louis XVI and, under the Revolution, had stood up to Robespierre and not only managed to save his own neck but those of his employees from the guillotine.

The minister of police, Fouché, was nothing if not independent, and he did communicate directly with Bonaparte. His position gave him information that made him invaluable to the first consul. He had created an independent source of funding by imposing taxes on brothels and gaming houses, 'making vice, which is endemic to all large cities, contribute to the security of the state', as he put it, and used the money to pay a web of informers of every rank and station. He made himself useful to many and wielded considerable influence. 'Fouché has a detestable reputation,' Bonaparte admitted to Cambacérès. 'He talks ill of everyone and well only of himself. I know that he has not broken off relations with his terrorist friends. But he knows who they are and that will make him very useful to us. I will keep an eye on him. If I discover any infidelity in him I will not spare him.' Fouché records that their meetings occasionally led to ugly scenes, but he valued Bonaparte for his ability to make things happen and impose order on chaos.[20]

Imposing order on the country was a challenge. Ten days after the coup, the consuls sent envoys to the twenty-two military districts into which the country was divided to sound out public opinion and 'explain' what had happened. The new government had received professions of loyalty and congratulations from many local authorities, but these were largely valueless, and twenty out of the ninety-nine departments had not reacted at all. The envoys found public opinion around the country indifferent or suspicious. In some areas the National Guard had refused to swear loyalty to the new authorities, there were protests from Jacobins, and the administration of the department of Jura proclaimed Bonaparte a 'usurping tyrant'. In the west and the south, where royalist sentiment was strong, news of the coup was greeted with hostility by those who assumed it to have brought republicans to power and with joy by those who fancied it heralded a Bourbon restoration.[21]

Bonaparte could take nothing for granted, not even the army, which was underpaid and on the brink of mutiny. 'The spirit of the army is not at all favourable to the events of 18 and 19 brumaire,' Masséna reported from the Army of Italy. He had recently had to conduct a military operation against a band of 1,200 deserters who had gone on the rampage. Marmont, who had been sent to ascertain the mood in the Army of the North, was badly received. Bonaparte had already instructed Berthier to carry out a gradual purge of politically unreliable officers and malcontents.[22]

A virtuoso of manipulation, he had been quick to take control of the levers of public opinion. 'If I give free rein to the press, I won't survive in power for three months,' he asserted. Fouché needed little prompting. 'Newspapers have always been the tocsin of revolutions,' he wrote. 'They foretell them, prepare them and end up making them inevitable.' Bonaparte nevertheless recognised the usefulness of an element of press freedom. On 17 January sixty out of the total of seventy-three papers were closed down, leaving a few to reflect the views of factions such as the royalists. Through the Interior Ministry he supported *Le Mercure*, a counter-revolutionary journal edited by the returned émigré and ardent royalist Louis de Fontanes, who as well as being the lover of Élisa Bacciochi was convinced Bonaparte was the only man who could reform not only France but the world. Another journal, *Le Moniteur*, was taken over and turned into the mouthpiece of the government, propounding Bonaparte's views and explaining his actions in unsigned articles.[23]

Fouché extended censorship to the theatre, and henceforth every word uttered on stage was strictly controlled. Bonaparte had pronounced views and tastes when it came to the theatre and was alert to its political potential. He despised comedy, with the exception of Molière's *Tartuffe*, and believed only grand tragedy worth watching, since it revealed truths about human nature and affairs. He held Corneille and to a lesser extent Racine to be the masters, and in his lifetime he saw the former's *Cinna* at least a dozen times, *Oedipe* at least nine, and *Le Cid* at least eight, and Racine's *Phèdre* and *Iphigénie en Aulide* at least ten times each. Wishing to avoid the representation of historical events that might suggest parallels with the present, he instructed Fouché not to allow any plays set after the fifteenth century. By flattering and favouring writers who knew how to please, Bonaparte would gradually nurture a literature of approval which bordered on adulation.[24]

He also looked to his own reputation by putting in hand a thorough search through the archives for all documents relating to his past, particularly his relationship to Paoli and his attempts to take over the citadel of Ajaccio from French government forces in 1792. Some papers were destroyed, others replaced by forgeries rewriting history, and some of his own writings were doctored in the process.[25]

The only other minister who had as direct access to Bonaparte and worked as closely with him as Fouché was Talleyrand. Although his loyalty was always in question, he had proved useful in the past, and as Bonaparte remarked to Cambacérès, who had warned him of Talleyrand's treacherousness and rapacious venality, 'his personal interests are our best guarantee'. Not only was Talleyrand a talented negotiator and an instinctive diplomat, he was also, for all his revolutionary past, an aristocrat of the ancien régime, and thereby well placed to conduct unofficial negotiations through his kin all over Europe. This was vital in securing peace within France as well as abroad, and the first was a high priority, essential not only for reasons of security but also for Bonaparte's credibility as the man who would bring all Frenchmen together and cauterise the wounds of the Revolution.[26]

Talleyrand had got wind of the arrival in Paris of two agents of Louis XVIII, the baron Hyde de Neuville and the comte d'Andigné, who had been sent to organise a royalist coup, or alternately to persuade Bonaparte to bring about a restoration of the monarchy. Bonaparte seized the opportunity this offered and bade Talleyrand arrange a meeting.

On 26 December Talleyrand duly picked up Hyde de Neuville in his carriage and drove him to the Luxembourg, where he was ushered into a room and told to wait. When 'a small insignificant-looking man dressed in a scruffy greenish tail-coat entered, his head lowered', Hyde took him to be a servant, but the man walked over to the fireplace and, leaning against the mantelpiece, looked up and, as Hyde notes, 'he appeared suddenly taller and the flaming light in his eyes, now piercing, announced Bonaparte'. The first consul accepted that the royalists had a right to resist what they saw as oppression and expressed his admiration for their loyalty to the cause of the Bourbons, but he told Hyde it was now time to accept the new reality. He dismissed him after a short interview (there was a session of the Institute he wished to attend), asking him to return the following day with his colleague. Andigné too was astounded at finding himself face to face with a 'small man of mean appearance' in an 'olive coloured' tail-coat when he called with Hyde. Bonaparte urged them to give up their struggle, proposing various concessions. 'I will re-establish religious practice, not for your sake, but for mine,' he promised among other things. 'We nobles have no great need of religion, but the people need it, so I shall re-establish it.' He angrily rebuffed their suggestion that he pave the way for a Bourbon restoration, for which he would be richly rewarded. He accused the Bourbon princes of cowardice, saying that if they had had the courage to land and lead their partisans in the Vendée he might well have embraced their cause himself. He urged Hyde and Andigné to rally to him, offering to make them generals, prefects, or whatever they liked.[27]

'In his disagreeable foreign accent, Bonaparte expresses himself with brevity and energy,' noted Andigné. 'A very lively mind causes him to run his sentences one into the other, so much so that his conversation is quite difficult to follow and leaves much to be guessed at. As animated in his conversation as he is nimble in his ideas, he continually leaps from one subject to another. He touches on a matter, leaves it, returns to it, appears to hardly listen to one while not missing a word of what one says....An immoderate pride which causes him to place himself above all that surrounds him leads him continually back to himself, and to what he has done. He then becomes prolix and listens to himself speak with visible pleasure, and does not spare one a single detail that could flatter his amour-propre....'[28]

The following day Bonaparte proclaimed an amnesty to those who laid down their arms and the freedom of religious practice. He opened negotiations with the royalist commanders through the militant monarchist Abbé Étienne-Alexandre Bernier, while declaring that troops would be deployed against those who continued to fight. The stick-and-carrot policy bore fruit, and on 18 January the royalist commander on the left bank of the Loire submitted, followed a few days later by his colleague on the right bank. They recognised that they were fighting for a lost cause and lost faith in their ally. 'England was inclined to furnish us with some of the means to resist, but refused us those which would have allowed us to triumph,' reflected Andigné. On 25 January, in response to a sally by diehard royalists further north, the army moved in and carried out savage reprisals. Within a couple of weeks all the remaining royalist forces capitulated, and in Normandy one of the most unrepentant leaders, Louis de Frotté, was shot. Isolated bands continued to resist, crossing the line into more or less outright brigandage, even if they did claim to be robbing 'in the name of the King'. Three weeks later Bonaparte made another move to pull the rug from under the royalists' feet by setting up a commission to vet émigrés wishing to return to France: in under two years, some 40 percent of them (around 45,000) would do so and accept the new regime. On 6 March he held an audience for the principal royalist commanders in the course of which he managed to impress them with his professions of national reconciliation, and indeed his charm. One who resisted this was the Breton Georges Cadoudal, and there were others in the country and among the émigrés who would carry their struggle underground. But Bonaparte had managed to achieve what successive governments had failed to for more than half a decade: to put an end to the civil war.[29]

'Even the most impartial will not hesitate to admit that it seemed as though a kind of predestination had called him to command men,' wrote the forty-two-year-old barrister François Nicolas Mollien. The veteran general Mathieu Dumas reflected that Bonaparte 'did not destroy liberty, because it no longer existed; he smothered the monster of anarchy; he saved France'. A much younger man, Mathieu Molé, declared that only one man could have achieved this, explaining that Bonaparte's origin, his exploits, his virtues, his vices, and 'the kind of magic that enveloped his life' 'made him the only instrument Providence could have employed for such a purpose'. The young aristocrat Philippe de Ségur did not deny his achievement, but felt that 'it was also the work of France'.[30]

20

Consolidation

ON 19 FEBRUARY 1800 the consuls transferred from the Luxembourg to the Tuileries. The move was dictated by the need to make room for the Senate at the Luxembourg and by the fact that the former royal palace was more centrally situated and easier to defend against mob violence. According to Cambacérès, Bonaparte was also concerned that if a use were not found for it, the building would fall into ruin. On inspecting the palace before the move he was disgusted to see revolutionary graffiti scrawled on the panelling.[1]

On the day, in fine spring weather, the three consuls left the Luxembourg in some pomp in a coach drawn by six white horses, with Roustam resplendent in his Mameluke gear riding alongside. They were preceded by the ministers, who had to make do with ordinary Paris cabs, their numbers papered and painted over for the occasion, and by a detachment of Bonaparte's Guides. Behind the carriage came the cavalry of the new Consular Guard and an escort of other troops. The cortège was cheered by a small crowd of onlookers as it arrived before the palace. The consuls alighted, and while Cambacérès and Lebrun entered the palace, Bonaparte mounted a horse and inspected three demi-brigades which were drawn up on parade in front of the building. He then installed the Council of State in one of the galleries and formally received the city's civil and military authorities.[2]

With the ceremonial over, Bonaparte and Josephine settled into their new abode. She was uneasy, as the place brought to mind the fate of its last occupant, Marie-Antoinette. Her apartment, which she had redecorated in yellow silk and filled with mahogany furniture, was on the ground floor. The windows opened on to the Tuileries gardens, from which the palace was separated only by a narrow terrace and a few steps. As the gardens were open to the public she made little use of them, but Bonaparte often did when he felt the need for some exercise.[3]

He took over a set of rooms above, linked to hers by a hidden staircase. He installed his study in a room with a single window overlooking the gardens which had been a queen's bedroom, decorated in the reign of Louis XIV with a fresco of Minerva being crowned by Glory on the ceiling and landscapes on the walls. With time he would tailor the quarters to suit his working needs, but to begin with he accommodated himself as best he could, using a desk that had belonged to the last king and converting a small oratory into a bathroom.

His household consisted of ten men, including a librarian, a groom, a cook, and a valet, and a dozen or so lesser staff, all marshalled by Bourrienne. He was also constantly attended by Roustam, who slept in the next room. At the end of March, Bonaparte took over from Josephine the twenty-one-year-old Belgian Constant Wairy, who became his principal valet.[4]

He usually rose at seven and had the newspapers and sometimes a novel read to him while he washed, had himself shaved (something he was slow to learn to do for himself), and dressed. He would then work with Bourrienne in his study, only leaving it to receive ministers or officials in an outer office. He usually ate lunch alone, seldom spending more than fifteen minutes over it and often less. He preferred simple dishes, although he had brought home from Egypt a taste for dates and enjoyed a 'pilaff'. He only ever drank a single glass of wine, always Chambertin, usually watered down. He would follow this with strong coffee. He was sometimes joined by Josephine and often employed the time talking to people such as artists or writers he wished to see, who stood around as he lunched.

The other two consuls had been meant to take up their quarters in the palace too, but while Lebrun obliged, Cambacérès preferred to stay in his own house. The prospect of being able to keep his own table probably played a part, as no doubt did the freedom to take his pleasure without censure from the prudish Bonaparte, but so did his

North Sea

DENMAR

UNITED
KINGDOM

Hamb

Atlantic
Ocean

BATAVIAN
REPUBLIC

HANOVER

H

London○

Brussels○

R

Brest○

○Paris

BADEN

BAVA

FRANCE

E   M

SWISS
CONFED.

Corunna○

PIEDMONT
(French occupation)

CISALPINE
REPUBLIC

PORTUGAL

○Madrid

LIGURIAN
REP.
Nice

TUSCANY

Lisbon○

S P A I N

Corsica

PAP

STATES
○Ro

Cadiz○

KINGDOM
OF
SARDINIA

Na

Gibraltar
(British)

M e d i t e r r a n e a n   S e a

Si

MOROCCO

ALGIERS

TUNIS

EUROPE
1800

Revolutionary France

French Puppet States

260

WEDEN

PRUSSIA

Y

ONY

AN

RE

USTRIA

o Moscow

o Königsberg

Danzig

o Minsk

R U S S I A N

E M P I R E

o Warsaw

Prague

o Cracow

o Kiev

o Vienna

Belgrade

O

O

T

T

O

M

A

N

o Sofia

driatic Sea

Black Sea

Constantinople

NGDOM OF
NAPLES
AND
SICILY

Ionian Islands
(French)

E M P I R E

Crete

Cyprus

Alexandria

Nile Delta

E G Y P T

o Cairo

261

wise prescience that he might with time have to face the indignity of being asked to vacate the palace, as Lebrun would one day.

On the morning after he moved in, Bonaparte held the first meeting of the three consuls in the former royal palace. By coincidence, that same day its would-be occupant, Louis XVIII, wrote to him from his Warsaw exile proposing he assist him in recovering the throne. Bonaparte did not reply. Cambacérès believed that at this stage he had no clear idea of the future, beyond the reconstruction of France. 'All the signs were that he wanted to be the master,' he wrote. 'Nothing suggested that the title of First Consul seemed insufficient to him.' In conversation with Roederer, Bonaparte said he would retire if he felt the French people were 'displeased' with him. 'As for me, I require little,' he told him. 'I have an income of 80 or 100,000 livres, a town house, one in the country: I do not need more.' But, he added, so far they seemed satisfied with him. He was there to stay and made a point of showing it.⁵

The next day the consuls held a reception for the diplomatic corps, headed by the ambassadors of the King of Spain and the Pope, then the various administrative bodies of the Republic. A former royal chamberlain was dug out of retirement, told to conduct the proceedings exactly as they had been under the last king, and handed a staff for the purpose. Bonaparte received the guests as head of state, after which they were offered coffee and hot chocolate before being conducted by Talleyrand to Josephine's apartment to be presented to her and a gaggle of women who were already behaving as though they were in waiting. She had slipped into the role of royal consort as effortlessly as he had adopted the attitude of a head of state.

Gone was the threadbare 'greenish' tail-coat. He had designed a uniform for the consuls which was a clear break with the togas and plumes of the Directory. It consisted of a blue tail-coat buttoned up to the chin, with a standing collar and cuffs enhanced by gold embroidery, white breeches, and stockings, and a more sumptuous version in scarlet velvet for ceremonial occasions such as this. Gone too were the lanky strands of hair limply framing his sallow face, replaced by a closer crop á la Titus. He also began to take greater care over his toilette, insisting on frequent changes of linen and manicuring his hands, of which he was inordinately proud. He bathed frequently and doused himself in eau de cologne.

A couple of days after this first reception, Bonaparte asked the minister of finance to locate the crown jewels; not long afterward, visitors to the Tuileries noted that the first consul's sword blazed with diamonds, its hilt topped by the famous *Régent*, the largest in the world. Stung by some amused comments, he felt it necessary to publish in *Le Moniteur* an article explaining that it was not merely a piece of jewellery but a symbol of the greatness of France.[6]

Bonaparte's new role meant he had to learn to behave. Until now, he had operated in a military environment with sallies into small-town politics and wartime diplomacy. He had never had to accommodate the niceties of convention or adapt to civil procedure and had not had the opportunity to develop normal social skills. He was tactless and had, according to one his ministers, all the grace of a badly-brought-up subaltern, using his fingers at table and getting up from it regardless of whether his companions had finished eating. His pronounced views, attitude, and character did not predispose him to begin a social apprenticeship at his age, and he suffered from one fundamental disadvantage in his relations with others, which Germaine de Staël perceptively identified as a total lack of the faculty of empathy.[7]

He was kind by nature, quick to assist and reward. He found comfortable jobs and granted generous pensions to former colleagues, teachers, and servants, even to a guard who had shown sympathy during his incarceration after the fall of Robespierre. He was generous to the son of Marbeuf, promoted his former commander at Toulon Dugommier and looked after his family when he died, did the same for La Poype and du Teil, and even found the useless Carteaux a post with a generous pension. Whenever he encountered hardship or poverty, he disbursed lavishly. He could be sensitive, and there are countless verifiable acts of solicitude and kindness that testify to his genuinely wishing to make people happy.[8]

He possessed considerable charm and only needed to smile for people to melt. He could be a delightful companion when he adopted an attitude of bonhomie. He was a good raconteur, and people loved listening to him speak on some subject that interested him, or tell his ghost stories, for which he would sometimes blow out the candles. He could grow passionate when discussing literature or, more rarely, his feelings. When he did, he was, according to Germaine de Staël, quite seductive, though the actress Ida Saint-Elme found 'more brusquery than tenderness' in his attempts to charm. Claire de Rémusat also found his gaiety 'tasteless and immoderate', and his manners often more suited to the barrack room than the drawing room. He was generally ill at ease with women, not knowing what to say and making gauche remarks about their dress or their looks, and allowing his lack of consideration for their sex to show. Only in the presence of Josephine was he less prickly.[9]

He was most at his ease with children, soldiers, servants, and those close to him, in whom he took a personal interest, asking them about their health, their families, and their troubles. He would treat them with a joshing familiarity, teasing them, calling them scoundrels or nincompoops; whenever he saw his physician, Dr Jean-Nicolas Corvisart, he would ask him how many people he had killed that day. His way of showing affection was giving people a little slap on the cheek or pinching their nose or ear. He was curiously unconscious of causing pain, even when a hard pinch of the nose brought tears to the victim's eyes, and since they regarded it as a mark of great favour, which it was, nobody objected. At the end of a stormy meeting in the course of which he roundly told off a minister about his handling of his brief, Bonaparte invited him to dine. The minister bowed, respectful but defiant, at which point he was seized by both ears, which he took as 'the most intoxicating sign of favour for him who is honoured enough to receive it'. It was a gesture of familiarity that defused many an awkward situation. Yet real familiarity was something Bonaparte seemed to fear, and only a select few, such as Duroc and Lannes, ever got away with addressing him with the familiar *tu*.[10]

He did lose his temper, but he was quick to calm down and forgive. He did on occasion lose control and break things or stamp on his hat. He once hit the interior minister Chaptal with a roll of papers and was known to use his riding crop, on one occasion striking a groom across the face for negligence which had led to a horse throwing him, for which he would make generous amends. Most of his rages were feigned, either to frighten people, to make an example of an officer in front of his men or a general in front of his peers, or just to test someone's reactions. His principal interest on meeting a man was to assess whether he would be of use. He expected quick and precise answers, appreciated a snap retort if it was in order, but according to his chamberlain General Thiard, 'his amour-propre was flattered if he noticed the signs of fear and confusion caused by his presence'. This is confirmed by Claire de Rémusat, who noted that in great as in small things, he applied the rule that 'people only showed zeal if they were scared'. Chaptal's assertion that 'Nobody was at ease in his company except himself' may sound harsh, but it is borne out by the testimony of others.[11]

'The fact is that for him human life was a game of chess,' reflected Mathieu Molé, 'and people, religion, morality, affections, interests were so many pawns or pieces which needed to be moved about and used as the occasion demanded.' According to Molé, 'he was quick to grasp an individual's character, to seek out each person's weak spot, and to address it with remarkable skill and perceptiveness'. This suggests, as does Bonaparte's behaviour in general, that he was no more at ease in the company of others than they in his.[12]

His new position aggravated the awkwardness, and his attempts to strike the right note as the head of government often went very wrong. As a token of thanks to Roederer, he decided to give him a jewelled snuffbox. On hearing of this through Talleyrand, Roederer felt offended, explaining that he would have gladly accepted a signed copy of a book on Bonaparte's Egyptian campaign, but this smacked of the classic royal gesture of giving tips to faithful servants. 'I have done nothing for Bonaparte,' he wrote. 'All I wanted was to help him do what he has done for us, I mean for all patriotic Frenchmen. It is for us to give him presents, and I have an oak-leaf ready.'[13]

Equally gauche were his attempts to position his family in a manner he deemed appropriate. He saw it, and his close military entourage, as an extension of himself, and felt an urge to direct and control its members, both for practical reasons and in order to project a suitable image of himself. He liked to arrange the marriages not just of his family but of his military entourage too and often selected names for their children—usually from antiquity or from the poems of Ossian; Leclerc's son was *Dermide*, Bernadotte's *Oscar*, Murat's *Achille*.

He ensured that Letizia was comfortably housed and gave her enough money to live and entertain like a grande dame, but her experience of penury had made her parsimonious and, not trusting to the permanence of her son's good fortune, she squirrelled away for a rainy day every penny he gave her, some of it in foreign banks.

Joseph continued to play a role in politics, and although he was generally supportive, he affected a degree of independence. He created his own court at Mortefontaine with literary figures and members of the old aristocracy. His wife, Julie, was charming and docile, universally loved for her kindness and amiability and endlessly tolerant of Joseph's infidelities.

Élisa, the least good-looking of the siblings but possibly the brightest, had moved to Paris and installed herself as hostess to the widowed Lucien, while her husband, Bacciochi, remained at his provincial military post. She held a salon with a literary flavour in which her lover, the poet Fontanes, held sway. Although she was admired by the writer René de Chateaubriand, whom she helped bring back to France and into favour with her brother, her salon was dull.

Despite having played a crucial role in bringing his brother to power, Lucien's attitude to him remained ambivalent. He made it clear that he regarded Joseph as the head of the family and disapproved of what he saw as Bonaparte's usurpation of that role. He was proving an able and suitably unscrupulous minister of the interior, but being a widower he felt at liberty to pursue women and abused his position to have his way.

Caroline had married Murat, in a civil ceremony at the Luxembourg in January, followed by a pseudo-religious one in a temple at Mortefontaine. Bonaparte had opposed the match. While he appreciated his military dash and his devotion, he considered the Gascon innkeeper's son, with his picaresque past, too coarse and low-born. 'I do not like these silly little love marriages,' he commented, speculating that one day she might be in a position to marry a monarch. But Caroline was headstrong and he could not afford to make an enemy of Murat. Paulette was also wayward, and Bonaparte felt obliged to lecture her on her marital duties to her husband. Louis, whom he loved most of all his brothers, he had the highest hopes for.[14]

Josephine was both his greatest asset and his greatest liability. She had all the necessary grace and polish to hold court, as well as the charm to win people over and soothe anger or hurt. She was, if anything, too kind and approachable, and she lent a sympathetic ear to a stream of petitioners begging her to press their case for favour or redress. Bonaparte expressed his annoyance but found it difficult to resist her pleas, which only encouraged others to join the queue. More of an irritant to him were the jewellers, dressmakers, hatters, glove-makers, cobblers, and other tradesmen who swarmed on her, indulging her insatiable appetite for luxury of every kind. This was an uncontrollable urge, possibly a disorder brought on by her experiences during the Terror, and the tradesmen knew it. However much he raged, often having them ejected physically and in one case having a dressmaker thrown in prison for twenty-four hours, they crept back when he was away or occupied with work.

One of her fancies that he shared was the house at La Malmaison, which she had bought while he was in Egypt. They drove down there at every opportunity, as she loved the privacy and he the fresh air. In November 1799, shortly after the coup, she brought the architect Pierre Fontaine to see it; he agreed the site was delightful and the gardens pleasant, but thought the house a mess. He started work on it in January 1800. He had to work around their visits so as not to interfere with their leisure, and he put up with criticism of his work and frequent changes of plan from Bonaparte. When he was first presented to Bonaparte on 31 December, Fontaine heard of his plans for Paris and was commissioned to embellish the Invalides, where Bonaparte intended to have the horses of St Mark's installed along with a statue of Mars brought from Rome. He was bombarded with new ideas and projects faster than he could work on them, and he found Bonaparte's impatience as well as his attention to detail and continual questioning of costs exhausting as well as irritating.[15]

Fontaine was not the only one to feel the strain of the first consul's manic urge to get as much done as quickly as possible. Berthier was pressed to purge the army of inefficient or politically suspect officers, improve conditions for the troops, see to it that they were paid and fed, organise the supply of uniforms and equipment, improve discipline, and stem the endemic desertion. Every minister was similarly harassed. Nor did Bonaparte spare himself. 'There were no fixed hours for his meals or his sleep,' recalled Chaptal. 'I saw him dine at five o'clock and at eleven. I saw him go to bed at eight o'clock in the evening and at four or five in the morning.' He generally slept about seven hours out of twenty-four, but often in three short bursts. His only means of relaxation was either violent exercise such as riding, when he would gallop furiously, or a hot bath, in which he might spend up to an hour.[16]

Between going to the theatre and the opera, attending sessions of the Institute, and inspecting troops, Bonaparte found the time to supervise such matters as the standardisation of the metre throughout French territory, appoint David as 'painter of the government', and give instructions concerning the next year's *salon*. He absorbed information rapidly, stripping it down to essential facts, and made snap decisions after a moment's reflection—usually the right ones. His secretaries could hardly keep up with him as he dictated, racing ahead as though he were talking to someone in the room, never pausing and intolerant of being asked to repeat anything. He treated his secretary 'like a machine, to which one does not speak', as one of them put it. He would become animated as he spoke, pacing up and down his study, either bent forward with his hands in his pockets or swaggering with his hands behind his back, his right shoulder occasionally jerking upward in a nervous tic, developing his train of thought as he went. Not the least of the difficulties was his propensity for malapropism, substituting 'amnesty' for 'armistice', 'convention' for 'constitution', 'session' for 'section', the Elbe for the Ebro, Smolensk for Salamanca, and so on. But since his writing was almost indecipherable, they nevertheless preferred to take dictation rather than copy his notes. They never stopped him to clarify a point, as his features would set in 'an attitude of imposing severity' when he was at work, and it was only when he stopped that he would smile 'with great warmth', as one of his secretaries recalled. 'He rarely laughed, and when he did, it was in a great burst, usually to show irony rather than great joy.'[17]

His contacts with others, whatever their station and whatever their relationship, were bedevilled by a mass of insecurities, social, intellectual, physical, and sexual. 'There was no kind of merit or distinction of which he was not jealous,' according to Mathieu Molé. 'He aspired to strength, grace, beauty, to the gift of being able to please women, and what is most curious is that his pride was so successful in containing his vanity, his real superiority in covering up his pettiness, that with so many opportunities to appear ridiculous he never did.' His insecurities were, however, reflected in the way life was lived in the Tuileries.[18]

Bonaparte felt it should be conducted according to a strict etiquette in order to add dignity to his person and office and, as he later put it, to stop people slapping him on the back—though there is no record of anyone ever having dared to do so even when he was a mere cadet. His close friend and aide since the Italian campaign, General Duroc, was put in charge of arrangements in the palace, and liveried footmen soon joined officers in uniform. Old courtiers were sought out, along with documents describing procedures at the court of Louis XVI, and quizzed about details of life at Versailles under the ancien régime. Madame Campan, former lady of the bedchamber to Marie-Antoinette, was consulted. Josephine acquired a series of noble ladies as companions. At the same time, the first consul clung to his familiar habits, walking into Josephine's dressing room to tell her what to wear. They shared the same bedroom and lived, as he put it, 'in a very bourgeois way'.[19]

He was aware how much the coterie of men of business and women of slight virtue that had gathered around Barras and other Directors had tarnished the image of the government, and he wanted that of the consular administration to remain untainted. This accorded with his personal dislike of what he saw as profiteers and his prudish morality and led to his banning Thérèse Tallien and other friends of Josephine's whom he regarded as morally sullied; he took a high tone when it came to any amorous activity, other than his own, and made plain his disapproval of revealing female dress.

The result was a stuffy parody of a court, which only Bonaparte seemed satisfied with as he strutted about making awkward conversation with the ladies or holding forth on some subject. Those of his entourage who had spent the past years on campaign found it difficult to comply with the imposed rules of behaviour and had to be called to order; Junot had an unfortunate habit of attracting a lady's attention by slapping her on the thigh. Bonaparte himself disregarded etiquette when it suited him and would on occasion escape the constraints of the Tuileries. He would put on an old overcoat, pull a scruffy hat over his face, and walk the streets of an evening with Bourrienne to observe, and sometimes to engage people in conversation to find out what they thought of his regime.[20]

In their retreats in the Faubourg Saint-Germain, the old aristocracy made fun of the parvenu court, which did lend itself to mockery; as the need to underline revolutionary credentials receded, old forms of dress revived, but lack of savoir-faire produced a mixture of fashions described by one as 'a real masquerade'. Republicans were no less scathing, and when in Josephine's drawing room people began addressing each other as 'Madame' rather than *Citoyenne*, they voiced their horror and predicted the worst.[21]

A routine was established, with two receptions a month for the diplomatic corps, one every second day of the *décade* for senators and generals, on the fourth for the members of the Legislative Body, and on the sixth for those of the Tribunate and the top judiciary. Once a *décade* there was a parade at which Bonaparte would review troops, dressed in his blue consular uniform, wearing boots rather than stockings and pumps. These parades became a popular spectacle for Parisians and tourists alike. For the first consul they were an opportunity to demonstrate the power and discipline of the new state, and his own. They also provided an opportunity for units which had not served under him to see Paris and their new master.

Though vanity undoubtedly played a part, these rituals were inspired principally by the need to create the institutions and framework which Bonaparte believed to be essential props of the nascent French polity. They were all of a piece with everything else he was doing, which he famously described as laying down blocks of granite on which the state would rest.

He was not insensible to the fact that the authoritative government and strong hand required to put France back together were in conflict with the ideals of the Revolution, most of which were his own. That it had degenerated into a series of murderous convulsions he ascribed to a lack of discipline and the pursuit of consensus through discussion, which ultimately led to the rule of the mob. The tensions between liberty and effective government had been one of the principal preoccupations of eighteenth-century thinkers; in the first sentence of *Du Contrat Social*, a seminal Enlightenment text, Rousseau sought a formula that could tailor good legislation to the imperfections of man. 'In this quest I shall everywhere try to reconcile what the law permits with what is required by the common good, in such a manner that justice and utility should not conflict,' he wrote, recognising that laws too rigid to adapt to developing events can prove pernicious in certain situations, even leading to the downfall of states.[22]

The Revolution, Bonaparte believed, had shown the way and then got lost. 'We have finished the novel of the Revolution,' he told the Council of State. 'We now have to write its history, to pick out only those of its principles which are real and possible to apply, and not those which are speculative and hypothetical. To follow a different course today would be to philosophise, not to govern.'[23]

Rousseau defined the man who usurps royal authority as a tyrant and the one who usurps the sovereignty of the people as a despot. 'The tyrant will break the law in order to take power and govern according to the law; the despot places himself above the law itself,' he explained. 'Thus a tyrant may not be a despot, but the despot is always a tyrant.' France needed a tyrant, and Bonaparte fitted Rousseau's definition, but he did not at this stage aspire to the role of despot. 'My policy is to govern people as the majority wishes to be governed,' he would explain to Roederer a couple of months later. 'That is, I believe, the best way to acknowledge the sovereignty of the people.'[24]

He had gone to great lengths to allow a voice and a forum to everyone who was not opposed to the state as it was constituted. The credibility of the four constitutional bodies was grounded in his nonpartisan appointments, which gave many who were ill-disposed to him a platform on which to air their views. As the various bodies met in different places—the Legislative at the Palais-Bourbon, the Tribunes at the Palais-Royal, the Senate at the Luxembourg, and the Council of State at the Tuileries—they were not in a position to form a nexus of resistance. And there were few prepared to stand in his way, if only out of fear. The prominent liberal Benjamin Constant had invited a number of friends to dinner at his house on 6 January 1800, but the previous day he had criticised one of Bonaparte's projects in the Tribunate, and in consequence only two turned up—and they only because he had bumped into them that afternoon, which left them no excuse. Such self-control provided no guarantee, and Bonaparte realised the necessity of building state structures of requisite strength and stabilising the political, economic, and social situation to the point at which the benefits of the status quo would outweigh any desire for change. A key element in this was local administration.[25]

A law of 17 February 1800 fixed the administrative structure of the country (which survives almost unchanged to this day). It was based on a project devised by Sieyès at the beginning of the Revolution in 1789, and its guiding principle was centralisation, with every department run by a single prefect. 'Discussion is the function of many, execution is that of one man,' was how he had introduced it. As with many of Sieyès's projects, it was theoretically sound but wanting in practice, and the new structure put in place by Bonaparte, Daunou, Roederer, and Chaptal was more effective. The administration of the country was divided up into ninety-eight departments, each with a prefect exercising full authority, assisted by a sub-prefect and a General Council (*Conseil général*). A department consisted of a number of districts (*arrondissements*), which grouped together the communes, run by a mayor and a municipal council. The new law abolished the election of prefects, sub-prefects, and mayors, who were henceforth to be nominated by the first consul. In the interests of stability, most incumbents were maintained, but as they now held their office by the grace of the first consul, he acquired a control throughout the provinces which the monarch under the ancien régime could only have dreamed of.[26]

Lying in the department of the Seine, Paris was granted special status, with twelve mayors overseeing the arrondissements, but the city's real mayor was the prefect of the Seine—an autonomous mayor of Paris would have been a potential focus for political opposition. Fear of the city's populace made Bonaparte act fast; barely a week after the coup d'état, some 70 percent of the municipal authorities had been sacked, with those of lower-class origins replaced by men of property, mostly shopkeepers, who were admonished to act in such a way as to 'extinguish all hatreds'.[27]

A month later, on 18 March, a new system of justice came into being, with 400 local courts, a high court (*cour de première instance*) for every department, and twenty-nine courts of appeal, all overseen by the highest court in the land, the Tribunal de Cassation. Before any case came to court, it was brought before one of 3,000 justices of the peace. The prestige of the law was enhanced by regulations which created a new class of magistrates who were given the robes and titles which had applied before the Revolution. This class, along with the wealthier and more active citizens in every locality, constituted what were termed as 'notables', a social grouping described by Thibaudeau as 'a kind of aristocracy destined exclusively for public office'. They would become the backbone of the new French state.[28]

As important as any political or administrative measures were those Bonaparte undertook to stabilise the economic and financial situation. The French state had been struggling to avoid bankruptcy for most of the eighteenth century, and the crisis of the late 1780s had led to the outbreak of the Revolution. The ensuing chaos and wars had wrought yet more havoc with the economy. Consecutive revolutionary governments had issued vast quantities of *assignats*, paper money backed by the supposed value of the confiscated *biens nationaux*. More and more notes were printed, precipitating a headlong fall in their value, leading to a monetary crisis which by 1793 had become endemic. The introduction of the silver franc in 1795 only served to underline the worthlessness of the paper currency (the printing costs of which exceeded its value), and in February 1796 the Directory attempted to halt the slide by holding a ceremonial smashing of the plates, hoping to convince people that no more would be printed. But in March it issued a new form of paper currency—which lost 80 percent of its value in the space of a month and had to be withdrawn within less than a year. It then resorted to a sleight of hand that made two-thirds of all paper currency valueless.[29]

The Directory just about managed to survive on the proceeds of successful wars which brought millions in specie as 'contributions' and straight looting from Italy, the Netherlands, Switzerland, and western Germany. But the majority of the people suffered. While the rural population could feed itself it could not sell its produce at a reasonable price, and the knock-on effect on manufacturing led to stagnation. The only sector which thrived was that of supplying the armies, and fortunes were made by unscrupulous entrepreneurs (members of the Bonaparte clan among them) who were paid in specie by the government, bought victuals and goods at knockdown prices, and often did not even pass them on to the troops but sold them to locals in occupied territories. The situation began to improve in the last year of the Directory, but this went largely unnoticed. In time, Bonaparte would take the credit, but when he took power the situation was dire. The coffers of the treasury contained no more than 167,000 francs. Expected receipts were 470 million, to cover a budget of 600 million and service a debt of 500 million.

Financial milieus, badly battered by the Directory's attempts to deal with the liquidity crisis, were ready to pin their hopes on any government that looked as though it might provide fiscal stability. Cambacérès's prestige stood high in these circles, and they were prepared to follow his lead. Shortly after the coup, on 24 November, Bonaparte received five leading financiers whom he assured that his government would respect private property, defend the social order, and provide stability. He then withdrew, leaving the finance minister Gaudin to ask them for a loan, which they readily subscribed.[30]

Gaudin instituted a lottery, sold off government property, and imposed a levy on the Sister Republics. He persuaded Bonaparte to introduce a range of indirect taxes, including duties on tobacco, alcohol, and salt—the very taxes which had done so much to provoke the Revolution and been repealed in 1789. In order to provide a new mechanism for raising credit for the government, on 13 February he established the Banque de France. Gaudin's work on enforcing the payment of arrears and bringing in efficient methods of collecting taxes gradually began to pay off.

Bonaparte had already gone a long way to destroy, disable, or disarm the political malcontents on both the right and the left. Their capability had been eroded by the general mood of contentment. He had managed to win over many without necessarily fulfilling their hopes or expectations. Hyde de Neuville admitted that the advent of the new regime had induced 'a sense of relief and acceptance', and that 'the desire for order and stability was so universal that people were delighted to find themselves taken in hand by one capable of re-establishing them'.[31]

'The favourable opinion of the talents and principles of the First Consul grows daily, and that opinion, along with his authority, is really held by the people,' reported the Prussian minister on 2 January. 'It is difficult to imagine in what a state of relief and happiness France soon found itself,' recorded the young Amable de Barante. 'After ten years of anarchy, of civil wars, of bloody discord, after the fall of an ignoble tyranny, we saw public order re-establish itself as though by miracle.' He did note that some far-sighted people were alarmed that these benefits all stemmed from the absolute power of one man, but the price seemed worth paying.[32]

Marengo

IF HE WAS to achieve his aim of rebuilding the French state, Bonaparte needed to put an end to the war. The enemies of France were preparing to resume hostilities in the spring of 1800, and the condition of the French forces did not inspire confidence. As Britain was the paymaster of the coalition, he believed that the road to peace lay through London. One of his first acts on taking office as first consul on 25 December 1799 was to write to George III professing his desire for peace and offering to open negotiations. He also sent Louis-Guillaume Otto to London to arrange the exchange of prisoners along with a brief to try to initiate peace talks.[1]

Writing a personal letter to the king was a breach of protocol, and the response, from the foreign secretary Lord Grenville, was haughty. Addressed to his counterpart Talleyrand rather than Bonaparte, it accused France of ten years of aggression and declared that since Britain did not recognise the present authorities in France as legitimate, it would only negotiate with the restored Bourbons. Bonaparte's response, delivered by Talleyrand, rejected the charge of aggression and challenged Grenville's attitude to the French government, given that every other state in Europe had recognised the Republic and Britain had itself conducted negotiations with it only two years before. Every nation had the right to choose its rulers, he went on, pointing out that the house of Hanover itself reigned in Britain thanks to a revolution. The point was picked up in the House of Commons by a member of the opposition who asked Prime Minister William Pitt what he would say if a victorious France were to declare she would only negotiate with the Stuarts. Pitt countered that there was no point in entering into negotiations with Bonaparte, an adventurer who would not last long, as he was 'a stranger, a foreigner, and an usurper'. Grenville replied to the second French note only to say that he would not accept any further correspondence.[2]

Pitt could see no reason to enter into negotiations. Victory appeared to be in sight: Nelson's destruction of the French fleet in the bay of Aboukir had established British dominance in the Mediterranean, the French force on Malta was besieged, and it was thought that the French occupation of Egypt was about to collapse.

Bonaparte's departure had caused consternation in the army he left behind, followed by an explosion of anger, but this soon died down as most of the men accepted that he knew what he was doing and would soon return with reinforcements or send ships to bring them home; they had grown to trust him, and Kléber had raged against 'that little bugger' for deserting his army mainly because he missed him and his firm command. He could hold out with the 20,000 or so men he had left, all of them seasoned troops. They were regularly resupplied with essentials by blockade-running despatch boats known as *avisos*, and by Genoese, Algerian, and Tunisian trading vessels, and from the moment Bonaparte came to power a fast sloop and two frigates began making regular runs out of Toulon. But Kléber lacked the will to carry on the enterprise. He entered into negotiations with Sydney Smith, and at the end of January 1800 signed the Convention of El Arish, by which the French would evacuate Egypt with their arms.[3]

Believing they could obtain an unconditional surrender, the British government disowned the convention and resumed hostilities. Kléber defeated an Ottoman army at Heliopolis and recovered control over the whole of Egypt. But British troops from India had landed on the Red Sea coast, and another force was preparing to come ashore at Alexandria. The letters of French officers writing home intercepted by the Royal Navy painted a picture of low morale. The ease with which the British were able to land small contingents of troops in areas of France where royalist feeling was strong suggested that France itself was vulnerable. Pitt took Bonaparte's peace overtures as a sign of weakness, believing that 'the whole game is in our hands now, and it wants little more than *patience* to play it *well, to the end*'.[4]

Bonaparte had also written to the emperor proposing peace negotiations, and although it was more diplomatic, the response from Vienna was just as clear as that from London. The emperor had every intention of pursuing the war. His armies had driven the French out of Italy and overthrown the Cisalpine Republic. In the north, they had pushed the French back across the Rhine. Like his British ally he misjudged the significance of what had taken place in France, seeing it as a sign of internal chaos, and was confident of victory. Austrian armies were preparing to launch a two-pronged attack in the spring, over the Rhine from Germany, and into the south of France through Italy, supported by the Royal Navy, which was to land British troops on France's south coast.

Bonaparte later admitted, 'This response could not have been more favourable to us'; if Britain had accepted his offer to negotiate, she would have used her position of power and France's weakness to force France out of Holland, almost the whole of Italy, and Malta. In order to entrench his political power, Bonaparte needed to make good some of France's recent losses and regain the initiative. 'The war was essential [to France] at that moment in order to maintain the energy and unity of the State, which was still weak,' he would explain, adding that as it also strengthened his own hand, he had received the news of the British refusal 'with secret satisfaction'.[5]

On 8 March he issued a proclamation stating that he had done everything he could to negotiate a peace, but since the allies were set on war, France must fight. 'The kings of Europe may well regret not having wished to make peace,' he said to Cambacérès as he faced up to the challenge. He meant to bring Austria to the negotiating table by a vigorous strike through Germany to defeat the 120,000 men massing there under Field Marshal Kray and then march on Vienna. He was building up a Reserve Army around Dijon which could be used either to move south against the Austrians in Italy or to reinforce the forces operating in Germany. His main problem was the condition of the troops at his disposal, which were in many cases little better than a mutinous rabble. He held parades, inspected barracks, talked to soldiers, and took an interest in their wants. He took every opportunity to enhance their self-esteem, signing off a letter to a grenadier who had distinguished himself with the words 'I love you like a son.' He wanted the author of the *Marseillaise*, Rouget de Lisle, to compose a new hymn that might galvanise them.[6]

The question also arose as to who was to command the armies in the field. Rulers had long ago ceased leading their troops into battle, delegating the task to professionals, and as virtual head of state Bonaparte might have been expected to do so too. Yet he considered himself best qualified for the task. Moreover, since he had achieved his position largely through military prowess, if he were to hand over command to another, their success might equal or even eclipse his past triumphs and thereby weaken his right to rule. Yet his setting off to war would raise all manner of possibilities, hopes, and fears; with Bernadotte in command of Army of the West and Moreau on the Rhine, a military coup could not be ruled out. There was also the possibility of his being killed in battle, and Joseph suggested he nominate him as his successor. Political considerations also impinged on his military planning.

The 100,000-strong Army of Germany was under the command of Moreau, whom Bonaparte could not very well replace, even though he was neither willing nor capable of carrying out the operation Bonaparte had in mind. He tried to stimulate him through flattery. 'I envy your good fortune, for you have a brave army with which you will do fine things,' he wrote to him on 16 March. 'I would gladly exchange my consular purple for the epaulette of a chef de brigade under your orders.' Moreau was unmoved.[7]

Since Moreau could not be relied on to deliver the main blow, Bonaparte would have to strike at the Austrians in Italy. 'What he doesn't dare do on the Rhine, I shall have to do over the Alps,' he concluded. 'He may soon regret the glory he is leaving to me.' He nevertheless kept his intentions secret. He had put Berthier in command of the Reserve Army, replacing him at the War Ministry by Carnot, who was dependable and competent and popular with the Jacobins. Ten days later the Consular Guard marched out of Paris in a southerly direction, but Bonaparte remained in Paris.[8]

On 6 April the Austrians went into action against Masséna's Army of Italy. Less than 40,000 strong, it was strung out in a defensive screen and the Austrian commander, Field Marshal Melas, had no difficulty in forcing a wedge through the middle, slicing it in two and driving one half under General Suchet back toward the Var while Masséna fell back on Genoa. Bonaparte ordered them both to hang on at all costs while he accelerated the formation of the Reserve Army, with which he would have to come to their aid. Despite his repeated pleas Moreau had still not made a move, and it was not until 25 April, after what amounted to an ultimatum, that he crossed the Rhine.

On his last day in Paris, 5 April, Bonaparte received news of a victory by one of Moreau's divisions under General Lecourbe at Stockach. After sending a letter replete with flattery and congratulation to Moreau, he went to the opera and at two o'clock in the morning climbed into a carriage with Bourrienne and left the capital. Officially, he was only going to inspect the Reserve Army, now about 36,000 strong.[9]

The following evening, at Avallon, he encountered a courier from Masséna who informed him that he could not hold out in Genoa for long. 'Are you not the brave, the victorious Masséna?' Bonaparte wrote back, urging him to stand firm. He sped on, inspecting the various units of the Reserve Army still on the march along the road. The next day, at Auxonne, he visited the artillery barracks and several erstwhile acquaintances came to see him. At Dôle he inspected the cannon foundry and saw the former chaplain of Brienne, Father Charles. But there was little time for banter, and at three o'clock in the morning of the following day, 9 May, he was in Geneva, where he joined Berthier. He had been enthusiastically cheered by the troops along the way and, tired as he was, appeared in high spirits.[10]

'The whole army is on the move and in the best condition possible,' he wrote to Cambacérès, from whom he had received a report on the situation in Paris. He was pleased to hear that the capital was quiet, but repeated his order to 'strike hard the first one, whoever he might be, who steps out of line'. 'The Italian campaign was a real trial for my colleague [Lebrun] and me,' Cambacérès later recalled.

'Even in the tumult of war, Bonaparte never took his eye off us.' Joseph reported their every move to his brother.[11]

Bonaparte lingered three days in Geneva. He was called on by its burghers, whom he edified with professions of pacifism and predictions of a general peace founded on justice and liberty. He also received a visit from the renowned Jacques Necker, minister of finance of Louis XVI before the Revolution and father of Germaine de Staël, who appeared to be fishing for an invitation to become his finance minister. Bonaparte had avoided seeing him on his previous passage through Geneva and remained unimpressed after a two-hour conversation with him.[12]

On 12 May he ordered Lannes to begin crossing the Great St Bernard Pass, which would bring him into the Austrian rear in Italy. He then left Geneva for Lausanne. On arriving there he wrote to Josephine telling her that she would be able to join him in ten or twelve days. His spirits were lifted by the news that Desaix had managed to get back from Egypt safely, 'good news for the whole Republic but more especially for me, who has vowed to you all the esteem due to men of your talent, along with a friendship which my heart, already very aged and knowing men all too well, bears for no other'. He urged him to make haste to join him.[13]

Taking the army over the pass was a difficult undertaking. Everything had to be carried, by man, horse, or mule. The ordnance had to be dismantled, the wheels and limbers transported on muleback, and the barrels dragged along in the hollowed-out trunks of trees, with as many as a hundred men pulling each one up the steep inclines.

Bonaparte made the ascent on the back of a mule led by a guide. Although he peppered his talk with references to Caesar, Alexander, and Hannibal, he did not cut much of a figure, his hat protected by an oilskin cover, his uniform hidden under a cloak. Impatient as always, at one point he tried to hurry his mount, which slipped and nearly pitched him down a precipice into the stream below. He was saved from this indignity by the guide (meaning to reward him, Bonaparte asked to know his dearest wish, which turned out to be a good mule of his own, so when he returned to Paris, he sent him the best mule money could buy). No more gloriously, on the descents he was obliged to imitate his men, who slid down the icy slopes on their bottoms.[14]

At the summit he visited the hospice and monastery of St Bernard and dined with the prior. On being shown the library he pulled out a copy of Livy and looked up the passage on Hannibal. His onward march was impeded by the fort of Bard, defended by a small force of Croat grenadiers with twenty-six cannon. They refused to surrender, and an attempt by the vanguard to storm the fort came to nothing. An attack commanded by Bonaparte also failed, so he decided to bypass the fort across country and press on, leaving the artillery to follow once it had surrendered. The next day he was at Aosta, from where on 24 May he reported to Cambacérès and Lebrun that events were moving fast. 'I hope to be back in Paris within two weeks,' he wrote. The following day, having ridden ahead of his escort with only Duroc at his side, he was surrounded and almost captured by an Austrian cavalry patrol, but he pressed on regardless, reaching Ivrea on 26 May. There he paused to take stock.[15]

Leaving a force of 25,000 men under General Ott blocking Masséna in Genoa, the Austrian commander Melas with some 30,000 men had driven the French forces under General Suchet back as far as Nice. He disposed of another 50,000 or so strung out along his lines of communication or manning fortresses in his rear. If Genoa were to fall, the Royal Navy would be able to supply him through that. As well as making it possible to land allied troops, this would free up those 50,000 guarding his communications with Austria, bringing his effectives up to around 100,000 men. With such a force he would be able to sweep into the south of France unhindered.

Bonaparte had only 54,000 men. He could have made for Genoa, defeated Ott, and delivered Masséna, but he decided instead to take Milan, where he would find Austrian guns to replace those he had left behind at Bard. He would also be able to join up with 14,000 men under General Moncey detached from the Army of the Rhine and another 3,000 who had crossed the Alps over the Mont Cenis pass. He calculated that on hearing of the fall of Milan, Melas would race back to dislodge him and would be caught between two fires, with Masséna free to act once the siege had been raised. 'I hope to be in the arms of my Josephine in ten days' time,' he wrote to her from Ivrea on 29 May, convinced that his strategy would yield a quick result.[16]

He reached Milan on the evening of 2 June, annoyed to find no cheering crowds. Before going to bed he dictated a Bulletin in which he reported that he had entered the city greeted 'by a people animated by the utmost enthusiasm'. Two days later, when he went to La Scala he really was cheered, and he spent the night with the prima donna Giuseppina Grassini, who was surprised he wanted her now, having rejected her when she was young and fresh. Then, he had had thoughts only for Josephine.[17]

At eleven on the night of 7 June a captured Austrian courier was brought to him, from whom he learned shocking news. Pressed by Ott on the landward side and bombarded from the sea by Admiral Keith's squadron, fearing an insurrection by the starving inhabitants, Masséna had capitulated, leaving Genoa in Austrian hands. This not only removed his force from the scene, it raised the possibility that Melas might ensconce himself behind the walls of the city, where, supplied by the Royal Navy, he would be able to hold out indefinitely, facing Bonaparte with an impasse similar to that of Acre. For political as well as military reasons, he must obtain a quick victory. He woke up his staff and began dictating orders. By the early hours his troops were on the move.

He followed on 9 June, in the rain, with a bad cold. 'I cannot stand the rain, and my body was drenched in it for hours,' he wrote to Josephine; while she had forfeited the exclusivity of his sexual interest, she still had his affection, and he wrote to her regularly, almost always including an impish message for 'Mademoiselle Hortense'. This apparent nonchalance could not disguise his anxiety. That same day the vanguard under Lannes had come across Ott's army returning from Genoa on its way to join Melas at Alessandria and defeated it at Montebello. But Bonaparte was no clearer as to where Melas was and what he intended to do next. At Stradella he was joined by Desaix, and the two sat up all night talking.[18]

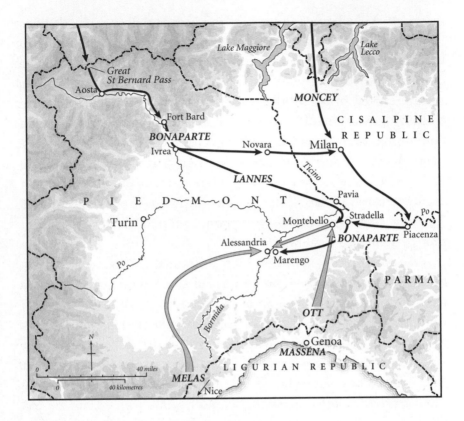

In the morning Bonaparte sent Desaix south with two divisions to get between Melas and Genoa, and another division westward to check him if he were intending to move on Turin instead. After another day without intelligence on the Austrian's whereabouts, he moved forward with the rest of his forces, reaching the small village of Marengo under pouring rain on 13 June. He went up a tower to survey the surrounding countryside, but came down none the wiser. From what he could tell, there was only a small Austrian force facing him at Alessandria on the opposite bank of the river Bormida. He dried his clothes and dined with a local nobleman, then made another attempt to assess the situation by counting the number of Austrian campfires. He slept badly and was up at five in the morning.

At seven, a large number of Austrians began crossing the river over three bridges, backed up by heavy artillery fire, at which point he realised he was facing Melas, who had concentrated 30,000 men and a hundred field guns at Alessandria. Bonaparte was down to 22,000, with only twenty guns. 'Come back, in God's name, if you still can,' he wrote to Desaix. Desaix received the order at one o'clock and immediately set off, his men occasionally breaking into a run as they covered the thirteen kilometres that separated them from the field of battle.[19]

Meanwhile, Bonaparte mounted up and led all his available reserves up to support Lannes and Victor, who were trying to hold on against the Austrian onslaught at Marengo. At two o'clock the division he had sent to cover the road to Turin returned, followed by the Consular Guard. But the best these reinforcements could do was to prevent the more or less orderly retreat from Marengo turning into a rout under pressure from the overwhelming Austrian artillery and cavalry. 'The battle appeared to be lost,' recalled Victor, and by three o'clock in the afternoon Bonaparte was preparing to disengage. Melas judged that he had won, and having had two falls from his horse that day, painful at his age of seventy-one, retired to Alessandria and lay down to rest, leaving it to his generals to finish off and pursue the French.[20]

Just as Melas had taken to his bed, around five o'clock, Desaix turned up and, after a brief exchange with Bonaparte, led his two divisions into the fray. Simultaneously, General Kellermann, son of the victor of Valmy, gathered up his cavalry and charged the Austrian flank. As the astonished Austrians faltered, the entire French line surged forward, causing them to fall back and then flee in disorder.[21]

It was not much of a victory. Although Austrian losses were almost twice as high as French ones, Melas could easily replace them, while the French could not make up theirs. A particularly painful loss was that of Desaix, who was killed leading his men into the attack. 'I feel the most profound grief at the death of the man I loved and esteemed the most,' Bonaparte wrote to Cambacérès. He took on his late friend's two aides, Generals Rapp and Savary, adding them to his own staff.[22]

Fortunately for Bonaparte, Melas was demoralised by the turn events had taken and requested an armistice. Bonaparte was good at browbeating his enemies in such circumstances and, aware that he must use his less than decisive victory to maximum effect, forced him to agree to evacuate Piedmont, Liguria, and Lombardy and retire behind the river Mincio. In order to keep up the pressure, and perhaps to sway his master the emperor while he was still under the shock of his defeat, Bonaparte wrote to him saying that it had been British perfidy that had prevented them coming to terms at his first request. 'The war has taken place,' he continued. 'Thousands of Austrians and Frenchmen are no longer.... Thousands of desolate families mourn their fathers, their husbands, their sons!... It is on the field of battle of Marengo, surrounded by suffering and 15,000 corpses [no more than about 2,000 were killed], that I conjure Your Majesty to listen to the cry of humanity and not allow a whole generation of two brave and great nations to go on murdering each other in the interests of others.' He argued that the interests of all the causes the emperor held dear were best served by peace, while the revolutionary ideals he was trying to contain were best spread by war. He followed this up with a letter to Melas on 20 June, bewailing the fact that their brave troops had to die in the interests of 'English merchants', complimenting him on his military talents and presenting him as a mark of his esteem with a fine sabre he had captured in Egypt. Unbeknown to him, that very day Austria signed a fresh subsidy treaty with Britain which bound her not to make a separate peace with France for another six months.[23]

Bonaparte could not afford to waste time in Italy. The next day he was back in Milan, where he attended a *Te Deum* at the Duomo on 18 June and enjoyed La Grassini. He also made arrangements for the reoccupied territories, leaving behind under Masséna's command a strong detachment of the Consular Guard in case he was forced to return. A week later he was hurrying back to Paris, greeted along the way like a hero. He hardly noticed as he raced on; a wheel came off his coach as it was hurtling down a hill, and he had to be pulled out of the wreckage of the vehicle through a window. At two o'clock on the morning of 2 July he drove up to the Tuileries.[24]

The French public had been treated to exciting blow-by-blow accounts of the campaign. The Bulletin describing the battle of Marengo is largely fantasy and reads like a bad novel. It describes Bonaparte galvanising the troops by his presence in the thick of battle and records the heroic modesty of the dying Desaix's last words and Bonaparte manfully holding back his tears on hearing them. The Bulletin of 18 June described in sentimental terms how the two black boys given to Desaix by 'the King of Darfur' had mourned him 'in the custom of their country, and in the most touching manner'. It related various glorious deeds and noble utterances of the dead hero in such a way that they fitted into and enhanced the overall narrative of Bonaparte's campaigns both earlier in Italy and in Egypt.[25]

In order to illustrate it, his propaganda machine produced a series of prints, and he commissioned a painting from David which was to become, like that of him on the bridge of Arcole, an icon. He was to be portrayed crossing the Alps, evoking memories of Hannibal and Caesar. David proposed depicting him sword in hand, but Bonaparte told him it was not with a sword that battles were won, and he should paint him looking serene on a fiery horse. The Brutus of Vendémiaire, the Hannibal of the first Italian campaign, and the Alexander of the Egyptian campaign had been superseded by Caesar. From now on painters would depict Bonaparte not as the flamboyant general, rather as a great captain absorbed in thought—pondering the sad necessity of making war, the horrors of which were inflicted on him by 'English merchants' and European monarchs in their pay. As Bonaparte would not sit for the portrait, David used his own son as a model.[26]

The thoughts that assailed the first consul on his return to Paris were not happy, and Josephine complained to a friend of daily 'scenes' poisoning her life. She ascribed his moodiness to the presence of La Grassini, whom he had invited to Paris and whom she correctly suspected him of visiting at night. But he had more serious reasons for displeasure: it had not taken him long to get an idea of what had been going on during his absence, and he did not like it.[27]

A few days after the battle of Marengo, rumours had begun to circulate in Paris of a French defeat and the death in battle of 'a great general'. Confidence plummeted, as did government stocks. It was not until 20 June that news of the victory reached the capital, confirmed two days later by the official report, announced by gun salutes. Confidence surged once more, and government stocks staged a dramatic recovery. Although there is some evidence to suggest that Bonaparte, Berthier, Talleyrand, Fouché, and others made a killing and may have been behind the original rumours, the episode was nevertheless unsettling, as it underlined the fragility of the consular government. That was not the only thing that bothered Bonaparte.[28]

Sieyès and other disgruntled ideologues met regularly at Auteuil just outside Paris, and with Bonaparte off to war the question of replacing him featured in their discussions. Other malcontents met at a restaurant in the rue du Bac and at the salon of Germaine de Staël, where the subject also came up. Among the candidates suggested as possible replacements were the hero of the American and French Revolutions Lafayette; the minister of war Carnot; Generals Moreau, Brune, and Bernadotte; and two émigré royal princes, Enghien and Orléans.

That in itself was understandable, but what upset Bonaparte was what he saw as the lack of faith in him amongst those he depended on. Fouché and Talleyrand had both known of the confabulations, and both waited anxiously, ready to swing either way. Although they detested each other, they were drawn together by the common interest of preventing a Bourbon restoration, which would entail their political, if not physical, death. Bonaparte's colleagues Lebrun and Cambacérès were also aware of what was going on, and while the latter assured him that in the event of his death he would have persuaded the Senate to nominate Joseph as his successor, they too had waited nervously to see which way to jump. There was nothing surprising or reprehensible in this. It was only natural for people to look to the future, and there was no evidence of any kind of plot against him, but Bonaparte's sense of insecurity made him touchy. He told Roederer that what he had feared most at Marengo was getting himself killed and being replaced by one of his brothers.[29]

The overblown accounts of the victory of Marengo had produced the wanted effect throughout the country, and he kept up the celebratory mood by staging a series of public ceremonies. On 14 July he held one to commemorate not the fall of the Bastille but the Fête de la Fédération held a year after that, on 14 July 1790. This had brought units of National Guards from every corner of France to Paris to participate in an act of nationwide solidarity which involved swearing an oath of loyalty to the king and the nation before an 'altar of the fatherland'. Bonaparte celebrated this tenth anniversary with a parade on the place de la Concorde (whence the statue of Liberty which had replaced that of Louis XV was discreetly removed). Captured flags were paraded and Bonaparte praised the bravery of generals and troops, likening them to the heroes of antiquity. Although there was no oath of loyalty to him, the message was clear as to whom France should place her trust in. He admitted to Roederer that it was a profound sense of insecurity, which his apparent popularity could not assuage, that made him seek to build up his image in the public imagination.[30]

On 20 July he received news that Kléber had been assassinated in Cairo by a native on 14 June, the day of the battle of Marengo and the day Desaix had died. Bonaparte made much of both generals and announced that he would erect a monument to them. On 22 September he used the celebration of the anniversary of the foundation of the Republic in 1792 to stage a ceremony in which the remains of one of France's greatest generals, Marshal Turenne, were laid to rest under the dome of the Invalides. They had been rescued from the desecration of the Basilica of Saint-Denis and stored in an attic at the Jardin des Plantes, and subsequently in a convent converted to a museum, to which Bonaparte had traced them.

The two ceremonies promoted the image of Bonaparte as a man prepared to acknowledge the merits of others, even to defer to them, but in doing so he arrogated a share of their fame and glory, which were thereby incorporated into his own legend. The ceremony at the Invalides was also notable for the speech made by Lucien, according to whom the new century would be the century of France, which was recovering a greatness she had not known since the days of Charlemagne. The reference to the first French emperor was no coincidence.[31]

Caesar

THE STATE OF France is greatly changed over the past year, a perfect tranquillity and general confidence have replaced civil war and despondency,' a former nobleman wrote to his son who was in Egypt with the Army of the Orient in September 1800. 'I do not know whether you realise how great is the enthusiasm of the French for the First Consul. We are as tranquil as under the ancien régime.' That was something Bonaparte would have been glad to hear; he himself was far from tranquil.[1]

On 7 September he answered the letter he had received from Louis XVIII six months earlier, thanking him for the flattering things he had written about him, but ruling out a restoration, as that could not be achieved without civil strife and bloodshed on a vast scale. He advised him to sacrifice his interests to those of France and activated Talleyrand's contacts with royalists and the Russian and Prussian governments to investigate the possibility of obtaining from Louis the abdication of his rights and those of his dynasty to the throne of France (Warsaw, where Louis had moved after being expelled from Mittau [Jelgava] by Tsar Paul I, was under Prussian rule). The options held out to him ranged from a generous pension and a grand residence in Russia to some minor kingdom in Italy. But Louis replied in a letter to Bonaparte which he had published in the British press, thanking him for recognising that he did have rights to the throne and rejecting the offer of a pension. The snub produced no effect in France.[2]

The royalist insurgents in the west had been defeated earlier that year. The British agent William Wickham, who had been coordinating espionage and plots against the French government from Switzerland, had been recalled to London. The royalist agency in Augsburg had been wound up due to lack of funds, and the British had ceased to finance the royalist émigré army under the prince de Condé, which gradually disintegrated.

Yet the question of who was to rule France was not one that could be easily settled, any more than other issues raised by the Revolution, and Bonaparte realised it. During a visit to Joseph's country house at Mortefontaine in August, he went over to the park of Ermenonville to see the tomb of Rousseau, now empty, in its picturesque setting on an island in the lake. 'It would have been better for the peace of France if that man had never existed,' he said to the owner, Stanislas de Girardin. 'Why do you say that, citizen consul?' asked the other. 'He paved the way for the French Revolution,' replied Bonaparte. Girardin pointed out that Bonaparte had only gained by that, to which the consul replied, 'History will tell whether it would not have been better for the peace of the world if neither Rousseau nor I had been born!'[3]

The younger brother of Louis XVIII, the comte d'Artois, now based in London, continued to foster plots through agents in France, supported by the British government. The first was in the spring of 1800, when Hyde de Neuville and Georges Cadoudal had planned to kidnap and assassinate Bonaparte while General Pichegru, who had escaped from Guyana, prepared to subvert elements of the army and march on the capital. Fouché had gotten wind of the plot, but proceeded slowly, hoping to find out more and, by giving the conspirators time, to catch as many as possible in the act. Lucien, who as minister of the interior had his own intelligence networks, became aware of what was going on and saw an opportunity of denouncing Fouché, whom he loathed, as a co-conspirator. Fouché was not to be caught unawares and arrested the ringleaders, revealing the plot to Bonaparte on 4 May, just before his departure for Italy. There would be more than thirty plots to kill him over the next decade, most of them by royalists.[4]

Bonaparte regarded the Jacobins as a greater threat than the royalists, as they had more supporters in the army. He contrived to keep these as far from the capital as possible: Augereau was in the Netherlands, Brune in Italy, Joubert had been sent to Milan as ambassador to the Cisalpine Republic. Potentially more dangerous than any of them was Moreau, who allowed himself to be courted by all parties—Jacobins, royalists, and ideologues—and, by making the right noises, playing the honest soldier concerned only for the good of his country and remaining all things to all men. The officers in his entourage enhanced the image of him as a guileless patriot and a brilliant commander, and at his headquarters Bonaparte was seen as a self-seeking usurper.[5]

Fouché foiled a number of attempts on the life of Bonaparte, most notably one to kill him at the Opéra. The plotters included Joseph Aréna, a Corsican Jacobin whose brother Barthélémy had allegedly tried to stab Bonaparte during the scuffle in the orangery at Brumaire, and Joseph Ceracchi, a sculptor and pupil of Canova. They were seized red-handed at the Opéra on 10 November, but were not brought to trial. Bonaparte believed in hushing up most attempts on his life, as news of them would only dent the image of his immense popularity and put in question the stability of his regime. In some cases the culprits were locked up for a few weeks or months and then let out. In this case, they were executed.[6]

He paid little attention to his own safety. 'He realised the impossibility of foreseeing an attempt on his person,' according to one senior policeman. 'To fear everything struck him as a weakness unworthy of his nature, to be guarded everywhere a folly.' He gave the impression of being remarkably detached. 'Well, see to it, it's your job,' he would say when informed of a threat to his life. 'It is up to the police to take measures, I haven't the time.'[7]

He really did not have the time. From the moment he returned from Italy he adopted a punishing work schedule, holding a meeting with his fellow consuls nearly every day and sessions of the Council of State several times a week through the whole of July, in the course of which he only managed one visit to Malmaison and one to Mortefontaine. In August there were only three days on which he did not have a meeting with the consuls, in September only one. He managed three days at Malmaison and one at Mortefontaine in the course of August. That month saw the achievement of one of his principal objectives and the initiation of a number of others.

For one who disliked 'men of business' as much as he did, Bonaparte was remarkably interested in money; having reflected on the causes of the Revolution, he appreciated its importance for the security of the state. His views on economics were unsophisticated. Like everyone else in France, he had seen the dire consequences of paper currency inflation. His personal experience contributed to a fear of penury, and he liked to have cash in hand. He did not understand or like the idea of well-balanced debt and government credit, which he saw as no more than betting on a favourable outcome. He liked specie and wanted to amass as much of it as possible.

One of the first things he did on coming to power was to charge Gaudin with reorganising the collection of tax. The next was to address the problem of the Republic's huge debt, which hindered attempts to balance the budget. Gaudin called in a friend, Nicolas Mollien, the son of a wealthy weaver of Rouen, who had started out as a barrister and who, in the course of a clandestine sojourn in England under the Directory, indulged a long-standing interest in economics. Brought down to Malmaison by Gaudin, in the course of a two-hour session in the presence of Cambacérès and Lebrun, he explained to a bewildered Bonaparte the workings of the stock market and the principle of a sinking fund, suggesting the creation of one as an agency for managing government debt. Mollien was not convinced that the first consul fully understood the concept, but Bonaparte was never slow to grasp a good idea, and Mollien was duly appointed director of the *Caisse d'amortissement*, the sinking fund.[8]

In a bold move, Bonaparte decreed on 11 August that interest on government bonds would henceforth be paid in specie rather than paper money. The effect was immediate; government bonds doubled in value. The 'men of business' were now firmly behind him, and the return of public confidence in the state finances stimulated economic activity and paved the way for the introduction of the silver franc in March 1803 (it would remain stable until 1914).[9]

Another measure initiated that August was the codification of the multifarious laws in existence. France had been waiting for over a century for this, and in 1790 the revolutionary National Assembly addressed the matter. A committee under Cambacérès came up with a project for a Civil Code consisting of 719 articles. This was discussed, amended, resubmitted, and rejected by the Convention in 1794. Cambacérès produced a third draft, of 1,104 articles, in June 1796, but only a few were promulgated and the commission was dissolved.

Shortly after his return to Paris, on 12 August 1800, Bonaparte appointed a commission consisting of Jean-Étienne Portalis, François-Denis Tronchet, Jacques de Maleville, and Félix-Julien Bigot de Préameneu to draw up a Civil Code of Laws. Its leading light was Portalis, a brilliant lawyer and a friend of Cambacérès. He was fifty-four, Bigot only a year younger, Maleville nearly sixty, and Tronchet seventy-four. They were products of the ancien régime (Maleville was a *ci-devant* marquis) and had all been active during the Revolution. They brought a wealth of experience and a heavy dose of pragmatism to the task and produced a draft which was passed for comment to the judges of the highest courts before being presented to the Council of State in January 1801, less than six months after their nomination.

Over the next year the Council of State would devote more than a hundred sessions to it, at least fifty-seven of them presided over by Bonaparte, who stamped his own views and personality on the final version. This was a marriage of Roman and common law, incorporating much of the legislative legacy of the kingdom of France but deeply marked by the spirit of the Revolution. It was in some ways more than a code of laws. As Portalis stressed in his introduction, it was a kind of rulebook for a new society, secular and modern. Bonaparte's contribution was considerable and is particularly evident in the Code's stress on property as the basis of social organisation, and even more so in the domestic sphere.

His background is detectable in the Code's assumption of the family as the basis of society and of the manner in which it should function. His personal experience is detectable in the clauses governing marital relations and the rights of women. According to the Code, the husband had a duty to provide for and protect the wife, but she must obey him in everything and could not perform any legal action without his authorisation. The husband could divorce an adulterous wife, but the opposite was only possible if he moved his mistress into the family home. A woman convicted of adultery was obliged to spend between three months and two years in a house of correction. The minutes of the meetings reveal Bonaparte's input, which is marked by his disenchantment with women caused by Josephine's infidelities and profligacy. 'Women need to be contained,' he declared, explaining that they were naturally more flighty than men when it came to sex and liable to spend their husband's money like water. 'The husband must have the absolute power and right to say to his wife: Madame, you will not go out, you will not go to the theatre, you will not see such and such a person.' At the same time, he was sensitive on matters such as divorce, making it easier for couples living in unhappy marriages. He also sought to elevate adoption into a secular sacrament, granting it solemnity.[10]

The *Code Civil des Français*, as it was called, would not become law until 21 March 1804 and would be known as the *Code Napoléon*. Bonaparte was immensely proud of it. 'Proud as he was of his military glory, he was no less so of his legislative talents,' according to Cambacérès. 'Nothing moved him more than the praise frequently bestowed on the merits of a code of which he liked to see himself as the creator.' He was neither its creator nor even its editor, but he was the catalyst, and without him it would not have come into existence.[11]

That was true of almost everything that was achieved during his consulship. In the Council of State he had gathered together the most brilliant minds and the greatest experts in the country, and he drove them like slaves. As one of them put it, 'one had to be made of iron' to work with him. In the course of 1800 alone, the Council of State dealt with 911 separate measures (in 1804 it would be 3,365). Over a period of not much more than five years it would create the entire framework of the state and, in its *auditeurs*, the young men who sat behind the councillors taking minutes and notes, a new administrative class to run it. It was not unusual for Bonaparte to keep them at it for eight or ten hours with only a fifteen-minute break for lunch. 'Come, come, citizens, wake up,' he would exclaim if he saw them flagging after midnight, 'it is only two o'clock, and we must earn the money which the people of France give us.'[12]

He would prepare himself before every session by reading up on the relevant subject. Taking his place at the head of a long table at which the councillors were seated, he would open the discussion, which he expected to be conducted without deference to him. 'Gentlemen, it is not to be of my opinion but to hear yours that I have summoned you,' he would say if he noticed a trace of complaisance. 'The Council was made up of people of very diverse opinions, and everyone freely supported his,' recalled Thibaudeau. 'The majority view did not prevail. Far from bending to that, the First Consul would encourage the minority.' He would listen to them attentively, toying with his snuffbox, opening and shutting the lid, occasionally taking a pinch, most of which fell on the white facings of his uniform, and, without looking, pass the snuffbox to an aide waiting behind his chair, who would hand him another. To help himself think, he would produce a pen-knife from his pocket and belabour the arm of his chair with it (this was regularly replaced by a cabinetmaker). He asked questions, demanded more precision, and sometimes applied the rules of mathematics to the process of arriving at a conclusion. He encouraged them to contradict and correct him, saying, 'We are amongst ourselves here, we are *en famille*.' Once a conclusion had been reached, however, he would close the discussion and quickly pass on to the next matter.[13]

His input was considerable. 'What he did not know he seemed to anticipate and divine,' according to one. 'He had a prodigious facility to learn, judge, discuss, and to retain without confusing an infinite number of things.' His extraordinary memory, combined with an ability to pinpoint the key idea, stimulated colleagues who were more learned, wiser, and more expert but needed to be pinned down, and in the words of Mathieu Molé, 'the most learned and most experienced legal minds would come out confounded by the sagacity of the First Consul and the illuminating insights he introduced into the discussion'. Roederer confirms that at the end of every session they would part feeling wiser. 'Under his governance, a rather extraordinary thing happened to those who worked with him,' he wrote. 'Mediocrities found they had talent, and men of talent felt their mediocrity, so much did he inspire the one and unsettle the other.

People hitherto thought to be incapable became useful, men who had been considered brilliant were confounded....' Even Lucien, who gave his brother little credit, admitted to being impressed by his brilliance when he first saw him in action at a session of the Council.[14]

His capacity for work was extraordinary. He would on occasion preside over a Council from ten o'clock at night until five in the morning, then retire to have a bath, after which he would get back to work. 'An hour in a bath is worth four hours' sleep,' he used to say. His work schedule outside the meetings of the consular council and the Council of State was equally punishing. He would sometimes wake up at one or four o'clock in the morning, summon his unfortunate secretary, and dressed in a white dressing gown with a scarf wrapped about his head, start dictating. He hardly ever wrote himself, mainly because his writing could not keep up with his thought process, but also because neither he nor anyone else could read it. He might take a break for some ice cream or sorbet, and sometimes for something more substantial, then resume where he had left off.[15]

As a man of action with a military background and a mathematical mind, Bonaparte had a clear idea of how to proceed with the task he had set himself. Following the Brumaire coup he had provided himself with the means of getting on with it, and after Marengo he acquired even greater power. Many welcomed this. Germaine de Staël was enthusiastic about the 'glorious dictatorship' of 'this great man' who according to her had the ability to 'uplift the world'. Lafayette too expressed his approval of the 'restorative dictatorship' he was exercising, seeing in it the only hope of repairing the state and safeguarding liberty. But there were many who disagreed.[16]

A decade of debate had encouraged speculation and discussion, as well as a sense of self-importance among the intellectual elites which had dominated politics from the start of the Revolution, at the expense of pragmatism. In the interests of including representatives of the whole spectrum of French politics, Bonaparte had given seats to them in one or other of the assemblies. As soon as they took their seats his opponents began to denounce him as a tyrant, emboldening the more moderate who were alarmed at the developments. His doings were also discussed and criticised in salons and at the Institute, toward which he had cooled markedly, no longer addressing its members endearingly as 'colleagues'. Much of it was harmless verbiage, but like many witnesses of the Revolution Bonaparte was wary of demagogy. Having got used to giving orders and brooking no discussion, he saw any dissent as a challenge to his authority. His sense of insecurity made him umbrageous, and he took obstruction or even delay personally.

There was also resistance in the army, which was highly politicised and clung to the ideals of the Revolution more tenaciously than the rest of society. Generals did not look favourably on one of their kind being placed above them, and there were some who felt equally entitled to such distinction. Bonaparte's best hope here, as in the political field, where he reached over the heads of the political class and appealed to the nation, was to bypass the generals and capture the hearts of the soldiers. That task was not going to be made any easier by his intention of bringing about a national reconciliation involving what he called a social 'fusion' of those who had served the ancien régime with those wedded to the Republic, which involved the reintegration into the mainstream of royalist dissidents and émigrés. This would both eliminate a threat to the state and capture a wealth of talent for it. It also involved something which was bound to offend most soldiers as well as the entire political class.

The Bulletin of 18 June from Milan had carried an unctuous account of the first consul's attendance at the *Te Deum* in the Duomo, where the clergy of the city had treated him with the utmost respect. It was not a gratuitous piece of self-promotion. Bonaparte's views on religion were influenced by the writings of the Enlightenment, and like many of his contemporaries he rejected much of Christian teaching—he found the divinity of Christ not credible, the resurrection physically impossible, and miracles ridiculous. He could not accept that, as he put it, Cato and Caesar were damned because they were born before Christ. He was also anti-clerical. But he displayed lingering attachment to the faith, making the sign of the cross at critical moments and admitting to a love of the sound of church bells. He pondered the meaning of life, seeking explanations which were not always rational, and with time even came to believe that he had a soul. 'I do not believe in religions, but in the existence of God,' he said to Thibaudeau in June 1801, adding, 'Who created all this?' 'Everything proclaims the existence of a God, that is beyond doubt,' he asserted to another.[17]

More important, he valued the role of religion itself. 'As for me, I do not see in religion the mystery of the Incarnation, only the mystery of the Social Order,' he told his councillors. 'How can one have order in a state without religion?' he challenged Roederer. 'Society cannot exist without inequality of wealth and inequality of wealth cannot exist without religion. When a man is dying of hunger next to another who is gorging, he cannot possibly accept this difference if he has not had it on good authority that: "God wishes it so: there must be poor and rich people in the world, but afterwards, and for eternity, things will be divided up differently."' A proper religion, he assured the Council of State, was 'a vaccine for the imagination', inoculating people against 'all sorts of dangerous and absurd beliefs'. He held atheism to be 'destructive of all social organisation, as it robs Man of every source of consolation and hope'.[18]

He also appreciated that religious observance lay at the heart of the spiritual and temporal lives of the rural masses which made up the overwhelming majority of the population, and that by attacking it the Revolution had alienated them from the state. Attempts at introducing new, supposedly rational, substitutes such as the cult of the Supreme Being and Theophilanthropy he dismissed as inept since they lacked a numinous dimension. He was convinced that France could only be 'restored' (and his domination firmly established) if the state could engage the acceptance, if not the affection, of the rural masses and the old nobility, and this meant re-establishing the Church. Circumstances favoured him in one way.

The death of Pope Pius VI in August 1799 was followed by a long interregnum, and it was not until 14 March 1800 that the conclave, sitting in Venice, elected a new pope in the fifty-seven-year-old Cardinal Barnaba Chiaramonti, who took the name Pius VII. Not only was he an open-minded and intelligent man not averse to republican forms of government, he was locked in conflict with Austria and Naples, which both had designs on the Papal States.

A week after the *Te Deum* in Milan, at Vercelli on his way back to Paris, Bonaparte encountered Cardinal Martiniana, to whom he expressed the wish to open negotiations with the Pope to regularise the status of the Church and religious practice in France. It was not going to be easy to achieve; most of the political class was dogmatically irreligious, while most of the military were 'cassock-haters' who had only ever entered churches in order to loot.

Many in Bonaparte's entourage were appalled when he mentioned the idea. Neither Cambacérès nor Lebrun relished it. Fouché and Talleyrand were horrified—the first had been a teacher in Oratorian schools, the second a bishop, and any reminder of their ecclesiastical past was unwelcome. Fouché argued that it would be unpopular among the people. Talleyrand, who was still technically in holy orders, did everything he could to discourage Bonaparte, but once he realised the process was unstoppable, he set about trying to get the Pope to release him from his sacerdotal vows—which Pius VII refused to do. On 5 November Monsignor Spina, Archbishop of Corinth, arrived in Paris to open negotiations. Bonaparte greeted him cordially and appointed the Abbé Bernier to prepare the ground, under the supervision of a squirming Talleyrand.[19]

Spina's arrival was overshadowed by another event, which caused a sensation: the publication on 1 November of an anonymous pamphlet titled *Parallèle entre César, Cromwell, Monck et Bonaparte*. 'There are men who appear at certain epochs to found, destroy or repair empires,' it proclaimed. 'For ten years we have been seeking a firm and able hand which could arrest everything and sustain everything [...] That man has appeared. Who can fail to recognise him in Bonaparte?' The author went on to say that where Cromwell destroyed, Bonaparte repaired, where Cromwell had made civil war, Bonaparte had united Frenchmen. As for Monck, how could anyone believe that Bonaparte would be happy with a dukedom and retirement under some indolent monarch? 'Bonaparte is, like Caesar, one of those characters before whom all obstacles and all opposition give way: his inspiration seems so supernatural that in ancient times when the love of the wondrous filled people's minds they would not have hesitated to believe him to be protected by some spirit or god.' By suggesting the parallel with Caesar, the pamphlet suggested Bonaparte's elevation to the ultimate authority, but also raised fears (the Aréna-Ceracchi conspiracy was fresh in people's minds). 'Happy republic *if he were immortal.* [...] If suddenly Bonaparte were lost to his country, where are his heirs?' The author feared that if he were to be killed they would find themselves back under either the 'tyranny of the assemblies' or a 'degenerate race' of kings. Without proposing anything, he suggested the need to give permanence to Bonaparte's authority and ensure its perpetuation.[20]

The author was Lucien, possibly encouraged by Bonaparte, in the interests of testing public opinion. This reacted with a predictable degree of outrage. The first consul affected to share it, ordering a thousand copies to be publicly burned. For the benefit of insiders who knew or suspected the identity of the author, he staged a dressing-down of his younger brother which culminated in Lucien throwing his ministerial portfolio onto the desk and flouncing out of the room. On 5 November Lucien was relieved of his post and replaced by a favourite of the ideologues, Jean-Antoine Chaptal. Letizia attempted to intervene on behalf of her favourite son, and Joseph tried to mediate, but Bonaparte was intractable. Lucien's wife had died, and he was leading a rackety life of promiscuity ill-suited to a leading minister (he would as good as rape any woman unwise enough to call at the ministry), which Fouché was avidly recording and publicising. Talleyrand suggested sending the delinquent to Madrid as ambassador, and he duly left Paris. Josephine and Fouché were exultant—Fouché because he hated Lucien, Josephine for even weightier reasons.[21]

Whatever the public reaction, Lucien's pamphlet had provoked discussion on how to ensure the survival of the stability achieved over the past year. It had made the connection between that and the person of the first consul and pointed the discussion in the direction along which he was thinking. What Bonaparte, and the country, needed above all was an end to the war. Whether he believed it or not, he argued that a republic by its very nature represented an affront to the hereditary monarchies of Europe, and therefore a fundamental *casus belli*. The only way of removing this source of conflict was to give the French state's political institutions a 'form', as he put it, 'a little more in harmony' with theirs. The Revolution's primary achievement had been to overthrow the feudal aspects of the ancien régime and establish a constitutional monarchy. The Republic had come into being as a result of untoward events which the majority of the population did not endorse. Turning the state back into a monarchy was unthinkable only to the relatively small number of dedicated republicans. 'The party which longs for a king is immense, enormous, although it is united by nothing other than the deep feeling that there should be one,' reported an informer in Paris to the court of Naples in the spring of 1798, adding that nobody wanted Louis XVIII, only a warrior king and a constitutional monarchy.[22]

The institution of monarchy may have still surrounded itself with anachronistic pomp, but it no longer required the kind of sacral aura it had in the days of divine right. Whereas the Bourbons had been on the throne of France for 300 years, the house of Hanover had reigned in Britain for only eighty-six, the same as the Bourbons in Spain, those of Naples only sixty-six, and the Habsburgs had entrenched themselves on the imperial throne as late as 1745. The elector of Brandenburg had decided to call himself king in Prussia less than a hundred years before, and the tsar of Muscovy emperor of Russia in 1721.

In the circumstances, there was no reason why France should not acquire a new dynasty. The question was who was to found it. There were potential candidates among the cadet branches of the French royal house, but they were too closely associated with the ancien régime. They were also unlikely to possess the qualities requisite to deal with the dangers of the French political scene. The man who had those was currently in charge, so there seemed little point in getting rid of him. But he had no heir. And since he had no ancient lineage, or other assets beyond his talents, military and administrative, there was no *a priori* reason to differentiate between him and any other capable general.

At the beginning of December, news reached Paris of a brilliant victory over the Austrians at Hohenlinden by Moreau. Bonaparte heaped praise on his general's military skills and presented him with a magnificent pair of pistols. But he was not impressed, or pleased. He had attempted to neutralise him, even going so far as suggesting he marry his sister Caroline, but Moreau was ruled by his mother-in-law, Madame Hulot, a harridan who hated Bonaparte and particularly Josephine. The feeling was mutual, and Bonaparte's cup overflowed when she made a snide remark about his alleged incestuous affair with Caroline.[23]

Following his victory, Moreau's reputation rode high, and while he was far from eclipsing Bonaparte, he was a reminder that there were alternatives, and his very existence heartened ideologues frightened by Bonaparte and royalists still searching for a 'Monck'. He might well have found himself playing that role if things had turned out differently on the night of 24 December.

That evening, Bonaparte went to the Opéra to listen to Haydn's *Creation*. As his carriage trundled down the rue Saint-Nicaise, it passed a stationary cart loaded with a large barrel. This was filled with gunpowder and exploded just after his carriage had passed it, devastating the street, killing four bystanders and wounding another sixty, some of whom would die, but inflicting no harm on Bonaparte. He carried on to the Opéra, where he was deliriously greeted by an audience who had heard the explosion and feared the worst.

On his return to the Tuileries after the performance, he found the palace teeming with concerned generals and officials. When Fouché turned up, Bonaparte taunted him for failing to forestall the attempt on his life, which he attributed to Fouché's Jacobin 'friends'. The minister assured him that it had been the work of royalist conspirators and promised to prove it within a week.

With his colleague Réal, Fouché carried out a forensic examination of the scene and what remained of the horse that had drawn the 'infernal machine' into position. Réal noticed that one of its legs was newly shod. They showed the shoe to every farrier in Paris, until one recognised it and was able to give a description of the men who had brought the horse to him. They took the nag's head to every horse-dealer, which led them to the man who had bought it. The arrests that followed established a direct link to Georges Cadoudal and to the British government.[24]

It was all of a piece with Hyde's earlier plan to kidnap Bonaparte, and his more recent one, uncovered by the police, of landing a force at Saint-Malo. But Bonaparte feared the Jacobins more than the royalists. 'The [royalist rebels] and the émigrés are a disease of the skin,' he said to Fouché a couple of days after the attempt, 'while [the Jacobins] are a malady of the internal organs.' He ordered Fouché to draw up a list of active Jacobins, whom he intended to have deported to the penal colonies of Cayenne and Guyana. It came to about a hundred names. The assemblies baulked at proscribing so many, some of them colleagues. In order to bypass them, Cambacérès and Talleyrand devised a legal ploy whereby the Senate, acting in its capacity as guardian of the constitution, issued a *senatus-consulte*, an edict dressed up as a constitutional safeguard, enacting the contested measure.[25]

The event had proved a godsend to Bonaparte. A number of royalists were shot, as were some Jacobins. A larger number of those were deported, including what Bonaparte called the sergeants of revolution, those capable of rousing the masses. 'From then on, I began to sleep peacefully,' he confided. More important, the episode had led to the invention of the *senatus-consulte*, a mechanism for making law on the hoof, which he would soon be using to force through a measure establishing special tribunals without juries to deal with certain categories of criminal activity.[26]

Most important of all, the attempted assassination had shocked public opinion, not only by its violence. It was seen as an attempt not just on Bonaparte's life, but on the future of the state just as it was emerging from ten years of anarchy and violence. It drew to Bonaparte all the sympathy a victim elicits, and at the same time brought home how fragile was the newfound stability, and how closely it was tied up with his person. It thereby bound the future of the country more closely to him and to his survival. After little more than a year in power, he had become the repository of the hopes of many, and he was about to make the dearest of these come true.

Peace

DEFEATED IN ITALY by Bonaparte and pushed back further by General Brune, and trounced in Germany by Moreau, Austria could not pursue the war any longer. The emperor had sent Cobenzl to Paris in the autumn of 1800 to prepare the ground, and on 9 February 1801, as soon as she was free to do so under the terms of her alliance with Britain, Austria made peace with France by the Treaty of Lunéville. News of its signature reached Paris on 12 February. The carnival was in full swing, and people reacted with joy.

The terms were less favourable to Austria than those of Campo Formio, as she lost some of the land she had then acquired in Italy. In addition, Austria recognised France's incorporation of Piedmont and the existence of the Batavian, Helvetic, and Cisalpine republics, the last expanded by the incorporation of Modena and the Legations. The former Habsburg fief of Tuscany was renamed the kingdom of Etruria and was to be ruled by the Bourbon Duke of Parma (which had been incorporated into the Cisalpine Republic). By the terms of a treaty negotiated with Charles IV of Spain, the new King of Etruria married one of his daughters, and his kingdom became a French satellite. Austria was also obliged to admit France as a party in the process of rearrangement of the Holy Roman Empire, made necessary by the dispossession of the former rulers of states on the left bank of the Rhine, which had been incorporated into France.

The settlement was hard on Austria, but it was an even more severe blow to Britain, which lost her principal ally and proxy on the

Continent. Worse still, by a separate treaty the kingdom of Naples ceded the island of Elba to France and closed its ports to British shipping, while further treaties with Algiers, Tunis, and Tripoli enhanced France's position in the Mediterranean. Malta and Egypt were still in French hands, and an agreement signed in February 1801 guaranteed France the support of the Spanish fleet.

The situation begged for a general settlement, to include all the powers involved since the outbreak of war in 1792, but that would not be easy to achieve, given the nature of the conflict; its roots reached into the second half of the eighteenth century, when traditional dynastic considerations were superseded by the need to keep up with rivals and seek security through a 'balance of power'. If one state made a gain, others felt they must make an equivalent one, precipitating a Darwinian process in which stronger states grew at the expense of weaker ones. Recent wars and the partition of Poland had demonstrated that no frontier could be considered immovable and no throne permanent. The process was accompanied by the disintegration of old networks of alliance and restraining rivalries—Franco-Austrian control over the smaller states of Germany, the French-Swedish-Polish-Turkish barrier against both Russia and Austria, the Franco-Spanish family compact to check British ambitions in the colonies, the Anglo-Dutch equivalent, and so on. The situation was complicated by the spirit of the times: anachronistic structures such as the Holy Roman Empire and feudal monarchies came under fire from the intellectual forces unleashed by the Enlightenment and from nascent nationalism.

Two powers were growing faster than the rest. To the east, Russia had moved her frontiers 600 kilometres into Europe in the space of fifty years while advancing eastward and reaching the Pacific Ocean. To the west, Britain was extending her overseas dominions. The only power to rival them was France, which alone could help Austria check Russia's westward expansion and, with her Spanish ally, stand up to Britain's drive for control of the seas.

The Revolution had curtailed French ambitions and its leaders had sent out pacific messages to all nations, but as their doctrines challenged the social order, they drew monarchs and ministers all

over Europe together in its defence. In August 1791 the Holy Roman Emperor Leopold II and King Frederick William II of Prussia
issued a declaration after a meeting at Pillnitz in Saxony in support
of the beleaguered Louis XVI. In France, this was received as a challenge and led to the outbreak of war in 1792 and an invasion by Austria and Prussia aimed at restoring the ancien régime. The invaders
were defeated and the French proceeded to 'liberate' the Austrian
Netherlands (Belgium). The French Convention issued an Edict of
Fraternity pledging to support all nations struggling for freedom
from feudal oppression. Britain, along with Sardinia, the United
Provinces, the Holy Roman Empire, and Spain, joined the coalition
against revolutionary France. The army of émigrés at Koblenz and
popular risings in the Vendée and the south of France were financed,
armed, and supported with troops. While Britain did not have a
standing army of any significance on hand, she paid others to fight
on her behalf. But while both sides made much of the ideological
crusades they were fighting, this thinly veiled what remained essentially opportunistic policies.

At the beginning of 1793 Georges Danton had put forward the
idea that France had 'natural' frontiers designated by the Channel,
the Atlantic, the Pyrenees, the Mediterranean, the Alps, and the
Rhine, which meant the annexation of large areas that had not lain
within the borders of 1789. While 'liberating' oppressed sister nations, the French Republic shamelessly relieved them of their riches.
Austria saw the possibility of reinforcing its grip on Italy and of helping itself, along with Russia and Prussia, to what remained of Poland. Russia acquired a longed-for naval base in the Mediterranean
by occupying the Ionian islands. Britain seized France's colonies and
those of her Dutch allies. Prussia was not averse to taking the British
royal family's fief of Hanover.

Although it was through war that he had achieved power,
Bonaparte knew that only peace could ensure his survival. His first
success came on 3 October 1800, with the signature at Mortefontaine
of a treaty with the United States brokered by Joseph. It took place
in the presence of Lafayette, who had fought alongside George Wash-
ington, and was celebrated with a banquet followed by theatricals and

fireworks. (A prolonged downpour marred the proceedings by turning the gardens into a sea of mud and delaying the building of the
stage, providing time for the workers to join the artificers in helping
themselves to the wine meant for the banquet, which did not begin
until midnight, to the accompaniment of an erratic firework display.[1])

The next step had been peace with Austria, then Naples, followed
by the signature of new treaties with Spain and Portugal, negotiated
by Lucien. That left Britain and Russia. Since Britain refused to enter
into negotiations, Bonaparte sought to apply pressure by isolating
her, which could best be done through alliance with Russia, which
resented Britain's command of the oceans and felt threatened by her
colonial reach in Asia.

The tsar, Paul I, had grown disenchanted with his partners in
the coalition and withdrawn his troops. Increasingly resentful of the
Royal Navy's high-handed searching and confiscation of neutral vessels, he combined with Sweden, Denmark, and Prussia in setting up
the League of Neutrals, which denied British ships access to the Baltic.
Using the opportunity provided by the presence in France of Russian
troops taken prisoner in Switzerland in 1799, Bonaparte opened negotiations and suggested a similar league in the Mediterranean. 'It is in
the interests of all the powers of the Mediterranean, as well as those of
the Black Sea, that Egypt remain in French hands,' he wrote to Paul
on 26 February 1801. 'The Suez Canal, which would connect the Indian seas with the Mediterranean, has already been drawn; the work is
simple and requires little time, and it would yield incalculable benefits
to Russian commerce.' He urged the tsar to pressure the Porte to allow
the French occupation of Egypt to continue.[2]

Bonaparte also pointed out that their two countries had no quarrel and many common interests and that only British perfidy had
turned them against each other. He even raised the possibility of joint
action to despoil the Ottoman Empire, and, knowing that Paul had
assumed the role of protector of the Order of St John, he threw in a
present for the tsar—the sword of Grand Master Jean de la Valette,
taken after his capture of Malta on the way to Egypt. It was a gesture
bound to appeal to the impetuous tsar with his chivalric fantasies.

Paul despised the French on account of the Revolution, but he was fascinated by Bonaparte, and he sent two envoys to Paris.[3]

At the beginning of March Paul ordered the British ambassador, Lord Whitworth, to leave St Petersburg. Before his departure Whitworth encouraged and gave funds to a group of noblemen who were conspiring against the tsar, and on the night of 23 March 1801 Paul was assassinated in his bedroom. Bonaparte had no doubt as to who was behind the act. On 2 April the Royal Navy bombarded Copenhagen and the Armed Neutrality rapidly unwound, the new tsar, Alexander I, making peace with Britain in June.

Britain was nevertheless isolated, internationally unpopular, and threatened with unrest at home. The Armed Neutrality had interrupted grain shipments, leading to a rise in the price of wheat and a number of 'bread or blood' riots. The crisis over the Act of Union with Ireland precipitated Pitt's resignation on 16 February 1801. He was succeeded by Henry Addington, whose foreign secretary Lord Hawkesbury began talks in London with the French envoy Louis Otto.

Coming to terms was made no easier by the role played in the wars by propaganda. British public opinion was moulded by the rhetoric of Edmund Burke, a raucous press, and a flood of scurrilous cartoons, all of which demonised the French Revolution as a disgraceful, bloodthirsty breakdown of civilisation. Its key figures were represented as degenerate, vicious, and ridiculous, and 'Boney' came in for the most vile, if often amusing, treatment. The French response was to represent the toiling masses of Britain as the slaves of the monster Pitt and the oligarchy of lords ruling the country. They were accused of wanting to dominate the world and behaving like, in Talleyrand's words, 'vampires of the sea' who needed to be 'exterminated' in the interest of 'civilisation and the liberty of nations'. The rhetoric on both sides incited hatred, and Nelson instructed his men that 'no delicacy can be observed' when making raids on the French coast. British treatment of French prisoners of war shocked Bonaparte. 'Is it possible that the nation of Newton and Locke has so far forgotten its standards?' he wrote to Talleyrand.[4]

The negotiations were complicated by the two countries still being engaged in military operations against each other, with minor stand-offs in various colonial outposts, continual clashes at sea, and a major confrontation in Egypt; Bonaparte was doing everything he could to supply and support his forces there. A British force had landed on the Red Sea coast, and on 1 March another 15,000 British troops landed at Alexandria. But Kléber had been succeeded by General Menou, who unlike his predecessor did believe that Egypt could be held. He had married an Egyptian woman and converted to Islam, taking the name Abdullah, which earned him some popularity with the locals, as did a number of sensitive improvements in the administration of the country. He managed to hold off the British force which had landed at Alexandria in an inconclusive battle but was hemmed in there while General Belliard was besieged in Cairo. On 31 August 1801 Menou capitulated, ending France's Egyptian venture.

This helped bring matters to a head, since the British cabinet had not wished to sign a peace with the French in Egypt, and there was now some urgency in London to conclude. Britain's ally Portugal had been forced by the Treaty of Badajoz on 6 June to give up the province of Olivenza to Spain, to cede part of her colony in Guyana to France, and to close her ports to British shipping. France had reached agreement with Russia, and a treaty would be signed in Paris on 8 October, further isolating Britain. Preliminaries of peace were signed in London on 1 October, and Lord Cornwallis was delegated to France to negotiate the treaty.

He was greeted at the Tuileries on 10 November with a splendid reception followed by a banquet for 200 people. The sixty-two-year-old Englishman, who had been in public service all his life, fighting in America and governing in India and Ireland, made a favourable impression on the first consul. He then went to Amiens, where he would flesh out the details with Joseph Bonaparte. Cornwallis thought Joseph 'a very sensible, modest and gentlemanlike man', and the negotiations assumed a cordial tone. In recognition of his military past, Bonaparte placed a regiment at Cornwallis's disposal so he could distract himself by making it parade and manoeuvre.[5]

Bonaparte sent his brother detailed instructions, providing him with arguments to use against the British, but Joseph was confident that with 'patience and firmness' he would be able to stand up to and wear down his opponent. He argued that the British 'have in previous treaties always triumphed over what they like to call French petulance' with their chief weapon, which he identified as 'imperturbability and inertia', and by keeping calm himself he would disarm his opposite number. The negotiations were complicated by Bonaparte, who had a habit of upping his demands on a matter just as it had been settled. He also introduced new ones, such as access to the Newfoundland fisheries and expansion of the French enclaves in India. Cornwallis stood firm on many of these points, but his superiors were impatient to conclude, as the country was exhausted and desperate for peace after nearly a decade of war during which the lower classes of the population had suffered serious hardship.[6]

Bonaparte would not allow considerations of foreign policy to distract him from his principal task of rebuilding the French state, and hardly a day passed during the first eight months of 1801 without a session of the Council of State or of the three consuls, dealing with everything from the legal system to the repair of roads, and including the reorganisation of the government itself, with the creation of a new Ministry of the Treasury. When the price of bread had risen because of shortages, causing discontent and even riots in the spring, he reacted not just with characteristic speed and decisiveness, purchasing large quantities of flour in order to produce subsidised bread, he also put in place a mechanism whereby such events could be anticipated and crises avoided in the future.

He had returned from Egypt with a pulmonary inflammation and was still afflicted with scabies contracted at Toulon. A succession of doctors had failed to alleviate his condition, which was aggravated by his punishing work schedule, not to mention the exertions of the Marengo campaign. His lifestyle, with its irregular eating and sleeping hours and frequent overnight travel by jolting carriage, cannot have helped. By the end of June 1801 he was so ill some thought him moribund. It was then that he engaged the services of Jean-Nicolas

Corvisart, an eminent physician with an empirical and holistic approach to medicine. Soon after, Josephine was delighted to note that his spots were clearing up. By means of poultices and other natural expedients, Corvisart cured Bonaparte of his ills, so much so that over the next months his appearance would be transformed, his complexion losing its sallow sickliness and his face its hollow look.[7]

Partly on account of his health, Bonaparte had spent most of the summer of 1801 at Malmaison. Thanks to Josephine, the house had acquired neo-classical interiors filled with furniture by Jacob and vases of Sèvres porcelain. She had transformed the gardens, filling them with roses and rare plants and landscaping the park in the English manner. She also collected animals in a menagerie, which would with time contain a kangaroo and an orangutan, while llamas and gazelles roamed the park. It was characteristic of Bonaparte that while he kept quibbling with the architect Fontaine over the expense of every bit of work he carried out there, he had installed as librarian his erstwhile French master, the ageing Abbé Dupuis, and as gate-keeper with a generous pension the man who had been the concierge at Brienne.[8]

Although he worked just as hard there as in Paris, holding meetings of the consuls and the Council of State, interviewing ministers and generals, and sometimes staying up at night dictating to Bourrienne, after dinner, which was usually at six o'clock, Bonaparte would take his leisure in a way that he never could in the Tuileries. There were several guest rooms, and there was usually a house party. They would put on amateur theatricals, stroll in the garden, or play children's games, with Bonaparte taking off his coat and rushing around to catch or get away from others like a schoolboy—and often cheating. He was amused to discover that the gazelles liked snuff and would regularly treat them to some. Glancing out of the window during his toilette one morning, he noticed some swans on the ornamental canal and told Roustam to bring his guns. He then started shooting at them, laughing like a child. When a horrified Josephine rushed in and snatched the guns away from him, he said, 'I was just having some fun.'[9]

At Malmaison he was approachable, relaxed and affable. 'I was expecting to find him brusque and uneven of temper,' recalled Joseph's secretary Claude-François Méneval, 'instead of which I found him patient, indulgent, easy in his manner, not remotely demanding, of a gaiety which was often boisterous and provocative, sometimes of a charming bonhomie, though this familiarity on his part did not encourage reciprocity.' It did not discourage the painter Isabey, who, seeing Bonaparte leaning over to inspect a flower one day, leap-frogged him.[10]

Bonaparte was now regularly having affairs—with Giuseppina Grassini earlier that year, then with Mollien's wife, then Adèle Duchâtel, the wife of one of his functionaries, not to mention the odd conquest among others of his entourage. Josephine was jealous and made her servants and ladies patrol the corridors in the Tuileries. With her husband's elevation and the talk of who might succeed him, she felt threatened by her thirty-seven years and her inability to produce an heir. She had consulted Corvisart, and that summer went to take the waters at Plombières in the hope of enhancing her fertility, accompanied by Letizia. Bonaparte himself did not attach much importance to the lack of an heir and showed no signs of dissatisfaction with his marriage. 'You should love Bonaparte very much,' Josephine wrote to her mother on 18 October. 'He is making your daughter very happy; he is kind, amiable, he is in every way a charming man, and he loves your Yéyette.'[11]

He had for years treated his younger brother Louis as more of a son than a sibling, and noticing this, Josephine had determined that he should marry her daughter, Hortense. She was eighteen, pretty, and endowed with her mother's charm (and bad teeth), and Bonaparte had immediately taken to her. She would keep him company when Josephine was away taking the waters, and a deep friendship developed between them. He had adopted her along with her brother, Eugène, and if she were to marry Louis their son would be as good as his grandson.

This incipient assumption of Bonaparte's heritage by the Beauharnais clan was not the least of the sources of discord between him and his siblings, who insisted on maintaining a degree of independence while riding on his success. Joseph, who had amassed immense wealth over the past few years and set himself up as a grandee, hosting house parties and hunts at Mortefontaine, maintained close links with many of those who voiced their opposition to Bonaparte and blocked his plans in the Tribunate. He was also, for family reasons, close to Bernadotte, whom Bonaparte despised and would long ago have destroyed had he not been married to Désirée Clary. Joseph considered himself the intellectual equal of his brother and, influenced by liberals such as Benjamin Constant and Germaine de Staël, often argued with him.

Lucien had returned from his posting as ambassador in Madrid vastly enriched, having won the favours of the queen of Spain and exacted bribes at every step in the negotiation of treaties with Spain and Portugal—along with twenty paintings from the Retiro collections (to add to his already impressive 300, including works by Rembrandt, Raphael, Michelangelo, Poussin, Caracci, Rubens, Titian, and da Vinci), a sack of diamonds, and a large quantity of cash (a portion of which he invested in London)—and he brought back a Spanish marqueza whom he installed in his Paris mansion and the château at Le Plessis he now acquired. Unlike Joseph's, his house parties there were anything but sophisticated, with childish games being played and guests subjected to apple-pie beds and itching powder. That did not stop him taking a high tone with Bonaparte, denouncing him as a tyrant and encouraging others in opposition to him.[12]

The tyrant still governed through institutions, and these were made up of people with ideas of their own. His inability to see things from the perspective of others meant that he could not discuss or persuade, only dismiss their views as 'metaphysical nonsense' and see criticism as opposition. In his view, expressed in a discussion of the plays of Corneille, the public good, which he described as 'the reason of State', was a higher aim which not only justified but demanded behaviour which in any other circumstance might be criminal. Corneille had understood this, and were he alive, Bonaparte declared, he would make him his first minister. Convinced of the rightness of the mission he had embarked on, and intolerant of those who could not see it, he was not inclined to waste time trying to persuade them.[13]

This came as a shock to early supporters such as Germaine de Staël, who had expected her salon to become the ideological powerhouse of the new regime. She had encouraged Benjamin Constant to provide constructive opposition on the English model in the Tribunate, but his criticism of the legislation presented to it enraged Bonaparte, who pointed out that since none of those sitting in the various assemblies had been elected they had no legitimacy, while he, whose assumption of power had been endorsed by the plebiscite on the constitution, was the elect of the nation. When Joseph tried to patch things up between him and the inconvenient bluestocking, Bonaparte merely told him to ask her what her price was for submitting. 'I do not know how to show benevolence to my enemies,' he snapped at Talleyrand when he suggested a more emollient approach. 'Weakness has never led anywhere. One can only govern with strength.'[14]

To Lafayette, he said that the people were 'fed up' with liberty. He had a point—the ideologues chattering away in their assemblies and salons were out of touch with the majority of the population. This was glaringly obvious when it came to Bonaparte's intention of reinstating the Catholic Church. The ideologues saw it as a betrayal of the Revolution, which had banished religious 'prejudice' and all the flummery that went with it. They tried to persuade him to abandon the idea, but he was adamant; when Volney tried to change his mind, their exchange flared into an argument in the course of which Bonaparte allegedly kicked the eminent philosophe.[15]

Talleyrand's negotiations with Spina were not going well. The principal stumbling blocks were the Pope's insistence that Catholicism be declared the religion of state, the return of or compensation for confiscated Church property, and the resignation of all existing bishops. To these he added a demand for the return of the province of the Legations. Bonaparte's response was to bully Spina, flying into one of his feigned rages, threatening to occupy the entirety of the Papal States, to found a national church in France, and even to become a Protestant if he did not sign an agreement within five days.[16]

The Pope replaced Spina with the more intelligent and skilful Cardinal Ercole Consalvi. Bonaparte welcomed him with great pomp at an audience for which he encouraged him to wear 'the most cardinalesque costume possible', but began bullying him too, setting an unreal ultimatum of five days. After much horse-trading, agreement was reached, and the Concordat (as it was named, after a twelfth-century precedent) was to be signed on 13 July 1801. At the last minute the Abbé Bernier warned Consalvi that Bonaparte had made some alterations, and the text he would be presented with was not the one agreed. When Consalvi declined to put his signature to it, a furious Bonaparte dictated yet another version, which Consalvi also rejected. Bonaparte threatened to act like Henry VIII of England, but he had met his match in Consalvi, who was not to be bullied. The Concordat was eventually signed at midnight on 15 July.[17]

Catholicism was recognised as the religion of the majority of the French. A new network of dioceses was created. The first consul would choose the bishops, who would then be invested by the Pope. Church property would not be returned, but the French state would pay for the upkeep of churches and salaries to priests, who would swear an oath of loyalty, effectively becoming its functionaries.

The Council of State voiced reservations about the agreement, and there was vociferous opposition in the Tribunate, the Legislative Body, and the Senate, which demonstratively coopted the former Abbé Grégoire, a revolutionary firebrand who denounced it. Reactions in the army were even more violent. Ever the opportunist, Bonaparte exploited the uproar to pressure Rome into accepting a number of changes, couched in 'organic articles' which altered the nature of the agreement in his favour.

As the opening of the second session of the assemblies approached in the autumn of 1801, it became clear that malcontents of every hue were preparing to unite in opposition to Bonaparte's increasingly autocratic rule. They were outraged that in a treaty with Russia the word 'subject' had featured with respect to French citizens and were determined to reject the Concordat. More distressing for Bonaparte was the Tribunate's critical reception of the projected Civil Code, which was close to his heart. To hear it picked apart piece by piece and criticised for being too old-fashioned and a betrayal of the Revolution was more than he could stand. He raged at the 'dogs' who had led the attack, likening them to lice infesting his clothes, and contemplated sending troops into the assembly. 'Let nobody think I will let myself be treated like Louis XVI,' he warned. 'I am a soldier, a son of the Revolution, and I will not tolerate being insulted like a king.'[18]

Cambacérès persuaded him to avoid confrontation and allow the Legislative Body to reject the Code; he had thought of a way round the problem, which Bonaparte adopted. On 2 January 1802 he declared that he was withdrawing all projects, which effectively closed the session of the assemblies, since they had nothing to do. On the same day he went to the Senate and berated its members, particularly Sieyès, whom he accused of trying to turn him into the ineffectual 'Great Elector' of his dreams. Bonaparte was a hard man to stand up to in a situation such as this, and they obediently coopted a number of his supporters, giving him a majority.

The following day he attended the marriage of Louis to Hortense. They had both resisted the match vigorously, but had been forced into it by Bonaparte and Josephine, who had set their minds on it, each for reasons of their own: he because he saw Louis as his possible successor, or the one who would sire his successor, she because it should guarantee her position against the onslaughts of the Bonaparte clan. Neither realised how psychologically damaged Louis was, and that this would lead to problems in time. Bonaparte had little time for reflection, and at midnight on 8 January he left for Lyon, where he had serious business to attend to.

After its resurrection following Marengo, the Cisalpine Republic, enlarged by the Treaty of Lunéville with the addition of the Legations and Parma, had been administered on the French model by a provisional government under Francesco Melzi d'Eril. He nurtured hopes of eventually extending it to embrace all of northern Italy and turning it into a strong buffer state between France and Austria, possibly ruled by either Bonaparte's brother Joseph or a Spanish Bourbon. But in the first instance he had to go to Lyon, along with 491 deputies, in order to have the constitution he had drawn up endorsed by Bonaparte and, he hoped, the republic's name changed from Cisalpine to Italian.

The deputies, many of whom had brought their wives and families, had a terrible time getting to Lyon. They crossed the Alps in blizzards, were holed up for long periods in poky inns and cottages—princes, bishops, and generals cheek-by-jowl with merchants and servants, all forced to eat the same meagre rations. One died along the way. They had finally reached Lyon on 11 December 1801, but their discomfort did not cease. Prince Serbelloni had brought his own cook, but most of them had to make do with local fare, which they found revolting, and nothing could lift the gloom of the winter mists as they waited for Bonaparte to arrive.

He was preceded, on 28 December, by Talleyrand. The deputies assumed they would at last be able to take their seats in the former Jesuit college church which had been turned into an amphitheatre of green leather chairs. They were disappointed. The last thing Bonaparte wanted was an assembly. He had instructed Talleyrand to divide the deputies up into five groups which were to discuss the proposed constitution separately. Talleyrand and Murat, who as commander of French forces in Italy was also present, circulated among the deputies, softening them up with a mixture of emollience and menace that made one of them think of the reign of Tiberius.[19]

Bonaparte arrived on the evening of 11 January 1802. He was met outside the city by an honour guard of young Lyonnais gentlemen accoutred in splendid pale-blue uniforms and plumed headgear of their own invention. As he approached the city he was greeted by artillery salvoes and the cheers of troops lining the streets. Despite the intense cold (the river Saône was freezing over) and the falling snow, a dense crowd waited to catch a glimpse of him sitting beside Josephine in his carriage.

The Italian deputies waited patiently to be convoked. There were two banquets and two balls, graced by Josephine and rushed through by Bonaparte, and on 20 January they finally took their seats in plenary session. But their hopes of a hearing by the first consul were dashed. Talleyrand appeared, to announce that Bonaparte wished them to select thirty of their number whom they considered worthy of a place in the future government.

When the thirty had been chosen by ballot, they were instructed to meet in two days' time, on 22 January, to elect a president of the Cisalpine Republic. Bonaparte had originally wanted Joseph to fill the post, but Joseph thought it beneath his dignity and realised that he would only be a placeman, so he refused. Bonaparte would not countenance any possibility of the new state drifting beyond his control, so he would have to fill the post himself.

When the votes of the thirty deputies were counted, three were blank, one was for Bonaparte, one for another Italian, and twenty-five for Melzi. Having been informed by Talleyrand that the first consul wanted the post for himself, Melzi declined it. A second vote produced another Italian, who also knew what was good for him, and the third an obscure Milanese deputy who was absent and could therefore not refuse. As they filed off to announce their choice to Bonaparte, who had already been informed, Talleyrand warned them that he was in an evil mood, like a lion with a fever. There are three versions of what happened. According to one, he refused to receive them, another has it that he would not address a word to them, a third that he threw a stool at them.[20]

Talleyrand explained that they must try harder, and after two days of agonising, they agreed. On 25 January they recommended to the assembly that it elect Bonaparte. There was predictable uproar and speeches by patriots demanding an Italian president. A vote was taken by asking the deputies to stand, and although some witnesses recorded that only a third did rise, according to the official record Napoleon Bonaparte was chosen by universal acclamation.[21]

The following day at one o'clock he entered the church in which the deputies were assembled, followed by Talleyrand, Murat, and the interior minister Chaptal. A podium had been erected for him, decorated with bronzes and bas-reliefs representing the Tiber and the Nile, surmounted by a canopy depicting a cloudless sky. He eschewed this for the humbler president's chair and addressed the assembly in his poor Italian. He told them that since the nascent state needed a strong hand and a wise head, and there was none among them with the requisite qualities, he graciously accepted their offer of the presidency. He was not put off by the barely polite applause and proceeded to present the new constitution. 'Let the constitution of the...' he began, and paused. Various patriots shouted 'Italian Republic!' With a wink to Talleyrand, Bonaparte smiled at the assembly and said, 'Very well, the Italian Republic!' The applause was deafening. The constitution was then read out, and Bonaparte nominated Melzi vice-president.[22]

The following day he reviewed the troops that had returned from Egypt and then left Lyon. He was back in Paris on 31 January and resumed his work on emasculating the legislative bodies.

As the Tribunate and the Legislative replaced one-fifth of their members at the end of every session, twenty tribunes and sixty legislators now had to be appointed. Instead of allowing the assemblies to choose who went and who came in, as the constitution specified, Bonaparte contrived to make the Senate intervene and decide for them. As a result, in the spring of 1802 the most cantankerous members of both assemblies would be replaced by men prepared to do Bonaparte's bidding. For good measure, Lucien, who despite his tendency to make trouble could be counted on to toe the line when necessary, was put back in the Tribunate to ensure its docility. In March, Bonaparte crowned his dominance with a triumph that silenced his critics.

24

The Liberator of Europe

PEACE WITH BRITAIN was signed at Amiens on 25 March 1802. The next day Joseph raced to Paris with the document, which he brandished as he entered his brother's box at the Opéra that evening. The performance was interrupted and Bonaparte presented his brother to the cheering audience as the able negotiator. He nevertheless took the credit when commissioning an allegorical painting depicting him leading Gaul and Britannia to cast their weapons into the flames. It was a triumph: when, exactly three months later, a new treaty was signed with the Porte, France was, for the first time in ten years, not at war with anyone. As a sign of the new era, Bonaparte appeared in civilian dress at the diplomatic reception on 27 March to formally announce the peace.

The terms of the treaty were that George III renounced his title of 'King of France', used by his predecessors since the Hundred Years War, and undertook to return all French colonies and those of her allies except for Ceylon (formerly Dutch) and Trinidad (formerly Spanish). France accepted the return of Egypt to the Porte and the Papal States to the Pope and recognised the independence of the Ionian islands. Malta was to be returned to the Order of St John and placed under the protection of Naples. France was to evacuate the Neapolitan ports, opening them to British shipping once more. What were considered minor points were left for subsequent agreement, including compensation for the dispossessed rulers of Piedmont and the Netherlands, the question of which side should pay for the upkeep of prisoners of war, and the signature of a trade treaty.

Once the preliminaries had been signed, mail coaches had carried the news 'Peace with France' chalked on their sides; they were greeted with rejoicing all over the country amid shouts of 'Huzzah for Buonaparte!' When General Lauriston arrived in London bearing the ratification, the horses were unharnessed from his carriage and it was pulled through the streets. The British press heaped praise on Bonaparte as the restorer of peace, and one Member of Parliament hailed him as 'the Great Man of the People of France, the Liberator of Europe'. Prints and busts of him sold like hot cakes.[1]

The euphoria could not last; the treaty had been a rushed job which would have required a remarkable degree of compromise and cooperation to implement properly, and both were in short supply. British mistrust of the French was embedded in the national psyche, while Bonaparte's attitude to the British had been radically altered by their hand in the assassination of Paul I and the attempts on his own life, which he saw as evidence of a disgraceful disregard of conventions governing international relations and typical of *perfide Albion*. Peace, however fragile, was nevertheless welcome. He still had much to do to rebuild France.

Ten days after the signature of the treaty, on 5 April 1802, the new session of the assemblies opened. Having lost its most vocal members, the Tribunate was further emasculated by a new measure proposed by Lucien: that instead of meeting in plenary sessions, it should henceforth divide into three sections which would deliberate separately. The measure was adopted, and Lucien took the chair in that designated to deal with the Concordat, which was passed on 8 April.

Easter Sunday, which fell ten days later, was chosen to proclaim the Treaty of Amiens and the Concordat. The twin achievements were to be celebrated by a pontifical high mass in the cathedral of Notre Dame, an occasion rich in allusion, irony, and farce. That morning the people of Paris could for the first time in ten years hear the tolling of the great bell of Notre Dame as well as the artillery salutes they had grown used to. The sermon would be delivered by Monsignor de Boisgelin, Archbishop of Tours, who had officiated at the funeral of Louis XV and the coronation of his successor.

The festivities opened with a parade at which Bonaparte presented newly created units with their standards. Then, dressed in their scarlet uniform, the three consuls drove to the cathedral escorted by a squadron of the newly formed 'Mamelukes', composed of exotically uniformed veterans of the Egyptian campaign. They were followed by the diplomatic corps, and then the senior functionaries, members of the assemblies, notables, court officials, and their ladies. The cathedral was crammed with clergy. An orchestra and choir conducted by Cherubini and Méhul lent solemnity as Bonaparte took his place, with the two consuls flanking him and Fouché and Talleyrand behind. It had been agreed that while he would go through all the motions as a good Catholic should, he would not, as had been the royal custom, kiss the paten. 'Don't force me to make a fool of myself,' he had snapped when the matter had been discussed.[2]

The element of farce entered the proceedings soon after, as Josephine arrived only to find her seat occupied by Madame Moreau (her husband showed his independence and contempt by refusing to attend, spending the morning sauntering around the gardens of the Tuileries puffing on a cigar). Things degenerated further when a number of generals and senior officers made their entry. They were almost to a man fiercely irreligious and furious at having been ordered to come. They swaggered in, chatting among themselves, shoving aside any priest who obstructed their passage. Finding all the seats taken, Masséna ousted a prelate from his chair with a 'Go fuck yourself!' His comrades followed suit and began cracking jokes and were only silenced by a glare from the first consul.[3]

Several generals angrily accused Bonaparte of betraying all those who had laid down their lives in the cause of the Revolution and its rejection of 'superstition'. He ignored them. Two days later he reconverted his bathroom in the Tuileries, which had been the private chapel of Marie de Médicis, and henceforth he would attend mass every Sunday and command his court to do the same. He dutifully went through the motions but did not take communion, since, as he explained, he 'was not enough of a believer for it to be of any benefit, and yet too much of one to wish to coldly commit sacrilege'.[4]

Many, particularly the soldiers, hated having to attend and would stand around chatting in the next room. 'These masses were little more than a travesty,' according to Thibaudeau. 'They could hardly have been more worldly, with the actresses of the opera singing the praises of God.' Some of the ladies nibbled chocolates as they listened. But Bonaparte had judged well, as a concurrent religious revival confirmed. Charitable and proselytising congregations sprang up around the country, and Chateaubriand's *Génie du Christianisme*, published that year, became an instant best-seller. If the Concordat caused indignation in the liberal salons, it was well received in the country at large.[5]

The measure would take much effort to implement, there would be acrimonious disputes over appointments of bishops, over property and money, and many ruffled feathers would have to be smoothed. But Bonaparte had pulled off a masterstroke. He had not only satisfied the rural population's attachment to the faith, thereby assuaging its resentment of the state and the government, he had also kicked away one of the principal supports of the Bourbon cause, as a return of the monarchy had until now seemed to be the only way of restoring the Church. Louis XVIII was quick to see the threat and protested vigorously to 'the criminal pope', as his brother Artois called Pius VII. Summing up, Archbishop Boisgelin declared that the consular regime was 'the legitimate government, both national and Catholic, and without it we would have neither the Faith nor the Fatherland'. More important as far as Bonaparte was concerned, he had achieved what Louis XIV had struggled in vain to do, namely to subject the Church entirely to the state. And to himself: his half-uncle and former archdeacon of Ajaccio Joseph Fesch became Cardinal Archbishop of Lyon and primate of the Church in France.[6]

A week after the ceremony, Bonaparte pulled another strut from under the Bourbon cause. He declared an amnesty for all émigrés bar about a thousand of the actively hostile (whom he wanted to see 'exterminated'), provided they returned to France by 23 September, the end of the year in the revolutionary calendar. Those whose property had not been sold would get it back. This measure too angered many, but Bonaparte paid little heed; it brought tens of thousands of educated and capable Frenchmen who loved their country back to serve it. Among them was his old friend Alexandre des Mazis, who came to see him and was warmly received. Napoleon gave him the position of chamberlain, which would provide him with an income. Assuming his friend to be penniless and knowing him to be too proud to accept charity, he sent an officer after him with a letter of credit for a large sum, saying it was something he must have left behind by mistake. Bonaparte did not stop at émigré nobles and explored the possibility of the return of Paoli. He also issued a proclamation inviting all the artisans and skilled workers who had emigrated to return; he aimed to bring all Frenchmen together in a new nation, the basis for the functional modern state he envisaged.[7]

One of the articles of faith of the Revolution had been the need to wrench education away from the Church and to create a new secular, rational man. Religious establishments had been closed down and education for all decreed, but, left to individual communes, this vision had failed to materialise. All children did benefit from some level of primary education, but little was available at secondary level. On 12 March 1802 Bonaparte set up a directorate within the Ministry of the Interior, with Roederer in charge. 'Public education can and must be a very powerful motor in our political system,' he instructed him. 'It is by this means that the legislator will be able to revive a national spirit. The department of public education is nothing less than the direction of minds by intelligence.'[8]

On 1 May 1802 a new law came into force, establishing 23,000 primary schools for children between the ages of seven and eleven to be administered by the communes. The communes could also open secondary schools, and private institutions were permitted if licensed by the local prefect. But the backbone of the new system were the forty-five *lycées* which were to teach the classics, rhetoric, logic, morality, and the elements of mathematics and physics. Although their pupils wore uniforms, underwent some military training, and answered to the sound of the drum rather than the bell, they were not strict and there was no corporal punishment—which Bonaparte strongly opposed. They were intended to turn out young men with the same morality and the same sense of service to society and the state—a new class of functionaries and soldiers beholden to it. Bonaparte maintained that this was the only way to instil a unity of purpose similar to that he imagined had existed in ancient Athens and Sparta; as Roederer frankly admitted, the new system was 'a political institution'.[9]

The seeds of another profoundly political institution were sown on 19 May, with the announcement of the creation of a 'legion of honour', a body of men, both military and civilian, who had distinguished themselves in the service of the state. It was to be made up of fifteen 'cohorts' of 250 each, but there were to be no insignia or other outward distinctions—among the first things to be thrown on the bonfire of vanities in the first stage of the Revolution had been the crosses and sashes of the royal orders of chivalry. Even so, the announcement aroused the ire of republicans, who denounced it as an assault on the principle of equality. They could hardly have imagined what was to come.

'People think me ambitious,' Bonaparte exclaimed one evening at the Tuileries. 'Ambitious!—for what? Ambitious, me? Listen to me, gentlemen, what I am about to say I authorise you to repeat. In three years, I shall retire from public affairs. I will have an income of fifty thousand livres, and with my tastes that is more than I need. I will have a country estate, because Madame Bonaparte likes the country.' He added that he would also like to be a justice of the peace. Whether or how much he meant it one cannot say, but he would not relinquish power before he had finished building his political edifice, and in order to do that, he believed he had to reinforce his position.[10]

Since the Brumaire coup, Berthier had been methodically purging the army of Jacobin officers and those hostile to Bonaparte—in the course of two years he had retired 72 colonels, 150 majors, and thousands of junior officers. But the army had preserved its revolutionary ethos, and Bonaparte was still not popular in those units he had not commanded himself. The Concordat and the amnesty for émigrés had revived residual hostility to him, and those generals who envied his rise to power sensed a new opportunity. Moreau, Brune, Masséna, Augereau, Gouvion Saint-Cyr, and Lecourbe were among many who felt varying degrees of outrage at the way things were going. Bonaparte either undercut them, as when he dissolved the Army of Batavia, thereby denying Augereau his command, or he sent them on distant missions: Gouvion to Madrid, Brune to Constantinople, others to the colonies where they could do no harm. That did not put a stop to the grumbling.[11]

From Italy, Murat reported revolutionary sentiment and shouts of '*Vive Robespierre!*' On 14 July troops stationed at Bologna refused to toast Bonaparte. At a dinner given by Moreau in June 1802, a chef de brigade felt he could spew out his hatred of the first consul in company which included Marmont and Berthier. Similar feelings were reflected in a number of conspiracies over the summer and early autumn of that year. One, connected to General Oudinot, never got off the ground. Another, more serious as it meant to assassinate rather than just depose the first consul, which a Captain Donnadieu vowed to do, was unusual in that it involved mostly non-commissioned and junior officers. But most of the plots, like an inept one involving Bernadotte, commander of the Army of the West, had more to do with the hurt pride of Bonaparte's former comrades than any serious purpose. 'As there is not one of them who does not believe himself to be his equal and to possess the same title as him to the first place,' reported Louis XVIII's agent in Paris, Antoine Royer-Collard, 'so there is not one of them who does not see his elevation as a wrong done to himself personally.'[12]

These plots were easily uncovered by Fouché's police and did not present a serious threat, but they did testify to a lingering sense of uncertainty as to the durability of the consular regime. Bonaparte felt he could not, for family reasons, make an example of Bernadotte by punishing him. Fouché advised against it, on the grounds that it was impolitic for the public to know that there was dissension at the heart of his entourage. Bernadotte was offered a command in Louisiana and an embassy to the United States, both of which he refused. The best Bonaparte could do was to gradually marginalise him. He was also growing wary of Fouché, whom he suspected of shielding his former Jacobin comrade. In September 1802 he abolished the Ministry of Police and gave Fouché a seat in the Senate. His former duties were split up and transferred to the Ministries of Justice and the Interior.[13]

The permanence of the new regime concerned not only Bonaparte. Cambacérès and Lebrun, Talleyrand, Roederer, and for reasons of their own, his brothers Joseph and Lucien had for some time been canvassing for a formal upgrade in Bonaparte's status, and many others had become resigned to what appeared to be inevitable. 'Power was encroaching with large strides behind the words *order* and *stability*,' as Thibaudeau put it. By the end of March 1802 a majority in the Tribunate had accepted the need to extend the first consul's tenure by another ten years.[14]

Among the opponents of this was Josephine, who understood that a man who rises to eminence and amasses an inheritance will sooner or later want an heir—the one thing she could not give him. With every step along a path that was beginning to look as though it would lead to a throne, her position grew more precarious. Bonaparte's family had been urging him to divorce her for years, and their case was growing stronger. She found an ally in Fouché, whose Jacobin instincts were reinforced by his recent loss of power and his hatred of Bonaparte's brothers. In an effort to deflect the Tribunate's expression of gratitude from extending Bonaparte's power, he proposed the erection of a monument. Others suggested a triumphal arch and the renaming of squares. Humble as ever, Bonaparte refused such honours. He showed the same modesty when a delegation of the Tribunate brought him the offer of an extension of his office for another ten years as a token of the gratitude of the French nation; he refused, saying that the love of the people was sufficient reward.

He nevertheless let his displeasure be known; he wanted an extension not for ten years but for life. Pretending to take his feigned modesty at face value, Fouché, Sieyès, Grégoire, and others persuaded the Senate to pass a *senatus-consulte* on 8 May extending his post for another ten years. The following day an irritated Bonaparte graciously thanked the Senate for its trust, but observed that as he had been invested with power by the will of the people, given voice in the plebiscite of February 1800, he would only accept its prolongation by a similar plebiscite. Outmanoeuvred, the Senate could only express its admiration for his reticence and respect for the will of the people. Bonaparte then left for Malmaison.[15]

The following day, 10 May, at an extraordinary session which Bonaparte demurely refrained from attending, the Council of State under the guidance of Cambacérès agreed that a plebiscite should be held, and since the will of the people could hardly be circumscribed by the imposition of a time limit, that the question to be put must be: 'Should Napoleon Bonaparte be consul for life?' Significantly, this was the first time his first name appeared in an official public document. Lucien (who saw himself as such) added a second question to be put to the nation: 'Should he have the right to designate his successor?'[16]

When the project was communicated to Bonaparte, he struck out the second question. 'The testament of Louis XIV was not respected, so why should mine be?' he said to Cambacérès. 'A dead man has nothing to say.' Only hereditary succession was possible, he asserted. What he did not say but probably anticipated was that while the answer to the first question was bound to be a resounding 'yes', the second would provoke debate in every village.[17]

Josephine spent most of June taking the waters at Plombières in a desperate effort to enhance her fertility. 'I am all sorrow, my dear Hortense: I am parted from you and my heart as well as my whole being suffer from it,' she wrote to her daughter on 19 June. 'I feel that I was not created for so much grandeur, my child....' In her absence, Hortense acted as lady of the house at Malmaison, where Bonaparte spent most of that summer, with occasional visits to Paris to preside over the Council of State. She was heavily pregnant, but Louis was not with her. He had become obsessed with his health and developed a number of neuroses which contributed to a complete estrangement from his wife. Combined with Bonaparte's evident affection for Hortense, this provided malicious tongues with material for gossip that Bonaparte was her lover and the father of her child.[18]

Bonaparte did philander, giving Josephine grounds not so much for jealousy as for anxiety, but not with her daughter. He wrote affectionately to Josephine, asking about her health, what she was doing and whom she was seeing (whenever she travelled without him, he would dictate a strict schedule which included travel arrangements, where she could stay, or even pause, and whom she could meet). He also sent news of what he was doing, telling her he had wounded his finger while shooting a boar at Marly, and reporting on a performance of *The Barber of Seville*, with Hortense playing Rosina, and Lauriston, Bourrienne, Eugène, and Savary among the other actors. He missed her and wrote that her forthcoming return 'will make the little man who is bored all on his own very happy', adding, 'It's all very sad here without you.'[19]

On 3 August he was at the Tuileries to receive a delegation of senators who called to present the results of the plebiscite. There had been 3,568,885 'yes' votes and only 8,374 against, with a turnout of close to 60 percent, which was a triumph considering that the three plebiscites held during the Revolution had never produced a turnout higher than 34 percent, and in one case below 20. Unlike in 1800, there is no real evidence of manipulation.[20]

There was much disapproval among liberals and ideologues. Lafayette, who had voiced his protest in the Senate, wrote to Bonaparte saying that while his 'restorative dictatorship' had yielded great benefits, a greater good now would be the restoration of liberty, and that he could not believe Bonaparte really wished to see the return of an arbitrary regime. Plenty of others voiced their fears of the encroaching tyranny, and even old comrades such as Junot felt they could no longer say what they thought, aware as they were of the tightening security net around Bonaparte—he was naturally suspicious, and his experiences had taught him to trust nobody, so he had everyone watched, even those closest to him.[21]

He had built up an extensive intelligence network stretching far wider and deeper than the ostensible ones: Fouché's efficient police, Réal's Paris police, Duroc's palace security network, Savary's Gendarmerie d'élite which supervised the army, and the Gendarmerie itself, a nationwide paramilitary police which not only maintained order but also reported on the political mood in every department. Bonaparte could also rely on the confidential reports of the prefects, and he had a web of correspondents, individuals scattered across the country who wrote to him directly, often anonymously (only he knew who they were), telling him what was being said in the provinces about what he did in Paris.

His increasing workload required an expansion of his secretariat. Bourrienne had not been able to resist exploiting his proximity to the first consul in blatant ways, and in the autumn of 1802 he had gone too far; fearing his venality would reflect on his own person, Bonaparte dismissed him. He was replaced by the mild-mannered twenty-four-year-old Claude-François Méneval, formerly a secretary to Joseph, who was presented to Bonaparte one evening and after a short conversation was instructed to come back at seven the following morning. When he did, he was told to sit down and start taking dictation. He was given quarters in the Tuileries and appointed as one of Bonaparte's aides de camp, but he never wore any kind of uniform, and many in the first consul's entourage never knew he existed, as he was rarely seen outside his private study. With time, he was joined by Agathon Fain and three others to deal with specific areas, but Méneval remained Bonaparte's right hand and constant companion, woken at all hours of the night to take dictation.

'The government is that of a military despotism, in most respects wisely, but not mildly administered,' was how Cornwallis described the governance of France. He was wrong. Bonaparte did not rule through the army, but through theoretically democratic institutions. Although he did manipulate them shamelessly, he had no intention of abolishing them. He meant rather to turn them into facilitators of his rule and preservers of his political edifice, by filling them with people dedicated to the good of France, as he saw it, and making them more pliable.[22]

The Directory had curtailed the unbridled democracy introduced by the Revolution, restricting the vote to property owners, but while this had introduced an element of stability, it had created the conditions for an unprincipled struggle for power and wealth which did little for the public good. The Constitution of Year III, inspired by Sieyès and edited by Bonaparte, had created something more efficient only in that it gave him the power to act decisively. What he now wanted was to create a class of people who would by instinct and interest work for the public good through the existing institutions. As they were nominated, not elected, they were not in a position to build an opposition by claiming to represent the people; they were to be a managerial class.

Bonaparte had been fostering the emergence of this governing caste from the moment he came to power. Although property was the fundamental qualification, his experience of the 'scoundrels' who had followed his army in Italy left him ambivalent about the rich. 'One cannot treat wealth as a title of nobility,' he said in the Council of State. 'A rich man is often a layabout without merit. A rich merchant is often so only by virtue of the art of selling expensively or stealing.' He wanted people whose wealth derived from honest service to the state, military as well as civil, and encouraged Freemasonry, which he saw as an instrument of civic formation. He aimed to fuse this new hierarchy with the old aristocracy by encouraging intermarriage. His growing court, to which he attracted members of the old aristocracy and returning émigrés, provided the framework for mixing them with his predominantly low-born military entourage. He introduced the court ceremonial that had existed before 1789, and for similar reasons insisted on attaching four *dames du palais*, drawn from the highest aristocracy, to Josephine. He encouraged young noblemen to join the army, frequently promoting them and giving them posts as aides. He would not have been human if he had not relished having young men with names redolent of the Crusades trotting along in his suite, but vanity was not the primary motive. Yet his desire to achieve social and political 'fusion' was ineluctably beginning to affect his own status.[23]

His nomination as consul for life demanded changes to the constitution, and he wasted no time in preparing a new one, which came into force on 5 August. 'A constitution should be fashioned in such a manner that it will not hinder the actions of the government, and will not oblige it to violate it,' he argued. 'Every day one is obliged to violate positive laws; one cannot do otherwise, or it would be impossible to proceed. [...] The government should not be tyrannical [...]; but it is impossible for it not to carry out some arbitrary actions.'[24]

The new constitution replaced Sieyès's pyramid democracy with an even more theoretical version of universal suffrage, since it was dominated by local electoral colleges of notables, which put forward candidates for the assemblies and other offices for the first consul to choose from. Even the justices of the peace were now nominated by him. The Tribunate was cut down by half, the Legislative Body shackled by procedural changes, while the Senate was expanded. The first consul chose five-eighths of its members and presided over it himself, which meant he could legislate by means of *senatus-consultes*. Both the Senate and the Council of State had become little more than administrative tools. He could make and break treaties without consultation or need for ratification by the chambers. He had arrogated the right to nominate his successor and the traditional prerogative of kings, the right of pardon, abolished in 1791.

Bonaparte's thirty-third birthday on 15 August was celebrated with royal pomp. In the morning the members of the assemblies came to the Tuileries with their congratulations, followed by the diplomatic corps. They were entertained with a concert by 300 musicians, after which all drove to Notre Dame for a *Te Deum*. Bonaparte then retired to Malmaison, where the evening ended with amateur theatricals and dancing while Paris was regaled with illuminations and fireworks.

On 21 August he drove alone in a coach drawn by eight horses (another royal attribute) to the Luxembourg to swear in the senators. The route was lined by a double rank of soldiers. He was escorted by a glittering group of aides and generals and followed by six carriages bearing his fellow consuls and the ministers. As his coach trundled into the courtyard it was greeted at the foot of the stairs by ten senators who conducted him to his seat, which resembled nothing less than a throne. In their reports, the Russian and Prussian ambassadors both remarked that there was but one more step left for him to take—to monarchy.[25]

The next step may not have taken him to Versailles, as Sieyès had once suggested, but Malmaison was a little far from Paris, and too small to be anything but a place for relaxation in intimate company. The road was difficult to police, and there had been more than one plot to abduct or assassinate Bonaparte between there and Paris. Yet he craved fresh air and felt constricted in the Tuileries. The solution was to provide him with an official residence in the palace of Saint-Cloud. The original idea had been to give him the palace and rename it Marengo, following the example of Blenheim in England, but he had rejected it as ridiculous. He moved into the palace on 20 September, and six days later, on Sunday, 26 September, the first court mass was held in the chapel, Bonaparte making his entrance with what was supposed to be the debonair gait affected by the later Bourbons, surrounded by courtiers, many of them regicides, who had frequently sworn to strike down any who reached for supreme authority.[26]

Bonaparte understood that ordinary people liked the idea of a head of state, the more exceptional and grander the better, and both he and those close to him had begun to see the new regime as inseparable from his person. That person must therefore be made dear to the people. At the end of October he set off with Josephine on a two-week progress through Normandy, meeting local authorities, functionaries, and notables; inspecting the National Guard and military garrisons; visiting factories, hospitals, and schools; reviewing building works; and planning infrastructure projects.

They travelled in only two carriages, attended by a small entourage, but one 'service' preceded them by twelve hours and another followed them with the same time lapse. Each consisted of a full, if reduced, replica of the establishment at the Tuileries which took care of all their needs. By the time they reached a given place, the accommodation provided had been adapted to their requirements, clothes were laid out, food was ready, a bath was waiting, and, most important, an office was ready, with papers, files, and a travelling library, so Bonaparte could get down to work immediately. As soon as he arrived, he would call in the local authorities and question them on the needs of the locality and their plans and often mount up immediately to ride out and see for himself.

He hated having to attend the accompanying receptions, and wanted to get them over with as quickly as possible, but realised their value. He instructed Josephine to wear all the jewellery she could physically display and to behave like a queen—she needed little prompting. Wherever they went they were mobbed by the people, who often travelled long distances to see them and would stand under his windows half the night waiting for him to show himself. 'The people do not know what to call him,' Josephine wrote to Joseph from Rouen. 'Some call him the pacification of the world, others the father of the people, one man came forward and said: "After God, it's you!" Another told him: "My soul belongs to God but my heart to You!"' He would soon belong to them in more traditional mode: on 12 March 1803, accompanied by Josephine, he went to the Paris mint to watch the first coins being struck with his effigy.[27]

The advent of peace had opened frontiers, and people from all over Europe came to Paris. The French capital had always attracted visitors avid for fashion and culture, and it was now made more enticing still by the frisson of seeing the battleground of the Revolution and the hero or ogre, depending on viewpoint, who had tamed it. The majority were British. They had been starved for a decade of the opportunity of making a Grand Tour, and an estimated 20,000 of them passed through Paris, some going on to Italy or Switzerland, but all stopping long enough to at least catch sight of the man of the moment. They included no fewer than eighty-one Members of Parliament who came to see how his new political system functioned, among them Charles James Fox. Scientists eager to assess the achievements in the field of building, engineering, and physics were able to visit an exhibition of French industry at the Louvre. Many noted artists, including Maria Cosway, Flaxman, Fuseli, Hoppner, Turner, and West came to see the museum in the Louvre, which provided them with a unique opportunity to study and copy the works of the masters. Few travelled the other way, from France to Britain, notable exceptions being the sculptor in wax Marie Tussaud and the portrait painter Elisabeth Vigée-Lebrun.

Bonaparte ordered Fontaine to ransack the royal furniture stores to fit out the Tuileries in splendour, as he was determined to show the visiting British that France was not bankrupt. He ordered him to clear the area around the palace and to place the horses of St Mark's on the pillars of the gates in front of it. He also had all the remaining liberty trees planted during the Revolution cut down. Foreign visitors were welcome in his apartments following his regular parades, and he encouraged his generals and ministers to give balls and entertainments for them.

The Russian Elizaveta Petrovna Divova thought Paris 'an earthly paradise', and found everything about Bonaparte and his court enchanting. The Polish Wiridianna Fiszerowa thought the court 'striking by its lack of manners and dignity'. Another Polish aristocrat remarked that the servants did not seem to know what they were supposed to be doing. Mary Berry was overwhelmed by the luxury of the first consul's apartments, which she thought surpassed Versailles and Trianon.[28]

Everyone who left accounts found Josephine charming and the atmosphere in her apartments and at her receptions 'very fine and princely', as one Englishman put it. Reactions to her husband were more varied. Divova found him 'amiable, charming, kind, honest, polite'; Maria Edgeworth was less complimentary about his 'pale woebegone countenance', and thought him 'very little'; the eccentric Bertie Greathead was disappointed to find him not as 'melancholy' and 'not so picturesque' as he had imagined, adding that 'his person is not only little, but I think, mean'. The landscape painter Joseph Farington noted, 'He picked his nose very much.' Fiszerowa thought he looked ill at ease, and noticed that 'When he spoke with the ministers of foreign courts, he twisted the buttons of his coat like a schoolboy.' Fanny Burney was transported by his face, in which 'care, thought, melancholy, and meditation are strongly marked, with so much of character, nay, genius, and so penetrating a seriousness, or rather sadness, as powerfully to sink into the observer's mind'.[29]

'The nations admire you. France, made greater by your victories, has placed her hope in you,' wrote Chateaubriand in the dedication to the second edition of *Génie du Christianisme*, which came out in May 1803. 'One cannot help but recognise in your destiny the hand of the Providence which has marked you out a long time ago for the fulfilment of its prodigious designs.'[30]

His Consular Majesty

I T IS CERTAIN that some of our travelling Nudes of Fashion intended to conquer the Conqueror of the Continent,' reported *The Times* of 12 January 1803. 'What glory would it have brought to this Country, if it could have boasted of giving a Mistress, or a Wife, to the First Consul.' It would have taken more than that to maintain a peace that many in Britain were beginning to see as little more than a truce. There had been five treaties signed between the two countries since 1697, and only one had lasted more than ten years.[1]

For Britain, the principal benefit of peace was access to European markets—without which dominance of the seas and colonial trade, not to mention its industrial primacy, were worthless. Shortly after the signature of the treaty, Cambacérès warned Bonaparte that it would not last without a commercial one. 'This suggestion appeared to displease him,' he noted. Bonaparte reminded him of the catastrophic effect on the French textile industry of the previous treaty, signed in 1783, which had opened French markets to British imports.[2]

Whether he wished the peace to last or not is impossible to establish, but his inability to see the other's point of view meant that he did not waste time developing good relations with Britain, concentrating instead on using the opportunities offered by the cessation of hostilities to rebuild France's economic and political power. He may not have been a great economist, but he did grasp one thing: whether they were formally at peace or not, France and Britain were in economic conflict. In peacetime, British manufactured goods undercut

French ones, hurting France's industries, particularly in the important textile sector. In wartime, British dominance of the seas wrought havoc with France's overseas trade.

As he believed in developing French industry and enriching the country by acquiring hard currency, Bonaparte wanted to export as much as possible while importing as little as possible. This inclined him to protectionism, in which he was backed by many in his entourage, such as his interior minister Chaptal, a chemist by training and a keen supporter of the textile industry. Given the possibility of war breaking out once more, France needed to provide itself with sources of raw materials and markets beyond the reach of the Royal Navy. This seemed possible, since a large part of the Continent was under greater or lesser French control. That in turn suggested the desirability of binding such areas into the French economic sphere and developing them in the service of the metropolis. This entailed the harmonisation of their administrative and judicial systems, and the implementation of infrastructure projects such as roads over the passes into Italy, all of which would in time make their incorporation into France seem no more than an administrative formality: Piedmont, for example, linked directly by the new Simplon road, would become essential to the manufacturing centre of Lyon, and vice versa.

Although France recovered her overseas empire by the Treaty of Amiens, reasserting control over it presented a challenge; the Revolution had encouraged local elites to assert their independence and seek greater autonomy, mainly to enable them to resist socially progressive and abolitionist tendencies emanating from Paris. In Saint-Domingue (Haiti) the local assembly had passed its own constitution. When the Convention had abolished slavery in 1794 many in the colonies refused to accept its authority and in some cases welcomed occupation by the British, who maintained it.[3]

Restoring France's authority was complicated by the existence of a powerful creole lobby defending the planters' interests in Paris. This opposed Bonaparte's intention of maintaining slavery only where it had not been abolished and accepting the status quo in colonies such as Guadeloupe and Guyana, where it had. His views on the subject were pragmatic. 'If I had been in Martinique, I would have opted for the English, because above all else one has to think of one's own life,' he told Thibaudeau. Such reasoning was not enough to resolve the conundrum presented by the colony of Saint-Domingue along with the Spanish one of Dominica (Santo Domingo), occupying the eastern half of the island, which was ceded to France by Spain in 1795.[4]

At the outbreak of the Revolution, Saint-Domingue produced three-quarters of all the sugar imported into Europe, as well as large quantities of coffee and indigo. It made up a significant element in the French economy and nourished the port cities of the Atlantic coast, with half of the trade of La Rochelle dependent on it. It is estimated that, directly or indirectly, one Frenchman in ten lived off the Saint-Domingue trade.[5]

The Revolution had unleashed animosities between the various strata of society, ranging from 'grands blancs' (white planters), through envious 'petits blancs' and various degrees of mulattos, quadroons, and octoroons, down to the black African slaves, which jostled against each other, often in bizarre alliances dictated by local politics. It inspired slave revolts which were savagely repressed. After much violence, the former slave Pierre-Dominique Toussaint Louverture assumed leadership of the blacks and gained control of the colony. In 1795 the Directory appointed him military governor of Saint-Domingue. He began acting as its master, expelling French officials and confiscating plantations, which he gave to his henchmen. He introduced a system of forced labour differing little from slavery, and opened the colony's ports to British and American shipping, thereby breaking the convention of the exclusivity of trade between colonies and their metropolis.

Shortly after coming to power, Bonaparte wrote Toussaint a flattering letter, confirming that France recognised the abolition of slavery, holding out a vision of a new 'pacte social', and calling on him to show loyalty to France by breaking off contact with its slave-trading enemies the British and Americans. He named Toussaint Captain-General and encouraged him to form a national guard and an army. These overtures were ignored by Toussaint, which strengthened the case of the creole lobby and soured Bonaparte's attitude to him. He nevertheless continued to make conciliatory gestures. 'Whatever your origins and your colour,' he wrote in a proclamation to the inhabitants of the colony on 8 October 1801, 'you are French, you are all free and all equal before God and the Republic.' His recognition of their freedom was confirmed by the assemblies and the Senate a month later. Toussaint defied France by invading the eastern part of the island, which was still administered by Spain pending the arrival of a French force. He entertained ambitions for his country and himself no meaner than those of Bonaparte, and the two were set on a collision course.[6]

The colonies France had recovered in the area included the islands of Guadeloupe, Martinique, Marie-Galante, La Désirade, Les Saintes, Saint-Martin, Saint-Lucia, and Tobago, and French Guyana on the South American coast. In 1795 she had also recovered from Spain the vast territory of Louisiana (comprising all of present-day Louisiana, Arkansas, Minnesota, Kansas, Nebraska, Colorado, North and South Dakota, Montana, Wyoming, and Oklahoma). This opened up the prospect of creating an important colonial empire which would enrich France by providing natural resources and a market for its manufactured goods, not only within its territory but in the neighbouring United States and New Spain (Mexico).

A week after the signature of the Treaty of Amiens, Bonaparte set out for the minister of the navy Denis Decrès his plan for the colonies. He was to show the flag in India, where France had recovered her five trading posts, and reoccupy or reinforce the islands of Réunion, Île de France (Mauritius), and the Seychelles, along with the colony of Senegal in Africa and the islands of Saint-Pierre and Miquelon off the North American coast. A force of 20,000 men was to take back control of Saint-Domingue, another 3,600 to do the same on Guadeloupe, and with time 3,000 in Louisiana.[7]

The Americans and the British did not warm to the prospect of a resurgence of French power in the area, but they relished even less that of the existence of republics ruled by rebellious slaves. There was also the possibility that if thwarted, France might subvert British colonies and the southern states of the United States by fomenting slave rebellions against their British and American masters.[8]

Bonaparte gave command of the expedition to Saint-Domingue to Paulette's husband, General Leclerc, who had a good track record not only as a soldier but also as administrator of Marseille and then Lyon—and he was diplomatic, which would be vital when dealing with Toussaint and later with Spanish and American neighbours: once Saint-Domingue had been secured, he was to sail on to Louisiana. Paulette would go with him, partly to prevent her from behaving scandalously if left to herself, partly to make sure he did not take it into his head to betray her beloved brother. Bonaparte notified Toussaint of Leclerc's impending arrival in a flattering letter holding out promises of honours and riches if he cooperated.[9]

His instructions to Leclerc were to support Toussaint and gradually get into a position in which he could decapitate the black liberation movement. There was nothing in them about slavery. 'The question is not whether one should abolish slavery, but whether one should abolish liberty in that part of Saint-Domingue,' he said to Roederer. 'I am convinced that this island would be in English hands if the negroes were not attached to us by their liberty.' It was therefore best to let things be. 'They will, perhaps, produce less sugar than they would as slaves, but they will produce it for us, and they will serve us, if need be, as soldiers.' As far as he was concerned, the only issue was to regain control of the colonies.[10]

When Leclerc's armada reached Saint-Domingue in February 1802, Toussaint tried to prevent him from landing. Leclerc came ashore, defeated him and forced him to come to terms. He then attempted conciliation, but this was undermined by developments in the neighbouring colonies. Under pressure from the creole lobby and business interests, slavery was being reimposed in Guadeloupe and Martinique, where the slaves had rebelled and thrown off their shackles. As Leclerc struggled to win over the black population of Saint-Domingue, news of this drifted in, arousing suspicion that the same would be done there. He urged Bonaparte to check this, arguing that Saint-Domingue being the most important part of the empire, he should give it priority.[11]

Leclerc's expedition had been under-equipped and under-financed, which limited his potential. But that was as nothing to the threat posed by yellow fever. Within a month of his disembarking, some 3,500 of his men had fallen victim, and they were soon dying at the rate of a thousand a month. Reinforcements could not keep up. By September 1802 only about 10,000 men, some 6,000 of them in hospital, remained of the 29,000 who had sailed from France.[12]

Hostilities had resumed, and Leclerc did his best to navigate the complicated internal politics dividing the black leadership. He succeeded in capturing Toussaint, who was sent back to France and imprisoned as a traitor to the Republic in the Fort de Joux in the Jura, where he would die of tuberculosis on 7 April 1803. Exactly three months earlier, on 7 January, Leclerc himself succumbed to the fever. 'Damned sugar, damned coffee, damned colonies,' Bonaparte burst out when he heard the news. By then the expedition had cost the lives of four other divisional generals, a dozen brigadiers, and 30,000 other ranks. He would later admit that he had committed one of the greatest mistakes of his life in not leaving Toussaint in place as a kind of semi-independent viceroy who would inevitably have sided with France and undermined British colonial power in the area.[13]

Meanwhile, relations between London and Paris were growing tense. The choice of Lord Whitworth as Britain's ambassador did not help. His connection with the assassination of Tsar Paul I was not calculated to endear him to Bonaparte. He was a professed Francophobe, ruthless and prepared to cross the bounds of diplomacy in what he saw as his country's interest, and he made no effort to ease tensions or inspire trust. Not that there was much he could do, given that his instructions, which were 'to state most distinctly His Majesty's determination never to forgo his right of interference in the affairs of the Continent on every occasion in which the interest of his own dominions or those of Europe in general appear to require it', were directly opposed to those of the French ambassador in London, General Antoine Andréossy, which were 'to prevent on every occasion any intervention of the British Government in Continental affairs'.[14]

The British cabinet regarded Bonaparte's unwillingness to open negotiations for a commercial treaty as evidence of bad faith. Bonaparte complained that Britain was harbouring thousands of hostile émigrés, some of them hatching plots against his life. He was incensed that apart from giving shelter to people who openly professed their desire to overthrow him by any means, the British government did nothing to prevent the publication of calumnies and slanderous articles vilifying him, as well as a slurry of scurrilous cartoons by the likes of Rowlandson. One London-based émigré paper openly called for his assassination. He could not accept the British excuse of the freedom of the press, as the Home Office regularly clamped down on the radical press and impounded the writings of those campaigning for parliamentary reform. The British press published lurid accounts of his poisoning plague victims and burying alive his own wounded, and titillated readers with scandalous stories on Josephine's past, on Bonaparte's alleged sexual orgies with his sisters and affair with Hortense, and even on his supposed African origins. His insecurity and limited sense of humour meant that he found this deeply hurtful as well as infuriating. He blamed the British cabinet for everything, for, as Cambacérès put it, 'he had the strange conviction that the greater part of the population of England was well disposed to him'.[15]

There had been much pro-French feeling in Britain in the 1790s, fuelled by the movement for parliamentary reform and the excessively repressive policies of Pitt's government, but this had now evaporated and would soon be succeeded by a new spirit of antipathy and belligerence, largely as a consequence of Bonaparte's behaviour. He had assumed that the return of peace meant France could resume the pursuit of her international interests with no thought of the effect of his actions on public opinion in Britain.

In August 1802 the Imperial Diet met at Ratisbon (Regensburg), as stipulated in the Treaty of Lunéville between Fance and Austria, to rearrange what was left of the Holy Roman Empire. Bonaparte had as a mark of courtesy (and to neutralise him) invited Tsar Alexander to participate as a fellow arbiter. But it was Bonaparte—through the agency of Talleyrand on the spot, who took hefty bribes from all concerned—who decided everything. The Pope was persuaded to cede the prince-bishoprics of Mainz, Cologne, and Trier to France, and that of Hanau to Austria, which would hand it to Ferdinand of Habsburg in compensation for Tuscany, which was now Etruria.

Rulers who lost territory to France on the left bank of the Rhine were compensated at the expense of others in Germany: by the Imperial Recess of February 1803, three electorates, twenty bishoprics, forty-four abbeys, forty-five free cities, and a number of smaller states, 112 in all, were disestablished and some three million people acquired new rulers. By favouring their claims, Bonaparte gratified Prussia and turned Hesse-Darmstadt, Bavaria, Baden, and Württemberg into French client states. The result was a considerable extension of French influence, mainly at the expense of Austria. It had all been done in accordance with the Treaty of Lunéville, but instead of being flattered the tsar felt offended, and the British government could only see French power expanding to an alarming degree. The pattern continued to unfold.

As the Treaty of Amiens had stipulated that all French troops should leave the Batavian Republic (the Netherlands), Bonaparte engineered a political crisis as a result of which the Dutch government requested they remain. To add insult to injury, the former ruler of the Netherlands had not been paid the financial compensation promised. French troops also remained in Etruria. In September 1802 Bonaparte turned Piedmont and Elba, both acquired under the Treaty of Lunéville, into departments of France. But he did not pay the promised indemnities to the King of Sardinia. Taken with the transformation of the Cisalpine into the Italian Republic, with Bonaparte as president, this amounted to a consolidation of French power in Italy acceptable neither to Austria nor to Britain.

It was his actions in Switzerland that tipped the scales for British public opinion. Ironically, this was an area where Britain was not blameless, since it had been using the country as a listening post and point of entry for secret agents, as well as fomenting anti-French feeling there. Switzerland had also been a convenient point of entry into France for Austrian and Russian armies. 'I can see no middle course between a well organised Swiss government friendly to France and no Switzerland at all,' Bonaparte explained to Talleyrand. In the autumn of 1802 the tensions between the pro-French authorities of the Helvetic Republic and anti-French reactionaries developed into armed conflict. The former appealed to France for support, the latter to Britain. British public opinion responded in favour of what it assumed to be the freedom-loving party of independence, and the British ministry felt impelled to act. Before it could do so effectively, French troops had restored order and the crisis was over. On 19 February 1803 an Act of Mediation created a Helvetic Confederation, of which Bonaparte assumed the role of guarantor and effective arbiter.[16]

On 17 October the British secretary of state for war, Lord Hobart, wrote to the commanders in Malta, the Cape, and India ordering them to delay implementing the terms of the Treaty of Amiens. The British cabinet was growing alarmed at French moves beyond Europe. A fleet commanded by General Decaen was on its way to reassert French authority over the Indian Ocean island colonies of Île de France and Réunion and the trading posts of Pondicherry, Karikal, Mahé, Yanaon, and Chandernagore in India itself, all of which was in accordance with the Treaty of Amiens. But Decaen's instructions included investigating the possibility of enlisting the support of local rulers in India in the event of war breaking out again.[17]

Bonaparte had sent General Brune as ambassador to the Porte, General Sébastiani to Egypt and Syria, and General Cavaignac to Muscat. He opened relations with the pasha of Tripoli, the bey of Tunis, and the dey of Algiers and established French consulates throughout the Middle East. A major gaffe was the publication of Sébastiani's report, in which he suggested that it would be easy to oust the British from Egypt and reoccupy it. Talleyrand and the French ambassador in London Andréossy dismissed the report as mere speculation, and Bonaparte attempted to placate an indignant Whitworth. But by then what trust there had been was gone.[18]

Britain felt its monopoly in India was under threat and suspected France of imperial designs in the Mediterranean. It could not countenance the banking centre of Amsterdam and the Dutch ports being in French hands. British trade was suffering, with France imposing tariffs on imports not only to France, but to all areas it controlled, such as the Netherlands and much of Italy. When pressed over Malta, which the British were supposed to hand over to the Order of St John, the foreign secretary Lord Hawkesbury declared that he would only do so if France evacuated Piedmont. Whitworth was subjected to a lambasting by Bonaparte, who pointed out that Piedmont had nothing to do with the Treaty of Amiens and had been ceded to France under a different treaty to which Britain had not been a party.

Whitworth's reports from Paris were consistently unfavourable to Bonaparte, often retailing gossip as fact. He nurtured an invasion scare that gripped Britain in March 1803 by exaggerating the number of French troops in the Netherlands. On 8 March the cabinet decided to enlist 10,000 more sailors and embody the militia, a move probably meant as a show of force and a signal to Bonaparte. All it did was provoke him, and Whitworth was given a second dressing-down at a diplomatic audience on 18 March 1803.[19]

Over the next two months both sides sparred over the issue of Malta, proposing a variety of solutions: Bonaparte suggested Britain hand it over to Russia, Prussia, or even Austria, then that Britain keep it for ten years provided the Neapolitan ports of Otranto and Taranto remained under French occupation for the same period, and so on.[20]

On 27 April Whitworth delivered a verbal ultimatum to Talleyrand demanding the immediate evacuation of the Netherlands, acceptance of a continued British occupation of Malta, and compensation for the King of Sardinia for Piedmont. He refused to put it in writing, so he may have been bluffing. He raised the temperature by reporting that Masséna had told him Bonaparte was about to invade Hanover, Hamburg, Naples, and Sardinia.[21]

This may have been idle gossip, but the thirty-three-year-old Bonaparte was certainly full of bluster and unwilling to back down. When the tsar's envoy told him that Europe could not accept his incorporation of Piedmont into France, he sneered that Europe could come and take it from him. He was in reckless mood. When he went riding or hunting in one of the former royal parks, at Versailles, Marly, Fontainebleau, or Rambouillet, he would gallop around madly, bent over his horse's neck with the reins held loosely in his right hand and his left swinging by his side (he was a bad rider and swayed about on horseback). His disregard for danger alarmed his entourage, who were often left behind, desperately trying to catch up. On other occasions he would leave Saint-Cloud incognito with

Hortense and go to a country fair, where he was easily recognised, without any escort or attendants. On 8 May, as he was being driven back to Saint-Cloud with Josephine, Hortense, his sister Caroline, and Cambacérès, he suddenly climbed onto the box, and taking the reins, insisted on driving the six-horse team himself, which he had never done before. He drove too fast, struck a bollard at the gate with one of the wheels, and the shock sent him flying so far he knocked himself out on landing; he later claimed he had died for a moment.[22]

The power he had amassed, the conquests he had made, and the praise being heaped on him cannot have failed to affect his judgement. He had seen his effigy on the first piece of solid currency the country had known in ten years. There was talk of according him the address of 'His Consular Majesty'. A statue was planned to top a column similar to that of Trajan in Rome. His military instincts inclined him to seize every opportunity and rebelled at the idea of retreat and were backed up by his innate sense of insecurity.

He was profoundly conscious of his origins. His youngest brother, Louis, had come up with the idea of exhuming the body of their father, who had been buried in Montpellier, where he had died, and interring it with some pomp in Paris. Bonaparte was horrified by the idea—the memory of his father was an embarrassment. (Louis did quietly exhume the body, sent it through the public *messageries* hidden in a grandfather clock, and had it laid to rest in a mausoleum on his estate at Saint-Leu.) Bonaparte believed his only claim to status derived from glory—his own and that of his associates. That is why when he heard of the death of Leclerc he declared an official period of mourning lasting ten days, as was traditional in royal courts. It singled out his former brother-in-law and brother-in-arms as a national hero and equated him with royalty, thereby subtly enhancing his own status.[23]

'A first consul is not like one of those kings by the grace of God who view their states as an inheritance,' Bonaparte said to Thibaudeau. 'He needs brilliant actions, and therefore war.' It was a theme he would return to more than once during his life. He believed that his only title to rule rested on his making France greater than she was when he had come to power. Whatever the failings of the Directory, France had at that point been in possession of a great deal of territory, and he felt he could not preside over the loss of any part. By the beginning of 1803, as the first anniversary of the Treaty of Amiens approached, he had enlarged France, which now counted thirty-seven million inhabitants, exceeding Austria with its population of twenty-four million, Britain with sixteen, and Prussia with nine. He had placed France where Richelieu and Louis XIV could only have dreamed of it—dominant in western Europe, checking Habsburg influence in Germany and excluding that of Britain from most of the Continent. He equated this with his right to rule.[24]

The probable loss of Saint-Domingue and the possibility of the resumption of hostilities put in question the continued control of other colonies, particularly that of Louisiana, which France would certainly not be able to defend. The United States was keen to acquire it, and since Bonaparte needed to refill his war chest, he agreed to sell it. On 10 April the former governor of Virginia and future president James Monroe disembarked at Le Havre, and before the end of the month Bonaparte had 'with the greatest distaste' sold him the territory for 15 million dollars, equivalent to 50 million francs.[25]

He was just in time. At the beginning of May 1803 the British prime minister, Addington, issued orders to all commanders in the area to prepare to capture French colonies. He was also planning to take New Orleans and hand it to the United States, as a bribe to join in the coming war on the British side. On 14 May Lord Hawkesbury received an offer to mediate from Tsar Alexander. He had previously advised the British cabinet against giving up Malta, a base that had been in Russia's sights for some time, but had become alarmed at the possibility of the outbreak of war. In the words of his ambassador in Paris, Arkadyi Morkov, the victory of neither side suited Russia, as it would lead to 'either despotism on the seas or despotism on land'. It was too late.[26]

On 15 May 1803 the Admiralty issued orders for the detention of all French ships in British or British-controlled ports and at sea. The following day the frigate HMS *Doris* attacked and took the French naval lugger *l'Affronteur* close to the French coast, as the Privy Council reached a decision to make war on France. The declaration of war was published on 18 May, by which time more than a thousand French and Dutch ships had been seized in British-controlled ports.

26

Toward Empire

BONAPARTE REACTED WITH fury to the unannounced resumption of hostilities. He decreed that every male British subject in France and its dependencies aged between eighteen and sixty was to be arrested as a prisoner of war, ordered General Mortier to invade the British royal family's fief of Hanover, and announced the formation of an Army of England. Riding a wave of anti-British feeling, he opened a public subscription for the building of boats which were to take it across the Channel to teach 'perfidious Albion' a lesson. 'The anger is extreme,' recorded the architect Fontaine. 'Everyone is eagerly offering the government voluntary subsidies.'[1]

Bonaparte set about the formation of the Army of England, complete with a corps of guides who spoke English, overseeing the building of barges to transport the men and gunboats to protect them. He made frequent trips to its main camp at Boulogne, looking into every detail of the preparations, riding about in all weathers, and getting drenched as he inspected and badgered. Soon a large force had assembled on the Channel coast, strung out in camps from Normandy to Antwerp, and hundreds of boats had been built. On the evening of 29 October he assured those gathered at Saint-Cloud that he would plant his flag on the Tower of London or die in the attempt. Two weeks later, from the heights above Ambleteuse, he surveyed the English coast through his telescope and could see people going about their business. 'It is a ditch which will be crossed if one dares to try,' he wrote. Ever the propagandist, he had an article placed in

Le Moniteur describing how, when pitching a tent for him, the men had uncovered medals of William the Conqueror and an axe-head left behind by the legions of Julius Caesar.[2]

Across the Channel, George III declared that he would never abandon the cause of the Bourbons, and the Aliens Office went into action once again with the aim of overthrowing Bonaparte. Funds began to flow once more, agents were activated, and émigré diehards smuggled into France. Georges Cadoudal landed on 20 August at Biville, with his servant Picot and several accomplices, two of whom had been involved in the explosion of the rue Saint-Nicaise. Ten days later they were in Paris. The next to be sent was General Pichegru, who had escaped from Guyana and had been living in London on a British pension. The plan was to kidnap Bonaparte and send him to the remote Atlantic island of St Helena, replacing him with Louis XVIII.[3]

In an attempt to provide moral justification for what was becoming an increasingly personal vendetta, Bonaparte was henceforth referred to by the British government as a 'usurper'. Despite having maintained official relations and signed treaties with the first consul as 'Bonaparte', it now referred to him only as 'Buonaparte', in an effort to demean him through the suggestion of 'foreign' origins. Encouraged by the government, the press went to town, regurgitating all the slanders and gossip about 'Boney' and his family and building up an image of him as a demonic figure hungry for British blood; the government used the threat of invasion as an excuse to repress dissent at home and wrong-foot the opposition, denouncing it as unpatriotic or even treasonable.[4]

The resumption of hostilities was useful to Bonaparte as well. The organisation of the Army of England provided an opportunity for disrupting cliques of the discontented in the army by moving around units and commanders, purging the lukewarm and promoting the loyal. But bringing together so many units had disadvantages, and, unbeknown to Bonaparte, a secret society of *Philadelphes* was formed by hostile officers. The war also strengthened his hand in the assemblies, so he was able to put through a number of projects without trouble. It also helped to distract public opinion from the debacle of his Caribbean enterprise.

In Saint-Domingue the fighting went on in a spiral of unspeakable cruelty, with Leclerc's successor General Rochambeau waging what can best be described as a racial war against the insurgents. On 19 November 1803 he was forced to capitulate and sailed off with his remaining 1,500 troops but ran into a British naval squadron. He managed to negotiate terms and a return to Europe for his men, but these were not respected, and they were imprisoned until 1811. They were more fortunate than the 800 men left behind in the hospital at Port au Prince under a guarantee of immunity, who were massacred.[5]

Paulette had shown remarkable courage and devotion, nursing her husband in his final illness. She had his body embalmed and wrapped like a mummy's, having cut off her hair to cover his face, and the whole sealed in a lead coffin. His heart she enclosed in a gold urn inscribed with the words: 'Paulette Bonaparte, married to General Leclerc on 20 prairial Year V, has enclosed in this urn her love with the heart of her husband, whose dangers and glory she shared'. As they watched hardy grenadiers straining to carry the heavy coffin on its return to France, cynics quipped that it must contain treasure she had amassed in the West Indies.[6]

Bonaparte was keen to get her married again before she could start misbehaving, but while many lusted, few had the courage to take her on. He offered her to Melzi, who politely declined. Another Italian, Prince Camillo Borghese, did marry her, at Mortefontaine on 5 November. Bonaparte was not present, as he was on a landing barge off Boulogne watching an engagement with British vessels. But he wrote instructing her to refrain from annoying the Romans by praising the pleasures of Paris and to behave as they did, however tiresome she found their customs, and to show respect for the Pope.[7]

He was himself being unfaithful to Josephine with, among others, the actress Mademoiselle George, according to whom he was tender and loving, even childlike at times. His philandering always upset Josephine, not least because when engaged on an affair he became irritable, but also because it exposed the inherent insecurity of her position. His siblings acted as little short of pimps, putting nubile women in his path in the hope that one of them might lead to his divorcing her. He protested that he did not want an heir, even going so far as to say that he was not 'a family man', but it was likely that one day he would feel the urge to procreate.[8]

On 11 November he wrote from Boulogne in response to Josephine's reproaches, assuring her that his feelings for her had not changed. 'The good, sweet Josephine cannot be effaced from my heart except by Josephine herself, and only by one who had become sad, jealous and tiresome,' he wrote, explaining that in order to bear all his troubles he needed a happy and understanding home life, and assuring her that 'it is my destiny to love you always'. 'My intention is to console you, my desire to please you, my wish to love you.' This had the desired effect. 'All my sorrows have vanished,' she wrote back, saying she was pressing his letter to her heart. 'It does me so much good! I shall keep it always! It will be my consolation in your absence, my guide when I am with you, because I wish to always remain in your eyes the tender Josephine who thinks only of your happiness.'[9]

He was less successful when it came to the feelings of potential allies. While Britain was engaged on a diplomatic offensive aimed at forming a new coalition against him, he showed few signs of concern. He ignored Talleyrand's suggestion of a rapprochement with Austria to balance British efforts to engage the support of Russia. At the same time, he mishandled Tsar Alexander. He had sidelined him in the process of reorganising the Holy Roman Empire. He then snubbed him when he attempted to mediate in the stand-off with Britain, and in October 1803 the exasperated Tsar recalled his ambassador, leaving only Peter von Oubril as chargé d'affaires in Paris. Relations with every country in Europe were about to be placed under even greater strain.

In October 1803 the police arrested a number of royalists, an advance party in a plot to assassinate Bonaparte. Ambushes laid along the Normandy coast to intercept the second wave came to nothing, as British ships bringing them were warned off by signals from land. Those already arrested were condemned to death by a military court, and faced with the firing squad, one of them confessed that Cadoudal was in Paris. Another revealed that Pichegru was on his way; the plan was to assassinate Bonaparte and stage a simultaneous rising in Paris, whereupon a Bourbon prince would come and, with Moreau's support, re-establish the monarchy. Pichegru reached France on 16 January 1804, accompanied by an aide to Artois, the marquis de Rivière, and Prince Jules de Polignac. He made his way to Paris, where on 28 January he had the first of several meetings with Moreau.[10]

Réal, who was in charge of the police in Paris, was scouring the city while Lavalette, now head of the postal service, kept his *cabinet noir*, the interception unit, busy reading suspect letters. Bonaparte's correspondence over the last month of 1803 and the first two of 1804 reveals a murky world of espionage and counter-espionage as his intelligence sources followed the movements of plotters and double agents. The British consul in Munich, Francis Drake, his counterpart in Hamburg, George Rumbold, and the royalist in the pay of Russia and Britain, d'Antraigues, currently in Dresden, handled agents in Paris, some of them in Josephine's entourage. Some of these were double agents, feeding disinformation supplied by Bonaparte. He monitored the situation, ordering the arrest of this one, the tracking of that one, and the interrogation of a third, as he and Réal gradually made sense of what was going on.[11]

On 8 February, Cadoudal's servant Picot was picked up, and under interrogation confirmed his master's presence in Paris. Réal was certain that Pichegru was also in the capital and in touch with Moreau. At a meeting of his privy council on the night of 14–15 February, Bonaparte decided to act. The following morning, as he sat by the fireside in Josephine's bedroom with Hortense's baby son Napoléon-Charles on his knees, he suddenly said, 'Do you know what I have just done? I have given the order for the arrest of Moreau.' Josephine burst into tears. He got up, went over to her, and taking her chin in his hand, asked her whether she was afraid. She replied that she was only afraid of what people would say. She was right to be. The news of Moreau's arrest caused outrage in many quarters, particularly the army. Some jumped to the conclusion that the talk of conspiracy was no more than a ploy to incriminate Moreau. Few remembered that it was he who had covered up Pichegru's treachery after he had betrayed the positions and strengths of the army under his command to the Austrians in 1795.[12]

In a letter to Bonaparte, Moreau admitted his involvement in the plot and explained that he had not committed himself to it since he thought it unlikely to succeed. He had been playing a waiting game, keeping his options open, as ready to assume the role of dictator if the royalists were to succeed in assassinating Bonaparte as to play that of a 'Monck' in the Bourbon cause. But unless Moreau could be definitively implicated in a conspiracy, the first consul would be viewed as a vindictive tyrant bent on eliminating a potential rival. The police combed the city for the evidence that would vindicate him.[13]

This came with the arrest two weeks later of Pichegru, whom the police had finally managed to locate, and on 4 March of Polignac and Rivière. On the evening of 9 March, Cadoudal too was arrested, with the help of a crowd of bystanders after a dramatic chase through the streets of Paris. That brought to forty the number behind bars, and people accepted that there really was a conspiracy. The persistence of these royalists in their determination to overthrow the state caused public opinion to swing back in support of the first consul. Police reports stressed the 'universal joy' expressed by the inhabitants of Paris. But that was not to be the end of the matter.[14]

On 1 March Bonaparte had received a report from a double agent which identified the 'royal prince' who was behind the conspiracy as Louis de Bourbon, duc d'Enghien, the thirty-two-year-old grandson of the prince de Condé, who had commanded the counterrevolutionary forces at Koblenz. After that army had been dissolved he had settled at Ettenheim in Baden, just across the Rhine. When questioned, Cadoudal confirmed that the conspiracy hinged on the arrival on French soil of a royal prince to act as figurehead, though he could not specify which one. Enghien seemed the obvious candidate. His connection to the conspiracy appeared to be confirmed by a report that a number of people had joined him at Ettenheim, including General Dumouriez, who had deserted the Revolution and gone over to the enemy in 1793, and a 'Lieutenant Smith', who was assumed to be the British agent Spencer Smith (the pronunciation of the German informers had turned a General Thumery and the prince's equerry Schmitt into the more dangerous Dumouriez and Smith).

That evening Bonaparte conferred with Cambacérès, Talleyrand, Réal, and the chief of the department of the *haute police* Pierre Desmarest. He was on edge, complaining that he felt like a hunted dog; for the past few months there had been talk only of conspiracy. According to his secretary Méneval, by January 1804 he was gripped by 'anxiety, agitation and painful insomnia'. Desmarest records that when Réal informed him that Pichegru was in Paris and Moreau was involved, Bonaparte surreptitiously made the sign of the cross. He knew that Pichegru and Cadoudal were prepared to risk their lives in order to take his, and he was convinced that the British cabinet was not just supporting them with funds but actively plotting his murder, as he believed they had that of Tsar Paul I. Various Jacobins were restive too, and one police informer had reported at the beginning of December that 'terrible' things were being said *'against him up there'*. Even the Russian chargé d'affaires was reporting to his court that 'the conspiracy is far advanced'. Roustam, who normally slept on a camp bed in the next room, placed it across the door of Bonaparte's bedroom (he was told off after, getting up in the night to check something in his study, his master tripped over him).[15]

On the afternoon of 10 March, the day after Cadoudal's arrest, Bonaparte held another extraordinary meeting, attended by Cambacérès, Lebrun, the supreme judge Claude-Ambroise Regnier, Talleyrand, Réal, Murat, and Fouché. Although at least two of those present later falsified their own part in it, there is little doubt as to what took place. In the evidence before him, Bonaparte spotted a golden opportunity to catch out all the major players and put an end to royalist plots, by having Enghien and his accomplices arrested and brought to trial. This would expose to the world the perfidy of the Bourbons and their British allies, and possibly that of Moreau. Cambacérès advised caution, but Talleyrand encouraged Bonaparte to act firmly. His personal desire to prevent a Bourbon restoration was in this case reinforced by a need to rehabilitate himself, as Bonaparte had recently been growing suspicious of his contacts with the royalists—Talleyrand always kept several options open. Fouché almost certainly backed up Bonaparte's arguments, for much the same reasons. Later that day, Bonaparte summoned the minister of war and two generals, whom he ordered to cross the Rhine with a small detachment, seize Enghien and bring him to Paris.[16]

Early on the morning of 15 March the duke's residence at Etten-heim was surrounded by French gendarmes and he was arrested. He was whisked across the border to Strasbourg and his papers sent to Bonaparte, who found in them a copy of a letter to the British ministry agreeing to serve under British orders against France, informing it that Enghien had supporters in French units stationed along the Rhine, and describing the French nation as his 'cruellest' enemy. Josephine attempted to plead for the prince, only to be told not to interfere, and later that day Bonaparte summoned Murat, who was military governor of Paris, instructing him to convene a military court.[17]

It was to sit at the fortress of Vincennes outside Paris, where Enghien arrived in a coach escorted by six mounted gendarmes at half past five on the afternoon of 20 March. That morning Bonaparte had signed an order for him to be tried by a military court on charges of having borne arms against France, of being in the pay of the British, and of involvement in a conspiracy to overthrow the French government.[18]

After dictating these orders, Bonaparte drove to Malmaison, where he was joined by Talleyrand. Some time later Joseph arrived from Mortefontaine, to be greeted by a worried Josephine who urged him to persuade Bonaparte to show mercy. According to Joseph, Bonaparte asked his advice, and after hearing Joseph's pleas for the prince's life, agreed to allow him to redeem himself by serving in the French army. This account can be safely ignored. In the afternoon, Bonaparte instructed Savary to go ahead with the trial. He also wrote to Réal ordering him to go to Vincennes to interrogate the prisoner beforehand.[19]

At eleven that evening Enghien was taken from his cell and brought before the military court. He pleaded guilty to all three charges but asked to be allowed to see the first consul. The request was denied. The verdict was delivered at two o'clock in the morning. A grave had already been dug and a firing squad was waiting; he was led out, shot, and buried.[20]

Savary, who had commanded the gendarmes making up the firing squad, went directly to Malmaison to report. According to him, Bonaparte was astonished that the act had been carried out so quickly, and that Réal had not been to Vincennes to question Enghien before the trial. 'There is something I do not understand,' he said to Savary. 'There is something I cannot grasp.... This is a crime, and one with no purpose.' Savary's account is probably coloured by the wish to show Bonaparte in a good light. Méneval and Cambacérès both write that he had been intending to reprieve Enghien, and Bonaparte himself in later years claimed that he had never wanted him shot. He may well have been intending a theatrical pardon, which would have left him with a bargaining chip in hand, but there is no real evidence, and all accounts of the event should be treated with the greatest suspicion.[21]

News that a distinguished person had been executed was spread through the city that morning by returning gendarmes and peasants from the locality of Vincennes bringing vegetables to market. When it became known who it was, royalists and aristocrats were horrified, and many would never forgive Bonaparte. But most accepted that the execution had been necessary—only a decade earlier that of an innocent monarch and his consort had been accepted as such. Most people wanted stability, not plots to overthrow the government, particularly as unemployment and the price of bread were both low. There was little sympathy for the Bourbons and their supporters, who, being in the pay of the British enemy in wartime, were seen as traitors. Many of those who were saddened by the execution actually felt sorry for Bonaparte, assuming that he had been regretfully obliged to carry out an act of severity.[22]

Whatever his true intentions, Bonaparte acted as though there had been a serious threat, but no danger, thanks to the solidity of his government. It had been necessary, as he put it, to demonstrate once and for all to the Bourbons, the royalists, and the British that he would no longer treat their plots as 'child's play'. To the outside world he took the opportunity to issue something of a challenge. Talleyrand wrote to every court not at war with France demanding the expulsion of all active French émigrés from their territory. One of the first to comply was the elector of Baden, who should have been the first to protest, his territory having been violated. But being so close to France, and having done well out of French support, he had no intention of doing any such thing. On 26 March, at Bonaparte's behest, Talleyrand held a reception at the foreign ministry, which every diplomat in Paris attended.[23]

In Warsaw on the same day, Louis XVIII, who had received news of Enghien's arrest but not of his execution, sent an appeal to all the courts of Europe urging them to intercede on the prince's behalf. His letters were returned, mostly unopened. The British government offered a reward to anyone who would free Enghien, and Tsar Alexander took the matter to heart; when he heard of the prince's death, he announced court mourning as for a monarch. As he was treating with Britain over an alliance with the aim of making war on France, he considered making the 'murder' of Enghien a *casus belli*. But the negotiations with Britain were not far advanced, and neither were his military preparations. Instead, he issued a protest against the violation of the territory of Baden and ordered his chargé in Paris to demand 'a satisfactory explanation'. Bonaparte responded with a taunt, referring in the most diplomatic terms to the fact that Alexander had been a party to the murder of his father and had ascended the throne over his body.[24]

Almost every person involved wrote up the events in colourful ways aimed at justifying their role in what later came to be seen as a heinous act. Both Talleyrand and Fouché asserted that they had opposed the execution, and both claimed to have said, 'It is more than a crime, it is a mistake.' But at the time neither regarded it as anything of the sort. They were as anxious as Bonaparte to put an end to royalist plots aimed at restoring a dynasty that would have shown them little kindness. Both had recently aroused his mistrust (and in Fouché's case fallen out of favour) and therefore needed to rehabilitate themselves. Bonaparte had shown a decisiveness and ruthlessness Machiavelli would have applauded, and they would have been of the same mind.[25]

Yet the unholy alliance of these three men sealed by this incident had a seamy side. According to the prefect of police Étienne Pasquier, Talleyrand's collusion with Bonaparte in the elimination of Enghien had revealed to each the degree of ruthlessness the other was capable of, and it frightened them both. 'From then on, they expected nothing but perfidy and betrayal from one another,' he wrote, and while Bonaparte henceforth treated Talleyrand with mounting disgust and hauteur, at the same time fearing him, Talleyrand grew more resentfully servile, while secretly undermining his master. Fouché, however, used the event to convince Bonaparte of the need for a ministry of police and got himself reinstated as minister. Instead of gratitude, he henceforth displayed greater arrogance and independence. Having seen his master dip his hand in royal blood, the regicide felt more confident. He extended his brief not only within France but abroad, creating a web of intelligence-gathering and quasi-diplomatic agents all over Europe through whom he entertained relations with most of France's and Bonaparte's enemies.[26]

Machiavellian calculation aside, Bonaparte was emotionally affected by the episode. He noted that people looked at him in a different way and revealed his unquiet conscience by alternately trying to put the moral case for the execution and making gratingly brutal comments about political necessities. He did not try to shift blame or admit he had blundered, but tried to brazen it out by acting as though nothing had happened. He ignored advice from his entourage to keep out of the public eye for a while, at some cost. One of Josephine's ladies-in-waiting remembered him entering his box at the opera for the first time after the event, with the air of a man leading an attack on a battery of guns. The audience applauded him as usual.[27]

Although he professed feeling no fear, Bonaparte did admit that the many plots against him made him shudder at the thought of what would happen to France were he to be killed. That fear was felt by the majority of the population. He was commonly referred to as 'the man called by Providence and protected by the heavens', and after the discovery of the Pichegru–Cadoudal plot, there was talk of 'the happy star which has saved the saviour of the fatherland from the assassins', and of 'the protective spirit which arrested the fatal stroke'. Although some termed him 'the hero, the idol of France, master of the elements, above all perils and all obstacles', there was an underlying fear that the motherland might lose him.[28]

Much the same was true for all those who had played a major role in the Revolution, who feared the consequences for themselves of a return of the Bourbons. Not only would all the achievements of the past decade and a half be overturned, they would at best find themselves obliged to seek safety in obscurity. Émigré nobles who had returned to France, thereby abandoning the Bourbon cause and accepting the legitimacy of the first consul, could also expect little understanding from a returning Louis XVIII, so they too looked for a consolidation of the existing regime. 'They want to kill the consul,' a worried Regnaud de Saint-Jean d'Angély wrote to Thibaudeau. 'We must defend him and make him immortal.' The form this would take seemed obvious to most. 'The question was not whether Bonaparte had those qualities which are most desirable in a monarch,' explained Talleyrand. 'He certainly possessed those which were indispensable....'[29]

'The feasibility of establishing in France a republic like those of antiquity had been dismissed long ago, but people had not given up hope of a government compatible with the dignity of man, with his interests, his nature and his aspirations,' in the words of Thibaudeau. 'People did not believe such a government to be incompatible with having a *single* head, and the one France had given herself seemed on the contrary to have been conjured up by Providence to resolve this problem so long discussed by writers and philosophers.' In a word, Bonaparte appeared to provide the ideal solution to the conundrum of bridging the ideological gap between monarchy and the sovereignty of the people. As this conviction grew, so did the desire to make his authority permanent, and therefore hereditary. 'Consul for a term, any coup could see him off like the others. Consul for life, it only needed one assassin...' explained Maret. 'He took hereditary government as a shield. It would no longer be enough to kill him; it would be necessary to overthrow the state.' When people spoke of heredity, they meant monarchy. During the negotiations over the Treaty of Amiens, Cornwallis had even suggested that since George III agreed to drop the title of King of France, the first consul should assume it.[30]

Fouché urged his fellow senators to create 'institutions which could destroy the hopes of conspirators by ensuring the survival of the government beyond the life of its head'. On 28 March the Senate duly delivered an address to Bonaparte stressing that every attack on his person was an attack on France, as he had rescued the country from chaos and brought huge benefits for all, and it was therefore his duty to guarantee the future. 'You have created a new era; you must perpetuate it. Glory is nothing if it is not lasting,' it ran. The only opposition came from Sieyès, Volney, and Grégoire. When the delegation of senators called to deliver the proposal, Bonaparte affected surprise but graciously agreed to consider it.[31]

In effect, his brothers Joseph and Lucien, Fouché and Talleyrand, and many others were canvassing hard, encouraging local authorities and military units all over the country to send in appeals begging him to accept supreme authority. He spent most of these months at Saint-Cloud, where he held sessions of his privy council and the Council of State, and received delegations from the assemblies like a monarch attended by his subjects.[32]

On 13 April his privy council directly addressed the question of his becoming emperor. No other title seemed appropriate. Louis XVI had been executed and declared to be 'the last of the Kings', so that title was out of the question. The kingdom of France had been abolished and superseded by the French Republic, which had grown into an empire. People at the time referred to the British and Ottoman empires, even though one was a kingdom and the other a sultanate. Given the size and power of France, her ruler could be compared only with Caesar or Charlemagne. The titles of the only two emperors in Europe both supposedly derived from Rome, the word 'tsar' being a Russian version of 'Caesar', while the title of Holy Roman Emperor spoke for itself. If the head of the French Republic were to take a title, it could only derive from Rome. He was consul, and would become Imperator.

Bonaparte did voice some reservations. 'So many great things have been achieved over the past three years under the title of *consul*,' he had said to Roederer in January 1803. 'It should be kept.' Cambacérès agreed. 'As First Consul, your greatness has no limits and the example of your success being a lesson to them, the kings of Europe will, if they are wise, seek to respect you and avoid all cause or war, so as to prevent French troops from spreading the principles

NAPOLEON

for war, so as to prevent French troops from spreading the principles of the Revolution in their possessions,' he warned. 'As Emperor, your position changes and places you at odds with yourself.' Although he had embraced the idea of the imperial title, Bonaparte clung to his revolutionary heritage. It would, it was understood, be a liberal parliamentary monarchy. 'The citizens will not become *my subjects*, and the French nation will not become *my people*,' he affirmed.[33]

On 30 April the Tribunate voted in favour of declaring France an empire, with Carnot among the very few dissenters. On 3 May this was communicated to the Senate, which had been working on how to bring it about for the past month. The following day it sent a delegation to Bonaparte which declared that circumstances had made it imperative he accept the dignity of hereditary emperor. It set out a number of conditions, insisting that liberty and equality must never be jeopardised and the sovereignty of the people safeguarded, ending with the hope that the nation should never be placed in the position of having to 'reclaim its power and to avenge its outraged majesty'. The address was accompanied by a long memorandum listing all the conditions in detail, such as the inviolability of laws, the freedom of institutions, of the individual, of the press, and others quite unacceptable to Bonaparte. It was he who was outraged, and he forbade publication of the document.[34]

At Saint-Cloud over the next few days he oversaw the work of a commission working on what was effectively a new constitution. The resulting document opened with the words: 'The Government of the Republic is entrusted to an Emperor, who takes the title Emperor of the French.' The state continued to be referred to as the Republic (and would be until 1809), and the sovereignty of the people was given its titular due. But the succession was to be by male descent in the Bonaparte family, and the master of France was now Napoleon I. It was presented to the Senate for approval and passed into law on the morning of 18 May. Following the vote, the senators climbed into their carriages and drove en masse from the Luxembourg to Saint-Cloud.

Bonaparte, in military uniform, was waiting for them in the Gallery of Apollo, in which he had addressed the Ancients on

19 Brumaire. He was surrounded by the male members of his family, his fellow consuls, ministers, and other dignitaries. When Cambacérès ushered in the senators, he addressed Bonaparte as 'Sire' and 'Majesty', words not used in France for over a decade. Many of those present felt uneasy on hearing them, but Bonaparte did not flinch. 'He seemed the least embarrassed of all those present,' recorded one.[35]

Lebrun made a speech, at the end of which he proclaimed Napoleon I Emperor of the French. Napoleon graciously accepted the honour. 'Anything that can contribute to the good of the motherland is closely bound up with my own happiness,' he said. 'I accept this title which you believe to be in the interests of the nation.' As they waited to file in to lunch, Duroc moved among the dignitaries informing them how they should henceforth address each other. They were no longer citizens.[36]

Napoleon I

T HIS NEW DIGNITY bestowed on the most insolent of all the usurpers who have ever mounted the world stage has accumulated and consummated our shame and our misfortunes,' the Austrian official and British agent Friedrich von Gentz wrote to the British minister in Berlin, Francis James Jackson, on 22 August 1804. 'The ease and indeed the joy with which this impudent procedure has been received and applauded at every court marks the extent of the world's decadence.' Frederick William of Prussia did indeed write a letter of congratulation to Napoleon which was nothing if not cordial. The other states of Europe were more or less grudging, but all except Britain, Russia, and Sweden recognised Bonaparte's elevation. Francis II, whose title of Holy Roman Emperor had grown meaningless with the dissolution of that political unit, proclaimed himself emperor of Austria as Francis I, citing as precedents the Russian monarchy and the elevation of 'the new sovereign of France'. He had sought Napoleon's approval first.[1]

Reactions in France were mixed. Scorn was poured on the enterprise by the people of the street in Paris, who were strangers to reverence. During the performance of a play about Peter the Great at the Théâtre Français on 19 May the words 'emperor' and 'empire' were hissed by the audience. But there were no disturbances, and according to a police report of 25 May the workers of Paris 'were making much of their right to vote [in the plebiscite held to sanction it] for the hereditary empire' and turning up at the Préfecture in large numbers to do so.[2]

Many in the army felt their past glories and the epic days of marching barefoot and beating the Austrians on empty stomachs would be submerged in the new pomp. General Rapp disliked the ceremonial, resented the growing number of nobles in Napoleon's entourage, and regretted his former familiarity with the great man, as did Lannes.[3]

'As for me,' wrote another veteran of Italy and Egypt, 'while regretting the austere yet noble trappings of the Consulship, which suited me better than the pomp of the Empire, along with my old comrades of the Pyrenees, of Arcole, Rivoli and the Pyramids I sincerely welcomed this great political event.' In an official address, General Davout assured Napoleon that the troops under his command saw in his elevation 'not so much an honour for you as a guarantee of future happiness for us'. In a private letter to his friend Murat, General Belliard, then stationed in Brussels, noted that his men were 'on the whole pleased with the new form of Government and the idea of heredity'.[4]

It was unfortunate that the trial of Moreau, Cadoudal, and the other conspirators opened only ten days after the proclamation of the empire. Pichegru did not feature, as he had been found strangled in his cell with his neckcloth. The official verdict was suicide, but many did not believe it. Moreau still elicited sympathy, and people were not convinced of his culpability; he defended himself ably and was acquitted. Napoleon put pressure on the judges and a retrial found him guilty. Sentence was passed on 10 June. Cadoudal and nineteen of his fellow conspirators were condemned to death, Moreau and others to two years in prison.[5]

That morning Josephine had brought the parents of the marquis de Rivière and Prince Jules de Polignac to the Tuileries, where they pleaded with the emperor. The mother of Polignac fainted and fell at his feet. Napoleon pardoned the two young men, along with two more nobles for whom his sisters had interceded. In doing so, he sent out a message to royalist nobles that they, unlike the Bourbons, did have a future in the new empire. Not so Moreau, whom he had hoped to see condemned to death so he could pardon him. As it was, Moreau could appeal against the verdict, which would lead to another trial, so Bonaparte quickly commuted the sentence to banishment from France and sent him to America. The episode had stirred powerful emotions. 'The animosity and outbursts of rage against the government were as violent and as widespread as any that I saw in the days leading up to the Revolution,' noted Roederer. But they did not affect the general acquiescence in the change of regime.[6]

Miot de Melito was surprised at the degree to which people found the idea of hereditary succession reassuring. 'It was not as if any surge of affection for the first consul inclined public opinion to favour this new increase in grandeur for him and his family—he had never been less popular—but the need for peace and stability was so pressing, the future so alarming, the fear of terrorism so great, the return of the Bourbons, who had so much to avenge, so fearsome, that people eagerly grasped anything that could to elude these dangers against which they could see no other means of defence.' Many assumed that Napoleon would, having first dealt with the impediment of Josephine by repudiating her, marry into the network of European royalty, to reinforce his legitimacy and guarantee France membership of the club. Some talked of the sister of the elector of Bavaria, which would have made Bonaparte the brother-in-law of Tsar Alexander.[7]

The marquis de Bouillé, an émigré who had returned during the peace of Amiens, was so struck by how strong and proud France had grown that he felt justified in switching his allegiance from the Bourbons to the man who had achieved this. Being a monarchist at heart, he believed Napoleon had a right to the throne. The ageing Cardinal Maury, a devoted adherent of the Bourbons, congratulated Napoleon on his accession. 'I am French,' he wrote. 'I wish to remain so always. I have constantly and loudly maintained that the government of France must be from every aspect essentially monarchical.'[8]

Most of the hierarchy welcomed anything that could consolidate the rule of the man who had restored France to the Church. The Imperial Catechism treated him as the representative of God on earth, and the clergy would celebrate his victories, read out his bulletins from the pulpit, and condemn desertion from the army as a sin. Bishops referred to him as 'a Hero preordained by Providence', an

This painting by Antoine-Jean Gros of General Bonaparte visiting victims of the plague at Jaffa during his Syrian campaign was commissioned to represent his compassionate nature, and at the same time to endow him with a Christ-like aura through the suggestion of his own immunity and of the healing nature of his touch.

According to Corsican custom Joseph was the head of the family, and
Napoleon tried to give him his due, but although he felt great affection
for him, he could not hide contempt for his weakness.

Jean-Baptiste Bernadotte, by Nicolas Joseph Jouy. Napoleon despised him, but since he married the sister of Joseph's wife (who had also been an early love of Napoleon's), he was part of the family.

Napoleon's mercurial younger brother Lucien saved his coup from failure and him from the scaffold, but their views soon diverged, and by the time this portrait was painted, around 1808 by François-Xavier Fabre, he would have nothing to do with the Napoleonic venture.

Bonaparte in the uniform of First Consul, 1800, by Louis Leopold Boilly.

The house in the rue de la Victoire where Napoleon first visited
Josephine and where the coup was planned.

The Tuileries, with the arch of the Carrousel, c. 1860. The area between
the palace and the arch was where the regular parades were held.

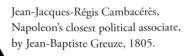

Jean-Jacques-Régis Cambacérès, Napoleon's closest political associate, by Jean-Baptiste Greuze, 1805.

The brilliant foreign minister Charles-Maurice de Talleyrand, seen here at the coronation in 1804, by Jacques-Louis David, was one of Napoleon's greatest supporters, but with time their ideas of what was best for France diverged, and he would betray him.

Joseph Fouché, the police chief who protected Napoleon, but he too eventually betrayed him.

Like her brother Eugène, Josephine's daughter Hortense de Beauharnais, portrayed by François Gérard, was adopted by Napoleon and treated as if she were his own daughter.

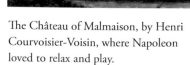

The Château of Malmaison, by Henri Courvoisier-Voisin, where Napoleon loved to relax and play.

Napoleon's favourite younger brother Louis (in 1809, by Charles Howard Hodges), whom he forced to marry Hortense against both their wishes.

This painting by Jacques-Louis David of Napoleon crossing the Alps in 1802 on his way to victory at Marengo is one of the icons of Napoleonic mythology: in fact, he crossed on a mule led by a guide, his hat and uniform covered in protective oilskin, and did not take the same route as Caesar or Hannibal. Nor could he be bothered to sit for the portrait, so David used his own son as a model. But he did insist that he should be depicted full of martial energy yet making a pacific gesture rather than brandishing a sword, as he was already trying to project an image of the ruler rather than the soldier.

'instrument of Divine mercy', 'another Moses', and even in one case described his return from Egypt as being ordained by God.[9]

'It was a unique moment in our history!' wrote the twenty-four-year-old hussar officer Philippe-Paul de Ségur, an aristocrat who had defied his family to join up and only reluctantly accepted Bonaparte's offer of the prestigious post of aide-de-camp. He had wept when he heard of the death of Enghien and condemned Napoleon. Yet he was swept along by enthusiasm for the enterprise of restoring France to greatness. 'We were living in a state of exaltation as though in a world of miracles. On that day of 18 May in particular, what enthusiasm, what splendour, what power!'[10]

'Today at last one can say that the Happiness of France is made forever!' ran a letter addressed to Napoleon by a group of soldiers of all ranks on 19 June 1804. 'Today the resounding Glory which envelops this Great Nation has been made imperishable [...] Your glory is immense: the Universe is barely great enough to contain it and posterity would find it difficult to believe the real deeds of your illustrious career if faithful history had not graven them.' Contemporary observers and historians of the times alike agree that these overblown addresses were not mere flattery or the docile mantras of a populace manipulated by Napoleonic propaganda, but the genuine expression of collective exaltation. Many believed he was so favoured by the gods that the sun always came out when he held a parade or some other outdoor ceremony.[11]

In 1807 the philosopher Claude-Henri de Saint-Simon would write that while there had been geniuses of action such as Alexander the Great, Hannibal, Caesar, Charlemagne, and Mohammed on the one hand, and geniuses of the mind such as Socrates, Plato, Aristotle, Bacon, and Descartes on the other, Napoleon was a miraculous conflation of both. This extraordinary combination of creativity with action and power meant that he made things happen, things that others could only dream of. He was the ultimate creator, a kind of human God. Seven years of propaganda had built up a sense of his superhuman nature and of his being the darling of fortune, providence, fate, or the gods. Paintings such as that by Gros of him visiting the plague victims in Jaffa, in which he is seen touching them while his aides cover their faces with kerchiefs, conveyed a subliminal message of his divine untouchability. And, as he pointed out himself, even the name 'Napoleon', unheard-of as it was, added to the mystique.[12]

Ironically, that mystique would be undermined by his attempts to institutionalise what had existed hitherto in the realms of the imagination. As Cambacérès had predicted, Napoleon was now at odds with himself. But the son of the parvenu noble Carlo Maria had been captivated by another mystique—a Romantic vision of a chivalric past. The constitution was amended by the addition of 142 clauses, and the words 'nation' and 'people' disappeared; Napoleon was emperor 'by the Grace of God and the constitutions of the Republic'. He was to be succeeded by his male heirs, natural or adopted, and failing that by Joseph or Louis. A point was made of guaranteeing the possession of property acquired during the revolutionary period. The Senate, which became the dominant body, was swelled by the addition of the Cardinal Archbishop of Paris and grandees of the ancien régime. Its members received grants of land with a significant income, so as to create a new senatorial aristocracy grounded in the regions but connected to Paris, turning it into a kind of *étatiste* version of the British House of Lords.

The new constitution surrounded the throne with offices copied from the French monarchy and the Holy Roman Empire. On 18 May Napoleon's brother Joseph became grand elector, Louis took the ancient title of *Connétable*, Cambacérès was named arch-chancellor, Lebrun arch-treasurer, Murat grand admiral. The following day fourteen generals were given the title of marshal of the empire, among them dissidents whom Napoleon wished to flatter such as Masséna, Augereau, and Bernadotte. Talleyrand became grand chamberlain, Fesch grand almoner, Duroc grand marshal of the palace, Berthier grand huntsman, and so on. There was confusion as people struggled to remember how to address the bearers of these new charges, whether as *Monseigneur*, *Votre Grandeur*, or *Altesse Sérénissime*, and their number did not cease to grow. An imperial *maison* was created, modelled on the former *Maison du Roi*, the official structure of the royal court. Napoleon had a *maison civile*, consisting of ninety-four officials, and a leaner *maison militaire*, to make up his court on campaign. Josephine had her own *maison* of twenty-seven officials, as well as twenty-nine *dames du palais* (Marie-Antoinette had twelve) and her own stables, a total of ninety-three people, including her grooms. Distinctive uniforms and liveries were designed, and a strict etiquette was established, as Napoleon believed that he must create greater distance between himself and other mortals in order to place his authority on a higher plane. The rules were published on 13 July, but people were still confused. Grand Chamberlain Talleyrand, who on being released from holy orders by the Pope was forced by Napoleon to marry his mistress, a lady of shady past, was firmly told that he could not bring his 'whore' to the Tuileries. The eminently sensible and tactful marshal of the palace Duroc was frequently called upon to deal with such delicate matters.[13]

The Legion of Honour, which had grown to a membership of some 6,000, was transformed into an order of chivalry which was to be a pillar of the throne. On 11 July it acquired insignia in the shape of a five-branched cross and was graded in five ranks: *chevalier, officier, commandeur, grand officier,* and *grand'croix.* As well as attributing prestige, inclusion in the Legion brought remuneration and perks such as free education of daughters at a new school in Saint-Denis. On Sunday, 15 July, after a solemn mass at Notre Dame, Napoleon proceeded to the Invalides, where, under the dome where his remains now lie, he handed out the crosses to and took the oath of the first to have been honoured. 'What I felt at that moment made me understand how a hundred thousand men went to their deaths to deserve it,' recorded the returned émigré General Thiard on receiving his.[14]

Symbols and festivals associated with the Revolution, such as the commemoration of the execution of Louis XVI on 21 January, were phased out; the commemoration of the fall of the Bastille on 14 July was replaced by a national holiday on Napoleon's birthday, 15 August, under the name of *la Saint Napoléon*—though there had never been any saint of that name. The *Marseillaise* was superseded by the bland *Veillons au salut de l'Empire.* Many wise heads were bowed over the problem of what insignia should distinguish the new state and dynasty; the lacklustre coat of arms awarded to Carlo Maria would not do. Lebrun suggested going back to the Bourbon fleur-de-lys, but was overruled. Among the proposals put forward were a resting lion, the cock of the Gauls, an owl, an elephant, an eagle, and an ear of wheat. The cock was a favourite, but Napoleon would not have it. 'The cock is a farmyard animal, it is too weak,' he protested. The eagle was too closely associated with other royal houses, such as the Russian, Prussian, and Austrian, but Napoleon was keen. He hesitated between that and the lion, but the association with ancient Rome prevailed, and the eagle became the emblem of the French Empire. It was Cambacérès who came up with the bee, a symbol of industry and community, as that of the dynasty.[15]

Napoleon had insisted that the change of regime be sanctioned, like the others, by a plebiscite to obtain the endorsement of the nation. The question related only to the hereditary nature of the monarchy, not to Napoleon's elevation. The turnout was less than that for the previous one, around 35 percent. The results were 3,572,329 for and 2,569 against. There was some vote-rigging, with possibly as many as half a million 'yes' votes being added, and it is also probable that many voted out of indifference or fear. But as far as Napoleon was concerned, it proved he held his position from the people. Having obtained their endorsement, he wanted to sanctify the new state of affairs with an act of God, by means of a religious coronation.[16]

He believed that this would crown his policy of fusion, by bringing Church and state together, and grounding his throne in tradition, lending his rule added legitimacy. He meant to outdo the Bourbons. The founder of the first French dynasty, Pepin the Short, elected king by the Franks in 751, had been crowned by the Pope, as had his son Charlemagne and grandson Louis the Pious. Napoleon had sounded out Pius VII before his elevation, and the Pope was prepared to overcome his distaste in the hope of obtaining in return for his presence some concessions on the terms of the organic articles that Napoleon had foisted on the Concordat at the last moment.

Napoleon considered holding the coronation away from Paris, whose populace he regarded with a mixture of fear and contempt, and whose educated classes he disliked for their irreverence and open-mindedness. He considered Aix-la-Chapelle, associated with Charlemagne, and Lyon, which he saw as the model modern industrial city. If it did have to be Paris, he favoured the Invalides over Notre Dame. Discussion of such details continued up to the last moment.

His physical environment had to be adapted. The area between the Tuileries and the old Louvre was being progressively cleared and turned into a monumental open space. Works began in the palace to accommodate his court, including a large chapel in which all its members would be expected to hear mass every Sunday. Saint-Cloud was also adapted, likewise acquiring a chapel large enough to accommodate not just the court but also a choir and orchestra, which Paisiello would conduct. The old royal palace of Fontainebleau, which had been turned into a military prison, was now restored so as to be able to receive the emperor and the court.[17]

If Paris was to be the seat of the new French Empire, the new Rome, it must reflect its glory and be turned into the most beautiful city in the world, as Napoleon had dreamed aboard the *Orient* on the way to Egypt. He had methodically bought up and demolished crumbling medieval hovels to create wide streets and prospects, with proper paving, guttering, and lighting. Since coming to power he had had fifty-six fountains repaired and fifteen new ones built; hospitals had been refurbished; hospices for the terminally ill and shelters for the indigent had been built. New cemeteries had been established outside the city. Two new bridges had been started and the Seine's banks were being cleared. A powerful impulse had been given to the arts, particularly painting and sculpture, with the biannual *Salon* showing works by David, Gros, Girodet, Fabre, Ingres, Isabey, Prud-hon, and others. The various museums, principally the Louvre, were a wonder the world had never seen before. Paris had also become the capital of music, with a conservatoire staffed by 115 teachers, three opera houses, and most of the prized composers of the day. There were also seventeen theatres, and despite censorship, literary life continued. The sciences flourished under the directorship of the Institute and the active encouragement of the state. Radiating out of the capital, utilities such as roads and bridges were being built. Since Paris was to be the centre of its universe, the telegraph, a system devised in the 1790s on the basis of a chain of wooden structures with moving arms which relayed messages by semaphore, was extended to carry news fast from the west coast, from the south, from Germany and Italy—and from Boulogne, where a giant one had been built to send signals across to the Army of England once it had landed.[18]

On 18 July, two months after becoming emperor, Napoleon left for Boulogne. Arriving at one o'clock the following afternoon, he immediately mounted up and rode about inspecting troops, harbour, and ships, then insisted on sailing out on one of them, and after being fired on by the blockading Royal Navy, returned to port. He was keen to see the transport barges in action, so the following day he gave orders for some to put to sea. Admiral Bruix pointed out that the wind was shifting, making it dangerous. Napoleon insisted and rode off, but Bruix did not carry out the order. On his return, Napoleon was so angry he raised his riding crop as if to strike Bruix, whereupon the admiral put his hand to his sword. Napoleon lowered his arm, but dismissed him and commanded his second to order the operation to commence. The wind did shift, and the vessels were thrown onto the rocks. Napoleon directed the rescue operations through the night, and evidently found the experience exhilarating after months of ceremonial in Paris. 'It was a grand sight: cannon firing warning shots, beacons lighting up the coast, the sea roaring with fury; the whole night spent anxiously anticipating whether we would save these poor wretches or see them perish!' he wrote to Josephine. 'At five o'clock in the morning the light came up, all was saved and I went to bed with the sensation of having lived through a romantic and epic dream.' His Ossianic dream had cost seven ships and twenty-nine lives.[19]

He was in fighting spirit. To Cambacérès he reported that the army and the naval units were in good shape. To Chaptal's successor as minister of the interior, Jean-Baptiste Champagny, he gave instructions for the Institute to study the American inventor Robert Fulton's plans for steamships and submarines. To Brune in Constantinople he wrote that he had 120,000 men and 3,000 barges and armed galleys 'only waiting for a favourable wind to carry the imperial eagle to the Tower of London'. When Marshal Soult told him that it was impossible to embark the whole army in under three days, he snapped back, 'Impossible, sir! I do not know that word, it is not French, remove it from your vocabulary!'[20]

Napoleon spent the next six weeks with the Army of England. Although a pavilion had been erected for him in the camp, he took up quarters in a small château at Pont-de-Briques just outside Boulogne. The main camp, on the heights above the city, had been established over a year earlier, and the men had made themselves at home, with 'very fine stone living quarters along regular lines to accommodate their officers, the administration, workshops, etc.', according to the commander of the 26th Light Infantry, even building cafés and laying out gardens. This and the other encampments, strung out along the coast from Étaples to Ostend, contained around 150,000 men. There were a further two corps, one under Marmont in Holland and the other at Brest under Augereau, which brought the total number of troops facing Britain close to 200,000.[21]

They were to cross in a variety of craft, mostly flat-bottomed barges powered by sail, some supplemented by oars. Each vessel was to carry its complement of infantry, cavalry and artillery, so that the loss of one would merely diminish the strength of a corps without disabling it. Much thought had gone into their design: cannonballs making up the ballast were covered in sand on which horses could stand attached to posts, arms were stored in the deck above the men's hammocks, gun carriages were suspended over the water fore and aft, while the gun barrels were mounted on deck so as to be able to fire. As it required five tides to get all the vessels out of harbour (which meant three days with ideal weather conditions and no interference by the Royal Navy), they were unlikely to be of much use. Yet over those six weeks Napoleon gave every sign of meaning to go ahead with the enterprise. He thought up an elaborate naval manoeuvre based on sending two fleets out to the Caribbean in order to draw off the Royal Navy, and then bringing all available ships into the Channel to shepherd the barges across. He was confident that once he had reached England he would sweep away any military defences he encountered and be in London within a couple of days. In that he was probably right, but given that the Royal Navy would by then have gathered in the Channel, he would have been completely cut off.

It seems extraordinary that Napoleon should have spent millions of francs on an enterprise he did not mean to carry out, yet everything points to that being the case. He had been actively engaged in the preparations, making frequent visits to Boulogne for over a year, but it was only in July and August 1804 that he busied himself with it most ostentatiously, telling all and sundry that he would be in London in a matter of days. By then he knew that Austria was in negotiations with Britain and Russia, which had massed a large army on its western frontier and was putting pressure on Prussia to join a new coalition against him. He could not possibly in such circumstances take the bulk of his forces off to England, leaving France and Italy exposed. He said as much in a letter to Champagny on 3 August.[22]

Many in Napoleon's entourage, beginning with Cambacérès, believed the exercise was a bluff aimed at draining British resources, which it did to a large extent, and drawing attention away from his real plans. Variants of this opinion can be found among the military and even foreign diplomats in Paris. But it is likely that there were moments when he did consider invading. His exasperation at the repeated attempts on his life and work, such as the recent conspiracy, may have acted as a spur to striking at what he saw as their source in Britain.[23]

Another spur to try a risky throw of the dice might have been the almost supernatural wave of success he was riding. According to Marmont, he was dreaming of achieving ever grander things. 'One has to live up to one's destiny,' Napoleon told one of Josephine's ladies-in-waiting. 'He who has been chosen by destiny cannot refuse.' He was so preoccupied with how he would go down in posterity that he had come to see his life as epic. It was as if the image he had so carefully been fashioning over the past years had begun to direct his behaviour. To Admiral Decrès he complained that he had reached a dead end where glory was concerned, as the modern world was too prosaic for truly transcendental acts. 'Take Alexander [the Great]: having conquered Asia and announced that he was the son of Jupiter, [...] the whole of the East believed him.' Yet if he, Napoleon, were to announce that he was the son of God, every fishwife in Paris would laugh at him, he told the astonished admiral.[24]

He was in fine spirits, riding up and down the coast, inspecting troops, weapons, and equipment, chatting with officers and men, putting them through their paces and basking in the reflected glory. On 16 August he held a ceremony in which he handed out decorations of the Legion of Honour. The massed troops looked magnificent, flags fluttered in the sea breeze, and bands played martial airs. Against a backdrop of war trophies, surrounded by his men, Napoleon distributed the insignia to the brave. 'No, never, in none of his grandest ceremonies was he so majestic!' in the words of an army physician. 'It was Caesar with his legions.' According to Miot de Melito, Napoleon told his brother Joseph that he believed he had been 'called to change the face of the world'. 'Perhaps some notions of predestination have affected my thoughts,' he admitted, 'but I do not reject them; I even believe in them, and that confidence provides the means of success.'[25]

'My health is excellent,' Caesar wrote to Josephine on 20 August. 'I am longing to see you, to tell you all about my feelings for you and to cover you in kisses. A bachelor's life is a mean one, and nothing like having a good, beautiful and tender wife.' He would soon be joining her at Aix-la-Chapelle, where she was taking the waters. 'As it is possible that I might arrive at night, let the lovers beware,' he wrote jestingly on 25 August, assuring her that he had been too busy for any philandering and dropping suggestive hints.[26]

On 1 September he was in Brussels, from where he set off on a breathless tour of inspection of the left bank of the Rhine. On 2 September, at Aix-la-Chapelle, he received news from Paris that the Russian chargé d'affaires, Oubril, had asked for passports and left, which forecast a state of war, yet Napoleon carried on as if nothing had happened. With Josephine he attended a *Te Deum* in the cathedral and was shown the relics of Charlemagne. On the evening of 9 September he reportedly suffered something that looked like an epileptic fit. But two days later he was on his way to Cologne, from where he went to Koblenz and on to Mainz, where he received a number of minor German rulers who came to pay their respects. Having finished inspecting French defences along the Rhine, he was back at Saint-Cloud on 12 October.

Although he knew Russia was by now well advanced in preparations for war and Austria was also arming, and Naples only waiting for a chance to strike, Napoleon showed no sign of concern. He spent the next weeks alternating between Paris and Saint-Cloud, hunting there or at Versailles or in the Bois de Boulogne, while maintaining his intent to invade England, chivvying troops and crews to practise embarking and landing. On 27 September he had written to Berthier that 'the invasion of Ireland has been decided', to be led by Augereau with 18,000 men supported by Marmont with another 25,000, while the rest of the army crossed the Channel to Kent. The operation was to begin on 20 October. Yet he now shifted his attention to preparations for his coronation—even taking the trouble to have his wet-nurse, Camilla Carbon Ilari, brought from Corsica to see Paris, detailing Méneval to look after her.[27]

His elevation had raised questions about the part his family were to play in the imperial structure. While they had for the most part been of little assistance to him, and felt no duty of obedience, they had all developed bloated ideas of their own worth and exorbitant pretensions—Joseph actually believed that as the eldest brother he had a better claim to the throne. He was proving such a nuisance that Napoleon gave him a regiment to command and sent him off to Boulogne. But a more permanent solution was needed, and as Napoleon could hardly be president of the Republic of Italy as well as emperor of the French, he decided to turn that into a kingdom and offered its throne to Joseph. Preliminary soundings in Vienna suggested such an arrangement might be acceptable. Joseph agreed but kept laying down conditions, mostly concerning what he considered to be his right to succeed to the French throne.[28]

Having been persuaded by Josephine that he was infertile, Napoleon had fixed on his step-grandson Napoléon-Charles, the two-year-old child of Louis and Hortense. He had a special fondness for Louis, whom he had largely brought up, and adored Hortense. But Louis had turned into a neurotic hypochondriac (among his bizarre 'cures' was bathing in tripe). His relationship with Napoleon was fraught, as Hortense explains: 'Brought up by him, perhaps too strictly, he conserved a kind of fear of him which robbed him of the strength to contradict him openly, as a result of which he had developed a habit of quiet defiance which hindered him in the expression of his wishes.' Matters were made no easier by the rumour circulating that Hortense's son was Napoleon's; he treated him as though he were his, sitting on the floor to play with him. Louis resented this and did everything to thwart Napoleon's plans. So did Napoleon's other siblings. One evening when he was playing with Napoléon-Charles, who was sitting on his knee, Napoleon addressed him, saying, 'I advise you, my poor child, if you wish to live, never to accept any food offered by your cousins.' Not surprisingly, Louis and Hortense protested against their son being designated as the heir apparent. But Napoleon had decided that if he failed to produce a legitimate heir himself, the succession would pass through Joseph (who had only daughters) and then through Louis.[29]

Letizia was given a court of her own, with an ancien-régime duke as chamberlain and Louis XVI's erstwhile first page as equerry. After much historical research, she was given the title of *'Madame, mère de sa Majesté l'Empereur'*, generally abbreviated to *'Madame Mère'*. She took the money Napoleon gave her but was uncooperative, siding with her favourite Lucien against him. He had meant Lucien to marry the recently widowed queen of Etruria, but Lucien had secretly married another widow, by whom he had a son. Napoleon refused to recognise the marriage and tried to get him to divorce, but Lucien stood firm. He took his wife and his art collection off to Rome, where he was joined by Letizia.

Caroline Murat was in a rage at not having been given a title she regarded as due to her and vented it on Hortense, whose children were princes while hers were not. She made such a scene, bursting into tears at table, that Napoleon relented and made her a princess. When Paulette realised that she was not going to be made one too, she stormed over to see her brother and screamed so much she actually fainted. Napoleon complied.[30]

The youngest brother, Jérôme, was arrogant, vain and fatuous. He was destined by Napoleon for the navy, but was a reluctant sailor, enjoying only the pleasures of life in port. He did eventually learn his craft and take command of a brig, in which he sailed to the West Indies. He was stranded there by the end of the peace of Amiens and aimed to return by way of the United States. In Baltimore he fell in love with Elizabeth Patterson, the daughter of a local merchant, and married. He had no right to do so, as French law required parental consent up to the age of twenty-five, and when he heard of it, Napoleon refused to recognise the union. He ordered him back to France, alone, as soon as possible, but Jérôme would not be parted from his wife. 'Inform your master,' she wrote to the French consul in Lisbon, where they landed, 'that Madame Bonaparte is ambitious and claims her rights as a member of the imperial family.'[31]

As the coronation drew near, his siblings made a concerted effort to make Napoleon divorce Josephine. That the new etiquette demanded they curtsey and bow before her was bad enough, but the idea of her being crowned was too much. Matters came to a head in an unholy row on 17 November at Saint-Cloud as the final arrangements were discussed; when they were told they would have to carry her train, his sisters mutinied. Napoleon lost his temper, threatening to strip them of all their honours if they did not behave and treat his wife with the respect due to her.[32]

'My wife is a good woman who has never done them any harm,' he said to Roederer. 'She's perfectly happy to play the empress, to have her diamonds, her fine dresses and the other consolations of her age! I never loved her blindly. If I made her empress it was out of a sense of justice. I am above all a just man. If I had been thrown into prison rather than mounting the throne, she would have shared my misfortune. It is only right that she should have a part in my greatness.' He had stopped nagging her about her spending on clothes and handing money out to friends in need, which was probably uncontrollable: even though she had a yearly clear-out, distributing discarded clothing to friends and servants, a surviving inventory of her wardrobe lists forty-nine grand court dresses, 676 dresses, sixty cashmere shawls, 496 other shawls, 498 blouses, 413 pairs of stockings, 1,132 pairs of gloves, more than a thousand heron feathers, and 785 pairs of shoes. He must have realised it was a compulsive disorder. According to Hortense, he was by then so exasperated by his siblings' attacks on Josephine that he asked her whether she would mind if he were to sire a child by another woman and pretend it was hers. He even consulted Corvisart on how this could be carried out, but the doctor refused to have anything to do with it.[33]

Other arrangements may have cost him less annoyance, but no less time and effort. Historians rummaged through records of early French coronations, noting symbols and traditions. Some, such as the vigil of prayer, were deemed too religious; others, like the ceremonial robing, might diminish the new emperor. The actual crowning could not be done by the Pope, as that would have implied Napoleon held his power from him. For similar reasons the pontiff would not be borne into the cathedral on the *sedia*, and would have to be in place by the time the emperor arrived. The question of what his throne should look like and the design of the coronation coach and robes were the subject of protracted discussion, as they had to be based on precedent but must not resemble anything pertaining to the previous dynasty. The result—a bizarre mishmash of the Graeco-Roman, the Merovingian, and the Carolingian, with a dash of Henri IV—beggars description.[34]

Napoleon had hoped to hold the coronation on 18 Brumaire, the anniversary of his seizure of power, but the Pope was not to be hurried, and the date was eventually set for 2 December. On 25 November Napoleon was at Fontainebleau and about to go hunting when news reached him that the Pope's coach was approaching. He mounted his horse and rode out to meet him, dressed as he was in his hunting clothes. When he sighted the Pope's travelling coach, he dismounted and walked over to greet the pontiff, who alighted. Shortly after, the imperial carriage drove up and took them the rest of the way to the palace. They spent three nights there and on 28 November drove into Paris together. The Pope was installed in the Pavillon de Flore of the Tuileries, and as soon as word of his arrival spread, crowds of the faithful gathered outside. When he appeared at the window they knelt and held out long-concealed rosaries and images for him to bless. Napoleon rushed over to share the aura by appearing alongside him on the balcony.

There was a last-minute hitch when Josephine let slip to the Pope that she and Napoleon had never married in church. The coronation ceremony could not go ahead unless they were wed in the eyes of God, so that evening, much to Napoleon's discomfort, Fesch conducted a secret religious marriage in the Tuileries.

The ceremonial for the coronation was devised by Louis-Philippe de Ségur, grand master of ceremonies, assisted by the prefect of the palace, Auguste de Rémusat. The logistics were in the hands of the grand equerry, General Armand de Caulaincourt, and the music was composed or selected by Paisiello and Lesueur. The cathedral of Notre Dame was decorated by Fontaine. To facilitate rehearsals, the painter Isabey drew floor plans of Notre Dame and painted a series of dolls to represent the principal figures. On 29 November he brought them to a delighted Napoleon, who began playing with them and then called over the major participants to rehearse their parts.

At eight o'clock on the icy morning of 2 December, while the capital resounded to the thunder of cannon and the pealing of bells, the legislative bodies arrived at Notre Dame and took their places. Two hours later the Pope arrived, in a gilded coach drawn by eight greys, preceded as custom demanded by a prelate mounted on an ass and bearing a processional crucifix. He took his seat and waited for nearly two hours in the freezing cathedral for Napoleon, who did not leave the Tuileries until eleven o'clock. He rode with Josephine in a gilded coach drawn by eight buckskin horses, escorted by several hundred cavalry with their bands blaring, followed by other members of his family and court in their carriages. The imperial couple and their attendants alighted at the archbishop's palace, where they donned their ceremonial robes, Napoleon's making him look even smaller than he was with its huge ermine cloak. He snapped furiously at his sisters when they staged a last-minute protest at having to carry Josephine's train.[35]

By the time they entered the cathedral, to a bombastic fanfare, the Pope and most of those present were stiff with cold. To a twenty-year-old guardsman who had slipped in to watch, the ceremony was 'everything that the most fertile imagination could conjure up in the way of beauty, grandeur and magic'. Captain Boulart, a fervent admirer of the emperor, thought it resembled a masquerade, 'and Bonaparte as Commander of the army of Italy seemed to [him] greater than the Napoleon who was having himself anointed in order to reign by virtue of some pretended divine right'. He did not enjoy the ceremony, which he considered a load of 'humbug'. Republicans raged and Christians were appalled by what they saw as a cynical manipulation of the faith for political ends and the humiliation of the Pope. Paisiello's music for the occasion echoed these contradictions: his usual light Neapolitan lyricism is in constant conflict with fanfares of brass and drums. Only Napoleon seemed sure of his purpose, though even he found it trying. The physician Joseph Bailly was seated quite close and had a good view of him. As he sat on the throne, with the crown on his head, clutching the orb in one hand and the sceptre in the other, Napoleon suddenly felt a sneeze coming on and made 'a singular grimace' as he attempted to quell it.[36]

'There was, in this saturnalia, plenty to laugh at and to weep over, depending on one's taste,' remarked the royalist baron de Frénilly. The English caricaturists certainly had a feast. In France there were pamphlets critical of the ceremony, and scurrilous jokes and graffiti scrawled on walls opposite the Tuileries. Most of the population showed more curiosity than enthusiasm as they watched the gilded carriages and brilliant troops of cavalry clatter past and made the most of the festivities and fireworks laid on for them that evening.[37]

There was to have been a grand parade the following day at which regiments were to be presented with eagle finials for their standards, but it was delayed by two days as a result of Josephine's indisposition. On the evening of 4 December a relentless downpour soaked the painted canvas of the stand that had been prepared for the imperial couple and the dignitaries, whose seats were drenched. The following day, dressed in his carnivalesque coronation robes, Napoleon presided over a painful ceremony as his marshals distributed the eagles to the regiments, which paraded 'covered in mud and drenched in the coldest rain' with no crowd to watch them. Their clothes were soaked, their hats flopped over their faces, their plumes drooped. 'We were up to our knees in mud,' recalled one guardsman.[38]

For once, the sun had let Napoleon down. Superstitious as he was, he might have reflected on this. He had radically altered his relationship to the French nation, a relationship which had brought him to power and restored its sense of identity. The invitations to the coronation proclaimed that Napoleon had been accorded imperial status by 'divine providence and the constitutions of the Empire'. When he received the members of the legislative bodies who had come to swear a new oath to him as emperor, in making a speech with more than his usual number of grammatical mistakes, he addressed them as 'My people' and his 'faithful subjects', which even his staunchest supporters did not consider themselves to be. In his pursuit of a national 'fusion' he had been sidetracked by the lure of aristocratic grandeur, which was leading him away from the republican spirit which had inspired and given him power. Far from reconciling French society as he had hoped, the implicit contradictions alienated republicans and royalists, agnostics and Christians, nobles and proletarians. And, as Cambacérès had foretold, they put him at odds with himself.

28

Austerlitz

O N 1 JANUARY 1805 Napoleon wrote to George III using the address '*Monsieur mon frère*', customary between monarchs, proposing a new peace settlement based on a division of spheres of interest. France was not interested in overseas empire, and if allowed a dominant role in Europe would not contest Britain's dominion over the seas. The world was large enough for both nations, he argued. The offer was dismissed in a letter addressed to 'the head of the French government'. An unintended consequence of Napoleon's activities at Boulogne was to make the war popular in Britain for the first time since hostilities had begun over ten years before. The threat of invasion by 'Boney' struck a chord in all classes of the population, and the government now had the support of the country.[1]

Napoleon had also written to Francis I of Austria to inform him that he had magnanimously ceded all his rights over Italy to his brother Joseph, who would ascend the Italian throne and renounce his claim to that of France, thereby ensuring that the two countries would never be united under one ruler. He expressed the hope that this sacrifice of his 'personal greatness' would be reciprocated by goodwill on the part of Francis, urging him to reverse the Austrian troop concentrations in Carniola and the Tyrol.[2]

The letter had hardly left Paris when Joseph declared that he would not, after all, renounce his right to the French throne. Napoleon then offered the crown of Italy to Louis, who also refused, equally jealous as he was of preserving his right to the imperial throne. Napoleon resolved to take the crown himself and to appoint his stepson, Eugène de Beauharnais, as his viceroy. On 16 January a sick and depressed Melzi agreed to offer him the crown, and in a ceremony at the Tuileries on 17 March he was acclaimed by a number of Lombard nobles. On 31 March he left for Fontainebleau on the first leg of the journey to Milan for his coronation as King of Italy.[3]

Marshalled by the grand equerry Caulaincourt, carriages, horses, and three sets of court officials and servants leapfrogged each other along the way, so that when the imperial couple reached a stop everything was ready for them, with a full complement of staff, while the second set raced ahead to prepare the next stage, and the third waited to clear things up once they had left. Napoleon himself now had a travelling *berline*, sometimes referred to as his *dormeuse*, as he could sleep in it, which maximised his capacity to work. The vehicle could be turned into a study, with a tabletop equipped with inkwells, paper and quills, drawers for storing papers and maps, shelves for books, and a lamp by which he could read at night. It could also be turned into a couchette, with a mattress on which he could stretch out, and a washbasin, mirrors, and soap-holders so he could attend to his toilette and waste no time on arrival, and naturally, a chamberpot. There was only room for one other person—Berthier on campaign, Méneval at other times.[4]

They left Fontainebleau on 2 April and stopped at Brienne the following day, staying the night at the château with the ageing Madame Loménie de Brienne and visiting the ruins of Napoleon's old school and other former haunts. On 14 March, Easter Day, they made an imperial stop at Lyon, where they attended mass celebrated by Fesch in the cathedral. By 24 March they were in Turin, and on 1 May reached Alessandria, from where Napoleon rode over to contemplate the field of Marengo. Four days later he reviewed 30,000 troops under Lannes on the battlefield, in the coat and bullet-holed hat he had worn during the battle.

The next day he met his youngest brother. Jérôme had reached the shores of Europe at Lisbon, but the French consul there refused to allow his wife ashore, and while he travelled on to plead with his brother she sailed to London. In July she would give birth in

Camberwell to a son, Jérôme Napoléon, who would never be recognised by the emperor. 'There are no wrongs that genuine repentance will not efface,' Napoleon told his brother when they met at Alessandria on 6 May. Elizabeth Patterson was granted a pension on condition she went back to America, and Jérôme was given command of a frigate, with the mission to sail to Algiers and retrieve French and Italian subjects imprisoned there.[5]

On 8 May 1805 Napoleon entered Milan. Although his entry was described by one French soldier as triumphal, with people weeping for joy in the streets, he was not satisfied. There followed nearly three weeks of receptions and festivities, culminating on 26 May, when he crowned himself with the iron crown of Lombardy once worn by Charlemagne, declaring, 'God has given it to me, woe to him that reaches for it!' The ceremony was greeted with enthusiasm by many who dreamed of a united Italy. It also made a lasting impression, with woeful consequences for much of South America, on a twenty-one-year-old Spanish creole who happened to be there, named Simón José Antonio Bolívar.[6]

The coronation could only be viewed in Vienna as a provocation. With the aid of British subsidies, Austria had been arming over the past year and had concentrated considerable forces in the Tyrol. They would be difficult to contain if other states on the peninsula were to join Austria. Napoleon had written to Queen Maria Carolina, the power behind the throne of Ferdinand IV of Naples, warning her not to allow herself to be drawn into a coalition against him; she was the sister of the late Marie-Antoinette, and hated the French. He rightly suspected that a plan already existed to land British and Russian troops in Naples.[7]

After the coronation he set off on a tour of the kingdom of Italy, inspecting fortifications and troops, meeting local authorities and nobles, going to the theatre and the opera, in a display of confidence and mastery. On 1 July he reached Genoa, which had been under French control for some time and was being administered, along with Liguria, Lucca, and Piombino, by Saliceti, and now requested to be incorporated into the French Empire. The act was accompanied by elaborate celebrations, with Napoleon and Josephine towed out into the bay on a floating temple surrounded by gardens from which they watched a firework display. He went aboard the flotilla which Jérôme had commanded, greeting the 231 liberated slaves as they came ashore to universal applause.[8]

A week later Napoleon was back at Saint-Cloud. He was expecting a new Russian envoy, Count Nikolai Novosiltsev, through whom he hoped to negotiate a separate treaty with Russia, but Novosiltsev had stopped in Berlin and sent back his French passports, on the grounds that Napoleon's encroachments in Italy had made negotiations pointless. The tsar had originally meant to avoid foreign entanglements and concentrate on reforming the Russian state. He secretly admired Napoleon but had been shocked by the execution of Enghien—and mortified by Napoleon's retort to his protest. Supported by his anti-French foreign minister Prince Czartoryski, he now put himself forward as a champion of ethical politics, with a far-reaching vision for the remodelling of the political arrangement of Europe.[9]

Napoleon affected to ignore the military preparations being made against him, and on 2 August he went to Boulogne. At the end of June he had given orders for the invasion force to be ready for embarkation by 20 July. He expressed frustration that his plan of drawing British ships off to the Indian Ocean and the Caribbean before sailing back to the Channel was proving difficult to implement. He was hoping to concentrate up to sixty-five ships of the line to protect the invasion craft. Impatient and accustomed as he was to overcoming any difficulty, he could not accept the delays imposed by the weather, blaming the admirals. They did indeed lack the dash he expected of them; hardly surprising, given the poor quality of the ships and the inexperience of the crews, which were no match for a Royal Navy in which Pitt had invested heavily during the late 1780s and early 1790s, and which had reached a peak of performance. The only French admiral with any initiative, Louis-René de Latouche Tréville, had died the previous summer. Napoleon urged Decrès to seek out younger men to command his fleets, but the real problem was, as he had already noted, lack of discipline among the crews, which could not be imposed in the British way, given his distaste for corporal punishment and the fact that, as he put it, 'for a Frenchman it is a principle that a blow received must be returned'.[10]

He kept up the appearance of intending to go ahead with the invasion, even though eight months earlier, on 17 January 1805, he had told the Council of State that the concentration at Boulogne was a pretext to build up an army to strike against any of France's enemies at a moment's notice. On 3 August he instructed Talleyrand to warn Francis that he only meant to attack England, but might feel obliged to turn about and fight Austria if she supported Britain. Ten days later he instructed Talleyrand to send what amounted to an ultimatum to Francis, repeating that his invasion of England did not constitute a threat to Austria, but that if Francis persisted in rearming there would be war, and he would be spending Christmas in Vienna.[11]

Throughout August Napoleon kept up a stream of instructions for the invasion of England, and on 23 August he wrote to Talleyrand saying that if his fleet arrived in the Channel in the next few days he would be 'master of England'. But on the same day he ordered supplies and rations to be stockpiled at Strasbourg and Mainz; two days later he sent Murat ahead along the Rhine to scout routes into southern Germany and gather maps of the area. 'The decisive moment has arrived,' he informed Berthier. A few weeks before, on 13 August, he had renamed the Army of England *La Grande Armée*. It was not only the name that had changed.[12]

The army Napoleon had inherited was a mixture of regulars from the royal army and untrained volunteers and conscripts. Each unit had coalesced in wartime conditions around its most competent officers, and each of the armies around their commanding general. Given the soldiers' aptitude for desertion, it was impossible to impose discipline in traditional ways. Incompetent and disloyal officers had been purged and generals moved about, undercutting loyalties forged on campaign; demi-brigades had been re-formed as regiments; the men were paid, clothed, and fed, and a sense of pride was instilled through parades. It nevertheless remained an unaccountable assemblage of men with idiosyncratic loyalties.

In May 1804 Napoleon had nominated fourteen marshals of the empire. While those singled out were all military men, this was in fact a civil rank, placing its bearer on a par with the '*grands officiers*' of the empire and giving them a position at court, with the privilege of being addressed as '*mon cousin*' by the emperor. The fourteen included close comrades such as Berthier and Murat, some awkward ones Napoleon needed to neutralise, such as Augereau and Bernadotte, as well as a number of capable generals whose loyalty he needed to capture. One such was Nicolas Soult, five months Napoleon's senior, the son of a small-town notary who had distinguished himself fighting under Moreau and later Masséna, a braggart and an opportunist who needed to be controlled. Another was the cooper's son from northeastern France, Michel Ney, seven months Napoleon's senior, who had also risen through the ranks under Moreau, brave but limited, and therefore in need of cousinly guidance; Josephine had taken the first step in 1802 by arranging his marriage to one of her protégées. A very different man was Louis Nicolas Davout, the scion of a Burgundian family that could trace descent from Crusaders, who, being almost a year younger than Napoleon, had just missed him at the École Militaire and had served as a cavalry officer in the royal army. He had been introduced to Napoleon in 1798 by Desaix, who valued him highly, and although he too had served under Moreau, he was not a man for factions; self assured and professional, a strict disciplinarian and unflinchingly brave, he was devoted to the service of France. But whatever their origins, attitudes, and sympathies, on receiving their marshal's baton such men became Napoleon's lieutenants, bound to him by far more than mere bonds of loyalty. They would allow him to operate in larger numbers on a wider theatre, and they would hold his army together.

The concentration of the greater part of the army at Boulogne for over a year transformed it. The idea of taking the war to the hated English aroused enthusiasm, and the rate of desertion dropped off. The cohabitation and frequent contact, both in drilling and exercises (although there was surprisingly little of either) and in off-duty activities, developed a wider esprit de corps and, in the words of one soldier, 'established relationships of trust between the regiments'. It had forged an army for Napoleon.[13]

By 3 September he was back at Malmaison. A couple of days later he learned that Austria had invaded Bavaria, an ally of France. Over the next three weeks he attended to matters that needed to be despatched before he went on campaign, including an edict abolishing the revolutionary calendar and reinstating the Gregorian. On 24 September, having instructed the Senate to put in hand the raising of 80,000 more men, and leaving Joseph and Cambacérès in charge, he left for Strasbourg to join the Grande Armée, which had been on the march since the end of August.

While the 90,000 Austrians in Carniola and the Tyrol under Archdukes Charles and John moved into Italy, on 8 September General Karl Mack with a corps of 50,000 Austrians under the titular command of Archduke Ferdinand had marched into Bavaria and taken up position in the west of the country to await a Russian army under General Kutuzov which was to join him in invading France. The Grande Armée had left the Channel coast in seven corps, commanded by Bernadotte, Marmont, Davout, Soult, Lannes, Ney, and Augereau, with a cavalry force of 22,000 under Murat, a total of some 180,000 men. They moved with astonishing speed, living off the land, allowing men to fall behind and catch up as best they could.

Napoleon left Strasbourg on 2 October in fine weather, cheered as he passed troops on the march, some of whom would present him with petitions. He would stop his horse or carriage alongside resting units and address the men; thanks to his extraordinary memory he could always name one or other of them and allude to their or their unit's battle records. On 4 October he was at Stuttgart with the elector of Württemberg, with whom he attended a performance of Mozart's *Don Giovanni*, and from whom he had to borrow fresh horses as his were all spent. Three days later he was directing the crossing of the Danube at Donauwörth, far to the east of Mack's positions, which enabled him to sweep round and attack him from behind. From Augsburg on 12 October he wrote to Josephine that things had gone so well that the campaign would be one of his shortest and most brilliant yet: 'I am feeling well, although the weather is dreadful and it's raining so much I have to change clothes twice a day.' He was always in the thick of the action, and when Murat and Berthier took his horse's reins to pull him away from an exposed position in which bullets were whistling around their heads, saying it was not the place for him, he snapped at them, 'My place is everywhere, leave me alone. Murat, go and do your duty.'[14]

'For the past eight days, rain all day and cold wet feet have taken their toll, but today I have been able to stay in and rest,' he wrote to Josephine from the abbey of Elchingen on 19 October, adding, 'I have carried out my plan: I have destroyed the Austrian army just by marching.' Archduke Ferdinand had managed to get away with a small force, but Mack had been checked by Ney at Elchingen and was left with no option other than to seek refuge in the town of Ulm, where he was bottled up with some 30,000 men while his cavalry fled back to join the Russians in Bohemia. On 19 October Mack had been obliged to capitulate, bringing the number of Austrian prisoners taken by the French in the space of two weeks to 50,000.[15]

It was an extraordinary feat. Sébastien Comeau de Charry, a fellow artillery officer who had emigrated and ended up serving in the Bavarian army, now allied to the French, could barely believe what he witnessed. He had watched what looked like a rabble pour into Germany, shedding men and horses but streaming on, suddenly turn into a fighting force. On the Austrian side there were beautiful uniforms and fine horses, on the French 'not one unit in order, just a compact mass of foot-soldiers' pouring down the road. 'It is only a superior man, a sovereign, who can bring unity and harmony to such a crowd,' he reflected. A young French officer in Ney's corps thought he had dreamed it all when he reflected that he had been at Boulogne on 1 September and was taking Mack's surrender in Bavaria on 20 October.[16]

Comeau de Charry had last met Napoleon at a mess table in Auxonne in 1791, when he had refused to sit next to him on account of his republican views, and was now astonished to see him adopt 'the tone and manner of an old, loved, esteemed comrade'. Attached to his staff, he was able to observe not only the emperor's extraordinary grasp of

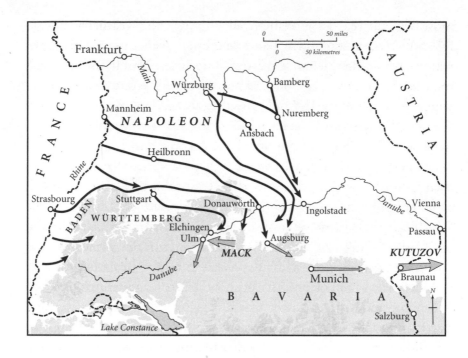

the situation but also the unorthodox behaviour of the French army. Where another general would have wished, and another army demanded, a few days' rest and resupply after a victory such as Ulm, Napoleon pressed on along the Danube toward Vienna and his troops surged on, stopping in groups to cook up something to eat, then resuming their march, dropping behind their units, getting mixed up with others, going off on '*la maraude*' in search of food and other necessities, but always ready at a moment's notice to form up columns, lines, or squares, without having to be directed by their officers. Colonel Pouget, commanding the 26th Light Infantry, noted that on the march soldiers of various units would get together in groups to scavenge, mess, and find comfortable overnight quarters, only rejoining their respective units in camp, but in an emergency they would integrate with the closest unit and fight as though they belonged to it.[17]

On 24 October Napoleon entered Munich and invited the elector of Bavaria to repossess his capital. On 13 November, after Murat, Lannes, and Bertrand had managed to fool the unfortunate Austrian colonel guarding it to let them cross a bridge over the Danube, assuring him that an armistice had been signed, Napoleon entered Vienna. He took up quarters outside the city in the imperial palace of Schönbrunn. He was in an evil mood, to judge by a letter to Joseph written the next day in which he raged against Bernadotte, who had failed to act on his orders and missed a valuable opportunity. He was also displeased with Augereau, who had been slow, and with Masséna, who had failed to pin down the Austrians in Italy. His mood would not have improved three days later, when he received news that instead of sailing into the Mediterranean and harrying British ships supporting Naples, Admiral Villeneuve had left Cádiz with the combined French and Spanish fleets only to be disastrously defeated off Cape Trafalgar by Admiral Nelson. He took his displeasure out on Murat, who had allowed a Russian unit to give him the slip.[18]

After Ulm, Napoleon had suggested peace negotiations to Francis, pointing out that Austria was bearing the brunt of the war and suffering on behalf of her British and Russian allies. Although he had lost an army, Francis remained sanguine, as Napoleon's position was precarious. In Italy, Masséna and Eugène had defeated the archdukes, but they could not pursue them as they had to turn about and face a Neapolitan attack supported by British and Russian troops. Forced out of Italy, the archdukes were now hovering on Napoleon's southern flank. Having been obliged to detach a force to head them off and leave men behind to cover his lines of communication, he was himself down to little over 70,000 men. A combined Russian and Austrian force of nearly 90,000 had gathered at Olmütz (Olomuc) to the north of Vienna, and there was a risk that Prussia might join the coalition and attack him from behind.[19]

King Frederick William had been wavering between the option of joining France and acquiring Hanover as a reward, and that of joining the anti-French coalition. News of Trafalgar lifted the spirits of every enemy of France and increased Napoleon's vulnerability. Tsar Alexander had visited Berlin on 25 October and, aided by the fiercely anti-French Queen Luise, managed to persuade the king to sign an accord promising to take the field against the French by 15 December at the latest. The pact was sealed by a night-time visit by the tsar and the royal couple to the tomb of Frederick the Great, where by the light of flaming torches they vowed to fight together and Alexander kissed the sarcophagus of the renowned warrior.

Napoleon's anxieties were compounded by the situation at home, where the fall-off in trade following the end of the peace of Amiens, a bad harvest, and a budget deficit caused by military expenditure had precipitated a financial crisis and a run on the Bank of France, which Joseph was barely managing to contain. The first successes of the campaign, reported in fulsome bulletins which were plastered on street corners and read out in theatres, had elicited enthusiasm and created a sense of national solidarity. But by the end of October there were scuffles outside the bank as people struggled to withdraw specie. By the beginning of November troops were being deployed to keep order outside the bank. Joseph and Cambacérès sent Napoleon daily pleas for good news to feed to the jumpy population. 'It is highly desirable that Your Majesty should send me news every day,' Joseph wrote on 7 November. 'You cannot imagine how easily anxiety rises when the *Moniteur* does not give any news of Your Majesty and the grande-armée; in the absence of real news, anxiety forges false news.' Although the official reports played down its significance (Napoleon would dismiss it with talk of gales dispersing and wrecking some of the fleet), news of Trafalgar further undermined confidence. By 9 November, Joseph warned that 'we must either support the Bank or let it fail immediately'. Napoleon tried to ease the tension by sending back more mendacious bulletins, but as he and his army marched further and further away, anxiety mounted, and by late November there was mild panic in Paris.[20]

Napoleon needed a quick victory. He marched north to confront the Austro-Russian concentration at Olmütz, reaching Brünn (Brno) on 20 November. He rode out with his staff and spent a long time surveying the vicinity, noting various features of the terrain. 'Gentlemen, look carefully at this ground!' he said to his entourage. 'It will be a field of battle! You will all have a part to play on it!'[21]

He was eager to bring on events, fearing the entry of Prussia into the war. Having ridden out and scouted the ground again, he began acting as though he wished to avoid an engagement. He withdrew units which had approached the enemy positions and instructed others to retreat if attacked, gradually drawing the enemy onto his chosen ground. On 26 November he sent a letter to the tsar through General Savary. Savary was snubbed at Russian headquarters by sneering aristocratic young aides, and although the tsar was more polite, his reply was addressed to 'the head of the French government'. Napoleon sent Savary back with a request for a meeting, to which Alexander responded by sending one of his aides, Prince Dolgoruky. Along with others in the tsar's entourage, the young man took these overtures as a sign of weakness, and when they met, out in the open, he looked down on Napoleon, whom he thought small and dirty, and declared that he must evacuate the whole of Italy and all Habsburg dominions, including Belgium, before any talks could take place. A livid Napoleon told him to leave. The exchange confirmed that Russian headquarters was dominated by inexperienced hotheads eager to prove themselves in battle, like the tsar himself, who would prevail over wiser counsels.[22]

Two Austrian delegates arrived at Napoleon's headquarters requesting an armistice, and two days later, on 27 November, the Prussian foreign minister Count Christian von Haugwitz also turned up. Napoleon recognised these moves for the delaying tactics they were and rudely sent them off to Vienna to confer with Talleyrand, to whom he wrote on 30 November saying he would be prepared to make far-reaching concessions to make peace with Austria. But he spent that day preparing for battle.[23]

Impervious to the alternating rain and hail, he again carefully surveyed the terrain and observed the Austro-Russian army's movements. He seemed preoccupied, but rubbed his hands together with satisfaction. That night he slept in his carriage. After a final reconnaissance on 1 December, he settled into a small round hut which his grenadiers had built for him near a cottage in which his staff put up. He was joined by Junot, who had travelled from his embassy in Portugal to be at Napoleon's side and was overjoyed to have arrived in time for the battle. That night, after lecturing his staff over dinner on the subject of the deficiencies of modern drama when compared with the works of Corneille, Napoleon rode out for a last look at the enemy positions. He then walked among the campfires around which the troops huddled against the bitter cold. The supply train had, as usual, failed to keep up with the army, and they had little food. They had been read a proclamation in which he assured them that he would be directing the battle throughout and would, if needed, be among them to face the danger. Victory on the morrow would mean a speedy return home and a peace worthy of them and him. As he walked through the bivouac, some soldiers lit his way with torches and were soon joined by others with twists of straw or flaming branches, so that soon a torchlight procession snaked through the camp, to shouts of '*Vive l'Empereur!*' 'It was magnificent, magical,' recalled one chasseur of what was now the Imperial Guard. The following morning seemed no less so.[24]

It happened to be the anniversary of Napoleon's coronation. The troops were roused long before daybreak and formed up in the thick mist of a wintry morning which muffled all sound. They stood to for some time in eerie silence. The sun rose, burning off the mist and temporarily blinding them before its rays glinted on the rows of bayonets and lance-tips facing them, giving the signal for the artillery to open up. The '*soleil d'Austerlitz*' would go down in legend.[25]

Napoleon's 73,000 men were outnumbered by the combined Russian and Austrian force of 86,000 facing them and seriously outgunned with 139 pieces of artillery to their opponents' 270. But having surveyed the ground and taken up what appeared to be defensive positions, he had anticipated the direction in which they would be tempted to attack and laid his plans accordingly. He instructed Davout on his right wing to fall back when the Russian left challenged him and to draw them on, off the high ground, in order to make their eventual retreat more difficult. The Russians responded as expected, and when they had overextended themselves, Napoleon launched a vigorous attack on the now exposed enemy's centre, while his left wing outflanked their right and forced it back, widening the gap at the centre. The manoeuvre worked as he had intended, and the enemy were thrown into confusion, with some units having to face about and others to fall back into the path of their advancing colleagues. But the Russians in particular fought doggedly, and there was a moment when a counter-attack by the Russian Guard

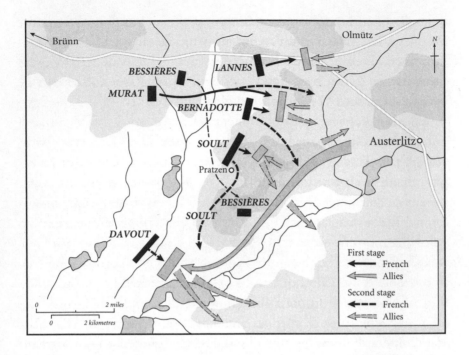

threatened the outcome. It was countered by a vigorous cavalry charge led by Bessières and Rapp. The allied army crumpled, and while individual units stood their ground, the majority took flight, with a humiliated Alexander galloping away from the field of battle.[26]

'The battle of Austerlitz is the finest of all those I have fought,' Napoleon wrote to Josephine on 5 December; 'more than twenty thousand dead, a horrible sight!' As usual, he exaggerated the enemy losses and diminished his own, but it had been a triumph. The French army had taken 45 enemy standards, 186 guns, and 19,600 prisoners, and although the number of dead was considerably smaller than 20,000, the allied army had been diminished by at least one-third and its morale shattered. 'I had already seen some battles lost,' wrote the French émigré Louis Langeron, a general in Russian service, 'but I could never have imagined a defeat on this scale.'[27]

The victorious troops lay down and slept around miserable smoking fires among the dead and dying, with nothing to eat except the odd crust they carried with them. Flurries of snow had made everything damp, and in the evening it began to rain. It was not until the following night that Napoleon himself slept in a bed for the first time in over a week, in a country house in the nearby village of Austerlitz, after which he named the victory. In his address to the troops he stressed that it had been entirely their work and announced that he would adopt the children of all the French dead.[28]

He only slept for a couple of hours. The Austrians had requested a ceasefire, and the following day he met the emperor, in the open at a prearranged place. Francis drove up in a carriage, from which Napoleon handed him down, and they spoke for over an hour as their aides watched. Francis conceded that the British were merchants in human flesh and abandoned the coalition. Napoleon agreed to an armistice, on condition he expelled the Russians from his dominions. It was signed on 6 December.[29]

Napoleon admitted to his secretary Méneval that he had made a mistake in agreeing to the meeting with Francis. 'It is not in the aftermath of a battle that one should have a conference,' he said. 'Today I should only be a soldier, and as such I should pursue victory, not listen to words of peace.' He was right. Davout, who had been in pursuit of the retreating Russians, had cornered them and was on the point of taking Alexander himself prisoner when he was informed by a note from the tsar that an armistice had been signed which included the Russians—which it did not. Davout retired and let them pass. On 5 December Napoleon had written to the elector of Württemberg, who was Alexander's brother-in-law, to use his good offices to persuade the tsar to lay down his arms and negotiate. But Alexander felt, according to one contemporary, 'even more thoroughly defeated than his army', and longed only for a chance to redeem his honour; he would fight on.[30]

On 12 December Napoleon was back at Schönbrunn. Three days later, on the very day by which it was supposed to have joined the anti-French coalition, he signed a treaty of alliance with Prussia, sanctioning its annexation of the British king's fief of Hanover and thereby stealing one of Britain's potential allies on the Continent.

Talleyrand had been trying to persuade Napoleon to be generous to Austria and turn her into his principal European ally, which would give France tranquillity in Italy and the Mediterranean and a bulwark against Russia, as well as a counterbalance to Prussian influence in Germany. But while Napoleon agreed with him that the only alternative, an alliance with Russia, was a poor prospect, qualifying the Russians as 'Asiatics', he had lost respect for Austria. He took no precautions as he moved about Vienna and its environs, and his soldiers noted that while the population was reserved, they treated them as tourists rather than enemies. On 17 December Napoleon had treated an assembly of Austrian generals and representatives of the estates to a two-hour admonition containing, according to the prince de Ligne, 'a little greatness, a little nobility, a little sublimity, a little mediocrity, a little triviality, a little Charlemagne, a little Mahomet and a little Cagliostro...' Napoleon did not consider them worthy allies.[31]

True to his threat, he spent Christmas in Vienna. By the Treaty of Pressburg, dated 27 December, Austria ceded the Tyrol and Vorarlberg to Bavaria, other territories in Germany to Napoleon's allies Württemberg and Baden, and Venetia, Dalmatia, Friuli, and Istria, gained by the Treaty of Campo Formio, to France. As well as losing Francis a sixth of his twenty-four million subjects, it destroyed what was left of the Holy Roman Empire. By the same treaty, Francis recognised Napoleon as King of Italy, the rulers of Bavaria and Württemberg were elevated to royal status, while that of Baden became a grand duke. Finally, Austria had to pay a huge indemnity to France to cover the cost of the campaign.

Napoleon could not afford to waste time in Vienna, as he had a country to rule, and he left the next day. On 31 December he was in Munich, where on 6 January he enjoyed a performance of Mozart's *La Clemenza di Tito* with the newly minted King of Bavaria, who was only too happy to give away his daughter Augusta in marriage to Eugène a week later. Josephine, who had come from Paris for the occasion, was 'at the height of happiness' according to Caulaincourt. The next stop was Stuttgart, where the new King of Württemberg, a man of legendary girth, laid on entertainments which included operas and a hunt. Wherever he went in southern Germany Napoleon was greeted with genuine enthusiasm. But he could not linger.[32]

From the frantic letters of Joseph and Cambacérès it was clear that the French financial crisis had not subsided. News of Austerlitz eased the tension, but Cambacérès urged Napoleon to return as soon as possible, as there was 'a torrent of bankruptcies' undermining confidence in the government. People had come to identify stability and order so much with the person of Napoleon that his absence was in itself cause for anxiety. He was back at the Tuileries at ten o'clock on the evening of 26 January. Before retiring for the night he summoned the Council of State and a number of ministers to meet in the morning.[33]

29

Emperor of the West

I F THE PEOPLE of Paris were relieved to hear that their master was back, the same could not be said of those summoned to appear at the Tuileries on the morning following his return. They were going to have some explaining to do, and it was with a sense of foreboding that they gathered at the palace.

Faced with the necessity of going to war with Austria in the summer of 1805, Napoleon had instructed his treasury minister, François Barbé-Marbois, to raise money. This could only be achieved by unorthodox means which involved a group of Paris finance houses and merchants along with one of the principal military and civil victuallers, Joseph Vanlerberghe. It did not take long for them to become insolvent, and in the case of Vanlerberghe bankrupt, but they were kept afloat by the financier and speculator Gabriel Ouvrard. He had lent money to the Spanish government, in return for the contract to bring gold and silver coinage and bullion from Mexico and other American colonies to Europe. Since the Royal Navy had captured the Spanish treasure fleet in October 1804 and another treasure ship in July 1805, Ouvrard devised an ingenious scheme involving North American and Dutch partners, but this unravelled. In order to avoid the domino collapse of all the finance houses in Paris, Barbé-Marbois had extended credit to Vanlerberghe and his associates through the Bank of France, which precipitated a run on the bank.[1]

Despite his distaste for 'men of business' and their ways, Napoleon had given his sanction to the operation before leaving to join the army. He now grilled his councillors and ministers in a session lasting a full nine hours, at the end of which he sacked Barbé-Marbois. 'I hope that Your Majesty does not accuse me of being a thief?' the minister asked, only to receive the reply, 'I would prefer it a hundred times if you were, for dishonesty has limits, stupidity has none.'[2]

The man Napoleon appointed to take over at the treasury, Nicolas Mollien, was a brilliant administrator who shared his distaste for financial wizardry while understanding the need for subterfuge. He would rebuild the finances of the French state, at the same time allowing his master to pillage them secretly and manage his own parallel finances. The first step was to alter the statutes of the Bank of France, in order to bring it under closer government control; the second to salvage whatever could be from the Ouvrard operation. Vanlerberghe, Ouvrard, and others were summoned and told they had to repay 87 million francs, but while some were forced to pay up, Ouvrard, had enough connections among Napoleon's family and entourage to negotiate his way out. Mollien contrived to involve the London banking house of Hope, based in Amsterdam, and over a period of time most of the Spanish bullion would be brought to France—some of it in British ships.[3]

Napoleon created a separate military treasury, under Pierre Daru, into which all the proceeds of war would be paid, beginning with the indemnity due from Austria under the Treaty of Pressburg. This provided him with a ready war chest of his own. In order to preserve it, he kept part of his army cantoned in Germany, at the expense of the local authorities, and he warned that he would still raise taxes in time of war. He also began building up a '*Domaine extraordinaire*', a private treasury from which he could dispense pensions, grants, and gifts. The cash was kept in a vault at the Tuileries and its contents closely monitored by means of two registers, one listing every source of income and its yield, the other every payment. Wherever Napoleon went, a '*cassette*' went with him, full of rolls of gold coins, to be distributed at will.[4]

When he returned from his first Italian campaign at the end of 1797 and discovered how much money Josephine had spent, Napoleon began investigating where it had all gone, and her continuing profligacy developed in him a reflex for checking bills and accounts.

He would find out independently the cost of fabrics and ribbons in order to query the prices charged by her dressmakers and milliners. When he moved into the Tuileries, he began checking the numbers and cost of candles, firewood, and food. He enquired how many of his household took sugar, how often, and then calculated how many kilograms that added up to, researched the price per kilo, and finally checked the amount spent over the past month. In order to cut down on expenses he introduced vouchers, *bons de repas*, with which members of the court were issued. The scheme was only abandoned after Hortense arrived for dinner and, as her ladies had forgotten to bring the appropriate vouchers, was denied coffee. He also issued regulations regarding candle-ends—if there were more than eight inches left, they were to be reused in the corridors, if between six and eight, they were to be sent to the private quarters of members of the court, and so on. He developed a quasi obsession when it came to linen, ordering Daru to make an inventory of the 12,671 pairs of bedsheets, 2,032 napkins, 500 'rags', and the other items. The cost of laundry did not escape his scrutiny either—not surprisingly, since he kept changing clothes himself: in the space of one month he sent 36 shirts, 14 waistcoats, 137 kerchiefs, and 9 dressing gowns to be washed.[5]

He began keeping notebooks in which he wrote down payments and expenditure in a given area, as well as decisions taken and observations on their execution. This helped him spot anomalies and fraud when checking accounts and to catch out ministers, functionaries, and officers. As he always wanted quick and precise answers to his questions they would sometimes invent facts or figures, but he would challenge them, often knowing more about their ministry or regiment than they did. Mollien noted that no amount of detail could overwhelm him, that he was always looking out for problems to solve, and that 'he was not content to reign or govern, he had to manage, and not as a prime minister, but more directly as any minister'.[6]

The unsatisfactory conduct of affairs by those to whom he had delegated during his absence suggested the need to be better informed and have greater control of what was going on in Paris when he was away. He therefore set up a new system of communication, '*estafettes*', whereby despatches contained in a briefcase to which only he and the director of posts, Lavalette, had a key were carried by postilions from one posting station to the next. They knew where they were going, they had fresh horses at their disposal, and they would write down the time of arrival and departure in a notebook that accompanied each briefcase. As there were sanctions for any delay, they acquitted themselves with diligence. This would permit him to control the administration in Paris more closely and to delegate less.

The Council of State met regularly when he was away, with his chair standing empty on its dais. Whoever was presiding, be it Cambacérès, Lebrun, Joseph, or one of the other grand dignitaries or princes, sat in another chair beside it. According to councilor Jean Pelet de la Lozère, as Napoleon grew older business progressed more rapidly when he was absent, as he would suddenly fall into a reverie or go off on some digression which, fascinating as it might be, did not advance the business in hand. Napoleon himself believed that things did not work properly unless he was present, and the members certainly paid greater attention when he was.[7]

Among the matters addressed on his return from Vienna were education, prison reform, the judiciary, the status of the Jews, the provision of free funerals for the indigent, and subsidy for the opera and the national theatre. What comes through all his ideas on these and other subjects is that he was now more interested in building a society than just the state. On 10 May 1806 he founded the University of France, 'a body exclusively concerned with the education and instruction of the public throughout the Empire', with a special brief to 'direct political and moral opinions'. It was a pyramidal establishment crowning the entire educational system, bringing under a single management all existing institutions of learning. While Napoleon was particularly keen on developing the sciences, as he hoped to build up a large cadre of technocrats, he appeared more concerned with the morality of the teachers and the uniformity of the curriculum than anything else. 'I prefer to see the village children in the hands of a monk who knows nothing beyond his catechism and whose principles I know than of a half-educated man with no moral base,' he declared on the subject of primary schools. As for teachers in higher education, they should be incorporated along semi-military lines and make a ceremonial commitment, like a priest taking holy orders. 'When it comes to education, I feel that the Jesuits have left a great void,' he told the Council of State. 'I do not wish to bring them back, nor any other corporation subject to a foreign power, but I feel I should organise the education of the next generation in such a way as to be able to control its political and moral outlook.' He therefore felt that teachers ought to remain celibate until such time as they had proved themselves to be mature and reliable, but they should marry with time, as marriage was in his eyes the perfect social stabiliser, and they should then go on to achieve status, even as high as the Senate. 'I wish to create a corporation not of Jesuits who would have their sovereign in Rome, but Jesuits who would have no other ambition than that of being useful and no other interest than the public interest.'[8]

A similar prejudice against individualism is manifest in his complaints about the members of the judiciary, whom he regarded as a kind of independent corporation. He wanted to see their sentencing standardised rather than left to their own judgement. He was also bothered by the Jews, of whose existence he had only become aware on his visits to northeastern France and western Germany. Aside from his natural dislike of 'people of business', which prompted him to see Jews as usurers preying on the innocent poor like 'veritable flocks of crows', 'sucking the blood of real Frenchmen' and 'a vile, degraded nation capable of every baseness', he did not like the idea of them as a nation apart and suspected them of disloyalty and spying. The fact that their presence was most notable in the border region of Alsace bothered him, and the best thing to do with them, he suggested, was to spread them more evenly over the territory of France. He would convene a great Sanhedrin, bringing together the rabbis and elders in a body, in consultation with which he would regulate their status.[9]

Much of Napoleon's most cherished legislation was aimed at integrating people into society. He introduced the '*livret*', which every worker had to carry, defining his profession. He was inordinately proud of having overseen the introduction of the '*cadastre*', the land registry, which he described as being tantamount to a new constitution in itself, since it fixed everyone's rights to the property they possessed but also because it fixed their taxable status and therefore their position in society. They no longer needed to fear having their property seized, but in return had to submit to the state, in which they thereby gained a stake.[10]

The grueling workload he assumed was reflected in the routines he had adopted, which were carefully recorded by Agathon Fain, who now joined Méneval in Napoleon's private office as archivist. After his coronation Napoleon no longer shared a bedroom with Josephine. He did on occasion visit her for the night, and sometimes he would ask her to come and read to him before he went to sleep. This left him free to follow his own routine, which involved rising at around two o'clock in the morning to work with his secretary, who had to be on call at all hours of the day and night. After a couple of hours' work he would take a hot bath, and sometimes go to bed for an hour or two of sleep, before rising at seven to begin his toilette and dress. In Paris he always wore the blue uniform of a colonel of the grenadiers of the Guard, with white stockings and buckled shoes, or if he were going hunting, his green hunting dress, and only occasionally the '*habit habillé*', the former court dress which he had reintroduced but hated wearing, referring to it as '*cet accoutrement*'. On campaign, he wore the green uniform of a colonel of the mounted chasseurs of the Guard, with high top-boots.[11]

He had not moved his quarters in the Tuileries, but they had been altered. His inner study was, in the words of Fain, 'but a dependency of his bedroom', and he would work there in his dressing gown. The outer study or salon he only entered when fully dressed. Between the inner study and the bedroom was a room containing a store of maps and a large table on which they could be spread. At one end there was a partition with a hatch, behind which was a staircase and a station manned twenty-four hours a day by a *garde de portefeuille* who passed incoming communications through it. There were two of them, working alternate shifts, eating and sleeping at their station, entering the private study only to tidy and to light the fire.[12]

Napoleon's study was dominated by a table designed by himself, with two indentations facing each other on the long sides so he could sit at it facing his secretary with plenty of space for papers on either side. He would sit with his back to the fire, facing the door to the outer study or salon. The room had one window, opening on the gardens, in the embrasure of which stood a small writing table, at which the secretary would take dictation with his back to the room. At the other end of the room was a bookcase with a clock mounted in it, and in front of that a long mahogany table on which spreadsheets and maps could be unfolded. Beside the fire was a comfortable settee with a small round occasional table beside it.

Having dressed, Napoleon was usually back in his study by eight o'clock, ready to start work. His secretary would sit opposite him at the desk, passing him papers to sign. He would then go over to the fireplace and read the despatches and letters piled on the table next to the settee. He would dictate replies to some, dropping them on the floor for filing, and place those which needed reflection on the table to be dealt with later. He also read various reports and letters from his correspondents, the 'friends' all over the country who kept him abreast of opinion and gossip, which he would throw into the fire after reading, and would sometimes peruse a book, which also went into the fire if it displeased him. He would also look through the red morocco briefcase marked '*Gazettes étrangères*', containing transcripts of letters intercepted by the *cabinet noir*, the postal intercept and decryption office.[13]

If there was need for a map, the emperor's cartographer, Louis Albert Bacler d'Albe, was summoned. After finding the requisite map in the cases of a room which was little more than a passage between the bedroom and the study, he would spread it on the large, sturdy table built for the purpose and produce a pincushion full of pins with different-coloured heads, together with coloured pencils and a pair of compasses to measure distances. If it was a large map, they would both climb onto the table and lie down on it. 'More than once I saw them both lying on that great table, interrupting their work with a sudden exclamation only when one of their heads hit the other too hard,' records Fain.[14]

At nine o'clock the chamberlain of the day would scratch on the door to announce that it was time for the *lever*. Napoleon would pass into the larger study or salon, where the *chefs de service* of the court would be waiting to receive their orders for the day, along with those of the ministers who had something to report or orders to receive. The room contained two tables covered in green cloth placed diagonally in the corners at the end nearest his private study, at which Napoleon would sit and interrogate a minister or make him sit and take dictation. But on the whole he would receive people standing up in order to save time. The minister of police and the prefect of the Seine were always there to regale him with the latest information and gossip on the night's doings. Unless he needed to discuss some matter at length, the *lever* might last as little as five minutes, after which he would go back to his study to work. He breakfasted in a few minutes, taking only one cup of strong coffee. On Thursdays there was a *grand lever*, to which all those who had entry would come, which included most of the court. The morning's work usually concluded in an interview with the secretary of state, Maret, a man some loathed but who was perfectly mannered and was one of the few who enjoyed Napoleon's complete confidence.[15]

Napoleon dined at six or seven, usually with Josephine, and with members of his family on Sundays. The dinner consisted of no more than two or three dishes, and usually lasted closer to fifteen than twenty minutes. Sometimes not a word was uttered. After dinner he might go back to work or join the empress in her salon. At the end of the evening there was a brief *coucher*, at which he would give the heads of the household services their orders for the next day. He was normally in bed by ten o'clock. 'In his private life, Napoleon was almost a military monk and everyone in his immediate service had to accommodate themselves to his rule,' recorded Fain.[16]

The workload did not prevent the military monk from going to the theatre, hunting, planning new works, and even philandering. The new sleeping arrangement gave him greater freedom, and he used it. He would take advantage of some of Josephine's young ladies-in-waiting, who were in no position to resist. He also liked going with Duroc to the public masked balls at the Opéra, where he acted as though nobody could recognise him, propositioning women and spreading salacious gossip. At one of these, early in 1806, he met Éléonore de la Plaigne, a nineteen-year-old protégée of Caroline Murat, newly married to a dragoon captain by the name of Revel, by all accounts an undesirable character. Shortly after Napoleon had noticed her, the captain was arrested, demoted, and roughly dealt with by the police before being pressured into divorcing her. Éléonore was taken in by the Murats as a member of their household and lodged in a small pavilion of their house at Neuilly, where Napoleon visited her.[17]

'He would sometimes spend a whole day without working, but without leaving the palace or even his study,' according to Méneval. 'He might go and spend an hour with the empress, then he would come back, sit down on his settee and either fell asleep or seemed to for a while. He would then come and perch on a corner of my desk, or on the arm of my chair, sometimes even on my knees. He would then put his arm around my neck and amuse himself by playfully pulling my ear or smacking me on the shoulder or on the cheek.' He would wander about the room, pull out a book, quote from it and discuss it, or declaim some verses by Corneille, and sometimes he would sing—horribly out of tune.[18]

In the course of the past year Napoleon had defeated the combined might of the two greatest powers on the Continent, reducing one emperor to begging for peace and the other to ignominious flight. The experience cannot have failed to give him a sense of almost limitless power—his troops enthusiastically proclaimed that under his leadership nothing was impossible. He had also gained closer experience of the other states of Europe, at the diplomatic, administrative, and military levels, and was not impressed. He had met rulers who were pusillanimous, ineffectual, corrupt, stupid, treacherous, weak, or just lazy. He had seen for himself how poorly and nonsensically most of Europe was administered, and how people were ill-treated and resources wasted, and had come to view all rulers with varying degrees of contempt.

One who fully deserved it was the King of Naples. Back in September 1805 he had signed a treaty with France pledging to remain neutral on condition French troops withdrew from the Neapolitan ports which they had occupied against British and Russian landings. Knowing through his spies that the king had already signed treaties with Britain and Russia against France, Napoleon wrote to Queen Maria-Carolina, warning her not to make any hostile moves. Three weeks after French troops started pulling out, in mid-October an Anglo-Russian squadron appeared and landed 12,000 Russian and 8,000 British troops which, along with the 40,000 strong Neapolitan army, began operations against the kingdom of Italy. On hearing news of Austerlitz, the Anglo-Russian contingent fell back and re-embarked. On 26 December Napoleon issued a proclamation from Schönbrunn declaring that by their faithlessness the Bourbons of Naples had forfeited their right to reign. On 6 January 1806 he put his brother Joseph in command of a French army with orders to occupy their kingdom. Maria-Carolina wrote an abject letter declaring that she had recovered from the blindness which had led her to act the way she had and appealing to Napoleon's generosity to leave her husband his throne. But Joseph was already making his entry into Naples, and on 30 March Napoleon nominated him King of Naples—for the sake, as he put it, of the tranquillity of Europe. This, in Napoleon's view, required curbing British and Russian ambitions in the Mediterranean. With the whole of the Italian and Illyrian coasts now in French hands, and Spain as an ally, it seemed possible.

Following the death of Pitt on 23 January and the formation of a ministry under Lord Grenville with Charles James Fox as foreign secretary, an accommodation with Britain also seemed possible. On 6 March Talleyrand received a letter from Fox passing on intelligence about a planned royalist plot against Napoleon and suggesting peace talks. The British cabinet appeared willing to proceed, but nevertheless imposed a blockade on the coast of Europe from the Elbe in Germany to Brest in France. Napoleon took the precaution of pre-empting any discussion of the status of the Netherlands by converting the Batavian Republic into the kingdom of Holland, with his brother Louis as king.

Ten days after Louis ascended the throne, on 5 June 1806, the Earl of Yarmouth arrived in Paris to negotiate a peace treaty. The

British were prepared to make peace, their only demand being that King Ferdinand be allowed to keep the Sicilian half of his former kingdom and that Joseph content himself with the mainland part of Naples. Napoleon declared that Joseph must also have Sicily and promised to find Ferdinand a replacement kingdom in northern Germany or possibly Dalmatia. Oubril, who had been sent to Paris by Tsar Alexander to negotiate a treaty, suggested that Ferdinand be compensated with the Balearic Islands. This set alarm bells ringing in London, where it was seen as a ploy to provide Russia with a naval base in the western Mediterranean. The new British negotiator, Lord Lauderdale, who reached Paris on 5 August, suggested Ferdinand be compensated somewhere in South America. For reasons that are hard to fathom, Napoleon kept changing his demands, undermining Talleyrand and eventually replacing him as negotiator with the less than diplomatic General Savary. Napoleon seems to have begun entertaining an entirely new vision of how Europe should be reordered, and of France's position in it.[19]

A striking aspect of his elevation of 'Joseph-Napoleon' to the throne of Naples and Sicily was that it entirely bypassed the French Senate. So did the transformation of the Batavian Republic into a kingdom with Louis as king. The Senate was simply informed that 'We have proclaimed Louis-Napoléon, our beloved brother, King of Holland.' He went on to redraw the political map of Europe and transform the manner in which a great swathe of the Continent was governed. Having reduced Austria and enlarged Bavaria, Württemberg, and Baden, he bound those three states, along with the remaining thirteen German political units, into the Confederation of the Rhine, of which he nominated himself protector. It was an updated version of the Holy Roman Empire, part of a Continental security system with each of the members obliged to provide a certain number of troops in the common defence: France 200,000; Bavaria 30,000; Württemberg 12,000; Baden, Cleves, and Berg 5,000 each; Hesse-Darmstadt 4,000; and the rest 4,000 between them.

There was a logic to this arrangement, insofar as it protected the German heartland from outside interference and invasion; but the logic required the successor to the Holy Roman Emperor, this

'Emperor of the West' as people had begun to allude to him, to govern in the universal interest. Yet France was not actually a member of the Confederation, although it was clear that the whole enterprise was to function in her interest. The same went for the supposedly sovereign kingdoms. 'Do not ever cease to be a Frenchman,' Napoleon instructed Louis after making him King of Holland.[20]

The internationalism of the Revolution had been gradually subsumed into the cult of the Nation, which had in turn been subjected by Bonaparte to that of the State, and this was now being transformed into a vision of empire. The terminology of the *Grande Nation* had been superseded by that of the *Grand Empire*. Buried somewhere in this was the ideal of a Europe without frontiers, a common *patrie* of the Enlightenment with a universal legal system and currency in which, as Napoleon put it, 'while travelling, everyone would never cease to be at home'. It was a dream that appealed to many and held out promise to millions, as most of the Continent was ruled in ways that were at best not benign, by corrupt and incompetent administrations geared to the benefit of the few.[21]

'One of these days, I am convinced, we will see the Empire of the West reborn as tired peoples rush to place themselves under the rule of the best-governed nation,' Napoleon told his Council of State. In this, as in other things, he was ahead of his time. Yet as he started constructing his new pan-European system, he unaccountably began to look back. Not only did he base his diplomatic strategy on that of Louis XIV—his new 'Empire of the West' resembled a medieval system of personal vassalage.[22]

He began at home, introducing statutes to govern the imperial family, of which he was 'head and father'. They were modelled on similar documents governing the ancient royal houses of Europe, but included concepts pertaining to Corsican family lore together with a dash of military discipline. They laid down rules of precedence, guidelines on conduct, restrictions on marriage and travel, so that nothing could be done or undertaken without his consent. They included a table of penalties, incarceration and exile among them.

The Continent was to be bound together not by a modern administration but by the Bonaparte dynasty and those established royal and ducal houses of Europe prepared to associate with it. Joseph was King of Naples, Louis King of Holland, Caroline's husband Murat Grand Duke of Berg, Élisa Bacciochi Duchess of Lucca and Piombino. Further layers of control were provided by those closest to the imperial throne, with Berthier becoming prince of Neuchâtel (a former Prussian fief), Bernadotte prince of Pontecorvo, and Talleyrand prince of Benevento in the kingdom of Naples. Other fiefs, such as Dalmatia, Istria, Friuli, Cadora, Belluno, Conegliano, Treviso, Feltre, Bassano, Vicenza, Padua, and Rovigo in what had been Venetian territory went to ministers and marshals.

In France itself, by a *senatus-consulte* of 14 August 1806, Napoleon created an imperial nobility, granting titles of prince, duke, count, baron, and knight. The language accompanying these acts and investitures was redolent of another age; the costumes, forms of address, and fabulous endowments were an insult to the spirit of the Enlightenment and all that was dear to most Frenchmen about the Revolution. 'Dare I say it, when in a full council he posited the question of whether the institution of hereditary titles was contrary to the principles of equality which we professed, almost all of us replied in the negative,' admitted the old revolutionary butcher of nobles Fouché. 'In fact, the Empire being a new monarchy, the creation of grand officers and dignitaries and the bulwark of a new nobility seemed indispensible to us.' He became Duke of Otranto.[23]

Human vanity had triumphed over the so-called Age of Reason. Murat, Louis, and Joseph instituted new orders of chivalry, exchanged decorations, designed refulgent uniforms for themselves, their regiments of Guards, and court officials. They published etiquettes and granted titles of nobility to their friends. They sent ambassadors to each other's courts and played the part of monarch to a degree that even Napoleon found ludicrous. Marshals, ministers, and generals, and particularly their wives, vied for titles and resented each other's, and former revolutionaries applied themselves to inventing arms to paint on their carriage doors. When Jérôme instituted an Order of the Union featuring the imperial eagle, a serpent eating its tail as a symbol of eternity, the lion of Hesse, the horse of Brunswick, and another eagle and lion, Napoleon told him there were 'too many beasts in that order'.[24]

'Few people in his position would have retained such a degree of modesty and simplicity,' maintained the prefect of the palace, Louis Bausset, and there was a grain of truth in this. When a group of people declared the desire to open a subscription for an equestrian statue of him, Napoleon forbade it. 'Very simple in his way of being, he liked luxury in his surroundings only because it seemed to him that great show was a way of imposing, which made the business of government easier,' according to Fain, who saw in him 'a sure friend and the best of masters'. He spoiled his servants and made sure they did not lack for anything, even after they retired. If he did lose his temper with them, or upset them in any way, he would make up for it royally.[25]

His view of himself and what he believed he embodied is reflected in his court ceremonial, which grew ever more ponderous, and in his artistic patronage, particularly his building programme and the monuments he erected. During his consulship, he wanted to celebrate soldiers. His early schemes included an ambitious rebuilding of the Invalides centred on a temple of Mars in which great French commanders would be suitably commemorated. Dead brothers-in-arms such as Desaix were immortalised in sculpture. In 1806 he laid the foundation stone of a triumphal arch to be built in front of the Tuileries on the place du Carousel, and of a column modelled on that of Trajan in Rome, to be cast from the bronze of the cannon captured at Austerlitz, on the place Vendôme. Another, larger triumphal arch was also projected for the other end of the Champs Élysées. These works were balanced by a concurrent project to rebuild the church of La Madeleine as a temple to the glorious dead, but this was to be the last of the monuments dedicated to soldiers.

His next plan was for a vast palace on the heights of Chaillot, effectively a new imperial city with military barracks, a university, archives, a 'palace of the arts' and other buildings. His programme did continue to benefit the public: between 1804 and 1813 he spent 277 million francs on roads; 122 on canals; 117 on sea-ports; 102 on embankments, roads, squares, and bridges in Paris; 30 on bridges elsewhere; and 62 on imperial palaces and buildings such as ministries and the stock exchange. Yet from 1806 onward the monuments centred not on the nation, the army, or even great victories, but on the person of the emperor. He does not, however, appear to have worked out in his own mind the ultimate purpose or the limits of the empire he was building.[26]

30
_____

Master of Europe

T HE PEACE NEGOTIATIONS in the spring and summer of
1806 with Britain and Russia were bedevilled by mistrust
on all sides. While professing its peaceful intent, the British
cabinet not only issued Orders in Council putting France and much
of Germany under blockade, it continued to support the Bourbon
King of Naples against Napoleon's brother Joseph, landing troops
in southern Italy and in July scoring its first mainland victory for a
century at Maida. Napoleon was also stalling. He had negotiated a
treaty with the tsar's envoy Peter von Oubril which had been sent to
St Petersburg for ratification; he was probably hoping that this would
put him in a stronger negotiating position vis-à-vis Britain.

It unsettled the King of Prussia, who feared that Napoleon would
make a deal at his expense. He had acquired Hanover by a treaty
with France in December 1805, and it seemed probable that an agreement between Britain and France would entail its loss. He also suspected that the price of peace between Napoleon and Tsar Alexander
might be the cession of some of his eastern lands to Russia. Having
marginalised Prussia, Napoleon had no wish to reduce it further, and
tried to reassure the king, going so far as to order at the beginning of
August the withdrawal of French troops still in Germany. Frederick
William wanted nothing more than a preservation of the status quo,
but he was being influenced by his belligerent queen and his minister
Karl August von Hardenberg, who played to a body of public opinion which felt that Prussia had been humiliated, and an officer corps
which believed its army was the best in Europe and longed to prove

it. On 9 August, in response to a false report by General Blücher of French troop concentrations threatening Hanover, Prussia began to mobilise.[1]

Although Napoleon responded with assurances of his desire for peace, he was outraged. When he learned of the publication in Bavaria of a violently anti-French pamphlet bemoaning the humiliation of Germany, he had its publisher, Johann Philipp Palm, tried by a military court and shot on 26 August. This provoked reactions among German nationalists and a surge of anti-French feeling in Prussia, where officers demonstratively sharpened their sabres on the stone steps of the French embassy in Berlin. Quick to take offence himself, Napoleon was seemingly incapable of appreciating that he could give it.

He also suspected there was more to Prussia's belligerence. 'The idea that Prussia can single-handedly engage against me seems to me so ridiculous that it is not worth discussing,' he wrote to Talleyrand. When on 3 September he learned that Tsar Alexander had rejected the treaty negotiated by Oubril he realised that Britain, Russia, and Prussia had reached an understanding. Failing to grasp that he had pushed them into each other's arms, he could see only perfidy. 'These kings will not leave me alone,' he said to Caulaincourt. 'They seem determined to convince me that I will have no peace and quiet until I have destroyed them.'[2]

He instructed Talleyrand and his ambassador in Berlin to assure Frederick William that he had no wish to make war, pointing out that it was not in his interests to disturb a peace he had just concluded. He may have been sincere in this, as it would have been difficult to see what advantages such a war could bring him. But he had taken umbrage at what he called 'a little kingdom like Prussia' defying him in front of the whole of Europe. It was, as he put it to Caulaincourt, 'like some little runt impudently raising its leg to piss over a Great Dane'. By this stage, peace could only have been maintained if the runt lowered its leg, but that was not going to happen.[3]

Buoyed by the prospect of 100,000 Russians marching to his aid, and anticipating that Austria, Bavaria, and Sweden would seize the opportunity to join in the fight against France, the usually undecided

Frederick William set his troops in motion. On 12 September they invaded Saxony in order to prompt its ruler into an alliance against the French. Two weeks later he issued an ultimatum to Napoleon to pull all his forces back behind the Rhine. 'They want to change the face of Europe,' Napoleon said to Caulaincourt. He went on to speculate that perhaps his 'Star' meant him to fight this senseless war which would, as he put it, 'open up a vast field for great questions'. He also intimated that since mere treaties could not guarantee peace, some new system would have to be put in place.[4]

He wrote a last letter to Frederick William on 12 September professing his peaceful intentions and warning him not to start a pointless war. But he had ordered his *maison militaire* to take the road two weeks earlier, and on 25 September he left Saint-Cloud for Mainz, accompanied by Josephine. On 2 October he was at Würzburg with his ally the King of Württemberg, aiming to confront the Prussians in Saxony.[5]

On 10 October Lannes, commanding the advance guard, attacked and defeated a Prussian corps at Saalfeld. Its commander, the Prussian king's cousin Prince Ludvig, was cut down and killed by a French hussar. Napoleon sent one of his aides with a letter for Frederick William proposing peace talks, but on reaching the Prussian lines the aide was held back, and the letter never reached its destination.

The Prussian corps manoeuvred erratically, and Napoleon had some difficulty in guessing their intentions, but he reacted with extraordinary speed and attacked what he believed to be their main force at Jena on 14 October. In fact it was a body of about 40,000 men under Prince Hohenlohe. Not realising in the thick morning mist (he was shot at by his own pickets as he reconnoitred) that he outnumbered them heavily, possibly by as much as two to one, Naopoleon operated cautiously and defeated them, putting them to flight by the early afternoon. Some fifteen kilometres to the north, Davout, with 30,000 men, who had been ordered to outflank what Napoleon took to be the left wing of the Prussian force, had run into the main Prussian army numbering some 70,000 men under the Duke of Brunswick and King Frederick William at Auerstadt. Bernadotte, who was marching alongside Davout with his corps, failed to

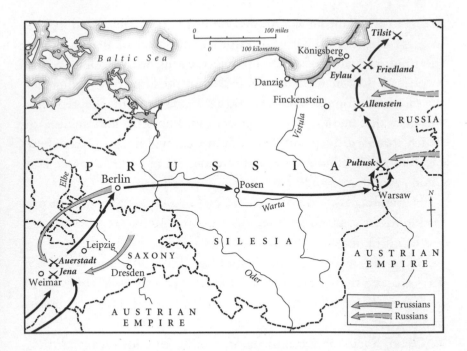

come to his aid. But although he suffered heavy losses, in a brilliant action Davout routed Brunswick, who was mortally wounded, and as the retreating remnants collided with those fleeing from the battle-field of Jena, the Prussian army disintegrated. Entire corps and for-tresses surrendered to advancing platoons of French cavalry, bringing Prussian losses in killed, wounded, and captured to 140,000 in the space of a few days.[6]

On 24 October Napoleon was at Potsdam, where like Tsar Alex-ander before him he visited the tomb of Frederick the Great, stealing his hat and sword to take back to the Invalides as trophies. He re-ported to Josephine that he was well and that he found Frederick the Great's renowned retreat of Sans-Souci 'very pleasant'. Davout made a triumphal entry into Berlin, where Napoleon joined him three days later, riding down Unter den Linden to take up residence at the royal palace, escorted by his Guard in parade-ground order.[7]

Frederick William had written him a pathetic plea for a suspen-sion of hostilities, but Napoleon was not in generous mood. He had been so incensed by Bernadotte's behaviour that he would have had him court-martialled and shot had he not been the husband of Dé-sirée. He did order the execution of the governor of Berlin, Prince Hatzefeld, as a spy. After an amiable meeting with Napoleon, the prince had written to Frederick William's headquarters giving details of French dispositions, and the letter had been intercepted. The prince's wife came to beg for mercy, and Napoleon pardoned him. But his mood did not improve. Riding along with his Mameluke Roustam at his side, he drew a pistol from his saddle-holster and aimed at some crows. The gun did not go off, so he angrily threw it to the ground and berated Roustam in the foulest language. He was obliged to apologise after the Mameluke reminded him he had ordered a new safety-catch fitted to the pistol.[8]

Napoleon was not impressed by Prussia. Its army had been little better than an eighteenth-century military machine, with the soldiers showing scant devotion to their officers or their country. 'The Prussians are not a nation,' he kept saying to Caulaincourt. He likened the desk of Frederick the Great at Sans-Souci to that of a French provincial notary, and having meant to take the four-horse chariot from the triumphal arch at Charlottenburg to adorn one in Paris, he was disgusted to discover that it was made of sheets of iron. He described Prussia and its monarchy as a tinsel stage-set hardly worth preserving and began turning over in his mind various options regarding the reorganisation of its territory.[9]

Count Metternich, the Austrian ambassador in Paris, believed that if Napoleon had made peace with Frederick William on the basis of a reduced Prussia incorporated into the Confederation of the Rhine, France would have been unassailable and Russian influence would have been entirely excluded from Germany. But Napoleon was slow to respond to Prussian overtures, and his conditions—that Prussia give up her possessions west of the Elbe, pay heavy war reparations, and join France in alliance against Russia and Britain—were too harsh. Negotiations never got going before Frederick William took refuge in Königsberg to await salvation by Russia.[10]

Meanwhile Napoleon decided to strike at the paymaster of all the coalitions against France. Like most Europeans at the time, he believed that the British economy, which was heavily reliant on credit, would implode if the trade supporting that credit were destroyed. Responding to the British Orders in Council of 16 May 1806, which decreed a blockade of French ports and seizure of French shipping, on 21 November he signed decrees which closed all European ports under his control to British ships, British goods, and British trade. The aim was to deny British industry its markets and cut off vital supplies of grain, timber and raw materials, particularly from the Baltic. Napoleon would increase the pressure the following year, when he ordered that any ship which had docked at a British port could be confiscated, and then broadened this to include any vessel which had been searched by the Royal Navy, and to allow French corsairs to confiscate British goods on neutral ships. The British responded in kind.

The Berlin Decrees had far-reaching implications, since they made it essential that France control, directly or indirectly, every port in Europe. Allies would have to be forced and neutrals coerced into what Napoleon would call his Continental System. As a first step he ordered General Mortier to occupy the Hanseatic towns of Hamburg and Lübeck, and Swedish Pomerania. But enforcing the decrees was going to take a great deal more than a few regiments. Napoleon had entered into an open-ended commitment which he was never going to be able to fulfil. As if that were not enough, he now opened a Pandora's box.

On 19 November he had received a delegation of Polish patriots from Posen (Poznań), the capital of a Polish province annexed by Prussia a decade earlier. The collapse of Prussian might had raised hopes throughout Poland of the re-creation of that country, which had been divided up by Russia, Prussia, and Austria in 1795. The Prussian part of it was now effectively free, and the patriots had come to find out his plans for the area. He had none.

Like most western Europeans, Napoleon felt residual sympathy for the Poles following the loss of their country. During his first Italian campaign he had come to value several Polish officers, and particularly his aide Sułkowski. When he realised that among the Austrian prisoners there were Poles who had been drafted by the Austrians and were keen to fight against them, he formed them up into a legion which fought alongside the French. But when they were no longer of any use he felt no compunction in sending them off to Saint-Domingue, where most of them perished. Back in March 1806 he had instructed Fouché to insert articles in the press describing Russian repression and violence against the Poles, probably only to embarrass Russia, with which he was then negotiating a treaty.[11]

Many Poles drafted into Prussian ranks had also deserted to the French, and Napoleon had them formed up into a legion under General Józef Zajączek, who had served under him in Italy and Egypt (1,500 were incorporated into a legion made up of Irish insurgents of 1798 who had been sold by the British government to the King of Prussia to work in mines, but had subsequently been pressed into the Prussian army). On 24 September Napoleon had instructed Eugène to despatch all Polish staff officers in the Italian army to join the legion under Zajączek. Less than a week after reaching Berlin, on 3 November, he wrote to Fouché in Paris instructing him to send the Polish general Tadeusz Kościuszko, the universally respected leader of a Polish national insurrection in 1794, along with any other Poles he could find in Paris, to join him in the Prussian capital. On 17 November, two days before his meeting with the delegates from Posen, he had given instructions for it to be said that he was intending to re-create a Polish state. Talleyrand was keen on the idea and had been sounding out Austria on the possibility of her giving up her Polish province of Galicia in exchange for the richer Prussian one of Silesia.[12]

By then the Grande Armée was marching through Poland to meet the oncoming Russians, and on 25 November Napoleon left Berlin to join it. Late on 27 November he drove into Posen, which was illuminated in his honour. He was greeted like a saviour, and young men rode in from the surrounding countryside hoping to fight for their country under his command. Murat, who rode into Warsaw on the following day, wrote that he 'had never seen such a strong national spirit'. The inhabitants were inviting officers and men into their houses, offering them food and drink. 'The Poles are all asking for arms, leaders and officers,' he went on. The following day, after talking to some of the locals, he wrote that he was convinced they were ready to rise and fight and would be prepared to accept any ruler he chose to give them. He asked for instructions on how to proceed.[13]

Napoleon wrote back from Posen that the Poles were superficial and unreliable, telling him to offer nothing. 'Make them understand that I have not come to beg a throne for one of my people, as I do not lack thrones to give my family,' he warned Murat, who was already being lined up by Paris gossip as the next King of Poland. He had always been a dashing dresser, never conforming to regulation uniforms, preferring to swagger in skin-tight buckskin breeches adorned with ribbons, embroidered dolmans, and turned-down buccaneer boots, but when he first saw traditional Polish noble dress, he stepped into another sartorial world. He had a new wardrobe run up in his version of the Polish model, with fur-trimmed velvet tunics, slashed hanging sleeves, and fur cap, in a variety of colours. 'He had all the majesty of an actor trying to play a king,' commented one Polish lady, but she admitted that the Polish people would have accepted him as such if it had meant independence.[14]

Napoleon meant to keep his options open as to how he would settle the 'great questions' raised by his victory over Prussia. While he encouraged Poles to join the ranks, in talks with local notables he did little more than demand supplies for his army. On 2 December he attended a ball given by the local nobility to mark the anniversary of his coronation, only to tell them they should be booted and spurred, not wearing stockings and pumps. After the ball he wrote to Josephine saying he loved and missed her, he found the nights long without her, and he would soon be sending for her to join him. He was frustrated, as he had devised a sweeping manoeuvre designed to destroy the Russian army now in Poland under General Bennigsen. He had sent detailed instructions to his corps commanders, but while his plan looked straightforward on the map, it was proving difficult to implement, and he realised he needed to be closer to the theatre of operations.

On 16 December he left for Warsaw, which he reached on horseback, having had to abandon his carriage because of the state of the roads. He entered the city at night in order to avoid having to face a reception committee, spent four days there making arrangements for what he hoped would be a decisive battle, then left to take charge of operations, crossing the Vistula and the Bug to join his army at Nasielsk on Christmas Day. Intelligence on the whereabouts of the main Russian forces was confused, and while Lannes with 25,000 men attacked what proved to be Bennigsen's main force of 40,000 near Pułtusk, Napoleon marched toward Gołymin, where Davout, Augereau, Ney, and Murat were engaged against other Russian units. By the time he realised what was going on and struggled back to join Lannes, it was all over. Lannes had beaten Bennigsen, who retired, but pursuit was out of the question due to atrocious conditions.

A sudden thaw had melted the snow and ice, turning the roads, mere tracks, into rivers of mud. The conditions were so bad that gun carriages sank into the sludge, dragging down their horse teams; even doubling the teams could not pull them free. Sunk to their bellies in mud overnight, the animals died, their crews helpless. Soldiers took off their boots and carried them, but it was not just boots that were swallowed up by the mud. According to the artillery officer Louis Brun de Villeret, 'in one single regiment, eighteen men drowned in this mud during a night march, their comrades being unable to help them without running the same risk'. Caulaincourt complained of 'mud up to one's ears', and Napoleon himself had to spend the night with only a few wisps of straw between him and the mud in an old barn. 'Regiments melted away by the day,' remembered Lieutenant Théodore de Rumigny.

Matters were not improved by a dire lack of supplies. 'No commander ever gave as many orders to provide victuals for his army as Napoleon,' remarked one infantryman, 'and none were more poorly executed.' What little supplies there were had got bogged down as well, and the underpopulated, poor countryside provided scant resources. Men died of hunger and exposure, and some took their own lives out of despair. The mud of Poland entered French military lore alongside the burning sands of Egypt.[15]

Napoleon's usual method of moving fast and seizing opportunities as they offered themselves proved useless in these conditions, but he had also fallen behind the army and could not coordinate operations. It is allegedly from this moment that he began to refer to his Guard as '*grognards*' on account of their grumbles over the conditions and lack of food. They had learned the Polish for bread, '*chleb*', and for 'There is none,' '*Nie ma.*' Whenever he passed marching troops they would shout '*Chleba, Chleba!*' to which he would shout back, '*Nie ma!*' They were not just grumbling over the lack of food; it was the first campaign on which he was not constantly in their midst. There was also criticism of his conduct of the campaign, and his prestige in the ranks was dented.[16]

Back in Pułtusk on 29 December, given the impossibility of fighting on, he ordered his army to take winter quarters. On his return to Warsaw on 1 January 1807 he declared that since they could not fight, everyone should enjoy themselves. He was certainly meaning to do so himself. On 31 December news had reached him that Éléonore de la Plaigne had given birth to his son—proof that it was not, as Josephine had always maintained, he who was infertile. In his letters there was no further mention of her coming out to join him.

He spent the whole of January in Warsaw. There were parades, balls, and concerts. Polish society fêted their French guests, and many women gave themselves to their putative liberators with patriotic fervour. 'The time we spent in Warsaw was magical,' recalled Savary. Major Boulart of the Guard Artillery remembered to the end of his days a pair of 'beautiful eyes' and the joy of flying around the sparkling, snowbound city in a sleigh.[17]

Napoleon was viewed with respect, and in some cases with genuine awe. 'He seemed to have a halo,' noted the thirty-year-old Countess Potocka, who was 'bedazzled' by the sense of power he exuded. But if he was expecting to enjoy the privileges of a conqueror, he was to meet with disappointment. At a ball he spotted the beautiful Princess Lubomirska and in the morning sent an aide to inform her he would call that evening. Fearing for her virtue, the princess ordered her carriages and left for the country, and when he called Napoleon found himself, as the Polish saying went, kissing the door handle. 'Silly woman,' he snapped.[18]

Josephine, still in Mainz, was eager to join him in Warsaw, but he put her off, using the distance and the bad roads as a pretext. He urged her to return to Paris and enjoy herself, promising to let her know when she could join him. His letter of 18 January was a little more impatient: 'I am very well and love you very much, but if you keep crying I will begin to think you have no courage and no character.' He did add a saucy phrase about kissing her breasts, but it was not hers he was thinking of.[19]

The evening before, at a ball given by Talleyrand in one of the Warsaw palaces, he had danced with a young woman he had spotted at a reception ten days earlier and was smitten. Her name was Maria Walewska. She was twenty and married to a seventy-one-year-old, and though she did not love her husband, she had strong principles and believed in the sanctity of marriage. Her two brothers, both officers in the French army, and various other Polish patriots who had noticed Napoleon's interest, urged her to at least humour the man on whom the future of their country depended. She appears to have given him some hope, and the following day he sent her a note through Duroc. 'I saw only you, I admired only you, I desire only you,' he wrote, demanding a prompt response 'to calm the impatient ardour of N'. She refused to go with Duroc to the ardent Napoleon. He wrote again. 'Have I offended you, Madame? I had the right to expect the contrary. Your emotions have cooled, while mine have grown. Thoughts of you do not let me sleep! Oh! Give a little joy, of happiness to a poor heart which is ready to adore you. Must it be so difficult to obtain a reply? You owe me two.' She did come to him at the royal castle that evening, but left at four in the morning without having given herself to him. That morning he wrote Josephine a testy note ordering her to be 'merry, charming and happy', and stop nagging him.[20]

Walewska's reticence was a novel experience for one who had grown used to submission. In his short, eager letters he cast himself as the lonely man at the top whose cares only she could dispel by allowing him to throw himself at her feet. 'Oh! Come to me, come to me! All your wishes will be granted. Your motherland will be dear to me if you take pity on my poor heart,' he cajoled, counting on her patriotism. The more she resisted him, the more loving the tone of his letters, the more he followed her around at receptions, watching her every move like a lovelorn teenager. At the same time his tone forbidding Josephine to even think of coming to join him grew imperious. Walewska did agree to call on him again, and after expending every argument he could, and faced only with her tears, he appears to have as good as raped her.[21]

He had set up a council of prominent Poles as a provisional administration, but it was firmly supervised by Talleyrand and Maret, and its brief was limited to raising a Polish army and providing victuals and horses for his troops. At the same time, he ordered the setting up of a French-style administrative structure and even the introduction of his Civil Code. He would not make further commitments until the military situation had clarified.[22]

He left Warsaw on 30 January, travelling north through Pułtusk, where he visited the sick Lannes, who told him the place was not worth fighting for and they should go home, a view echoed by many in his entourage. Three days later he watched a skirmish between Soult's corps and Bennigsen, who fell back, and on 4 February himself attacked Bennigsen at Allenstein, forcing him to retreat in a northerly direction and, on 7 February, to abandon the little town of Eylau. The weather had changed again, and it was snowing. The troops had not had any bread since leaving Warsaw a week earlier, and that evening Napoleon sat by a bivouac fire baking potatoes along with his grenadiers. Bennigsen counter-attacked in the morning, and there followed a chaotic battle fought in a blizzard, in which Napoleon himself was nearly captured. Both sides fought with determination, and although Bennigsen retired and his losses were greater, it could hardly be termed a French victory, and there was little doubt that Napoleon had not been fully in control.[23]

'The victory was mine, but I lost many men,' he wrote to Josephine at three o'clock in the morning after the battle. 'The enemy's losses, which are even greater, are no consolation to me.' Many of his best troops had been killed, and the sub-zero temperatures meant that most of the wounded who could not move froze to death in the night. The sight of the battlefield the next day had a demoralising effect on the survivors: the dead lay so close that it was difficult not to walk over them. Napoleon himself was horrified by the carnage. 'This is not the pretty aspect of war,' he wrote to Josephine a couple of days later. 'One suffers and one's soul is oppressed by the sight of so many victims.' The army shared his feelings, and the men were anxious, knowing the losses could not be easily made good so far from home. The weather and the mournful landscape made them homesick, and morale plummeted as they once more went into winter quarters at Osterode. According to some accounts, over 20,000 men were suffering from dysentery.[24]

As usual, the bulletins proclaimed a decisive victory and minimised French losses, but letters from husbands, brothers, and sons spread anxiety in Paris. Josephine expressed it and wished he would come home, not least because rumours of his romance were beginning to circulate. He wrote telling her she had no grounds for sorrow. 'I do know how to do other things than making war, but duty comes first,' he chided her. 'Throughout my life, I have sacrificed everything—tranquillity, interest, happiness—to my destiny.'[25]

On 1 April Napoleon moved into the nearby castle of Finckenstein, where he was joined by Maria Walewska. She was delivered at night in an unmarked carriage by one of her brothers and having been shown to her quarters would not leave them for the next six weeks. Her presence was supposed to have been a secret, and only Napoleon's valet Constant and his secretary Méneval were allowed to see her, but there was talk in the surrounding camps of '*la belle polonaise*', and Warsaw society knew she was there.[26]

She later admitted to a friend that her scruples had vanished, for Napoleon made her feel as though she were his wife. Innocent and uncomplicated, she was unlikely to have been critical of or dissatisfied with his sexual prowess, and seems to have fallen in love with him. They behaved as a married couple, even taking their breakfast together in her red-damask upholstered bed. He found the castle 'very fine', and its numerous fireplaces suited him, as he liked to see a fire burning when he got up in the night. He was in good health, he assured Josephine, noting that the weather was cold but fine. He inspected troops almost every day and took exercise on horseback, and in the evenings played cards.[27]

His strategic position was not good. He had some 70,000 men at Osterode, but many were sick, the rest hungry and dispirited, and rates of desertion were alarming. He was facing a constantly growing Russian force. The last fortress in Prussian hands, Danzig, had fallen to Marshal Lefèbvre (who became duc de Danzig), but although the Prussian army had all but disintegrated, many of its officers were making their way to take service with Russia. On 26 April Frederick William signed the Convention of Bartenstein with Russia, by which both powers vowed not to make a separate peace. At his back, Napoleon had Austria, which was only being held in check by the presence of an Italian army under Eugène on its southern border. He had recently got wind of contacts between the Spanish minister Godoy and the British concerning the possibility of Spain joining the anti-French coalition. In May Napoleon concluded the Treaty of Finckenstein with Persia, which he hoped would result in military action on Russia's southern border. He was also encouraging the Turks to make a move that might divert Russian forces; he had received a Turkish envoy at Finckenstein in this spirit. But a British fleet had sailed into the Dardanelles, accompanied by a British invasion of Egypt, to pressure the Porte to make peace with Russia and expel the French ambassador.

At the beginning of June Bennigsen attacked Ney's corps, and with a couple of deft manoeuvres managed to sow confusion among the other French corps. Napoleon rallied them and followed Bennigsen, who fell back on the little town of Friedland in a curve of the river Alle, where on 14 June he was forced to accept battle. With no room to manoeuvre and no possibility of falling back when two of the three bridges over the river were destroyed by French artillery, his army was cut to pieces, losing by some estimates as much as 50 percent of its effectives. It was the anniversary of Marengo, and Napoleon made much of this, saying the battle had been as decisive as Marengo, Austerlitz, and Jena.[28]

The tsar, who was close by, had no option but to request an armistice, and Napoleon, who was keen to make peace and take his homesick army home, agreed to one on 21 June. Three days later, at his headquarters in the small town of Tilsit, he received a note from Alexander stating that for the past two years he had longed for an alliance with France, as only that could guarantee the peace and well-being of Europe, and requesting a meeting.[29]

Alexander had been humiliated and lost an army at Austerlitz, and now another at Eylau and Friedland. He could raise more men, but his officer corps was not up to doing much with them. If he retreated he would be drawing the French into an area taken from Poland only ten years before, in which they would be welcome and he not. He was single-handedly supporting the crushed and ineffectual Frederick William and felt abandoned by his British ally; British gold had bought nothing but Russian blood and embarrassment. Something of a fantasist, he fancied he would be able to seduce Napoleon.

Napoleon for his part had begun to reflect on a possible alliance with Russia, against the advice of Talleyrand, who consistently pressed for a strategic alliance with Austria. On the day he received Alexander's note he had received a report from his ambassador in Vienna, General Andréossy, that Austria was hostile and only waiting for a chance to take revenge. The other news Napoleon had that day was that there had been a palace revolt in Constantinople, and the sultan Selim III, with whom he had been negotiating, had been deposed, so he could expect no support against Russia from that quarter. He agreed to Alexander's offer and invited him to a meeting on the following day.

He ordered his sappers to construct a raft with a tented structure on it, decorated with the arms and ciphers of the two monarchs, and to moor it midstream on the river Niemen (Neman). When Alexander arrived with his suite on the opposite bank, he was rowed out to the raft, where Napoleon greeted him with an embrace as his troops, drawn up on the western bank, cheered. Frederick William, who had come with Alexander, was left sitting on his horse on the east bank, pointedly left out. Symbolism was the order of the day, and the showman in Napoleon had taken over.

'My Dear, I have just met the emperor Alexander,' he wrote to Josephine that evening. 'I am very pleased with him; he is a very handsome and good young emperor, he is more intelligent than is commonly thought. He is coming to stay at Tilsit tomorrow.' Over the next two weeks he entertained Alexander to dinner, had his troops parade before him, and held private conversations with him, sometimes lasting long into the night. As they strolled arm in arm he played the part of the great conqueror who appreciated the hidden qualities of the younger man and graciously treated him as an equal, taking him into his confidence as he discoursed on weighty matters of state. This was balm to the young tsar, a man of complexes, weak, unsure of himself, desperate to cut a figure as a military leader. He was intelligent enough to appreciate what Napoleon had achieved in rebuilding the French political edifice and society, something he dreamed of doing himself in Russia. Although a part of him resisted (strongly supported by his mother and his sister Catherine), he could not help falling under the spell of Napoleon, who tempted him with prospects of being able to play a part in the affairs of the Continent and even to fulfil the Russian monarchy's dream of conquering Constantinople, and of a combined march on India to expel the British and extend their own empires. This was accompanied by typically Napoleonic gestures, such as his asking the Russian guards parading before him to name their bravest, and presenting him with the Legion of Honour.

The troops of both sides fraternised, the French guards inviting their Russian counterparts to banquets in the open air. At a higher level, Murat teamed up with Alexander's younger brother Constantine in orgies of drunkenness and debauchery. When Murat appeared in his 'Polish' dress, Napoleon told him to go home and change, saying he looked like a comedian. More decorously, parades were held and uniforms inspected and compared—on one occasion two battalions of French infantry displayed the new white uniforms with which Napoleon was thinking of replacing the blue, on account of the shortage of indigo dye following the loss of France's West Indian colonies.[30]

Although Alexander did persuade him to meet the King of Prussia and to admit him to the festivities, Napoleon continued to treat him as an irrelevance. He even failed to show much interest in the beautiful Queen Luise when she came to plead the Prussian cause. He adopted a tone both flirtatious and mocking, promised to do something for Prussia, and then broke his word, reducing her to tears. He had already prepared the text of a proclamation dethroning Frederick William and only relented at the request of the tsar.[31]

The upshot was a treaty, signed on 7 July 1807, by which Russia lost nothing except its protectorate over the Ionian islands and gained in return a small piece of territory from Prussia, seemingly a miraculous outcome after having been roundly defeated. She also bound herself to withdraw from the Danubian principalities over which she was in conflict with the Turks, but was given licence to capture Finland from Sweden instead. Furthermore, Russia bound herself to bring Britain to the negotiating table by 1 November 1807, and if this proved impossible, to join France in alliance against her. In return, Russia endorsed all of Napoleon's arrangements in Europe, which included the dramatic reduction of Prussia, whose Polish possessions were turned into a grand duchy of Warsaw, ruled over by the King of Saxony, and the creation of a kingdom of Westphalia, mostly out of former Prussian provinces, with Napoleon's brother Jérôme as king.

The treaty effectively negated Russia's designs on Constantinople, excluded her from influence in Germany, and left in the shape of the grand duchy of Warsaw a French outpost on her border and an embryonic Polish state that might one day recover, or at least subvert, many of Russia's recent western conquests. The treaty humiliated Prussia, whose population was reduced from nearly ten million to less than five by the removal of its Polish conquests and provinces absorbed into the kingdom of Westphalia. It was obliged to join the war against Britain and pay a crippling indemnity to France—and to remain under French military occupation until that was settled. Furthermore, Denmark, Sweden, and Portugal would be asked to close their ports to the British and recall their diplomats from London. If they refused, they were to be considered enemies of France and Russia.

Napoleon had got his way in everything, and there was now no state independent enough to act as proxy for Britain on the Continent. But by committing his allies to the trade war, he forced an unpopular and in some cases suicidal policy on them—and on himself the obligation to ensure that no port in any part of Europe remained beyond his control.

31

The Sun Emperor

ON HIS RETURN to Paris Napoleon was greeted with a sixty-gun salute. When, on 15 August, his birthday, he drove across the city to Notre Dame he was cheered by people who believed they could now expect prolonged peace and prosperity. France had never seemed so great, and people began referring to him as *Napoléon le Grand*, an epithet last bestowed on Louis XIV. There was by now much more of the Sun King about him than of the 'necessary dictator' whom so many had welcomed on his return from Marengo eight years earlier.

He had been away for nine months, but every couple of days he received an *estafette* with most of the news and information he would have had in Paris, so he was able to hold the reins of government throughout that time, with Cambacérès regularly sending one of the *auditeurs* of the Council of State off to his headquarters with a batch of papers for him to sign along with the relevant minutes and reports. Everything had functioned smoothly, and while enjoying the carnival in Warsaw or sitting by the fireside at Finckenstein he had been able to continue implementing public works and supervising projects such as the Commercial Code, which was to form part of the Civil Code. He was kept abreast of the meetings of the Grand Sanhedrin, which he had summoned to discuss the status of the Jews in the empire. He inspected accounts and queried the smallest expenses. His presence haunted Paris, if only by the never-ending stream of letters, instructing, admonishing, reproving, and always firm. This, combined with the institutions he had put in place contributed to a remarkable sense of stability. Few states could have survived, let alone functioned efficiently, with their absolute ruler so far away for so long. British naval bombardments of French ports and attempted landings had been seen off. News of Eylau had caused despondency and a recrudescence of anti-government and even royalist feeling in the west, but this had been contained, and although there was still much banditry on the roads, the country functioned normally. Cambacérès and Fouché had ensured that the press, the theatre, and literature all followed the official line.

Yet on his return Napoleon felt a need to take matters more firmly in hand. He made a number of ministerial changes and named new senators, and on 19 August he abolished the Tribunate, allowing some members to retire and others to join the Legislative. The closing down of the 'chattering chamber' did not cause much surprise or alarm, and many felt the system would function better without it. Whatever people thought of it, the Napoleonic regime delivered stability and prosperity, and that was what most people wanted. Yet he seemed to be gradually losing sight of that crucial fact, and his vision was beginning to diverge from that of the majority of his subjects.

His latest victories had not produced the same effect on public opinion as earlier ones, partly because people no longer believed the bulletins—the phrase 'to lie like a bulletin' had entered common parlance—but mostly because they could see no point to them. As the Austrian ambassador put it, they felt no excitement at the news of a victory, only relief that it was not a defeat. Napoleon expressed disappointment when he was made aware of this, but did not reflect on the cause, which was that his role as the longed-for victorious hero and saviour of France had been played out; what the people now wanted was a strong ruler who could safeguard what had been achieved. That was not how he saw things.[1]

His triumph over Russia and Prussia had opened up limitless new vistas to his imagination, in which mirages of eastern conquest now fought with concepts of a grand new arrangement of Europe. The exhilarating experience of Tilsit, and possibly also of knowing that he was not after all sterile, was not calculated to make him settle down to a quiet life. On 3 August Frederick William wrote him a letter,

UNITED
KINGDOM

*North
Sea*

London○

KINGDOM OF
HOLLAND

GRAND DUCHY OF BERG

KINGDOM OF
WESTPHALIA

Berlin

CONFEDERATION

SAXONY

Brussels○   Cologne○

Seine

Paris○

F R E N C H

Loire

OF THE

RHINE

Rhine

KINGDOM OF
WÜRTTEMBERG

E M P I R E

Basel○

KINGDOM OF
BAVARIA

NEUCHÂTEL

Bordeaux○

Geneva○

Lyon○

HELVETIA

Turin○   Milan○

Venice○

KINGDOM
OF ITALY

Bayonne○

Rhône

Genoa○

Montpellier○

Marseille○   Nice○
Toulon○

LUCCA

Pisa○   ○Florence

ETRURIA

PAPAL

S P A I N

Barcelona○

Ajaccio○

Corsica

STATES

Rome○

PONTECORVO

BENEVENTO

Naples○

KINGDOM
OF
SARDINIA

KINGDOM
OF
NAPLES

M e d i t e r r a n e a n   S e a

Cagliari○

Palermo○

Sicily

EUROPE
1808

French Empire

French Dependencies

Tunis○

PRUSSIA

GRAND DUCHY
OF WARSAW   Warsaw

Vistula

Cracow

RUSSIAN
EMPIRE

Kiev

Dnieper

Elbe

Prague

AUSTRIAN

Vienna

Danube

Buda Pest

EMPIRE

MOLDAVIA

Belgrade

WALLACHIA

Danube

OTTOMAN

Sofia

Black
Sea

Constantinople

EMPIRE

Smyrna

addressing him as 'the greatest man of the century' and begging for an alliance, but Napoleon did not answer; he preferred to bleed Prussia dry. Thanks to the huge sums she was forced to disburse, the war had largely paid for itself, and there was more to be squeezed out. Estates seized by the Prussian government when it had taken over its part of Poland were not returned to the government of the grand duchy of Warsaw but given to French marshals and dignitaries instead—part of a plan to bind Napoleon's growing imperium in a great web controlled by himself. He distributed titles of nobility to faithful servants and potential enemies alike, in the conviction that all men could be bought, creating 3,263 princes, dukes, counts, barons, and knights by the end of the empire. Fifty-nine percent of them were soldiers, and most of the rest either state functionaries or notables; 22.5 percent were from the old nobility, 58 from the middle class, and 19.5 from the working classes.[2]

Since they owed everything to him, he believed he was their master. Pontécoulant was struck by the change that had taken place in his manner during his absence, noting that 'there was in his deportment a kind of constraint, a sort of stiffness, which inspired fear rather than respect and seemed to put distance between him and those closest to him'. He also found his conversation less scintillating, and felt that in the Council of State he seemed 'more intent on imposing than convincing'. The court of the Tuileries reflected this process: 'it was no longer the tent of the hero crowned by victory, but the ridiculous show of an old-fashioned royal court with all the exaggerations of the past, without the politeness, the urbanity and the good manners'. As Josephine's lady-in-waiting Claire de Rémusat pointed out, the entire brilliant structure of Napoleon's power 'rested on an authority whose foundations were in opposition to the irresistible march of the human spirit'. Not only was he no longer in tune with the spirit which had brought him to power, he seemed to be regressing in time.[3]

Perhaps the most significant change he made on his return was to remove Talleyrand from the Ministry of Foreign Relations. This was not a mark of disgrace or even displeasure, and he was honoured with the rank of vice-grand elector, which kept him at the heart of the court. It was a question of policy. Talleyrand may have been an opportunist by nature, but he was also a strategist. He had repeatedly and forcefully given Napoleon his opinion that he was moving in the wrong direction and urged a reorientation of French foreign policy based on a strategic alliance with a strengthened Austria.

Napoleon wanted to direct foreign policy himself, and as Talleyrand's successor he appointed Jean-Baptiste de Champagny, previously minister of the interior, a conscientious executor of his will without much experience of the outside world. Unwilling or unable to take into account the interests and aspirations of others, Napoleon could not develop a fixed strategy. Most of his actions were henceforth dictated by a determination to bring Britain to book by destroying her economic power, while encouraging industrial development in mainland Europe by eliminating British competition, which was to be achieved by closing Russian, Prussian, and Danish ports to her shipping. The Royal Navy would suffer for lack of supplies of Baltic timber, hemp, and tar; there would be food shortages for lack of Polish wheat; and British industry would lose some of its most lucrative markets. With Louis reigning in Holland, Jérôme in Westphalia, and Murat in the grand duchy of Berg, the entire coastline from St Petersburg to France was in theory secure, and Central Europe out of bounds to British commerce. This hurt the British economy, as some 36 percent of exports had gone there.[4]

An early setback in Napoleon's economic war came at the beginning of September 1807. Acting on intelligence that Denmark was being pressured by France to join in alliance against Britain with her large fleet, the British cabinet ordered an attack on Copenhagen which resulted in the capture of the entire Danish fleet. Fouché noted that he had not seen Napoleon react to any news with such fury since hearing of the assassination of Tsar Paul I. But he quickly realised he had to secure the other weak link in his alliance against Britain.[5]

Ruled since 1700 by Bourbon kings descended from Louis XIV, Spain had been France's closest political and commercial partner. Along with the Bourbon kingdom of Naples and Sicily, it had formed part of the *pacte de famille*, a defensive alliance against principally

Austrian and British designs. This had been shaken by the outbreak of the French Revolution, and following the execution of Louis XVI, his Spanish cousins invaded France. They were soon expelled, and fearing the contagion of revolution, Spain made peace, and by the Treaty of Basel in 1795, became an ally of France once more.

The King of Spain, Charles IV, was an amiable but foolish man more interested in hunting and making things—particularly shoes—than affairs of state. More interested in these was his wife, Maria Luisa of Parma, commonly referred to as *la puta* for her supposedly insatiable sexual appetite. She was governed by her favourite, the minor noble Manuel de Godoy, two years older than Napoleon, who had been showered with rank and honours, becoming virtual ruler of the country by 1792. Insofar as he had any principles beyond accumulating as much power and wealth as possible, he was a conservative and ill-disposed to France. He was widely hated. Most of his enemies and those of the status quo pinned their hopes on the heir to the throne, Ferdinand Prince of the Asturias, a dim-witted but treacherous twenty-four-year-old.

Because of its geographical position and colonial empire, Spain was of immense importance to France, and Napoleon did not trust Godoy to keep the country from falling under British influence. When he reached Berlin after Jena he found letters from Godoy to the King of Prussia offering to attack France in support of Russia and Prussia. The risk of such an attack would not have worried Napoleon much, even when he was occupied in Central Europe, but the possibility of the British getting a foothold on the Iberian Peninsula did, because it would breach the commercial blockade. As an ally of France, Spain was committed to it, but Portugal was not.

In September 1807 Napoleon wrote to the regent of Portugal, Dom João, telling him to choose between France and Britain. He responded favourably and declared war on Britain, but he was too late. On 27 October an impatient Napoleon had concluded the Treaty of Fontainebleau with Charles IV, by which France and Spain would jointly take over Portugal.

To carry out the operation Napoleon had chosen Junot, telling him his marshal's baton was waiting for him in Lisbon. Among his reasons for sending him was that during Napoleon's nine-month absence Junot, who was military governor of Paris, had been having an affair with Napoleon's sister Caroline Murat (who some thought was thus positioning herself for the struggle over the succession were her imperial brother to meet with disaster on campaign). Napoleon did not wish Paris to witness the confrontation between Junot and a returning Murat. He could count on Junot, whose devotion since their first meeting at Toulon some compared to love. What he did not appreciate, or chose to ignore, was that the swashbuckling *bravoure*, the hard drinking and the happy-go-lucky manner of the handsome, curly-headed Junot, concealed the beginnings of mental problems.

Junot crossed the border into Spain with 20,000 men on 17 October, with no maps and only a hazy idea of where he was going. His force was made up of young French conscripts unused to the rigours of war, supplemented by detachments of Swiss, Italians, and Germans. They were inadequately equipped and supplied, and while they were unopposed by the bemused Spanish garrisons they passed on their way, they could not count on their assistance. Men soon began to fall behind and die, so that when he entered Lisbon on 30 November after a forced march of over a thousand kilometres, Junot had only 1,500 left, no cavalry, and not one piece of artillery. It was a feat, but it misfired: the British had sailed into Lisbon, embarked the Portuguese royal family and taken them to their colony of Brazil, along with the Portuguese fleet which Napoleon had counted on seizing. Junot did not get his marshal's baton, only the title of duc d'Abrantès.

The situation in Spain itself was deteriorating rapidly as supporters of Ferdinand had begun plotting to overthrow Godoy, encouraged by the French ambassador in Spain, Josephine's brother-in-law François de Beauharnais, acting independently of Napoleon. Charles IV arrested his son on charges of treason, but then pardoned him and wrote to Napoleon asking on his behalf for the hand of a princess of the house of Bonaparte, something Ferdinand's supporters had been urging for some time.

At the end of November 1807 Napoleon began a tour of his Italian dominions, which were of key importance if he was to exclude the British from the Mediterranean and keep Spain allied to France.

He had set in motion an ambitious shipbuilding programme which would over the next years produce seventy ships of the line, and while he had not given up hope of recovering some of France's colonies, his first priority was the Mediterranean, where he ordered the fleets at Brest, Lorient, and Rochefort to join that of the Adriatic, based in Venice. He was already making new plans concerning the Middle East and India. Having, by the Treaty of Tilsit, recovered the Ionian islands, he was preparing to turn Corfu into a naval base to rival Malta. In the interests of making Italy secure against British interference, he pressed Joseph to invade Sicily and expel the British who were using it as a base. He dislodged the queen of Etruria, who did not apply the rules excluding British trade rigorously enough. He added her kingdom, which reverted to its name of grand duchy of Tuscany, to the French Empire as a fief for his sister Élisa, and gave the ex-queen a piece of Portugal in exchange (it was done quite amicably, and they went to the opera at La Scala together afterward). Similarly, he annexed the papal province of Le Marche to the kingdom of Italy; that and the other Papal States had several strategic ports, and the Pope could not be relied on to deny use of them to the British or the Russians, as his relations with Napoleon had soured.

Napoleon's doings in Germany had affected the status of the Church by boundary changes and the introduction of French-style administration, not to mention financial extortion and outright looting of Church property. This was compounded by the extension in January 1806 of the Civil Code to Italy, which impinged on areas governed by the Church. The Code established the primacy of civil over religious marriage, and legalised divorce. The Pope's protests over this and over the French occupation of Ancona during the Austerlitz campaign angered Napoleon, who assumed he was siding with the allies at a moment when it looked as though they were winning. 'Your Holiness is sovereign in Rome, but I am its emperor,' he had reminded him in a brusque letter in February 1806. He insisted that 15 August, the feast of the Assumption of the Virgin, be henceforth celebrated as that of St Napoleon, and that the Imperial Catechism be taught in schools. At every opportunity he drove home the message that as temporal ruler of the Papal States, the Pope was vassal of the emperor of the French. He had not forgotten Rousseau's thesis that Church and state were in fundamental conflict.[6]

Another point of discord was Napoleon's nomination of Joseph to the throne of Naples. Traditionally, the kings of Naples had been invested by the Pope, so Napoleon's action caused offence. When he insisted the Pope recognise the new monarch the Pope refused, prompting Napoleon to send troops in to occupy all the ports in the Papal States, purportedly to prevent communication between the Vatican and the exiled Bourbons, now in Sicily.[7]

Napoleon kept making demands of the Pope as though he were one of his ministers, requesting, for instance, that he annul the marriage of Jérôme to Elizabeth Patterson. As the couple had never been married in church, the Pope could not oblige, which annoyed Napoleon, who was intending to marry Jérôme to Catherine of Württemberg and wanted to make him look as acceptable as possible to the family of the bride. On his return from Tilsit he sent more troops into the Papal States and demanded the Pope withdraw his religious objections to his Code and apply it in his states.

As he sped around Italy, reviewing troops, inspecting fortifications, and lecturing local authorities, Napoleon managed to fit in operas at La Scala and La Fenice, and to go to the theatre in smaller cities. Joseph came from Naples to confer with him in Venice, and on 13 December Napoleon had a six-hour-long meeting with Lucien at Mantua. He needed his younger brother to rejoin the family enterprise and offered him any kingdom he wanted, but, stuck in the rut of his self-inflicted conventions, he insisted Lucien must first divorce his wife, whom he deemed both too common and, as a divorcée, unsuitable. Lucien retorted that Napoleon had also married an unsuitable woman, adding, 'and at least mine isn't old and stinking like yours'. Napoleon undertook to recognise Lucien's daughters, Lolotte and Lilli, and make them princesses of France, but not his son, who was born out of wedlock. Lolotte would marry the prince of the Asturias and become queen of Spain. Lucien could carry on living with his wife, but she could only have the status of concubine. To sweeten the pill Napoleon offered to make her Duchess of Parma. But Lucien, who disagreed with the course Napoleon was taking, refused.[8]

Three days later, in Milan, Napoleon signed yet another decree concerning the blockade. Britain had responded to his Berlin Decrees by ruling that any ship belonging to a neutral nation which had not put into a British port and had its cargo taxed (at 25 percent) was liable to seizure. Napoleon reacted by ordering the seizure of any vessel that had conformed to the British decrees. This prompted President Thomas Jefferson of the United States to place an embargo on British and French vessels entering American ports.

Napoleon was back at the Tuileries on 1 January 1808. Three days later he visited David's studio to see the monumental painting of his coronation in progress. On 9 January he inaugurated the new theatre he had ordered Fontaine to construct in the Tuileries, with a performance of Paer's *Griselda*, but at the second performance, of Corneille's *Cinna*, the room was so cold the ladies in their scanty dresses had to flee at the interval, and he vented his rage on the unfortunate architect. In between hunting, attending performances of tragedies by Racine, presiding over the council of the university, and inspecting public works, he fitted in visits to Maria Walewska, whom he had brought to Paris and installed in a discreet house. He also decreed the introduction of full military discipline into the navy, sent Joseph a plan for the invasion of Sicily, and gave orders for the military occupation of the Papal States.

In the course of a meeting with the Austrian ambassador, Metternich, he broached the subject of combined Franco-Austrian operations against Turkey. One can only wonder at how he thought he would represent this to his ally Alexander, given the Russian monarchy's age-old dream of conquering Constantinople. Napoleon wrote to him on 2 February dangling another prospect before him, presumably meant to distract him: 'An army of 50,000, Russian, French, perhaps even partly Austrian troops, marching into Asia through Constantinople would need to get no further than the Euphrates to make England quake and fall to its knees before the Continent.' But while he dreamed of dealing British power a blow in the east, he was going to have to defend himself against it closer to home.[9]

By the beginning of 1808 it had become obvious that drastic action was required if Spain was not going to disintegrate. Aside from the struggles for power revolving around its dysfunctional royal family, there were broader tensions as well as local animosities simmering all over the country, between peasants and nobles, nobles and clergy, peasants and clergy, traditionalists and reformers, and within the clergy between those who supported the Inquisition and those who wanted it abolished; most historians agree that the manifold passions agitating Spanish society were about to boil over into extreme violence. France could ill afford to have a failing state on its border, particularly one open on three sides to seaborne British attack.[10]

Along with most Europeans, the French viewed Spain as an archaic state ruled by an imbecile dynasty, populated by a lazy and decadent people marshalled by obscurantist priests—in a word, a society that badly needed the benefits of the Enlightenment. In the course of his recent tour of Italy, Napoleon had formed the impression that on the whole its inhabitants had accepted the new order he had imposed, and many had embraced it with enthusiasm. There seemed little reason to doubt that the same could be done in Spain.

His primary concern was to keep the British out, and he had been gradually sending troops into northern Spain under the pretext of guarding the supply lines of Junot in Portugal. By the beginning of 1808 Generals Dupont and Moncey had some 20,000 men each at Valladolid and Burgos respectively. In order to keep his options open, Napoleon deflected Charles IV's proposal of a dynastic marriage to Lucien's daughter on grounds of the disgraceful behaviour of the prince of the Asturias. On 20 February he sent Murat in with another 80,000 men while he considered what to do next.[11]

Talleyrand argued that France would never be safe unless she could rely on the alliance with Spain, and that the solution imposed by Louis XIV a century earlier was the only sensible one: the throne of Spain should be occupied by a member of the same dynasty as that reigning in France. Cambacérès warned against getting involved in yet another country, but while Napoleon considered the options, events in Spain sucked him in.[12]

On the night of 18 March 1808, supporters of Ferdinand stormed Godoy's palace at Aranjuez and imprisoned him, then forced Charles IV to abdicate in favour of his son, whom they proclaimed King

Ferdinand VII. They assumed that they had the support of France and were surprised when Murat, who had occupied much of the country by stealth and installed himself in Madrid, took the unfortunate Charles under his protection. Charles wrote to Napoleon informing him that he had been forced to abdicate and in effect placing himself at his disposal. Napoleon began to think his own presence in Madrid was necessary, and at the end of March he ordered horses, pages, and cooks to be sent there. At the same time, he invited Ferdinand to France. It is difficult to deduce his ultimate goal, or whether he had one at this stage.[13]

On 2 April he left Saint-Cloud, ostensibly on a tour of inspection of the southwest, stopping at Orléans, Bordeaux, and other towns to inspect troops and meet local notables. Along the way he encountered three Spanish grandees sent by Ferdinand to announce his accession to the throne, but refused to receive them. On 14 April he reached Bayonne and three days later took up residence nearby at the grim château of Marracq.

Massively built but small, it barely contained Napoleon and Josephine, who joined him there later with her *maison*, which huddled uncomfortably in a series of small upstairs rooms. Napoleon's numerous staff were accommodated in nearby houses and cottages, while his military escort camped on the lawn in front of the house: a battalion of grenadiers of the Guard first; next to them a detachment of Basque *gardes d'honneur* in red dolmans, black berets, breeches, and stockings; and 500 metres away a fancily uniformed squadron of the newly formed Polish *chevau-légers* of the Guard.[14]

The day after taking up residence Napoleon wrote to Ferdinand, reserving his decision on whether to recognise him and inviting him to Bayonne. The same day he wrote to his brother Joseph warning him that in five or six days he might write again asking him to leave Naples and come to Bayonne. When Ferdinand arrived, on 20 April, Napoleon had a short interview with him and discussed matters with members of his entourage. Six days later Napoleon met Godoy, who had also arrived; he told him the Bourbons had lost all credit in Spain, and the people wanted Napoleon as their ruler. 'If I am not mistaken,' Napoleon wrote to Talleyrand, 'this play has reached its fifth act, and we are about to see the dénouement.' It began with the arrival on 30 April of Charles and Maria-Luisa, who trundled into the town in a convoy of magnificent state coaches of another age, 'huge gilded boxes with glass in front and behind as well as on the doors', suspended on wide leather straps attached to outsize gilded wheels. After dining with them that evening, Napoleon could begin to make his own assessment of the Spanish royal family.[15]

He had taken little time to rule out Ferdinand. 'The Prince of the Asturias is very stupid, very wicked, very hostile to France,' he wrote to Talleyrand. As well as being an imbecile, he was untrustworthy— he had expressed regret that when forcing Charles to abdicate his partisans had not followed the example of Tsar Paul's assassins. He would also be easy for the British to manipulate. Further, a couple of meetings with Charles and his consort sufficed to persuade Napoleon that he too was incapable of ruling effectively. 'King Charles is a good man,' he thought, while 'the queen has her heart and her past written all over her face; no more need be said'. He persuaded Charles to revoke his abdication and appoint Murat as his lieutenant pending a resolution of the crisis.[16]

This had a taken on a new dimension with the outbreak on 2 May of a riot in Madrid. Supposedly a protest against the departure for Bayonne of two more members of the royal family, it turned into an attack on all Frenchmen, principally soldiers, stationed in the capital, between 150 and 200 of whom were murdered. Murat restored order with savage repressions involving the execution of around a thousand rioters. When it reached Bayonne, the news contributed to a scandalous royal row in front of Napoleon, as Charles accused Ferdinand of treachery and Maria-Luisa urged Napoleon to have him executed. An exasperated Napoleon declared he could not recognise anyone as despicable as Ferdinand and bullied him into renouncing his claim to the throne and acknowledging his father as king. Whether under pressure from Napoleon or not it is not clear, but Charles then renounced his own right to the throne, which he placed at the disposal of Napoleon, on the grounds that only he was in a position to restore order.[17]

Napoleon returned to Marracq that evening in a state of agitation and walked around the park with his chaplain, the Abbé de

Pradt, discussing the diminishing options. He could see only one: 'The old dynasty is used up, and I have to rebuild the work of Louis XIV,' as he put it to General Mathieu Dumas. The next day he wrote to Talleyrand instructing him to prepare the château of Compiègne to receive the ex-king of Spain and his consort. The prince of the Asturias and his brother Don Carlos were to be put up at Talleyrand's château of Valençay, a punishment for Talleyrand, who was given the additional job of finding him a woman. 'I believe the most important part of the job to have been done,' Napoleon wrote, adding that although there might be a few disturbances, the firm lesson given by Murat in Madrid would prevent further trouble. He waited another four days before writing to Joseph instructing him to come and take the throne of Spain, encouraging him with the argument that while Naples was 'at the ends of the earth', 'In Madrid, you are in France.'[18]

Another four weeks passed before Joseph arrived, and during that time Napoleon visited local garrisons and ports. At Biarritz he bathed in the sea, watched over by mounted chasseurs of the Guard. Presumably in consequence of a lack of reading matter, he gave orders for the creation of a thousand-volume travelling library, in the small duodecimo format with large print fit to be read in a carriage. It was to include sections on religion and the classics, a hundred novels, history, memoirs, and the great classics of French drama. He also instructed his librarian to make extracts and précis of the campaigns of Crassus, Trajan, and other Roman emperors against the Parthians on the Euphrates, and to have maps and plans of the area drawn up. When the weather grew warm, he and Josephine were plagued with flies and other insects and slept together under a mosquito net. He was affectionate with her and did everything to scotch the gossip about a possible divorce.[19]

Joseph reached Bayonne on 7 June, and the two brothers began setting up the new monarchy. They drew up a constitution which enshrined many Spanish traditions and recognised Catholicism as the religion of state. Napoleon refrained from introducing the Code as he had insisted on doing in Italy. On 22 June, at Valençay, Ferdinand swore an oath of fealty to Joseph, who was proclaimed King

José I on 8 July by a hastily convened Cortes consisting of ninety-one members. He was congratulated by the other members of the former dynasty and began issuing proclamations styling himself 'Don José, by the Grace of God, King of Castille, Aragon, the Two Sicilies, Jerusalem, Navarre, Grenada, Toledo, Valencia, Galicia', and a sackful of other titles which had accrued to the Spanish monarchy, including sovereignty over the Canaries, the Eastern and Western Indies, those of Archduke of Austria, Duke of Burgundy, Brabant, and Milan, and many others even more abstruse. Napoleon told him not to be so silly and packed him off to Madrid the following day.[20]

Joseph looked forward to his new role with confidence. In his two years on the throne of Naples he had proved himself a competent and generally popular king, displaying tact, behaving as a good Catholic, and respecting local traditions. He had reformed the corrupt administration and modernised the army, cleared out gaols filled with people festering for forgotten crimes, and suppressed much of the endemic banditry, eventually capturing the most notorious bandit, Fra Diavolo. He admitted that he had been naïve and idealistic in believing that people would respond well to reasonable and benign rule and occasionally had to resort to firmness. But he did understand something Napoleon did not—that Naples could not be ruled as a colony.[21]

Despite the apparent similarities, Spanish society and the Spanish political edifice differed fundamentally from those of Naples, and the cauldron of complex and contradictory hatreds had boiled over as a result of recent events inside and outside the country. The French military incursion had provoked resistance, to which the French responded with reprisals which in turn produced savage reactions, releasing a spiral of cruelty which spun out of control as the French razed villages and looted churches, and the inhabitants disembowelled or crucified French soldiers in retaliation.

The French Revolution, which had combined the destruction of the Catholic Church and religious persecution with that of the monarchy and the nobility, had branded all Frenchmen as enemies of Church and throne, while Napoleon's recent persecution of the Pope had turned him in the Spanish popular imagination into the Anti-Christ. Priests proclaimed that to kill a Frenchman was not a sin but a step on the path to heaven. Ferdinand, however, was miraculously transformed into a sacred symbol. Although he had not a drop of Spanish blood—of his sixteen great-great-grandparents, four were Bavarian, three French, two Polish, two Italian, one Austrian, and the rest German (two of them Protestant)—he had become a national hero, *el Deseado*, the Desired One.

Joseph's enthusiasm evaporated long before he reached Madrid. 'The fact is that there is not one Spaniard who is on my side apart from the small number of people who made up the junta and are travelling with me,' he wrote to his brother only three days after setting off from Bayonne. Even they began leaving him as he travelled on, and less than a week later he had to face the fact that 'I have not one single supporter here.' A couple of days later he made his solemn entry into Madrid: bells pealed and cannon saluted, but there was nobody in the streets or at the windows. 'I was not received by the inhabitants of this city as I was by those of Naples,' he reported.[22]

In a succession of letters he assured his brother that they had been deluded and that to pacify the country was an almost impossible task, given that he was facing an exasperated nation of twelve million people. He changed his approach, as in the circumstances 'kindness would appear as cowardice', and only overwhelming force could produce results, though he regarded it as 'a repulsive task'. He demanded an extra 150,000 troops and overall command of them—beginning with Murat, who had fallen ill with dismay at having been passed over, all the military commanders were ignoring him and acting independently of each other.[23]

Napoleon made light of his brother's warnings. He had left Bayonne on 21 July after receiving reports of Bessières's rout of a Spanish army at Medina del Rioseco, confident in the effectiveness of French arms to deal with the situation. He made a stately progress, inspecting military units and attending receptions with the civil authorities as he went, and reached Bordeaux on 31 July. Joseph's literary pretensions had always annoyed him, and in his jeremiads he read only cowardice. He wrote back telling him the Spaniards were cowards, and he must show resolution and apply force. But his tone faltered after, on 2 August, he received news which profoundly shocked him.[24]

A French force of 20,000 men under General Pierre Dupont was marching to relieve the remnants of the French fleet stranded at Cádiz after Trafalgar when it was itself encircled by a larger Spanish army under General Francisco Castaños at Bailén on 22 July. Dupont, whose mostly raw conscripts were suffering from severe shortages of food and supplies, capitulated on the promise that he and his men would be allowed to return to France with their arms and artillery. Once the act of capitulation had been signed, all but Dupont and a handful of senior officers were driven off as prisoners and treated with brutality.

The French setback gave heart to their enemies throughout the country, and on 31 July, after only twelve days in the capital, Joseph was obliged to evacuate it and fall back on Burgos. He wrote to Napoleon that he was not prepared to rule over a people who loathed him and begged to be allowed to go back to Naples, arguing that Spain had become ungovernable. 'Your Majesty cannot have any idea, because nobody will have told him, to what extent the name of Your Majesty is reviled here,' he added for good measure. But Joseph had nowhere to go, as Napoleon had given his Neapolitan kingdom to Murat, who promptly declared himself Joachim-Napoleon, by the Grace of God King of Naples and Sicily. Two weeks later, Joseph wrote from Burgos giving his opinion that Spain could only be ruled 'by treating the Spaniards as they had treated the subjects of Montezuma', which would require 200,000 troops and 100,000 scaffolds 'to support the prince condemned to rule over them'.[25]

Napoleon agreed, and on 5 August he directed half of the French troops still stationed in Germany to Spain, and sent Marshal Ney to take command. But the situation in the peninsula continued to deteriorate; in Portugal, Junot had attacked a newly landed British force under General Arthur Wellesley at Vimeiro on 21 August, only to be beaten and forced to capitulate. He was more fortunate than Dupont, and the terms of the capitulation were respected, his whole force being shipped back to France by the Royal Navy. With most of the peninsula cleared of French troops, Ferdinand VII was proclaimed king by a junta in Madrid.

Napoleon continued his tour of inspection, visiting the ports at Rochefort and La Rochelle, but he was in a bad mood. When, at

Napoléon-Vendée, he discovered that his project supposed to revit-alise a rundown village and transform it into an industrial town had barely got off the ground, he erupted. He had taken Bailén as an insult to French arms, and by extension to himself. When Mathieu Dumas reported to him at Saint-Cloud, he fumed at what he termed the cowardice of Dupont and, seizing Dumas's uniform by the fac-ings, shook him, saying with concentrated rage that the French uni-form would have to be washed in blood. He had determined to do that himself, but before he could send all available troops to Spain to drown it in blood, he had to parry a looming threat from another quarter.[26]

32

The Emperor of the East

ON THE DAY following his return to Paris, 15 August 1808, Napoleon held the customary audience for the diplomatic corps to receive their good wishes on his birthday. In the absence of a papal nuncio, the diplomats were headed by the handsome and urbane Austrian ambassador Count Metternich, who, in the interests of intelligence-gathering, was having an affair with Napoleon's sister Caroline, the new queen of Naples, having already consulted several other ladies in the same manner. Napoleon took him to task for over an hour on a quite different matter—that of recent Austrian armaments which had come to his notice. Emperor Francis was also dragging his feet in recognising Joseph as King of Spain.[1]

The harsh terms imposed after Austerlitz had left Austria smarting, while anti-French feeling had been growing throughout Germany, stimulated by a wave of nationalist literature and a folkloric revival, as well as French exactions and the arrogance of French officials; even within the Confederation of the Rhine, Napoleon's highhanded treatment of his allies generated resentment. News of Bailén gave heart to all those who longed for revenge, and many felt it was time to rebel against French domination. Austria had been rearming in anticipation of war with France, assuming the rest of Germany would rise up and join it.[2]

In the circumstances, Napoleon could not afford to denude Germany and the grand duchy of Warsaw of troops in order to send them to Spain unless he could cover his back, and the only way of doing that was to call on his ally Russia. Yet her reliability was open to question; his ambassador in St Petersburg, Caulaincourt, warned him that the Tilsit settlement was unpopular in Russia, being associated in the public mind with the defeats of Austerlitz, Eylau, and Friedland, and the blockade was having a damaging effect on the economy.

Napoleon's inability to see things from another's perspective helped him ignore this and other warnings, as did his tendency to believe he could obtain results by dint of trying. When Alexander's ambassador was due in Paris after Tilsit, Napoleon bought Murat's sumptuous residence—pictures, furniture, silver, china, bedding, and all—to provide him with a comfortable embassy and went out of his way to honour him. But the ambassador, Count Tolstoy, remained aloof and barely concealed his dislike of Napoleon. In an attempt to revive Alexander's enthusiasm for the alliance, Napoleon had earlier that year returned to the subject of a joint expedition against the British in India, with the accompanying promise of an extension of the Russian empire in the east. Caulaincourt and the Russian foreign minister, Count Nikolai Rumiantsev, duly pored over maps, and General Gardanne calculated marching distances through Aleppo, Baghdad, Herat, Kabul, and Peshawar. But while Napoleon never ceased dreaming of India, he had no intention of embarking on the venture, as Alexander probably realised.[3]

Before parting at Tilsit, they had agreed to meet again the following year, and this encounter was to take place at Erfurt in Westphalia at the end of September 1808. Napoleon hoped that by deploying his usual mixture of charm and implied threat he would be able to reassert his ascendancy over the tsar. The meeting would also provide the opportunity to propose a dynastic marriage; such a union would kill two birds with one stone, as it would cement the alliance and at the same time provide Napoleon with an heir, which had become a pressing issue once again. The question had resurfaced when, on 5 May 1807, his nephew and adopted son Napoléon-Charles, the child of Louis and Hortense, died of croup. Now that he knew he could sire a child himself, many in his entourage, including Fouché and Talleyrand, urged him to divorce Josephine and marry a woman of childbearing age.[4]

One day in November 1807, with the court at Fontainebleau, Fouché had called on Josephine in her apartment and suggested she go before the Senate and request a divorce in the interests of the empire. He even produced a prepared text of the speech she should make. She asked him whether he had been sent by Napoleon, which he denied, so she dismissed him, saying she would do only what her husband asked of her. When she informed him of Fouché's visit Napoleon made a show of rebuking his minister, though it seems unlikely Fouché would have acted without his knowledge. He also reprimanded him when he read a police report which mentioned that people were discussing the divorce as though it had been agreed. To Josephine it seemed as though it had. 'What sadness thrones bring!' she wrote to her son, foreseeing the inevitable.[5]

Alexander had two unmarried sisters, and Napoleon did not see any reason why he should not embrace the idea if he could put it to him directly. 'An hour together will suffice, while the negotiations would last several months if it were left to the diplomats,' he said to Cambacérès as he left Paris. He had ordered Erfurt to be cleaned up, its buildings repainted and its streets lit, and he had sent out tapestries, pictures, and china to adorn his apartments there. He had also arranged for the best actors and the prettiest actresses of Paris to be sent out to entertain the company in the evenings, and, if possible, to find their way into Alexander's bed.[6]

To impress Alexander and lend weight to their meeting, he had also invited all the rulers of the Confederation of the Rhine and the King of Saxony. He had carefully selected the plays to be performed. According to Talleyrand, by staging heroic scenes he meant to disorient the ancient royals and aristocrats present and 'transport them in their imagination into other realms, where they would see men who were great by their deeds, exceptional by their actions, creating their own dynasty and drawing their origin from the gods'. The themes of immortality, glory, valour, and predestination which recur in the plays he chose were meant to inspire admiration in all who approached him, and Corneille's *Cinna* delivered the punchline in the phrase 'He who succeeds cannot be wrong'. Voltaire's *Mahomet* treats of the need for a new faith and a new master of the world;

its protagonist owes everything to his own qualities, and nothing to ancestry. Napoleon did not bring Josephine or a numerous suite, but as Talleyrand had been at Tilsit and was a good courtier who knew everyone in Europe, he brought him along. This turned out to be a mistake.[7]

When Alexander announced his intention of going to Erfurt, most of his entourage expressed fears that he would allow himself to be cajoled by Napoleon into further engagements unfavourable to Russia, and even, given recent events at Bayonne, that he might never come back. In reply to his mother, who had written begging him not to go, he explained that despite the setbacks at Bailén and Vimeiro, Napoleon was still strong enough to defeat any power that defied him. Russia must build up her military potential while pretending to remain his ally. He must go to Erfurt to persuade Napoleon of his goodwill, and his presence there should send a signal to Austria not to try anything rash before time. To his sister Catherine, who had also implored him to have nothing to do with the Corsican ogre, he replied more succinctly: 'Napoleon thinks that I'm just a fool, but he who laughs last laughs longest.'[8]

As soon as he heard that Alexander had set out, Napoleon left Paris, arriving at Erfurt on the morning of 27 September, and after dealing with some administrative business he called on the King of Saxony, who had preceded him. At two o'clock, having been alerted to Alexander's approach, he rode out to meet him outside the town. On seeing him ride up, Alexander alighted from his carriage and the two emperors embraced, after which they mounted up and rode into the town, greeted with full military honours, and spent the rest of the day together, only parting at ten that night.

Napoleon hoped to re-create what he called 'the spirit of Tilsit', having his troops parade before Alexander and spending hours in conversation with him on every subject that could flatter his vanity, while displaying his power over the other assembled sovereigns by ordering them about and telling them where to sit at table—'King of Bavaria, keep quiet!' he snapped at one point.[9]

As Alexander was hard of hearing in one ear, Napoleon had a dais built for the two of them close by the stage at the theatre. This meant that, as Talleyrand remarked, 'People listened to the actors, but it was him they were looking at.' During one performance, at the lines 'To the name of conqueror and triumphant victor, He wishes to join that of pacifier,' Napoleon made a show of emotion noticed by all. When, during a performance of Voltaire's tragedy *Oedipe*, the actor spoke the line 'The friendship of a great man is a gift from the gods,' Alexander stood up and took Napoleon's hand in a gesture meant for the audience.[10]

Napoleon acted the charming host one moment, running down the stairs to greet Alexander as he arrived for dinner, and putting him in his place the next. He arranged an excursion to the nearby battle-field of Jena, where, as one military man to another, he explained the battle to him, no doubt meaning to remind him of his own military prowess. He invited Alexander to a parade in the course of which he decorated soldiers with the Legion of Honour; since each man called forward had to give an account of his heroic exploit, and these had all taken place at Friedland against the Russians, the tsar was openly humiliated by having to listen to stories of his troops being beaten. Napoleon had even in the course of a discussion resorted to staging one of his rages, throwing his hat on the floor and stamping on it.[11]

On 6 October there was a hunting party in the forest of Etters-berg, for which stags were driven into a funnel of canvas screens so that by the time they reached the hunters they were disoriented, and so close that even the inexperienced Alexander with his poor eyesight managed to bag one trotting past eight feet from him. The hunt was followed by a dinner, a short concert, a play, and a ball. Napoleon did not dance because, as he put it in a letter to Josephine, 'forty years are forty years'. Instead, he had a two-hour discussion about German lit-erature with the poet Wieland, whom he had invited for the purpose, showing off his knowledge to the surprised and flattered German literary men listening to him. He then walked over to Goethe and had a long conversation with him. One can but admire his stamina, given that all the while he was manipulating the various rulers of the Confederation of the Rhine, each of whom had to be cajoled and bullied by turns, running the government of France, and overseeing operations in Spain, not to mention fighting a severe cold. Goethe, with whom he had a long meeting over breakfast on 1 October, was overwhelmed by the power he sensed in Napoleon's gaze and fascinated by his seemingly superhuman qualities.[12]

One day, when Alexander had forgotten his sword, Napoleon handed him his own, at which Alexander declared, 'I accept it as a mark of your friendship, and Your Majesty may be quite sure that I shall never draw it against you.' He did not, as Napoleon had hoped, promise to draw it against Austria if she were to attack while he was occupied in Spain. Alexander adopted an attitude of stubborn neutrality, refusing nothing and promising nothing. Napoleon's position was identical, since he wanted to oblige Alexander to bind himself further while offering nothing in exchange, except for a vague promise to withdraw French troops from the grand duchy of Warsaw and Prussia and, in return for the tsar's acceptance of his doings in Spain, to allow his annexation of Finland. The lack of any mutual interest in their alliance was glaring. Yet it was crucial to Napoleon not only to keep Austria in check but also to maintain the blockade against Britain, which was beginning to take effect.[13]

It was impossible to exclude British goods from the Continent entirely. Even while paying lip service, Russia had been contravening the terms of the blockade by allowing some neutral ships into its ports. British merchants had established entrepots at Heligoland, from where small ships could dart into creeks or minor harbours all over northern Europe, and at Malta, to do the same in the Mediterranean. British ships also defied the blockade by putting into the Austrian port of Trieste, from where their merchandise could reach Central Europe. There was plenty of clandestine trade, and there were even cases of French merchants from Bordeaux supplying the British forces in Portugal with wine and brandy. In Hamburg, the city authorities were surprised at a curious rise in the number of funerals, only to discover that coffins were being used to transport smuggled coffee and indigo—from which Bourrienne, now a commissioner there, was taking a cut. Even Napoleon's family flouted the blockade, Louis in Holland almost blatantly, Jérôme in Westphalia passing on goods, and Josephine buying smuggled silks and brocades. Cambacérès actually ordered the chief administrator of the grand duchy of Berg, Jean-Claude Beugnot, to send him cured hams by clandestine means in order to avoid paying customs duties aimed to back up the blockade. On the march back from Germany following Tilsit, Captain Boulart of the Guard artillery and his fellow officers and men happily bought quantities of English merchandise in Frankfurt and Hanover which they smuggled into France in their ammunition wagons, which they would not allow the customs officials at Mainz to inspect, arguing that the falling snow would soak the powder.[14]

Nevertheless, by the first months of 1808 the blockade was having a crippling effect on the British economy and, crucially, threatened to impinge on the political situation. Imports of much-needed cereals had plummeted by a staggering 93 percent, and Napoleon calculated that if the pressure could be kept up, the country would not be able to feed itself and there would be bread riots which would force the government to its knees. He was therefore desperate to keep Russia within the system, and with Alexander visibly cooling the surest means of doing that seemed a dynastic alliance. The subject was broached, and the tsar gave all the appropriate signs of delight but declared he had to obtain the assent of his mother before he could give a definite answer. He had no intention of going along with the idea, as he had already resolved to undermine Napoleon.[15]

On the day after his arrival at Erfurt, Talleyrand had found a note from Princess Thurn und Taxis, a sister of the queen of Prussia, inviting him to take tea with her. There he met Alexander, who had set up the meeting. The two met there several times over the next few days, having quickly entered into an understanding—Talleyrand told Alexander that he was the only civilised ruler capable of saving Europe and France from Napoleon and declared himself ready to serve him in this cause. Whether it was mentioned then or not, the service would not come free of charge.[16]

On his return to Paris, Talleyrand would remain in touch through the secretary of the Russian embassy, Karl von Nesselrode. He was already in secret contact with the Austrian ambassador Metternich, who summed up Talleyrand's position thus: 'The interest of France herself demands that the powers capable of standing up to Napoleon must unite to oppose a dyke to his insatiable ambition, that the cause of Napoleon is no longer that of France, that Europe itself can only be saved through the closest possible alliance of Austria and Russia.'[17]

'I am very satisfied with Alexander, and he must be with me,' Napoleon wrote to Josephine on 11 October, convinced that he had seduced the tsar. The following day they signed an agreement reaffirming their alliance, as well as a joint letter to George III professing their wish to make peace and appealing to him to enter into negotiations. Three days later, they rode out of Erfurt together to the spot on which they had met two weeks before, embraced and took their leave of each other. Napoleon then rode back, slowly, into town, apparently deep in thought. He had plenty to reflect on.[18]

He had come to Erfurt to consolidate the alliance forged at Tilsit, only to see cracks developing in it. He had held court, surrounded by cringing monarchs, but, as he once confessed to his interior minister Chaptal, he felt they all despised him for his low birth and would gladly topple him from his throne. 'I can only maintain myself on it by force; I can only accustom them to see me as their equal by keeping them under my yoke; my empire is destroyed if I cease to be feared.' He was aware that the higher he rose the greater his vulnerability. It is tempting to think that the reason he was drawn to Alexander, the most unlikely and inconvenient ally for him, was that he sensed the tsar's insecurities and did not feel such a parvenu in his company. However much he may have boasted about them, Napoleon lacked faith in the value of his own achievements. 'Military glory, which lives so long in history, is that which is most quickly forgotten among contemporaries,' he admitted to one of Josephine's ladies. He also feared that his state-building and other achievements would not survive. Josephine remonstrated with him, maintaining that his genius gave him his title to greatness, to no avail. He was, according to Rapp, lamentably obsessed with what the aristocratic milieu of the Faubourg Saint-Germain thought of him and ridiculously susceptible to gossip. It is ironic that while, as Talleyrand had noted, he used the theatre to drive home the message to the mostly idle and ineffectual sovereigns that he stood above them as the man of action, he lacked confidence in his own achievements and felt the need to adorn them with the trappings of royalty. 'Simplicity does not suit a parvenu soldier such as myself as it does a hereditary sovereign,' he said to one Polish lady.[19]

To Chaptal, he complained that it was only ancient dynasties that could count on unconditional popular support, and while a hereditary monarch could lie around being dissolute, he could not afford to, as 'there is not one general who does not believe he has the same right to the throne as me', which was patently not true. Mollien was struck by 'his insatiable need to be the centre of everything', which he believed to be dictated by 'the fear lest any particle of power escape him'. He also noticed in Napoleon an obsessive need 'to represent himself as the only essential man, to establish in the public perception an exclusive superiority, to belittle anything that might threaten to share it', and he was convinced this was the result not of calculation, but of a kind of instinctive reaction—which suggests deep psychological insecurities. 'Don't you see,' Napoleon used to say to members of his family, 'that I was not born on the throne, that I have to maintain myself on it in the same way I ascended to it, with glory, that it has to keep growing, that an individual who becomes a sovereign, like me, cannot stop, that he has to keep climbing, and that he is lost if he remains still.' He could certainly not afford to remain still now.[20]

The day following his arrival at Erfurt, he had received a special envoy from the Emperor Francis, General de Vincent. Although the audience had been courteous, with declarations of goodwill on both sides, it was obvious from Vincent's tone and the Austrian armaments that Vienna was preparing for war. Napoleon could not conceive that Francis would be foolish enough to make war on his own, and this led him to suspect the existence of a secret agreement between him and Alexander.[21]

This made it all the more imperative to pacify Spain as quickly as possible. He was back at Saint-Cloud at eleven o'clock on the night of 18 October. On 22 October he visited the Salon (the painters who wished to submit had been given to understand that it would be desirable to show Napoleon visiting the battlefield of Eylau and casting a 'consoling eye' over it which would 'soften the horror of death'; the winner, Antoine Gros, evidently achieved this, having managed to 'give Napoleon an aura of kindness and majestic splendour'). In the course of the next few days he opened the session of the Legislative, held receptions, and inspected public works, orphanages, and hospices before leaving on 29 October. Travelling day and night, stopping only to dine briefly and meet officials along the way, sometimes taking to his horse, by 3 November he was at Bayonne, where in a letter to Joseph he admitted that he was 'a little tired'. That did not stop him sitting up all night with Berthier dictating orders. By the evening of the next day he was in Tolosa, where he delivered a tirade to a group of monks, telling them that if they meddled in politics he would cut their ears off, which, not knowing French they could only judge the gist of by his tone. Much the same was true when, at Vitoria two days later, Joseph presented his ministers to him; he harangued them in a mixture of Italian and French, accusing them of incompetence and their clergy of being in the pay of the British, and poured scorn on the Spanish army. He declared that he would pacify the whole country in the space of two months and treat it like conquered territory.[22]

He took command of the Army of Spain, consisting of some 200,000 men spread across the country. While Marshal Soult on his right wing pushed back a British force of 40,000 under Sir John Moore, and on his left Lannes drove General Castaños back to Saragossa, Napoleon made for Madrid. On 12 November he reached Burgos, which had just been captured and was being put to the sack. One of his aides, Ségur, had been sent ahead, and selected the residence of the archbishop as the most suitable for his quarters. He was closely followed by Napoleon, accompanied only by Savary and Roustam. They went off in search of food and drink while Ségur lit a fire. Napoleon told him to open a window, and when Ségur pulled back the heavy curtains he was confronted by three Spanish soldiers, still fully armed, who had taken refuge there and now pleaded for their lives. Napoleon laughed at the danger he had run.[23]

He spent ten days in Burgos inspecting troops and then pressed on, forcing strong Spanish positions at the pass of Somosierra on 30 November, and arrived before Madrid two days later. He ordered the attack for the next day, and on 4 December the city surrendered. Napoleon took up residence in a country house at Chamartin outside the city, leaving that to his brother to repossess. From the moment he had joined Joseph at Vitoria he had ignored him, and Joseph was reduced to following in the wake of the army. He complained, with some reason, that this undermined his authority in a country which was difficult enough to rule as it was, and on 8 December he wrote to Napoleon renouncing his rights to the throne of Spain.[24]

Napoleon did not reply for ten days, when he sent him a short note concerning finances, and a few days later a flurry of instructions through Berthier. He found time to write to Josephine frequently, mainly short affectionate notes assuring her that he was well, that his affairs were going splendidly, and that she should not worry. In one, he discussed the wisdom of Hortense dismissing members of her domestic staff. He wrote to Fouché saying the Spaniards were not 'wicked' and the British only a minor irritant. He had a young virgin procured for him, but according to his valet Constant she wore too much scent for his keen sense of smell, so he sent her away untouched—having paid her.[25]

He issued decrees and orders for the administration of the kingdom as though Joseph did not exist, abolishing feudalism and the Inquisition, closing down convents, and confiscating as much property as he could to pay for his campaign. He also attended to the administration of the empire, going into details and checking figures, and specifying, for instance, what quantities of quinine should be distributed to the health services of each of the empire's forty-two major cities.[26]

He reviewed the main body of his army and on 22 December set off to confront Moore, hoping to at last have an opportunity of fighting his British enemy in the field. 'The weather is fine, my health is perfect, do not fret,' he wrote to Josephine before leaving. The weather changed dramatically not long after he set off, and his march over the Sierra de Guadarrama in sleet and snow proved an ordeal for the troops, which not only grumbled but in some cases actually showed their feelings by shooting at him as he passed. He thought it best to ignore the incidents and pressed on, hoping that a battle would restore morale.[27]

Moore retreated, making for the port of La Coruña, where the Royal Navy could evacuate his force, with Napoleon in pursuit. But on the evening of 1 January 1809, halfway between Benavente and Astorga, Napoleon was informed that an *estafette* from Paris was trying to reach him, so he stopped and waited by the roadside until it arrived. When he had read the despatches, his mood grew sombre and he proceeded to Astorga in silence. Those around him noted with surprise that the urge to catch up with Moore at all costs had left him. After spending a day at Astorga and handing over command to Soult, he went back to Benavente and thence to Valladolid. The despatches confirmed that Austrian rearmament was proceeding fast, but that was not what troubled him.

He was aware that there was much discontent in France. At Bayonne in June he had been notified of an inept conspiracy involving a General Mallet which had been uncovered and the plotters imprisoned. Bailén had emboldened his critics in the Senate and the Legislative, but he knew he only had to crack the whip to silence them. A slip made by Josephine while receiving a delegation of the Legislative, addressing them as the representatives of the nation, had annoyed him, but it had also given him his cue; he gave instructions for *Le Moniteur* to carry a notice explaining that her speech must have been wrongly reported, since she was too well-versed not to know that 'In the order of our constitutional hierarchy, the prime representative of the nation is the emperor, and the ministers, who are organs of his decisions.' Now he was informed of what looked like an altogether more sinister machination—by two of his closest associates.[28]

During a reception given by Talleyrand on 20 December, just as the guests had assembled, the usher announced the minister of police. It was no secret that Talleyrand and Fouché loathed each other and were seen under the same roof only when official functions required it, yet here was Talleyrand eagerly hobbling forward to greet the new arrival and then taking him, arm in arm, through the reception rooms for all to see, deep in conversation. News that two of the most consummate practitioners of the political pirouette had combined flew round Paris and reached the emperor at Astorga.[29]

What also reached him, thanks to postal intercepts by Lavalette, was an idea of what they were up to. With alarming reports of the exceptionally savage nature of the war in Spain reaching Paris, the possibility of Napoleon being killed had resurfaced, and this had drawn together the two men most concerned at the possible consequences for themselves. Both had for some time been in close touch with his sister Caroline and were now preparing a contingency plan to put Murat on the throne if Napoleon were killed. Lavalette had passed the incriminating letters from Murat on to Napoleon.[30]

His exasperation showed. When he heard soldiers of the Old Guard grumbling about conditions in Spain, he made a scene on parade, accusing them of laziness and of just wanting to get back to their whores in Paris. All officers passing through the town were obliged to call on him, and when one day General Legendre, who had been Dupont's chief of staff and signed the capitulation of Bailén, presented himself, he vented his fury on the man. He accused him of cowardice, of having defiled the honour of France, called the capitulation a crime as well as a crass show of ineptitude, and said the hand with which he had signed it should have withered. In a letter to Josephine on 9 January he urged her not to fret but to be prepared to see him appear unexpectedly at any moment. A week later he raced back to Paris, at one stage covering 120 kilometres on horseback in five hours.[31]

He reached Paris at eight o'clock on the morning of 23 January. That afternoon he visited the works on the Louvre and the rue de Rivoli; over the following days he received the diplomatic corps, went to the opera, and on 27 January, wrote to Talleyrand instructing him to hand his key of grand chamberlain over to Duroc. Talleyrand complied and wrote Napoleon a letter brimming with sweetness and submission, expressing the extreme pain with which he had done so: 'My only consolation is to remain tied to Your Majesty by two sentiments which no amount of pain could overcome or weaken, by a feeling of gratitude and of devotion which will end only with my life.'[32]

The twenty-ninth of January was a Sunday, and after the usual parade, Napoleon held a privy council attended by Cambacérès, Lebrun, Gaudin, Fouché, Admiral Decrès, and Talleyrand. Toward the end of the meeting he suddenly grew agitated and, turning to Talleyrand, who was leaning against a console, unleashed his fury. 'You're a thief, a coward, a faithless, godless creature; you have throughout your life failed in all your duties, you have deceived and betrayed everyone; nothing is sacred to you; you would sell your own father,' he ranted, pacing the room while Talleyrand remained perfectly still in his nonchalant pose, 'pale as death' according to one witness, his eyes half-closed. 'You, sir, are nothing but a pile of shit in silk stockings!' Napoleon concluded. Although he remained superciliously calm as he left the room, Talleyrand said quietly to grand master of ceremonies Ségur, who was just entering, 'There are some things one can never forgive.' And later he added, 'What a shame that such a great man should be so ill-bred.' He informed Metternich that he now felt free to act in the common cause. No doubt not wishing to give the impression of instability, Napoleon left Talleyrand with his rank of vice-grand elector. He did not penalise Fouché, whom he still needed, particularly as it was by now certain that he would have to go to war.[33]

This was a war for which neither Napoleon nor France had any appetite. It also elicited little enthusiasm outside Austria, which was getting nowhere in its search for allies. Russia was opposed to it and Prussia fearful, as were most of the German states, however much they may have resented French dominance. Even Britain was only prepared to come up with a meagre subsidy. But Austria was eager to wipe out its humiliations of Ulm and Austerlitz. And despite the lack of interest in Germany, for the first time in its history the Habsburg monarchy was going to play the German national card. A powerful influence was Emperor Francis's third wife, Maria Ludovica, a German nationalist with a hatred of all things French, whom he had married in January 1808. Another was the chief minister, Count Johann Philipp Stadion, who encouraged nationalist propaganda through the press and government-sponsored pamphlets, in which the coming war was represented as one of liberation, and parallels were drawn with that raging in Spain.[34]

The thirty-seven-year-old Archduke Charles had been reorganising the army, introducing conscription and giving it a more national character. In March 1809 he appointed the nationalist writer Friedrich Schlegel as his military secretary. His brother Archduke John also struck a national note, declaring himself to be 'German, heart and soul'. By the spring of 1809 Austria had mustered around 300,000 men. A force of 30,000 was deployed in Galicia under Archduke Ferdinand to check the Polish forces in the grand duchy of Warsaw and deter the Russians from supporting their French allies. Another 50,000 under Archduke John were poised to stop a French move out of Italy. The main army of nearly 200,000 under Archduke Charles invaded France's ally Bavaria on 10 April and entered Munich. This coincided with a planned insurrection in the Tyrol led by the partisan Andreas Hofer which forced the French and Bavarian troops stationed there to capitulate. The Austrian advance was accompanied by an appeal to the people of Germany to rise. It was answered by a Prussian officer, Major Schill, who led his regiment out to attack Westphalia, and by the Hessian Colonel Dornberg, an officer in Westphalian service who sallied forth at the head of 6,000 men to raise a general rebellion. With his main forces tied down in Spain, Napoleon could only muster 100,000 French troops, along with a total of 150,000 less reliable and certainly less motivated men supplied by his various allies. As soon as news came on the telegraph that the Austrians had invaded Bavaria, he went into action.[35]

Although he still moved fast, travelling at all hours of the day and night, Napoleon had introduced a modicum of comfort into his campaigning, as his age no longer permitted subjecting himself to the rigours of sleeping out in all weathers and going without food. His travelling carriage was equipped with every comfort, and he kept adding resources. He loved *nécessaires* of one sort or another, cases containing every conceivable utensil required for their purpose, be it washing or writing. He was followed or preceded by fourteen wagons and a train of mules bearing a set of five tents of blue-and-white-striped ticking—two of them, his bedroom and study, private; the other three also used by his staff. The wagons also carried everything else he might need, from spare uniforms and linen to dining silver and a supply of Chambertin. Closer to hand, one of his pages carried a telescope and another maps, which Napoleon would spread out on a table, or sometimes on the ground, and lie down on it, pincushion in hand, then stand up, surveying the picture and dictating orders briskly. His Mameluke was always in attendance, as was a small group of orderlies, *officiers d'ordonnance*, some of them civilians, dressed originally in green and later pale-blue uniforms. Not far behind was a supply of spare horses, mostly Arabs. He was always escorted by a couple of dozen mounted chasseurs or chevaux-légers of the Guard, while Berthier and the general staff were escorted by his own guards from his principality of Neuchatel, uniformed in bright Serin yellow. Napoleon always seemed at his happiest when on campaign, spending much of the day in the saddle, surrounded by his staff and cheered by his troops, whom he would stop and talk to. The exercise invigorated him, and his high spirits were contagious. When he paused for something to eat, a picnic would be deftly spread out by his *maison militaire* and all would share. 'It was really a party for all of us,' recalled his prefect of the palace Bausset.[36]

In a series of three engagements between 19 and 21 April he tried to encircle part of the Austrian army, eventually scoring successes at Eckmühl and Ratisbon (Regensburg). He would later claim that Eckmühl was one of his finest manoeuvres, but these were not the victories he had been used to. The Austrians had learned to move and fight well and retreated in good order. Riding over the battlefields Napoleon was unpleasantly struck by the carnage involved in achieving victory. He had himself been lightly wounded in the foot by a spent musketball at Ratisbon. In his proclamation issued after the battle, he praised his troops for having once more demonstrated 'the contrast between the soldiers of Caesar and the rabble of Xerxes', and listed fictitious numbers of guns, standards, and prisoners taken. To Cambacérès he wrote that it had been a finer victory than Jena. Few were fooled. Cambacérès replied that everyone was delighted by the news of the victories. 'Yet, Sire, in the middle of the general happiness your people are greatly alarmed at the dangers to which you expose yourself,' he wrote on 3 May.[37]

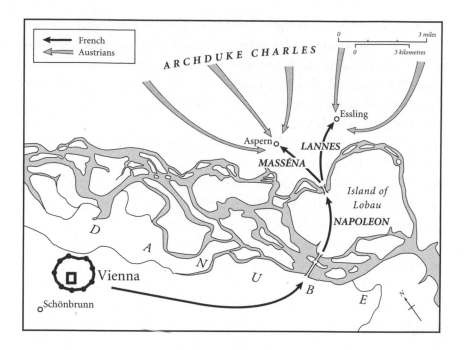

Napoleon's attempts to outflank and cut off the retreating Arch-duke Charles came to nothing, and although he reached Vienna on 11 May and took up residence at Schönbrunn once more, he had little to rejoice over. His army had been bloodied and it had under-performed, largely because his seasoned troops and some of his best commanders, such as Ney and Soult, were in Spain, while Murat was in Naples. This time he had had to make a show of bombarding the city before Vienna opened its gates; the inhabitants neverthe-less showed their admiration for him by cheering as he rode up to the walls. Archduke Charles had regrouped on the north bank of the Danube, and getting the French army across was not going to be easy.

Napoleon chose the stretch where the Danube divides into two narrower streams around the large island of Lobau, and on 19 May his engineers began building pontoon bridges. The following af-ternoon he was on Lobau, and began moving his troops across the second branch of the river. By the morning of 21 May some 25,000 to 30,000 had made it across and taken up positions in the villages of Aspern and Essling, facing about 90,000 Austrians. At this point the Austrians destroyed his bridges by floating heavily loaded barges down the river, which was in spate. The engineers struggled to repair them, but with more heavy objects being floated downriver Napoleon's army was stranded in three places, while Archduke Charles seized his chance and opened up on the French positions with heavy artillery. Fierce fighting developed as he tried to get between Masséna's corps at Aspern and the river, while Napoleon himself clung on at Essling. With the bridges repaired, more men got across, bringing French numbers up to around 60,000 on the morning of 22 May. Napoleon launched an attack which was returned, and the two villages changed hands several times. Although the French had held their ground, the bridges at his back had been set alight by incendiary barges, preventing reinforcements from coming up, so at nightfall Napoleon pulled all his forces back onto the island. Both sides claimed victory, the Austrians naming it Aspern and the French Essling, but there was little to celebrate on either side. Losses had been heavy—more than 20,000 Austrians and upwards of 15,000 French.[38]

A harrowing personal loss for Napoleon was that of Marshal Lannes, who had both legs crushed by a cannonball. Larrey amputated in an attempt to save his life, and the physicians struggled to keep him alive. Napoleon visited him every evening, but Lannes had been badly concussed. 'My friend, don't you recognise me?' Napoleon allegedly asked. 'It's your friend Bonaparte.' He died on 31 May. On hearing the news Napoleon hurried over and embraced the lifeless body. He was in tears and had to be dragged away by Duroc. Lannes had been one of his closest and, according to Fouché, the only one of Napoleon's friends who was still able to tell him the truth. He ordered the body to be embalmed and taken back to France.[39]

Napoleon was cheered by the news from the south, where Eugène had forced the Austrians out of Italy, and General Étienne Macdonald had ousted them from Dalmatia. He turned the island of Lobau into a fortress and a launchpad for his next offensive and spent most of June bringing up reinforcements. He would go there nearly every day and often, donning a soldier's overcoat and carrying a musket, venture out to observe enemy positions. On 14 June Eugène and Macdonald defeated Archduke John at Raab and joined forces with Napoleon, giving him a comfortable superiority over Archduke Charles. On the night of 4 July, in a violent thunderstorm, Napoleon began crossing to the north bank of the Danube.

33

The Cost of Power

ON THE MORNING of 5 July 1809 a powerful artillery barrage opened what was to be the largest and longest-lasting battle Napoleon had fought. Over the next two days his forces, totalling nearly 190,000 men drawn from all over Europe, supported by more than 500 guns, fought it out with an Austrian army of up to 170,000 with 450 pieces of ordnance in what was more a battle of attrition than his usual decisive manoeuvre.

While the bombardment of their defences at Enzersdorf distracted the Austrians, the French army turned their left wing, forcing them to fall back on the village of Wagram. Archduke Charles managed to repel an attempt by Masséna's corps to outflank him on his right—helped by the fact that following a bad fall from his horse the day before, Masséna was commanding from a reclining position in his carriage. French attacks by Bernadotte, Eugène, and Davout ground to a standstill in fierce fighting at close quarters which continued late into the evening and only died down at around eleven, when Bernadotte and then the others fell back.

Late that evening Napoleon conferred with Berthier, Davout, Oudinot, and others, preparing a plan for the next day. The nature of war had changed, and so had his style; it was a far cry from the days of his first Italian campaign, when he told Costa de Beauregard that a council of war was a coward's resource. He went to bed in his tent at one o'clock in the morning and rose at four. At five he was in the saddle, astride a fine grey called Cyrus on which he would cover almost the whole ten-kilometre stretch of the battlefield, often within range of enemy guns, which took a heavy toll on his staff. As one of his aides lifted his hat, which was the form on receiving an order, it was blown away by a cannonball, causing Napoleon to smile and say, 'It's lucky you're not taller.'[1]

While Archduke Charles made a bold attempt to encircle Masséna, still in his carriage, on the French left, Napoleon ordered Davout to turn his left wing, while he himself launched a massed attack on his centre at Wagram. Ineptly led by Bernadotte, after having triumphed over stiff resistance the Saxon corps, which had led the attack, fell back, and all the advantage gained was lost. After exchanging vigorous words with Bernadotte (whom he later said he ought to have had shot for cowardice, but now just ordered back to Paris), Napoleon reorganised his forces. He combined a massive cavalry attack led by Bessières with a second assault on the Austrian centre, preceded by a heavy barrage, with the French artillery bringing over a hundred guns up to within a few hundred metres of the Austrian lines and pounding them at short range.

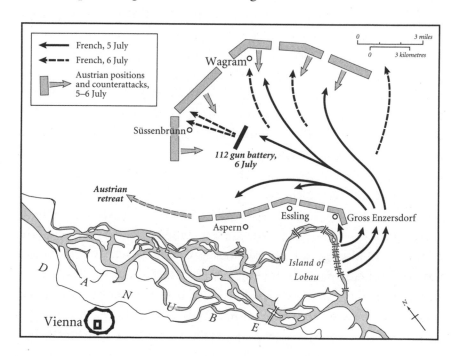

When he saw the attack drive home, Napoleon lay down on the grass to sleep for an hour, undisturbed by the thunder of nearly a thousand cannon. The exertions of the past two days were telling on his health, and he had what he called 'an overflow of bile' that evening. He was better in the morning. 'My enemies are undone, beaten and fleeing in complete disorder,' he wrote to Josephine. 'They were very numerous, but I crushed them.'[2]

This was nonsense; the Austrians may have been defeated, but they withdrew in relatively good order, with most of their artillery. Assessments of the losses differ widely, but they were heavy both in men and horses, and greater on the French side. Although the French took as many as 15,000 prisoners, the Austrians lost fewer flags and cannon, and the battle had been neither tactically masterful nor decisive. Yet Napoleon's bulletin claimed exactly that and described the Austrian retreat as a 'rout', which it was not, since the French were too exhausted to pursue the advantage. When they did, two days later, they caught up with the Austrians at Znaïm, where after an inconclusive engagement on 11 July the Austrians proposed an armistice. Dismissing the wishes of his entourage, who were keen to finish them off decisively, Napoleon agreed to it, saying too much blood had been spilt already; he had been shocked by the heavy casualties incurred by both sides in the course of the campaign.[3]

That was not his only worry as he returned to Schönbrunn on 13 July. Whatever he wrote in his bulletins, he could see for himself that none of the battles he had fought over the past three months were in any sense decisive. Others could see it too. Even though it had earned him his marshal's baton, Marmont called Wagram 'a victory without consequence'. 'The days when swarms of prisoners would fall into our hands, as in Italy, at Ulm, at Austerlitz, at Jena, were past,' he reflected. In those days, when they encountered the lightning-bold tactics of the still young Napoleon and the dash of the French soldier fledged in the ranks of the Revolution, the Austrian or Prussian commanders and soldiers did not know what had hit them and threw up their hands in a natural reflex. But much had changed since then. It was not just that Napoleon and his generals had grown older, though that was certainly a factor.[4]

Although Austria was obliged to sue for peace, Germany was by no means subdued. The indecisive nature of the battle of Aspern-Essling had reverberated through Europe in much the same way as news of Bailén the previous year, further denting the myth of Napoleon's invincibility. It had encouraged the Duke of Brunswick-Oels, whose father had been vanquished at Auerstadt, to march out in June at the head of his 'Black Legion of Vengeance' of 2,000 men raised with money from the Austrian government. He had joined up with a force of 5,000 Austrians and marched on Dresden and Leipzig before being seen off by Jérôme's Westphalians. The rising in the Tyrol had also revived at the news, forcing Napoleon to send Marshal Lefèbvre to pacify the area, but this only inflamed local feeling and fuelled a *guerrilla* which would take time to put down.

Perceptions of Napoleon had shifted dramatically. From having been widely viewed as a liberator and a friend of the oppressed, he was now coming to be seen as the oppressor. The failure of his attempt to play the national card by calling on the Hungarians to rise up against the Austrians was eloquent evidence of this. They had good reason not to trust him: in order not to ruffle Russian sensibilities, he let down his own party in Poland. Commanded by the nephew of the country's last king, Prince Joseph Poniatowski, the army of the grand duchy of Warsaw had, after an initial defeat by Archduke Ferdinand, beaten the Austrians back and occupied most of their Polish province of Galicia. Instead of letting the Poles add it to the territory of the grand duchy, Napoleon ceded half of it to Russia, which had barely pretended to support him against Austria. He thereby forfeited the support of a large part of a nation prepared to be his most devoted ally.

The young Buonaparte, who had lived to hate the oppressor of his nation and dreamed only of liberating it, had grown out of his island patriotism and espoused the cause of a France that had embraced the progressive values of the day and offered greater promise to his people. Bearing the standard of that France, he had shattered the chains of feudalism and overthrown tyranny in northern Italy and subsequently bestowed the benefits of rational administration there and in western Germany, earning the gratitude and even love of millions.

But a growing cynicism had led him to sacrifice the aspirations of those millions to what he had come to see as higher priorities. The dreams of a German emancipation which he had done much to foster were methodically doused by his arrangements within it, as well as his own and his agents' behaviour.

A prime example is Westphalia, which could serve as a microcosm of what was wrong with Napoleon's imperial policy. 'What the people of Germany ardently desire is that those who are not noble and who have talent should have an equal right to your respect and to employment, that all kinds of servitude and all other bonds separating the sovereign from the lowest class of the people should be entirely abolished,' Napoleon wrote to Jérôme as he took his throne. 'The benefits of the Code Napoléon, the openness of procedures, the establishment of juries will be among the distinguishing marks of your monarchy. And if I am to be quite open with you, I am counting on such measures more than on the greatest victories to extend and establish your monarchy. Your people must enjoy a liberty, an equality and a well-being unknown to the people of the rest of Germany, and may this liberal government in one way or another lead to the most salutary change in the whole Confederation and the enhancement of your monarchy.'[5]

The kingdom, which had a population of two million, was made up of territory taken from Prussia and eighteen minor German principalities. With its capital at Kassel, it was organised in departments along French lines and given a constitution drawn up by Cambacérès and Regnaud de Saint-Jean d'Angély based on that of France but incorporating local law. Although at the outset it was run by ministers brought in from Paris, the administration was gradually taken over by locals. But while the kingdom was supposed to be independent, Napoleon could not help treating it as a department of France. He demanded from it a tribute of 49 million francs per annum, and awarded estates there to French generals and officials who sucked another 7 million francs a year out of it.[6]

The twenty-four-year-old Jérôme was not lacking in intelligence or other qualities, but he was lazy, vain, and dissolute. His career as a naval officer had been a fiasco and his military role as commander of an army corps in Silesia during the campaign against Prussia of 1806–07 was less than brilliant; in Breslau in January 1807 he and his staff had kept themselves warm with eighteen bottles of Champagne and 208 of other wines each day. He was married to the plain and plump Catherine, daughter of the King of Württemberg, and although he was copiously unfaithful to her, he developed real love for his 'Trinette'.[7]

He established a court modelled on Napoleon's, created a new nobility, and instituted an order of chivalry. Palaces were rebuilt and hung with state portraits of the new royal couple, splendid uniforms were designed for royal guards, and even a new unit of currency, the Jérôme, was introduced—to be spent lavishly on court entertainments, jewellery, and the trappings of royalty. He ordered a statue and over fifty busts of himself, and twelve of his wife, from Carrara. He nevertheless managed, with the help of a few competent French officials, to rule not much worse than most monarchs. As Countess Anna Potocka put it, 'With a little more legitimacy and a little less puerile vanity, he would have passed for a distinguished ruler.' But as well as making endless demands for more money and troops, many of which were sent to Spain, Napoleon kept interfering in his conduct of affairs, undermining his authority. He also kept rearranging the territory of his kingdom along with his changing plans; provinces were shunted between vassal states or incorporated into the French Empire, which not only disorganised the administration but also sapped any feelings of loyalty that might have developed to the new state and its ruler. Therein lay much of the weakness of Napoleon's system: he undermined the authority of the siblings he placed on thrones by treating them as his lieutenants, yet out of a combination of fondness, family solidarity, and the inability to put anyone more trustworthy in their place, was unable to control or discipline them.[8]

There was an inherent contradiction at the heart of the whole Napoleonic imperium: its mission was to enlighten, liberate, and modernise. Feudalism was swept away, along with all disabilities imposed by guilds and corporations, Jews were liberated, and all forms of servitude abolished, yet new hierarchies were created and political constraints imposed on the economy. Since most of the inhabitants of the Continent recognised only monarchy as a principle of govern-ment, Napoleon abandoned republican models in favour of imperial and royal ones, with all their trappings of titles, honours, decora-tions, and courts. In August 1811 he would institute an *Ordre de la Réunion*, intended to bind prominent people from all parts of the French dominion into a confraternity—which necessarily excluded all the inhabitants of Napoleonic Europe who did not belong to his newly created elite.

What undermined the whole enterprise, particularly in Germany, was that while the benefits of emancipation, equality before the law, and a functioning administration based on a solid constitution, not to mention the spread of education for all, were generally appreci-ated, those who had bestowed them were increasingly resented for their arrogance and their financial demands. As Jacques Beugnot, who had been sent to Dusseldorf to run the grand duchy of Berg after the generally popular Murat had moved to Naples, noted, he and other French officials in Germany were in the same positions as proconsuls in the Roman Empire. 'Do not forget that in the states of the King of Westphalia you are the minister of the Emperor,' the finance minister Gaudin reminded Beugnot as he set off on his mis-sion in 1807. 'His Majesty is very keen that you should not lose sight of that.'[9]

The situation was not much better in those states of the Confed-eration of the Rhine ruled by their own sovereigns. While the people were emancipated and constitutions brought in, the process allowed the rulers to sweep away anachronistic rights and exemptions and gave them far more power than they had enjoyed hitherto. Liberated from their Habsburg overlords, they now had armies, and many had been promoted in status, while their subjects gained little. And with time, the rulers too began to resent the constant demands from Na-poleon for money and troops. Something which affected all the areas outside France, whether they were kingdoms governed by one of Na-poleon's siblings or allied states, was Napoleon's stationing of French troops there. The commanders tended to behave as though they were in conquered territory, helping themselves to what they needed, be-having badly and ignoring or even browbeating local officials. As

Rapp once said to Napoleon, 'Unfortunately, Sire, we do a lot of damage as allies.'[10]

They did a great deal more damage in the case of Prussia, which was not an ally, and which had been subjected after Tilsit to humiliating conditions. It was obliged to pay a levy of 600 million francs to France in penalties for having started the war, and to support a French army of occupation numbering 150,000 men and 50,000 horses. French military authorities supervised the administration of the country, sucking more money out and reducing much of the population to poverty and even starvation. Houses in towns and villages were abandoned, thousands of beggars wandered the land, and suicides were common. Originally welcomed as a liberator, by 1809 Napoleon was seen as an oppressor. Resentment of all things French grew, and the ribbon of the Legion of Honour was referred to as 'the sign of the Beast' in some quarters. Young men dreamed of revenge.[11]

All those who for one reason or another hated French rule or Napoleon looked to Spain, where the outbreak of variously motivated violence provoked by French intervention coalesced around the symbols of God and Ferdinand. Wishful thinking turned the 'little war', *guerrilla*, waged by small regular units and armed bands against the French into an archetype; in the popular imagination all over Europe as far as Russia, the figure of the heroic *guerrillero* assumed mythical proportions, arousing the enthusiasm of conservative Catholics and revolutionaries alike, who dreamed of emulating him. In Prussia many young men joined the *Tugendbund*, the 'League of Virtue', to prepare themselves and Prussian society for the struggle to liberate Germany from the Napoleonic stranglehold. The extent to which Napoleon's credibility as a liberator had fallen can be gauged from the failure of Augereau's attempt to play the anti-Spanish card in Catalonia, usually open to suggestions of separatism.

The situation in Spain had actually shifted in favour of the French. Joseph had re-entered Madrid on 22 January, and ignoring his brother's advice to act with firmness, he played to Spanish national feelings by attending mass every day, appointing Spaniards to key posts and indulging local customs. He created a functioning administration and gradually built up a body of adherents among Spaniards who wished to modernise their country. He even managed to raise Spanish regiments which demonstrated a modicum of loyalty to him. The area under his control expanded, and the first burst of insurgency subsided. Saragossa had fallen to the French on 20 February, and Soult had taken Oporto on 27 March. Victor defeated a Spanish army at Medellin on the following day, and Suchet managed to pacify Aragon.

But there was no unity of command, as none of the commanders in the field paid any attention to orders issued by Joseph or his commander-in-chief, General Jourdan. Napoleon had encouraged a spirit of emulation among his marshals which had turned into rivalry, and they were not disposed to cooperate, as each tried to wrongfoot the other. The situation was particularly bad between Ney and Soult, whose mutual animosity dated back to their service on the Rhine in the 1790s. General Wellesley outmanoeuvred Soult and Victor, broke out of Portugal, and marched into Spain. He scored a minor success at Talavera at the end of July before being forced to retreat back into Portugal. After a French victory at Almonacid two weeks later, things began to look good for the French. A victory by Soult at Ocaña in November would open up Andalucia, and by the following spring the French were in control of most of the country.

Wellesley showed himself to be the equal of Napoleon in terms of propaganda, sending home a report of Talavera representing it as a great victory which was printed in the British press. This came to Napoleon's notice in Vienna, and he fumed at the incompetence of his brother and the commanders in the field. An officer sent by Joseph explained that the report in the British press was exaggerated, listing as regimental colours and eagles what were only *guidons*, and pointed out that all the eagles were still in French hands, but Napoleon would have none of it. He had little faith in his brother's capabilities. His ambassador in Madrid, Antoine de Laforest, disliked Joseph and retailed what he knew his imperial master would like to hear. Each of the commanders also criticised Joseph, as well as each other, in their reports. Joseph's attempts to explain the realities of the situation and justify his policy make painful reading. Napoleon dismissed his arguments, ignored his request to be allowed to abdicate, and stopped answering his letters altogether.[12]

This silence should have been caused by a period of reflection. Cambacérès had written after Essling informing Napoleon, with all the emollient tact that had kept him in office so long, that public opinion in Paris did not reflect his triumphs, and that people did not feel they were worth the cost in blood. He added that there was anxiety at the possibility of his being killed, but made it clear that there was much discontent at the continuing war, the dispiriting news from Spain and a deteriorating economic climate. He received in reply what he described as 'a rather dry letter' demanding more specific information. In his next report Cambacérès could not hide that there was also much criticism of his treatment of the Pope.[13]

It had long been Napoleon's conviction that France's security rested on denying other powers influence in Italy and the Mediterranean and that the Papal States represented a strategic security risk for the kingdoms of Naples and Italy. As all subsequent rulers of Italy would accept, logic demanded they be liquidated. Logic was reinforced in Napoleon's view by the fact that the College of Cardinals was mostly made up of aristocrats sympathetic to every anti-Napoleonic coalition and that Rome had become a refuge for many of his enemies.

He also believed that the clergy should be loyal citizens of the state and politically neutral. Since most of them were his subjects, they should obey him, yet the Pope exercised a rival authority over them, inspiring them to resist some of his arrangements, which he found intolerable. He could not or would not see that there were some measures which the Pope could not sanction on theological grounds, which is why he opposed the introduction of the Code into the Papal States. As Napoleon saw it, the Pope was using spiritual weapons in defence of his temporal interests, which justified disarming him by confiscating these.[14]

Shortly after reaching Vienna, on 17 May, Napoleon ordered the Papal States' incorporation into the French Empire. He justified this by arguing that the Pope had only acquired temporal power through the generosity of Napoleon's 'august predecessor' Charlemagne and that he now no longer required it.[15]

In response, on 10 June the Pope issued a bull excommunicating all the despoilers of the Holy See. Just in case he might be in any doubt, two days later he wrote to Napoleon informing him that he had been excommunicated and anathemised. Napoleon made light of this but sent orders to the commander on the spot, General Miollis, to deal severely with the pontiff, without specifying what he meant. On the night of 6 July Miollis sent General Radet to Rome. Radet entered the Castel Sant'Angelo, seized the Pope, bundled him and Cardinal Pacca into a travelling coach, and drove them off under escort of gendarmes to Genoa and thence to Grenoble, where they were held incommunicado. Napoleon was annoyed when he heard of this, saying the Pope should have been left in peace in Rome, but concluded that 'what is done is done'; he was not going to back down. On the pages of *Le Moniteur* he lectured that Christ had preached poverty and rejected temporal power, quoting His saying that His kingdom was not of this world, and the passage about rendering unto Caesar. But the good work of the Concordat had been undone, and royalist sentiment revived in France. His actions also alienated public opinion throughout Catholic southern Germany, which included his allies Bavaria, Baden, Württemberg, and Saxony, in Poland and Italy, and inflamed the situation further in Spain.[16]

Many of Napoleon's oldest supporters were growing anxious at the turn events were taking, and some of his closest collaborators, even among the military, were beginning to have their doubts. There was criticism of his conduct of the last campaign, and particularly of Wagram, as well as anxiety at the cost in life. Napoleon relied more and more on brute force and artillery—an estimated 96,000 shots were fired by the French at Wagram.[17]

As he relied on tactics and movement for his successes, Napoleon saw little reason to innovate equipment. While other armies perfected theirs—the Prussians brought in a slicer on their muskets which saved the time taken biting off the top of the cartridge with one's teeth and increased firepower, the British brought in rifles which increased accuracy—the French stuck with the musket model of 1777. While the British developed rockets and the Russians sophisticated gunsights, the French stuck with the Gribeauval cannon designed in 1765. Although Napoleon founded officers' schools at Fontainebleau, La Flèche, and Saint-Germain-en-Laye, promotion still operated on the revolutionary principle of peer selection, with Napoleon nominating officers after a battle on the recommendation of their comrades, which often yielded poor results. And, as the commander of one light infantry regiment noted, awarding the Legion of Honour was often counterproductive, as it gave the recipient a pension to protect, an incentive to avoid danger.[18]

While his enemies learned from him, Napoleon failed to learn from them. After the battle of Heilsberg in 1807, Lannes commented that the Russians were beginning to fight better, and Napoleon agreed, allegedly adding that he was teaching them lessons that would one day make them his masters. It was not just a question of weapons and tactics. Many on the French side were astonished as they surveyed the battlefield of Eylau to see Russian dead lying in ranks as they had stood and fought, and at Friedland Russian soldiers were seen to throw themselves in the river and risk drowning rather than surrender. Napoleon paid no attention to this, nor to the other lessons of the campaign of 1806–07.[19]

He failed to take into account that the tactics he had used in his Italian and south German campaigns, where the theatre was relatively small, densely populated, rich in provender, and easily crossed on relatively good roads, were entirely inappropriate to the open spaces and quagmires that passed for roads in Poland and Russia. More important, he had failed to take stock of another factor which he had not encountered before.

Until then he had commanded troops motivated by national feeling or local loyalties against imperial or royal armies of drafted peasants or professional soldiers who differed little from mercenaries. This had gradually been reversed. By 1807 the Grande Armée contained contingents of Poles, Germans, and Italians, and even the French soldiers were beginning to question what they were doing so far from home, while the Russian army he faced was composed of determined Russian peasants doggedly defending theirs. This reversal became more pronounced over the next two years, in the fighting against a more nationally conscious Austrian army, and above all against the Spanish regulars, not to mention the *guerrilleros*. Just as he had mutated from liberator into oppressor, so his troops had become agents of imperial power while their adversaries had changed roles from being the upholders of feudalism to that of defenders of the people.

According to one member of the Council of State, Achille de Broglie, at Vienna after Wagram all the generals and marshals longed for peace, 'cursing their master' and contemplating the future with 'great apprehension'. Many were astonishingly outspoken. 'He's a coward, a cheat, a liar,' General Vandamme burst out in front of his comrades. Admiral Decrès did not mince his words either. 'The Emperor is mad, completely mad, and he'll send us all, every one of us head over heels and it'll all end in an appalling catastrophe,' he said to Marmont. There were plenty more who shared such views.[20]

Napoleon ignored them, resorting as he increasingly did to cynicism. During the Wagram campaign he turned to General Mathieu Dumas, who had fought for the American as well as the French Revolution, and asked him whether he was 'one of those idiots who still believed in liberty'. When Dumas affirmed that he was, Napoleon told him he was deceiving himself and that he must be driven by personal ambition like everyone else. 'Look at Masséna,' he went on. 'He has acquired enough glory and honours, but he's not content: he wants to be a prince like Murat and Bernadotte, he's ready to go out tomorrow and get himself killed just to be made a prince.' Masséna did accept the title of prince of Essling, but he and his fellow marshals were appalled when Napoleon floated the idea of instituting a new military order of the Three Golden Fleeces.[21]

Napoleon spent the next two months at Schönbrunn, where he made himself at home, even erecting a couple of obelisks capped with imperial eagles at the entrance. He held parades which people would drive out of Vienna to watch, as they were both splendid and theatrical. Napoleon would speak to the soldiers, inspect their knapsacks and question them about their experiences. While reviewing a pontoon company he went up to one *caisson*, asked what was inside, and after having its contents listed in detail, had it opened and personally counted the axes, saws, bolts, nails, and other equipment, even climbing up onto the wheel to inspect the inside, to the delight of soldiers and onlookers. He would make regiments execute various manoeuvres and adopt battle formation, praising or criticising, and personally correcting. When the splendidly uniformed Polish Chevau-Légers of the Guard broke ranks around a pile of building materials blocking the entrance to the parade ground, he flew into a rage and ordered them off, snapping, to the delight of onlookers, 'That lot are good for nothing except fighting!'[22]

In the evenings there were theatrical performances, usually Italian opera, which Napoleon found 'rather mediocre'. There was also more intimate entertainment. Soon after reaching Schönbrunn, before Essling, he had written to Maria Walewska inviting her to join him. While he waited, he distracted himself with what was noted down in the accounts of his *cassette* as 'Viennese adventures'. When Walewska arrived, Duroc installed her in a cottage in the village of Mödling a short distance from Schönbrunn, and Napoleon's valet Constant would come to collect her at night. In mid-August he developed a persistent rash on his neck, so he summoned Corvisart from Paris. The rash had largely cleared up by the time he arrived, and it may be that the reason for the summons was not the rash, but to check whether, as Maria thought, she was pregnant, which Corvisart confirmed. Yet in his letters to Josephine, Napoleon made out that he was bored and looked forward to getting back to Paris, and to her, expressing himself with his usual hints of intimacy.[23]

During one of the parades at Schönbrunn, on 12 October, a young man approached him and managed to get quite close before Rapp, noticing that he had a hand in his pocket, ordered a gendarme to arrest him. He was found to be clutching a kitchen knife with which he meant to murder Napoleon. When questioned, he said he would only talk to the emperor himself. Intrigued, Napoleon interviewed him. Friedrich Staps, the seventeen-year-old son of a pastor, had decided to assassinate Napoleon for the harm he was doing to Germany. Napoleon could not understand him and concluded that he was mad. He passed him to Corvisart, who examined him and declared him to be quite sane. Napoleon told him that if he apologised he would be forgiven and allowed to go free, but the young man said that would be a mistake, as he would only try again. Napoleon was nonplussed and had him shot.[24]

On 16 August Cambacérès wrote reporting that Napoleon's birthday had been celebrated in Paris with 'prodigious' attendance. But his letter crossed one from Vienna with a stricture on his behaviour over something he had viewed as no more than a local difficulty, but which had caused alarm in his unquiet master.[25]

While Britain had only contributed a modest subsidy to Austria's war effort, it did attempt to take advantage of Napoleon's absence, and on 7 July, just as the battle of Wagram was drawing to a close, a British force of 1,000 men landed at Cuxhaven at the mouth of the river Weser. It was quickly contained and forced to re-embark by Westphalian troops, but on 30 July a larger force landed on the island of Walcheren in the Scheldt estuary, took the port of Flushing and threatened Antwerp.

As the minister of the interior Émmanuel Crétet was ill and Cambacérès dithered, it fell to Fouché to deal with the threat. He called out the National Guard and delegated the only marshal of France at hand, Bernadotte, to take command of the troops in the area, which he did, arriving at Antwerp on 13 August. Bernadotte had left the battlefield of Wagram in disgrace, and on hearing of the nomination a furious Napoleon despatched Bessières to take over from him. The British, incompetently led and suffering from swamp fever, re-embarked a few days after his arrival and sailed away.

As minister of police, Fouché was aware of the discontent simmering in various quarters and worried by the continuous landings in France of royalist agents from England. There were also occasional raids by the British on coastal forts, possibly rehearsals for an invasion to coincide with a royalist rising. News of the substantial landing on Walcheren may have caused him to overreact in calling out the National Guard. To Napoleon in Vienna it looked as though he was providing himself with the necessary force to take over Paris, and the connection with Bernadotte conjured sinister thoughts, but what seems to have particularly annoyed him was the ineffectual role of Cambacérès in the crisis.[26]

The Treaty of Vienna was signed on 14 October. The terms were harsh, but not as drastic as Napoleon had originally intended. His first thought had been to force Francis to abdicate in favour of his

brother Ferdinand and to break up the empire by creating an independent kingdom of Hungary and using other provinces to cement
his failing alliance with Russia. The negotiations, conducted by Metternich and Champagny, resulted in Austria losing access to the sea
by the cession of Trieste, Ragusa, Istria, Fiume, and Carniola, which
were added to French possessions along the Dalmatian coast to make
up the new department of Illyria. Austria also lost Salzburg, which
went to Bavaria, and Galicia, which was divided between the grand
duchy of Warsaw and Russia. In all, Austria lost about three and a
half million subjects. She also had to reduce her army to 150,000 and
pay a heavy indemnity. Two days after the signature of the treaty,
Napoleon left Schönbrunn for Paris.

He travelled by easy stages, pausing for two days at Nymphen-
burg to go hunting with a grateful King of Bavaria and flirt with his
wife, to whom he had taken a fancy. He also stopped at Stuttgart
to visit the King of Württemberg, though his visit there was more
Napoleonic—he arrived at seven o'clock in the morning and left at
ten the same evening, after having attended a play in the court theatre. On the evening of 26 October he was back at Fontainebleau,
where the following morning he gave Fouché a dressing-down. He
spent the best part of the next three weeks there, stag-hunting on
horseback and shooting, and enjoying a dalliance with a plump little
blonde lady-in-waiting to Pauline, Christine Ghilini. She had only
recently been married to a Piedmontese nobleman, so she resisted
his advances at first, but Pauline wore her down, and although she
could be difficult and moody, the affair would go on for a couple of
months. Never ungenerous, Napoleon granted her father a title.[27]

He had for some time been coming round to the view that he
must divorce Josephine but hesitated to make the move, perhaps because he had got used to her and feared being alone. She was always
sensible when he sought her advice. She understood him and the
world they lived in—and from where they had come. He was a man
of habit, and he had passed his fortieth birthday. There had been no
more talk of divorce during the first half of 1808, although he was
already considering marrying a Russian princess. Josephine's letters
reveal that their relations had been particularly close during the time

they spent at Bayonne and in the autumn of 1808. It was not until a full year later, on the evening of 30 November 1809, that he openly broached the subject with her at the Tuileries. She burst into tears, then collapsed, writhing in a paroxysm, and appeared to lose consciousness. Napoleon called Bausset, who had been in the next room, and together they carried her down to her bedroom.[28]

The process of divorcing Josephine was not going to be easy. The Code Napoléon permitted divorce by mutual consent only up to the age of forty-five, which she had passed, while the Statutes of the Imperial House which he had invented himself forbade it outright. The matter was handed over to Cambacérès to sort out, which he accomplished with the legal acrobatics he excelled at. Louis, who had taken the opportunity to seek permission to divorce Hortense, was told he could not as there were no grounds for it.[29]

Meanwhile, life went on as usual, and the morning after her fainting fit Josephine presided over a reception in honour of the kings of Naples, Württemberg, and Holland who had come to Paris to celebrate the peace with Austria. On 3 December there was a *Te Deum* at Notre Dame, the following day a reception at the Hôtel de Ville followed by a banquet, a concert, and a ball at the Tuileries. The banquet was a tense affair, with Napoleon in full coronation robes with his plumed hat on his head looking uneasy and impatient, while Josephine sat opposite covered in diamonds looking as though she might faint at any moment. She would not have enjoyed the presence of Letizia, Caroline, and Pauline, who had never looked happier. Whether she received much comfort from her husband is doubtful, as he spent the night of 5 December with another. Once he had decided on the divorce, he had begun to philander more, which Hortense saw as a means of both making himself more interesting to women and of fortifying himself against the forthcoming separation. 'His mind was made up, but his heart still hesitated,' she wrote. 'He was trying to distract it elsewhere.' He had broken down and wept when he had informed her of his intention to divorce her mother. On 8 December Eugène arrived in Paris and the divorce was discussed with him and Josephine by Napoleon. Three days after that she had to take her place at Napoleon's side at a party at Berthier's estate of Grosbois.[30]

On 15 December, at a special meeting attended by all the family members currently in Paris—Letizia, Louis and Hortense, Jérôme and Catherine, Joseph's wife Julie, Eugène, Murat and Caroline, and Pauline—in the presence of Cambacérès and the secretary of state for the Imperial House, Regnaud de Saint-Jean d'Angély, Napoleon and Josephine each read out prepared texts announcing their wish to divorce, and stating their reasons. The minutes of the meeting taken by Regnaud were signed by those present and passed to the privy council, which that same evening drew up the project of a *senatus-consulte*. This was presented to the Senate the following day by Regnaud. The meeting was presided over by Cambacérès, and Josephine's son, Eugène, read out the family's wish that 'the founder of this fourth dynasty should grow old surrounded by direct descendants'. There was no debate, and the *senatus-consulte* was passed by seventy-six votes, with seven against and four abstentions. The same day, Josephine left the Tuileries.[31]

There then arose the delicate matter of annulling the religious marriage. There could be no question of involving the Pope, who was in solitary confinement at Grenoble. Cambacérès argued that the ceremony conducted by Cardinal Fesch had been 'clandestine', since there had been no witnesses present, and was therefore invalid. This could be attested by the diocesan authorities in Paris, and the marriage being invalid, there was no need of an annulment. The diocesan council ruled accordingly, fining Napoleon six francs (to be distributed to the poor) for having contracted an illegal marriage. The ruling was endorsed by a bishop who had no authority, since he had not been approved in office by the Pope.[32]

Two days after she drove away from the Tuileries, Napoleon dined with Josephine at Trianon. 'My love, I found you weaker today than you should be,' he wrote afterward. 'You have shown courage, and you must find enough to support you and not to let yourself go to a fatal melancholy, and to be content, and above all to keep up your health, which is so precious to me.' He wrote frequently, expressing his concern and professing his enduring love for her. He visited her at Malmaison on 24 December, and she dined with him at Trianon the following day. She could barely eat and looked as though she were about to faint. Hortense, who was present, saw Napoleon wipe away his tears more than once. When he returned to the Tuileries three days later he found the palace empty without her and wrote saying he felt lonely there.[33]

He was determined to treat her well. She retained her titles and arms as Imperial Majesty. He gave her the Élysée Palace in Paris, Malmaison, and the château of Navarre near Évreux. She had a settlement on the civil list of 2 million francs per annum, and he threw in another million from his private chest. When it came to his notice that people were keeping away from her he made it plain that such behaviour would incur his displeasure.[34]

34

Apotheosis

THE QUESTION OF whom Napoleon should marry had resolved itself. Tsar Alexander had no intention of cementing his alliance with him, let alone letting him marry one of his sisters. Even if he had, he would have been powerless to do so. Shortly before his death his father, Paul I, had issued an *ukaz* giving his consort power to decide over his daughters' marriages. The dowager empress loathed the very idea of Napoleon, and as soon as she heard of his intention she encouraged her elder daughter to marry Prince George of Holstein-Oldenburg. Alexander's other sister Anna was two months short of her fifteenth birthday when, at the end of November 1809, Napoleon instructed Caulaincourt in St Petersburg to make the request for her hand. Alexander made a show of pleasure but did nothing. When pressed a few weeks later he asked for two weeks to consider the matter and gain his mother's approval. At the end of the two weeks he asked for another ten days, then for another week. He was still stalling at the beginning of February 1810, by which time Napoleon, fearing the snub of a refusal, had changed his mind.

A meeting of his privy council at the Tuileries on Sunday, 28 January, had reviewed the three possible candidates: the Grand Duchess Anna, the twenty-eight-year-old Maria Augusta of Saxony, and the eighteen-year-old daughter of the emperor of Austria, Marie-Louise. Napoleon never seriously considered the Saxon option. His first choice would have been the Russian, as it would have cemented his alliance with Russia against Britain—and it would have tickled his vanity that his heirs could then claim descent from the Paleologue rulers of the Roman Empire of the East. Cambacérès, Murat, and Fouché also favoured the Russian, but given the difficulties being made by Alexander, they concurred with Talleyrand and the others, who supported the no less grand Austrian candidate, who was descended from Louis XIV and Charles V. Informal talks had been taking place between Talleyrand and Metternich, now Austria's chancellor, and both had come to the conclusion that such a match might distract Napoleon from his pursuit of dominion. Metternich had authorised his ambassador in Paris, Prince Karl von Schwarzenberg, to accept the offer if it were made. A week later, during a shoot at Fontainebleau, Eugène went up to Schwarzenberg and formally requested the hand of the archduchess on Napoleon's behalf. Napoleon ordered the marriage contract to be drawn up that very day, taking as a template that between Louis XVI and Marie-Antoinette.[1]

The news was greeted with horror by Louis XVIII in England and with delight in Austria. 'What a joy for mankind!' exclaimed the ultimate Habsburg courtier the prince de Ligne, expressing a view held by many that the match would 'settle' Napoleon and that, by joining him to a descendant of the 'real Caesars', 'his edifice will become stable at last'. As well as promising peace and stability, the forthcoming union would go some way to restoring Austria's position among the great powers, even though Napoleon did not envisage returning any of the territory he had taken. Public opinion in Vienna was not even put out when Berthier, recently named Prince of Wagram, arrived there to marry the archduchess by proxy. The news had also gone some way to soothe anti-French feeling elsewhere in Germany.[2]

Reactions in France were more mixed. The aristocracy which had rallied to Napoleon were delighted. Many welcomed the promise of a lasting peace settlement. But many were haunted by memories of that other Austrian marriage and its unhappy end. Others did not like the idea of what looked like yet another step back to the ancien régime. The army mostly disapproved, not so much for ideological reasons as out of sympathy for '*la vieille*', 'the old girl', whom they saw as a good French wife to Napoleon and whom many even considered to have brought him luck—old soldiers could be highly superstitious.[3]

The proxy marriage took place in Vienna on 11 March 1810, and two days later Marie-Louise left for France. Napoleon was in a state of childlike excitement in anticipation of her arrival and insisted on overseeing down to the last detail the arrangements for her reception at Compiègne. He went there a week before she was due, followed by his sisters Caroline and Pauline, Joseph's wife, Julie, and, later, Murat, Fesch, and others. They were joined over the days by members of the court and Austrian dignitaries. To keep fit, Napoleon went hunting, enjoyed the favours of his current mistress, and took dancing lessons from Hortense, whom he asked to help him appear less grave.[4]

Following the protocol of 1770, Napoleon had Davout's engineers run up a building on the frontier with three chambers representing, respectively, Austria, neutral territory, and France. When she arrived there on 16 March, Marie-Louise entered the first room, in which she shed everything associated with her Austrian past and changed into a dress of gold brocade. She then entered the central chamber with her Austrian attendants and seated herself on a dais. A French reception party entered from the other side, bringing the number of those present to around a hundred. An act of translation was read out and signed, after which her Austrian attendants departed one by one, kissing her hand as they took their leave. She was then ushered into the French chamber, where Caroline Murat took charge and she was dressed in the French fashion.[5]

Taking things one step further than the Bourbons, Napoleon had invented another ceremony, to take place in a specially designed tent at Soissons not far from Compiègne, in the course of which Marie-Louise was to kneel before him. But his impatience was such that it never took place. Taking only Murat with him, he drove out to meet her and had reached the village of Courcelles when one of his coach wheels broke. It was pouring with rain, so he and Murat took shelter in the porch of the village church, and when the carriage bringing Marie-Louise drove up the coachman, recognising him, stopped. Napoleon rushed up to the carriage, opened the door and leapt in. Dripping wet in his grey overcoat, he sat down next to his astonished bride and kissed her. He then told the coachman to drive straight to Compiègne, where they arrived at half past nine in the evening.[6]

The little town had been illuminated, but the rain had extinguished most of the lights. There was to have been a banquet, but Napoleon decided otherwise. They supped lightly together with Caroline, after which, having ascertained from Fesch that they were actually married, instead of retiring to his prescribed quarters he quickly freshened up with eau de cologne, changed into a dressing gown, and followed Marie-Louise into hers, where he exercised his marital rights. In the morning they took breakfast and lunch in her bedroom and were hardly parted for the next forty-eight hours. Both appeared ecstatically happy, and Napoleon later reminisced that she kept asking for more. In a letter to her father she confessed that the Corsican ogre was 'very engaging and very eager, and almost impossible to resist'. On the evening of 29 March, only forty-eight hours after she arrived, during a concert at which La Grassini sang for them accompanied by Paër, Napoleon kept falling asleep. 'From time to time, the empress would wake him up by saying something to him, he would give her a sweet look, adopt a serious air to reply, and then fall asleep again,' according to an Austrian courtier present.[7]

The next day the couple transferred to Saint-Cloud, where on 1 April they were married in a civil ceremony (the irony of the date did not go unnoticed). The following day, in bright sunshine, they drove into Paris in two separate coaches, each drawn by eight horses, followed by another thirty-eight carriages drawn by six horses each. Escorted by detachments of all the mounted regiments of the Imperial Guard, they drove under two specially erected wood and canvas triumphal arches, one of them covering the half-built Arc de Triomphe at the Étoile, and down the Champs-Élysées to the Tuileries. The onlookers showed little interest.[8]

Napoleon wore a white satin version of court dress designed by himself, with a black velvet toque covered in diamonds topped by three white plumes, making him appear even shorter and fatter than he was, looking, according to one witness, like the king of diamonds from a pack of cards. Beaming with satisfaction he led his bride down the long gallery, lined on either side by the ladies of the court standing on three tiers. There had been the usual family rows, with his sisters balking at being made to carry Marie-Louise's train, and

Pauline took her revenge by pulling faces behind her back. Delighted as they were to see the end of Josephine, they did not welcome a new interloper. The grand salon with a ceiling depicting Apollo had been converted into a chapel, and there Cardinal Fesch married them, after which he performed the traditional royal ceremony of blessing the bed.[9]

By then, Napoleon was furious. Thirteen of the cardinals he had brought to Paris by force in January had failed to attend the ceremony, on the grounds that his marriage to Josephine had not been annulled. When the ceremony was over, he was heard threatening to have them shot. The following day, when he and Marie-Louise seated on their thrones received the compliments of the Senate, the Legislative, the marshals, the diplomatic corps, and all the other bodies, and the cardinals' turn came, he had them thrown out. He ordered them to be exiled to provincial towns where they were forbidden to wear their robes.[10]

That night Paris was illuminated and decorated as never before. Public buildings were adorned with painted canvas panels or, like the seat of the Legislative across the bridge from the place de la Concorde, turned into a 'Temple of Hymen', with an allegorical figure representing Peace blessing the newlyweds. Trees were decked with lanterns and private houses with candles in every window and braziers outside. But the festivities did not live up to the décor. In preparing the public fête for the people of Paris Napoleon had deliberately abandoned the tradition of having food served in the street and fountains running with wine, on the grounds that it led to brawls, and replaced it with more organised celebrations, including having food and wine delivered to the poor in their houses. But, as one contemporary noted, even the public festivals Napoleon gave were somehow stilted, and people were beginning to be made to feel their station. Those who were admitted to the more august festivities felt little different. Thibaudeau found the marriage ceremony 'as cold and sad as a funeral', while Capain Coignet, who had been present at the banquet, commented that 'It may have been grand, but it was not fun.'[11]

Having dealt with the essentials in a session of the Council of State, on 5 April Napoleon took his bride back to Compiègne, where they spent the next three weeks. He hunted and occasionally received someone on business, but otherwise devoted all his time to his wife, petting her and showering her with presents. Aside from the fact that she liked to sleep with the window open and he with it closed, they were well suited, and he particularly appreciated her innocence and truthfulness, which contrasted with Josephine's depravity and deviousness, which had both excited and annoyed him.[12]

On 27 April 1810 the imperial couple set off on a tour of Belgium and the Low Countries, inspecting canals, public works, and factories along the way. In Antwerp they launched a ship of the line and watched the Festival of the Giant, which included a carnivalesque procession with a huge dummy whale squirting water, a chariot of Neptune, and an outsize elephant. On 5 May they attended a reception given by Louis, King of Holland. But in the course of a conversation between the two brothers Napoleon learned something that enraged him.[13]

He had been aware that for some time the banker Ouvrard had been in contact with the British government through his associate Pierre-César Labouchère's cousins, the Barings of London; he had used the connection to make informal peace proposals himself. When these were rejected he lost interest, but his brother Louis did not, as he was desperate for some kind of settlement with Britain; the Dutch economy was heavily dependent on overseas trade and banking and was crippled by the state of war. Another who was keen for an end to the conflict with Britain was Fouché. He had been sending out feelers through his own contacts in London, and sometime in 1809 he had also begun to use the Ouvrard/Labouchère channel. One of his agents had been received at the Foreign Office by Lord Wellesley. This came to Napoleon's notice at Antwerp, and he jumped to the conclusion that Fouché was plotting behind his back. 'Not only has the man been meddling in my family affairs without my permission [a reference to the minister's bringing up the subject of divorce with Josephine], he now wants to make peace behind my back,' he raged. The next day he vented his ill-humour on a deputation of Belgian clergy which had come to greet him, for having dropped regular prayers for him from the liturgy.[14]

He ordered Savary to investigate and continued on his tour, taking in Breda, Berg-op-Zoom (where he boarded a yacht after a copious lunch and was seasick), and Flushing, where he made his displeasure felt that the town had capitulated to the British the previous year. They visited Middleburg, Brussels, where they attended a grand reception, Ghent, Bruges, where they visited the cathedral, Ostend, Dunkirk, and Lille, and then went via Calais, Boulogne, Dieppe, Le Havre, and Rouen back to Paris, where they arrived on the night of 1 June. Napoleon held a council of his ministers in the morning, and the following day he sacked Fouché.

As Napoleon had left the capital for Compiègne immediately following his marriage, it was only now that the various festivities that would normally have accompanied it were held. Marie-Louise was awkward and did not possess Josephine's charm. Unlike Josephine, she could not remember people or their names, which led to embarrassing situations. Her awkwardness was contagious, and a sense of constraint reigned whenever she was present.[15]

The city of Paris gave a fête at the Hôtel de Ville for the notables of the capital to meet the new empress, but it was a joyless occasion, spoiled as much by Napoleon's evident impatience and inability to enjoy such events as by her manner. More successful was a fête given by Pauline at her property in Neuilly, in the grounds of which she arranged magical tableaux and illuminations. Actors of the Théâtre-Français acted out a play in one part, dancers executed a ballet in another, both vying for the attention of the guests. Two orchestras placed at opposite ends of the park played as though one were the echo of the other. There were temples with goddesses, a hermitage with a hermit, and a cherub who offered the empress a garland. At the end of the park there was a replica of Schönbrunn, with fountains and dancers in Tyrolean costume, at which point Marie-Louise burst into tears, whether out of homesickness or exhaustion nobody could tell.[16]

Two weeks later, on 28 June, while they were at dinner in the Tuileries, Eugène was announced and Napoleon rose from the table while Marie-Louise was still eating her ices. She protested, but he ignored her, sensing the news was important. It was: Louis had decided to give up the Dutch throne. Napoleon expostulated, gesticulating 'like a real Corsican' according to one witness, but the news should not have come as a surprise.[17]

While he too enjoyed festooning himself with trappings of monarchy, Louis had taken his job as King of Holland seriously. He worked hard to mould the disparate and traditionally republican elements he was given into a modern constitutional monarchy with a national identity. He introduced fiscal and administrative reforms and a new educational system. Holland was economically devastated by the blockade, yet with its innumerable estuaries, creeks, and islands it was impossible to seal against smuggling, so goods still got through, but the state could not control or tax them. In December 1808 Napoleon closed its frontier with France in order to keep them out, compounding the problem for Holland. He demanded that Louis supply another 40,000 troops over and above the 12,000 already serving France in Germany and the 3,000 fighting in Spain. In 1809 he refused to allow him to introduce a version of the Code he had painstakingly adapted to Dutch conditions and insisted on imposing his own.[18]

Using the pretext of the British landing on Walcheren the previous year, Napoleon had sent French troops to take control of the coastal areas and then annexed the provinces of Brabant, Zealand, and Guelders to France. In March 1810 he had forced Louis to place all Dutch troops under French command, and in June Marshal Oudinot set off for Amsterdam, where Louis was instructed to put on a triumphal ingress for him. Napoleon had made his younger brother's position untenable, yet he was upset by his decision to abdicate and took it as a personal affront. 'The folly of the King of Holland has upset me,' he wrote to Josephine, 'but I have grown used to the ingratitude and the fickleness of my brothers; they serve me poorly, as they have little love for France or me.' He had been stung by the behaviour of Lucien, who had ignored his wishes and set off for America but had been caught by the Royal Navy and taken to England as a prisoner of war.[19]

Louis abdicated formally on 2 July in favour of his son Napoleon-Louis and fled, taking refuge at Gratz in Austria. A week later Napoleon decreed the incorporation of Holland into France, arguing that 'it is complementary to the empire, the estuary of its rivers; its navy, its ports, its commerce and its finances can only prosper if combined with those of France'. The move went down badly with public opinion in France, as people feared it might provoke another war and could see no point to it.[20]

Paris was in a sombre mood. On 1 July the Austrian ambassador Prince Schwarzenberg had given a ball in honour of the newlyweds. After they had watched 'a charming ballet' performed on a lawn against the backdrop of a *trompe-l'oeil* of the gardens at Laxenburg, when the ball had started and the dancing was in full swing one of the marquees caught fire. Panic ensued as people rushed for the exits and men tripped over their swords while struggling to carry out fainting ladies. Napoleon managed to lead Marie-Louise out and drive her to safety, and then returned to help, earning praise for his handling of the situation. 'Heart-rending cries of pain and despair could be heard on all sides as mothers called out to daughters and husbands their wives,' in the words of one officer. 'The garden lit up as though it were daylight, filled instantly with people shouting as they searched for each other and running to extinguish their clothes which were on fire.' The ambassador's sister-in-law Princess Schwarzenberg rushed back into the marquee in search of her daughter but died as it collapsed on her. Several others died of burns, and many were permanently scarred. People did not fail to draw analogies with the celebrations of the marriage of Louis XVI and Marie-Antoinette in 1770, when a firework display went wrong, precipitating a panic in which over 200 people were crushed to death.[21]

Analogies with the ancien régime were not out of place. A new court etiquette was introduced, consisting of 634 articles, based on that of 1710. Colonel Lejeune was astonished when he came with reports from Spain to find himself instructed by the ballet master from the Opéra on how to perform three courtly bows when introduced into the imperial presence. The efforts of broad-shouldered proletarian warriors to submit to the new etiquette often ended in ridicule. The eighteenth-century silk *habit habillé* obligatory for court balls looked absurd on men with a military gait and scarred faces, sometimes still bandaged or with an arm in a sling.[22]

Having married a niece of the last King of France, Napoleon began referring to his 'uncle Louis XVI', and adopted a kind of walk he had been told the Bourbons had affected, which in his case turned into an unflattering waddle. He had the slogan '*Liberté, Égalité, Fraternité*', which had been painted over the entrance to every public building in Paris during the Revolution, effaced. He considered going back on his plan to refashion the Madeleine into a Temple of Glory dedicated to French heroes and turning it instead into an expiatory chapel dedicated to the guillotined Louis XVI. He carried his policy of social fusion to bizarre lengths, at one point issuing a circular to all prefects to draw up lists of nubile girls from noble families suitable for marriage to soldiers and officials—the purpose was not so much to conjoin as to subsume and legitimise. Yet it had not worked in his own case, and he had lost nothing of his social awkwardness. 'It is difficult to convey how gauche he was in a drawing room,' recalled Metternich, who had come to Paris to represent Francis I at the marriage.[23]

'The court had grown rigid and lost everything it still conserved of social ease,' recalled Victorine de Chastenay, adding that Marie-Louise made people regret Josephine. She had possessed a grace and an ancien-régime *savoir-vivre* tempered by all the experiences of the Revolution, and created an atmosphere in which all could feel at ease. She had also exerted a humanising influence on Napoleon, often bringing him down to earth from his flights of fancy. Now Napoleon was grander and more distant, and even more prudish. In Josephine's day he would banter with the ladies and on occasion talk of past conquests. Now, young men were afraid of addressing ladies in his presence for fear of being ticked off for what he assumed were salacious proposals, or even just frivolous talk. 'I do not think there could have been a court where the morals were more pure,' recalled Hortense. The notoriously homosexual Cambacérès was instructed to pay regular ostentatious visits to an actress in the Palais-Royal, which fooled nobody and only provoked ribaldry.[24]

Napoleon's civil list and other sources of income (he was not averse to diverting some taxes and state revenues to his private treasury) made him the richest monarch in Europe, with a vast stack of gold in the vault of the Tuileries which allowed him to adorn his court with unprecedented splendour. His views of himself and of France were well reflected in his public works and monuments, which were increasingly grandiose and closely bound to his person. He had been so struck by the magnificent royal palace in Madrid that on his return he instructed Fontaine to draw up plans for the aggrandisement of the Louvre, which he wanted 'to equal in magnificence everything he had seen', and to incorporate a church dedicated to St Napoleon. He also gave instructions for the former royal residences of Rambouillet, Meudon, and Chambord to be restored to splendour, along with more than forty other palaces around the empire. When Fontaine came up with a plan for the Louvre which involved linking up the two extended wings, Napoleon protested. 'What is great is always beautiful,' he declared, 'and I cannot agree to dividing a space whose principal feature is its extent.' Instead, the space was embellished with the triumphal arch of the Carrousel, on which were placed the four horses of St Mark's in Venice, drawing a Roman chariot in which the spirit of flattery had led to a statue of himself being placed. Even he balked at this and had it removed. No such restraint was in evidence when, as soon as it was known that Marie-Louise was pregnant, he put in hand plans for a monumental palace complex for his presumed son on the heights of Chaillot.[25]

This infatuation with all things aristocratic and the accent on grandeur worried most of those who had helped bring Napoleon to power and worked with him at rebuilding a France that would incorporate the best of all worlds. Even Cambacérès, despite being bedecked with imperial and Austrian decorations, was uneasy. The country seemed to them to be drifting back to a mongrel version of the ancien régime. Yet those who had come of age under the empire did not share such reservations, and the symbols of Napoleon's power and glory made them feel proud to be French and to serve him.[26]

The departure of Fouché from the centre of political life broke yet another link with the Revolution, and not just because of his Jacobin past, which had acted as a sort of guarantee against a Bourbon restoration. As had been the case with Talleyrand, his presence at the centre of public affairs and his ability to act as a restraining influence on Napoleon had provided a dose of wisdom to his conduct. Cynical and often perfidious as it was, his method of policing had been based on surveillance rather than punishment, on making people behave because they thought they were being watched rather than on the detention of suspects. This light touch changed overnight with the appointment in his place of Savary, who admitted to being astonished on taking over at how little real power he found at his disposal. He also found very little information, as Fouché had deftly removed or destroyed all his more sensitive papers.[27]

'I inspired fear in everyone; people started packing their bags and talking of exile, imprisonment and worse still,' wrote Savary. 'I do not think that an outbreak of the plague on one of our coasts would have caused more fear than my appointment to the ministry of police.' This was hardly surprising. He was a strict executor of Napoleon's wishes, which were growing increasingly despotic. On his return from Vienna after Wagram, he had reorganised the workings of the courts in the interests of what he saw as efficiency, and in March 1810 he re-established prisons of state in which people could be locked up without trial, in effect reinstating the infamous *lettre de cachet* and creating half a dozen new Bastilles. According to Savary, there were just over 600 inmates, a significant number of them 'deviants' of one kind or another whose families preferred to avoid the publicity of a trial.[28]

The Penal Code, introduced that year, made assemblies of twenty or more illegal, although religious confraternities and Freemasonry were exempt. There was also a growth of scientific societies around the country. But the number of theatres, where the themes of plays could only too easily suggest unfavourable parallels and provoke discussion, was reduced. Although he supposedly instructed Savary to 'treat men of letters well', Napoleon tightened censorship. His reactions to any disorder or infraction had grown more peremptory and included in one case ordering soldiers to be shot for no more than a drunken brawl. Yet when a young man from Saxony turned up in Paris and after being arrested confessed to the intention of assassinating him, Napoleon instructed that he be locked up with plenty of books to read so he could cool off and released him after a few weeks.[29]

Napoleon was still capable of showing his human side—usually with people of the lower orders. When they were caught by rain during the tour of the Low Countries the imperial party took shelter in a farmhouse whose owner, not knowing who his guests were, sat in his armchair while Napoleon and the others perched on benches, and proceeded to talk freely, dispensing old man's wisdom. The emperor chatted with him affably, and it was only as they were leaving that he gave an inkling of who he was, by offering to provide a dowry for the man's daughter. He often did this when travelling, dispensing gifts to astonished serving girls and grooms at wayside inns.

Nor did he forget those he loved. He set up Maria Walewska in a townhouse in Paris elegantly furnished in the Empire style, gave her a villa in Boulogne, and provided for their son by giving him estates in the kingdom of Naples. 'No sovereign has ever given more than the Emperor, yet none has left so many resentful,' remarked Chaptal, explaining that the manner in which he gave smacked of charity or reward rather than generosity, but the former minister was by then ill-disposed to him. Josephine turned to Napoleon whenever she needed help or money with the plea, 'Bonaparte, you promised never to abandon me; now I need your advice', and he never failed her. 'He would charm everyone around him whenever he let himself go to his bonhomie,' recalled Hortense. Even Metternich had to admit that in private or in intimate company, Napoleon's conversation 'possessed a charm difficult to define'. He could also be clear-sighted and candid. One day, he asked those around him what people would say when he died. As each began saying something flattering, he interrupted them. 'People will just say: Ah! at last we can breathe! We're rid of him, what joy!' He also admitted that his becoming emperor was really something of 'an accident'.[30]

But that did not correspond to any sense of humility. Napoleon noticed that when writing to her father his wife addressed her letters to 'His Sacred Imperial Majesty', and he asked Metternich about this form he had not come across before. Metternich explained that it was accepted usage when addressing the Holy Roman Emperor. 'It is a fine and fitting custom,' said Napoleon with a solemn air. 'Power derives from God, and it is only on account of that that it can be placed beyond the reach of men. In time, I shall adopt the same title.'[31]

Metternich had attempted to resolve the conflict with the Pope, but Napoleon's views had hardened. To the sculptor Antonio Canova, whom he had brought to Paris to make a bust of Marie-Louise, he said irritably that 'these priests want to control everything, meddle in everything and be masters of everything'. He reasoned that St Peter had chosen Rome rather than Jerusalem because that was the metropolis of the time, but Rome had fallen, and the papacy had ended up being a minor state subject to the temporal require-ments of the rulers of 'a very small corner of Italy', and that it was the resulting political entanglements which had led to the Reformation. He argued that the Pope should move to Paris, and in preparation he began rebuilding the archiepiscopal palace beside Notre Dame, mov-ing the Vatican archives, and in January 1810, forcing the cardinals of the Sacred College to take up residence in the new Rome.[32]

Meanwhile, in the former Papal States the French authorities dis-solved monasteries and convents, rationalised parishes, and expelled recalcitrant priests and monks. The text relating to their incorpo-ration into the French Empire underlines 'the independence of the imperial throne from any authority on earth'. The custom among Catholic monarchies which maintained the belief that they ruled by the grace of God had been to defer to His vicar on earth, the Pope. Napoleon had paid lip service to this by insisting on the Pope being present at his coronation, even though he then still based his right to rule on the will of the nation. Now he needed neither the Pope nor the nation. Arguing the point with Fesch at Fontainebleau one evening, Napoleon led him out on to the terrace and, pointing to the heavens, asked him whether he could see God, to which the cardi-nal replied in the negative. 'Well, then, you had better keep quiet,' snapped the emperor. 'I can see my star, and that is what guides me.'[33]

35

Apogee

NAPOLEON WOULD LATER blame his marriage to an Austrian archduchess for his downfall, referring to her as 'that bank of roses obscuring the abyss'. There was something in that, as its joys did distract him and its fruits deceived him, with fatal consequences. He was besotted with his new bride and seemed to revel in the possession of this fresh, young, submissive yet lusty girl with her imperial blood.[1]

In a report to his emperor, Metternich had characterised Napoleon as a 'good family man, with those accents which one finds most often in middle-class Italian families', but the Latin paternalism had given way to deference and become tinged with Austrian *Gemütlichkeit*. He ordered paintings of battles fought against the Austrians to be removed from the imperial palaces and commissioned views of Schönbrunn and Laxenburg, where Marie-Louise had grown up. Where he had chided Josephine for being late, he waited obsequiously for his new bride. He who had never spent more than twenty minutes at table now sat patiently as she munched her way through seven courses. She was bored by the tragedies of Corneille and Racine that he loved, so he sat through comedies that he despised. He was so deferential that she confessed to Metternich that she thought he was a little in awe of her.[2]

He went hunting more often than before, mainly to get some exercise and exhaust himself; he dashed about on his horse wherever his fancy took him, to the exasperation of Berthier, who as grand huntsman planned the hunt with his usual thoroughness. It did not prevent him putting on weight, and those around him felt he had slowed down and declined physically. He was not eating more than usual, so there must have been another cause to his slide into obesity. It has been convincingly argued that it was probably the failure of his pituitary gland, which can affect men around the age of forty, leading to weight gain and genital shrinkage, from which he also suffered according to post-mortem examinations.[3]

His workload remained impressive, but less strenuous. In the past he had been continually on the road, obsessed as he was with taking matters in hand and judging on the spot before making decisions. He was now travelling less; he had never before spent such a long time in Paris and its environs. Many saw in this an encouraging development. At the marriage banquet in April 1810, Metternich had proposed a toast 'To the King of Rome!'—the title traditionally borne by the heir to the Holy Roman Empire. The Austrian chancellor's toast suggested that the Habsburg monarchy had ceded its rights to the new emperor of the West, and the age-old struggle between the House of Austria and France was at an end. It implied that the birth of a King of Rome would seal a lasting peace, and as soon as it was confirmed that the empress was pregnant people began to pray for it.[4]

As she went into labour on the evening of 19 March 1811, the court gathered at the Tuileries, while doctors Corvisart and Dubois took charge, attended by two surgeons. Expectation gripped the city. The stock exchange closed, and many employers gave their workers the day off. The birth would be announced, as were victories and major events, by the firing of cannon: twenty-one shots for a girl and one hundred for a boy. On the esplanade in front of the Invalides, the gunners of the Imperial Guard primed their pieces and waited for the order to fire.

They had to wait all night, as the birth proved a difficult one. Napoleon remained at his wife's bedside from the moment the labour started at about seven in the evening, showing signs of distress at her pain. This subsided at around five o'clock in the morning and she fell asleep, so he went to have a bath. It was not long before a nervous Dr Dubois came hurriedly up the hidden staircase to tell him that there were complications, as the baby was presenting itself badly. Napoleon asked whether there was any danger, and the doctor replied that the empress's life was threatened. 'Forget she is the empress and treat her as you would a shopkeeper's wife from the rue Saint-Denis,' Napoleon interrupted him, adding, 'And whatever happens, save the mother!' He dressed and joined the doctors at her bedside, calming her as Dr Dubois took out his forceps. The baby came out feet first, and it took some time to get the head clear, during which Marie-Louise screamed so much Napoleon was in tears. At around eight in the morning the child was born. Having satisfied himself that the mother was out of danger, Napoleon took the child in his arms and stepped into the adjoining salon where the dignitaries of the empire were waiting, bleary-eyed after their long vigil. 'Behold the King of Rome!' he declared. An aide ran through the rooms and out to his waiting horse to give the gunners their orders.[5]

At the first shot, the city came to a standstill. People opened their windows and came out of shops, carriages and wagons pulled up, pedestrians stopped. The first twenty-one were fired at intervals of several seconds so everyone could count them. When the twenty-second was heard, 'there rang out across the town a long shout of joy which ran through it like an electric current', in the words of one lady. It was accompanied by the remaining seventy-eight shots delivered in quick succession, and the pealing of bells from every church in Paris. A police report noted that two porters at Les Halles who were on the point of coming to blows paused at the first shot and embraced at the twenty-second. Even opponents of the regime and enemies of Napoleon felt joy. To many it seemed as though the future was secure, and a *pax gallica* would descend on Europe. In a poem dedicated to Marie-Louise, Goethe represented her union with Napoleon in cosmic terms, referring to her as 'the beautiful bride of peace'.[6]

That evening, while the people of Paris celebrated, the child was baptised according to the rites of the French royal family—he had already been assigned as governess the same comtesse de Montesquiou who had brought up the children of Louis XVI. The next morning, seated on his throne, Napoleon received the congratulations of the Senate, the Legislative and other bodies of the government and administration, the diplomatic corps, and the municipal authorities, after which they accompanied him to view the infant as he lay in a cradle donated by the city of Paris, featuring a figure of Glory holding a crown, with an eagle ascending toward a star representing Napoleon. Over the next days congratulations poured in from every corner of the empire, and from every foreign court except that of St James's.

Aside from the satisfaction he felt at the birth of an heir, Napoleon was as moved as any man by the experience of fatherhood; he immediately sent a page to inform Josephine of the birth. He may even have taken the child later to Malmaison for her to see. He still felt deep affection for her, and every year after the divorce he would send her a million francs in addition to her settlement. When Mollien informed him that she wanted three more officers to attend her, Napoleon told him 'not to make her cry' and let her have them. He had hoped that Marie-Louise would come to accept her as a friend, and that he would be able to accommodate them both in his life, and was, according to Hortense, put out by the younger woman's jealousy.[7]

The notion that the blessings of peace were about to descend on France was enhanced by numerous depictions of Napoleon as a father figure of the nation and a pacific family man. An engraving published in Vienna showed a nativity scene, with Marie-Louise as the Virgin, Napoleon's son as the infant Christ, the kings of Saxony, Bavaria, and Württemberg as the three wise men, and the other rulers of the Confederation of the Rhine as the shepherds, and, hovering on a cloud, Napoleon himself as God the Father declaring, 'This is My Son, in whom I am well pleased.'[8]

On 9 June 1811 Napoleon and Marie-Louise drove in the coronation coach to Notre Dame for the ceremonial christening of their son. The two-month-old baby was baptised by Cardinal Fesch in a church packed with marshals, members of the court, the public bodies, representatives of all the cities of the empire, foreign princes, and the diplomatic corps. This was followed by a banquet at the Hôtel de Ville at which Napoleon, his consort, and the royals present sat at table wearing their crowns. There followed a court ball and, in the

Champs-Élysées, fireworks and free food, wine, and dancing for the people of Paris.

'Now begins the finest epoch of my reign,' Napoleon declared shortly after the birth of his son, and appearances seemed to bear this out. Miot de Melito, who came to Paris for the baptism after an absence of five years, was astonished at the change the city had undergone. Everywhere he saw new buildings, bridges, and monuments, he drove down elegant *quais* and across open spaces, visited the Louvre and other museums, and was overwhelmed by the city's magnificence.[9]

Paris, with its wide streets, grand buildings, fountains, and gardens was only the centre, from which fourteen grand imperial roads and as many improved lesser ones, supported by 202 subsidiary ones, radiated to the furthest points of the empire. Travel time was cut by at least half in the course of Napoleon's rule, and with a network of 1,400 posting stages and 16,000 horses, the *Messageries impériales* could carry people and post at unprecedented speed. The telegraph had been extended to Amsterdam, Mainz, and Venice. There was a plan to link the river Seine to the Baltic with a new canal. Decrees had been issued for the cleaning of the Roman Forum and the dredging and banking of the Tiber and, after the birth of the King of Rome, for a new imperial quarter on the Capitol. Antwerp, Milan, and other cities throughout the empire were improved or, as in the case of La Roche-sur-Yon, built from scratch in deprived areas. Paris boasted the greatest library on earth, but dozens of public libraries had sprung up in medium-sized towns, each the seat of a literary and/or scientific learned society. The empire and its allied states had seen spectacular industrial growth, encouraged by the blockade which excluded outside competition, with the development of metallurgical industries in northeastern France, Belgium, and Saxony, of textile industries in France and northern Italy, and of the sugar-beet industry across northern Europe.

The French empire, with its 130 departments stretching from Amsterdam to Rome and its population of 40 million out of a European total of 170, was the greatest power on the Continent, and to the outside observer looked set to remain so. But in effect, it was a deeply flawed structure with profound problems.

While it had continued to grow on the Continent, it had been shrinking overseas, losing its last colonies to the British: La Petite Terre in 1808; La Désirade, Marie-Galante, Guyana, Saint Louis, Santo Domingo, Saint Lucia, Tobago, Martinique, and the Danish Antilles in 1809; Réunion (renamed Bonaparte in 1806), Guadeloupe, and Île de France in 1810; and Mauritius, Tamatave, and the Seychelles in 1811. Napoleon planned to build up to a hundred ships of the line, but in the hurry to achieve this poor timber was used, while the cannon were of such poor quality, and so prone to explode, that the British did not use captured guns. French privateers did prey on British shipping, taking 519 prizes in 1806, and 619 in 1810, but that was only a pinprick to the British sailing stock, and with the introduction of convoys even that was reduced.[10]

The real problems were economic: Napoleon's grand projects and imperial splendour required money, and his need kept growing. His budget went up from 859 million francs in 1810 to 1,103 million the following year. The cost of the land army rose from 377 to 500 million. His court was taking a greater share of government income than that of Louis XVI before the Revolution. He raised taxes and imposed customs duties and other means of indirect taxation (these had more than doubled in the past five years), while looking for economies by eliminating imagined waste. He spent hours inspecting accounts, adding up figures, and delighting in discovering a discrepancy of a few francs; he discussed the necessity of every expense and quibbled with architects, engineers, and builders, accusing them of trying to cheat and insisting that any, even the smallest, extra-budgetary expense be authorised by himself, even in dependent territories such as the grand duchy of Berg. He went through the court accounts looking for waste and haggled with suppliers. He kept lists in his notebooks of everything he had authorised and referred to them to check that nothing had been slipped in without authorisation. At the same time, the published budgets and accounts were as fictitious as his bulletins.[11]

His military expenditure was enormous. In the past, war had paid for it, and the treaty signed after Wagram had yielded a huge sum in indemnities. Part of the reason for the harshness of its terms was that the campaign had been more costly than previous ones on account of the size of the armies and the quantity of ordnance involved. It had also been more costly in terms of casualties. The war in the Iberian Peninsula was proving equally costly and brought in nothing. Napoleon had raised a loan on the income of the grand duchy of Warsaw to finance his foray into Spain in 1808 ('Bayonne-like sums' is still a proverb in Poland today to denote untold riches), looted whatever he could, and sold off as much Church property as he could lay his hands on. He sent as many non-French units as possible to fight there in order to reduce the expense—Westphalian, Dutch, Polish, and Italian troops were equipped and paid by their respective governments, and their casualties did not have an impact on public opinion in France. But the war dragged on, and the cost to his treasury was growing.[12]

He had meant to return to Spain in the autumn of 1809 to take charge, drive out the British, and impose order. But his divorce and remarriage had distracted him, and when in the spring of 1810 he discovered the joys of life with his new bride, he put off going. There seemed to be no urgency, as the military situation did not look bad: Joseph and Soult had occupied Andalucia and Seville, where they recovered all the standards lost at Bailén, Suchet had taken control of Aragon, and Masséna had pushed Wellesley, now Lord Wellington, back into Portugal. But Napoleon's policy of sending German, Dutch, and Italian troops to serve in Spain had a deleterious effect, as many of them took the first opportunity to desert, creating a climate which communicated itself to their French comrades who also went over to the enemy.[13]

Joseph had no control over the French troops supposed to support his rule. Berthier was nominally in command of the Army of Spain but remained in Paris. In February 1810 Napoleon divided Spain into military provinces whose commanders had extraordinary powers, which, since there was nobody in overall command, only dispersed the military effort further. The administration put in place by Joseph was undermined, taxes collected by his officials were seized, and his attempts to impose his authority were ineffectual. By the middle of 1810 he was in conflict with every one of the commanders operating in Spain, and Napoleon ignored him, not bothering to reply to his letters.

Joseph was so exasperated that one day in August he emptied a pair of pistols at a portrait of Napoleon. He wrote to his wife, Julie, saying he had decided to leave Spain, sell Mortefontaine, and find a place far from Paris to retire to. He begged Napoleon to allow him to abdicate, arguing that his health could no longer stand the strain. He came to Paris unbidden for the christening of the King of Rome to plead his case, only to be told to go back to Madrid and wait for Napoleon to come and take things in hand.[14]

But the possibility of his doing so was receding, as other, financial and political problems loomed. One was a severe economic crisis at the beginning of 1811 which caused a recession across northern Europe and hit France badly, with multiple bankruptcies, a rise in unemployment and strikes, along with riots against conscription and anti-war slogans daubed on walls. Napoleon took measures to provide emergency food for the poor, but he had to look further for additional sources of income, which aggravated an already difficult international situation.

The economic war with Britain was damaging both sides while failing to deliver a result. Just as Britain began to suffer, the French intervention in Spain provided her with a lifeline; the Spanish colonies in Central and South America took advantage of the change of dynasty in Madrid to declare independence and open their ports to British shipping, creating a market for British manufactured goods. And if Britain was economically damaged by the Continental blockade, the effect on France was hardly better: maritime trade had withered, French ships rotted in port, and the treasury was starved of customs revenue. Under pressure to find new sources of income, in 1809 Napoleon allowed merchants to purchase licences to trade with Britain, and not long afterward the British government did the same with regard to France, as the country was running short of grain. Thus, by the end of the year France was exporting brandy, fruit, vegetables, salt, and corn to England and importing timber, hemp, iron, quinine, and cloth. This made a mockery of the Continental System and had profound political consequences, as it was an insult to France's principal ally, Russia.[15]

As soon as his marriage to Marie-Louise had been agreed, Napoleon had written to Alexander tactfully announcing his intention. His letter crossed one from Alexander informing him that while he still hoped their two houses would one day be united, the dowager empress had ruled out his marrying the Grand Duchess Anna for another two years on the grounds of her age. It was a polite refusal, and it should have been Napoleon who felt affronted. Yet it was Alexander who was made to look foolish; he had championed the entente with France in the face of hostile public opinion at home, and it now looked as though his ally had snubbed him. The announcement of the Austrian marriage also suggested that Napoleon had been conducting parallel negotiations with Austria, which raised the question of what else might have been agreed. 'Russia acts only out of fear,' Metternich had said to Napoleon during his visit to Paris for the wedding in March 1810. 'She fears France, she fears our relations with her, and, with fear generating more fear, she will act.' He judged correctly.[16]

At Tilsit, Napoleon had declared to Alexander that there were no points of friction between the interests of France and those of Russia and that he had no wish to extend French influence beyond the Elbe, adding that the area between that and the Niemen should remain a neutral buffer zone. Yet he had established a French satellite there, and a provocative one at that; the creation of the grand duchy of Warsaw in 1807 was seen in Russia as the first step in a restoration of the kingdom of Poland, which raised the possibility of Russia's having to give up some if not all of the 463,000 square kilometres, with a population of some seven million, acquired when Poland was liquidated. Many Poles, whether they were citizens of the grand duchy or not, did see it as the nucleus of a restored Poland. When Austria went to war with France in 1809 and the Polish army of the grand duchy invaded Galicia, the part of Poland ruled by Austria, local patriots rose in support. In the peace settlement, Napoleon allowed only a small part of the liberated territory to be added to the grand duchy and awarded the greater part to Russia. It was a typically Napoleonic compromise: it disappointed the Poles without pacifying Russian public opinion, which saw it as a second step in the restoration of Poland.[17]

Napoleon never intended to restore Poland. All his statements to the contrary date from later, when he was trying to keep the Poles on his side or salvage his reputation. At the time he dismissed the idea firmly and frequently; he regarded Poland as 'a dead body' and did not think the Poles capable of reviving it as a viable state. But he could not deny himself a vast pool of soldiers (most of them to fight in Spain), so he encouraged the Poles in thinking he favoured their cause.[18]

Alexander wanted Napoleon to sign a convention pledging not to allow the restoration of Poland and to take up arms against the Poles should they attempt it. Napoleon replied that while he could declare his opposition to such a revival, he would not and could not undertake to hinder it. To sign the text suggested by Russia would 'compromise the honour and dignity of France', as he put it to his foreign minister Champagny; tens of thousands of Poles had fought alongside the French for over a decade, inspired by hopes of a free motherland and convinced of France's sympathy for their cause.[19]

On 30 June 1810, when he received a communication from St Petersburg with a list of complaints and a renewed demand that he sign the convention on Poland, and hinting that Russia might not be able to keep up the blockade against Britain without it, Napoleon lost his temper. He summoned the new Russian ambassador, Prince Kurakin, a ridiculous and ineffectual man known in Paris as 'le prince diamant', since he never appeared otherwise than covered in decorations and jewellery, who was eloquent testimony to how little Alexander valued developing good relations with France. 'What does Russia mean by such language?' Napoleon demanded. 'Does she want war? Why these continual complaints? Why these insulting suspicions? If I had wished to restore Poland, I would have said so and would not have withdrawn my troops from Germany. Is Russia trying to prepare me for her defection? I will be at war with her the day she makes peace with England.' He then dictated a letter to Caulaincourt in St Petersburg telling him that if Russia was going to blackmail him and use the Polish question as an excuse to seek a rapprochement with Britain, there would be war. It was an idle threat, as war with Russia was the last thing he wanted.[20]

Alexander, conversely, was coming to see war as inevitable. Russian society resented the alliance with Napoleon as it associated him with the Revolution and godlessness, as well as fearing that he intended to restore Poland. Orthodox Russian traditionalists regarded the Catholic Poles as the rotten apples in the Slav basket, and the Polish inhabitants of what were now the empire's western provinces as a fifth column of western corruption within it. Such feelings turned to paranoia when, in the summer of 1810, the Swedish people elected a Frenchman as their crown prince and de facto ruler.

The Swedish king, Charles XIII, was senile and childless, and in their search for a successor, the Swedes looked for a distinguished French soldier who might help them recover Finland, lost to Russia in 1809. They turned to Napoleon, who suggested Eugène. He declined, not wishing to abandon his Catholic faith, so, encouraged by Champagny, they suggested Bernadotte. Napoleon was not best pleased, realising that he might prove less than cooperative, but assumed that he would behave as a Swedish patriot if not a Frenchman—Sweden's natural enemies were Russia and Prussia and France her traditional ally. The Swedes' friendly feelings toward France were strained by the Continental System, but their long coastline and their Pomeranian colony on the northern coast of Germany permitted them to breach it. It would also have been a relief to Napoleon to have Bernadotte out of the way.

In Russia, Bernadotte's election was greeted with uproar. 'The defeat of Austerlitz, the defeat of Friedland, the Tilsit peace, the arrogance of the French ambassadors in Petersburg, the passive behaviour of the Emperor Alexander I with regard to Napoleon's policies—these were deep wounds in the heart of every Russian,' recalled Prince Sergei Volkonsky. 'Revenge and revenge were the only feelings burning inside each and every one.'[21]

Such feelings were reinforced by the economic hardships caused by the Continental System. Russia had little industry and was dependent on imports for a variety of everyday items. These now had to be smuggled in via Sweden or through smaller ports on Russia's

Baltic coastline. Her exports—timber, grain, hemp, and so on—were bulky and difficult to smuggle. The Russian ruble fell in value against most European currencies by as much as 25 percent, which made the cost of foreign goods exorbitant. Between 1807 and 1811 the price of coffee more than doubled, sugar became more than three times as expensive, and a bottle of champagne went from 3.75 to 12 rubles. This cocktail of wounded pride and financial hardship produced ever more violent criticism of Alexander's policy, and the only way he could deflect it was to break free of Napoleon. He had been building up and modernising his army since Tilsit, and back in December 1809, while still pretending to favour Napoleon's marriage to his sister, he began trying to subvert the Poles with promises of autonomy under Russian aegis.[22]

The summer of 1810 yielded a poor harvest in England, which coincided with a dramatic fall in the value of sterling. Napoleon tightened the economic screw by raising tariffs further on licensed imports. Britain was struggling economically, and he was convinced he could bring her to the negotiating table (on his terms). He therefore, in October 1810, instructed Caulaincourt to order Russia to raise tariffs too. This left Alexander with little option but to defy the system openly. On 31 December he opened Russian ports to American ships, and imposed tariffs on French manufactured goods imported overland into Russia. British goods were soon pouring into Germany from Russia; the Continental System was in tatters.

Napoleon could not accept it. 'The Continental System is uppermost in his mind, he is more taken up with it than ever,' noted his secretary Fain. In his determination to control all points of import, Napoleon annexed the Hanseatic ports. In January 1811 he did the same with the duchy of Oldenburg, whose ruler was the father of Alexander's brother-in-law. He did offer him another German province as compensation, but this was refused. Alexander was outraged and felt personally insulted—his supposed ally was now despoiling members of his family. He had to act, if only to save face. 'Blood must flow again,' he told his sister Catherine.[23]

At the beginning of January 1811 he renewed attempts to win over the Poles, or at least ensure their neutrality, while his minister of war,

General Barclay de Tolly, drew up plans for a strike into the grand duchy followed by an advance into Prussia. Alexander had 280,000 men ready and calculated that if the Poles and the Prussians were to join him, he could be on the Oder with a force of 380,000 before Napoleon could react. Napoleon was well informed and took the threat seriously. He ordered Davout, in command of the French forces in northern Germany, to prepare for war and ordered the Poles in the grand duchy of Warsaw to mobilise. 'I considered that war had been declared,' he later affirmed. In a report to Francis on 17 January 1811, Metternich stated his opinion that war between France and Russia was inevitable.[24]

In the same report, he argued that the restoration of Poland would be desirable if, in return for giving up the rest of Galicia, Austria were to recover the Tyrol, part of Venetia and Illyria. That would strengthen her position in the Balkans, improve her defences in the south, and give her Trieste and access to the sea, while a restored Poland would act as a buffer against Russian aggression. Austria rejected Russian diplomatic overtures aimed at securing support against France, fearing Russian expansion in the Balkans and increased influence in Central Europe; a strategic alliance between Austria and France was in the cards. The treaty Austria would sign with France on 14 March 1812 had as its aim the return of the Danubian Principalities to the Porte and left open the possibility of re-creating a kingdom of Poland. In Paris, gossip had it that Murat would be made King of Poland.[25]

'I have no wish to make war on Russia,' Napoleon declared to the Russian count Shuvalov during an interview at Saint-Cloud in May 1811. 'It would be a crime on my part, for I would be making war without a purpose, and I have not yet, thanks to God, lost my head, I am not mad.' To Colonel Chernyshev, whom the tsar had sent to Paris with letters for Napoleon, he repeatedly stated that he had no intention of fatiguing himself or his soldiers on behalf of Poland, and 'he formally declared and swore by everything he held holiest in the world that the re-establishment of that kingdom was the very *least* of his concerns'. But such professions of goodwill would not suffice.[26]

When Caulaincourt returned to Paris from St Petersburg on the morning of 5 June 1811, he drove straight to Saint-Cloud and within minutes of arriving was ushered into Napoleon's presence—in which he spent the next seven hours in a discussion whose course he noted down that evening. He explained Alexander's position and warned that the tsar would fight to the end rather than submit to Napoleon's demands. Napoleon dismissed this as bravado, asserting that Alexander was 'false and weak'. He could not believe Russian society would accept the implied sacrifices—the nobles would not want to see their lands ravaged for the sake of Alexander's honour, while the serfs would as likely revolt against them as fight for a system of slavery.

He viewed the Russian abandonment of the Continental System as a betrayal and her troop build-up as a threat to his influence in Central Europe. He had convinced himself that Alexander was using the Polish question and the subject of trade as excuses to break out of the alliance and draw closer to Britain and that he would invade the grand duchy of Warsaw the moment an opportunity presented itself.

Caulaincourt pointed out that Napoleon had only two options: he must either give a significant part, if not the whole, of the grand duchy of Warsaw to Alexander, or go to war with the aim of restoring the kingdom of Poland. He advised him to take the first course, which in his opinion would guarantee a stable peace. Napoleon declared that such a betrayal of the Poles would dishonour him and lead to further Russian expansion into the heart of Europe.[27]

He wanted to maintain his alliance with Alexander, yet would not pay the necessary price, and wanted to keep the Polish question open without committing to it. But this was no longer possible. By making his alliance with her the linchpin of his plan to defeat Britain, Napoleon had inflated Russia's significance, and his continued attempts to make Alexander do his bidding had spurred the tsar to assume an even greater role in European affairs.

Napoleon's exasperation erupted on 15 August 1811, his forty-second birthday. At midday he strutted into the throne room at the Tuileries, filled with court officials and diplomats perspiring in their uniforms and ceremonial dress on what was a particularly hot day. After receiving their good wishes, Napoleon stepped down from the throne and walked among the guests. When he reached the Russian ambassador, he accused Russia of massing troops with the intention of invading the grand duchy of Warsaw, describing it as an open act of hostility. The unfortunate Kurakin kept opening his mouth to reply but could not get a word in edgeways, while sweat poured down his face. After bullying him for a while, Napoleon walked away, leaving him in a state of shock.[28]

The following morning, after a conference with Maret, who had succeeded Champagny as foreign minister, in the course of which they reviewed every document concerning Russia since Tilsit, Napoleon concluded that France wanted Russia as an ally against Britain and had no wish to fight her, since there was nothing she wanted from her, but that she could not buy Russia's friendship by betraying the Poles. France must therefore prepare for war in order to prevent Russia from going to war. Caulaincourt's successor in St Petersburg, General Lauriston, was instructed to explain this.[29]

Napoleon could not see that he had put Alexander in an impossible situation, and he would not believe what he did not wish to see—that unless he stepped back, war was inevitable. Nor did he wish to face the fact that Russia was strategically invulnerable, as it was too vast to overrun and subdue. France, conversely, was highly vulnerable, since it was already engaged in a war in the Iberian Peninsula and was open to attack from Britain along its entire coastline. French possessions in Germany and Italy were unstable, as Napoleon kept moving boundaries and rearranging their administration, and satellites such as Naples were not dependable. Nor were his allies in the Confederation of the Rhine loyal other than by necessity. The whole Napoleonic system was a work in progress, whose final arrangement was contingent on an outcome with Britain, which now depended on solutions in both Spain and Russia. Acting tactically, without an overall strategy, Napoleon had got himself into an impasse from which the only way out was back—not a step he was used to contemplating.

'It would have been difficult to imagine any new obstacle to the Emperor's prosperity, and, whatever he undertook, people expected of the magician what no man would have undertaken,' wrote Victorine de Chastenay. Surrounded by his *maison*, which had grown to include 3,384 people, he was cut off from the real world. Beugnot,

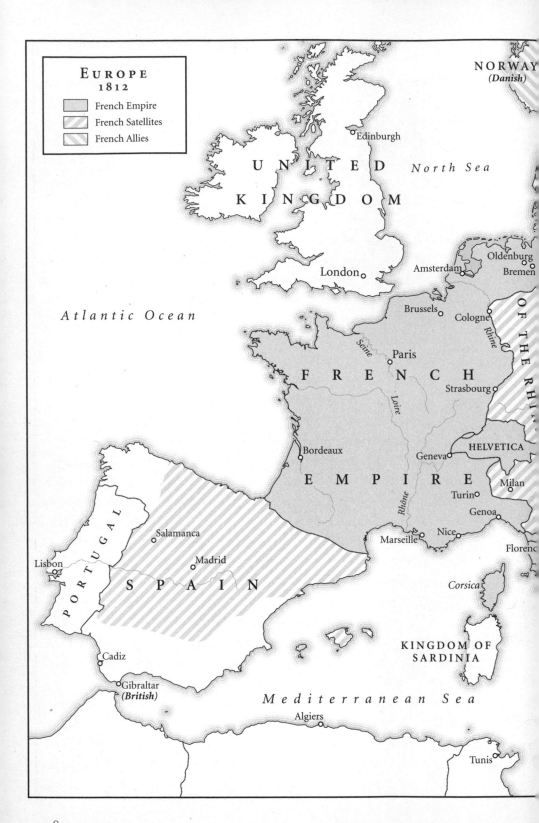

who had returned to Paris after an absence of three years, was struck by the luxury of the court, but noted that at Napoleon's table and those of his ministers, which were 'sumptuously served and attended by valets shimmering with gold', boredom reigned, as nobody discussed matters of state as they had in the past. Although there were few guards in evidence at the Tuileries, and security surrounding the emperor was light, fear and self-censorship proclaimed despotism; people whispered or kept silent, and Napoleon could ignore unpleasant truths. He must have read, as he always did, the police report from Lille relating to 2 December 1811, the anniversary of Austerlitz and his coronation, one of the major national feast days of the Napoleonic calendar, which found that 'the inhabitants appeared not to know for what reason' the city was illuminated and festivities were taking place. But it clearly made no impression deep enough to make him reflect. From where he sat, his power seemed limitless. On 3 November 1811, the fourteen-year-old Heinrich Heine watched him ride into Düsseldorf. He thought 'his features were noble and dignified, like those of ancient sculptures, and on his face were written the words: "Thou shalt have no other gods beside me." '[30]

He was defying God himself; when, back in June, the Council of French bishops, headed by Fesch, had sworn allegiance to the Pope, Napoleon had closed it down and imprisoned a number of its members in the fortress of Vincennes. On 3 December he issued another ultimatum demanding the acquiescence of the Pope, whose behaviour had 'wounded' his imperial authority, and imprisoned or exiled more clerics. The Pope himself would soon be dragged off in a closed carriage, travelling by night to house arrest at Fontainebleau, and even Fesch would be exiled.

By that time, troops were on the move all over Europe, recruits were being drilled, and arms, uniforms, and supplies of every kind stockpiled. Yet Napoleon still denied he intended to make war. To Metternich and many others it now seemed inevitable, and the only question was what the outcome would mean for Europe. 'Whether he triumphs or succumbs, Europe will never be the same again,' Metternich wrote to Francis. 'This terrible moment has unfortunately been brought on us by the unpardonable conduct of the Russians.'[31]

36

Blinding Power

NAPOLEON STILL HAD no fixed policy at the beginning of 1812. 'I am far from having lost hope of a peaceful settlement,' he wrote to Jérôme on 27 January. 'But as they have adopted towards me the unfortunate procedure of negotiating at the head of a strong and numerous army, my honour demands that I too negotiate at the head of a strong and numerous army. I do not wish to open the hostilities, but I wish to put myself in a position to repulse them.'[1]

Yet to one of his aides he explained that he was 'propelled into this hazardous war by political reality', as the fertile and civilised south of Europe would always be threatened by uncivilised ravenous hordes from the north, and 'the only answer is to throw them back beyond Moscow; and when will Europe be in a position to do this, if not now, and by me?' According to some in his entourage, he feared that his military talents and powers of endurance were in decline and felt he must deal with Russia while he still had the energy. 'One way or another, I want to finish the thing,' he said to General Vandamme, 'as we are both getting old, my dear Vandamme, and I don't want to find myself in old age in a position in which people can kick me in the backside, so I am determined to bring things to a conclusion one way or the other.' As he began regrouping his forces and preparing for war, the soldier seems to have awoken in Napoleon. And according to Mollien, he even thought that, as in the past, a war might refill his coffers. In effect, he did not really know what to do. 'I feel myself propelled towards some unknown goal,' he admitted to his aide Philippe de Ségur, adding that his fate was 'written'.[2]

He had assembled the largest army the world had ever seen. The Frenchmen in its ranks were outnumbered by Poles, Germans, Austrians, Belgians, Dutchmen, Swiss, Italians, Spaniards, Portuguese, and Croats, all of whom had differing interests and loyalties. Yet military instinct and the spirit of emulation bound them together. French rabbis exhorted young Jews: 'You will fight and vanquish under the command of the God of armies. Go, and return covered in laurels which will attest to your valour.' Valour, as tested in battle, was considered the prime virtue at the time, and young men felt a strong urge to prove their worth. 'Whatever their personal feelings towards the emperor may have been, there was nobody who did not see in him the greatest and most able of all generals, and who did not experience a feeling of confidence in his talents and the value of his judgement,' in the words of one aristocratic German officer. 'The aura of his greatness subjected me as well, and, giving way to enthusiasm and admiration, I, like the others, shouted "*Vive l'Empereur!*"' A Piedmontese cavalry lieutenant to whom Napoleon had addressed a few words during a parade felt the same. 'Before that, I admired Napoleon as the whole army admired him,' he wrote. 'From that day on, I devoted my life to him with a fanaticism which time has not weakened. I had one regret, which was that I had only one life to place at his service.'[3]

The size of the army obscured its quality. In March 1812 an inspection of the cavalry revealed that a third of the horses were too weak to carry a man. Only about the same proportion of the men were fit for action in most of the contingents. Napoleon made light of this. 'When I put 40,000 men on horseback I know very well that I cannot hope for that number of good horsemen, but I am playing on the morale of the enemy, who learns through his spies, by rumour or through the newspapers that I have 40,000 cavalry,' he argued. 'Passing from mouth to mouth, this number and the supposed quality of my regiments, whose reputation is well known, are both rather exaggerated than diminished; and the day I launch my campaign I am preceded by a psychological force which supplements the actual force that I have been able to furnish for myself.'[4]

Buoyed by the enthusiasm of the younger men, he chose to ignore the state of mind of many of those with greater experience. Much of the revolutionary ardour that had fired the French armies of the 1790s and early 1800s had been quenched by 1812. 'From the moment Napoleon came to power, military mores changed rapidly, the union of hearts disappeared along with poverty and the taste for material well-being and the comforts of life crept into our camps, which filled up with unnecessary mouths and numerous carriages,' in the words of General Berthézène. 'Forgetting the fortunate experiences of his immortal campaigns in Italy, of the immense superiority gained by habituation to privation and contempt for superfluity, the Emperor believed it to be to his advantage to encourage this corruption.' He had given his marshals and generals titles, lands, and pensions; they became less willing to forsake their warm beds and palaces, their wives and families for the rigours of the bivouac and the uncertainties of war. Many were entering middle age; they could hardly expect to win greater glory, but could lose everything they had and leave their families destitute.[5]

Napoleon's marshals, senior generals, and entourage were mostly opposed to the war for specific reasons: the distances involved, the terrain, the nature of the enemy, the pointlessness, the lack of any advantage to be gained from it, and the possible consequences on the political situation back in France. Even the commander of the Polish contingent, Poniatowski, warned him against invading Russia. Yet such was Napoleon's extraordinary aura that even the most sceptical submitted to the spell and believed in his 'star'. 'It was so sweet to abandon oneself to that star!' reminisced Ségur. 'It blinded us, it shone so high, so brilliant, it had worked such miracles!'[6]

While Napoleon was involving half the states of Europe in the forthcoming war, he was determined not to enlist them as real allies, because he meant to keep his options open. Nor did he bother to prepare the ground at the diplomatic level—quite the contrary. On 27 January 1812, under the pretext that the Continental System was not being enforced rigorously there, he sent his armies into Swedish Pomerania and took possession. He followed this up with a demand to Sweden for an alliance against Russia and a contingent of troops. When this was rejected, he offered to return Pomerania and threw in Mecklemburg as well as a large subsidy. But it was too late. His high-handed seizure of Pomerania had been taken as an insult in Sweden, and within two weeks of the news reaching Stockholm, Bernadotte's envoy was in St Petersburg asking for a treaty with Russia, which was duly signed on 5 April.

Napoleon failed to encourage the Turks to carry on fighting the Russians in the Balkans, with the result that they would soon make peace, allowing Russia to transfer troops from there to face him. His treatment of Austria and Prussia meant he had two disgruntled allies at his back only waiting for a chance to abandon or even turn against him. This was careless in view of the rising tide of anti-French feeling in Germany. Throughout 1811 reports from French commanders and diplomatic agents there alerted him to the growing danger. In Prussia, the king was barely able to contain the national feeling, particularly strong in the army. 'The ferment has reached the highest degree, and the wildest hopes are being fostered and cherished with enthusiasm,' reported a nervous Jérôme from neighbouring Westphalia in December. 'People are quoting the example of Spain, and if it comes to war, all the lands lying between the Rhine and the Oder will be embraced by a vast and active insurrection.'[7]

Napoleon's lack of contingency planning accords with other evidence that he was confident war could be avoided and that the military build-up was aimed principally to cow Alexander into submission. In this he misjudged the situation catastrophically; he knew Alexander was weak and stubborn, and with his wide experience of men he should have known that stubborn men, however weak, grow more stubborn when pushed. Alexander could not step back from the brink without discrediting himself forever in the eyes of his subjects, thereby exposing himself to a fate like his father's. By now, even a face-saver over Poland would not have sufficed, as the tsar had rallied to his side an impressive array of Napoleon's enemies, representing a spectrum of causes. They included Germaine de Staël, who lent him the intellectual credibility of supporting liberalism, the fiercely anti-French German nationalist Baron Karl vom Stein, who hoped to bring about the regeneration and unification of Germany, and Napoleon's old enemy Carlo Andrea Pozzo di Borgo, pursuing his vendetta. Alexander also dreamed of playing a grand part on the world stage and was beginning to see his duel with Napoleon as not just a challenge, but an opportunity.

If it did come to war, Napoleon needed to inflict such a shattering blow that the Russian army would lose all ability and will to resist, as the Prussian had following Jena. But his campaign of 1807 had shown that speed was not achievable in this part of the world, and that of 1809 had revealed that his enemies had got wise to his tactics and become deft at slipping out of the traps he set for them. In a sparsely populated area where he had no spies, he would be operating in the dark. And by concentrating such a huge force he cancelled out any possibility of swift manoeuvring.

The enterprise presented a logistical nightmare. Napoleon had read every book he could lay his hands on regarding the topography, climate, and characteristics of the theatre of operations. He had pored over maps, calculating distances and imagining the conditions in which he would have to operate. The starting point, the Russian frontier on the Niemen, was some 1,500 kilometres from Paris, and the two principal Russian cities, St Petersburg and Moscow, were respectively 650 and 950 kilometres beyond that. The stretch of 300 kilometres on the western side of the border and 500 beyond it was very poor, sparsely populated country with rudimentary roads and bridges, few towns, numerous rivers, bogs and forests to get lost in, and scant resources. The Grande Armée would have to take with it everything it needed.

Perhaps more important than any of these considerations was that a change had taken place in the nature of war, and the kind of brilliant victories he had achieved in the past would no longer yield the same results; the verdict of the battlefield had ceased to be decisive. Napoleon still believed that if an enemy's army was defeated and its capital occupied, it would be forced to sue for peace and then to abide by its terms, however onerous, even though Spain had revealed this not to be so. And although he had seen the Russian soldiers let themselves be hacked to pieces at Eylau and Friedland rather than surrender, he had not drawn the conclusion that, given the size of the country, there would always be more to take their place, and he was therefore bound to lose a war of attrition.

There were only two areas in which the Russian state was vulnerable. Having recently conquered a huge amount of territory and not had time to absorb or fully pacify its indigenous populations, it could be challenged by multiple national insurrections. And, based as it was on serfdom, it could be destabilised by revolution. Yet these were two options that Napoleon did not wish to use, since they would undermine his preferred outcome—a renewal of his alliance with Alexander.

On 24 April Kurakin delivered a letter from Alexander in which the tsar declared that no more talks could take place unless Napoleon withdrew all his troops west of the Rhine, which was tantamount to a declaration of war. In his reply, delivered three days later, Napoleon expressed regret that the tsar should be ordering him where to station his troops while he himself stood at the head of an army on the frontiers of the grand duchy. 'Your Majesty will however allow me to assure him that, were fate to conspire to make war between us inevitable, this would in no way alter the sentiments which Your Majesty has inspired in me, and which are beyond any vicissitude or possibility of change,' he ended.[8]

He could delay no longer. He had to go and take command of his armies. Before doing so, he made arrangements for the defence and the administration of France. Although he had, as a long shot, made a peace offer to Britain, suggesting a bilateral withdrawal of French and British troops from the Iberian Peninsula, with Joseph remaining King of Spain and its former rulers being allowed back into Portugal, he expected nothing to come of it. He therefore strengthened France's coastal defences and organised a national guard of 100,000 men who could be called out in an emergency. To remind people of their duty, he had the man who had capitulated at Bailén, General Dupont, retried and given a stiffer sentence. He also put in hand public works projects including five abattoirs, two aqueducts, three fountains, a canal, eleven markets, three bridges, a granary, a university, an observatory, a college of art, and refurbishments to or further work on an opera, a conservatoire, the national archives, a ministry, several palaces, a temple, a church, cemeteries, embankments, and streets.[9]

At their last meeting, on the eve of Napoleon's departure, the prefect of police Étienne Pasquier voiced fears about the possibility of an attempt by his enemies to seize power while he was so far away. 'Napoleon seemed to be struck by these brief reflections,' recalled the prefect. 'When I had finished, he remained silent, walking to and fro between the window and the fireplace, his arms crossed behind his back, like a man deep in thought. I was walking behind him, when, turning brusquely towards me, he uttered the following words: "Yes, there is certainly some truth in what you say; this is but one more problem to be added to all those that I must confront in this, *the greatest, the most* difficult, enterprise I have ever undertaken; but one must accomplish what has been undertaken. Goodbye Monsieur le Préfet." '[10]

Napoleon knew how to hide any anxiety he may have felt. 'Never has a departure for the army looked more like a pleasure trip,' noted Fain as the emperor left Saint-Cloud on Saturday, 9 May, with Marie-Louise. At Mainz he reviewed troops and received the Grand Duke of Hesse-Darmstadt and the prince of Anhalt Coethen, who had come to pay their respects. At Würzburg, where he stopped on the night of 13–14 May, he found the King of Württemberg and the Grand Duke of Baden waiting for him like faithful vassals.[11]

On 16 May he was met by the king and queen of Saxony, who had driven out to greet him, and together they made their entry into Dresden by torchlight as the cannon thundered salutes and the church bells pealed. His *lever* the next morning was graced by several ruling princes. The queen of Westphalia and the Grand Duke of Würzburg arrived later that day and the emperor and empress of Austria the next. They were joined a couple of days later by Frederick William of Prussia and his son the crown prince.

Napoleon had taken over the royal palace, obligingly vacated by the king, in which he held court attended by all the crowned heads present, 'whose deference to Napoleon went far beyond anything one could imagine', in the words of his aide Boniface de Castellane. After they had cringed at his *lever* every morning, they followed him to attend the *toilette* of Marie-Louise. They watched her pick her way through an astonishing quantity of jewellery, trying on and discarding one piece after another, and occasionally offering one to her barely older stepmother the Empress Maria Ludovica, who simmered with shame and fury; she loathed Napoleon for the upstart he was and for having thrown her father off his throne of Modena some years earlier.[12]

In the evenings they dined off the silver-gilt dinner service Marie-Louise had been given as a wedding present by the city of Paris, which she had thoughtfully brought along. The company assembled and entered the drawing room in reverse order of seniority, each announced by a crier, beginning with mere excellencies, going on to the various ducal and royal highnesses, and culminating with their imperial highnesses the emperor and empress of Austria. A while later, the doors would swing open and Napoleon would stride in, with just one word of announcement: *'L'Empereur!'* He was also the only one present who kept his hat on. 'Napoleon was indeed God at Dresden, the king amongst kings: it was on him that all eyes were turned; it was to him and around him that all the august people brought together in the King of Saxony's palace gathered,' in the words of one observer.[13]

There were balls, banquets, theatrical performances, and hunting parties, all focused on Napoleon in a choreographed display of power intended to remind his allies of their subjection to him. He was still hoping that when he saw himself isolated and faced with such an array of power, Alexander might agree to negotiate. He still felt what Méneval described as 'an extreme repugnance' for going to war and clung to the delusion that the tsar's resolve would crumble. 'Never have the reason and judgement of a man been more deceived, more led astray, more dominated by his imagination and his passions than those of the Emperor in some matters,' noted Caulaincourt after one of their meetings.[14]

Napoleon had convinced himself that Alexander was being manipulated by his entourage, and believing that if only he could talk to him directly or through some trusted third party they would reach an understanding, he despatched his aide Louis de Narbonne to the tsar's headquarters at Vilna (Vilnius). Alexander received him coolly and sent him back to Dresden. Napoleon then sent a courier to Lauriston in St Petersburg, instructing him to go to Alexander at Vilna and talk sense into him, but he was denied permission and told to leave Russia.

Napoleon had left himself with no option other than to fight, and he put on a brave face. 'Never has an expedition against them been more certain of success,' he said to Fain, pointing out that all his former enemies were now allies. 'Never again will such a favourable concourse of circumstances present itself; I feel it drawing me in, and if the Emperor Alexander persists in refusing my proposals, I shall cross the Niemen!' Yet he had no fixed idea as to what he would do after that.[15]

'My enterprise is one of those to which patience is the key,' he explained to Metternich. 'The more patient will triumph. I will open the campaign by crossing the Niemen, and it will end at Smolensk and Minsk. That is where I shall stop. I will fortify those two points, and at Vilna, where I shall make my headquarters during the coming winter, I shall apply myself to the organisation of Lithuania, which is burning to be delivered from the Russian yoke. I shall wait, and we shall see which of us will grow tired first—I of making my army live at the expense of Russia, or Alexander of nourishing my army at the expense of his country. I may well myself go and spend the harshest months of the winter in Paris.' And if Alexander did not sue for peace that year, Napoleon would mount another campaign in 1813, into the heart of Russia. 'It is, as I have already told you, only a question of time,' he assured Metternich. He said much the same to Cambacérès, whom he assured that he would restore Poland up to the river Dnieper, and would go no further.[16]

He was nevertheless open to every possibility. 'If I invade Russia, I will perhaps go as far as Moscow,' he wrote in his instructions to one of his diplomats. 'One or two battles will open the road for me. Moscow is the real capital of the empire. Having seized that, I will find peace there.' He added that if the war were to drag on, he would leave the job to the Poles, reinforced by 50,000 French.[17]

He still refused to see Alexander as an enemy to be defeated, thinking of him as an ally to be brought back to heel, which he wished to do with as little unpleasantness as possible and a minimum of damage. 'I will make war on Alexander in all courtesy, with 2,000 guns and 500,000 soldiers, without starting an insurrection,' he explained. But he still clung to the hope that he would not have to do even that. 'I may even not cross the Niemen,' he wrote to Cambacérès; his aide Dezydery Chłapowski was convinced that he was only bluffing and had no intention of invading Russia at all.[18]

Talleyrand, Narbonne, and Maret were among those who advocated creating a Polish state as a bulwark against Russian expansion, and Napoleon did not rule this out. He did have to keep the Poles on his side, and he needed to prime, even if he did not come to fire it, the weapon of Polish national insurrection in Russia's western provinces. In order to do this, he must send a clever man to Warsaw as an unofficial personal ambassador. He had originally selected Talleyrand for this purpose, but his choice now fell on the Abbé de Pradt, Archbishop of Malines. He was to encourage the Poles to proclaim the resurrection of the Polish state, without committing himself or his imperial master to backing it.[19]

Napoleon gave some thought to the question of whom to put on the Polish throne if he did decide to restore the kingdom. It would be too important a place for Murat or Eugène, both of whom believed themselves to be in line for the job. He did consider Davout, a good soldier and administrator popular with the Poles, but the example of Bernadotte raised questions as to future loyalty—and Napoleon never entirely got over his jealousy at having been outshone by Davout's feat at Auerstadt. 'I'll put Jérôme on it, I'll create a fine kingdom for him,' he told Caulaincourt. 'But he must achieve something, for the Poles like glory.' He duly put Jérôme in command of an army corps and directed him to Warsaw, where he was supposed to win the love of the Poles.

Thrilled at being given a command, Jérôme kitted himself out with helmet and breastplate emblazoned with the insignia of his Order of Union, with its eagles, lions, and serpents. He made a regal entry into the Polish capital and announced that he had come to spill his blood for the Polish cause. He sent back the mistress he had brought from Kassel and took a Polish one. The Poles found him overbearing and ridiculous and were put off by the behaviour of his troops. More important, most reasoning Poles sensed the lack of commitment, and indeed of purpose, in Napoleon's policy. He had assembled the greatest army the world had ever seen, with no specific goal; by definition, aimless wars cannot be won.[20]

After thirteen days in Dresden, where he had achieved little more than blinding himself with his own display of power, Napoleon bade an affectionate farewell to the King of Saxony and a tearful one to Marie-Louise and climbed into his travelling carriage. Two days later he was in Posen, which he entered under an arch inscribed with the words *Heroi Invincibili*, greeted deliriously by its Polish citizens, who had illuminated the city and festooned it with flags and garlands. But after a conference with Daru, who was overseeing the provisioning, he had to face up to the fact that his preparations had proved ineffective, and as he continued his journey he could see for himself the dire supply situation. There was a shortage of draught horses, which meant that supplies could not be brought forward fast enough, and men and horses were dying in large numbers. The situation was growing worse with every passing day; the ground was burning under his army's feet, and Napoleon had to move fast before it starved.[21]

The Russian forces were divided into three armies, positioned so as to be able to either defend Vilna or move out and attack. The First, deployed in advance of the city under General Mikhail Bogdanovich Barclay de Tolly, numbered about 160,000 men. The Second, under General Piotr Ivanovich Bagration, consisted of just over 60,000. It was poised to either support an advance by the First by outflanking the enemy, or to assist its defence by threatening the enemy's flank. A Third Army consisting of nearly 60,000 men under General Tormasov was positioned south of the Pripet Marshes, guarding the approaches to the Ukraine.[22]

Napoleon proposed to attack Barclay's First Army while Eugène's and St Cyr's corps drove a wedge between that and Bagration, and further south, Jérôme took him on with three other army corps. The attack was to be spearheaded by Murat with a huge body of cavalry, a great battering-ram of four divisions. In the north, Marshal Macdonald with the Prussian contingent was to advance on Riga with Oudinot in support. South of the Pripet, Schwarzenberg's Austrians were to mark Tormasov. 'The wings of our army were thus entrusted to the two nations which had the greatest interest in seeing our enterprise fail,' remarked an officer on Berthier's staff.[23]

It is impossible to determine the real strength of the Grande Armée. In theory, it consisted of 590,687 men and 157,878 horses, with another 90,000 or so men in various parts of Poland and Germany. On 14 June Napoleon issued a circular insisting that the commanders of every corps provide honest figures on the able-bodied, the sick, deserters, as well as the dead and the wounded. 'It has to be made clear to the individual corps that they must regard it as a duty towards the Emperor to provide him with the simple truth,' ran the order. But Napoleon reacted angrily when provided with dwindling figures, particularly if these could not be explained by battle casualties, so unit commanders concealed losses from him. 'He was led astray in the most outrageous way,' wrote General Berthézène. 'From the marshal to the captain, it was as if everyone had come together to hide the truth from him, and, although it was tacit, this conspiracy really did exist; for it was bound together by self-interest.' According to him, the true strength of the Grande Armée was no greater than 235,000 when it crossed the Niemen. That was still a considerable force, and this added urgency to the need for a quick victory; every day increased the difficulty of feeding it.[24]

In two bulletins, on 20 and 22 June, Napoleon explained how, since Tilsit, he had bent over backward to accommodate Russia, but she had been taken over by 'the English spirit' and begun arming against him and the whole of Europe. 'The vanquished have adopted the tone of the conquerors,' he concluded. 'They are tempting fate; let destiny take its course.'[25]

37

The Rubicon

OMENS OF DESTINY were not in short supply. Having reached the furthest outposts, in the early hours of 23 June Napoleon borrowed a Polish lancer's cap and cloak and rode out, with his staff similarly disguised as a regular patrol, to scout the river Niemen for a good crossing point. A hare started from under his horse's hooves and he was thrown. Instead of cursing and blaming the horse as he usually did, he remained tight-lipped and remounted without a word. Berthier and Caulaincourt, who were in attendance, took it as a bad omen and said they should not cross the river.[1]

Napoleon spent the rest of the day working in his tent, in a sombre mood. This contrasted sharply with the elation he normally displayed at the start of a campaign, and his entourage noted it with apprehension. He issued a proclamation to the army which announced the commencement of 'The Second Polish War', assuring his men that as well as being 'glorious for French arms', it would bring about a lasting peace and 'put an end to that arrogant influence which Russia has been exerting on the affairs of Europe over the past fifty years'.[2]

At three on the morning of 24 June he was in the saddle once more, mounting a horse named Friedland, and as the sun came up he could see three pontoon bridges which had been thrown across the river, and one division taking up defensive positions on the other side. He took his place on a knoll overlooking the scene and watched, a telescope in his right hand and his left behind his back. The huge army, dressed as for a parade, was crossing the river, the morning sunshine glinting on the helmets and breastplates of cuirassiers and dragoons, and on every polished cap badge and belt buckle, and lighting up the blue, white, yellow, green, red, and brown uniforms of the various allied contingents. He seemed in a good mood and hummed military marches as he contemplated what one witness described as 'the most extraordinary, the most grandiose, the most imposing spectacle one could imagine, a sight capable of intoxicating a conqueror'.[3]

'*Vive l'Empereur!* The Rubicon has been crossed,' noted a captain of grenadiers of the Guard in his diary at a bivouac outside Kowno (Kaunas) on 26 June, adding that some 'fine pages' would be added to the annals of the French nation. Four days later Napoleon entered Vilna, which had just been evacuated by the Russians. He was greeted by a municipal delegation, but the inhabitants had not had time to prepare the usual trappings, and his entry into the city was anything but triumphal. And as he bedded down for the night in the former archbishop's palace, where Alexander had slept the night before, a primeval storm burst on the area to the south and west of the city.[4]

Men and horses exhausted by lack of food and fodder, as well as by the intense heat of the past weeks, were suddenly drenched by a downpour of cold rain which lasted through the night. The morning sun revealed a landscape littered with dead or dying horses and men; of wagons, guns, and gun carriages mired in mud; and those still alive struggling to get free. Some artillery units lost a quarter of their horses, and the cavalry did not fare much better, but it was the supply services which suffered the most; at a conservative estimate the French army lost around 50,000 horses that night.[5]

The psychological damage was hardly less significant. As the men trudged on through the quagmire that had replaced the dusty roads, they could see dead and dying men and beasts by the roadside, and rumours of grenadiers having been struck by lightning passed from rank to rank. Had they been Greeks or Romans in ancient times they would undoubtedly have turned about and gone home after such an augury, quipped one of Napoleon's aides.[6]

Napoleon was baffled by the behaviour of the Russians, who had shown every sign of meaning to defend Vilna, yet decamped at his approach, leaving behind stores accumulated over months. It made no sense, and he instructed his commanders to proceed with caution, expecting a counter-attack. He need not have bothered. Barclay was a fine general, but although he was also minister of war, Alexander had not given him overall command and hovered at his side, limiting his freedom of action. In the absence of any fixed plan, he thought it best to fall back.

On 1 July Napoleon received an envoy from Alexander, General Balashov, who brought a letter proposing negotiations conditional on a French withdrawal. 'Alexander is making fun of me,' Napoleon retorted: he had not come all this way in order to negotiate, and since Alexander had refused to do so before, it was time to deal once and for all with the barbarians of the north. 'They must be thrown back into their icy wastes, so that they do not come and meddle in the affairs of civilised Europe for the next twenty-five years at least.'[7]

Balashov could hardly get a word in as Napoleon paced the room, venting his frustration in a monologue which veered from whining complaints to squalls of anger. He professed his esteem and love for Alexander and reproached him for surrounding himself with 'adventurers'. He could not understand why they were fighting instead of talking as they had at Tilsit and Erfurt. 'I am already in Wilna, and I still don't know what we are fighting over,' he said. He shouted, stamped his foot, and when a small window which he had just closed blew open again, tore it off its hinges and hurled it into the courtyard below. But in the reply to Alexander which he handed to Balashov he professed continuing friendship, peaceful intentions, and a desire to talk, without accepting the precondition of a withdrawal behind the Niemen.[8]

'He has rushed into this war which will be his undoing, either because he has been badly advised, or because he is driven by his destiny,' he declared after Balashov had gone. 'But I am not angry with him over this war. One more war is one more triumph for me.' On 11 July he issued a mendacious bulletin announcing great military successes, achieved at the cost of no more than 130 French casualties.[9]

On the same day as Napoleon's interview with Balashov, the Polish patriots of Vilna had held a *Te Deum* in the cathedral, followed by a ceremony of reunification of Lithuania with Poland. Napoleon had hoped that he would be able to defeat the Russians and reach an agreement with Alexander before he had to confront the Polish question, since that would probably have been part of the deal. But now he was being pressed to commit himself. In an attempt to duck the issue, on 3 July he set up a government for Lithuania, to administer the country, gather supplies, and raise troops, and instructed his foreign minister, Maret, whom he had brought to Vilna, to string them along.

On 11 July, eight delegates from the national confederation which he had called for in Warsaw arrived in Vilna. The emperor kept them waiting three days, then listened impatiently to their request that he announce the restoration of the kingdom of Poland. 'In my position, I have many different interests to reconcile,' he told them, but added that if the Polish nation arose and fought valiantly, Providence might reward it with independence. With this speech, he cooled the ardour of the Poles and robbed himself of what would have been a powerful weapon; the investigation conducted by the Russians after the war revealed that the population of the area in which he was operating was on his side, yet he would not engage its support or even sanction popular initiatives to act behind enemy lines lest it hinder chances of a reconciliation with Alexander.[10]

In his proclamation launching his 'Second Polish War', he had written that he was taking the war into Russia, giving his troops the impression that from the moment they crossed the Niemen they were in enemy territory and therefore licensed to behave as they liked. 'All around the city and in the countryside there were extraordinary excesses,' noted a young noblewoman of Vilna. 'Churches were plundered, sacred chalices were sullied; even cemeteries were not respected, and women were violated.' With no fighting to do and no palpable purpose to the campaign, tens of thousands of men had deserted and were roaming the countryside in gangs, attacking manor houses and villages, raping and killing, sometimes in collusion with mutinous peasants. 'The path of Attila in the age of barbarism cannot have been strewn with more horrible testimonies,' in the words of one Polish officer. In view of their numbers there was no way of enforcing the law, and those rounded up deserted again at the first opportunity. Officials were not safe, and *estafettes* were attacked.[11]

Apart from cooling the ardour of the local patriots, this complicated what was already a challenge. Napoleon was operating with huge army corps at distances that would have presented a problem in well-mapped areas with good roads. Couriers and staff officers struggled to find their way down sandy tracks, through boggy wildernesses and interminable forests. It was difficult for them to locate the commanders they were seeking, as these were themselves on the move, and many of the troops encountered along the way were not familiar enough with the marshals and generals to recognise them, while many could not speak French. Napoleon could not act or react as fast as he was wont to, which frustrated his plans.

He had managed to drive a wedge between Barclay's First Army and Bagration's Second and had sent Davout with two divisions and Grouchy's cavalry corps to cut Bagration's line of retreat and crush

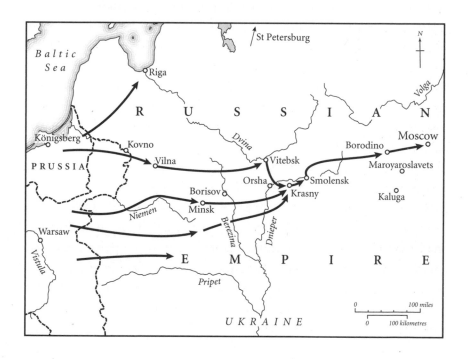

him against Jérôme's advancing corps. But Jérôme had got off to a slow start and failed to pin down Bagration, who was able to swerve south and get clear before the French pincers closed. Napoleon berated him, reprimanded Eugène, and insulted Poniatowski, both of whom were under his orders.[12]

The failure to destroy Bagration was his own fault; it had been his idea to give Jérôme such an important role. He had quickly come into conflict with his corps commanders and his own chief of staff. Napoleon had instructed Davout to oversee the combined operation but had failed to notify Jérôme, so Davout and Jérôme also fell out. Jérôme decided to go home, and taking with him his royal guards and his only trophy of war, a Polish mistress, on 16 July began his march back to Kassel. 'You have made me miss the fruit of my cleverest calculations, and the best opportunity that will have presented itself in this war,' wrote a furious Napoleon. For good measure, he reproved Davout for his handling of the situation.[13]

'I am very well,' Napoleon wrote to Marie-Louise that day. 'Kiss the little one for me. Love me, and never doubt my feelings for you. My affairs are going well.' They were not. Having himself wasted two weeks at Vilna, he had allowed the Russians to retreat in good order to a previously fortified camp at Drissa. When he got news of this, he decided to sweep round into their rear and trap them in it. But by the time he set off they had changed their plan and abandoned the camp, robbing him of his chance of a battle. On 21 July he nevertheless wrote a triumphant letter to Cambacérès announcing the capture of the camp.[14]

He resumed his pursuit and took heart when Murat engaged the Russian rearguard at Ostrovno. 'We are on the eve of great events,' he wrote to Maret on 25 July, and he sent off a note to Marie-Louise brimming with optimism. Two days later he caught up with Barclay, who was preparing to give battle before Vitebsk. It was midday, and he could have engaged him immediately. Instead he decided to wait for all his troops to catch up and postponed the attack to the following morning. That evening Barclay received news that Bagration, whom he had been expecting, could not make it, so he decided to strike camp silently in the night and resume his retreat. The French rose early and prepared for battle only to find the Russians had vanished.[15]

Napoleon was baffled and spent a day scouting the surrounding area before deciding to pause and give his army a rest. The men had marched under scorching sun, in temperatures recognised only by the veterans of the Egyptian campaign, along dusty roads through swarms of mosquitoes and horseflies, suffering agonies of thirst, since wells were few and far between. Many had wandered off in search of victuals and never been seen again, some had died of heatstroke or dehydration, others had fallen ill from drinking from brackish puddles or even horses' urine. The cavalry had been concentrated in a great body under Murat, which meant that even when they did find water, the tens of thousands of horses could not all be watered, and as there was no forage, they were lucky to find some old thatch to eat off a cottage roof. Some units were down by a third, and Napoleon had lost as many as 35,000 men without a battle since leaving Vilna.[16]

He took up quarters in the governor's residence at Vitebsk, where he spent the next two weeks, undecided as to what to do next. He contemplated stopping there and turning Vitebsk into a fortified outpost. He wrote to his librarian in Paris requesting 'a selection of amusing books'. It was still extremely hot, and while his troops bathed in the river Dvina he sweated as he worked at tidying up his army. He issued confident-sounding bulletins, wrote to Maret in Vilna instructing him to publicise non-existent successes, and blustered in front of the men, but in the privacy of his own quarters he was irritable, shouting at people and insulting them. He received news of the treaty between Russia and Turkey and details of that between Russia and Sweden signed in March. What he did not know was that Russia had also signed a treaty of alliance with Britain on 18 July. But he was cheered by the news of the outbreak of war between Britain and the United States of America.[17]

He had been greeted in Vitebsk by local Polish patriots and evaded their questions as to his intentions by heaping abuse on Poniatowski and the alleged cowardice of the Polish troops, which, he claimed, was largely responsible for the failure to catch Bagration. 'Your prince is nothing but a c—,' he snapped at one Polish officer. To Maret in Vilna he sent contradictory instructions regarding the Polish question. Many argued that this was the moment to send Poniatowski south into Volhynia. This would have raised an insurrection in what had been Polish Ukraine, which would have yielded men and horses as well as supplies. More important, it would have tied down the Russian forces in the south, under Chichagov and Tormasov. But, as he admitted to Caulaincourt, he was more interested in using Poland as a pawn than in restoring it.[18]

Unusually for him, Napoleon consulted a number of generals on what to do next. Berthier, Caulaincourt, Duroc, and others felt it was time to call a halt. They cited losses, provisioning difficulties, and the length of the lines of communication and expressed the fear that even a victory would cost them dearly, on account of the lack of hospitals and medical resources in the area. But Napoleon hankered after a battle to show for his pains and hoped that now they were on the borders of Russia proper, Barclay would have to fight. 'He believed in a battle because he wanted one, and he believed that he would win it because that was what he needed to do,' wrote Caulaincourt. 'He did not for a moment doubt that Alexander would be forced by his nobility to sue for peace, because that was the whole basis of his calculations.' Leaping out of his bath at two o'clock one morning he suddenly announced that they must advance at once, only to spend the next two days poring over maps and papers. 'The very danger of our situation impels us towards Moscow,' he said to Narbonne. 'I have exhausted all the objections of the wise. The die is cast.'[19]

He marched out of Vitebsk on 13 August, meaning to cross the Dnieper and take Smolensk from the south before the Russians could prepare a defence, and then use its bridges to recross the river into Barclay's rear. As a result of confused manoeuvring caused by differences between Barclay and Bagration, who had now joined forces, Smolensk was full of Russian troops. There was no value in taking this thickly walled fortress, and Napoleon could have recrossed the river further east and forced Barclay to give battle by coming between him and Moscow. He nevertheless decided to storm it. The murderous battle cost him 7,000 casualties and reduced Smolensk to a scorched charnel house strewn with the corpses of the defenders and citizens who had died in the bombardment and fire that engulfed it.

Barclay resumed his retreat, with Ney in pursuit. Napoleon had sent Junot to cross the river further east, and he was in a position to cut the Russian line of retreat, but Junot had a mental blackout and his generals could not get an order out of him, and since Napoleon did not bother to ride out to see what was going on, the manoeuvre came to nothing. Ney, supported by Davout and Murat, fought hard but could not stop the Russians from making good their retreat.

The following morning Napoleon rode out to the scene. 'The sight of the battlefield was one of the bloodiest the veterans could remember,' according to a lancer of his escort. The troops paraded on the field of battle, and he awarded the coveted eagle that topped the colours of regiments which had earned it to the 127th of the Line, made up largely of Italians, which had distinguished itself the previous day. 'This ceremony, imposing in itself, took on a truly epic character in this place,' in the words of one witness. Napoleon took the eagle from the hands of Berthier and, holding it aloft, told the men, their faces still smeared with blood and blackened by smoke, that it should be their rallying point, and they must swear never to abandon it. When they had sworn the oath, he handed the eagle to the colonel, who passed it to the ensign, who in turn took it to the elite company, while the drummers delivered a deafening roll. Napoleon dismounted and walked over to the front rank. In a loud voice, he asked the men to name those who had distinguished themselves in the fighting. He promoted those who were named and gave the Legion of Honour to others, dubbing them with his sword and giving them the ritual embrace. 'Like a good father surrounded by his children, he personally bestowed the recompense on those who had been deemed worthy, while their comrades acclaimed them,' in the words of one officer. 'Watching this scene,' wrote another, 'I understood and experienced that irresistible fascination which Napoleon exerted when he wished to.' By this means he managed to turn the bloody battlefield into one of glory, consigning those who had died to immortality and caressing those who had survived with words and rewards. But many asked what, if anything, had been achieved by the past four days of bloodletting.[20]

Napoleon had beaten the Russians and taken a major city, but while he had inflicted heavy losses, he had lost as many as 18,000 men in the two engagements, with nothing to show for it. According to Caulaincourt, over the next few days he behaved like a child who needs reassurance. 'In abandoning Smolensk, one of their holy cities, the Russian generals have dishonoured their arms in the sight of their own people,' he claimed. He fantasised about turning it into a base, from which he would attack either Moscow or St Petersburg the following year. But the burnt-out city represented no military value. Yet to retreat now was politically unthinkable. He had walked into a trap from which he could see no viable issue.[21]

He vented his frustration on anything that came to hand. He blamed the Lithuanians for failing to raise enough troops and supplies, he reprimanded the corps commanders, and when he came across some soldiers looting one day, he attacked them with his riding crop, yelling obscenities. In his desperation to find a way out, he tried to persuade a captured Russian general to write to the tsar. 'Alexander can see that his generals are making a mess of things and that he is losing territory, but he has fallen into the grip of the English, and the London cabinet is whipping up the nobility and preventing him from coming to terms,' he lectured Caulaincourt. 'They have convinced him that I want to take away all his Polish provinces, and that he will only get peace at that price, which he could not accept, as within a year all the Russians who have lands in Poland would strangle him like they did his father. It is wrong of him not to turn to me in confidence, for I wish him no ill: I would even be prepared to make some sacrifices in order to help him out of his difficulty.'[22]

Most of his entourage begged him to go no further, but he felt he could not return home without a victory. Moscow was only just over two weeks' march away, and the Russians would surely make a stand in its defence. 'The wine has been poured, it has to be drunk,' he told Rapp. When Berthier nagged him once too often on the subject, he turned on him. 'Go, then, I do not need you; you're nothing but a...Go back to France; I do not force anyone,' he snapped, adding a few lewd remarks about what Berthier was longing to get up to with his mistress in Paris. The horrified Berthier swore he would not dream of abandoning his emperor, but the atmosphere between them remained frosty, and Berthier was not invited to the imperial table for several days.[23]

While senior officers shook their heads, the younger ones were excited by the prospect of a march on Moscow. 'The whole army, the French and our foreign auxiliaries, was still full of ardour and confidence,' according to the twenty-one-year-old Lieutenant de Bourgoing. 'If we had been ordered to march to conquer the moon, we would have answered: "Forward!"' recalled Heinrich Brandt of the Legion of the Vistula. 'Our older colleagues could deride our enthusiasm, call us fanatics or madmen as much as they liked, but we could think only of battles and victories. We only feared one thing— that the Russians might be in too much of a hurry to make peace.'[24]

As they penetrated Russia proper, the character of the war changed. The retreating Russians adopted a scorched-earth policy, forcing the population out of their homes and burning them, along with standing crops and anything that might provide shelter or provender to the advancing army. 'At night, the whole horizon was on fire,' in the words of one soldier. They poisoned wells with dead animals. They felled trees and left overturned carts in the road, and, as their retreat grew less orderly, corpses of men and horses, which rotted in the sweltering heat. Yet the men marched on, confident in what one soldier called 'the vast genius' of their 'father, hero, demi-god'.[25]

Napoleon was uneasy at the sight of the burning villages but concealed his feelings by heaping ridicule on the Russians and calling them cowards. 'He sought to avoid the serious reflections which this terrible measure raised as to the consequences and duration of a war in which the enemy was prepared to make, from the very outset, sacrifices of this magnitude,' explains Caulaincourt. He nevertheless continued to clutch at every straw; on 28 August he seized an opportunity to write to Barclay, hoping to open up a channel of communication with Alexander.[26]

Two days later, when he and his entourage stopped for lunch by the roadside, Napoleon walked up and down in front of them, holding forth about the nature of greatness. 'Real greatness has nothing to do with wearing the purple or a grey coat, it consists in being able to rise above one's condition,' he declaimed. 'I, for instance, have a good position in life. I am emperor, I could live surrounded by the delights of the great capital, and give myself over to the pleasures of life and to idleness. Instead of which I am making war, for the glory of France, for the future happiness of humanity; I am here with you, at a bivouac, in battle, where I can be struck, like any other, by a cannonball. . . . I have risen above my condition. . . .' But the following day an *estafette* from Paris brought news that in Spain Marmont had been defeated by Wellington at Salamanca on 22 July. 'Anxiety was clearly visible on his usually serene brow,' according to General Roguet, who lunched with him that day.[27]

The Russians were as desperate as Napoleon for a battle, but the speed of the French advance had prevented Barclay from getting his troops into position. Under pressure from public opinion Alexander replaced him with the popular Mikhail Ilarionovich Kutuzov, a sly, gout-ridden, fat sixty-six-year-old with a talent to rival Napoleon's for falsifying facts to build up his image. It was not until 3 September that Kutuzov chose a defensive position in which to stand and fight, in front of the village of Borodino.

Napoleon reached the scene two days later. He ordered an exposed Russian redoubt to be captured, then spent a day reconnoitring and preparing for battle. Kutuzov had built a formidable earthwork redoubt on a slight rise at the centre of his line, covered on his left with three *flèches*, earthworks in the shape of chevrons. Napoleon decided to deliver a frontal assault on the redoubt while Ney, Davout, and Junot took the *flèches* and penetrated into the Russian rear, and Poniatowski made a deeper flanking movement in support. Davout suggested that his corps be added to the Polish one so as to drive deeper into the Russian rear, but Napoleon feared engaging such a large force too deep. He had between 125,000 and 130,000 men, so he was outnumbered by the Russians with their 155,000 (about 30,000 of whom were poorly trained militia), and he was outgunned, in calibre as well as in numbers, by the 640 Russian guns to his 584.[28]

Napoleon was unwell. He was suffering from an attack of dysuria, an affliction of the bladder which made it almost impossible for him to urinate, and when he did only a few dark drops came out, heavy with sediment. He may also have had a fever, as he was coughing, shivering, and breathing with difficulty. His spirits were lifted by the arrival of Bausset with a case containing a portrait of the King of Rome just painted by Gérard, which he immediately had unpacked. 'I cannot express the pleasure which the sight gave him,' noted Bausset. The proud father had the picture displayed outside his tent so his generals and soldiers could come up and admire it, and he wrote a tender note to Marie-Louise thanking her for it.[29]

A less welcome arrival was Colonel Fabvier, who had come from Spain with details of Wellington's victory over Marmont at Salamanca and of the worsening military position of the French in the Peninsula. News of the French defeat would give heart to all Napoleon's enemies—not just those facing him, but, more alarmingly, those at his back. He slept badly, waking several times. At three in the morning he got up and drank a glass of punch with Rapp, who was on duty and had spent the night in his tent. 'Fortune is a fickle courtesan,' Napoleon suddenly said. 'I have always said so and now I am beginning to feel it.' After a while he added, sighing, 'Poor army, it is much reduced, but what is left is good, and my Guard is intact.' He then rode out to show himself to the troops.[30]

The army had spent the previous day buffing up, and some said it looked as fine as on a parade before the Tuileries. The men were read a proclamation which exhorted them to fight and assured them that victory would lead to a prompt return home. It contained a reference to Austerlitz, which was not out of place, since that was the last time the Grande Armée had faced Kutuzov, and when the sun came up Napoleon exclaimed, '*Voilà le soleil d'Austerlitz!*' He then rode up to a vantage point from which he could see almost the whole field of battle, where a tent had been pitched for him, surrounded by his Guard in formation. He took the folding chair that had been set out for him, turned it back to front and sat down heavily, his arms on its back.[31]

At six o'clock the French guns opened up and the attack began. Assault followed assault as the Russian positions fell, only to be re-taken in fierce hand-to-hand fighting. The *flèches* were murderous traps for the troops who took them, as their only escape was forward, into the next Russian line of defence. Napoleon listened impassively as officers rode up to report. He refused all offers of food, only taking a glass of punch at around ten o'clock. He watched two assaults on the grand redoubt at the centre but failed to reinforce the successful one, while his cavalry stood idle. 'We were all surprised not to see the active man of Marengo, Austerlitz, etc.,' noted Louis Lejeune, an officer on Berthier's staff. Napoleon appeared curiously remote.[32]

His state of health undoubtedly played a part, but so did his state of mind; unsettled by an unexpected sortie by Russian cavalry on his left wing and afraid of playing his last card so far from home, he would not commit the Guard when Davout reported that the way was open for it to sweep into the rear of the Russian army and destroy it completely. He hesitated for a couple of hours before ordering the general assault. When he did, his cavalry, which was being gradually

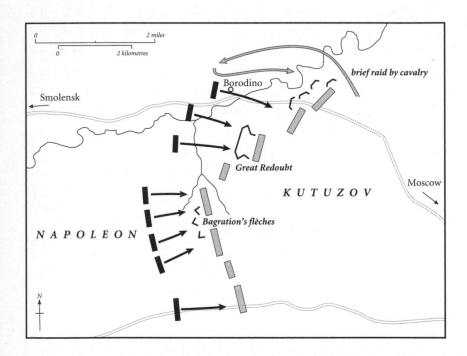

shot to pieces by the Russian guns, surged forward and, charging up the hill, swarmed into the great redoubt, and the Russian line crumpled. Napoleon then rode over the battlefield, which presented what one of his generals describes as 'the most disgusting sight' he had ever seen. Russian casualties were around 45,000, including twenty-nine generals, the French 28,000 and forty-eight generals. The bodies of nearly 40,000 horses littered the ground.[33]

The French victory was complete; Russian losses were such that most of the units had ceased to be operational, and nothing stood between the French and Moscow. But there had been no trace of Napoleonic genius in evidence in what had been little more than a slogging match. The Russians did not flee, and there was no pursuit, as the French cavalry was exhausted. At dinner that evening with Berthier and Davout, Napoleon said little and ate less. He did not sleep that night.

Kutuzov badly needed to get the remnants of his army out of the path of the French and to fall back to the south, where he could be fed and resupplied. Instead of doing so directly, he cleverly retreated to Moscow and out the other side, guessing that the city would act as a 'sponge' which would absorb the French and permit him to get away. He was right. Napoleon followed, and on the afternoon of 14 September from the Poklonnaia Hill he surveyed his prize—a huge and beautiful city glittering with its many gilded onion-shaped domes. But it was empty, and no delegation came out to submit to him. 'The barbarians,' he exclaimed. 'They really mean to abandon all this? It is not possible.'[34]

38

Nemesis

THE FOLLOWING MORNING, 15 September, Napoleon rode into Moscow and took up residence in the Kremlin. 'We were surprised not to see anyone, not even one lady, come to listen to our band, which was playing *La Victoire est à Nous!*' a disappointed Sergeant, Bourgogne noted as they marched in. Some two-thirds of the city's inhabitants had left, and the remainder, including many foreign tradesmen, servants, and artisans, cowered in their homes. Even members of the several-hundred-strong French colony kept out of the way. The shops were closed; and what little traffic there was in the streets was mainly Russian stragglers.[1]

The surrender of a city was normally negotiated so that the authorities assigned the occupying troops billets and made arrangements for feeding them, but in this case there was a free-for-all to obtain the necessities of life. Generals and groups of officers selected aristocrats' palaces and noblemen's townhouses, while their men settled in as best they could in the surrounding houses, stables, and gardens. Napoleon had appointed Marshal Mortier governor, with orders to prevent looting, and the occupation began in a relatively civilised manner. But as the shops were closed and most of the houses abandoned, the men helped themselves to whatever they needed, and chaos ensued, aggravated by the action of the Russian governor of the city, Count Rostopchin, who had ordered it to be put to the torch and removed the fire pumps before leaving. By nightfall large parts of it were on fire, and as a significant proportion of the houses were made of wood, it proved impossible to bring under control.

By the following morning the flames came dangerously close to the Kremlin, and Napoleon thought it prudent to leave the city with his Guard and move to the nearby palace of Petrovskoe. The city turned into an inferno in which French looters were joined by local criminals, Russian deserters, and others eager to save something for themselves from the flames. A drunken bacchanalia accompanied the pillage, rape, and murder, shattering the bonds of military discipline.

Once the fire had abated, on 18 September Napoleon rode back into Moscow, but the smouldering remains of the city no longer represented much of a prize, and he began to make plans to leave. The question was where to go. A withdrawal to Vilna would mean losing face and admitting that all the exertions since crossing the Niemen and the deaths of Borodino had been in vain. He considered leaving the main body of his army in Moscow and marching on St Petersburg with Eugène's corps and a few other units, which might persuade Alexander to treat. Eugène was apparently keen on the plan, but others raised objections, and according to Fain, 'they managed for the first time to make him doubt the superiority of his own judgement'. Some wanted to fall back and take winter quarters in Smolensk, others suggested a march south on the industrial cities of Tula and Kaluga, followed by a foray through the Ukraine. But that would mean abandoning his bases at Minsk and Vilna.[2]

Napoleon tried to make contact with Alexander, in the hope that the fall of Moscow might have made him more amenable. In his letter, sent through a Russian gentleman who had remained in the city, he castigated Rostopchin's burning of Moscow as an act of barbarism; in Vienna, Berlin, Madrid, and every other city he had occupied the civil administration had been left in place, which had safeguarded life and property. 'I have made war on Your Majesty without animosity,' he assured him, saying that a single note from him would put an end to hostilities. He sent another letter through a minor civil servant, and on 3 October suggested sending Caulaincourt to St Petersburg. Caulaincourt excused himself, on the grounds that Alexander would not receive him. Napoleon then decided to send Lauriston. 'I want peace, I need peace, I must have peace!' Napoleon told him as he set off two days later. 'Just save my honour!'[3]

According to Caulaincourt, Napoleon realised his repeated messages would, by showing up the difficulty of his position, only confirm Alexander in his purpose. 'Yet he kept sending him new ones! For a man who was so politic, such a good calculator, this reveals an extraordinary blind faith in his own star, and one might almost say in the blindness or the weakness of his adversaries! How, with his eagle's eye and his superior judgement could he delude himself to such a degree?'[4]

He may have been trying to pressure Alexander by giving the impression that he was prepared to sit it out in Moscow and spend the winter there if necessary; he talked of bringing the actors of the Comédie-Française to entertain him and his men through the winter months. But lingering in Moscow only undermined his own position; although enough had survived in cellars and buildings that had escaped the flames to feed and clothe his army for some months, and there were large quantities of arms, shot, and powder left in the city's arsenal, there was no fodder for the horses, and without horses he would be able neither to keep his lines of communication open nor to launch a fresh campaign in the spring. The whole area in his rear had been ravaged in the advance and was awash with deserters, many settled in bands along the way. The behaviour of these, and of foraging parties sent out from Moscow, was beginning to turn an originally indifferent population against the invaders; isolated French soldiers and even small units were being attacked.

While Kutuzov gradually rebuilt his forces in his fortified camp at Tarutino south of Moscow, Murat's corps, camped nearby to check him, wasted away. The 3rd Cavalry Corps, consisting of eleven regiments, could only muster 700 horsemen. The 1st Regiment of Chasseurs could only field fifty-eight, and that only thanks to some reinforcements that had reached it from France. Some squadrons in the 2nd Cuirassiers, usually 130 strong, were down to eighteen men. The backs of many of the horses were so worn through that in some cases when riders dismounted and unsaddled they could see their entrails. 'We could see that we were slowly perishing, but our faith in the genius of Napoleon, in his many years of triumph, was so unbounded that these conversations always ended with the conclusion that he must know what he is doing better than us,' recalled Lieutenant Dembiński.[5]

Napoleon's apartment in the Kremlin overlooking the river Moskva and part of the city consisted of a vast hall with great chandeliers, three spacious salons, and one large bedroom, which doubled up as his study. It was here that he hung Gérard's portrait of the King of Rome. He slept on the iron camp bed he always used on campaign; his desk had been set up in one corner and his travelling library laid out on shelves. He had two burning candles placed at his window every night, so that passing soldiers would see he was watching and working.

He had set up a skeletal administration of the city, and a semblance of normality was established. People travelled 'as easily between Paris and Moscow as between Paris and Marseille', according to Caulaincourt, if it took them a little longer. The post took up to forty days, but the *estafette* only fourteen. Its arrival was the high point of Napoleon's day, and he would grow restless if, as happened once or twice, it was a couple of days late.[6]

News from Paris was welcome, particularly when it flattered Napoleon's vanity. He read with pleasure that his birthday, which he had spent before Smolensk, had been celebrated by the laying of foundation stones for the Palais de l'Université, a new Palais des Beaux-Arts, and a building to house the national archives. He was informed that 'the enthusiasm of the Parisians, on hearing of the emperor's entry into Moscow is tempered only by their fear of seeing him march out of it in triumph on a conquest of India'. News that Wellington had taken Madrid was less welcome.[7]

Napoleon attended to affairs of state as well as those of his army with a punctiliousness that may have helped him avoid facing up to the realities of his situation. He badgered Maret to put pressure on the American minister, the poet Joel Barlow, who had just arrived in Vilna, to negotiate an alliance with the United States against Britain. He gave instructions for horses to be sent from France and Germany and for rice to be purchased and shipped to Moscow. He held parades on Red Square before the Kremlin, at which he awarded crosses of the Legion of Honour and promotions earned at Borodino. He was not looking forward to a winter away from home. 'If I cannot return to Paris this winter,' he wrote to Marie-Louise, 'I will have you come and see me in Poland. As you know, I am no less eager than you to see you again and to tell you of all the feelings which you arouse in me.'[8]

While he reviewed the troops stationed in Moscow, he showed little interest in those elsewhere. When Murat sent his aide-de-camp to inform him of the dire state of the cavalry, Napoleon dismissed him, saying his army was 'finer than ever'.[9]

Each day he spent in Moscow made it harder to leave without loss of face, and the usually decisive Napoleon seemed paralysed by the need to choose between an unappealing range of options on the one hand, and belief in his star on the other. He only really had one option, and he was reducing the chances of its success with every day he delayed. The weather was unusually fine, and he teased Caulaincourt, accusing him of telling tales about the Russian winter. 'Caulaincourt thinks he's frozen already,' he quipped, dismissing suggestions that the army provide itself with gloves and warm clothing. As soon as they reached Moscow, all the Polish units had set up forges to produce horseshoes with crampons in preparation for winter. A few Dutch and German officers followed their example, but not the French. Luckily for Napoleon, Caulaincourt had the horses of his *maison* properly shod.[10]

On 12 October the *estafette* from Moscow to Paris was captured, and the following day that coming from Paris was intercepted. General Ferrières, who had travelled all the way from Cádiz, was captured almost at the gates of Moscow. These events shook Napoleon, as did the first shower of snow, on 13 October. 'Let us make haste,' he said on seeing it. 'We must be in winter quarters in twenty days' time.' It was not too late. Smolensk, where he had some supplies, was only ten to twelve days' march from Moscow, his well-stocked bases at Vilna and Minsk only another fifteen to twenty from there. If he could reach these, his army would be fed and supplied, safe in friendly country, and able to draw on reinforcements from depots in Poland and Prussia.[11]

His chances of an orderly withdrawal were reduced by his hope that he might sway Alexander by appearing to occupy Moscow indefinitely; instead of sending the lightly wounded of Smolensk and Borodino back to where they could safely convalesce, he had left them where they were or had them brought to Moscow. Rather than send the thousands of horseless cavalrymen back to Poland where they could be remounted, he kept them in Russia. He did not send back unnecessary members of his *maison* or other civilians and did not evacuate the trophies—banners, regalia and treasures from the Kremlin, and the great silver-gilt cross he had had wrenched from the dome of the tower of Ivan the Great. It was not until 14 October, the day after the first snowfall, that he gave orders that no more troops were to be sent forward to Moscow and that the wounded in the city be evacuated, a pointless and fatal decision; the badly wounded, possibly as many as 12,000, should have been left where they were, as Dr Larrey intended (he had organised medical teams to care for them).[12]

Napoleon could go back the way he had come, which had the advantage of being familiar, guarded by French units, and punctuated with supply depots, as well as being the most direct route. But that would smack of retreat. He considered marching northwestward, in a sweep back to Vilna, and defeating a Russian army on the way. This option had the merit of threatening St Petersburg, which might just cause Alexander's nerve to snap. Or he could march southward, strike a blow at Kutuzov, and then go back to Minsk another way. He did not make up his mind until the last moment, further delaying preparations.[13]

Having decided to strike at Kutuzov, he still entertained the option of returning to Moscow. He therefore left part of his *maison* there and gave orders to stockpile three months' worth of rations, to improve the defences of the Kremlin, and to turn all the monasteries into strongpoints. He overruled General Lariboisière, inspector-general of the artillery, who wanted to start evacuating equipment; as a result 500 caissons, 60,000 muskets, and quantities of powder, not to mention a large number of cannon, were left in the city. Napoleon seemed incapable of committing to any course, as though he were waiting for some chance to present itself. He ended a letter to Maret in which he sketched out his probable plans with the words: 'But in the end, in affairs of this kind, what takes place in the event is sometimes very different from that which is foreseen.' He affected a confidence which had seen him through in the past. 'Today is 19 October, and look how fine the weather is,' he said to Rapp as he set out from Moscow. 'Do you not recognise my star?' Rapp felt this was no more than bravado and noted that 'his face bore the mark of anxiety'.[14]

His forces numbered no more than 95,000, and probably less, but they included a nucleus of tested troops, including the Guard, which had not been blooded during the campaign. They marched out singing, but while they looked martial enough, their baggage carts were loaded down not with military supplies, but with loot. Behind them came less disciplined troops, stragglers and civilians driving carriages and carts loaded with booty, looking like a grotesque carnival. The high spirits flagged three days later when a downpour transformed the road into a morass. Vehicles had to be abandoned, cumbersome objects jettisoned from knapsacks, and the line of march lengthened as stragglers fell behind.[15]

They marched south, but found the road blocked by Kutuzov at Maloyaroslavets. After fierce fighting in the course of which the town changed hands several times, Eugène and his Italians drove out Kutuzov. Losses were heavy, with at least 6,000 casualties, and that night, in a squalid cottage whose single room was divided in two by a dirty canvas sheet, Napoleon asked his marshals for their views on what to do next. He listened in silence, staring at the maps spread before him. At dawn he rode out to reconnoitre. He narrowly missed being captured by cossacks, and after riding through the burnt-out ruins of Maloyaroslavets, whose streets were strewn with corpses, many of them hideously mutilated by the wheels of guns or shrivelled in grotesque poses by the blaze, he was visibly shaken. He decided to retreat by the most direct route and sent orders to Mortier in Moscow to abandon the city, bringing all the wounded, and make with all speed for Smolensk. Before he left he was to blow up the Kremlin and torch the townhouses of Rostopchin and Count Razumovsky, the Russian ambassador in Vienna, as well as destroying all the stores left in the city.[16]

Mortier also brought with him two prisoners, General Wintzing-erode and his aide-de-camp, who had unwisely ridden into Moscow to verify that the French had left, only to be captured. When Napoleon saw Witzingerode, a native of Württemberg in Russian service who seemed to epitomise the *internationale* that was forming against him, he erupted into a rage. 'It is you and a few dozen rogues who have sold themselves to England who are whipping up Europe against me,' he ranted. 'I don't know why I don't have you shot; you were captured as a spy.' That did not exhaust his anger, and on seeing a country house that had escaped destruction, he ordered it burnt down. 'Since *Messieurs les Barbares* are so keen on burning their own towns, we must help them,' he raged (he soon countermanded the order).[17]

When they passed Borodino, he was annoyed to find many wounded still in the makeshift hospitals. Against the advice of Larrey and the medical teams caring for them, he insisted they be placed on every available vehicle, including gun carriages. The order killed many who might have lived; they were in no condition to survive the jolting and buffeting, and those who were not killed by it soon either fell off or were thrown off. Progress was slow due to lack of horsepower. Shortage of fodder had debilitated the horses—guns normally drawn by three pairs were now hitched to teams of twelve of more, and even these had to be helped up inclines by infantry. Powder wagons were blown up and shells jettisoned to lighten the load. Private carriages and loot-laden wagons were seized and burnt by the artillery, which commandeered the horses, but this did not solve the problem. As the nights grew colder more horses died, and the artillery took those that had been drawing wagons with wounded men.

Napoleon saw himself as carrying out a tactical withdrawal rather than a retreat, so although his generals advised abandoning some of the guns in order to free up horses with which to draw the rest and save time, he would not hear of it, fearing the Russians would claim the abandoned guns as trophies. The same went for the 3,000 or so Russian prisoners, who only encumbered the army.[18]

The army corps were marching one behind the other, so only the leading one had a clear road; the others had to move through the mess left behind by preceding ones. Their path was churned by tens of thousands of feet, hooves, and wheels into a sea of mud if it was wet, and into a sheet of ice when it froze. Such supplies as there might have been along the way were devoured, and any available shelter was dismantled for firewood by those who had gone before. The road was littered with abandoned vehicles, dead horses, and jettisoned baggage and clogged by slow-moving stragglers and civilians—French and other foreign inhabitants of Moscow who feared the return of the Russians; Russians, particularly women and petty criminals, who had thrown their lot in with the French or been forcibly enlisted as wagoners or bearers; functionaries attached to the army; and officers' servants. Soldiers fell behind and became separated from their units by a mass of people, horses, and vehicles. After a time, most of them threw away their weapons and joined the crowd of stragglers, demoralised and guided by herd instinct, easy prey for pursuing cossacks.

The new moon on the night of 4 November brought a drop in temperature, and by the morning hundreds of undernourished men and horses had frozen to death. The men began adapting their dress to the cold: furs, shawls, and costly textiles brought along as gifts for wives or sweethearts were put on over uniforms, giving the retreating army a carnivalesque aspect. It did not protect them from frostbite, and as the inexperienced inhabitants of warmer climes had no idea how to restore circulation, many lost fingers, toes, ears, and noses. Cavalrymen had to dismount to prevent their feet freezing, and Napoleon, who had abandoned his uniform for a Polish-style fur-lined green velvet frock-coat and cap, got out of his carriage at intervals and tramped alongside his troops, with Berthier and Caulaincourt at his elbow.

On 6 November he was met by an *estafette* from Paris which brought news of an attempted coup aimed at overthrowing him. It had been quickly foiled, but it brought home to him the frailty of his rule, and he began to contemplate leaving the army and racing back to Paris. When he reached Smolensk on 9 November, the blanket of snow concealing the charred ruins allowed him to entertain for a while the feeling that he had reached safety. He set about organising winter quarters for the army, but found only a fraction of the stores he expected, barely enough for the 15,000 sick and wounded left behind after the storming of the city. Bad news poured in from all sides. Vitebsk had been taken by the Russians, a division had been forced to surrender south of Smolensk, and Eugène's Italian corps had lost almost a quarter of its effectives and fifty-eight guns while crossing a river. As his columns trudged in he could see how depleted they were; there were now no more than about 40,000 left with their colours.[19]

He took out his frustration on his marshals. 'There's not one of them to whom one can entrust anything; I always have to do everything myself,' he complained, refusing to accept responsibility for his predicament. 'And they accuse me of ambition, as though it was my ambition that brought me here! This war is only a matter of politics. What have I got to gain from a climate like this, from coming to a wretched country like this one? The whole of it is not worth the meanest little piece of France. They, on the other hand, have a very real interest in conquest: Poland, Germany, anything goes for them. Just seeing the sun six months of the year is a new pleasure for them. It is they that should be stopped, not me.'[20]

The retreat would have to go on, and fast, as two Russian pincers were converging in his rear, and Kutuzov was overtaking him to the south. Schwarzenberg had fallen back, not on Minsk, where he would have joined forces with Napoleon, but westward, back into Poland, leaving Napoleon's line of retreat exposed. Desperate not to lose face and not wishing to withdraw further than he absolutely had to, he refused to accept that he would not find winter quarters in Russia, and so put off until the last minute every decision to retreat further. He only left Smolensk on 14 November. Eugène, Davout, and Ney were to follow at one-day intervals.

As they set off the temperature dipped further, to as low as minus twenty degrees, and conditions deteriorated. Those who were still with their colours managed to provide themselves with food and shelter; when they could not get hold of rations they ate horses, then dogs and cats, and anything else they could lay hands on; sometimes no more than hot water with some axle-grease. But the growing number of stragglers were caught up in a desperate struggle for survival; they began to steal food and clothing from each other, callously stripping those too weak to resist. The cold was such that what food could be obtained froze so hard it could not be eaten, so horses were sliced up while still alive.

Napoleon himself had a regular supply of food and wine. An officer would ride ahead to select a place to stop for the night, sometimes a country house, sometimes a hut. The iron camp bed would be set up, a rug spread on the floor, and the *nécéssaire* containing razors, brushes, and toiletries brought in. A study would be improvised, in the same room if no other could be found, with a table covered in green cloth, his travelling library in its case, and the boxes containing maps and writing instruments. A small dinner service would be unpacked, so he could eat off plate. Even though he did have the luxury of a change of clothes, and despite the resources of the *nécéssaire*, he was infested with lice like the rest of his army. And despite the comforts of his camp bed, he suffered from insomnia. The night after leaving Smolensk, he called Caulaincourt to his bedside and discussed the necessity of his going back to Paris. He had just heard that the Russians had cut the road ahead near Krasny, and he could not rule out the possibility of being taken prisoner, so he had his physician Dr Yvan prepare him a dose of poison, which he kept in a black silk sachet around his neck.[21]

He fought his way through to Krasny, where he paused to allow the other corps to catch up, keeping the Russians at bay. 'Advancing with a firm step, as on the day of a great parade, he placed himself in the middle of the battlefield, facing the enemy's batteries,' in the words of Sergeant Bourgogne. Eugène's and Davout's corps got through, but Ney was still some way behind. Napoleon could not afford to wait any longer, as Kutuzov was by now threatening to cut his line of retreat to Orsha, and set off at the head of his grenadiers. 'The shells which flew over were bursting all round him without his seeming to notice,' recalled one of the few cavalrymen left in his escort.

The Emperor Napoleon I, painted in 1805 by Jacques-Louis David in the classic convention of the royal portrait established by the Sun King Louis XIV.

A fragment of Jacques-Louis David's painting of the coronation, showing, from left to right, Joseph, Louis, Napoleon's three sisters and Hortense, holding the hand of her son Napoléon-Charles.

Napoleon's youngest brother, the feckless Jérôme, 1805.

This depiction of Napoleon on the battlefield of Eylau by Antoine-Jean Gros was painted to strict instructions – that the emperor be represented casting 'a consoling eye' over the field of carnage in order 'to soften the horror of death' and exuding 'an aura of kindness and majestic splendour'. Note the fantastic 'Polish' costume of Murat, which Napoleon said made him look like a circus-master.

One of Napoleon's closest and dearest real friends, Marshal Jean Lannes, by François Gérard.

General Armand de Caulaincourt, who became a close and loyal confidant, sketched in 1805, by Jacques-Louis David.

Perhaps Napoleon's closest friend, General Géraud-Christophe Duroc, by Anne-Louis Girodet-Trioson.

Napoleon I on the Imperial Throne, painted in 1806 by Jean-Auguste-Dominique Ingres,
by which time the emperor was projecting the image of himself as a latter-day Charlemagne,
replicating the style and attributes recorded on Carolingian seals.

View of the proposed Palace for the King of Rome, by Pierre-François Fontaine.

This painting by Alexandre Menjaud of Napoleon *en famille* hugging the King of Rome is part of an iconography that sought to reassure ordinary Frenchmen that an era of peace and stability had dawned, yet it was strikingly at odds with his escalating imperial programme.

Napoleon in his study at the height of his power, in early 1812, by Jacques-Louis David.

Napoleon on the bridge of HMS *Bellerophon* after giving himself up to the British in 1815, by an evidently unimpressed witness, Charles Lock Eastlake.

The house at Longwood on the island of St Helena, where Napoleon spent his last years and died, photographed *c.* 1940.

Napoleon on St Helena, drawn in June 1820 by a clearly unsympathetic British visitor.

That morning he had told Roguet it was time he stopped playing the emperor and became the general once more.[22]

On reaching Orsha on 19 November, he set about rallying the remains of his army. He ordered everything surplus to requirements to be burnt—including the portrait of the King of Rome. He forced stragglers to rejoin their regiments and distributed the supplies stored in the town. He was overjoyed when Ney, who had cleverly circumvented the Russian force blocking his path, rejoined him at Orsha. The five days of fighting around Krasny had cost him possibly as many as 10,000 of his best remaining soldiers and more than 200 guns, but he refused to give in to despair.[23]

'Although this man was rightly regarded as the author of all our misfortunes and the unique cause of our disaster,' wrote Dr René Bourgeois, who held profoundly anti-Napoleonic political views, 'his presence still elicited enthusiasm, and there was nobody who would not, if the need arose, have covered him with their body and sacrificed their lives for him.' One of his aides, Anatole de Montesquiou, explains that they owed everything to Napoleon's ability not to show his feelings. 'In the midst of the overwhelming horrors which seemed to be pursuing or rather enveloping us with the perseverance of fatality, we recovered peace of mind and hope by turning our eyes on the Emperor,' he wrote. 'More unfortunate than any of us, since he was losing more, he remained impassive.' He represented their best chance of getting out of the mess they were in, and his stoicism gave them comfort. 'His presence electrified our downcast hearts and gave us a last burst of energy,' wrote Captain François. Whatever their nationality and their political attitude, men and officers alike realised that only he could keep the remains of the army together and snatch some shreds of victory from the jaws of defeat.[24]

Napoleon's glory was their common property, and to diminish his reputation by denouncing him would have been to destroy the fund they had built up over the years, which was their most prized possession. According to the British general Wilson, who was attached to the Russian army, even when taken prisoner, they 'could not be induced by any temptation, by any threats, by any privations, to cast reproach on their emperor as the cause of their misfortunes and sufferings'. These were about to increase dramatically.[25]

On 22 November Napoleon learned that his supply base at Minsk had fallen to the Russians. He was momentarily 'struck with consternation' and sat up all night talking to Duroc and Daru, admitting that he had been foolish to invade Russia. Another piece of bad news came two days later: the only bridge over the river Berezina at Borisov had been burnt, and a Russian force held the far bank. 'Any other man would have been overwhelmed,' wrote Caulaincourt. 'The Emperor showed himself to be greater than his misfortune. Instead of discouraging him, these adversities brought out all the energy of this great character; he showed what a noble courage and a brave army can achieve against even the greatest adversity.'[26]

Having learned of a ford some twelve kilometres north and upstream from Borisov, he made a feint to the south and managed to convey false intelligence to the Russians on the opposite bank that he was aiming to make a crossing there, then marched north to the ford

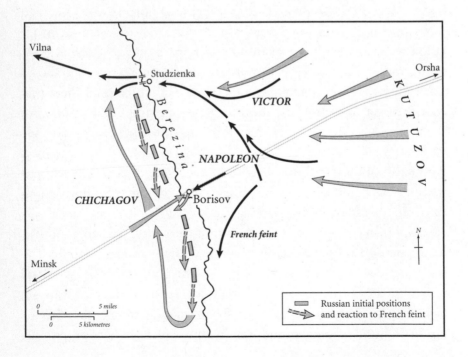

at Studzienka. 'Our position is impossible,' Ney said to Rapp. 'If Napoleon succeeds in getting out of this today he is the very Devil.' Napoleon had regained his composure and inspired his shattered army to one last act of heroism. He stood on the bank as his sappers dismantled the wooden houses of the village, and 400 Dutch engineers began building a trestle bridge across the river. Stripping off, they worked up to their necks in the icy water, battling the current and avoiding the large blocks of ice being carried along by it. They completed one bridge, a hundred metres long and four wide, and began work on a second as units still capable of fighting crossed and took up defensive positions on the opposite bank, shouting '*Vive l'Empereur!*' as they marched past. He himself crossed on 27 November, along with most of the units still with their colours. The infantry and cavalry used the first bridge, while the artillery, baggage train, and carriages carrying the wounded took the second. The crush of men and horses on the frail structures resulted in many ending up in the water, and when the Russian guns on the eastern bank opened up that afternoon, confusion and panic added to the casualties. Over the whole of that day and the next, the remnants of the army, followed by the mass of stragglers and civilians, struggled across while Marshal Victor's depleted but still battleworthy corps held off the converging Russian armies. But it could not prevent them from shelling the crush of people and vehicles on the bridges and those waiting their turn to cross, turning the scene into one of indescribable horror, with people being shot, trampled, or pushed into the icy water. The Russian forces on the western bank had also come up by now, but they were held off by units of Swiss, Dutch, Poles, Italians, Croats, and Portuguese under Oudinot and Ney. That night, Victor crossed with his corps, and in the morning the bridges were destroyed, leaving a considerable number of stragglers and civilians to their fate.[27]

Napoleon's bold manoeuvre had extricated him and most of the remaining army from a seemingly fatal trap. Over the three days of the crossing the French had lost up to 25,000, many of them civilians or non-combatant stragglers, and inflicted losses of at least 15,000 on the Russians, all of them soldiers. The operation was not only a magnificent feat of arms; it was an extraordinary demonstration of the resilience of the Napoleonic military machine and of his ability to inspire men of well over half a dozen different nations to fight like lions for a cause which was not theirs.

Buoyed by the miraculous escape and the feeling that they had once more triumphed over the odds, the remnants of the Grande Armée made a dash for Vilna, where they would be safe and where there were abundant victuals. But at this point the temperature sank to a new low, recorded by some as minus thirty-five and a half degrees. Many froze to death during this last march, and those who did not walked in a state described by some as akin to drunkenness, while others were struck with snow-blindness and had to be led.

Napoleon instructed Maret to send away any foreign diplomats, so they should not see the condition of his army, and badgered him for news from Paris, demanding to know why no *estafette* had reached him for eighteen days. Maret was to spread news of a victory at the Berezina, in which the French had taken thousands of prisoners and twelve standards. Ironically, the next day Alexander held a service of thanksgiving in St Petersburg, having been informed by Kutuzov that he had won a resounding victory on the Berezina. Napoleon could no longer hope to fool people, and on 3 December he dictated the 29th Bulletin of the campaign, in which he described the disaster, finishing off with the phrase: 'His Majesty's health has never been better.' He had to stop playing the general and become emperor once more—which meant he must get to Paris as quickly as possible to reassure his subjects.[28]

Against the advice of Maret, who said the army would fall apart without him, he decided to leave immediately. Ignoring advice to put Eugène in command, he chose Murat, fearing that his brother-in-law would not obey him and would seize the perceived insult as an excuse to march back to Naples. Napoleon set off on the evening of 5 December, with Caulaincourt, Duroc, and a couple of other officers, and Roustam, Constant, and Fain, escorted by Polish and Neapolitan cavalry. The cold was intense, shattering the wine bottles in Napoleon's carriage as their contents froze and cutting a swathe through the escort, which lost all of its Italians along the way. At one point they narrowly missed being intercepted by marauding cossacks. Napoleon had a pair of loaded pistols with him and instructed his companions to kill him if he failed to do so himself in the event of capture.[29]

Two days later, having recrossed the Niemen, he felt safe. He transferred to an old carriage mounted on runners and chatted to Caulaincourt as they sped along with snow blowing in through the cracks around the ill-fitting doors. He went over the events that had led up to the war, which he repeatedly insisted never having wanted. 'People do not understand: I am not ambitious,' he complained. 'The lack of sleep, the effort, war itself, these are not for someone of my age. I love my bed and rest more than anyone, but I have to finish the work I have embarked on.' His conversation kept drifting back to the subject of Britain, the one obstacle to the desired peace; he was fighting the fiendish islanders on behalf of the whole of Europe, which did not realise that it was being exploited by them.[30]

He had talked himself into a good mood by the time they reached Warsaw on the evening of 10 December, and in order to stretch his legs he got out at the city gate and walked through the streets to the Hôtel d'Angleterre, where the sleigh had been sent on. Nobody took any notice of the small, plump man in his green velvet overcoat and fur hat, which covered most of his face. He seemed almost disappointed.

He continued to talk with animation while dinner was prepared and a servant girl struggled to light a fire in the freezing room they had taken. Caulaincourt had been sent to fetch Pradt, who was struck by the jolly mood of the emperor when he arrived. Dismissing his own failure with the phrase 'From the sublime to the ridiculous there is but one step,' he berated Pradt for having failed to galvanise Poland, raise money, and furnish men. He said he had never seen any Polish troops during the whole campaign and accused the Poles of being ineffectual and cowardly.[31]

His tone changed with the appearance of the Polish ministers he had summoned. He admitted to having suffered a major reversal but assured them that he had 120,000 men at Vilna, and that he would be back in the spring with a new army. In the meantime, they must raise money and a mass levy in order to defend the grand duchy. They stood around getting progressively colder as he paced up and down, warmed by his fantasy. 'I beat the Russians every time,' he told them. 'They don't dare to stand up to us. They are no longer the soldiers of Eylau and Friedland. We will hold Wilna, and I shall be back with 300,000 men. Success will make the Russians foolhardy; I will fight them two or three times on the Oder, and in six months' time I will be back on the Niemen....All that has happened is of no consequence; it was a misfortune, it was the effect of the climate; the enemy had nothing to do with it; I beat them every time....' And so it went on, with the occasional self-justificatory 'He who hazards nothing gains nothing,' and the frequent repetition of the phrase he had just coined, and which he appeared to relish: 'From the sublime to the ridiculous there is but one step.'[32]

Having had dinner, Napoleon climbed back into his sleigh and set off for Paris. When he realised they were passing not far from the country house of Maria Walewska, in a sudden surge of gallantry he decided to call on her. Caulaincourt had the greatest difficulty in convincing him that not only would this delay their arrival in Paris (and increase the danger that some German patriot might get to hear of their passage and ambush them), it would be an insult to Marie-Louise, and public opinion would never forgive him for going off to indulge his lust while his army was freezing to death in Lithuania.

As they sped on, Napoleon turned over the whole political situation again and again, as though he were trying to convince himself that the Russian campaign had been only a minor setback. 'I made a mistake, *Monsieur le Grand Écuyer*, not on the aim or the political opportunity of the war, but in the manner in which I waged it,' he said, giving Caulaincourt's ear an affectionate tug. 'I should have stopped at Witepsk. Alexander would now be at my knees. [...] I stayed two weeks too long in Moscow.'[33]

This was true. Two weeks before Napoleon left Moscow, Kutuzov had no more than about 60,000 men and was in no condition to engage him; he could have withdrawn down any road he chose. He would have been able to evacuate his wounded and equipment and get back to Minsk and Vilna before the temperature dropped. Most Russians at the time, as well as observers such as Clausewitz, agreed that the French defeat had nothing to do with Kutuzov and everything to do with the weather. 'One has to admit,' wrote Schwarzenberg, who referred to the field marshal as *'l'imbécile Kutuzov'*, 'that this is the most astonishing kick from a donkey any mortal has ever had the whim to court.'[34]

39

Hollow Victories

NAPOLEON REACHED DRESDEN in the early hours of 14 December 1812 and stopped at the French minister's lodgings. He dictated letters to his German allies and sent an officer to the royal palace to summon the King of Saxony. Frederick Augustus dressed hurriedly and arrived by sedan chair at the French minister's residence. Napoleon, who had managed to snatch an hour's sleep, was sitting up in bed. He reassured the astonished king that he would be back in the spring with a new army and asked him to raise more troops. He also borrowed a comfortable carriage from him in which he resumed his journey, pausing only to change horses. At some stops he would not even leave the carriage. At Weimar he leaned out of the window to ask someone to convey his respects to 'Monsieur Gött'. At Verdun he bought some sugar-coated almonds, the regional speciality, for Marie-Louise, saying that one could not return to one's sweetheart without a gift. He asked the serving girl whether she had one, and on hearing that she did, asked what was locally considered to be a respectable dowry, promising to send her the sum once he reached Paris.[1]

Four days after leaving Dresden his carriage trundled up to the Tuileries. It was a few minutes before midnight, and although he was unshaven and barely recognisable in his fur overcoat and cap, he marched into the apartment of Marie-Louise, who was preparing for bed. Before allowing Caulaincourt to go home and rest, he ordered him to call on Cambacérès, to inform him of his return and tell him to announce that there would be a regular *lever* in the morning.

The twenty-ninth Bulletin had been published three days earlier. For over a decade these had contained only tidings of victory, and people were stunned to read an admission of failure. Before they could recover from the shock or start drawing conclusions, on the morning of 19 December the cannon of the Invalides notified them with an imperial salute of Napoleon's return. The master was back, behaving as though the events of the past few months had been no more than a minor difficulty. 'I am very pleased with the mood of the nation,' he wrote to Murat, addressing the letter to Vilna. But by the time he was writing out that address, Vilna was in Russian hands and Kutuzov was attending a gala organised in his honour by the nervous inhabitants.[2]

On leaving the Grande Armée, Napoleon calculated optimistically that he still had some 150,000 men holding the eastern wall of his imperium, with 60,000 under Murat at Vilna, 25,000 under Macdonald to the north, 30,000 Austrian allies to the south under Schwarzenberg, Poniatowski's Polish corps and the remainder of the Saxon contingent covering Warsaw, and over 25,000 men in reserve depots or fortresses from Danzig on the Baltic down to Zamość. He was confident of being able to raise 350,000 men and come to their aid in the spring.[3]

The fiery Murat was magnificent when given a tall order on the battlefield, but, as Berthier pointed out, 'The King of Naples is in every respect the man least capable of overall command.' He had failed to hold Vilna, declaring to Berthier before leaving that he was not going to let himself be besieged in that 'pisspot'. The resulting confusion had prevented an orderly evacuation even by those units still capable of action, and a couple of days later not many more than 10,000 men recrossed the river Niemen. For political reasons it was expedient to keep the King of Naples on-side, so instead of a reprimand, Napoleon sent him a friendly note saying that the mood in Paris was positive and reinforcements were on their way.[4]

He told anyone who would listen that the outcome of the campaign was due to extraneous factors. 'My losses are substantial, but the enemy can take no credit for them,' as he put it in a letter to the King of Denmark. The losses were more than substantial, since some 400,000 French and allied troops had perished or gone missing during the campaign—less than a quarter of them combat casualties. Among those losses were some of the most experienced soldiers, non-commissioned officers (NCOs) and officers, the backbone of the army, without whom it would be difficult to rebuild a new one. They included cavalrymen whom it had taken years to train, not only to fight on horseback but also to look after horses. It would take years to replace the more than 100,000 horses, along with the hundreds of thousands of muskets and swords, not to mention the cannon, gun carriages, ammunition wagons, and the vast quantity of harness and other essential equipment.[5]

The losses did not end there. Méneval's constitution had been so undermined that he could no longer work, Junot returned a broken man, and many others were badly maimed, mentally as well as physically. It had required all his powers of self-possession, Napoleon explained to Molé, to repress all signs of emotion, but he too had been tried by the experience. 'I showed a serenity, I might even say gaiety throughout, and I do not think anyone who saw me then could deny it,' he said to Molé. But it had cost him. 'Without such command over myself, do you think I could have achieved all I have done?'[6]

To Hortense, who saw him shortly after his return, he seemed 'tired, preoccupied but not crestfallen'. Mollien was astonished when he called at the Tuileries: a few days before Napoleon left for Russia, Mollien's wife had fallen dangerously ill, and Napoleon's first words to him on his return were to enquire of her health. Another who was struck by the emperor's serenity was Frederick William's envoy Prince Hatzfeldt. 'In general, I can assure Your Majesty on my honour that on no other occasion when I have been with the Emperor have I found him so gay, so affable and so pronounced in his opinions and his hopes than on this,' he reported.[7]

Napoleon meant to show that nothing had changed, so he rode out inspecting public building works with Fontaine and insisted that the carnival go ahead as usual, even though tens of thousands were mourning their dead or anxiously waiting for news of loved ones who had gone missing. The balls were not calculated to spread merriment, as so many of the dancers had no arms, wooden legs, or lacked noses, ears and fingers lost to frostbite. His feeling did show on occasion, and as he took leave of him in March, the prefect Joseph Fiévée noted 'a dark sadness' in his eyes.[8]

While the immediate reason for leaving his army and returning to Paris was to muster fresh forces with which to march out in the spring and relieve those he had left behind, what really preoccupied Napoleon on his return was something entirely different.[9]

On the night of 23 October, as he was beginning his retreat from Moscow, General Claude-François Malet and a handful of others had made an audacious attempt to seize power by calling on key officials, announcing that the emperor was dead and brandishing faked documents authorising them to take over. They had managed to fool a number of people, including the prefect of Paris, Nicolas Frochot, and arrested the minister of police, Savary, before they were stopped. They were promptly tried, and twelve were shot, before Napoleon even came to hear of the attempted coup, which made some wonder whether the speed had not been dictated by the wish to prevent further investigations, a suspicion fuelled by the enmity between the two ministers conducting them, Clarke and Savary. Malet had already conspired to mount a coup in 1808 but had been caught and sent to a madhouse. When asked by the general presiding over the court-martial whether he had any accomplices, he had replied, 'The whole of France and you yourself, if I had been successful.' The police had stumbled on another conspiracy in the Midi, which involved a number of republicans, among them Barras, and there was undoubtedly much discontent with Napoleon's rule. But that was not what shocked and disturbed him.[10]

On hearing the news of his death in Russia, those who believed it had not reacted in the appropriate manner, which, he pointed out to the Council of State and the Senate when they came to greet him, would have been to proclaim the accession of his son. 'Our fathers rallied to the cry: "*The king is dead, long live the king!*"' he reminded them, adding that 'these few words encompass the principal advantages of monarchy'. The fact that they had not been uttered on the night of 23 October spelled out to him that for all its trappings, the monarchy he had created lacked credibility. It was a severe blow to his self-esteem as well as to his political edifice, calling into question the very basis of his right to rule.[11]

From Dresden on his way back to Paris, Napoleon had written to his father-in-law asking him to double the contingent of Austrian troops defending the grand duchy of Warsaw and to send a reliable ambassador to Paris. Francis sent General Ferdinand Bubna, whom Napoleon knew and liked. At their first meeting, on the evening of 31 December 1812, Bubna made an offer on the part of Austria to mediate in peace negotiations between France and Russia. Napoleon debated with Cambacérès, Talleyrand, and Caulaincourt, as well as Maret, on whether it would be better to accept this offer or to try and strike a deal directly with Russia, over the heads and possibly at the expense of Austria and Prussia. He listened to their opinions without committing to either course.[12]

He wanted peace, probably more than any of his enemies. He was forty-three years old. 'I am growing heavy and too fat not to like rest, not to need it, not to regard the displacements and activity demanded by war as a great fatigue,' he confessed to Caulaincourt. He knew that Austria, Prussia, and all his other German allies also longed for peace and that they feared the involvement of Russia in German affairs even more than they disliked his dominance. From certain statements it is clear that he had come to appreciate that the terms of Tilsit were too hard on Russia and that he might be prepared to make concessions, particularly if a general settlement including Britain could be agreed. But he had an innate reluctance to negotiate from anything other than a position of strength. He also believed, as he explained to Mollien, that if he were to sign a peace he himself had not dictated, nobody would believe in his sincerity. Perhaps more important, he felt a need to restore his credentials as a ruler, called into question by the Malet affair, and as he believed these were based on military glory, the only way to do so was to re-establish his reputation as a general.[13]

The Senate agreed to raise 350,000 fresh troops, 150,000 of them to be conscripted in advance from those normally eligible in 1814, another 100,000 from those who had been eligible in previous years but had not been called up, and a further 100,000 from the ranks of the National Guard. In the event, probably no more than two-thirds of that number would join the colours, many of them of doubtful quality. They could not all be provided with uniforms and arms, and despite enormous effort, no more than 29,000 horses could be found, which would not provide for the needs of cavalry, artillery, and transport. The improved situation in Spain allowed Napoleon to withdraw four Guard regiments, the mounted gendarmerie, and some Polish cavalry from the Peninsula.[14]

'Everything is in motion,' he wrote to Berthier on 9 January 1813. 'There is nothing lacking, neither men, nor money, nor good will.' He appears to have elicited more sympathy than blame for what had happened in Russia, and he received many marks of support. Not all were of much use: Louis, who had just published a crass novel titled *Marie, ou les peines de l'amour*, wrote to his brother from his retreat in Gratz offering to return to Holland and galvanise the Dutch. Lucien, who had settled in England to write a new version of the *Odyssey*, had approached the foreign secretary, Lord Castlereagh, with a proposal to broker an alliance between Britain and Joseph in Spain. Jérôme had whiled away his time since leaving Napoleon in Russia with his three mistresses, and in November he unveiled a nine-foot-tall statue of himself on the Place Royale of Kassel.[15]

The perceived danger threatening France helped the mobilisation. There was much discontent and grumbling about the call-up, but, as even a declared enemy of Napoleon had to admit, once conscripted the young men marched out shouting '*Vive l'Empereur!*' The conscripts, known as '*les Marie-Louise*' (as she had signed the call-up decree in Napoleon's absence), were kitted out in a simplified uniform, with trousers rather than breeches, and no waistcoat. There were not enough officers to lead them, but Napoleon hoped to find these among the remains of the Grande Armée recuperating in Poland and Germany, since it was officers and NCOs who made up the majority of the survivors.[16]

He worked tirelessly, not only forming up the new army, but also shoring up his authority and tidying up affairs neglected during the retreat from Moscow. More than a thousand letters of his survive from the first four months of 1813, most of them long and detailed.

Quite a few of them relate to the situation in Spain, where although the military position had stabilised, Joseph and Soult were at logger-heads. A more pressing issue was that of finance: juggle the figures as he might, he could not find enough money for his needs, and mili-tary expenditure was now absorbing around 65 percent of state rev-enue. He put on a brave face, but the situation was not good, and on his return from a performance at the Théâtre Français on the evening of 9 January 1813 he received more unwelcome news.[17]

On 30 December 1812 General Yorck von Wartemburg, com-mander of the Prussian corps in the Grande Armée, detached it from the French units and effectively signed his own alliance with Russia. Following fast on this news came the assurance that Frederick Wil-liam had denounced the move and dismissed Yorck, but that was a meaningless gesture, since he and his men had already joined the Russian army.

Frederick William was in an unenviable position. The French garrison in the fortress of Spandau paraded through Berlin, remind-ing him that there were more French than Prussian troops in the country. The probability was that Napoleon would be back in the spring with a fresh army with which he would crush the Russians. In the circumstances, both he and his chancellor, Baron August von Hardenberg, agreed that alliance with Napoleon was the lesser of two evils. He sent Prince Hatzfeldt to Paris with the proposal of a closer alliance against Russia, to be sealed by the marriage of the Prussian crown prince to a princess of the house of Bonaparte. But Napoleon did not mean to tie himself to Prussia.[18]

He believed that his father-in-law, the Emperor Francis, would stand by him: Napoleon was so besotted by Marie-Louise and his son that he assumed Francis must share those feelings for his favourite daughter and grandson. 'Our alliance with France is so necessary that if you were to break it off today, we would propose to re-establish it tomorrow on the very same conditions,' Metternich had told Na-poleon's ambassador in Vienna, explaining that only France could counterbalance the threat presented by Russia.[19]

Kutuzov and most senior Russian officers were against carrying the war into Germany, and most of the Russians around the tsar felt that Russia should do no more than help herself to East Prussia and much of Poland, providing herself with some territorial gain and a defensible western border. But Alexander had undergone a spiritual awakening and had come to see himself as an instrument of the Almighty destined to free Europe from the spirit of Godlessness, of which Napoleon was the epitome. He pressed on, occupying East Prussia and the grand duchy of Warsaw, bringing in his wake a bevy of German nationalists bent on raising the whole of Germany against Napoleon.[20]

In the absence of any encouragement from Napoleon, and as most of his army was by then operating in defiance of him, Frederick William was obliged to accept Alexander's offer of an alliance and on 16 March declared war on France. The two monarchs accompanied this with a proclamation calling on Germans everywhere to rise up and help them overthrow the Confederation of the Rhine and warning its German rulers that if they did not join in this venture they would lose their thrones.[21]

Nobody was more alarmed by this than Metternich. While he and Francis were eager to exclude French influence from Germany, they did not wish to see it replaced by a Russian hegemony, and the proclamation threatened to arouse revolutionary and nationalist passions that could undermine the Habsburg state. Although Metternich had lamented the abolition of the Holy Roman Empire, he could appreciate the usefulness of the Confederation of the Rhine. And he did not agree that Napoleon must be got rid of at any cost.[22]

He hoped the Russian campaign had sobered him enough to make him realise his best option was to make peace—a peace Metternich would broker, with attendant advantages to Austria. First, he had to extricate Austria from her alliance with France. Only then could he cast Austria in the role of honest broker (and forestall the possibility of Russia and France reaching a deal over his head). To strengthen his position, he ordered the mobilisation of Austria's armed forces.[23]

Metternich had been in secret communication with the Russian court throughout the past year, and although obliged to send an Austrian corps into Russia as part of Napoleon's invasion force, he had instructed its commander, Schwarzenberg, to avoid fighting. When the Russians began to advance, Schwarzenberg pulled back into Poland, and in January 1813 he began evacuating the grand duchy of Warsaw, which he was supposed to defend in common with Poniatowski's Polish army. Schwarzenberg signed a secret convention with the Russians and withdrew from their path, forcing Poniatowski to fall back, opening Poland and the road west to the Russians.

Metternich also wanted to involve Britain, and in February 1813 he sent an envoy to London to sound out the British cabinet on whether it would agree to participate in negotiations under Austrian mediation. Since Marie-Louise's marriage to Napoleon, the view in London was that Austria was a close ally of France, and Metternich's move was viewed as some kind of intrigue. What neither Metternich nor Napoleon appreciated was that Alexander was on a mission; negotiations were far from his mind, and his troops were on the move.[24]

Before he could march out to face them, Napoleon needed to prepare the ground at home. At the opening of a new session of the Legislative Assembly, he astonished its members with an extraordinary speech asserting that he had 'triumphed over every obstacle' during his Russian campaign. He assured them that he desired peace and would do everything to further it, but that he would never make a dishonourable one. He painted a reassuring picture of the state of affairs: the Bonaparte dynasty was secure in Spain, and there was nothing alarming about the situation in Germany. 'I am satisfied with the conduct of all my allies,' he stated. 'I will not abandon any of them; I shall defend the integrity of their possessions. The Russians will be forced back into their horrible climate.' For good measure, he nominated a dozen new members solidly loyal to him to keep an eye on the others.[25]

Having at last accepted that his treatment of the Pope was alienating people all over Europe and undermining his standing in France, on 19 January he went to Fontainebleau, where the pontiff had been confined. After a preliminary meeting at which good intentions were professed on both sides, he returned on 25 February with a protocol which amounted to a partial climbdown, the details of which were to be determined at a later date. The Pope was ill and in no condition to resist, so he agreed to it. Napoleon promptly announced that a new concordat had been signed. The Pope abrogated the agreement three days later and issued a formal retraction on 24 March, but Napoleon ignored it, and since the retraction was not published his version stuck.

He then turned his attention to the coming campaign. Following his failure to rally the remnants of the Grande Armée at Vilna and then at Königsberg in East Prussia, on 16 January Murat had left his post and gone back to Naples. He had already opened secret negotiations with Austria as, sensing the possibility of further French defeats, he was determined to ensure the survival of his own throne; when Davout tried to stop him, reminding him that he had only acquired it 'by the grace of Napoleon and French blood', Murat retorted that he was king by the grace of God.[26]

Eugène, who had taken his place, managed to stabilise a front along the Vistula but was gradually obliged to pull it back to the Oder and then the Elbe, leaving behind French garrisons in fortresses such as Danzig, Modlin, and Magdeburg. They would be of use to Napoleon, who planned to take French forces back across the Niemen into Russia. On 11 March he sketched a bold plan for a sweep through Berlin and Danzig into Poland. From Krakow, Poniatowski supported by the Austrians would strike northward and cut the Russian army's lines of communication.[27]

These plans were disrupted, but Napoleon's confidence was not shaken when, on 27 March, the Prussian ambassador in Paris announced Prussia's declaration of war. Napoleon's reaction was to instruct his ambassador in Vienna, Narbonne, to offer Austria the Prussian province of Silesia (which the Prussians had captured from Austria in 1745) as a prize if she stood by France. Metternich could do without Silesia and did not mean to go to war again at the side of France. In order to persuade Napoleon to negotiate, he sent Schwarzenberg to Paris with instructions to make clear that while Austria would support France in pursuit of a fair peace, she did not feel bound to do so unconditionally and that Napoleon's marriage to Marie-Louise counted for nothing. Napoleon ignored these warnings as he prepared to restore his position by military means before entering into any negotiations.[28]

How sure of himself he felt is open to question; unnerved by the implications of the Malet coup, he had set the Council of State the task of devising a mechanism that would ensure the survival of his dynasty if anything were to happen to him. Accordingly, a *senatus-consulte* of 5 February 1813 gave Marie-Louise the status of regent for the King of Rome, with a Regency Council made up of the principal grand officers of the empire.

Schwarzenberg, who had a long interview with Napoleon at Saint-Cloud on 13 April, found him less belligerent than in the past and genuinely eager to avoid war. 'His language was less peremptory and, like his whole demeanour, less self-assured; he gave the impression of a man who fears losing the prestige which surrounded him, and his eyes seemed to be asking me whether I still saw in him the same man as before.' Thirty-six hours later Napoleon left for the army, which he joined at Erfurt on 25 April. He was hoping to defeat the Russians and Prussians before tackling negotiations with Austria and instructed Marie-Louise to keep her father from making a move prematurely. 'Write to Papa François once a week,' he wrote to her from Mainz, 'inform him of the military situation and assure him of my fondness for him.'[29]

Alexander and Frederick William had already taken the offensive. With the Prussian army under General Gebhard Blücher in the van, they invaded Saxony, denouncing its king as a tool of Napoleon and a traitor to their cause. As Alexander was intending to hold on to Prussia's former Polish provinces, he had promised to compensate Frederick William with territorial 'equivalents' at the expense of Saxony. Both therefore hoped that Frederick Augustus would not declare for the allies.

Frederick Augustus was one of the few European monarchs endowed with a sense of honour and was genuinely attached to Napoleon. He was both unwilling to cast off his alliance with him and afraid of doing so. He sidestepped the issue by taking refuge in Austria, which promised to protect him and his kingdom. Not long after he left his capital, Dresden was occupied by Alexander and Frederick William, who marched in at the head of their troops, some 100,000 Russians and Prussians commanded by the Russian general Wittgenstein and the Prussian Blücher. They then moved out to face the French forces concentrating around Erfurt.

Napoleon's appearance there exerted the old magic on the troops. 'The joy of the army was extraordinary and each of us, forgetting the sufferings we had experienced, was already looking forward to victory and, after that, to the longed-for peace,' recalled a lieutenant of the Lancers of the Vistula. 'The army is superb,' General Bertrand wrote to his wife, Fanny. Colonel Pelleport found his men 'confident, looking forward to meeting the enemy'.[30]

Napoleon advanced swiftly, making for Leipzig. The allied army attacked his right flank at Lützen on 2 May, where Ney held it off while Napoleon doubled back to take charge and lead the young conscripts into the attack. They showed remarkable enthusiasm and advanced on the enemy guns fearlessly, throwing the allies back in disorder. The victory was not decisive, as shortage of cavalry prevented Napoleon from pursuing the enemy and turning it into a rout. Although he trumpeted the news of a great victory for propaganda purposes, he was not satisfied. To Eugène he admitted that in view of the insignificant number of prisoners taken it was no victory at all.[31]

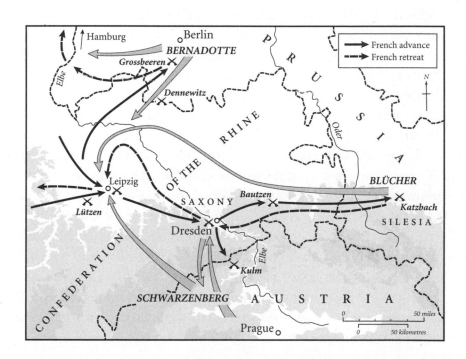

Alexander, who had been present along with Frederick William, made light of the defeat, but it cast a pall over the allied army. The Prussians had suffered painful losses, and mutual recriminations followed, as they blamed the Russians for not holding firm and vice-versa. Although the retreat was orderly, Alexander and Frederick William had to abandon Dresden and take refuge in Silesia. The King of Saxony hurried back to his capital to greet Napoleon. 'I am once more the master of Europe,' Napoleon declared to Duroc.[32]

Metternich assumed that their defeat would have sobered the allies and made them realise they needed the support of Austria, while its limited nature would not have given Napoleon enough confidence to make him intransigent. This raised the Austrian chancellor's hopes, but he believed the only way he could persuade Napoleon to agree to negotiate was by suggesting he would only have to make minor concessions to obtain peace. Narbonne correctly surmised that Metternich was hoping to get Napoleon to agree to negotiations in principle, and then start upping the terms, thereby forcing him to either accept these or break off the negotiations, which would allow Austria to declare their alliance null. Sensing that he was getting nowhere with Narbonne, Metternich resolved to address Napoleon through Bubna.[33]

Napoleon fortified Dresden, which he intended to use as the base from which he would strike at the allied armies converging on the Elbe. Wishing to dispense with etiquette, he put up not in the royal palace but in the Marcolini Palace, set in extensive gardens on the outskirts of the city. Here he could behave as though he were on campaign, working and resting to a rhythm set by the demands of war and diplomacy. A daily *estafette* from Paris brought news of everything that was going on not merely in the capital but throughout his realm. Agents all over Germany reported on events and morale.

Bubna arrived on 16 May with Metternich's suggested bases for negotiation: Napoleon should give up the grand duchy of Warsaw, cede German territory east of the Rhine, and return Illyria to Austria. The interview quickly turned into a harangue as Napoleon accused Austria of duplicity and of arming and negotiating with France's enemies while pretending to remain her ally. He pointed out that

Schwarzenberg's withdrawal from Poland had been a betrayal of their alliance; at their last meeting in Paris, Schwarzenberg had sworn that the 30,000-strong Austrian auxiliary corps was still at his disposal, only to withdraw it when the Russians appeared.

As for the suggested bases for negotiation, Napoleon declared that they were both insulting to him and obviously too minimal to satisfy his enemies. Narbonne had warned him that there was 'an underground connection' between Vienna and the Russian headquarters, and he realised a trap was being set for him. He told Bubna that he regretted having married Francis's daughter and declared that he would not give up a single village.[34]

At one point during the five-and-a-half-hour meeting, Napoleon launched into a diatribe about the importance of maintaining his honour, arguing that if the people of France were to conclude he had failed them, or worse, betrayed them as Louis XVI had done under the influence of his Austrian consort, he and Marie-Louise might end up just as they did, hinting at the possibility of her and her son being murdered by the Paris mob. While this may have been a crude attempt at blackmailing Francis, he does appear to have worked himself into a genuine frenzy on the subject. Less than two months later, when berating the Leipzig authorities over their poor handling of some anti-French disturbances in the city, he mentioned the September massacres of 1792 in language which suggests that he still feared the mob.[35]

Although he blustered at Bubna, he was far from confident and realised that if he refused to go along with the proposed negotiations he would be isolating himself, so at a final interview he told Bubna he was prepared to make peace, on terms to be discussed. As soon as Bubna had left Dresden, Napoleon despatched Caulaincourt to the Russian front lines with the request for an immediate ceasefire and for one-to-one talks between France and Russia. If he were going to be forced to give up the grand duchy of Warsaw, he might as well use it to bribe Russia into ditching Prussia and Austria. His instructions to Caulaincourt were to offer to 'destroy Poland forever'; his Polish aide, Chłapowski, who escorted Caulaincourt and stole a glance at them, was so appalled he resolved to leave Napoleon's service as soon as the fighting was over.[36]

The offer was rejected, so on 20 May Napoleon struck again. He outflanked the new allied defensive positions behind the river Spree around Bautzen, forcing them to abandon the field and beat a retreat. Had Ney not wasted an hour getting into position in the allied rear, their army would have been all but annihilated. Once again Napoleon had demonstrated that he was still the greatest general in Europe. The sureness of his touch impressed everyone, as did his decision to take a two-hour nap in the middle of the battle. 'Lulled by the sound of artillery and musketry the Emperor lay down on a cloak laid on the ground and gave orders that he was not to be woken before two hours, and in the calmest way went to sleep before us,' noted one of his aides. He did not even wake when a shell landed and burst close by. Although his shortage of cavalry once again prevented him from exploiting his victory, morale on the allied side plummeted as the Russians and Prussians trudged back into Silesia.[37]

The Russian army, some of whose units were down to a quarter of their nominal strength, was in poor condition. The rank and file, mostly drafted in 1812 to resist the foreign invader, had been promised they could go home once the fatherland had been liberated. Only junior officers avid for glory and promotion wanted to take the war into Germany. As far as the rest were concerned the conquest of Poland was enough of a prize. Tensions were mounting between them and their Prussian allies, and there were instances of individual commanders refusing to carry out orders given by allied superiors.

If Napoleon continued his advance, the Russians would be forced to fall back into Poland while the Prussian forces would have to retreat northwards, as Oudinot operating on Napoleon's left flank threatened Berlin. This would split the allied army in two, making it easy to defeat separately. Although the French lines of communication would be stretched by such an advance, that would be made up for by the troops Napoleon would release from fortresses in Poland. Morale in the Russian army might well be tipped over the edge. The retreat would also dampen the enthusiasm of the German nationalists. As it was, the number of volunteers coming forward to fight for the liberation of Germany was disappointing; it was proving difficult to raise troops, and desertion was on the rise, even among officers.[38]

But Napoleon was worried by the state of his own forces. French losses had been heavy. Shortage of cavalry restricted reconnaissance as well as pursuit. Paucity of draught animals meant there was a shortage of food and supplies. To add to the misery, the spring of 1813 was unusually cold and wet. Rates of desertion rose, particularly in the contingents contributed by Napoleon's German allies. Most of his marshals had had enough. 'What a war!' Augereau complained. 'It will do for us all!'[39]

At a more personal level, Napoleon had been deeply saddened by the death, during the opening shots of the battle of Lützen, of Marshal Bessières, one of his most loyal and capable commanders. He had been profoundly shaken three weeks later when his old friend Duroc was killed at Bautzen. Napoleon sat at his bedside for hours that night until Duroc breathed his last. Those two deaths revived muttering in the army that Napoleon had forfeited his 'star' when he divorced Josephine. 'When will it all end? Where will the Emperor stop? We must have peace *at any cost*!' was a common refrain.[40]

Instead of pursuing the allies, Napoleon decided to call a halt and wait for reinforcements, so he sent an envoy to allied headquarters with the offer of an armistice of seven weeks. The offer was eagerly accepted and the armistice concluded at Plesswitz on 4 June. The armistice 'saved us and condemned him', as one Russian general put it. Hardenberg agreed. Not only did Napoleon save the allies from almost certain defeat, he threw away the initiative, which he would never regain.[41]

40

Last Chance

NEWS OF THE armistice was greeted with joy throughout the empire; from every department prefects reported that people were desperate for peace. The pursuit of glory no longer held any appeal outside some sections of the army, and most of Napoleon's marshals and senior officers were begging him to conclude peace at almost any price. 'You are no longer loved, Sire,' General Belliard told him frankly, 'and if you want the whole truth, I would say that you may be cursed.' He assured Napoleon that if he were to make peace he would be blessed. Napoleon listened but said nothing.[1]

Even Poniatowski, who had been obliged to evacuate Poland and had joined Napoleon at Dresden with his Polish corps, told him he should make peace now on the best terms available in order to be able to make war from a better position in the future. 'You may be right,' Napoleon replied, 'but I will make war first in order to make a better peace.' In similar vein, Berthier suggested that Napoleon take advantage of the armistice to pull out his far-flung garrisons and concentrate all his forces on the Rhine. But Napoleon saw the presence of his troops in places such as Hamburg, Stettin, and Danzig, and his own in Dresden, as an indication of his determination to stand by his German allies and any retreat as a sign of weakness that would give heart to his enemies. In letter after letter Cambacérès urged him to make peace, saying that everyone was desperate for an end to the war and that his reputation would not suffer if he were to make concessions. But Napoleon clung to his conviction that the people of

582

France would not respect him if he failed to come up with something which could be dressed up as a victory, and what he called his '*magie*' would be dispelled, as he explained to Fouché.[2]

It was a measure of his insecurity that he had drawn Fouché out of retirement and was sending him to take up the post of governor of Illyria—in Paris he might be tempted to engineer a coup against him; in Trieste he was safely out of the way. The post had become vacant as its previous holder, Junot, had begun displaying dramatic symptoms of neurosyphilis dementia and had to be retired.

Metternich arrived in Dresden on 25 June. When he went to the Marcolini Palace the following day, he was struck by the look of despondency on the faces of the senior officers in the emperor's anterooms. He found Napoleon standing in a long gallery, his sword at his side and his hat under his arm. The emperor opened the conversation with cordial enquiries about Francis's health, but his countenance soon grew sombre. 'So it is war you want: very well, you shall have it,' he challenged Metternich. 'I annihilated the Prussian army at Lützen; I beat the Russians at Bautzen; and now you want to have your turn. I shall meet you at Vienna. Men are incorrigible; the lessons of experience are lost on them.' He accused Austria of treachery and said he had made a mistake in marrying Francis's daughter. When Metternich tried to make him see that this was his last chance to make peace on favourable terms, Napoleon declared that he could not give up an inch of territory without dishonouring himself. 'Your sovereigns, born on the throne, can afford to let themselves be beaten twenty times and still return to their capitals; I cannot, because I am a parvenu soldier,' he said. 'My authority will not survive the day when I will have ceased to be strong, and therefore, to be feared.'

He did not trust Metternich and saw the bases for negotiation suggested by him as a trick, since they would not be acceptable to Russia, let alone Britain, so that in agreeing to them he would be entering an open-ended negotiation. He was right, as although Metternich was sincere in trying to salvage what he could for Napoleon, his prime concern was to disengage Austria from alliance with him and give himself freedom of action. Napoleon tried to browbeat him, accusing him of treachery and of being in the pay of Britain, ridiculing

Austria's military potential and threatening to crush her. He lost his temper more than once, threw his hat into a corner of the room in a rage, only to resume the conversation on polite, even friendly terms. The meeting lasted more than nine hours, and it was dark outside when Metternich left.[3]

He returned that evening at Napoleon's invitation to see a play put on by the actors of the Comédie-Française, who had been brought over from Paris. He was astonished to find himself watching the famous Mademoiselle George (with whom he had had an affair in Paris) playing Racine's *Phèdre*. 'I thought I was at St Cloud,' he wrote to his wife before going to bed, 'all the same faces, the same court, the same people.' The weather had turned fine, and there was a festive atmosphere in the baroque city. The armistice had cheered all those who longed for peace, and there were balls and parties for the French officers and Napoleon's entourage.[4]

Further meetings having proved fruitless, Metternich was about to leave, on 30 June, when he received a note summoning him for an interview with Napoleon. He ordered his horses to be unharnessed and went to the Marcolini Palace, dressed as he was, expecting to have to listen to the same complaints and threats. To his surprise, Napoleon agreed to a peace congress under Austrian auspices, to be held at Prague in the first days of July. He suggested including Britain, the United States of America, and Spain, but Metternich demurred, seeing this as an unnecessary complication.[5]

A few days after his departure, Napoleon received unwelcome news from Spain. Wellington had gone over to the offensive at the end of May, and Joseph had been forced to abandon Madrid. The British caught up with him and the retreating French army at Vitoria and routed it on 21 June. It was a humiliating defeat, rendered all the more shameful to French arms by the loss of over a hundred cannon as well as all the army's and the king's baggage. Napoleon gave Soult overall command of the Army of Spain and ordered Joseph to go to Mortefontaine and not show himself in Paris.

He did not put much faith in Metternich's mediation but hoped he might be able to strike a deal with Alexander. 'Russia has the right to an advantageous peace,' he told Fain. 'She will have bought it with the devastation of her lands, with the loss of her capital and with two years of war. Austria, on the contrary, does not deserve anything.' Yet Alexander was the one monarch least likely to treat with Napoleon on any terms, while Metternich did still favour a peaceful outcome.[6]

The armistice was extended to 10 August; if terms were not agreed by midnight on that date hostilities would resume, with Austria in the allied camp. But the congress, which convened at Prague, never got beyond procedural questions. 'At heart, nobody truly wanted peace,' wrote Nesselrode, adding that the congress was a 'joke' which Alexander and Frederick William had opposed from the start, and the tsar sabotaged the proceedings by sending an envoy who would not be acceptable to Napoleon. Caulaincourt and Narbonne struggled to get negotiations going, but they were hamstrung; Caulaincourt had done everything to avoid being nominated to represent Napoleon, whose intransigence would make it impossible for him to negotiate. When he suggested making concessions, Napoleon burst out, 'You want me to pull down my trousers to get a whipping,' and stormed out of the room. Caulaincourt was instructed to take the line that Napoleon had never been beaten in Russia and only 'sustained some losses through the inclement weather'. He was so exasperated that he appears to have told Metternich he wished Napoleon would lose a battle, as only that could bring him to his senses.[7]

Napoleon was determined to brazen it out and in a show of nonchalance set off on 25 July for Mainz, to spend ten days with Marie-Louise. It was not a joyous occasion. He arrived to find her tired out by her journey and nursing a cold. The weather was bad, with heavy rain. After reviewing the troops in Mainz, he took her with him as he reviewed those camped in the vicinity. He made a show of confidence, putting in hand works for the refurbishment of the imperial residence in the city and declaiming about the apparent success of the negotiations going on in Prague. He also made elaborate plans for her to attend the flooding of the new harbour at Cherbourg, which was to provide a large sheltered basin for the fleet that would threaten Britain. But he was often silent and moody at dinner and on one occasion even snapped at her.

He was back in Dresden on 4 August, only to discover that the negotiations in Prague had not begun. He wrote to Metternich asking him to state his terms and received the answer on 7 August: the grand duchy of Warsaw should be divided between the three allies, Austria should recover Illyria, Hamburg and Lübeck should regain their independence, and France should give up her protectorate over the Confederation of the Rhine and her other German conquests.

Given Napoleon's position, the terms were acceptable; there was no mention of Holland, Belgium, or Italy, which left plenty of room for manoeuvre when peace talks began in earnest. His acceptance would have prevented Austria from joining the allies in the war against him, which was important, since he continued to entertain thoughts of defeating the Russians and Prussians before then, which would, he believed, allow him to split the allies and play them against each other. But determined not to appear too keen, Napoleon delayed his reply accepting the terms.[8]

The showman was determined to keep up his act. As his birthday fell after the end of the armistice, he had ordered the festivities to be brought forward by five days to 10 August, and it was celebrated with pomp in every unit, and imperially in Dresden itself, with a parade, a ball, a banquet, and fireworks. 'One could not imagine anything under the sun more martial; everything exuded confidence, ardour, enthusiasm,' wrote one of the actors of the Comédie-Française who had been performing in Dresden. 'My God, what a show!' It did not impress his generals, many of whom saw disaster looming.[9]

'The great moment has arrived at last, my dearest friend,' Metternich wrote to his wife the same day. That evening, while fireworks lit up the sky above Dresden, the Russian and Prussian negotiators had gathered at his residence in Prague. Watches were consulted with impatience, and when the chimes of midnight rang out over the sleeping city Metternich announced that the armistice was over and Austria was now a member of the alliance. He ordered a beacon to be lit which, by a chain reaction, carried the news to allied headquarters in Silesia. By morning, Russian and Prussian troops were on the march to join the Austrian army outside Prague.[10]

On 12 August, just as Caulaincourt and Narbonne were preparing to leave Prague, a courier arrived from Dresden with Napoleon's instructions to accept Metternich's terms. Caulaincourt called on Metternich without delay but was told it was too late; Austria had issued her declaration of war. Napoleon instructed him to delay his departure in the hope of being able to obtain an interview with Alexander, who was due a couple of days later. On 18 August Maret wrote to Metternich arguing that the congress had not been given a chance and proposing a fresh one to be convoked in some neutral city to include all the powers of Europe, great and small. But Metternich had by then ruled out peace, and Alexander had been against it all along. The tsar had gone so far as to conceal Britain's agreement to join the negotiations, knowing it would have strengthened Austria's case for peace and encouraged Napoleon to take the negotiations seriously—he would probably have been prepared to make concessions in such circumstances; a general peace with the participation of Britain, involving as it would not only huge economic relief but also the return of French colonies, could have been dressed up as a victory and allowed Napoleon to claim that he was making peace with honour.[11]

The only victory he could hope for now was on the battlefield, and that was going to be difficult to achieve. Facing him was the main allied army under Schwarzenberg, consisting of 120,000 Austrians, 70,000 Russians under Barclay de Tolly and 60,000 Prussians under General Kleist, a total of 250,000. Behind it stood Blücher's army of Silesia, consisting of 58,000 Russians and 38,000 Prussians. In the north Bernadotte commanded an army of 150,000 Swedes, Russians, and Prussians. That added up to well over half a million men and did not include Wellington's Anglo-Spanish army, which was approaching France's southwestern frontier. More significantly, the allies had agreed to a plan which consisted in refusing battle to Napoleon and only taking on individual corps commanded by his marshals. The idea was to wear down his forces without risking defeat. His resources were diminishing, while theirs were on the increase; the vast war effort Alexander had put in motion as soon as the French had been expelled from Russia was beginning to produce spectacular results in men, equipment, and, crucially, horses.[12]

'I have an army as fine as any and more than 400,000 men; that will suffice to re-establish my affairs in the North,' Napoleon boasted to Beugnot, but later in their conversation he complained that he was short of cavalry and needed more men, particularly seasoned troops. His forces were in fact greatly inferior to those of the allies. His garrisons in Germany and Poland accounted for 100,000 of his calculation, and they were beyond his reach. His best marshal, Davout, was stuck in Hamburg with a body of seasoned troops, Rapp was besieged in Danzig with over 20,000 veterans, many of them officers and NCOs, while the bulk of the 300,000 or so men at Napoleon's immediate disposal were mostly conscripts with rudimentary training. Much the same was true of the Army of Italy which Eugène had been forming up to threaten Austria's southern flank.[13]

Morale was surprisingly good among the troops as they marched out of Dresden on 16 August, boosted by the arrival of Murat, whom Napoleon had persuaded to come from Naples and take command of the cavalry. Napoleon's plan was to drive back Blücher and then, leaving Macdonald to cover him, veer south and outflank the main allied army under Schwarzenberg, which was moving on Dresden. The first part of the operation went according to plan, but at Lowenberg on 23 August, as he was taking a hurried lunch standing up, a courier arrived with a message from Gouvion Saint-Cyr, whom he had left to hold Dresden, warning that the main allied army under Schwarzenberg was threatening the city from the south. Napoleon smashed the glass of wine he was holding against the table as he read the despatch. The fall of Dresden would have political repercussions, so he turned about and marched back, detaching a force under General Vandamme to move south into the allies' rear while he took them on at Dresden.

He arrived outside the city on 26 August, and the next day, in pouring rain with mud up to their knees, his forces began pushing the allied forces back and eventually put them to flight. It was a fine victory; he had inflicted around 15,000 casualties, taken 24,000 prisoners, 15 standards, and a number of guns. But he failed to follow it up as he would have done in the past. He marched back to reinforce Vandamme, who was now in a position to cut off the allied retreat, but unaccountably stopped and turned back. The result was that Vandamme was himself caught in a trap and forced to capitulate at Kulm with around 10,000 men. If Napoleon had come to his assistance he would have destroyed the allied army and probably captured all three allied sovereigns and their ministers.[14]

Napoleon's sluggish behaviour has been variously blamed on a bout of food poisoning and on the depressing news he received on 30 August. Oudinot, whom he had ordered to march on Berlin, had been defeated by the Prussians at Grossbeeren. 'That's war,' Napoleon said to Maret that evening after hearing of the disaster of Kulm. 'Up there in the morning, down there in the evening.' He was increasingly prone to making fatalistic comments and quoting lines of poetry about destiny; it was as though he were giving himself up to it rather than, as in his youth, trying to forge it. News of the death of Junot, who had leapt out of a window and killed himself on 29 July, would not have helped. In his last letter he had compared his worship of Napoleon to that of 'the savage for the sun', but begged him to make peace. In Lannes, Duroc, and now Junot, he was losing men who had served him with devotion since Toulon, nearly twenty years before.[15]

A curious twist of fate had brought two of his long-standing rivals out against him. Moreau had been persuaded to return from America and had joined the tsar's headquarters, entertaining dreams of a military and perhaps political comeback. These were shattered by a French shell outside Dresden on 27 August; he died four days later. To the north, as Sweden had joined the coalition, Bernadotte was leading a combined Swedish and Prussian corps, entertaining more clearly stated dreams of succeeding Napoleon as ruler of France. To that end, he avoided coming face to face with French troops and badgered the allies to allow him to attack Denmark instead. The allies did not trust him (Blücher only ever referred to him as 'the traitor', and Hardenberg described him as 'a bastard that circumstances have obliged us to legitimise') and kept a wary eye on him.[16]

A couple of days after hearing of the defeats of Kulm and Gross-beeren, Napoleon received news that Macdonald had been repulsed with heavy losses by Blücher on the river Katzbach, and not long after, that Ney had been defeated at Dennewitz on 6 September. He was breaking his own golden rule, never to divide his forces but always to concentrate them at the decisive point. And while 'the Bravest of the Brave', as Ney was referred to, was a fine cavalry commander with all the panache one could hope for on the field of battle, he lacked judgement and, like most of the marshals, was not up to operating on his own. It did not help that Berthier was showing signs of age and despondency, which affected his management of operations. Napoleon too hesitated and kept changing his mind, meaning to march on Berlin one moment and into Bohemia the next. With the Austro-Russian army of Schwarzenberg licking its wounds in Bohemia, he decided to take on Blücher, but the Prussian refused to give battle, and Napoleon was obliged to trudge back to Dresden; the allies had drawn him into a game of blindman's buff as he lunged at one and then another.

Soon after hostilities began, the weather turned wet and cold. The roads were morasses of mud, reducing his mobility as well as the effectives of every unit with each march. Communications were impeded by shortage of cavalry and by the large numbers of cossacks roaming the country; staff officers were reluctant to carry orders and proceeded with caution when carrying out reconnaissance for fear of being captured. The persistent rain often rendered muskets useless, so the troops had to resort to the bayonet. The marches and counter-marches exhausted the men and depleted the ranks. 'Whenever we left a bivouac in the morning, having spent the night either only partially or not at all sheltered from the rain, the wind and the cold, we almost always left behind exhausted men, undermined by fever, hunger and misery, and that was almost always so many men lost, as in our incessant marches we did not have the possibility of having them moved,' wrote Sergeant Faucheur. Dresden was filling up with sick and wounded soldiers and the supply situation was dire. 'Never had my duties been more difficult or my efforts less fruitful,' recalled the man in charge, General Mathieu Dumas.[17]

Morale dipped, particularly among senior officers, who could see the situation growing desperate. None felt that more than Napoleon, whose exasperation was evident; he alternated between spells of lethargy and sudden bold decisions which his marshals considered too rash. He also lost his temper, calling into question their competence and their loyalty. When he accused Murat of treason (with good reason), Berthier tried to intervene, only to have Napoleon tell him to mind his own business and snap, 'Shut up, you old fool!'[18]

He could no longer hold on to his exposed position at Dresden and on 13 October decided to fall back on Leipzig, where Frederick Augustus had preceded him. Political considerations made him commit a fatal error: fearing that abandoning Dresden would make a poor impression, he left Saint-Cyr there with more than 30,000 men, thus depriving himself of a significant number of troops at a moment when the allies were gaining in strength. Reaching Leipzig two days later, he repelled an attack by Schwarzenberg, and the following day he scored significant success, at one point coming close to capturing the three allied monarchs. But toward the end of the day Blücher, whom he had assumed to be far away, appeared in his rear, and he was forced to call off the attack.

By then the allies had some 220,000 men facing his 150,000 on three sides, outgunning him with over a thousand pieces of artillery. He had lost the initiative and admitted as much by sending an Austrian general captured the previous day with an offer to negotiate—which was rejected out of hand. Their recent successes had buoyed the allies, and the tensions between them had been worked out by the signature on 9 September of the Treaty of Töplitz, which committed them to the common struggle. The only thing that could have saved Napoleon would have been a rapid withdrawal of all his forces in Germany and a concentration on the Rhine, but he continued to put strategy second to what were by now entirely irrelevant political considerations. The allies held off on 17 October as they prepared their concerted attack, but he did not seize the opportunity to make good his escape or even prepare for it; he did not evacuate the wounded or supplies of ammunition, or even have adequate crossings prepared over the rivers.

On 18 October, by which time they outnumbered the French by well over two to one with some 360,000 men and a vast artillery, the allies launched their attack. The French fought with determination, but the sheer numbers facing them told, and matters were not helped when the Saxon contingent in the French army suddenly turned around while advancing on the enemy and began firing on its French comrades who were coming up in support. Other German contingents also defected, sowing confusion and affecting morale. The number of men and guns on the field of battle meant that the slaughter was unprecedented. The corps commanders who could see the pointlessness of the situation were also losing heart. 'Does that b— know what he's doing?' Augereau fumed to Macdonald two days later. 'Haven't you noticed that in the recent events and the catastrophe which followed he lost his head? The coward! He abandoned us, he sacrificed us all. . . .'[19]

Napoleon really did not appear to know what he was doing. On the evening of 18 October he gave the order to withdraw, and columns of troops began a disorderly retreat through the narrow streets of Leipzig. The allies stormed the city the following morning, sowing confusion. A sergeant left guarding the single bridge over the river Elster with orders not to blow it until the rearguard had crossed panicked and lit the fuses too early, cutting off at least 12,000 men with 80 guns and leading to the death of Poniatowski, who drowned trying to get across the river despite being severely wounded. Napoleon had been asleep in a windmill outside the city and was woken by the explosion. Macdonald, who had managed to get across, reported the event. Napoleon seemed stunned as much as distraught and apparently unaware of the extent to which his lack of foresight had been to blame for a debacle of monumental proportions. The losses of the Grande Armée in the fighting around Leipzig were 70,000 and 150 guns, not counting the 20,000 German allies who had changed sides. Allied losses were 54,000.[20]

Before leaving Leipzig Napoleon went to the palace and offered Frederick Augustus refuge in France, but the Saxon king declined the offer, saying that he could not leave his subjects at such a time. Frederick Augustus sent officers to each of the allied monarchs but received no response. Alexander snubbed him when he rode into Leipzig, and after some argument the unfortunate Saxon royal couple were bundled into a carriage and sent under armed escort to captivity in Berlin. Murat, however, was allowed to sneak off to Naples, where he had an army of around 25,000 men, magnificently uniformed but inadequately trained and led. Metternich, who may also have been influenced by fond memories of the affair with Caroline he had enjoyed in Paris a couple of years before, seems to have believed that his forces were stronger and to have been impressed by his military reputation. He thought it politic to detach him from Napoleon by offering to leave him on the Neapolitan throne.

Napoleon fell back on Erfurt, where he spent two days, in the same rooms in which he had held talks with Alexander less than five years earlier, 'in an attitude of deep meditation', in the words of Macdonald. He briefly thought of making a stand there, but his marshals baulked at this, pointing out that the Bavarians, who had now joined the coalition, were about to cut them off from France. Listless and undecided, he had to be urged to move on by his marshals and made for the Rhine. Aside from the Guard, which was still disciplined, most of his remaining forces were no more than a crowd marching without order; one officer was reminded of the retreat from Moscow. No effort was made to rally the troops, and many were abandoned to die by the roadside.[21]

At Hanau, their road was barred by 50,000 Bavarians. The Guard managed to defeat their erstwhile allies, but Napoleon barely directed the action, sheltering in a wood and seeming to those around him to have lost his nerve. Ségur, who had arrived from Paris and had not seen him for six months, was shocked by the change that had taken place in him. 'The impression he made on me was so strong and so painful that I still feel it today,' he wrote more than a decade later. When Napoleon addressed the remnants of Poniatowski's Polish corps, releasing them from their oath but begging them to stay with him, promising to fight again one day for their country's cause, many were so moved to pity that they did.[22]

He crossed the Rhine on 30 October with no more than 30,000 men and some 40,000 stragglers. He spent two days at Mainz, from where he sent optimistic reports and captured standards to Paris, assuring Marie-Louise that people in Paris were 'unnecessarily alarmed': 'My troops have a decisive superiority over the enemy, who will be beaten sooner than he thinks.' To Savary, he wrote that the alarmist talk in Paris was ridiculous and made him 'laugh'. But the situation was nothing short of catastrophic.[23]

His empire was crumbling. The network of control over Germany built up since 1806 unravelled. As other rulers of the Confederation of the Rhine joined the allies, Jérôme fled Kassel, 'accompanied by his ministers of foreign affairs and war, and still surrounded by all the tattered trappings of royalty', in the words of Beugnot, who saw him pass through Düsseldorf, escorted by 'lifeguards whose theatrical uniforms heavy with gold were wonderfully inapposite to the situation' and a court which 'resembled nothing so much as a troupe of actors on tour rehearsing a play'. The 190,000 or so French troops still holding out in fortresses such as Dresden and Hamburg, not to mention points further east, were now beyond Napoleon's reach and isolated in a hostile sea and would capitulate one by one. Private scores were settled as his regime imploded, unruly Prussian and Russian troops bent on rapine swarmed over the area, and a typhus epidemic spread rapidly as people fled in all directions, turning military hospitals into morgues and striking down exhausted and underfed stragglers.[24]

The situation further south was little better. Austrian troops had invaded the Illyrian provinces, forcing the weak French garrisons to evacuate them. Eugène could do little to stem their advance and fell back on Milan. In November he was approached on behalf of the allies by his father-in-law, King Maximilian of Bavaria, who urged him to safeguard his future by changing sides, but he refused and remained loyal to Napoleon, firmly supported by his wife.[25]

As he contemplated the defence of France itself, Napoleon did what he could to improve her defences by closing off potential points of entry. He pressed the Diet of the Helvetic Republic to declare its neutrality (without going so far as to recall the Swiss troops in his own ranks), withdrew all French forces and renounced his role as Mediator.

He also belatedly tried to lance the Spanish ulcer, instructing Joseph to abdicate (which he at first refused to do, waxing indignant about being forced to 'sacrifice' sacred rights to 'his' throne, and complaining that he was not accorded the honours due to his royal rank), and freed Ferdinand, still a guest of Talleyrand at Valençay. He was to return to Spain, having first married Joseph's twelve-year-old daughter Zenaïde and signed an alliance with France promising to expel British troops from the Peninsula. By the time Ferdinand set off, in March 1814, he could no longer be of any use to Napoleon, even if he had wished to be. Soult at Bayonne and Suchet further south, with 50,000 and 15,000 men respectively, faced a combined Anglo-Spanish force three times that number.[26]

Eugène was only just holding out in Italy, with 30,000 troops of questionable quality and allegiance against a more numerous Austro-Bavarian army. Only Augereau's reserve of about 20,000 stationed in the region of Lyon stood between that and Paris. In the north-east, apart from the troops besieged in fortresses in Holland, Belgium and along the Meuse, Napoleon had only around 70,000 men. They faced at least 300,000 allies who had reached the Rhine and threatened to cross it at any moment.

While he was still at Dresden he had instructed Cambacérès to make the Senate bring forward the call-up of 1815, and on 12 November, after his return to Paris, it voted the conscription of another 300,000 men. Napoleon estimated that he would soon have 900,000 under arms, but his calculations were as fictitious as those concerning available funds. As the area under his control shrank, so did his manpower pool, and resistance to conscription increased; the number evading it by going into hiding rose drastically, and according to some estimates reached 100,000. Few of the class of 1815 ever reached the ranks. Even if they had, they would not have been of much use, as there was nothing to arm them with. Given an annual production of 120,000 muskets, the losses of 500,000 in 1812 and 200,000 in 1813 could not easily be made up. At the end of 1813, the 153rd Regiment of the Line had 142 muskets for 1,100 men, the 115th regiment 289 for 2,300 men. The situation in the cavalry was no better, with the 17th Dragoons having to share 187 sabres and even fewer horses between 349 men.[27]

Napoleon was back at Saint-Cloud on 10 November. The following day he held a Council of State during which he complained that he had been betrayed by everyone, venting particular rage against King Maximilian of Bavaria and vowing vengeance. 'Munich shall be burned!' he ranted repeatedly. He put on a brave face, and only a few days after getting back to Paris he went hunting. Ten days later he rode around with Fontaine inspecting the new post office and corn market and progress on the extravagant project of a palace for the King of Rome at Chaillot. Nobody was fooled. 'Despite his efforts to hide them, it was evident to all those accompanying him that other thoughts were occupying him more than these grand building projects,' noted Bausset. He relieved his stress with outbursts against people and also used his feigned rages to show that he was still the roaring lion. He tried to bully the Pope into accepting his 'new concordat'; when he refused, the old man was bundled off back to detention in Savona. Seeing Talleyrand at the first *lever*, Napoleon threatened him that if he were brought down, Talleyrand would be the first to die. On 9 December at the opening of the Legislative body he lectured it on the need for more men, more money, and more determination. Court life continued as usual; the receptions were as glittering and crowded as ever, but Joseph and Jérôme were kept away, as Napoleon did not want dethroned monarchs spoiling the show.[28]

'The master was there as always, but the faces around him, the looks and the words were no longer the same,' recorded one official who attended the imperial *lever* at the Tuileries. 'There was something sad and tired about the demeanour of the soldiers, and even the courtiers.' The mood in Paris was despondent. 'People were anxious about everything, foreseeing only misfortune on all sides,' wrote Pasquier. 'The court was gloomy,' wrote Cambacérès. 'With the exception of a very small number, all the men with positions anticipated the impending catastrophe and were secretly occupied in trying to avoid it and secure their political existence.' Many were expecting a change of regime.[29]

Napoleon only confided in a very few. 'In the evenings, he would call me to his apartment, as he sat in his dressing gown warming himself by the fire,' recalled Lavalette. 'We would chat (I can find no other word for this hour-long talk which preceded his sleep). The first days I found him so prostrate, so despondent, that I was horrified.'

Marmont, who saw him often, noted that he was 'gloomy and silent', but would always buoy himself up with hopes that the allies would pause on the Rhine long enough for him to raise a new army; he could envisage no other means of salvation.[30]

'Come back to France, Sire, identify yourself with the French and every heart will be yours, and you will be able to do what you wish with them,' Josephine had written to him on hearing news of Leipzig. But Napoleon could not bring himself to trust the French people. He knew that Bernadotte had contacted his Jacobin friends in the hope of taking power, and he saw the despair to which his entourage had given way as weakness at a moment when the state they had all laboured to build was about to crumble like the Bastille. He was convinced that only he could safeguard the new order he had created, and that only by a show of force.[31]

He desperately wanted peace, but he had based his right to rule so exclusively on glory and his supposedly miraculous 'star' that he felt he would be betraying it by making what he saw as a humiliating peace. 'In that, he underestimated the generosity of the French and was not able to trust in a quality which was alien to his own character,' commented Pasquier. 'He did not even do himself justice, for he possessed, in the memory of his brilliant record, and even in his mistakes and his reversals, an *éclat* and a grandeur that would always have sustained him.' He could envisage only one way of reasserting his right to rule, by redeeming himself on the battlefield, and as a result threw away his last chance of keeping the throne of France.[32]

The Wounded Lion

U P TO NOW, the allies had concentrated on forcing Napoleon out of Germany and only envisaged military operations as far as the Rhine. Having reached that, they hesitated; to carry the war into France would lend their enterprise a different character. Alexander was keen to keep going and take Paris, but neither his ministers nor his generals were, and his troops were more interested in going home. Frederick William was also wary of continuing, and although Blücher was bent on dealing further damage to the French, his army was in poor condition. Metternich, who was now in Frankfurt with the other allied ministers, did not wish to weaken France further and was wary of the tsar's plans, while Francis wanted peace.

Through a returning French diplomat, the baron de Saint-Aignan, Metternich sent Napoleon a peace proposal on the basis of France giving up her conquests in Italy, Spain, and Germany and returning to her so-called natural frontiers on the Rhine, the Alps and the Pyrenees, thereby keeping Belgium and Savoy as well as the left bank of the Rhine. The status of the rest of the Netherlands was left unspecified, and there was talk of negotiation on the subject of colonies and maritime matters. Although the British representative in the allied camp, Lord Aberdeen, was aware of it, the initiative was taken by Metternich and Nesselrode, so it had only a semi-official character.

Saint-Aignan reached Paris on 14 November and the following day presented these proposals to Napoleon. He was quick to spot that as there was no mention of maritime matters, and as Belgium was left in French hands, they would not be acceptable to Britain. They therefore represented an opportunity to split the allies, so he responded positively; but, not wishing to appear too eager, and encouraged by Maret, one of the few who still trusted that his 'genius' would triumph, he did so in the vaguest terms, suggesting a peace congress and bringing up additional points.[1]

It did not take him long to realise that this was a mistake. He moved Maret back to his old job as secretary of state and, after briefly considering Talleyrand, replaced him with a reluctant Caulaincourt. Caulaincourt spent the best part of a week persuading Napoleon to accept the Frankfurt proposals as they stood, and it was not until 2 December that he was able to write to Metternich that he had. His letter arrived too late. On 19 November the allies had agreed to a plan of campaign, and on 7 December they published their 'Frankfurt Declaration', which suggested that the 'natural frontiers' were no longer on offer, and, more ominously, that they were fighting not France but Napoleon.[2]

Had he accepted the proposals immediately, the allies would have been obliged to halt their offensive and a peace conference would have been convened, at which he could have bargained and played for time. It would have given him the breathing space he needed to rebuild his forces, and even if he did not manage to get his way at the conference (he had already drawn up all his demands, which were extensive), he would be in a position to start extending his influence again once peace had been made. Above all, he would have avoided the crucial development of his fate being separated from that of France.

'The strange thing is that Napoleon, whose common sense was equal to his genius, could never discern at which point possibility ended,' noted Mathieu Molé, who had worked closely with him since 1809. He went on to say that on encountering an obstacle Napoleon would look no further than surmounting it, seeing in the process a test for his will, and thinking only of the present, not the future. These characteristics were on display in the speech he made on 19 December, opening the session of the Legislative. He described the 'resounding victories' he had won in the recent campaign, which had only been annulled by the defection of his German allies. Ten days later, in the course of a debate on the unfortunate outcome of the Frankfurt negotiations, one member made a speech suggesting that peace should be made on the basis of the interests of France, not those of the emperor. An outraged Napoleon wanted to close down the assembly. 'France needs me more than I need France,' he ranted. Cambacérès managed to calm him, but a number of members were invited to leave Paris.[3]

The allied advance had resumed: in the north Blücher's Prussians crossed the Rhine between Mainz and Cologne, in the south the Austrians moved against Eugène in Italy, and in the centre Schwarzenberg with the main Austro-Russian forces crossed into France from Switzerland to deploy on the plateau of Langres. Metternich, who hoped to avoid unnecessary fighting, had suggested fresh talks, with the participation of Britain, whose foreign secretary Lord Castlereagh was on his way, and Napoleon had agreed; only the venue still needed to be fixed. As the allied advance had not been halted, Napoleon meant to strengthen his hand with a military victory. On 4 January 1814 he decreed the *levée en masse* in the departments threatened with invasion, mobilising customs officials, police officers, gamekeepers, foresters, and veterans to organise a territorial defence. He showed a degree of reluctance to call up the Paris National Guard, as he was no longer sure whom he could trust.

A few days later, on 7 January, unbeknown to Napoleon, Murat signed a treaty of alliance with Austria. As recently as 12 December 1813 he had written asking for instructions, assuring the emperor that 'I will for the rest of my life be your best friend'. Napoleon had been aware of Murat's contacts with the Austrians, but he realised that he and Caroline had only been hedging their bets, and would revert to him in the event of a change in his fortunes. Murat was being pressed by Austria to take the field openly but delayed as long as he could. Napoleon had sent Fouché to Naples in November to keep an eye on him, but Fouché was looking to his own future and advised Murat to join the Austrians. The decision was probably made by Caroline, who was more intelligent and hard-nosed, as was Élisa, who did her best to hang on to Lucca by breaking off relations with France. Meanwhile, Eugène continued to give Napoleon assurances of loyalty but resisted his suggestion that his pregnant wife come to Paris—where she would have been a hostage to his good behaviour. Napoleon asked Josephine to write to him, which she did, enjoining him to remain loyal to Napoleon and to France.[4]

On Sunday, 23 January, after attending mass, Napoleon made his way to the Hall of Marshals in the Tuileries. There he presented the King of Rome to the officers of the Paris National Guard. The same day he signed letters patent naming Marie-Louise regent in his absence. The next morning he nominated Joseph Lieutenant-General of the Empire, and that evening, after burning his most secret papers, he embraced his wife and son; at six in the morning on 25 January he rode out of Paris to join the army. 'He appeared in a good mood, determined and in perfect health,' noted Lavalette. To Pontécoulant he declared that unless a cannonball struck him down, within three months there would not be a single foreign soldier on French soil. He rebuked those around him who thought the war lost. 'They think they can already see cossacks in the streets,' he had quipped over dinner a few days earlier. 'Well, they're not here yet and we haven't forgotten our trade.' He assured his wife that he would defeat the allies and dictate peace to her father. 'I'll beat Papa François again,' he repeated as he hugged her for the last time. 'Don't cry, I'll be back soon.' He would never see her or his son again.[5]

Before leaving Paris he dictated a letter to his father-in-law suggesting that he make a separate peace. He pointed out that if the allies were to lose, Austria would lose more than the others, while every allied victory only diminished her influence, since it increased that of the other allies disproportionately. He meant to drive the point home with a victory, and having narrowly escaped being killed on the way by a patrol of cossacks, he took command of the 45,000 men camped at Châlons-sur-Marne. 'Despite the disasters of the campaign in Saxony, despite the allies' passage of the Rhine, the army was convinced that it would defeat the enemy,' recalled the colonel of one of the Guard regiments, noting at the same time that the senior commanders were more sceptical. They had good reason to be: while the allied generals could be defeated, the allied statesmen had become accustomed to defeat, and each new one confirmed them in their conviction that the only way to obtain a lasting peace was to be rid of Napoleon. He was sanguine that he could rout the allies and drive them back and thereby recover the 90,000 men stuck behind their lines in fortresses along the Rhine or just beyond the borders of France.[6]

Blücher had drawn ahead of the other allied forces, and Napoleon attacked him near Brienne, where he had begun his military career. He dealt him a heavy blow and drove him back, but, reinforced by Schwarzenberg, Blücher counter-attacked and, outnumbered by more than two to one, Napoleon was defeated at La Rothière on 1 February. He fell back on Troyes behind the Seine.

This emboldened the allies, and when Caulaincourt met their plenipotentiaries at Châtillon for negotiations a week later, he was flatly told that the best he could expect was France's pre-revolutionary frontiers. When Napoleon heard of this on the evening of 7 February

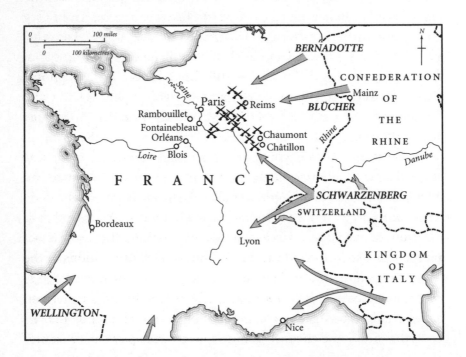

he protested that he could never agree to such terms, as he would be breaking his coronation oath and giving his enemies grounds to dethrone him. He was in a desperate mood and did not sleep. When, in the early hours, a messenger brought news that Blücher had drawn away from Schwarzenberg and was marching on Paris, he decided to take him on a second time. Maret, coming in with a letter to Caulaincourt for him to sign, found him lying on a map with a pair of compasses, all thoughts of negotiation banished. Napoleon moved fast, gathering up every unit he could find along the way. On 10 February he defeated Blücher's advance guard at Champaubert, the following day another of his corps at Montmirail, and the day after that a third at Château-Thierry. On 14 February he defeated Blücher himself at Vauchamps. He was in fine spirits, and all who saw him took heart. On 18 February he scored another victory at Montereau, in the course of which he aimed a cannon himself.

'They thought the lion was dead and it was safe to piss on him,' he exclaimed. He sent instructions to Caulaincourt at Châtillon to settle for nothing less than France's 'natural' frontiers, to hold out for Italy, to give as little ground as possible, and above all to refer back before agreeing to anything. He wrote to Francis once again, hoping to persuade him to make a separate peace, but he himself had only thoughts of war. On 21 February he wrote to Augereau, chiding him for dragging his heels: 'If you are still the Augereau of Castiglione, keep your command; if your sixty years weigh on you, leave it and hand over to the most senior of your general officers. [. . .] we must recover our boots and our resolve of '93!'[7]

Blücher's defeat had come as a shock to the allies, and panic spread through some units. Schwarzenberg fell back and requested an armistice as the allied monarchs and their ministers raced for safety. Bernadotte was in contact with his French friends, raising fears of his defection. Morale on the French side soared, despite the heavy losses and the exhausting forced marches in the atrocious conditions of the winter campaign, and in the countryside in which he operated Napoleon was greeted with enthusiasm. The behaviour of the German troops, seeking revenge for years of humiliation, had aroused the anger of the locals, and there was some spontaneous partisan resistance in the areas affected by the war. But while Napoleon made sure that the cannon of the Tuileries thundered out the good news of every victory and enemy prisoners were paraded through the streets along with captured standards, the Parisians were increasingly fatalistic. 'Everyone is hiding their most precious possessions, burying them in the ground, sealing them up in the thickness of walls or up their chimneys,' noted the architect Fontaine. The director of the Louvre was badgering Joseph to have its treasures safeguarded.[8]

Napoleon bombarded Joseph with instructions on how to manage public opinion, sending him material, such as accounts of atrocities committed by foreign troops, to be inserted in *Le Moniteur*. He was furious when he heard that Marie-Louise, remembering what she had done in Vienna when it was being bombarded by him, proposed holding public prayers for the success of the campaign. He was alert to anything that might weigh in the propaganda war, and, realising that detachments of cossacks were roaming the countryside, instructed Joseph to have the silver, the portraits of the imperial family, and 'anything that could be made to look like a trophy' at Fontainebleau packed up and removed to a place of safety.[9]

Napoleon agreed to Schwarzenberg's request for an armistice, but when negotiations opened on 24 February he tried to use them to affect the subsequent peace talks by suggesting a demarcation line close to France's 'natural frontiers', and after days of fruitless talks, on 5 March the negotiations broke down. By then he was in a much weaker position.

On 20 February he received news of Murat's defection. Ten days later he heard that on 27 February Soult had been beaten at Orthez by Wellington, who was marching on Bordeaux. Assuming that Murat might be swayed by news of his recent successes, Napoleon instructed Joseph to send someone to talk to him. He also suggested he make a renewed effort to bring Bernadotte over to the French side. He wanted Eugène to forget about defending Italy, which could be easily reconquered at a later stage; instead, he should march into France, collect the 5,000 men at Chambéry, another 8,000 at Grenoble and Augereau's force at Lyon, which would give him at least 50,000 men with which he could sweep into the enemy rear and up into Lorraine.[10]

The negotiations had resumed at Châtillon, but they were ineffectual, since Caulaincourt did not have a free hand and Napoleon was in no mood to give way. The situation had revived his deepest insecurities, and he could not face Paris otherwise than as a victor. Molé records him saying that he was in bond to his glory: 'If I sacrifice that, I am nothing, it is from her that I hold all my rights.'[11]

The desperate situation also brought out his finest qualities as a tactician and a leader of men and galvanised his faculties. General Ricard was astonished when he called at headquarters to hear Napoleon tell Berthier, 'Sit down and write!' and proceed to dictate orders enumerating the strength and giving the position of nineteen different units, and the time it would take each of them to concentrate at a given point, without referring to a single note.[12]

Spotting a chance to defeat Blücher, who was moving away from Schwarzenberg, he pursued him and attacked him at Craonne on 7 March, and after one of the bloodiest battles of the campaign drove him back. He was able to exploit intimate knowledge of the terrain by seeking out his old friend from Auxonne, Belly de Bussy, who lived nearby. Two days later he came up against Blücher's main force at Laon. He had underestimated the Prussian's strength, which was twice his own, and was forced to retreat after an inconclusive engagement. He refused to accept the hopelessness of his situation, and accused those who advised suing for peace of cowardice. 'Today, I am the master, like at Austerlitz,' he wrote to Joseph on 11 March. That was not how it looked in Paris, where those who had supported him in the interests of rebuilding France were growing disenchanted as they watched him bring her to her knees.[13]

'The situation is grave, and becomes worse with the passing of every day,' Cambacérès wrote the same day. 'We are in dire poverty and surrounded by people who are either spent or angry. Elsewhere it is even worse; official reports and private correspondence alike make it clear that we can no longer defend ourselves, that despondency has become general, that signs of discontent are evident in various quarters and that we are about to witness the most sinister events if the strong arm of Your Majesty does not come promptly to our aid.' Like some frantic gambler, Napoleon clung to the hope that another throw of the dice could still reverse the situation; now, more than ever, he needed to establish his right to rule.[14]

Two days earlier, on 9 March, the allies had signed the Treaty of Chaumont, which bound Britain, Russia, Prussia, and Austria, henceforth identifying themselves as 'the Great Powers', to fight Napoleon to the end and oversee the reorganisation of Europe after his removal. They were divided as to who should succeed him, Britain and Austria favouring the Bourbons, and Alexander supporting Bernadotte, who now made a dash for Paris, adopting an equivocal pose that left it open for him, if he failed to gain the throne, to become an enabling lieutenant either for a republic or for a Bourbon restoration—either a Cromwell or a Monck.

On 13 March Napoleon routed an isolated Russian corps at Reims. He then went after Schwarzenberg and caught up with him at Arcis-sur-Aube, but when the Austrian turned about and brought his 90,000 men to bear against Napoleon's 20,000 the following day, Napoleon had to withdraw. He saved the day when retreating French cavalry had threatened to cause panic in the ranks; when a shell landed in front of them and they drew back, he rode forward and stopped his horse over it, and although the horse was killed he escaped unscathed. Some believed he may have been seeking death; there were other moments in this campaign when he led from the front, sword in hand, apparently courting a glorious end.

On the retreat, 'discouragement overwhelmed our spirits', recalled General Boulart. On 25 March Marmont and Mortier were mauled at La Fère Champenoise; Augereau had surrendered Lyon. The troops were still capable of flashes of enthusiasm, but the mood in the higher ranks was defeatist, and generals talked openly of the hopelessness of further action. According to one police source, there was even a plot by a group of generals to do away with Napoleon.[15]

Cambacérès's advice that he return to Paris was based on sound calculation: the inhabitants of the poorer *quartiers* were overwhelmingly loyal and patriotic, and the allies would not have dared attempt to storm the city, with its huge population and its revolutionary legacy (and no Bourbon would be mad enough to agree to ascend a throne over the bodies of the capital's defenders). More important, as it turned out, his presence would have prevented his enemies from making a deal with the allies behind his back. But Napoleon did not heed it.

Instead, he decided to slip past the allied armies, penetrate into their rear, disorient them and oblige them to halt their advance, collect troops from the fortresses along France's eastern border, and strike at them from the rear. It was a bold plan which would have worked back in 1797, but the allies did not panic, and when a messenger carrying a note to Marie-Louise which revealed his plan was caught, along with others carrying various orders, they immediately moved on Paris. Realising his mistake, Napoleon hastened back, racing ahead on horses and vehicles borrowed along the way, leaving his troops to follow. He could hear the sound of guns in the distance as he hurried on, but he was too late.

Paris had been without news of him since 25 March, and as the enemy drew near Joseph grew nervous. Marmont's and Mortier's corps were on their way, but all the city's military governor General Moncey could muster in its defence was a mixed bag of troops, veterans, national guards, armed firemen, and gendarmes totalling no more than about 25,000. On 28 March Joseph held a meeting of the Regency Council to decide whether the empress and the King of Rome should leave the capital for a place of safety. Most of those present felt they should remain, fearing the instability that might follow their departure. Joseph then read out letters he had received from Napoleon in February instructing him to make sure that his wife and child did not fall into enemy hands. '*Do not leave my son*, and remember that I would prefer to see him drowned in the Seine than in the hands of the enemies of France; the fate of Astyanax as a prisoner of the Greeks has always seemed to me the most unhappy one in history,' he had written on 16 March, adding that every time he watched Racine's tragedy *Phèdre* he wept over the fate of the grandson of the King of Troy. In light of this, most of those present gave way and agreed that the empress should leave. She protested but was persuaded, and on the following day she and her son left for Rambouillet, accompanied by Cambacérès and other members of the Regency Council, as well as a number of other dignitaries and ministers, and most of her *maison*.[16]

Joseph, who remained in Paris, issued a call to arms and went to the heights of Montmartre to oversee the defence of the city, which began with the first allied attacks in the early morning of 30 March. It soon became evident that the situation was desperate, and he conferred with Marmont and others on what to do. The troops were determined to defend the city to the last man and were joined by volunteers from every class of the population, and a stiff resistance was put up at various points. At the same time, ladies in carriages drove out to watch as though going to a day at the races. Late that afternoon, judging the situation to be hopeless, against the advice of Lavalette, who expected Napoleon to arrive at any moment, Joseph sent Marmont to allied headquarters to negotiate a capitulation. He then left to join Marie-Louise and the rest of the Regency Council. Not long afterward, news arrived from Napoleon announcing that he was on his way, so Marmont asked for a twenty-four-hour cease-fire, but Alexander, who was at headquarters, refused and threatened to sack the city unless it capitulated immediately. Terms were agreed, and Marmont's units began withdrawing in the direction of Fontainebleau while his aides attended to the formalities.[17]

At ten o'clock that evening at La Cour de France, a couple of hours' drive from Paris, Napoleon met General Belliard, leading Marmont's cavalry, who informed him that Paris had capitulated. He was stunned. His immediate reaction was to go on, but after a short distance he turned back. He walked up and down along the road, giving way to conflicting emotions, raging against the 'coward' and 'cunt' Joseph, against his marshals and against fate, alternating between exaltation and despair, between the determination to march on Paris and to negotiate peace. He then went back to the post house, where he sat down with his head in his hands and remained motionless for some time.[18]

Around three o'clock in the morning he roused himself, wrote to Marie-Louise and despatched Caulaincourt to Paris to see the tsar. He then drove to nearby Fontainebleau, where over the next few days he was joined by the remnants of his army. Along with the units that had come out of Paris, they amounted to no more than 40,000 operational troops, but wishful thinking inflated their number in his mind (he kept writing down Marmont's corps, which now amounted to no more than 5,200 effectives, as being 12,400 strong). On 1 April he held a council of war to consider the options. Most of those present were for withdrawing behind the Loire, linking up with the remains of Soult's Army of Spain and Augereau's corps, and joining the empress and the King of Rome. Napoleon again wanted to march on Paris, convinced that his appearance would galvanise the population, and ordered Marmont, whose corps was camped in forward positions at Essonnes, to prepare for action. The following morning, as he was reviewing troops in the great courtyard of the palace, Caulaincourt returned from Paris with a gloomy countenance. Napoleon dismissed the parading troops and went inside to hear his news.[19]

Manipulated deftly by Talleyrand, who had avoided leaving the capital with the rest of the Regency Council, Alexander had accepted that the Bourbons should be reinstated. Talleyrand was forming a provisional government and, fearing any resurgence of Napoleon's influence, was exploring the possibility of having him assassinated. The tsar had succumbed to his influence and was determined not to negotiate with Napoleon, but did give assurances that he would be provided with a refuge in which he could continue as a sovereign, mentioning Corfu, Sardinia, Corsica, and Elba as possibilities. All that afternoon and late into the night Napoleon listened impassively as Caulaincourt went over every detail of his interviews with Alexander and everything he had seen and heard in Paris, where most people were busy looking to their future under the new regime, without a thought for him. 'I do not care about the throne,' Napoleon said. 'Born a soldier, I can, without feeling sorry for myself, become a citizen again. My happiness is not in grandeur. I wanted to see France great and powerful, and above all happy. I prefer to leave the throne than to sign a shameful peace. I am glad that they did not accept your conditions, as I would have been obliged to subscribe to them, and France and history would have reproached me for such an act of weakness. The Bourbons alone can accommodate themselves to a peace dictated by the cossacks.' Caulaincourt told him his only option was to abdicate, warning him that he was about to be toppled.[20]

Napoleon was outraged, and the next day, as the Old Guard paraded before him, he told them that traitors had handed over Paris to the enemy and they must go to its rescue. The men shouted 'To Paris!' and appeared keen to fight, so he began making plans. That evening news arrived that Talleyrand had assembled a rump of the Senate, sixty-four members out of 140, which had voted his deposition on the grounds that he had violated the constitution and subjected the interests of France to his own. It had also approved the formation of a provisional government under Talleyrand, whose first action was to release all Frenchmen from their oath of loyalty to the former emperor.

The following morning, 4 April, after the usual parade he conferred with Marshals Berthier, Ney, Lefèbvre, Moncey, Oudinot, and Macdonald, along with Caulaincourt and Maret. He kept bringing up the possibility of marching out and inflicting a stinging defeat on the allies, if only to be in a better position to negotiate. They all frankly told him the troops were no longer up to fighting, and that even if they had been, a victory would yield nothing. They were unanimous that he should abdicate. He told them he would think about it and give them an answer the next day, but afterward in conversation with Caulaincourt he again suggested carrying out military operations alongside peace talks. In the end he was persuaded to sign a proposal to present his abdication to the Senate once the Powers had recognised the succession of his three-year-old son as Napoleon II, with Marie-Louise as regent. The proposal was to be carried to Alexander by Caulaincourt as foreign minister, assisted by Marshals Ney and Macdonald to make it clear to Alexander that the army was behind the Bonaparte dynasty and opposed to the Bourbons. The three of them set off, accompanied by a numerous escort of senior officers.[21]

Along their way, at Essones, they called on Marmont, only to discover that he had been engaged in negotiations of his own. Having been fed misinformation by Talleyrand and others, he had been in touch with the Austrian commander, Schwarzenberg, to arrange the defection of his corps from Napoleon's side to that of the allies. The operation was to be carried out that night. He pretended that it had merely been discussed and gave instructions for nothing to be done, while volunteering that he join Caulaincourt and his two comrades on their mission to Paris, where they arrived late that night.

Despite efforts on the part of Talleyrand to prevent it, they were accorded an audience with Alexander at three o'clock on the morning of 5 April. He listened for half an hour to their arguments and showed some sympathy, as he despised the Bourbons and felt no enthusiasm to reinstate them. He told them to come back after noon the next day, which would give him time to consider the matter, and they left in positive mood, enhanced by the worried looks of Talleyrand and his colleagues whom they encountered on the way out (Alexander had put up at Talleyrand's residence). They went off to sleep and agreed to meet for breakfast at eleven at Ney's house.

As the four of them began their breakfast they were interrupted by the arrival of a breathless Colonel Fabvier, who announced that during the night Marmont's corps had gone over to the enemy. Marmont went pale, jumped up, and seizing his sword, blurted out that he must go and 'repair' things. He then rushed out, leaving his colleagues gaping with astonishment. By the time they called on Alexander the whole of Paris knew of Marmont's defection, and their argument that the army was solidly behind Napoleon no longer held. The tsar told them that Napoleon must abdicate unconditionally. In return he would be given the Mediterranean island of Elba to rule in full sovereignty, and generous provision would be made for him and his family.[22]

As Alexander was speaking, Napoleon was making alternative plans. He had attended his usual parade that morning, and the sight of his troops had filled him with military ardour once more. He began dictating orders for a withdrawal behind the Loire, where he would join the empress and the King of Rome, who had taken up residence in the Renaissance château at Blois with her *maison* and enough silver to fill a palace, as well as the entire imperial treasure from the Tuileries. Napoleon's brothers were also lodged in the castle, while Cambacérès, Molé, Clarke, Montalivet, Regnaud, and other members of the Regency Council and various dignitaries accommodated themselves as best they could in the small town.

Cambacérès valiantly kept up his standards, sticking to his official dress and having himself carried around the old town, whose streets were too narrow for carriages, in a sedan chair. The others tried as best they could not to show that they realised they had been outmanoeuvred and sidelined by their former colleague Talleyrand. Savary had already entered into negotiations with him regarding his own future. Marie-Louise was hoping to join Napoleon and wrote to him asking for guidance and support, and to her father for help. The Buonaparte men reverted to their native instincts as they contemplated a future in which they would not be able to rely on their brother for a life of grandeur and luxury. Joseph attempted to play the head of the family and make all the decisions, seconded by Jérôme. Napoleon had for some time suspected him of wishing to seduce Marie-Louise, and he now seized the opportunity to try and rape her. For his part, Louis added a sudden surge of religious zeal to his neurotic behaviour.[23]

Napoleon was woken at two o'clock on the morning of 6 April by Caulaincourt, Ney, and Macdonald, who had just returned from their mission to Alexander. After listening to their report he announced that he would never abdicate unconditionally and dismissed them. But nobody slept much; at six o'clock in the morning Caulaincourt was back with him, and the two of them talked at length. Napoleon had been taken aback by Marmont's defection and deeply hurt by such an act of treachery by one of his oldest friends. More than that, it had undermined his position by calling into question his hold on the army.

On that morning of 6 April, Napoleon wrote out the four and a half lines of his abdication in his own hand, making a large ink-stain in the process. He then dictated the formal instructions for Caulaincourt and the two marshals, empowering them to negotiate the details of the settlement. What he did not know as they took their leave that evening was that, persuaded by his ardently royalist wife, Ney had already written to Talleyrand pledging his submission to the new government. As Caulaincourt noted, 'everyone was turning their eyes to the rising sun and seeking to approach it; the sun of Fontainebleau no longer warmed, . . .'[24]

42

Rejection

HAVING SIGNED HIS abdication, Napoleon lapsed into a
state of listlessness punctuated by occasional bursts of anger
and a kind of bewilderment; for the first time in many years
he had lost control not only of events, but also of people whom he
had come to regard as elements of a well-oiled machine. For years he
had triumphed by daring to dare, refusing to give up, and eventually
finding a way to surmount or circumvent obstacles, and by making
failures disappear by writing a version of events in which they did
not figure. He now faced a reality which was entirely impervious to
his will.

'The well-being of France appeared to be in the destiny of the Emperor,' he wrote in his declaration to the army following the defection
of Marmont. That was true for a long time. What he had lost sight of
was that his destiny had been to save France from chaos and rebuild
the state. Ironically, what was happening now was a testimony to the
success of his endeavours; it was precisely because the state he had
built was so well grounded in the institutions he had created that a
change of regime was taking place without the political chaos, not to
mention the bloodshed, that would have accompanied it fifteen years
earlier. It was his own work that was standing up to him.[1]

For years he had exerted control over people around him through
a simple formula of fear and favour, and in the rare cases in which
these did not yield the desired results he would simply banish the
person from his sight, thus avoiding the unwelcome reality that

there could be limits to his power over others. Those he had brushed aside had, like Alexander, Talleyrand, and the members of the Senate whose views he had ignored, now been able to stand up to him, again partly as a result of the administrative structures he had put in place and the social stability these had encouraged; he had created a new hierarchy of notables whose first duty was to the state. Even the army, which worshipped him, felt its first duty was to France, and as soon as it became clear that it was not just foreign allies he was up against, pronounced itself against civil war in his cause.

The narrative he had spun in his propaganda from the beginning of his first Italian campaign had given him faith in himself as well as projecting an image which spoke to the people of France and enabled him to carry them with him on his political enterprise. But with time it had deformed his sense of reality, leading him to believe that he really did have the power to make things happen simply because he willed it. This tendency to wishful thinking, combined with his unwillingness to formulate a long-term strategy, had led to disastrous results in Spain and Russia. For a long time, his ability to manipulate facts and people had allowed him to avoid facing the consequences. He continued to write inconvenient truths out of the narrative, and even now, when they had so rudely invaded it, he instinctively fought against them.[2]

Every morning one of the regiments of the Guard paraded before him, and their acclamations revived his fighting instinct; while even his most devoted generals had come to accept the inevitable, he kept revisiting various military options. On 7 April, the day after he sent off his act of abdication, the commander of the Old Guard, Marshal Lefèbvre, wrote his submission to the new government and left to take his seat in the Senate. He was followed by Oudinot, leaving only Berthier and Moncey at Fontainebleau. Yet on 10 April, having received a report based on gossip picked up from an Austrian officer to the effect that Francis was prepared to support the accession of his son, Napoleon sent to Caulaincourt revoking his credentials to negotiate the abdication and began checking his troop numbers.[3]

Caulaincourt ignored Napoleon's recall. Supported by Ney and Macdonald, he was fighting to secure the best possible terms for him. He was now having to deal with not only Alexander but also Metternich and Castlereagh, both of whom had been appalled on reaching Paris at the promises made by the tsar, and, in the background, Talleyrand and Fouché, who had also turned up, both of them determined on the elimination of their former master. Talleyrand even engineered an intrigue aimed at provoking him to make a military move which could then be used by the allies as a justification for withdrawing from the engagements made by Alexander.[4]

Caulaincourt wrote explaining the situation, but on receiving the letter Napoleon fumed about betrayal, and at five in the morning wrote back ordering him not to sign anything. It was too late; agreement had been reached that night, and on 11 April the Treaty of Fontainebleau was signed by Castlereagh, Metternich, and Nesselrode for the allies, and by Caulaincourt, Ney, and Macdonald for Napoleon. The three of them arrived at Fontainebleau the following morning with the document for him to ratify. He listened gloomily to their report and the terms of the treaty, which were that he was to be given the island of Elba to rule in all sovereignty, be provided with an annual subsidy by the French government, allowed to take a small contingent of his Guard with him, and that his family would be provided for.

He still attended the daily parades, but he had been spending his days in his own rooms, occasionally walking in the garden, sometimes taking out his frustration by swishing with his stick at the flowers. He was sickened by what he saw as the desertions of members of his staff and his *maison*, who went off on invented errands, never to return, or simply vanished. Constant and Roustam had gone, and of those who still hovered many could barely disguise their impatience for the end to come. He complained bitterly of the ingratitude of his marshals, saying he had underestimated the baseness of men in general. Yet a handful remained faithful, most notably Maret and the marshal of the palace General Bertrand, and since the first rumours of plots against the emperor's life some of his aides slept on mattresses laid out in passages leading to his rooms to protect him. At the same time, his pistols and powder had been discreetly removed.

That day he wrote to Josephine expressing his despair, and those around him could sense it.[5]

Late that night he asked his valet Hubert to revive the fire in his bedroom and to bring writing implements and paper. Having done so, Hubert kept the door between Napoleon's bedroom and that in which he slept ajar. He heard him begin a letter several times, scrunching up the paper and throwing it into the fireplace. 'Farewell, my kind Louise,' ran the final version. 'You are what I love the most in the world. My misfortunes affect me only by the harm they do to you. You will always love the most loving of husbands. Give a kiss to my son. Farewell, dear Louise. Your devoted.' Hubert then heard him go over to the commode, on which there was always a carafe of water and a bowl of sugar, and was surprised to hear the sound of water being poured into a glass and something being mixed in with a spoon, as he had noticed that the valet in charge had failed to put any sugar in the bowl. After a moment's silence Napoleon came to the door of his room and asked Hubert to call Caulaincourt, Maret, Bertrand, and Fain.

Caulaincourt was the first to arrive. He found Napoleon looking sick and haggard, having evidently taken the poison he had been wearing in a sachet around his neck since the retreat from Moscow. He began a self-justificatory ramble and asked Caulaincourt to do various things on his behalf, but Caulaincourt called for Dr Yvan. By then Napoleon was doubled up with stomach pains and complaining how difficult it was to die. When Yvan arrived he asked him to prepare a stronger poison, but the doctor instead administered a potion which made him vomit up the original dose. By morning he was out of danger.[6]

'Since death doesn't want to take me either in my bed or on the battlefield, I shall live,' he said to Caulaincourt. 'It will take some courage to bear life after such events. I shall write the story of the brave!' He then told him to prepare everything for the signing of the treaty, which he did in the presence of Caulaincourt and Maret. At nine o'clock Macdonald, who was to take it to Paris, came into the room. He found Napoleon 'sitting in front of the fire, wearing only a simple white cotton dressing gown, his naked legs in slippers, with nothing around his neck, his head in his hands and his elbows on his knees'. He did not stir at Macdonald's entrance and seemed lost in his thoughts. Caulaincourt roused him and he stood up, went over to Macdonald, took his hand, and apologised for not having noticed him enter. 'As soon as he had lifted his face, I was struck by the change in it; his complexion was yellow and olive-coloured,' continues Macdonald. Napoleon told him he had had a bad night and sat down again, once more drifting off into a reverie, from which he had to be roused again. He then presented the marshal with the scimitar of Murad Bey, captured in Egypt, and embraced him, apologising for not having recognised before what a fine, loyal man he was.[7]

Macdonald set off for Paris bearing Napoleon's ratification, while Napoleon set about dictating letters to some of those who had served him. He had transferred command of the army to the new minister of war, General Dupont, the 'coward of Bailén', and there were only 1,500 grenadiers of the Old Guard left in attendance. Berthier had gone to Paris to finalise the arrangements, and on his return he took up residence in his private residence in the park. Although he and Napoleon had worked closely for more than fifteen years they had never been friends, and following the Wagram campaign the marshal had begun to feel old and tired. He had disapproved of the war with Russia and continually urged Napoleon to make peace, which had soured relations between them.

The once-great *maison* had dwindled to no more than a dozen or so, and the vast Renaissance palace resounded only to the step of sentries. When Maria Walewska turned up on 14 April to show her sympathy, she found the palace deserted and walked through several rooms before encountering Caulaincourt, who went to inform Napoleon of her presence. He seemed not to hear and remained lost in his thoughts. She waited for several hours before going back to Paris. He wrote to her the following day apologising for not having been able to receive her and thanked her for her feelings, saying he would love to see her when he reached Elba. The probable reason he had not received her was that he was hoping to be reunited with his wife and son, and if it were known that he was seeing his mistress it might affect Marie-Louise's and her father's views on the subject.[8]

On 9 April he had written to Marie-Louise asking her to leave Blois and go to Orléans, whence he was hoping to bring her and his son to Fontainebleau. The reason he had not sent for her earlier was that while he believed there was a chance of his son succeeding him he felt he must keep his distance; the principal argument against allowing the King of Rome to succeed was that it would be tantamount to leaving Napoleon in power, so it was imperative he underline his detachment.[9]

Marie-Louise and her entourage at Blois were taken aback by news of Napoleon's abdication, and her first instinct had been to join him, partly in order to get away from his brothers. Seeing in her person a form of insurance for themselves, Joseph and Jérôme planned to take her and seek refuge with Soult's Army of Spain, encamped nearby. Understanding nothing of the politics being played out, she felt disoriented and defenceless. She had seen less of Napoleon from the time he had set off for Russia two years earlier and had been subjected to a sustained campaign by his enemies in her entourage, who fed her stories of his supposed infidelities and tried to find her a lover. Her chief lady-in-waiting, Lannes's widow, the duchesse de Montebello, actually intercepted letters to her from Napoleon.[10]

The court at Blois melted away, the chamberlains, ladies-in-waiting, maids, valets, and the 1,200-strong contingent of guards going off to Paris or elsewhere, many of them heaving sighs of relief that it was all over. Commissioners arrived from the provisional government in Paris to claim the imperial treasure which had followed them to Blois, consisting of over 20 million francs in gold and a hoard of jewellery and plate. Marie-Louise's desire to join her husband was mitigated by the prospect of accompanying him into exile, as she feared his family would congregate around him and make her life unbearable. She told Caulaincourt that she wanted to die with Napoleon but not to live with him surrounded by them.[11]

The matter was resolved when on 9 April a Russian officer sent by Francis arrived at Blois and took her off to Orléans, where she was robbed first by roving cossacks and then by a government official who tried to tear from her throat the diamond necklace she was wearing. Dr Corvisart, who examined her, wrote a report that she was suffering from breathing difficulties, rashes on her face, and fever and prescribed the waters of Aix. On 12 April she was taken to Rambouillet, where on 14 April she met Metternich and a couple of days later her father. 'It is impossible for me to be happy without you,' she wrote to Napoleon, but she appeared to be little concerned at his fate, according to Anatole de Montesquiou, whom he had sent to her. Whatever her feelings, she was easily persuaded to follow her father's wishes (which, unbeknown to her, were that she and her son should never see Napoleon again).[12]

By then, arrangements were being made for his departure. He was to be accompanied by marshal of the palace Bertrand, General Drouot, his physician Dr Foureau de Beauregard, his treasurer Peyrusse, and his valets Marchand, who had replaced Constant, the Swiss Noverraz, and the Mameluke 'Ali', alias Saint-Denis. He was allowed to take a small contingent of his Guard to supplement the Corsican battalion he would find on Elba. After fierce competition between volunteers, around 600 grenadiers of the Old Guard had been selected, commanded by General Cambronne, and eighty Polish Chevaux-Légers lancers under Colonel Jerzmanowski.

On 16 April Napoleon wrote to Josephine reassuring her that he was reconciled to his fate. 'I will in my retirement substitute the pen for the sword. The story of my reign will be interesting; I have only been seen in profile, and I shall reveal myself entirely. How many things I have to tell. How many people of whom the public has a false opinion!...I have showered with favours thousands of wretches! What have they done for me at a moment like this? They have betrayed me, yes, all of them....' He excepted Eugène, whom he believed to have remained loyal, and assured her that he would love her always and never forget her. His trust was misplaced. 'It is all over,' Josephine had written to Eugène on 8 April. 'He is abdicating. As far as you are concerned, you are no longer bound by any oath of loyalty. Anything you might do on his behalf would be pointless. Look to your family.' She and Hortense received Alexander to dinner at Malmaison, and Hortense even met Bernadotte.[13]

That evening, the four allied commissioners who were to escort him to Elba arrived at Fontainebleau, and he received them the following morning. Colonel Sir Neil Campbell represented Britain, Count Shuvalov Russia, General Franz Köller Austria, and Count von Truchsess-Waldburg Prussia. Campbell, who had an informal meeting with him that evening, found him unshaven and dishevelled, and 'in the most perturbed and distressed state of mind'. Tears poured down his face when he spoke of being separated from his wife and child, and he paced up and down the room 'like a caged beast'.[14]

The next day, 20 April, he rose early and had a final conference with Maret, who was to stay behind and who would be his main correspondent in France. He then wrote to Caulaincourt, whom he had sent on a mission to Paris the previous day, thanking him for his loyal service. He also wrote a letter to Marie-Louise, which he handed to Bausset, who was to accompany her to Vienna, expressing his hope that once she had recovered and he was installed on Elba she would join him there.

He then received the commissioners. He was cool with the Russian, expressing anger at Alexander's fawning over Josephine at Malmaison, saying it was an insult to him, and appearing jealous of the tsar's popularity with the Parisians. He also protested at having to go to Elba without his wife and child and stated that he would insist on being taken to captivity in England instead. He ignored the Prussian but was consistently polite with Köller, meaning to maintain the best possible relations with his father-in-law, and cordial with Campbell, as he had never quite shed his admiration for the British. He had demanded to be taken to Elba on a British ship, as he did not wish to place himself in the hands of the provisional government, with some reason.[15]

Just before midday he came down into the grand courtyard of Fontainebleau, in which the first regiment of grenadiers of the Old Guard was drawn up. Beyond, a crowd was gathered at the railings to catch sight of him for the last time. He made a short speech, reminding his men of the glory they had shared and asking them never to forget him. Saying he could not embrace them all, he embraced their colours and kissed the eagle that topped the shaft. Everyone, including the allied commissioners, was in tears. 'Farewell, my children,' he concluded. Captain Coignet 'shed tears of blood', while Colonel Paulin admitted that he 'cried like a child who has lost his mother'.[16]

Napoleon climbed into his carriage, followed by Bertrand. He was in tears himself. The convoy of fourteen carriages drawn by sixty horses set off for the south coast, escorted by mounted chasseurs, cuirassiers and grenadiers of the Guard. Another convoy, consisting of baggage wagons and simple carriages, bearing furniture, furnishings, china, table silver, and 695 books, under the supervision of Peyrusse and a skeleton staff, had been despatched already. The 700 or so troops who had volunteered to accompany their emperor into exile took a different route.[17]

Napoleon was cheered wherever they stopped to change horses, but after Valence, where they were received by a less than enthusiastic guard of honour, they entered traditionally royalist country. The French cavalry escort was to have been replaced by Austrians and Russians, but Napoleon had refused to be escorted by his enemies like a prisoner. On 24 April outside Valence he met Augereau, whose corps was stationed along the road. He went up to his old comrade-in-arms, removed his hat and embraced him, but the other only tipped his forage cap and did not return the embrace. They exchanged a few words, but Augereau showed no wish to prolong the encounter.[18]

At Orange they were met with shouts of '*Vive le Roi!*' and stones were thrown at his carriage. At Avignon there was no more than a sullen crowd hissing, but at Orgon he and his party were treated to the sight of a dummy representing Napoleon in a uniform covered in red paint swinging from a gibbet with a placard saying that was how the tyrant would end up. The carriage was besieged by a crowd of people 'drunk with hatred and some with wine', in the words of Shuvalov, who, along with with Köller and the powerfully built Noverraz, fought them off with fists while Napoleon cowered in the carriage. The event had been orchestrated by local royalists, probably with the support of the authorities, and Shuvalov was convinced that it was only a matter of luck that Napoleon himself had not replaced the dummy on the gibbet.

Napoleon lost his nerve. Once they had left the town he stopped to relieve himself, then put on a blue cloak and a round hat with a white Bourbon cockade, mounted a horse and rode on ahead of the conspicuous convoy. When the commissioners caught up with him at an inn at La Callade, they found him slumped at a table with tears pouring down his face; he had not been recognised, and the innkeeper had told him that Napoleon was travelling down the road and would be lynched, as he deserved to be, being responsible for the deaths of her son and her nephew. Thereafter he wore Köller's uniform, and an escort of Austrian hussars was provided.

The party stopped for the night at a château outside Le Luc, where Pauline was staying. The two siblings spent the evening together, and she promised to visit him on Elba. The journey continued without incident to Fréjus. On the evening of 28 April he boarded the British frigate HMS *Undaunted*, commanded by Captain Ussher, where he was greeted by a twenty-one-gun salute. The Prussian and Russian commissioners took their leave, and only Campbell and Köller went aboard with him.[19]

The crossing took five days, and it was not until 3 May that the *Undaunted* arrived off Portoferraio, Elba's principal port and town. The 245 square kilometres of rocky island, fifteen kilometres off the Tuscan coast, was not the most hospitable place, and its 12,000 inhabitants, who had been Napoleon's subjects since 1802, were not well disposed—there had been minor revolts against French rule recently and some of the garrison had mutinied, so both Napoleon and the British officers accompanying him were nervous. The islanders had no inkling of recent events in France, but when they discovered the war was over and they were to host the great Napoleon, they assumed a golden era had dawned for them. They greeted him with all the pomp that an island port town of 3,000 inhabitants could muster.

The day after coming ashore, Napoleon was up at four in the morning inspecting the city's defences, a presage of what was to follow; over the next few months he would apply himself to what he referred to as his 'little cabbage-patch', as he had to rebuilding France after 1799. He identified a suitable building, the Villa Mulini, for his 'palace' and had it refurbished and extended with another floor (to accommodate Marie-Louise and the King of Rome). He did the same to a smaller summer retreat in the hills, at San Martino. He designed a flag for his new kingdom, a white square with a left-to-right diagonal red band with three of his armorial bees on it. He set up a court under the marshal of the palace Bertrand, nominating chamberlains from among local notables, and a military establishment under General Drouot. Bertrand, a military engineer by profession, had been campaigning with him since the Egyptian expedition; he had succeeded Duroc in his charge and was utterly devoted. The same was true of Drouot, a talented gunner who had commanded the hundred-piece battery that had tipped the scales at Wagram.

Within a week of landing, Napoleon had scouted the whole island in detail. He set about making roads, which were almost entirely lacking, and from there went on to building aqueducts, organising drainage, sanitation, wheat cultivation, dictating letters on the subject of poultry farming, tuna fisheries, and horticulture with the same concentration with which he had treated matters of state at the Tuileries. His principal collaborator was André Pons de l'Hérault, the director of the island's only major resource, its iron mines. Pons was a former Jacobin and artillery officer whom Napoleon had met at Toulon in 1793; he was then twenty and had treated Buonaparte to his first taste of the local speciality, bouillabaisse. Originally a supporter, he had disapproved of Napoleon's assumption of the imperial title and become a declared enemy, but within a few weeks of working with him was won over and became one of his most devoted supporters. For Napoleon it was essential to get the mines working as efficiently as possible, since they were practically the only source of revenue of the barren island.

Money was a major preoccupation, and on reaching the island Napoleon had sat down with his treasurer, Pierre Guillaume Peyrusse, to take stock. Elba's taxes brought in 100,000 francs a year, and the iron mines yielded no more than 300,000. That would barely pay for the administration of the island. Napoleon had brought with him 489,000 francs in his *petite cassette*. Peyrusse had managed to save 2,580,000 from the imperial treasury which had followed the Regency Council to Blois, and to bring it to Fontainebleau. Marie-Louise had withdrawn another 911,000 at Orléans and despatched it to her husband. But according to their calculations, the total of just under 4 million francs would not last beyond 1816, given that along with his own household Napoleon had to pay for the upkeep of military personnel totalling 1,592. Under the terms of the Treaty of Fontainebleau he was to receive an annual subsidy of 2.5 million francs from the French government, but nobody was under any illusion that Louis XVIII, who had assumed the throne of France, would honour them.[20]

Napoleon would say to anyone he met that he was 'dead to the world', and he appeared content in the role of Lilliputian monarch. Although he held receptions and balls, receiving the wives of the local functionaries as though they had been those of French notables and the numerous tourists who called at the island (over sixty Britons alone dropped in as part of their grand tour) as though they had been visiting princes, he lived a quiet and, by his own admission, a very 'bourgeois' life. He felt the absence of female company keenly, and was anxious to have his wife and son join him. He kept writing, urging her to come, but she only received some of the letters he sent through trusted secret channels to Méneval, whom she had kept on as her secretary; those sent openly were confiscated. Letters from her only got through sporadically. At the end of June she was still declaring her intention to join him (by now it was clear that his brothers were not going to settle on Elba), but within a month she had succumbed to various pressures that changed her mind. One was that while the Treaty of Fontainebleau had awarded her the duchy of Parma, it was now clear that she would not be getting it, and the only way she could assure her future and that of her son was by staying close to her father at Vienna. Another was that an Austrian officer assigned to act as her equerry with a brief to dissuade her from going to Elba had been so successful as to become her lover (and, in time, husband). She was being urged to make a public declaration against Napoleon and was gradually being worn down by various people telling her to be reasonable.[21]

At the beginning of June news reached him that Josephine had died at Malmaison. He was so upset that he would not see anyone for two days. But a few days later he received a rare mark of affection and loyalty when Jérôme's wife, who was the daughter of the King of Württemberg, wrote asking him to stand godfather to the child she was carrying. 'Circumstances can have no bearing on our feel-ings, and we will always take pride in regarding you, Sire, as the head or our family, and I, for myself, will never forget that Your Majesty never ceased to give us proofs of his friendship and that you made my happiness by uniting me with the King,' she wrote. The arrival of Pauline at the beginning of July also cheered him; she only stayed for two days, but would be back for good in October. His mother ar-rived on 2 August and settled into a house close by the Villa Mulini, and they often dined together and played cards afterward. She was the only person who dared confront him about his cheating, where-upon he would, according to Peyrusse, shuffle all the cards on the table around, scoop up the money and reply that he had played fair, but later hand it to his valet Marchand, who would give it back to its rightful owners. With the return of Pauline in October the little court grew merrier, although her hypochondria often put everyone to inconvenience. She also contrived to have the furniture from her husband's palace at Turin brought to Elba, adding some splendour to the 'palace' of Mulini.[22]

At the beginning of September, Maria Walewska arrived with their son, accompanied by her younger sister Antonia and her brother Theodore Łączyński. Napoleon made elaborate plans to house them in an abandoned hermitage next to which he had erected a tent in which he occasionally spent the night. The party arrived at dusk on a small vessel which put into a quiet bay far away from Portoferraio and were discreetly taken up to the hideaway, where Napoleon spent a couple of idyllic days playing with his son and visiting his mistress at night. But a small island is no place for secrets, and word soon got around that Marie-Louise and the King of Rome had arrived. The population grew excited, and Napoleon realised that if news of the visit were to leak out it would both scupper any remaining chances of Marie-Louise coming and damage his reputation. So after two days the little party were smuggled off the island.[23]

Napoleon could not keep anything secret for long, as he was sur-rounded by spies. Talleyrand had a network of informers based in Livorno, with an agent in Napoleon's household. The French gov-ernment had another based on nearby Corsica, and another handled from the south of France. The British had one run by a former con-sul in the area, and Metternich had a formidable web of spies all over northern Italy which extended to the islands. Napoleon had his informers in Tuscany and on Corsica and was the recipient of a great deal of information from sympathisers in France. He also gleaned much from visiting Britons.[24]

He knew of a number of plans by French royalists and govern-ment agents to remove or assassinate him and felt dangerously ex-posed; the seas around were infested by pirates operating from North Africa for whom he would have constituted a rich prize, and this greatly facilitated anyone bent on landing in order to assassinate him. At one point he became so nervous that he slept in a different room every night. His contingent of grenadiers and lancers were a defence, but as it was now almost certain that the French government was not going to pay him his due, he would soon have to let them go, and then he would be defenceless. Colonel Campbell believed Napoleon was resigned to his fate and warned his superiors in London that the only thing that might make him restive was lack of funds.[25]

Whether Napoleon was temperamentally capable of remaining the sovereign of a tiny island or not is academic, as the allies would not let him. Louis XVIII would not provide him with the means of support, and Francis had no intention of letting him see his daugh-ter and grandchild again. To deprive a man of an income and the company of his wife and child is to deny him the basics of a settled life, and in this case it was also to rob him of his last remaining sta-tus symbol. The message was clear: he had been allowed to possess a princess as a conquering Attila, but now he had been defeated he was to be put in his place as the undesirable upstart he was. With a Habsburg princess at his side he had to be treated with a modicum of respect. Without, he could be treated as the allies wished.

From the moment they heard of Alexander's gesture of giving him Elba, the allied ministers determined to remove him to a more remote place. The British had presciently weaselled out of ratifying the Treaty of Fontainebleau with a bizarre formula whereby they 'took notice' of it, even though Castlereagh had signed it along with the other ministers. The prime minister Lord Liverpool had already mooted the possibility of imprisonment on some more distant island, such as St Helena in the South Atlantic. By October 1814, as the ministers and monarchs gathered at Vienna for the peace congress that had been convoked to settle the affairs of Europe, it was no secret that they intended to move him; it had even been mentioned in the press. Napoleon brought up the matter with Campbell, protesting that lack of funds and the intentions of the Great Powers were making his position untenable.[26]

He was not the man to sit tight and wait to be assassinated or incarcerated, and he began considering his options. Short of evading the Royal Navy and making a dash for the United States, where he could settle as a private citizen, there was nowhere he could go. Only France seemed a possibility. He had never entirely accepted what had happened; when they met on his arrival at Portoferraio, he had spoken to Pons de l'Héruault of recent events as though they had nothing to do with him, and he appeared to have persuaded himself that if Marmont had not betrayed him he would still be emperor. In conversation with Campbell, he sometimes gave the impression that he was expecting to be called back to France at any moment.[27]

In royalist parts of the country the restoration of the Bourbons was welcomed; elsewhere it was accepted with varying degrees of relief and hope. But the behaviour of Louis XVIII, and particularly of his brother Artois and the émigrés who returned with them, soon began to offend. The hierarchy that had grown up to manage France over the past decade and a half was humiliated and often penalised, there were demands for property to be returned to its former owners, the Church began a religious crusade to recapture the soul of the country, and an atmosphere of hatred and revenge entered village as well as Paris life. The army was the object of particular vindictiveness, with men and officers being humiliated and retired on half-pay. Its glorious achievements were denigrated, its regiments renumbered, its colours changed. Within six months of recovering the throne, the Bourbons had alienated a considerable proportion of the population and almost the entire army.

Active and retired officers and men began to talk of the good old days and to conspire to bring them back. News of this reached

Napoleon, and a return to France presented itself as the only way to avoid being deported to a grim island prison. It was a gamble, but daring had always worked for him in the past, and his return from Egypt must have haunted his thoughts. He began taking note of the movement of the British ships on station in the area and of the comings and goings of Campbell, who was acting as an informal gaoler, visiting the island for days at a time and then going off to mainland Italy. By the beginning of February 1815 Napoleon had made up his mind.

He repaired the French brig *Inconstant*, which he had inherited, and improved the seaworthiness of a number of smaller vessels, on which he surreptitiously loaded stores. He had his grenadiers lay out new gardens near the port and invented excuses for his other troops to ready themselves. They received their order to embark on 26 February. It was a Sunday, and that morning at the *lever* he had informed those present of his plans, after which he heard mass as usual in a provincial simulacrum of the Saint-Cloud custom. His mother, who along with Pauline had been informed on the previous day, expressed severe reservations, but Napoleon ignored them. As his men marched down to the harbour, accompanied by the townsfolk, who had no idea what was happening but warmed to a spectacle, he prepared a proclamation to the troops and to the French people. In the evening he went down to the harbour and, after a brief speech to the local authorities who had assembled and who expressed grief at his departure, he went aboard.[28]

43

The Outlaw

A

T NINE O'CLOCK on the evening of 26 February 1815
the *Inconstant* slipped out of Portoferraio followed by six
smaller craft. Temporarily becalmed, the flotilla spotted the
sails of a British ship and in the course of its onward journey crossed
the paths of three French naval vessels, but the soldiers lay down on
deck to keep out of sight, and it reached the coast of France without
incident, sailing into the Golfe Juan on 1 March.

A few curious locals came to gawp at the unusual number of ships
in the bay, but there was little interest even when Napoleon came
ashore late that afternoon and made camp on French soil once more.
Twenty men sent off to nearby Antibes were arrested. Napoleon had
instructed his soldiers not to use their weapons, and it is doubtful
they would have even if he had wished; when questioned later they
admitted that they were delighted to be back in France but had no
stomach for fighting fellow Frenchmen. In the event, they had no
need to. They set off at midnight, along side roads in order to avoid
confrontation, attracting little attention as they went. The soldiers
had grown unused to long marches, and they had to carry all their
equipment as they had brought only a few horses, so the column
soon stretched into an untidy string of small groups struggling along
as best they could. They bought horses along the way, but these were
passed to the lancers, who had been lugging their saddles as well as
their arms.[1]

In two proclamations, from his Guard calling on former comrades to join them and from him to his people, in which he branded

Marmont and Augereau as traitors, Napoleon portrayed himself as coming to the rescue of suffering France, whose laments had reached him on Elba, and announced that 'The eagle bearing the national colours will fly from belfry to belfry all the way to the towers of Notre Dame.' There was no eagle and no national colours—until in one small town someone produced a gilded wooden bedpost or curtain-rail finial in the shape of one which was attached to a pole and adorned with strips of blue, white, and red cloth.[2]

They met no resistance until they reached Laffrey on 7 March, where they found the road barred by infantry. Napoleon rode forward and addressed the soldiers. He was answered with silence, so he unbuttoned his grey coat and, baring his breast, challenged them to shoot, at which, encouraged by his grenadiers who had stepped forward and started cheering, the royal troops burst into shouts of '*Vive l'Empereur!*'[3]

A larger force drawn up outside Grenoble would have presented a greater obstacle had it not been for Colonel La Bédoyère leading his regiment over to Napoleon's side. The royalist commander of Grenoble closed the gates of the city, but they were hacked open by workers, who ushered Napoleon in to a delirious welcome. At Lyon the populace tore down the barricades blocking the bridges and led him into the city in triumph. From then on the eagle did fly on to Paris with astonishing speed. Ney, who had been sent out to capture Napoleon and had solemnly promised Louis XVIII to bring him back in a cage, realised that his troops were wavering and, swayed by the prevailing mood, joined his former master.

By 20 March Napoleon was at Fontainebleau. At Essones later that day he was met by Caulaincourt and a multitude of officers and men who had driven out of Paris or from the surrounding area. The previous night Louis XVIII had left the Tuileries and fled for the Belgian frontier. As the news spread, supporters of the emperor came out all over the capital and the tricolour flag was hoisted on the palace and other public buildings. As Napoleon raced on to Paris his former staff and servants took over the Tuileries, so that by the time he arrived at nine o'clock that evening all was ready, and the salons were thronged with members of his erstwhile court. When he alighted, he had difficulty in making his way through the waiting crowd. As he mounted the staircase to repossess the palace, he closed his eyes and a smile lit up his face.[4]

Within an hour of reaching the Tuileries he was working in his study with Cambacérès and Maret, putting together a new government. He had some difficulty in persuading his old ministers to take up their jobs again, as most of them were feeling their age and were tired out by what they had been through. The memory of the uncertainties of 1814 was still fresh, and when they heard of his landing, some, like Pasquier and Molé, despaired for France, foreseeing more of the same. But most let themselves be swayed by the old charm. Daru, reluctant at first, soon melted. 'I felt I was back in my world, where my memories and my affections lay,' he recalled. 'At no other moment had I felt more affection, more devotion for the emperor.' But some, like Macdonald, resisted despite repeated efforts by Napoleon.[5]

Cambacérès agreed to serve as minister of justice, Maret took up again as secretary of state, Caulaincourt (under severe pressure) as foreign minister, Carnot took the Ministry of the Interior, Davout that of the army, and Decrès resumed his old post at the navy, as did Gaudin and Mollien at finance and the treasury respectively. Napoleon appointed Fouché minister of police, with Savary and Réal briefed to keep an eye on him. 'It was an extraordinary sight to see things put back in their place so quickly,' reflected Savary. When he called on the evening of the next day, Lavalette felt as though he had gone back ten years in time; it was eleven o'clock at night, Napoleon had just had a hot bath and put on his usual uniform, and was talking to his ministers.[6]

But the appearances did not hold up for long. When the legislative bodies came to present their addresses of loyalty on 26 March, Miot de Melito, now a member of the Council of State, noticed that 'the faces were sad, anxiety was etched on every feature, and there was general embarrassment'. The enthusiasm caused by the unexpected and almost miraculous return of Napoleon subsided, as, in the words of Lavalette, 'it was not so much that people wanted the emperor; it was just that they no longer wanted the Bourbons'. Napoleon realised this. 'My dear,' he replied when Mollien congratulated him on his remarkable return to power, 'don't bother with compliments; they let me come just as they let the other lot leave.' Few felt much confidence in the future.[7]

Taking in hand the administration of the country presented a formidable challenge. Napoleon's authority did not reach far outside the *mairie* in many areas, and not even there in the north and west, where royalist sentiment was strong. In the Midi, the king's nephew the duc d'Angoulême gathered 10,000 troops and national guards and marched on Lyon. He was forced to capitulate by Marshal Grouchy on 8 April and allowed to leave the country, but civil war simmered below the surface. In these circumstances, raising men for the army and funds to equip it would not be easy—Louis XVIII had emptied the coffers, leaving only 2.5 million francs in the treasury.

Napoleon was no longer the man to galvanise the nation. He was forty-five years old and not well; his physical condition had been aggravated by haemorrhoids and perhaps other ailments. He had grown fat and had slowed down. 'Great tendency to sleep, result of his illness,' noted Lucien, who had turned up in Paris to support his brother. Napoleon himself admitted to being surprised that he had found the energy to leave Elba at all. 'I did not find the emperor I had known in the old days,' noted Miot de Melito after a long interview. 'He was anxious. That confidence which used to sound in his speech, that tone of authority, that loftiness of thought that was manifest in his words and in his gestures, had vanished; he already seemed to feel the hand of adversity which would soon weigh down on him, and he no longer appeared to believe in his destiny.' Most noticed the change, and it did not inspire confidence; all they could see was a small, fat, anxious man with an absent look and hesitant gestures.[8]

His hesitancy was partly a consequence of his not being able to find the right persona to adopt and image to project, as he had so successfully done on his returns from Italy and Egypt, after Tilsit, and even following the disaster of 1812. He now had to be all things to all men. He left the Tuileries, which required a large *maison* and formal etiquette, both of which were expensive and inappropriate; Letizia, Fesch, Joseph, Lucien, and Jérôme had all turned up to support the family business but were given no formal status. He moved into the Élysée Palace, where he was freer to see whom he wished without the complications of a large court. His only regular company was his family, a few of the more faithful ministers, and Bertrand. He saw Hortense frequently and soon after his return called in Dr Corvisart to enquire about Josephine's illness and last moments. These less formal surroundings made it easier for him to engage the support of people he had previously disdained. He was more affable than in the past and, according to Hortense, more open, extending a warm welcome to anyone who wished to see him, even to the extent of receiving Sieyès. He expressed his regret at having alienated Germaine de Staël, in the hope that she might rally to him.[9]

In the course of his march on Paris, aside from the army and former soldiers, those greeting him with the greatest enthusiasm were those most offended by Bourbon rule. From Lyon, where he paused, he had decreed the abolition of the two legislative chambers set up by the Bourbons, proscribed all émigrés who had returned with them, announced the confiscation of lands recovered by them, and voiced phrases about stringing up nobles and priests from lampposts. This won him support among former Jacobins and republicans. But galvanising the revolutionary masses flew in the face of his wish and need to keep on his side the nobles and former émigrés whom he had involved in his 'fusion', and it also opened up the prospect of a return to the civil war that had ravaged the country before he came to power in 1799. He felt he must enlist the support of all those moderate republicans and constitutional monarchists he had consistently bullied and pushed aside. In order to achieve that, he must bring in a new constitution.

To this end, he invited his former critic Benjamin Constant, who enjoyed a strong following and a Europe-wide reputation as a moderate liberal. Their collaboration was not an easy one; Constant noted that in conversation Napoleon displayed libertarian instincts, yet when it came to the question of power, he stuck to his old views that the only way of getting anything done was through variants of dictatorship. 'I do not hate liberty,' Napoleon told him. 'I brushed it aside when it got in my way, but I understand it, as I was nourished on it.' Constant was frustrated by his contradictory instincts and the continual swings they produced; Napoleon was still marked by the influence of Rousseau and his admiration for Robespierre.[10]

He intended the new constitution to derive from the imperial one, in order to ensure continuity and give it what he considered to be a deeper legitimacy. It therefore took the form of an 'Additional Act' to it, passed on 23 April. This was a compromise, which had the unfortunate effect of provoking a public debate (liberty of the press had been restored) that opened up the old animosities he had sought to reconcile since 1799. The elections, held in May, satisfied no one. Turnout was little over 40 percent, and the new hierarchy Napoleon had sought to create with his fusion did not triumph. No more than 20 percent voted in the plebiscite to endorse the Additional Act.[11]

Napoleon attempted to galvanise the nation through a '*Champ de mai*', a version of the Federation of 1790, held on 1 June on the Champ de Mars in front of the École Militaire where he had been a cadet, watched by some 200,000 spectators. It was a ceremony in the mould of the old revolutionary festivals, with a stand for the dignitaries, graded seating for the members of the two chambers and other bodies of state, and an altar of the fatherland. But in attempting to also associate it with ceremonies of allegiance held by Charlemagne and the Capetian kings, he struck a false note. He arrived in a state coach drawn by eight horses, accompanied by his brothers, who, having no constitutional status, appeared as members of a royal family. He had designed fantastic costumes for them; they were decked out in white velvet tunics with lace frills and velvet bonnets surmounted by plumes (Lucien had protested vociferously before agreeing to wear it). Napoleon himself was encased in a similar costume, pink with gold embroidery, so tight he could hardly walk, and weighed down by an ermine-lined purple cloak.

The ceremony opened with a mass, with too many priests, after which Napoleon made a speech in which he hinted that he would recover France's 'natural frontiers' and assured his people that his honour, glory, and happiness were synonymous with those of France, enjoining them to make the greatest efforts for the good of the motherland. He then swore to abide by the constitution. A *Te Deum* was sung, after which he proceeded to distribute eagles to the regiments, and the ceremony ended with a parade, the only part the spectators enjoyed. He had failed to galvanise anyone. 'It was no longer the Bonaparte of Egypt and Italy, the Napoleon of Austerlitz or even of Moscow!' noted one observer. 'His faith in himself had died.' So had that of the crowd: for every '*Vive l'Empereur!*' there were ten '*Vive la Garde Imperiale!*'[12]

On his return to Paris, Napoleon had written to all the monarchs of Europe announcing that he was by the will of the people the new ruler of France, that he accepted the frontiers fixed by the Treaty of Paris of 1814, that he renounced any claims he might have previously made, and that all he wanted was to live in peace. He followed this up with personal letters to Alexander and Francis, and to Marie-Louise, asking her to join him. Hortense, who had been befriended by the tsar when he was in Paris in 1814, also wrote to Alexander supporting Napoleon. Caulaincourt wrote to Metternich assuring him of France's peaceful intentions. In an attempt to endear himself to the British, Napoleon abolished the slave trade.[13]

The news of his escape from Elba had sown astonishment and terror among the representatives of the Great Powers gathered at the congress in Vienna. With less than a thousand soldiers, he should have been no match for Louis XVIII's army of 150,000. But within hours of hearing the news they began mustering their forces: 50,000 Austrians in Italy; 200,000 Austrians, Bavarians, Badenese, and Württembergers on the upper Rhine; 150,000 Prussians further north; 100,000 Anglo-Dutch in Belgium; and, on the march from Poland, up to 200,000 Russians. The reappearance of Napoleon had re-established a solidarity which had been fraying in the course of the congress.[14]

Talleyrand, now foreign minister of Louis XVIII representing France in Vienna, was quick to realise that if Napoleon were to reach Paris and become ruler of France, there would be no legal basis for the Powers to do anything about it, unless he were to make a hostile move. If the allies were to accept this new status quo, Talleyrand's career would be over. He therefore prepared the text of a declaration which he proposed the plenipotentiaries of the Powers should make, according to which by leaving Elba Napoleon had broken his only legal right to exist and was therefore an outlaw and fair game for anyone to kill. Metternich and others protested at such a drastic step, but after much heated argument, an amended text was adopted. While it stopped short of sanctioning his murder, it did declare Napoleon to be outside the law and closed the door to any negotiations.[15]

Fouché was also a worried man. He had hedged his bets while serving Louis XVIII by setting up a conspiracy among the military to bring Napoleon back from Elba. He had hoped Napoleon would make him foreign minister but accepted the Ministry of Police, which he would exploit to his own ends. Using his contacts in England, he sounded out the chances of the British cabinet agreeing to leave Napoleon in power, at the same time negotiating asylum for himself were he to need it. He also persuaded his old Jacobin friend Pierre Louis Guingené, now living in Geneva and in close contact with Alexander's old tutor, the philosopher César de la Harpe, to write to the tsar. Guingené had been purged from the Tribunate by Napoleon, but like many like-minded colleagues, he now saw in Napoleon the only hope for France. 'Oppressed, humiliated, debased by the Bourbons, France has greeted Napoleon as a liberator,' he wrote to Alexander. 'Only he can pull it out of the abyss. What other name could one put in place of his? May those of the allies who are most capable of it reflect on this and attempt to address this question in good faith.'[16]

Fouché had been approached by an agent of a Viennese banking house at the behest of Metternich, who had been growing increasingly alarmed at Russian interference in European affairs and the lack of a reliable ally on the Continent to stand up to it—he had always sought one in France. He did not like war and was not happy at the prospect of a huge Russian army marching through Central Europe while Austrian forces were engaged in Italy and France. He also knew that Alexander, who had never liked the Bourbons and had grown to despise them, might wish to take the opportunity to replace Napoleon with someone of his own choosing.

The invitation for both sides to meet, at an inn in Basel, was intercepted, and Napoleon substituted his own agent for Fouché's. What transpired from this and subsequent meetings was that Austria and Russia might be prepared to treat with Napoleon on condition he abdicate in favour of his son. It might not have been what Napoleon wanted, but it was an opportunity to retrieve something from a venture that was beginning to appear doomed. But Napoleon had learned nothing from his experiences; in this tiny ray of hope he saw great promise, reading into Metternich's tentative offer a sign of weakness. If the allies were split and no longer felt sure of themselves, then he would not step down and accept humiliating terms, he would play for higher stakes. He therefore cut short the negotiations and resolved to stand firm.[17]

'I have been too fond of war, I will fight no more,' Napoleon said to Pontécoulant on his return from Elba, but the man who had helped launch him on his military career believed he had not changed and that 'war was still his dominant passion'. Part of him undoubtedly would have preferred to be left in peace, and he made similar pacific statements to others. He admitted to Benjamin Constant that he had been lured by ambition but said he now only wanted to lift France from her state of oppression. But war loomed, whether he liked it or not.[18]

France faced invasion by a formidable array of enemies, which suggested two possible courses of action for Napoleon: either assuming dictatorial powers and using them to regiment the country into an efficient military machine or harking back to 1792 and calling out the nation in arms. That was something he recoiled from. He trusted in his army, which he liked to believe was as good as ever and burning to fight. This was true of subaltern officers and the older men of the lower ranks, but not at the top. The marshals had not opposed him because they could not be bothered to fight for the Bourbons (only Marmont, Victor, and Macdonald followed Louis XVIII into exile). That did not mean they could be bothered to fight for him, particularly in what looked like a lost cause. Typical was Masséna, commanding the region of Marseille, who had not lifted a finger to stop Napoleon but was living in a state of semi-retirement and just wanted to be left in peace. Most of them tried to avoid service, on either side. Much the same was true among the generals and senior officers, who were not wholly committed to Napoleon and merely went with the flow. Even where there was enthusiasm and devotion to Napoleon, there was no longer the dash of youth to support it.[19]

He also robbed himself of a major asset in not calling on Murat, who had washed up in the south of France at the end of May. Fearing that the allies at the congress in Vienna were going to depose him, Murat had seized the opportunity offered by Napoleon's escape from Elba to march out and proclaim his intention of uniting Italy, calling on all Italian patriots to join him. Few did, and he was defeated by the Austrians at the beginning of April. He fled to France while Caroline took refuge on a British ship in the bay of Naples, from whose deck she listened to the crowds acclaiming the Bourbons returning from Sicily. Murat had betrayed Napoleon more than once, but at this stage he could do no damage, and his presence on the battlefield would have been a considerable asset.

According to Maret, Napoleon considered two possible plans. 'One consisted in remaining on the defensive, that is to say letting the enemy invade France and to manoeuvre in such a way as to take advantage of his mistakes. The other was to take the offensive [against the allied armies concentrating] in Belgium and then act as circumstances suggested.' Maret claimed that Napoleon wanted to adopt the first, but all the civilians invited to express an opinion were opposed to this, warning that the Chamber of Representatives would not support him in it.[20]

It seems extraordinary that Napoleon should have given way to such pressures, as the first option was clearly the best: by the beginning of June he had over half a million men under arms around the country including the National Guard, and by keeping them close together in a central position he could have brought shattering force to bear on individual armies venturing into France, as he had done in his Italian campaign. There were also weighty political implications to the first option: if the allied invasion of ancient French territory could be represented in the same terms as that of 1792, it might elicit the same patriotic *élan*, with similar results. Napoleon never tired of representing himself as the beloved of the people. 'The people, or if you wish the masses, want only me,' he boasted to Benjamin Constant. 'I am not only, as has been said, the emperor of the soldiers, I am the emperor of the peasants, the plebeians of France.... That is why despite the past, you can see the people gather to me. There is a bond between us.' This was largely true, certainly of Paris and of central and northwestern France.[21]

It is also possible that, faced with an entirely pacific Napoleon and the prospect of invading a country at peace, the allies might have paused for thought. Their own troops were tired after years of war, and the desire to have a go at the French had been assuaged in the previous year. And if, as some suggested, the people had been called to arms, visions of 1792 might have haunted them too; they were only too aware of the smouldering embers of revolution in France and Europe.

But so was Napoleon, and his memories of 1792 had never left him. He bowed to reasonable counsel. 'The sensible middle course is never the right one in a crisis,' remarked General Rumigny, who believed a national call to arms would have revived a revolutionary fervour that would have saved the day. But the mood in the upper echelons of society was not one to build hopes on. After dining at Savary's house and later calling at Caulaincourt's on 15 June, Benjamin Constant noted 'discouragement and a wish for compromise' wherever he went. 'Anxiety, fear and discontent were the predominant sentiments; there was no attachment or affection for the government in evidence,' noted Miot de Melito, adding that only the poorer quarters of the city were firmly behind Napoleon.[22]

Whether or not he was just putting on a brave face, as Hortense believed, Napoleon was merrier than usual on the day of his departure to join the army, talking of literature during dinner with Letizia, Hortense, and his siblings, and saying as he took his leave of General Bertrand's wife, 'Well, Madame Bertrand, let's hope we don't live to regret the island of Elba!' Lavalette was also struck by his apparent optimism. 'I left him at midnight,' he recalled. 'He was suffering from severe chest pains, but as he climbed into his carriage he showed a gaiety that suggested he was confident of success.' But the strategy he had chosen, to take the war to the enemy, doomed him in the long run, as France would not be able to stand up to the vastly superior allied forces in a prolonged war.[23]

The campaign opened well. Napoleon had some 120,000 men, with which he intended to defeat Blücher with his 125,000 Prussians and Wellington with an Anglo-Dutch force of 100,000 before they could join up and outnumber him. 'Our regiments are fine and animated by the best spirit,' Colonel Fantin des Odoards of the 70th Infantry of the Line, a veteran of many campaigns and a survivor of the retreat from Moscow, noted in his diary on 11 June. 'The Emperor will lead us, so let us hope that we will take a worthy revenge. Forward then, and may God protect France!'[24]

Napoleon went for Blücher first and dealt him a heavy blow at Ligny on 16 June. It would have been a rout if General Drouet d'Erlon had acted as Napoleon intended—not the first instance where the absence of Berthier to oversee and check orders were carried out made itself felt. Soult, who was acting as chief of staff, had neither the aptitude nor the authority required. The battle might also have eliminated the Prussians from the scene had it not been for the courtesy of some French cuirassiers who, returning from a charge which had swept over him, found Blücher himself lying helpless, pinned down by his dead horse, which his aide was unable to shift on his own. With soldierly gallantry they refrained from killing him or taking him prisoner.[25]

Napoleon detached Marshal Grouchy with over 30,000 men to pursue Blücher and make sure he did not veer west to join Wellington. He himself marched north along the road to Brussels, on which, on the next day, Wellington took up position on a slight rise just south of the village of Waterloo, anchored to two heavily fortified farms at Hougoumont and La Haye Sainte. Heavy rain had turned the roads to mud and it took a long time for the French forces to come up. They spent a cheerless, cold night, and on the morning of 18 June the ground was so sodden that it was not possible to go into action, so Napoleon waited till noon for it to dry out.

The younger Napoleon would have tied Wellington down frontally and outflanked him, pinning him in a trap of his own making. But he had long since abandoned such manoeuvres in favour of frontal confrontation and heavy fire. With his forces reduced by detaching Grouchy to around 75,000 men and about 250 guns, he did not have much to spare, and little time, as superior Prussian forces might appear on his right flank at any moment. He meant to pin down the British forces in their strong points of Hougoumont and La Haye Sainte and to deliver a strong blow at Wellington's centre. He was unwell and somnolent, and, as at Borodino, did not direct operations actively.

Jérôme, commanding the left wing, wasted time and lives on trying to capture Hougoumont instead of merely neutralising the British forces there. The main attack on the British centre petered out. With some urgency, since Prussian troops were approaching, Napoleon mounted a second assault on Wellington's positions, to be driven home by a massive cavalry charge. But the attack faltered and the cavalry went into action prematurely, allowing the British infantry to form squares and repel it.

Grouchy had been negligent in his pursuit of Blücher and lost touch with him when the Prussian changed course and moved

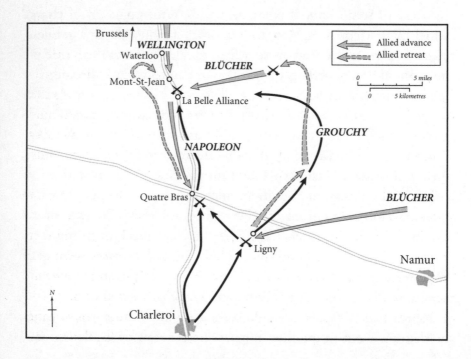

westward to join Wellington. Instead of marching on the sound of the guns, as some of his generals pleaded with him to do, he carried on, moving away from the battlefield. As a result, Blücher appeared on Napoleon's right flank and rear in the late afternoon. In a last desperate attempt to break Wellington's line, Napoleon sent in the Guard, but this was poorly directed and strayed off its prescribed course. Coming under fire from front and flank, it wavered and some units fell back, shaking the morale of the rest of the army, which began a retreat that quickly turned into rout under pressure from swarming Prussian cavalry. As a moonless night fell, the chaos and fear only increased. It was not just a military defeat; it was a morale-shattering humiliation, with standards, guns, supplies, and even Napoleon's famous *dormeuse* abandoned in the flight.

The roads were so clogged with fleeing troops that he had to make his escape on horseback, riding all night and only stopping the next morning at an inn at Philippeville, where he dictated two letters to Joseph, one for public consumption, the other more honest, and two long bulletins, one on Ligny, the other on what he called the battle of Mont-Saint-Jean, which made out that it had been hard-fought and was to all intents and purposes won when a moment of panic caused by the retreat of a single unit of the Guard caused a general retreat. It ended with the words: 'That was the result of the battle of Mont-Saint-Jean, glorious for French arms, yet so fatal.' He was utterly exhausted, and tears ran down his face, but he tried to sound optimistic. 'Everything is not lost,' he wrote to Joseph, since he had received reports that Jérôme and Soult had managed to rally some of the fleeing troops, while Grouchy was retreating in good order to join them, and he urged him to 'above all, show courage and firmness'.[26]

He himself was in a state of shock. It had been a bloody encounter—he had lost up to 30,000 men and the allies little short of 25,000. He had also left most of his artillery and a huge number of prisoners on the field and during the flight. The losses were one thing, but the blow to his reputation as a general and to his *amour-propre* and that of the French army was what really felled him.

He reached Paris around eight o'clock on the morning of 21 June and drove straight to the Elysée, where he was met by Caulaincourt, who was distressed that he had come back, believing he should have stayed with the army; without it, in Paris, he was politically vulnerable. Napoleon ordered a hot bath and summoned his ministers. The first to arrive, while he was still in it, were his paymaster Peyrusse, from whom he wanted to find out how much money was available, and Davout, whom he questioned about troop numbers. Davout assured him that all was not lost if he acted with determination and took the field as soon as possible with a fresh army. But Napoleon was in a state of shock. 'What a disaster!' he had exclaimed to Davout. 'Oh! My God!' he cried out with 'an epileptic laugh' as he greeted Lavalette.[27]

At ten o'clock he sat down to a meeting with his ministers. He told them that to defend the country from invasion he needed dictatorial powers but wished to be invested with them by the Chamber of Representatives and the Senate. He had already been informed by the president of the first and by his brothers Joseph and Lucien that news of the disaster at Waterloo had spread, and the mood in the Chamber was defeatist and strongly against him; Lafayette was calling for him to be deposed. Cambacérès, Caulaincourt, and Maret urged him to confront the Chambers and make his case, but he bridled at this. Regnaud expressed the opinion that he should immediately abdicate in favour of his son. Davout, Carnot, and Lucien advised him strongly to prorogue the Chambers, seize dictatorial powers, and declare 'la patrie en danger', the battle cry that had galvanised France in 1792. Fouché said there was no need for that, as, he assured them, the Chambers would be only too happy to support him. Decrès stared in astonishment; he, and Savary, knew that to be nonsense and could see that Fouché was trying to mislead Napoleon. Before giving him the job, Napoleon had told Fouché that he should have had him hanged long ago, but he seemed blind to what his minister of police was up to.[28]

Formerly so alive to any threat and so quick to see how to snatch a winning card from an unpromising deal, Napoleon appeared curiously detached and incapable of reaction. He would not concentrate on the matter in hand, going over the available troop numbers and the possibility of calling out the *levée en masse* one moment, asking for reports on the mood of the country the next, blaming people and events, speculating on possible manoeuvres, and confusing his own predicament with an apparently sincere conviction that he was the only person who could save France. 'It is not a question of myself,' he said to Benjamin Constant, 'it is a question of France'; if he were to retire from the scene, France would be lost.[29]

By midday, Davout felt he had missed his chance and there was no hope left, but the emperor remained calm. 'Whatever they do, I shall always be the idol of the people and the army,' he declared on being told the Chambers were now preparing to force him to abdicate or to depose him. 'I only need to say a word, and they would all be crushed.' He was right, but he would not say the word. A crowd of workers and soldiers had gathered outside the Élysée, calling for arms, and Napoleon had only to lead them across to the Palais-Bourbon, where Fouché was working for his demise in the Chamber, and the representatives would have been scampering quicker than on 19 Brumaire.[30]

When various family members called on him that evening, along with Caulaincourt and Maret, they advised him to abdicate. Only Lucien still begged him to act. 'Where is your firmness?' he urged him. 'Cast aside this irresolution. You know the cost of not daring.' 'I have dared only too much,' replied Napoleon, truthfully for once. 'Too much or too little,' snapped back Lucien. 'Dare one last time.' But he could not overcome his reluctance to unleash civil unrest. 'I did not come back from Elba in order to flood Paris with blood,' he said to Benjamin Constant. He continued to dither, and with every hour that passed his chances of saving anything from the debacle diminished. Savary advised him to leave and make a dash for the United States; Napoleon had already summoned the banker Ouvrard to ask him whether he could make sufficient funds available for him in America against a promissory note issued in France. He may also have tried to commit suicide that night; the evidence is patchy, but he was certainly out of sorts when he got up at nine o'clock on the morning of 22 June.[31]

He had still not made up his mind how to proceed, but by that time a council of ministers and delegates of the two Chambers which had convened that night under the direction of Cambacérès had decided to send a deputation to allied headquarters, effectively sidelining him. Buoyed by news of the numbers of troops Jérôme and Soult had been able to rally and the good spirits of other units around the country, Napoleon started considering various military options. But at eleven o'clock a deputation from the Chamber demanded his abdication. When it had left, he erupted into a rage and declared he would not abdicate, but Regnaud observed that in doing so he might be able to obtain the succession of his son. His advice was endorsed by all the other ministers present except for Carnot and Lucien, who both strongly urged him to seize power, reminding him of Brumaire. But Napoleon no longer had it in him. He dictated to Lucien a 'Declaration to the people of France', in which he stated that he had meant to ensure the nation's independence, counting on the support of all classes, but since the allies had vowed hatred to his person and pledged that they would not harm France, he was willing to sacrifice himself for his country. 'My political life is finished, and I proclaim my son Emperor of the French, under the name of Napoleon II,' he declared, going on to delegate powers to his ministers. Carnot wept, Fouché glowed.[32]

The declaration was delivered to the Chamber of Representatives shortly after midday, and although it was clear that nobody would accept the succession of his son, it was debated at length; Fouché and others still feared that, pushed too far, Napoleon might yet rouse himself and stage a coup. He influenced the choice of the delegates to negotiate with the allies, which alarmed those closest to Napoleon, who began to fear for his life; those chosen would not resist handing him over to the enemy as a mark of good faith. It became clear that he must get away to America as quickly as possible.

Napoleon requested Decrès to provide two frigates at Rochefort, and his librarian began preparing cases of books for him to read on the voyage and to help him in the writing of his memoirs. He went through his private papers, burning many, but, curiously, collecting together his youthful writings, including *Clisson et Eugénie* and the description of his first sexual encounter, in a box which he entrusted to Fesch. He seemed in no hurry to get away. 'He speaks of his circumstances with surprising calm,' noted Benjamin Constant, who also came to see him on 24 June. 'Why should I not stay here?' he kept saying. 'What can the foreigners do to an unarmed man? I shall go to Malmaison, where I shall live in retirement, with a few friends who will certainly only come to see me for myself.' He nevertheless repeated his request to Decrès that a couple of frigates be made ready to take him to America.[33]

On 25 June he left for Malmaison, going out by a side entrance to avoid the crowd that had been keeping a vigil in front of the Élysée. He would stay there four days, waiting for news that the ships were ready. Decrès replied that he required authorisation from the Commission of Ministers, effectively the provisional government. Under the influence of Fouché this sent General Becker with a contingent of troops to guard Napoleon at Malmaison, where he had been joined by Letizia, Hortense, Lucien, Joseph, Bertrand, Savary, General Lallemand, his aides Montholon and Planat de la Faye, the councillor Las Cases, and Caulaincourt. He received visits from old friends and saw his son by Éléonore de la Plaigne, whom he said he would bring over to America once he was established there. He admitted to Hortense to have been deeply moved by the child.[34]

The allied armies had paused, checked by smaller but still battleworthy French forces. Confused informal negotiations were going on between Fouché and Louis XVIII, who was still in Belgium, and between Talleyrand, who had joined him there, and various of his contacts in Paris. The allies were also discussing among themselves whether to reinstate Louis XVIII or install another ruler. Units in various parts of the country continued to fight. Some officers planned to kidnap Napoleon from Malmaison and rally the army to him in order to fight on—there were still 150,000 men under arms around the country, and others would have joined them.[35]

On 29 June, when he heard that the allied armies were on the move once more, Napoleon offered his services to the provisional government, promising to retire into exile once victory had been achieved. Fouché dismissed the idea, as it had become clear that one of the preconditions of any negotiation was that Napoleon was to be handed over. Not wishing to provoke any violent moves on his part or that of his entourage, the provisional government sent Decrès to Malmaison to inform Napoleon that two frigates were waiting at Rochefort. That same day, after taking his leave of Hortense and others, and pausing for a while in the room in which Josephine had died, he left Malmaison for Rochefort, escorted by Becker and his men.[36]

The two frigates were ready, but the port was blockaded by the Royal Navy, so there was no possibility of their sailing without a safe-conduct, which Napoleon was assured would be obtained by the government negotiators, a blatant lie; Fouché had let him reach Rochefort, where he was cut off from any support he might have found in Paris, and once he had boarded one of the frigates he was trapped. As he vainly waited for the safe-conduct, he was allowed to visit the island of Aix, next to which his vessel was anchored, and inspect the works he had commissioned; he was cheered by the troops stationed there, but that could not alter the fact that he was effectively a prisoner.

The allies had entered Paris on 7 July, and Napoleon did not relish the idea of being dragged back there as a captive, so the next day he sent Savary and his chamberlain Las Cases over to the British man-of-war blockading the port, HMS *Bellerophon*. At the same time, a number of plans were discussed for his escape. Joseph found a merchantman which would take him to America incognito, but Napoleon refused this subterfuge, judging it undignified. Captain Maitland, the commander of the *Bellerophon*, had given Savary and Las Cases to understand that Napoleon would be offered asylum in England, which seemed a more fitting solution. Napoleon wrote the prince regent a letter declaring that, trusting in his magnanimity and that of his subjects, he wished, 'like Themistocles, to come and sit by the fireside of the British people'.[37]

In the early hours of 15 July he put on his campaign uniform of colonel of the Chasseurs of the Old Guard, and at four o'clock in the morning he boarded the French brig *l'Epervier*, which took him out to within a cannon-shot of HMS *Bellerophon* and dropped anchor. To Becker, who had suggested escorting him, he replied, 'No, General Becker, it must not ever be said that France delivered me to the English.' He drank a cup of coffee and conversed calmly about the technicalities of shipbuilding while a launch came over from the British ship. Madame

Bertrand acted as interpreter during the exchange that then took place with the British naval officer, and Napoleon ordered his party to get into the launch. He got in last and sat down. As it pulled away, the crew of the *Epervier* shouted '*Vive l'Empereur!*', at which Napoleon scooped up some seawater in his hand and blessed them with it.[38]

It was 137 days since he had landed in the Golfe Juan, but supporters of the returning Louis XVIII tried to belittle the interlude by referring to the 110 that had elapsed between the king's evacuation of the Tuileries in March and his return at the beginning of July as a mere 'hundred days'. As with so much else in his extraordinary life, Napoleonic propaganda turned this into 'The Hundred Days', a tragic-glorious chapter in the emperor's march through history.

He was piped aboard the *Bellerophon*, and he declared to Captain Maitland that he had come to throw himself on the protection of the prince regent and the laws of England. The British naval officers had doffed their hats and addressed him as 'Sire', as did Admiral Hotham, who sailed up in HMS *Superb* that day and invited Napoleon to dinner. He felt respected and, ironically, safe as he returned to the *Bellerophon*, which set sail for England the same day. His Hundred Days in France were over.

As the *Bellerophon* rounded Ushant on 23 July, Napoleon looked on the land of France for the last time, not yet knowing that Louis XVIII had resumed his place on the throne with a ministry under Fouché and Talleyrand. What he would never know was that on hearing the news Marie-Louise wrote to her father saying that it had caused her great relief, as it put paid to 'various silly rumours that had been circulating'—that her son might be made emperor of the French.[39]

44

A Crown of Thorns

O N 24 JULY the *Bellerophon* dropped anchor in Torbay, and as soon as news got round that Napoleon was on board it was surrounded by a multitude of small craft full of locals eager to catch a glimpse of the great man. Themistocles obliged, appearing on deck and at the poop windows, tipping his hat to the ladies, evidently enjoying the attention and taking heart from the fact that it was not hostile. The newspapers wrote of his probable exile to St Helena, but that had been in the air for over a year, and the more ordinary English people saw him the more likely it seemed that he might be allowed to retire by their fireside. On 26 July *Bellerophon* weighed anchor and sailed for Plymouth, where it was flanked by two frigates with the aim of keeping away the tourists, but more than a thousand boats ferried people out to see the illustrious captive.[1]

The blow fell on 31 July, when Admiral Lord Keith came aboard accompanied by the under-secretary for war, Sir Henry Bunbury, to inform him that he was to be taken to St Helena as a prisoner of war. Napoleon protested vehemently, saying he had been tricked into believing he would be allowed to stay in England. Captain Maitland had certainly been equivocal, allowing him to think what he wished, and some of the officers of the *Bellerophon* felt he had been deceived. He objected that the British had no right to imprison him, as he had made war legally on the King of France, who had defaulted on a binding treaty. He retired to his cabin, from which he hardly emerged over the next three days, and on the fourth wrote out a formal protest at the manner in which he had been treated.[2]

By then *Bellerophon* had sailed from Plymouth to rendezvous with the flotilla under Rear Admiral Sir George Cockburn that was to escort him to St Helena. He was to travel on the flagship, HMS *Northumberland*, and the transfer would take place at sea, as the government was keen to get him away as quickly as possible. There had already been an attempt by British sympathisers to use legal means to bring him ashore by issuing a subpoena for him to attend court. If Napoleon had been allowed on English soil it would have been very difficult to get him off, and the British penchant for making a hero out of a loser might well have turned him into Themistocles.[3]

A limit was set to the number of people who could accompany him, and Savary and others were not allowed to go. Those permitted to share their master's captivity were Bertrand with his wife and young son, General Tristan de Montholon with his wife and five-year-old son, General Gourgaud, and the former chamberlain and member of the Council of State Emmanuel de Las Cases with his son. Napoleon's service consisted of his valet Louis Marchand, his Mameluke Louis-Étienne Saint-Denis, his second valet Noverraz, his butler Cipriani, his grooms the Archambault brothers, another valet, a cook, and a pastry-cook, and a man in charge of the silver. Servants attached to the other members of the party brought the total up to twenty-seven, and since Napoleon's physician had baulked at the prospect of going, the Irishman Barry O'Meara, surgeon of the *Bellerophon*, agreed to go along in his stead.

After a cordial farewell from the officers of the *Bellerophon* Napoleon was drummed off with the honours due to a general, but on coming aboard *Northumberland* he and his party had their baggage searched unceremoniously. A large sum of money was confiscated without any pretext being given. Having foreseen something of the sort, Napoleon had entrusted cloth belts full of gold coins to each of his entourage, and in that manner saved a small amount.

He seemed resigned to his fate and remained remarkably serene throughout the long passage. He bore the discomforts of shipboard life well, often remaining in his cabin to read. He chatted with the sailors, asking technical questions and trying to improve his English, and during dinner treated the ship's officers to reminiscences and accounts of his campaigns. Although they were unimpressed by his table manners, he got on well with most of them, whiling away the time in conversation or games of cards and chess. He was occasionally indisposed and sometimes irritable, which is understandable, given that from the moment he came aboard the *Bellerophon* at Rochefort to the day he stepped off *Northumberland* at St Helena, he would have spent three months at sea.[4]

On 14 October they sighted their destination, a volcanic outcrop rising out of the waters of the South Atlantic, accessible only at Jamestown, a small settlement nestling in a cleft which goes down to the sea. The island has a surface area of 122 square kilometres, and lies 1,900 kilometres off the coast of Africa, the nearest land. The climate is tropical but mild, and damp for much of the year. Discovered by the Portuguese in 1502, it was currently in the possession of the East India Company, serving the vital purpose of watering ships bound for India and Southeast Asia. In 1815 the population consisted of 3,395 Europeans, 218 black slaves, 489 Chinese, and 116 Indians and Malays. The island produced little and depended heavily on the import of food from Cape Town, a three-week trip away. There was a military governor and a small British garrison manning strategic forts and batteries, which was hugely inflated by the arrival of Cockburn's fleet, with 600 men of the 53rd Regiment of Foot and four companies of artillery totalling another 360, which, along with the sailors now permanently on station, brought to about 2,500 the number who had come to guard Napoleon.[5]

He came ashore at seven o'clock on the evening of 16 October and was put up in provisional quarters in Jamestown. By six o'clock the next morning he was on horseback with Cockburn and off to inspect the place that was to serve as his residence, a former farmhouse situated on a remote plateau at Longwood. Described by one English observer as 'an old extremely ill-built barn', it was virtually derelict and too small, so there could be no question of his moving there for some time. The British government had ordered a prefabricated wooden house to be shipped out along with some furniture, but this would take months to arrive and erect, so Cockburn set his ship's carpenters and sailors to work on patching up the existing structure and adding further accommodation.[6]

On their ride back, just over a mile short of Jamestown, they passed a bungalow set in flourishing gardens and known as 'The Briars' for its multitude of roses, the residence of the agent of the East India Company, William Balcombe. As there was nowhere else to put him, Napoleon was billeted in a small pavilion Balcombe had erected to serve as a ballroom, with an adjacent marquee. His campaign bed and *nécessaire* were installed at one end, and a makeshift study was arranged at the other, with a curtain dividing the two. Las Cases and his son moved into the garret and a skeleton staff of Marchand, Saint-Denis, and Cipriani accommodated themselves as best they could. The rest of his suite remained at Jamestown.

Napoleon would spend the next seven weeks there, working in the mornings with either Las Cases or Montholon, Bertrand, and Gourgaud, who would take it in turns to come up from Jamestown to take dictation of his accounts of the principal episodes of his life: Las Cases the Italian campaign, Bertrand Egypt, Montholon the empire, and Gourgaud the revolutionary period, the Consulate, Elba, the Hundred Days, and Waterloo. He took exercise by riding out with Captain Poppleton of the 53rd, who was detailed to keep a constant watch over him, or walking around the extensive gardens of the Briars, which were filled with fruit trees, including mangoes and figs, as well as shrubs and flowers. In the afternoons he would go for a drive with one or other of his entourage. He sometimes dined with the Balcombes and often spent his evenings with them, playing cards and other games with the children—two girls and two boys.

The second daughter, the fourteen-year-old Betsy, was pretty and vivacious and remarkably precocious. She spoke French, and once she had got over the fear of meeting the dreaded Bonaparte and the awe of seeing 'the most majestic person [she] had ever seen', captivated by his 'fascinating smile', she began chatting away with him. He delighted in her impish ways and happily joined in whatever games his 'Mademoiselle Betsee' chose to play, displaying unexpected talents at mimicry and blindman's buff; one day when a young friend of hers called to catch a glimpse of the Corsican Ogre he obliged by acting a grimacing, howling monster. Betsy treated him like a companion or a brother. 'He seemed to enter into every sort of mirth or fun with the glee of a child, and though I have often tried his patience severely, I never knew him lose his temper or fall back upon his rank or age,' she later reminisced, only dimly aware of the pleasure he derived from moments spent with his '*bambina*' or 'leettle monkee', as he referred to her.[7]

He had not been on the island a week when the full implications of his position sank in. Not only was he a prisoner, he was lodged in a miserable shed without curtains or furniture, he was watched day and night, and separated from his companions, who could only visit him accompanied by a guard. The food was inadequate and revolting, with no good bread and a shortage of fresh meat and vegetables. He was soon going to be put in an uncomfortable barn in the most dismal part of the island, damp and either windswept or enveloped in cloud. He was to be treated with the barest civility by his gaolers and, what rankled most, could expect not the slightest recognition of his former status.

On 24 October, in the presence of all four of his officers, he gave vent to his bitterness, saying that he had never treated any of his enemies with such heartless contempt. They had all been only too happy to call him their brother when he was in power and were now assuaging their shame by humiliating him. The Emperor Francis tried to bury his grandson's origins by giving the King of Rome an Austrian title and bringing him up accordingly; the man Napoleon had made King of Württemberg was doing his utmost to get his daughter to divorce Jérôme, as was the similarly crowned King of Bavaria with regard to his daughter and Eugène.[8]

Napoleon declared that he would make no more public protests himself, it being below his dignity, and would let others speak on his behalf. In a note he prepared for the captain of one of the accompanying ships who had come to take his leave before returning to Britain, he set out a number of points he wished him to make known there. The first was that the British government had declared him to be a prisoner of war, which was incorrect, since he had not been taken but had voluntarily placed himself under the protection of the laws of England; and if it had been true, then he should have been released as all prisoners of war are at the cessation of hostilities. The second was that by subjecting him to an unsuitable climate and harsh conditions, refusing him the consideration he deserved and preventing him from communicating with his wife and child, or even getting news of them, the British government was not only breaking international law but denying him basic human rights.[9]

On 9 December Cockburn took him to see Longwood, which had undergone extensive work. The stone barn had been partitioned to create living quarters for Napoleon consisting of a small bedroom, a study, a bathroom and a small room for the valet on duty, a dining room and pantry, and a library. A long wooden structure had been added on to the front at right angles, containing a parlour and a sitting room. Further additions at the back provided a kitchen, servants' quarters, various utility rooms, and accommodation for the Montholon family, Gourgaud, and in a loft reached by a ladder, Las Cases and his son (the Bertrands were to be lodged separately in a cottage halfway between Longwood and Jamestown). The building work on the annexes was still in progress, and Napoleon complained that the smell of paint made him feel sick, but even though the rooms were small and there was hardly any furniture, on the whole the accommodation was an improvement on the pavilion in the Balcombes' garden. The following day he put on his uniform and, after thanking the Balcombes for their hospitality, set off on horseback with Cockburn for his new residence, where he was greeted with military honours by a detail of the 53rd.

His campaign bed had been installed in his bedroom, a portrait of Marie-Louise had been hung on the wall, with a bust of the King of Rome beneath it, and that day he was able to relax for an hour in his first hot bath since leaving Malmaison. As their quarters were not yet ready, the Montholons, Gourgaud, Dr O'Meara, and others had to make do with tents in the garden. It was not long before the disadvantages of Longwood made themselves felt. The climate on the plateau was the worst on the island and the desolate surroundings the least appealing. The buildings were entirely unsuited to the conditions. They were roofed with paper covered in pitch, which soon began letting in the rain, and damp seeped through the walls of the annexes, which were of wood covered with the same, permeating clothes, bedding, books, and everything else. The house was full of flies and mosquitoes and infested with rats. The floors were of cheap pine, and as there was no cellar or underpinning, they rotted, occasionally giving way to reveal the damp earth beneath. The smoking chimneys did not give off enough heat to dry the rooms out.

The conditions depressed Napoleon and his entourage, who were used to a dry climate, good food, and a modicum of luxury. They also brought into sharp relief the reality of their situation and aggravated tensions which had been mounting since they left Europe. Each of the four officers who had chosen to come out with Napoleon had reasons of their own for their decision, which had been made under pressure at a moment of uncertainty. Bertrand's wife, Fanny, a beautiful, well-born creole of Irish descent, had threatened to drown herself when her husband declared his intention of going. Pangs of regret at what had seemed at the time the right gesture of loyalty were not long to hit all of the men, and their spouses even more so, as they contemplated limitless exile in such conditions. The spirit of emulation in these soldiers and courtiers, possibly manipulated by Napoleon, had aroused jealousies and animosities between them during the voyage, and these only grew with time. The Bertrands and Montholons, and particularly their wives, were locked in rivalry. Las Cases, a forty-nine-year-old minor nobleman of no evident talents, was generally referred to as 'the Jesuit'. Gourgaud was a product of the Napoleonic system: the son of a court violinist, he had fought his way up from the ranks at Austerlitz and Saragossa, been wounded at Smolensk and swum the Berezina, ending up with the rank of general, the title of baron, and the position of orderly officer to Napoleon. But he was excessively sensitive and histrionic, and they all took pleasure in baiting him.[10]

They nevertheless constituted a court around Napoleon, observing imperial etiquette and routine. Unless he was receiving a formal visit, during the day he usually wore his green hunting coat or a 'colonial' costume of white linen coat and trousers. In the evenings the company assembled for dinner in full uniform, the ladies in court dresses and bejewelled, and after dinner they played cards, conversed, or listened as Napoleon read from a book. He revisited his old favourites—*Paul et Virginie*, Racine, and Corneille—discussed other works, and went over his life in endless monologues on what he should have done or not done, passing severe judgement on people, making unpleasant comments about the women in his life, blaming others and particularly bad luck, treachery, or 'fate' for his failures. The house was furnished with whatever had come to hand, but shards of splendour were on display—imperial silver, a magnificent Sèvres coffee set depicting the salient events of his life, a few portraits and miniatures.

He took pleasure in laying out a garden at Longwood which he kept embellishing with the aid of two Chinese workers and which he enjoyed watering himself. He received visits from the Balcombes, particularly Betsy, who sometimes brought some local lady to see him. But they had to obtain authorisation beforehand and present a chit at the guardhouse at the outer limit of Longwood, as though they were visiting an inmate in prison.

His detention was anomalous, as he was neither strictly speaking a prisoner of war nor a convicted criminal, and while he was freer to move about than either, he was also forbidden a number of privileges guaranteed to both. Its conditions said more about the fears and insecurities of the cabinets of Europe than about any threat he might have posed. He was not allowed to walk or ride beyond certain limits without being accompanied by a British officer, and even within them he was watched by 125 sentinels during the day and 72 by night. In addition, there were pickets of soldiers placed on every hill in the area. Twice a day an officer had to ascertain his presence face to face. A telegraph was set up to alert Jamestown instantly of his movements (with a signal for 'escaped'). Nobody could visit him without authorisation, and a curfew applied to the immediate area. The 53rd was encamped nearby and patrolled incessantly. Two ships circumnavigated the island continuously, one clockwise, the other anti-clockwise. Dr O'Meara was enlisted by Admiral Cockburn to spy on Napoleon and report on his actions, his words, and even his mood. He was not allowed any newspapers. Ships calling at

Jamestown to take on water were boarded and searched, their crews and passengers screened. In June 1816, high-ranking commissioners sent by the French, Russian, and Austrian governments arrived to invigilate. 'The Island of St Helena is the point on which our telescopes must be unceasingly trained,' Louis XVIII's prime minister, the duc de Richelieu, wrote to his ambassador in London, anxious about whether the British were taking enough precautions. It was as if some dangerous force was being contained on the remote island, a plague that needed to be quarantined.[11]

There is no evidence that Napoleon ever contemplated or even wished to escape. On the contrary, he applied himself to making what he could of his predicament in such a way that at times he almost seemed to revel in it; the consummate actor and manipulator was gradually developing a new strategy.

Whatever his feelings about their government's actions, he had gone out of his way to be amiable to all the British officers, military and naval, during the crossing (he never cheated at cards with them). When the sailors put on their ceremony at the crossing of the Equator, he distributed money to them. He charmed the Balcombes during his stay at the Briars. He was polite and comradely toward the colonel and officers of the 53rd when they called. He received British inhabitants of the island graciously, and on the whole succeeded in engaging their sympathy, or at least in conveying the impression that he was being shabbily treated. To visiting Britons—and there were many of them, as after weeks or months at sea on their way to or from India, a glimpse of the fallen ogre was an irresistible attraction—he was charming and appeared to bear his misfortunes with good grace. It was not long before accounts were published, and people in England began criticising the unnecessarily harsh conditions to which he was being subjected.[12]

He applied himself to making them appear harsher than they were. While he had been on relatively cordial terms with Admiral Cockburn during the crossing, on St Helena he began to treat him as his gaoler. Rather than seek a *modus vivendi*, he challenged him. Knowing perfectly well that all officers and officials had been instructed to accord him no more honours than those due to a general, he would nevertheless order Bertrand to inform the admiral that the emperor wished this or that, which naturally elicited the response that the admiral knew of no emperor on the island and was therefore unable to comply. When an invitation was issued to 'General Buonaparte' to attend a function, Napoleon instructed Bertrand to answer that the person in question had last been seen in Egypt in 1799. This kind of behaviour soured the admiral's view of Napoleon and encouraged him to carry out his duty with greater zeal, leading to a further deterioration in relations between them and an accumulation of grievances on either side.[13]

In April 1816 the military governor who was to supervise his captivity reached the island and took over from Admiral Cockburn, who stayed on as commander of the naval station. Major General Sir Hudson Lowe had served mainly in the Mediterranean, taking part in the British capture of Corsica and commanding a regiment of pro-British Corsicans, and spoke French and Italian as a result. Although he was a capable soldier and a competent administrator, he was not popular, and Wellington thought him a fussy fool. Punctilious, narrow-minded, and lacking in imagination, let alone human sympathy, he was the worst possible choice for his new appointment.

Napoleon was pleased at the news that his new gaoler was to be a soldier. But things got off to a bad start when, shortly after his arrival, on 15 April the new governor called at Longwood unannounced, only to be told that the emperor was unable to receive him. It was agreed that he should return the following day, when Napoleon did receive him but took an instant dislike to him. Lowe was not interested in him as a person or a historical figure and could see no further than the limits of his instructions, which were to guard the prisoner according to guidelines laid down in London by the war secretary Lord Bathurst, who had no idea of local conditions and therefore piled on unnecessary precautions. Lowe saw no reason to question these and carried them out to the letter. Napoleon felt affronted and showed his feelings with characteristic rudeness. Lowe responded with officious detachment and an extreme interpretation of his instructions, meaning to teach the French upstart a lesson. This furnished Napoleon with the perfect target for his bitterness and frustration and, by extension, with the ideal means by which to fight his final battle against the British.

A couple of weeks after their first meeting, the ship carrying furniture and the materials for building the new house arrived at Jamestown, and Lowe came to enquire where Napoleon thought it should be erected. This carried an unwelcome suggestion of permanence regarding his captivity, and Napoleon flew into a rage about the way he was being treated, accusing his gaoler of having been sent to kill him. Lowe barely contained his anger and retired. The furniture was brought to Longwood (absurdly, since Napoleon did not play, a billiard table was installed in the parlour), and no more was said about the new residence.[14]

In mid-June Admiral Cockburn was relieved by a new squadron under Rear Admiral Sir Pulteney Malcolm, whose wife, Clementine Elphinstone, owed Napoleon a debt of gratitude; he had saved her brother's life by getting his wounds dressed at Waterloo. They brought presents from her brother (which Lowe attempted to prevent being handed over) and French newspapers and treated him with consideration. In the course of repeated visits this developed into cordiality, with Napoleon indulging his old fascination with Ossian by questioning her about her native Scotland. This profoundly irritated the governor, whose relations with the admiral became strained.[15]

The new fleet also brought the commissioners designated by Russia, Austria, and France to watch over Napoleon, and he briefly thought that, at least in the case of the Russian and the Austrian, they might provide a channel of communication with Alexander and Francis. When it became clear that they were only additional gaolers, he refused to receive them in their official capacity, as in doing so he would be accepting his position as a prisoner of their sovereigns. At the same time, he let it be known that he would gladly see them as private individuals. When, after having consulted their governments on the matter, they agreed, Lowe prohibited it, going so far as to forbid them to walk, ride, or drive in the vicinity of Longwood, or to exchange greetings with any of its inhabitants they might meet, including servants (he issued similar injunctions on the soldiers of the

53rd, who had run out to cheer Napoleon as he passed their camp on one of his morning rides). Having intercepted a note from Bertrand to the French commissioner, the marquis de Montchenu, whom he knew to have seen his sick mother in Paris, asking for news of her, Lowe rebuked him and declared that all correspondence must pass through him. He even prevented the Russian commissioner, Count Balmain, from any contact with a passing Russian ship, presumably fearing an attempt to kidnap his prisoner.[16]

Accompanying the Austrian commissioner, Baron Stürmer, was a young botanist employed in the gardens of Schönbrunn, Philipp Welle. He discreetly contacted Napoleon's valet Marchand and handed him a letter from Marchand's mother, who had been in service with the King of Rome and had accompanied him to Vienna. The letter contained a lock of his hair, and Welle, who had often seen the child in the gardens, was able to give news of him, which was all passed on to Napoleon; he was deeply affected and put the lock of hair away in his *nécessaire*, next to one of Josephine's.[17]

Another ray of sunshine in his life was the arrival of two cases of books, along with letters from Letizia and Pauline. He was so eager to get at the books that he opened the cases himself with hammer and chisel. But his mood was spoiled when Lowe confiscated two volumes sent by an English admirer stamped on the binding with the words *Imperatori Napoleoni*, as he refused to acknowledge his prisoner's imperial title. Napoleon had a number of well-wishers in England, most notably Lord and Lady Holland, who sent him books and other creature comforts—most of which were sent back by Lowe or by pettifogging officials in London. 'Napoleon cannot need so many things,' Lord Bathurst exclaimed when Pauline attempted to send him some necessities.[18]

Not surprisingly, Lowe met with a frosty reception when he called to discuss Napoleon's accommodation; Longwood was already showing signs of decrepitude and was fast becoming uninhabitable. Napoleon could see no point in building a new house, believing that by the time it was ready there would have been a new ministry in Britain or a change of regime in France, or he would be dead. He was reluctant to accept any favour which might give the impression that his lot had been eased. There ensued a difficult meeting lasting two hours (Napoleon would stand throughout, forcing Lowe to do likewise, fearing that if he were to sit down Lowe would do so too, a breach of etiquette in the presence of the emperor). Since the materials for the new house had arrived, Lowe was determined to erect it, but in the first instance remedial works to the existing one were put in hand.[19]

The Russian commissioner reported to his superiors that as well as being 'the saddest place in the world', St Helena was impossible to attack or to escape from. Yet the British government was obsessed with the possibility of his doing so and gave credence to every report and rumour of a plot to liberate Napoleon—including some absurd ones involving submarines. It therefore maintained the ludicrous number of troops and a naval squadron on permanent station, which, given the necessity of shipping in almost all victuals and supplies from Cape Town or even further afield, brought the cost of Napoleon's confinement up to, according to some estimates, as much as £250,000 a year.[20]

Rather than scale down the military establishment, Lord Bathurst ordered Lowe to reduce the expense of keeping the prisoner and his household. While on Elba Napoleon had skimped and saved, but here he was only too profligate with the British treasury's money (it had, after all, robbed him of a large sum when he came aboard the *Northumberland*). He insisted on being supplied with meat and vegetables which were unavailable on the island and often arrived spoiled, and Longwood consumed an astonishing 1,400 bottles of wine a month (assisted by Poppleton and other officers of the 53rd, who either scrounged or bought it from the servants). Lowe called at Longwood to discuss savings, but was not received, and was told to address himself to Napoleon's butler. He went to see Bertrand, who sent him to Montholon, who told him to go to the devil.[21]

On 18 August 1816 Lowe called at Longwood once more, in the company of Admiral Malcolm, who would at least gain him access to Napoleon. As they rode up they found him walking in the garden with Las Cases and Albine de Montholon. Lowe apologised for having to bring up the matter of finances but complained that he was obliged to communicate directly with Napoleon since Bertrand had insultingly refused to discuss it. Napoleon could not contain his antipathy toward the general; he reminded him that Bertrand had commanded armies in the field, while he was nothing but a staff clerk who had only ever commanded 'Corsican deserters', a man without honour who read other people's letters, a gaoler not a soldier, who was treating them 'like Botany Bay convicts'. He railed at the conditions he was being kept under, at the climate which was undermining his health, at his mail being read, his books being confiscated, and other indignities. 'My body is in your hands, but my soul is free. It is as free as it was when I commanded Europe....And Europe will in time come to judge the treatment inflicted on me. The shame will rebound on the people of England,' he said to Lowe. If he was not prepared to feed him, Napoleon would go to the camp of the 53rd, whose officers would surely not refuse to share their meagre mess with an old soldier. Red in the face, Lowe could barely contain his fury at the insulting references to his not being a real soldier and acting dishonourably when he was only following orders; he salvaged his honour by telling Napoleon that he was ridiculous and his rudeness pathetic and left, followed by Malcolm. He would never see Napoleon alive again.[22]

Napoleon admitted to Las Cases and Albine de Montholon that he had gone too far, but he was not one to apologise, and the hostilities continued. Faced with further demands to reduce the expense of his establishment, and a refusal to let him write to bankers who held his funds (a plot was feared), he had his servants gather up a large quantity of his table silver, hammer it out of shape and remove imperial devices, and sent it to be sold off for scrap in the square at Jamestown, in full view of the inhabitants and visiting Britons.[23]

Lowe retaliated by reducing the limits within which Napoleon was allowed to move and ordered the number of his servants to be reduced by four. At the end of November 1816 Las Cases was arrested, having been caught trying to smuggle out a couple of letters— apparently a ploy to get himself sent back to Europe with the four servants who were being sent away. This diminished the miniature court which was a psychological support for the fallen emperor.

Observing the routine etiquette became more difficult. A combination of monotony, boredom, bad weather, worse food, the sight of the sentries at every door and window, the petty restrictions and minor vexations, along with frequent indispositions caused by all of these, sapped morale as well as their health.

As a protest against Lowe's restrictions on his movements, Napoleon isolated himself further. He stopped riding and even going for walks; the constant attendance of a British officer spoilt the pleasure. The lack of activity told on his physical condition. His dysuria had got worse, and according to Saint-Denis he would sometimes stand over his chamberpot for long periods, his head leaning against the wall, trying to urinate. By the end of 1816 he was also suffering from protracted coughing fits and fevers.[24]

On some days he did not bother to dress at all, keeping to his rooms and reading, usually one of his old favourites. He still dictated accounts of his campaigns, to Albine de Montholon who had taken over from Las Cases, and it seems that in the spring of 1817 he began an affair with her—presumably with her husband's acquiescence, since there could have been no secrets in the confined space inhabited by so many (in January 1818 she would give birth to a daughter, Josephine, who was probably his).

After one of his visits to Longwood, Admiral Malcolm noted that Napoleon was 'not displeased' at the vexations being visited on him by Lowe and derived some satisfaction from his accruing grievances. At a later meeting, Napoleon explained the reason to Lady Malcolm. 'I have worn the imperial crown of France, the iron crown of Italy; England has now given me a greater and more glorious than either of them—for it is that worn by the Saviour of the world—a crown of thorns. Oppression and every insult that is offered to me only adds to my glory, and it is to the persecutions of England I shall owe the brightest part of my fame.'[25]

He composed a protest against the way he was being treated, listing all the petty indignities and legally dubious procedures, which was written out on a piece of satin from one of Albine de Montholon's dresses and sewn into the lining of the coat of one of the departing servants, the Corsican Santini, who on reaching London would contact the prominent radical General Sir Robert Wilson and get it published. It would fuel a debate initiated in the House of Lords by Lord Holland attacking the government for its shameful treatment of the captive emperor.[26]

Napoleon was aware that his companions were making notes and recording events for posterity, and he made sure they did not lack material. He reminisced about his childhood, his family, his love for Corsica, his time as a cadet and his later military and political exploits. He expounded his views on everything from religion to music, from women to war, reflected on what he had done and why, and discoursed on what he would have done if he had not been prevented. His monologues contain a deal of self-justification and blame of those who had supposedly failed or betrayed him, of circumstances and of 'fate'. He returned time and again to subjects such as his Russian campaign, blaming treachery and bad luck. He denigrated most of his marshals and dismissed the women he had loved with coarse comments on their attractions and desires. Unpleasant as much of it is, to anyone who does not know better the overall image that emerges from the material noted down by his four 'evangelists' is that of a man who meant well, tried to achieve the impossible, and was being horribly punished, indeed martyred, for it. Waterloo is reinvented as a kind of expiatory moral victory. And St Helena was the ideal Golgotha.

In June 1817 Malcolm and his wife sailed away, and the 53rd was also replaced. In July Dr O'Meara was expelled by Lowe, who suspected him of spying for Napoleon; the governor was increasingly suspicious of everyone, and having got wind of the meeting between Marchand and Welle, even had the Austrian commissioner expelled.

The monotony of life on the island affected everyone, and Napoleon's entourage could not hide their longing to leave. Gourgaud, who had grown neurotic and constantly feuded with Montholon, left in March 1818. Although it was something of a relief to be spared his mawkish tantrums, it further diminished Napoleon's court. The Balcombes left the same month, which upset him, as even though he had been seeing less of them recently they were a friendly presence, and Betsy always cheered him when she called. A more affecting loss was the death from appendicitis of Cipriani, whom Napoleon was fond of and who had managed to maintain a certain standard when it came to his table.

Napoleon was grateful to the Anglican chaplain who consented to give him a Christian burial and sent him the gift of a gold snuffbox. Hearing of this, Lowe forced the chaplain to return it, on the grounds that it represented an attempt by the prisoner to bribe a British official. When, as the Balcombes were about to leave, Napoleon wished to give their Malay slave Toby, whom he had befriended when staying with them, the money to buy his freedom, he was prevented from doing so on the grounds that he was fomenting a slave rebellion. Lowe did not give a political reason for not allowing the piano at Longwood to be tuned, but he did find a sinister one behind Montholon's offer to the French commissioner Montchenu of some beans, explaining in a report to Bathurst that Montchenu should only have accepted the white ones, since white was the colour of the Bourbons, and refused the green ones, since green was associated with Napoleon, the implication being that the commissioner was politically unsound.[27]

Three months after O'Meara had been sent away, Napoleon fell ill. Bertrand requested a replacement, but the governor did not believe there was anything wrong with Napoleon and offered to send one of the available military and naval medics. Napoleon refused, on the grounds that they would be no more than the governor's spies. He kept to his bedroom, which meant the British officer who was supposed to establish his presence twice a day could not see him, despite trying to peer through cracks in the shutters. Lowe insisted he be admitted into his bedroom. Napoleon refused. Lowe suggested sending a doctor to ascertain his presence. Napoleon would not admit him. Lowe threatened to have the door broken down, and Napoleon did eventually allow John Stokoe, surgeon of HMS *Conqueror*, to examine him. In January 1819 Stokoe diagnosed severe hepatitis, and was ill-treated by Lowe, arrested and dismissed, the governor being convinced that his captive was shamming. In April, Napoleon sent a plea to the prime minister Lord Liverpool through a relative of his who was passing through, but he too was persuaded by Lowe that there was nothing wrong with him.[28]

Bertrand contrived to contact Fesch in Rome, with a request for a doctor and a Catholic priest. Neither Fesch nor Letizia liked spending money (though she had sent her son some), and she appears to have been convinced by a soothsayer that Napoleon had been spirited away from St Helena and was safe in some undisclosed location; they therefore selected two decrepit Corsican priests and a young doctor with little experience who came cheap. The three of them reached the island in September 1819, and on the Sunday following their arrival, mass was celebrated in the sitting room of Longwood. Napoleon had the now largely redundant dining room turned into a chapel, and henceforth attended mass every Sunday.[29]

Albine de Montholon had left that summer, taking her children with her, and her husband was desperate to follow. The Bertrands were also keen to get back to Europe, and Napoleon, who understood their predicament but felt he could not do without the moral support of at least one high-ranking officer, considered finding replacements among his old faithfuls such as Savary and Caulaincourt. He was deluding himself if he thought they would be allowed to come; Pauline had sought permission without success, and in the previous year Jérôme and his wife, Catherine, had written to Lord Liverpool and the prince regent begging to be allowed to visit Napoleon, only to meet with refusal. In the event, he was coming to depend more on the twenty-eight-year-old Marchand, for whom he felt great affection and called 'mon fils', and who cared for him with truly filial devotion.[30]

Although he was now gravely ill, he had moments of enthusiasm and activity; toward the end of 1819 he decided to take more exercise and, spade in hand, took up gardening, which he seemed to enjoy. In January 1820 he went out for a ride, which laid him low for several days, and he repeated the exercise in May. That summer he drove out for a picnic, but on his return had to be carried into the house, and by the autumn he was in the terminal stages of what was either cancer or gastric haemorrhage due to his stomach wall being perforated by ulcers. The Corsican doctor sent by Fesch and Letizia, Francesco Antommarchi, was out of his depth and remarkably feckless with it, but there was little he could have done.[31]

Napoleon no longer left the house, and often not even his room, not bothering to shave on some days. He had grown very weak and unsteady, tripping over a rat in his room on one occasion, and fainted if he made an effort. He suffered from sweats and fevers, and vomited frequently, and by the end of the year it was clear to all around him that he was dying. Lowe refused to believe it and kept insisting on his presence being verified by a British officer, again threatening forcible entry. Dr Thomas Arnott, surgeon of the regiment which had taken over to guard the ogre, was admitted at the beginning of April 1821; he confirmed that Napoleon was still there and reported that there was nothing much wrong with his health.[32]

In the last week of April Napoleon was vomiting blood and complaining of searing pain in his side. He asked for his bed to be moved to the drawing room, which had more light and air. He was growing weaker and seemed to lose consciousness at times; on 29 April he muttered incomprehensibly about 'France', 'the army', and 'Josephine', and then about bequeathing his house in Ajaccio and the Salines to his son. On 3 May he was given extreme unction by one of his Corsican chaplains, Abbé Vignali, whom he instructed to follow the French royal tradition of the '*chapelle ardente*', a lying-in-state with mass celebrated daily. By the next day he was delirious, and at around ten minutes before six on the evening of 5 May 1821 he died.[33]

On hearing of Napoleon's death, the Italian poet Alessandro Manzoni felt a sense of shock and a powerful urge to write. He sat down and in the space of two days composed one of his greatest works, *Il Cinque Maggio*, an ode in which he portrays the deceased emperor as a heroic and superhuman being whose death he likens to that of Christ on Golgotha, since it raises him to immortality. Goethe, who translated the ode into German, also made analogies between Napoleon and Christ, and his continuing fascination with the emperor's Promethean nature had a profound influence on his work, particularly on his masterpiece, *Faust*. Napoleon's talent for self-promotion had yielded its highest achievement.

'He was neither good nor bad, neither just nor unjust, neither mean nor generous, neither cruel nor compassionate; he was *wholly political*,' wrote Matthieu Molé, who had worked closely with him for years. That was as true of his death as of his life. When he felt death approaching, on 12 April Napoleon began dictating his last will and testament, which he would later laboriously copy out in his own hand, as his Code demands. It was to be much more than just a will. It expressed affection for his family, to whom he left no money, only personal mementos. It bequeathed his heart in an urn and a lock of his hair to Marie-Louise (who would refuse to accept them). It rewarded seventy-six of his most faithful friends and followers, high and low. It gave generous grants to the men who had followed him to Elba, to foreign soldiers who had fought for France, and to the wounded of Waterloo. As he did not possess a fraction of the sums necessary, he effectively turned tens of thousands of people into creditors of the French government and therefore enemies of the Bourbons. The document is a political manifesto around which supporters of his son and the Bonaparte dynasty could unite.[34]

It opens with a number of declarations, about himself, his family, and his country and states that he is dying, 'assassinated by the British government and its hired executioner'. He had been working on this theme from the moment he reached St Helena, representing himself as a martyr, and he was unfailingly assisted by Hudson Lowe to the very end—he was buried in a picturesque spot about a mile from Longwood, but his gravestone was left blank, because the governor would not permit any inscription suggesting imperial status, and neither Bertrand nor Montholon would allow 'General Buonaparte'.[35]

Two years after his death, Las Cases published his *Mémorial de Sainte-Hélène*, an account of the emperor's slow martyrdom after Waterloo, a best-seller which spread the gospel of Napoleon throughout the world. The spirit of the age was highly receptive, and poets across Europe and beyond embraced Napoleon's carefully crafted propaganda. 'Britannia! you own the sea,' wrote the German poet

Heinrich Heine. 'But the sea has not water enough to wash away the disgrace that this great man bequeathed to you as he died.'[36]

Napoleon had finally triumphed over his British enemy, and in the process he had achieved something else. From his earliest years he had sought role models and braced his ego by casting himself in the image of a Hannibal, Alexander, Caesar, or Charlemagne, but after briefly considering Themistocles, he had lighted upon an entirely new model, one just as mythical as any of the others, which would gain far greater resonance than all of them put together—that of Napoleon the godlike genius who, misunderstood, betrayed, and martyred by lesser men, would triumph over death and live on to haunt the imagination and inspire future generations; he had begun a new life as a myth.

Notes

N.B. In some cases I have used different editions of the same title, because I have worked on this book in different places and the same edition was not always available

PREFACE

1. Franz Grillparzer, *Sämmtliche Werke*, vol. I, Stuttgart 1872, 192–4

2. Beyle, *Vie de Napoléon*, 1; see also Salvatorelli; Gueniffey, *Bonaparte*, 257

3. Bodinier, 328–9; see also Lefèbvre, 207; Lignereux, 213

CHAPTER 1:
A RELUCTANT MESSIAH

1. Bailleu, I/163; Williams, 8–9

2. Staël-Holstein, *Considérations*, XIII/192–3; Bourrienne, 1831, II/216; see also Jomard, 17–18

3. Espitalier, 52; Bailleu, I/165; Dumont Romain, 2

4. *Recueil*, 3

5. *Recueil*, 4; Dumont Romain, 3; Staël-Holstein, *Considérations*, XIII/199; Bailleu, I/164; Gueniffey, *Bonaparte*, 257

6. Williams, 8–9; Espitalier, 50

7. *Recueil*, 4; Espitalier, 49

8. Mallet du Pan, II/356; Espitalier, 56–7; Bourrienne, 1831, II/216; Mallet du Pan, II/371–2

9. *Recueil*, 6

10. Staël-Holstein, *Considérations*, XIII/199; Gueniffey, *Bonaparte*, 310; Napoleon, *Mémoires*, I/507

11. *Recueil*, 7

12. Ibid., 9

13. Ibid., 13

14. Ibid., 18

15. Ibid., 23

16. Bailleu, I/155

17. Ibid., 159; Bourrienne, 1831, II/219; Pontécoulant, II/489

18. Dumont Romain, 4; *Recueil*, 25; Pasquier, I/134

19. Bailleu, I/162; Espitalier, 143–7

20. Espitalier, 62; Mallet du Pan, II/384; Bailleu, I/167

21. Waresquiel, 232

CHAPTER 2:
INSULAR DREAMS

1. Branda, *Secrets*, 25–7 (Gerard Lucotte's study)

2. Defranceschi, 46–60; see also Vergé-Franceschi, *Napoléon*; Paoli; Carrington, *Portrait*, 17; Gueniffey, *Bonaparte*, I/27

3. Vergé-Franceschi, *Paoli*, 183–283

4. Vergé-Franceschi, *Paoli*, 183–4, 188, 283, 295, 9; Vergé-Franceschi, *Napoléon*, 73; Boswell

5. There are differences of opinion on the subject. See Simiot, 5; Gueniffey, *Bonaparte*, 29; Branda, *Le Prix*, 19–20; Carrington, *Napoleon*,

14, 19–20; Carrington, *Portrait*, 11–14; Charles Napoléon, 66; Vergé-Franceschi, *Napoléon*, 43–51, 55ff.; Bartel, 17

6. There is no evidence for the story in Carrington, *Portrait*, 15–17, 26–8; Vergé-Franceschi, *Napoléon*, 54, 73; Paoli, 27, etc., of Carlo going to Rome and living it up there

7. Boswell, 96

8. On the alleged authorship of the proclamation, see Carrington, *Portrait*, 37; Paoli, 29; Vergé-Franceschi, *Napoléon*, 76. See also Carrington, *Napoleon*, 78, 44–5; Vergé-Franceschi, *Paoli*, 376; Gueniffey, *Bonaparte*, 41

9. Paoli, 30–1; Carrington, *Portrait*, 46, 42–3; Carrington, *Napoleon*, 43

10. Versini, 21; Vergé-Franceschi, *Napoléon*, 90, 95; Carrington, *Portrait*, 43

11. Vergé-Franceschi, *Napoléon*, 30; On stories surrounding his birth, see also Charles Napoléon, 92; Carrington, *Napoleon*; Vergé-Franceschi, *Napoléon*, 13

12. Versini, 26; Carrington, *Napoleon*, 53–5; Defranceschi, 70

13. Vergé-Franceschi, *Napoléon*, 107–11, 121; Carrington, *Portrait*, 58; Versini, 33

14. Bartel, 38; Versini, 60–1; Carrington, *Portrait*, 48

15. Carrington, *Portrait*, 50–2

16. Paoli, 43

17. Carrington, *Portrait*, 57, 55–6; Carrington, *Napoleon*, 65, 78

18. Vergé-Franceschi, *Napoléon*, 48; Versini, 86; Charles Napoléon, 98; Defranceschi, 72

19. Versini, 64; Bartel, 40–3; Chales Napoléon, 105; Carrington, *Portrait*, 66, 72–3; Carrington, *Napoleon*, 103

20. Larrey, *Madame Mère*, 528–9; Masson, *Jeunesse*, 36; Chuquet, I/50; Bertrand, *Cahiers 1818–1819*, 137

21. Larrey, *Madame Mère*, 528, 530

22. Larrey, *Madame Mère*, 529; see also Vergé-Franceschi, *Napoléon*, 294–5; Paoli, 45, 50; Chuquet, I/78; Defranceschi, 79–80

23. Vergé-Franceschi, *Napoléon*, 319; Carrington, *Portrait*, 48–9

24. The story that he travelled through Italy, related by Coston, I/17–18, has been disproved by Versini, 78–9; Marcaggi, 65; Carrington, Paoli, and others

25. Masson, *Napoléon Inconnu*, I/49

26. Defranceschi, 82

CHAPTER 3:
BOY SOLDIER

1. Bartel, 61; Masson, *Napoléon Inconnu*, I/54

2. Paoli, 68–73; Chuquet, I/113–14

3. Bartel, 62–4

4. Vergé-Franceschi, *Napoléon*, 335

5. *Some Account*, 24; Bartel, 259; Bourrienne, 1829, I/25. Des Mazis seems to place this at the École militaire; see also Thiard, 51–2

6. Belly de Bussy, 235; *Some Account*, 27, 13

7. Bourrienne, 1829, I/30; Bartel, 255; Gourgaud, I/252–3

8. Napoleon, *Oeuvres*, I/xx; *Some Account*, 29–31; Chuquet, I/118, 129

9. Carrington, *Napoleon*, 103; Vergé-Franceschi, *Napoléon*, 49; Versini, 72–4; Defranceschi, 85–6

10. Vergé-Franceschi, *Napoléon*, 50; Versini, 74–6

11. Garros, 25; Tulard & Garros, 20–1

12. Carrington, *Napoleon*, 129; Versini, 174–6; Defranceschi, 72

13. Bertrand, *Cahiers 1818–1819*, 136–7

14. Napoleon, *Correspondance Générale* (henceforth CG), I/43–4

15. Ibid.; Lucien Bonaparte, I/24–5

16. Bartel, 87

17. Paoli, 84; Tulard & Garros, 24

18. Masson, *Jeunesse*, 110; Chuquet, I/200–3; Bartel, 119

19. Chuquet, I/200ff.; Bartel, 107ff.; Masson, *Jeunesse*, 90–1; Bien, 69–98

20. Marcaggi, 62; CG, I/49; Pachoński, 243–6

21. CG, I/45. See also Las Cases, 1905, I/94

22. The supposedly prophetic story of Carlo crying out as he was dying that Napoleon would avenge him (Chuquet, I/212; Joseph, *Mémoires*, I/29) can be safely dismissed

23. CG, I/47

24. Masson, *Jeunesse*, 113

25. Bartel, 255–6

26. Ibid., 256, 258, 136

27. Ibid., 258, 257

28. Ibid., 257–8

29. Marcaggi, 67; see also Claire de Rémusat, *Mémoires*, I/267

30. Bartel, 79, 256, 259, 261; Avallon, 10–17; Las Cases, 1905, I/95

31. Masson, *Jeunesse*, 129, 139; see also Abrantès, I/112–13

32. Bartel, 260

CHAPTER 4:
FREEDOM

1. Paoli, 108–9; Simiot, 39–40

2. Las Cases, 1905, I/100

3. Bartel, 148–9, 261; Paoli, 113; Las Cases, 1905, I/102; Masson, *Napoléon et les femmes*, 8

4. Paoli, 112, 109; Beyle, *Vie de Napoléon*, 28; Napoleon, *Oeuvres*, I/xxi

5. Napoleon, *Oeuvres*, I/37–8

6. Paoli, 102; Joseph, *Mémoires*, I/33

7. Joseph, *Mémoires*, I/32–3; Charles Napoléon, 137–8; Paoli, 128, 133

8. Paoli, 133, 138; Garros, 32; see also Branda, *Le Prix*, 19–20

9. Napoleon, *Oeuvres*, I/68–9; Joseph, *Mémoires*, I/38

10. Branda, *Secrets*, 35

11. Napoleon, *Oeuvres*, I/55–6

12. Paoli, 163; CG, I/65; Chuquet, I/308; Napoleon, *Oeuvres*, I/85ff.

13. Paoli, 29–30, 247, 43–9

14. Ibid., 67, 237, 451

15. CG, I/67, 70; Simiot, 50; Bartel, 261

16. CG, I/68, 72, 74; Thiard, 37–8

17. Chuquet, I/357; CG, I/72–3

18. CG, I/74, 72

19. Ibid., 76; Napoleon, *Oeuvres*, I/67, II/53 (According to Defranceschi, 20–1, the text was later heavily doctored by Napoleon)

20. Napoleon, *Oeuvres*, II/69; Masson, *Jeunesse*, 196

21. CG, I/77, 78–9; Coston, II/92–3

22. CG, I/81

23. Paoli, 178; Coston, 92–3

CHAPTER 5: CORSICA

1. Masson, *Napoléon Inconnu*, II/107–15

2. Paoli, 193; Garros, 41

3. CG, I/83; Paoli, 198; Chuquet, II/103; Napoleon, *Oeuvres*, II/70. See also Defranceschi, 126

4. Chuquet, II/129–34; CG, I/84

5. Gueniffey, *Bonaparte*, 86; Chuquet, II/103, 109

6. Marcaggi, 134, 162, breaks this down into two events, placing the confrontation in the Olmo in July, which is almost certainly wrong; Masson, *Napoléon Inconnu*, II/107–15

7. Masson, 105–6; Chuquet, II/110–24. The story of Napoleon making a sarcastic remark about Paoli's command at Ponte Novo can be dismissed

8. CG, I/89; Napoleon, *Oeuvres*, II/133–5

9. Paoli, 198; CG, I/97; Napoleon, *Oeuvres*, II/133–5

10. CG, I/100

11. Ibid., 97

12. Masson, *Jeunesse*, II/349

13. Napoleon, *Oeuvres*, II/225ff., 229, 231

14. Chuquet, II/217; Masson, *Jeunesse*, II/262; Napoleon, *Oeuvres*, II/254

15. Napoleon, *Oeuvres*, II/243, 249, 260, 293–4

16. Masson, *Jeunesse*, II/251

17. According to Branda, *Le Prix*, there was money; Defranceschi, 154–5, believes Luciano left only debts; see also Gueniffey, *Bonaparte*, 96. Joseph's story (*Mémoires*, I/47) that Luciano prophesied Napoleon's greatness on his deathbed can be dismissed

18. Schuermans, 11; Chuquet, II/246; Nasica, 175; Garros, 48

19. Nasica, 183–5; Marcaggi, 220–1; Chuquet, II/248

20. Gueniffey, *Bonaparte*, 97–9 (Charles Napoléon (190) believes it was Saliceti); Chuquet, II/359–75; Nasica, 211ff.; Masson, *Napoléon Inconnu*, II/357ff., 385; Marcaggi, 229–50; Napoleon, *Oeuvres*, II/305

CHAPTER 6: FRANCE OR CORSICA

1. Chuquet, III/90; Marcaggi, 253

2. Chuquet, III/16–18

3. Bourrienne, 1829, I/48

4. CG, I/110, 112

5. Bourrienne, 1829, I/49–50; CG, I/113; quoted in Garros, 50; CG, I/114

6. CG, I/116, 112

7. Masson, *Napoléon Inconnu*, II/397, 394–5

8. Ibid., 397

9. CG, I/116

10. Las Cases, 1983, II/114

11. Ibid., 114–15; see also Claire de Rémusat, *Mémoires*, I/269

12. Gueniffey, *Bonaparte*, 102; Paoli, 302

13. Lucien Bonaparte, I/74–6

14. Napoleon, *Oeuvres*, II/333; CG, I/123; see also Tulard & Garros, 55

15. Defranceschi, 192ff.

16. See Gueniffey, *Bonaparte*, 108

17. CG, I/124–5, 126; Paoli, 343; Tulard & Garros, 56; Masson *Napoleon Inconnu*, II/426

18. See Chuquet, III/133–5; probably the leanest account is in Defranceschi, who (158–60, 210–11) believes most of it is nonsense

19. Paoli, 345–6

20. Ibid., 359–60

21. Chuquet, III/142–3; Charles Napoléon, 215

CHAPTER 7:
THE JACOBIN

1. Gueniffey, *Bonaparte*, 109

2. Simiot, 69

3. Masson, *Jeunesse*, claims he did, but as Garros, 59–62, points out, this is doubtful

4. The various possibilities are summed up in Tulard & Garros, 60–6; Schuermans, 15–17; Chuquet, III/159–61. According to Masson, *Napoléon et sa Famille*, I/81, he wrote to the war ministry requesting promotion to lieutenant-colonel in the artillery of the navy; according to Chuquet, III/160, he requested a post in army of the Rhine. There is no trace of these letters in CG

5. Napoleon, *Oeuvres*, II/388, 369–75

6. Gourgaud, II/273; see also Abrantès, *Mémoires*, I/38. For Saliceti's attitude, see Garros, 63

7. Quoted by Gueniffey, *Bonaparte*, 126

8. Victor, 26, 30

9. Chuquet, III/176; Napoleon, *Mémoires*, I/7–12

10. CG, I/129, 133, 136

11. Chuquet, III/194; Garros, 64; Napoleon, *Mémoires*, I/16–17

12. CG, I/131–142; quoted in Garros, 64

13. Marmont, I/40–1

14. Masson, *Napoleon et sa Famille*, I/83

15. CG, I/142–7; Chuquet, III/203–4

16. Coston, II/237

17. Chuquet, III/212, 213; Poupé, 64

18. Napoleon, *Mémoires*, I/29

19. Las Cases, 1983, I/118–19; Victor, 70–1; Marmont, I/44–5

20. Quoted by Dwyer, *Napoleon*, 143; Poupé, 92; Tulard, Fayard, Fierro, 152

21. Gueniffey, *Bonaparte*, 133; Dwyer, *Napoleon*, 145

22. CG, I/154

23. Chuquet, III/229–30; Coston, II/242–4, 245–50

24. Victor, 28

25. On his catching scabies, see Gourgaud, I/302; Gueniffey, *Bonaparte*, 169; Roberts, *Napoleon*, 49 and 50 (note)

26. Masson, *Napoléon et sa Famille*, I/834; Simiot, 76; Barras, I/288; Des Genettes, II/357–8; Metternich, *Mémoires*, I/312

CHAPTER 8:
ADOLESCENT LOVES

1. Simiot, 79

2. Napoleon, *Oeuvres*, II/399–404

3. Ibid. For his views on Robespierre, see Casanova, 141–4; Englund, 68; Bertrand, *Cahiers, 1818–1819*, II/272; Joseph, *Mémoires*, I/111–12

4. Napoleon, *Oeuvres*, II/399–404; also, Gueniffey, *Bonaparte*, 170

5. Coston, II/278–80

6. Masson, *Napoléon et sa Famille*, I/97. For the story that Joseph had wanted to marry Désirée and been told to marry Julie instead by Napoleon, see Haegele, 72–3

7. CG, I/196

8. Coston, II/285–6

9. CG, I/197; Coston, II/292; Garros, 73; Dwyer, *Napoleon*, 154–5

10. Gueniffey, *Bonaparte*, 145

11. Masson, *Napoléon et sa Famille*, I/97; CG, I/201–2

12. Las Cases, 1983, I/122

13. Garros, 75

14. Napoleon, *Mémoires*, I/62–3

15. Gueniffey, *Bonaparte*, 145

16. CG, I/221, 218–20

17. Marmont, I/60–1; Chastenay, 203

18. Chastenay, 203–4

19. Ibid., 206, 206–8

20. See Fraser, *Venus*, 1–18

21. CG, I/243

22. Lavalette, 117; see also Frénilly, 235

23. Marmont, I/88; CG, I/246 (in Las Cases, 1983 I/598, he says he was horrified at the 'Babylon' and the perversions of Paris)

24. CG, I/224–6

25. Ibid., 226–7, 232–3

26. Ibid., 233–4, 235–6, 238–9, 241, 242; Marmont, I/64; see also Haegele, 76–82, and Branda, *Le Prix*, 30–3

27. CG, I/230–1, 237–8, 235–6, 246, 248–9; Haegele, 85–6; CG, I/233

28. CG, I/248

29. On the Clary family, see Girod de l'Ain, 19

30. Girod de l'Ain, 51, 54, 55

31. CG, I/227–9

32. Ibid., 229

33. Ibid., 231–2, 232–3; Girod de l'Ain, 70; CG, I/246; Haegele, 86; Bruce, 119

34. Marmont, I/62; see also Abrantès, *Mémoires*, I/275–6

35. Abrantès, *Mémoires*, I/254, 265; Bourrienne, 1829, I/78–81

36. Barras, I/242, 285; Ouvrard, I/20–2; see also Masson, *Napoléon et les Femmes*, 17

37. Pontécoulant, I/325; CG, I/244–5, 246, 248–9

38. Napoleon, *Oeuvres*, II/442–51

39. Pontécoulant, I/326, 327–35; CG, I/254; Gueniffey, *Bonaparte*, 151; see also Roederer, III/327

40. CG, I/254

41. Ibid., 256, 257, 258–62

42. Ibid., 262, 263

43. Ibid., 262, 268, 252; Pontécoulant, I/343–4

CHAPTER 9:
GENERAL VENDÉMIAIRE

1. CG, I/265

2. Barras, I/242

3. Napoleon, *Mémoires*, I/80; Barras, I/250, 303, maliciously claims that Napoleon discussed with the insurgents the possibility of joining them if they would give him command. See also Cambacérès, *Mémoires*, I/352, on his dislike of the existing authorities

4. Barras, I/250; Napoleon, *Mémoires*, I/81

5. Napoleon, *Mémoires*, I/84; Dwyer, *Napoleon*, 174

6. Napoleon, *Mémoires*, I/84–6, 523–6; CG, I/269

7. Barras, I/253–5, 261ff., 282; Dwyer, *Napoleon*, 176; Coston, II/342–5; Dwyer, *Napoleon*, 174; see also Pontécoulant, I/365–9

8. Barras, II/26; Marmont, I/95

9. Marmont, I/86; Coston, II/423–4; Las Cases, 1983, I/125; Gourgaud, I/254

10. Tulard, Fayard, Fierro, 380; Simiot, 98, 100–1; Dwyer, *Napoleon*, 178

11. CG, I/271–2; Le Nabour, 60; CG, I/280, also 287, 291, 293–4

12. Barras, I/348–58; CG, I/270, 280, 281

13. Gourgaud, II/263–4; Beauharnais, I/31–2; also Hortense, I/42; Lavalette, 127–8; Napoleon, *Mémoires*, I/87–8

14. Barras, II/56

15. Barras, II/52–3, 60, 60–1; Josephine, 50

16. CG, I/277–8, 290, 283; Barras, II/27; Lavalette, 129; Barras, II/60. See also Bertrand, *Cahiers, 1818–1819*, 262

17. Barras, II/58

18. CG, I/285

19. There was gossip about his having paid court to various young women at Auxonne and Valence, but no evidence, and the story that he had proposed to Panoria Permon (Abrantès, II/47) can be dismissed. See also Marmont, I/94–5

20. Coston, II/347–9. The letter is almost too good to be true in the way it expresses so graphically everything we know or can infer of Josephine's feelings and the nature of her relationship with Buonaparte, but it is hard to believe that anyone would have had the information in 1840 required to forge something so convincing. It also contradicts both Hortense I/43 and Eugène, I/32, who state that they were against their mother remarrying. Eugène claims they saw it as 'a profanation, an insult to the memory of my father'. Napoleon himself later recalled (Gourgaud, II/264) that Eugène was for and Hortense against the match. But the time and circumstances in which they were recording events might well explain this discrepancy

21. Pontécoulant, I/335; Gueniffey, *Bonaparte*, 168; Dwyer, *Napoleon*, 181

22. Dwyer, *Napoleon*, 183

23. Coston, I/438–40; Barras, II/66

24. Branda, *Secrets*, 41–4

25. Ibid., 44

26. Joseph, *Mémoires*, I/136; Louis Bonaparte, *Documents*, I/47

27. Masson, *Napoléon et les Femmes*, 17; Girod de l'Ain, 96

28. CG, I/298

CHAPTER 10:
ITALY
1. Bouvier, 47; Pelleport, I/38
2. CG, I/305, 310
3. Napoleon, *Mémoires*, I/130
4. Bodinier, 285; CG, I/305, 328; Bouvier, 19
5. Gourgaud, II/319; CG, I/304, 305
6. CG, I/303. See also Napoleon, *Mémoires*, I/130
7. Vigo-Roussillon, 29; Pelleport, I/37–8
8. Bodinier, 297
9. Bouvier, 15, 39
10. CG, I/315
11. Collot, 10; CG, I/310
12. CG, I/318–19, 323, 326
13. Bouvier, 209–11
14. Arnault, 423
15. Bouvier, 244
16. Ibid., 254; Napoleon, *Les Bulletins*, 20–2
17. Bouvier, 281; De Jaeghere & Graselli, 26; for Napoleon's expression of regret, see Costa de Beauregard, 336
18. De Jaeghere & Graselli, 28; Bouvier, 431
19. Costa de Beauregard, 341
20. CG, I/357, 361–2
21. Collot, 13; Bulletins, 30–2; Collot, 11
22. Collot, 13; The story of a Gascon grenadier dubbing Bonaparte 'the little corporal' is almost certainly apocryphal. Most accounts, e.g., by Lejeune in Petiteau, 36, or Collot, 13, were written after the *Mémorial* was published, and they probably took it from there—see Bouvier, 533–6
23. CG, I/343–5

24. Joseph, *Mémoires*, I/61
25. Bouvier, 316–17; Collot, 14
26. CG, I/359, 357, 371–2

CHAPTER 11:
LODI
1. See Chaptal, 296–7
2. Fugier, 35; CG, I/389
3. Bouvier, 527; Dwyer, *Napoleon*, 213; Napoleon, *Mémoires*, I/156–7, as usual exaggerates the number of prisoners taken and puts French losses at less than 200
4. Bouvier, 538; CG, I/392, 393; Fugier, 35; Dwyer, *Napoleon*, 216
5. CG, I/396–7
6. Ibid., 377; Napoleon, *Mémoires*, I/154–5; CG, I/357, 370–1
7. CG, I/398–400, 397–8; Dwyer, *Napoleon*, 217; Bouvier, 556
8. Méneval, I/427; Bertrand, III/77; Marmont, I/322–3, 353; Costa de Beauregard, 354, 340
9. Beyle, *Vie de Napoléon*, 3
10. Lavalette, 112; Marmont, I/22–3
11. Staël, *de l'influence*, 37, 48, 23–4
12. Fugier, 34–40; Marmont, I/180ff.
13. Vigo-Roussillon, 34–5
14. Beyle, *Vie de Napoléon*, 126–8
15. Bulletins, 43; Bouvier, 634–5
16. Fugier, 36; Bouvier, 589
17. CG, I/403; Coston, II/325; Miot de Melito, I/91
18. CG, I/416, 422, 443
19. Marmont, I/180–1
20. Bouvier, 538; Fugier, 38; see also Dwyer, *Napoleon*, 225
21. Launay, 149

22. CG, I/428, 433–4
23. Ibid., 407–8, 414, 435
24. Ibid., 443, 441, 448, 451, 453
25. Arnault, 392
26. Bruce, 180
27. Chevallier & Pincemaille, 137
28. CG, I/505, 506, 505–7, 517

CHAPTER 12:
VICTORY AND LEGEND

1. These and other figures in this chapter are taken from De Jaeghere & Graselli and Beraud and should be considered as approximate
2. Bulletins, 57
3. Marmont, I/314; Dwyer, *Napoleon*, 246, 247
4. Pelleport, I/47
5. Reinhard, 207–8; Chaptal, 296–7
6. Marmont, I/296; Roguet, I/30
7. Napoleon, *Mémoires*, I/206; Vigo-Roussillon, 37; Gourgaud, II/127; Napoleon, *Mémoires*, I/208, 217; Pelleport, I/80
8. Reinhard, 108; CG, I/569
9. Napoleon, *Mémoires*, I/225
10. CG, I/553
11. Josephine, 47; CG, I/638
12. CG, I/610–13; Bulletins, 75–6; CG, I/621
13. CG, I/631–2, 447; Reinhard, 194–5
14. Fugier, 51; Gueniffey, *Bonaparte*, 219; CG, I/664
15. Napoleon, *Mémoires*, I/239
16. Reinhard, 167
17. Bulletins, 76
18. Gueniffey, *Bonaparte*, 220. The number of Croats varies from 1,000

supported by two guns, to 2,000 with a battery: see also Pelleport, I/71, and Reinhard, 177
19. See Louis Bonaparte, I/59–61; Marmont, I/236–7; Napoleon, *Mémoires*, I/248; Vigo-Roussillon 42–3. See also Reinhard, 177–8
20. Bulletins, 78–80. See also Napoleon, *Mémoires*, I/256; Dwyer, *Napoleon*, 250–1
21. Dwyer, *Napoleon*, 4
22. See Dwyer, *Napoleon*, 255–62, for the best coverage of this subject
23. CG, I/671, 672–3, 675–6
24. Ibid., 680, 681; Garros, 105
25. Garros, 106; Fugier, 63
26. Fugier, 52–4
27. Ibid., 54; CG, I/778–9
28. Defranceschi, 13–14; CG, I/638
29. CG, I/790, 791
30. Ibid., 834, 838, 841, 852
31. Ibid., 897, 902
32. Ibid., 917–18; Dwyer, *Napoleon*, 292

CHAPTER 13:
MASTER OF ITALY

1. Gueniffey, *Bonaparte*, 245; Miot de Melito, I/159; Napoleon, *Mémoires*, I/425; Arnault, 421
2. Pontécoulant, II/470–2; Arnault, 421
3. Miot de Melito, I/159
4. Lavalette, 138
5. Miot de Melito, I/108, 184; Josephine, 50
6. Arnault, 431; Claire de Rémusat, *Mémoires*, I/204
7. Dwyer, *Napoleon*, 296

8. Gueniffey, *Bonaparte*, 230–1; Branda, *Le Prix*, 35–7

9. Lareveillère-Lépaux, II/39–40; Bartel, 149

10. Dwyer, *Napoleon*, 304

11. Gueniffey, *Bonaparte*, 273–4; Branda, *Secrets*, 159–69

12. CG, I/1058

13. Gueniffey, *Bonaparte*, 273–4; Pontécoulant, II/474; see also Barras, III/99

14. CG, I/1071–3; Lareveillère-Lépaux, II/101ff.

15. Niello-Sargy, I/4–5; Martin, I/130

16. Gueniffey, *Bonaparte*, 333–4; Alexander Rodger, 31

17. CG, I/957–8

18. Lavalette, 170, 110; Gueniffey, *Bonaparte*, 341; Marmont, I/295

19. Dwyer, *Napoleon*, 337–8, 340–1; CG, I/1119

20. Pontécoulant, II/473

21. Fugier, 61–2; Pelleport, I/96

22. Miot de Melito, I/163–6, 182–4

23. Pontécoulant, II/474; Collot, 15–17; see also Casanova, 158–69

24. Gueniffey, *Bonaparte*, 279; Pontécoulant, II/463; Barras, III/47–9, 62

25. CG, I/1081

26. Ibid., 1171; Napoleon, *Mémoires*, I/474–5

27. CG, I/1209, 1213

28. Ibid., 1244

29. Gueniffey, *Bonaparte*, 292; Gourgaud, I/115; Napoleon, *Mémoires*, I/493

30. Dwyer, *Napoleon*, 315; Lavalette, 172

31. CG, I/1249

32. Miot de Melito, I/195

33. Bourrienne, 1831, II/211

34. Lavalette, 174

35. Garros, 120

CHAPTER 14:
EASTERN PROMISE

1. Talleyrand, *Mémoires*, 40; Espitalier, 32–4

2. Pontécoulant, II/489–94

3. Garros, 122

4. Barras, III/138; Bailleu, I/166; Espitalier, 98

5. CG, I/1316–17; quoted by Gueniffey, *Bonaparte*, 317; see also Espitalier, 59, and Launay, 181

6. Lareveillère-Lépaux, 339; Bailleu, I/163–4

7. Bailleu, I/165

8. Garros, 123; Gueniffey, *Bonaparte*, 326; Bailleu, I/162, 176, 178, 182–3; Espitalier, 96; Jomard, 25; Cambacérès, I/407; Miot de Melito, 230–1; see also Barras, II/136, 161

9. Arnault, 595; Napoleon, *Mémoires*, I/509

10. Dwyer, *Napoleon*, 326

11. Ibid., 328; Garros, 125, also Espitalier, 114–19; Bourrienne, 1831, II/234

12. Arnault, 607; Dwyer, *Napoleon*, 328; Joseph, *Mémoires*, I/70–1; Bourrienne, 1831, II/222–3; Espitalier, 99

13. Waresquiel, 244; Gueniffey, *Bonaparte*, 344; Dwyer, *Napoleon*, I/339–40; Espitalier 129, 136, 156–7, 163; also Jomard, 102, and Bailleu, I/182–3

14. Garros, 127; Lareveillère-Lépaux, 345–6

15. Launay, 192

16. Bourrienne, 1831, II/231–4; Launay, 192; Fleury, 278

17. Josephine, 60

18. Napoleon, *Mémoires*, I/517; see also Bourrienne, 1831, II/234, 231

19. Guitry, 6

20. Geoffroy Saint-Hilaire, 23–4; Pelleport, I/107–9

21. Guitry, 5; Gueniffey, *Bonaparte*, 354

22. Niello-Sargy, 18; Moiret, 19–20; Bernoyer, 14; Espitalier, 238–9

23. Bernoyer, 20; Saint-Hilaire, 25

24. Arnault, 633, 621

25. Ibid., 629, 631; Des Genettes, *Souvenirs*, 1–2; Arnault, 630

26. Miot, 13; Pelleport, I/111; Bernoyer, 33

27. Bernoyer, 17; Dwyer, *Napoleon*, 354; Pelleport, I/112

28. CG, II/160–1

29. Lacorre, 23–4

CHAPTER 15:
EGYPT

1. Pelleport, I/115; Beauharnais, I/140; Guitry, 97; also Bielecki & Tyszka, I/56, and Guitry, 101–2

2. Niello-Sargy, 58; Pelleport, I/112

3. Marmont, I/374; Millet, 55; *Copies of Original Letters*, 75, 5

4. Guitry, 116

5. Miot, 39; Moiret, 25, 40; Pelleport, I/120–1, 115

6. Guitry, 97, 96; Vigo-Rousillon, 64; Moiret, 46

7. Gourgaud, I/244; Reiss, 248–50; Murat, I/26–7; Napoleon, *Mémoires*, II/133

8. Guitry, 107, 111

9. Beauharnais, I/41; Moiret, 47; Guitry, 111–14; Moiret, 48

10. CG, II/195

11. CG, II/158; Josephine, 63, 67, 69–71

12. Beauharnais, I/42; CG, II/199–200

13. Niello-Sargy, 115; Marmont, I/389; Des Genettes, *Souvenirs*, 6; see also CG, II/307

14. CG, II/298; Lavalette, 185; *Copies of Original Letters*, 33; CG, II/297

15. Bulletins, 107; Guitry, 200

16. Bernoyer, 104, 76

17. Geoffroy Saint-Hilaire, 52; Andy Martin, 67; Bulletins, 108–9

18. Claire de Rémusat, *Mémoires*, I/274

19. Pelleport, I/129, also Guitry, 150–2

20. Pelleport, I/130; Moiret, 65. See also Bernoyer, 79–80, and Guitry, 162

21. Moiret, 58, 53; Garros, 139; Lavalette, 188; Guitry, 117; Miot, 98–9; Bielecki & Tyszka, I/56

22. Guitry, 181

23. Bernoyer, 94, 100; Moiret, 33–4, 54; Niello-Sargy, 194–5; Gueniffey, *Bonaparte*, 389; Abrantès, III/69–70; Niello-Sargy, 194–5; see also Gourgaud, I/106, 218

24. Masson, *Napoléon et les Femmes*, 57–62; Niello-Sargy, 199–204; Napoleon, *Mémoires*, II/158–9; Fourès, 165–6; Launay, 215; Beauhearnais, I/45. For various versions of the event: Gourgaud, II/115; Bernoyer, 118–23; Garros, 140

25. CG, II/399–400, 513
26. Napoleon, *Correspondance*, V/221

CHAPTER 16: PLAGUE

1. Moiret, 64, 78
2. CG, II/867; Lavalette, 109; Gueniffey, *Bonaparte*, 411. See also Vigo-Roussillon, 81, and Des Genettes, *Souvenirs*, 29
3. Bernoyer, 139–40; Guitry, 250–1
4. Bernoyer, 142–3; Pelleport, I/140
5. Millet, 83; Niello-Sargy, 253–7; Bernoyer, 146; Guitry, 266; Lacorre, 90
6. Des Genettes, *Souvenirs*, 15; Miot, 145–7; Vigo-Roussillon, 83–4
7. Gueniffey, *Bonaparte*, 419–23
8. Des Genettes, *Histoire Medicale*, 49–50; Garros, 143; Geoffroy Saint-Hilaire, 87; Dwyer, I/424
9. CG, II/872–3; Gueniffey, *Bonaparte*, 425; Bernoyer, 153
10. Gueniffey, *Bonaparte*, 395; CG, II/874
11. Gueniffey, *Bonaparte*, 424; Bernoyer, 153
12. Des Genettes, *Souvenirs*, 17
13. Bernoyer, 163–4. His later claim that he was intending to take Constantinople and come at Austria through the Balkans, or become a Muslim and lead an army to India, can be dismissed as the hot air of an ageing bore
14. CG, II/910–16, 920; Napoleon, *Mémoires*, II/560–1
15. Beauharnais, I/64; Pelleport, I/155
16. Vigo-Roussillon, 87; Bernoyer, 180–1; Niello-Sargy, 295, says Bonaparte suggested it but doesn't confirm it was carried out at Acre and reports what he heard about events at Jaffa, 319–23; Marmont, II/12, defends Bonaparte's action; Larrey, in Guitry, 317–19, claims all the wounded were evacuated; Pelleport, I/156, claims the wounded and sick were evacuated on boats from Jaffa; Lavalette, 215, says the whole story is an atrocious calumny; see also *Documens particuliers*, 120–2; Bernoyer, 164–5, who claims to have had the story from Des Genettes himself, thought it praiseworthy; Bourrienne, 1831, II/336–40, is typical, admitting he never saw anything, but making various claims. According to Bonaparte (Las Cases, 1983, I/150–2), there were only seven men involved
17. CG, II/918–21; Lavalette, 215. See also Bourrienne, 1831, II/335, and Niello-Sargy, 291–99
18. Millet, 128–9
19. Dwyer, *Napoleon*, 437; Gueniffey, *Bonaparte*, 431, estimates it was one-fifth. On opinions of those who lamented Napoleon's decision to march out of Egypt, see for instance, Lavalette, 217
20. Niello-Sargy, 306–7; Bernoyer, 168; Vigo-Roussillon, 89 claims it fooled nobody
21. CG, II/849, 941
22. Ibid., 952–4, 972, 1032 passim
23. Niello-Sargy, 324–7

24. Englund, 131
25. CG, II/1042
26. Vigo-Roussillon, 96–7, 91, 101; Guitry, 342
27. See Guitry, 354–5, for the classic version, propounded by Bonaparte himself; Niello-Sargy, 343–57; For a full discussion of this, see Gueniffey, *Bonaparte*, 437–42
28. Launay, 222, erroneously claims she sailed with him; see also Masson, *Napoléon et les Femmes*, 62–3, and Gueniffey, *Bonaparte*, 442
29. Vigo-Roussillon, 102
30. Guitry, 361
31. Launay, 224
32. Denon, *Voyage*, 340; Bourrienne, 1829, III/7–8; Lavalette, 221
33. Launay, 225
34. Carrington, *Portrait*, 82; Le Nabour, 70–1; Denon, *Voyage*, 340–1; ·Méneval, I/11

CHAPTER 17:
THE SAVIOUR
1. Gueniffey, *Bonaparte*, 453; Marmont, II/51–2; Raza, 24
2. Boulart, 67–8
3. Coston, I/511; Marbot, I/45–8
4. Barante, I/44; Béranger, 70; Dwyer, *Napoleon*, 462; Tulard, *Brumaire*, 67
5. Molé, 122
6. Barante, I/40
7. Andigné, I/404; Barante, I/44; Ségur, *Histoire*, II/1
8. McMahon, 109, 77, 97
9. Dwyer, *Napoleon*, 458–61
10. Thibaudeau, 1
11. Chastenay, 311; Tulard, *Brumaire*, 79

12. Gueniffey, *Bonaparte*, 448; Vandal, *l'Avènement*, I/244; CG, II/1089
13. Collot, 20; Vandal, *l'Avènement*, I/244; Gueniffey, *Bonaparte*, 459
14. Masson, *Napoléon et sa Famille*, I/259–60; see also Le Nabour, 74–5
15. Barras, IV/31–3; Bourrienne, 1829, III/38, claims it was him; Collot, 33, gave him similar advice
16. Bourrienne, 1829, III/37, insists Bonaparte would not let her in for three days
17. Cambacérès, *Mémoires*, I/429–31
18. Fouché, 1957, 61
19. Vandal, *l'Avènement*, I/233
20. Ibid., 258
21. See Bourrienne, 1829, III/43–6
22. Gueniffey, *Bonaparte*, 465; Tulard, *Brumaire*, 88–90; Joseph, *Mémoires*, I/77
23. Vandal, *l'Avènement*, I/272–4
24. See Lavalette, 228–32
25. Talleyrand, *Mémoires*, 49–50; Arnault, 748
26. Vandal, *l'Avènement*, I/292–3; Lavalette, 227–8; Lucien Bonaparte, I/297; Gueniffey, *Bonaparte*, 469; see also Thibaudeau, 3
27. Vandal, *l'Avènement*, I/293–4; Tulard, *Brumaire*, 103

CHAPTER 18:
FOG
1. Vandal, *l'Avènement*, I/304
2. Ibid., 305; see also Barras, IV/70–2, and Bourrienne, 1831, III/68–9
3. Vandal, *l'Avènement*, I/314

4. Ibid., 316
5. Ibid., 317
6. Ibid., 325; Gueniffey, *Bonaparte*, 479
7. Vandal, *l'Avènement*, I/337–9, 344
8. Ibid., 340–3
9. Tulard, *Brumaire*, 127; Tulard, *Fouché*, 115–16; also, Bourrienne, 1831, III/82; Savary, I/241; Fouché, 1957, 79
10. Dwyer, *Napoleon*, 491; Tulard, *Brumaire*, 128
11. Vandal, *l'Avènement*, I/364
12. Joseph, *Mémoires*, I/79
13. Vandal, *l'Avènement*, I/367; Gueniffey, *Bonaparte*, 483; Girardin, I/170; Napoleon, *Mémoires*, II/561; Bourrienne, 1829, III/83–5
14. Vandal, *l'Avènement*, I/371–2; see also Bourrienne, 1829, III/91
15. Vandal, *l'Avènement*, I/373–5
16. Ibid., 378
17. Ibid., 381
18. Ibid., 386–7
19. Ibid., 387–9; according to Lucien Bonaparte, I/365, Bonaparte shouted, 'And if they resist, kill! kill!'
20. Dwyer, *Napoleon*, 503; one hundred according to Tulard, *Brumaire*, 146; eighty according to Collot, 28
21. Lentz, *Le Grand Consulat* (henceforth GC), 83–4
22. Vandal, *l'Avènement*, I/394–9; on Brumaire, see also Cambacérès, *Mémoires*, I/433–47; Roederer, III/296–306; Napoleon, *Mémoires*, II/367–401
23. Vandal, *l'Avènement*, I/393
24. Tulard, *Brumaire*, 153–4
25. Vandal, *l'Avènement*, I/276

26. Bourrienne, 1829, III/105–6; Lentz, GC, 13
27. Vandal, *l'Avènement*, I/400–1; also Bourrienne, 1831, III/105–8, and Abrantès, II/383

CHAPTER 19: THE CONSUL

1. Roederer, III/2–3
2. Napoleon, *Mémoires*, II/405; Cambacérès, *Mémoires*, I/442
3. Napoleon, *Mémoires*, II/411–12; Garros, 157
4. Napoleon, *Mémoires*, II/405–7; Fouché, 1957, 85; Cambacérès, *Mémoires*, I/490; Gueniffey, *Bonaparte*, 507; Tulard, *Brumaire*, 157
5. Fouché, 1957, 87; Cambacérès, *Mémoires*, I/443–4; Roederer, III/320–1; CG, II/1094
6. Lentz, GC, 196
7. Bourrienne, 1829, III/129–32
8. Napoleon, *Mémoires*, II/433
9. Fouché, 1957, 90; Napoleon, *Mémoires*, II/436; Tulard, *Brumaire*, 155
10. Napoleon, *Mémoires*, II/439
11. Garros, 159; Lentz, GC, 109; Lareveillère-Lépaux, II/423; Napoleon, *Mémoires*, II/438
12. Tulard, *Napoléon ou le mythe*, 120; Lentz, GC, 164; see also Gueniffey, *Bonaparte*, 525
13. Boudon, 50; Lentz, GC, 112
14. Lentz, GC, 112
15. Ibid., 119
16. Garros, 160
17. Roederer, III/305–6
18. Chaptal quoted in Boudon, 55; Bourrienne, 1829, III/129–32
19. Ernouf, 217

20. Fouché, 1957, 48, 97; Cambacérès, *Mémoires*, I/469
21. Bouillé, 405–6; Lentz, GC, 166
22. Lentz, GC, 153–4, 159–61
23. Hauterive, *Napoléon et sa Police*, 143, 197; Tulard, *Napoléon ou le mythe*, 136
24. Healey, *The Literary Culture of Napoleon*, Appendix B
25. Defranceschi, 14–25
26. Waresquiel, 284; Lentz, GC, 101
27. Hyde de Neuville, I/269
28. Andigné, I/414–16, 417–18, 420; Hyde de Neuville, I/270–2
29. CG, II/1118–19; Tulard, *Napoléon ou le mythe*, 132, 134; Lentz, GC, 322
30. Mollien, I/24; Mathieu Dumas, III/168; Molé, 174; Ségur, *Histoire*, II/1–2

CHAPTER 20: CONSOLIDATION

1. Cambacérès, *Mémoires*, I/470
2. Garros, 163–4; Barante, I/54; Cambacérès, *Mémoires*, I/488; Lentz, GC, 209; Thibaudeau, 2–7; Chastenay, 297
3. Hortense, I/69
4. Garros, 164; see also Bourrienne, 1829, IV/3
5. Cambacérès, *Mémoires*, I/464; Roederer, III/335
6. Molé, 175
7. Claire de Rémusat, *Mémoires*, I/103–4; Staël, *Considérations*, XIII/194
8. Fain, *Mémoires*, 291; Chaptal, 195; Chuquet, III/233–4; Saint-Denis, 170; Abell, 235

9. Choiseul-Gouffier, 100; Abrantès, III/194, 363; Staël, *Considérations*, XIII/195, 206–7; Marmont, I/297; Claire de Rémusat, *Mémoires*, I/101–2, 116–17, 112; Saint-Elme, 354; Bourrienne, 1829, XIII/228
10. Beugnot, I/457
11. Lentz, GC, 359; Las Cases, 1983, II/304–5; Thiard, 41; Bigarré, 152; Claire de Rémusat, *Mémoires*, I/224
12. Molé, 137, 243
13. Roederer, III/302–3
14. Lucien Bonaparte, I/384; Masson, *Napoléon et sa Famille*, I/319
15. Fontaine, *Journal*, I/7; Fontaine, *Les Maisons*, 318–19, 330
16. Chaptal, 329; Fain, *Mémoires*, 287–9
17. CG, II/1099, 1106; Fain, *Mémoires*, 289, 456–9; Chaptal, 225; Fleury de Chaboulon, III/176; see also Bourrienne, 1829, IV, 60–1
18. Molé, 158
19. Las Cases, 1983, I/416, 652, 618–19; Las Cases, 1905, II/567; Thiard, 33–4
20. Abrantès, *Roman Inconnu*, xv; Bourrienne, 1829, IV/36–7
21. Thibaudeau, 14–16
22. Rousseau, 25, 141
23. Gueniffey, *Bonaparte*, 625
24. Rousseau, 106; Roederer, III/334
25. Constant, *Journal Intime*, 224
26. Lentz, GC, 428; Lefèbvre, 84
27. Lentz, GC, 156
28. Thibaudeau, 69
29. Lentz, GC, 132
30. Garros, 158
31. Lentz, GC, 97; Andigné, I/407; Hyde de Neuville, I/252
32. Bailleu, I/357; Barante, I/50–1

CHAPTER 21:
MARENGO

1. CG, II/1114–15
2. CG, III/43–4; Lentz, GC, 220; Rose, 14, 288–9
3. Guitry, 362–3, 366–8; Savary, I/183; Pelleport, I/163; Moiret, 119–22; Des Genettes, *Souvenirs*, 37; Alexander Rodger, 131; Napoleon, *Mémoires*, III/247; see also Las Cases, 1983, II/169–72
4. CG, III/241, 308; Tombs, 394
5. Méneval, I/88–93; see also Lucien Bonaparte, I/377
6. Lentz, GC, 227; Cambacérès, *Mémoires*, I/474; CG, III/98, 41, 120; Gueniffey, *Bonaparte*, 547
7. CG, III/148
8. Gueniffey, *Bonaparte*, 550
9. CG, III/216; Gueniffey, *Bonaparte*, 548
10. CG, III/168–70; Garros, 169–70
11. CG, III/222; Cambacérès, *Mémoires*, I/522
12. Napoleon, *Mémoires*, III/37
13. CG, III/235, 238
14. Napoleon, *Mémoires*, III/38; Griois, I/120
15. Bourrienne, 1829, IV/91–2; Napoleon, *Mémoires*, III/39, 40; Savary, I/253–4; CG, III/271
16. CG, III/278
17. Bulletins, 136; Masson, *Napoléon et les Femmes*, 84; Gourgaud, I/217, II/92, claims it was after Marengo
18. CG, III/300
19. Lentz, GC, 234
20. Victor, 179

21. Savary, I/265–80; Marmont, II/125–36; Napoleon, *Mémoires*, III/33–69; Victor, 160–89
22. CG, III/301
23. Ibid., 303, 312
24. Ibid., 318
25. Bulletins, 145, 147
26. Lentz, GC, 230
27. Josephine, 101
28. Lentz, GC, 377–8
29. Cambacérès, *Mémoires*, I/524
30. Roederer, III/330–1
31. Savary, I/313; Lentz, GC, 261; Cambacérès, *Mémoires*, I/530

CHAPTER 22:
CAESAR

1. Bertrand, *Lettres*, 29
2. CG, III/386; Waresquiel, 320–1; see also Tulard, *Fiévée*, 126–7; Cambacérès, *Mémoires*, I/714; Remacle, 368; Westmorland, I/50ff.; Méneval, I/226–32; Bourrienne, 1829, V/107–8; Miot de Melito, II/157–8; Desmarest, 273–4; Masson, *Napoléon et sa Famille*, I/323
3. Girardin, I/189; see also Roederer, III/336
4. Desmarest, 33
5. Ségur, *Un aide de camp*, 47
6. Hauterive, *Napoléon et sa Police*, 48
7. Castanié, 231; Réal, I/359
8. Mollien, I/221–2
9. Bergeron, 29
10. Branda, *Secrets*, 70–6; see also Saada, 25–49
11. Cambacérès, *Mémoires*, I/567
12. Thibaudeau, 77; Lentz, GC, 370–1; Pelet de la Lozère, 8; Roederer, III/382

13. Rapp, 20; Thibaudeau, 257; Las Cases, 1983, I/207

14. Thibaudeau, 77; Molé, 411–12; Roederer, III/382; Lucien Bonaparte, I/373

15. Pelet de la Lozère, 11; Méneval, I/412–21

16. Gueniffey, *Bonaparte*, 567; Lafayette, V/248, also 117, 138, 143–4, 146–7, 153

17. Thibaudeau, 152; Casanova, 26–8; Gourgaud, I/323; Bourrienne, 1829, IV/276–81; Las Cases, 1983, I/688–9

18. Pelet de la Lozère, 223; Roederer, III/335; CG, V/882

19. Tulard, *Fouché*, 159

20. Lentz, GC, 264–6; see also Lucien Bonaparte, I/421–32

21. Chastenay, 310; Masson, *Napoléon et sa Famille*, I/335; Lucien Bonaparte, I/385–6

22. Tulard, *Napoléon ou le mythe*, 157; Espitalier, 292–3

23. Cambacérès, *Mémoires*, I/535–7; Decaen, II/292; Claire de Rémusat, *Mémoires*, I/192; Abrantès, II/372–3

24. Castanié, 17–18; Sparrow

25. Marquis, 211, 257–8; Castanié, 26–7

26. Barante, I/72

CHAPTER 23: PEACE

1. Gueniffey, *Bonaparte*, 601

2. CG, III/588

3. Ibid., 664–5

4. Bertaud, Forrest & Jourdan, 40; Uglow, 282; CG, III/509, 136

5. Las Cases, 1905, II/516; Cornwallis, 406; Grainger, 60

6. CG, III/913–16; Joseph, *Mémoires*, I/231; see also Cornwallis, 389–9

7. Josephine, 110

8. Méneval, I/132, 145

9. Raza, 188

10. Méneval, I/142; Bigarré, 128; Gueniffey, *Bonaparte*, 603; Ségur, *Un aide de camp*, 70–1; see also Abrantès, IV/326–62

11. Gueniffey, *Bonaparte*, 571; Josephine, 121–2

12. Bonaparte, CG, III/71–2, regarded the treaty as not favourable enough; Masson, *Napoléon et sa Famille*, II/96–7; Lucien Bonaparte, II/107, 113, 122, 219

13. Staël, *Dix Années*, 65

14. Ibid., 18; Girardin, I/236

15. Lafayette, V/164; Lentz, GC, 317

16. Consalvi, 100–1; Lentz, GC, 311

17. Consalvi, 130–6, 147, 151–7, 342ff.

18. Lentz, GC, 320

19. Fugier, 121

20. Ibid., 122

21. Ibid., 124

22. Ibid., 25

CHAPTER 24:
THE LIBERATOR OF EUROPE

1. Grainger, 50–2; Uglow, 282; Bouillé, II/468; Tombs, 396

2. Roederer, III/430

3. Gueniffey, *Bonaparte*, 669

4. Las Cases, 1983, I/690

5. Thibaudeau, 13; see also Bourrienne, 1829, IV/280

6. Lentz, GC, 330

7. Ibid., 332–3; Bartel, 254; Charles Napoléon, 224; CG, III/1178

8. Lentz, GC, 448

9. Napoleon, *Vues Politiques*, 211–13, 228; Ségur, *Histoire*, II/233–4; Lentz, GC, 450

10. Réal, I/38–9

11. Lentz, GC, 347

12. Murat, II/30; Remacle, 30–1; Gueniffey, *Bonaparte*, 670

13. Lucien Bonaparte, II/107

14. Thibaudeau, 237

15. Lentz, GC, 339; Molé, *Souvenirs*, 234–7

16. Lentz, GC, 340

17. Ibid.

18. Josephine, 97; Masson, *Napoléon et sa Famille*, II/150ff.

19. Josephine, 98–100; Chevallier & Pincemaille, 312–13

20. Lentz, GC, 341; Lentz, Nouvelle Historie du Premier Empire (henceforth NHPE), I/59; Gueniffey, *Bonaparte*, 675

21. Lafayette, V/199

22. Cornwallis, 406

23. Lefèbvre, 144

24. Ibid., 123

25. Gueniffey, *Bonaparte*, 680

26. Miot de Melito, I/317–18; Girardin, I/286

27. Fain, *Mémoires*, 224–6; Méneval, III/43; Chevallier & Pincemaille, 303

28. Fontaine, I/26–8, 38, 53; Divov, 51, 72, 88, 128; Fiszerowa, 245–6; Pamiętnik Stanislawa Zamoyskiego, in Biblioteka Uniwersytetu Adama Mickiewicza, etc., p. 200; Berry, 163

29. Edgeworth, 55; Greathead, 11–13, 55–6; Farington, 1906; Fiszerowa, 245–6; Burney, 271

30. Sédouy, 36

CHAPTER 25:
HIS CONSULAR MAJESTY

1. Alger, 53; Grainger, 81–2

2. Cambacérès, *Mémoires*, I/569

3. CG, III/1225

4. Thibaudeau, 120–1

5. Branda & Lentz, 19–22, 192

6. CG, III/600; Branda & Lentz, 120

7. Branda & Lentz, 84–5

8. Ibid., 168; Gourgaud, I/278

9. Branda & Lentz, 72–3, 86–7; CG, III/853–4

10. Roederer, III/334; CG, III/837–43, 850–1, 1227

11. CG, III/957–8; Branda & Lentz, 131

12. Branda & Lentz, 139–40

13. Ibid., 171; see also Napoleon, *Mémoires*, III/259–76; Las Cases, 1905, II/522–3; Gourgaud, I/278

14. Alexander Rodger, 287

15. Cambacérès, *Mémoires*, I/680; Grainger, 147, 161; for the plots against Bonaparte, see also Desmarest, 10, Marquis, and Sparrow

16. Marquis, 135, 142ff.; quoted in Lentz, GC, 297

17. Grainger, 125; CG, IV/30–2

18. Grainger, 153, 160

19. Ibid., 171, 175, 185

20. CG, IV/122, 127, 131–2, passim; see also Girardin, I/291–5

21. Miot de Melito, II/73; Grainger, 188–9; Browning

22. Thibaudeau, 21; Hortense, I/326

23. Versini, 118–19

24. Thibaudeau, 391–2; see also Bourrienne, 1829, III/214; Lentz, GC, 401–2

25. Branda & Lentz, 181; Grainger, 184–5

26. Alexander Rodger, 293; Miot de Melito, II/119–20

CHAPTER 26: TOWARD EMPIRE

1. Uglow, 340–5: Many managed to avoid arrest through their connections, and while some were locked up in fortresses, most remained on parole and continued to enjoy the pleasures of Paris; Fontaine, II/63

2. Tulard & Garros, 244; CG, IV/291ff., 426–7, 448; Claire de Rémusat, *Mémoires*, 285

3. Lentz, GC, 517–18

4. Uglow, 335ff., 367–71; Zamoyski, *Phantom Terror*, 58–75

5. Branda & Lentz, 164–7

6. Masson, *Napoléon et sa Famille*, II/229–33

7. Ibid., 241; CG, IV/439

8. George, 81, 95, 116–17, 126; Claire de Rémusat, *Mémoires*, I/206, II/88; Roederer, III/332

9. CG, IV/439; Josephine, 137

10. Lentz, GC, 518

11. CG, IV/583–8, 594, 598, 601, 604–5, 610–12, 616, 621–7, etc.; Tulard, *Fouché*, 203ff.; Lentz, GC, 514–15

12. Lentz, GC, 532; Claire de Rémusat, *Mémoires*, I/33–1; Thibaudeau, 322–3; Ségur, *Un aide de camp*, 80

13. Lentz, GC, 538, 530–1; Desmarest, 102

14. Lentz, GC, 538

15. Méneval, I/264; Desmarest, 99; see also Girardin, I/322–35;

Cambacérès, *Mémoires*, I/738; Lentz, GC, 510–11, 517; Raza, 208; see also CG, IV/646–7

16. CG, IV/633–4; Pasquier, I/178, 200; Desmarest, 116–25; Waresquiel, 320–34; Talleyrand, *Mémoires*, 62–5; Bertrand, *Cahiers, 1818–1819*, 248; Fouché, 135; Méneval, I/305–6; Cambacérès, *Mémoires*, I/711–12; Lentz, GC, 543

17. Garros, 215

18. Lentz, GC, 540–1

19. Joseph, I/97–9; Ségur, *Un aide de camp*, 94–7

20. Savary, I/48–65, 337–479; Murat, *Lettres*, III/83–103

21. Savary, I/66; Méneval, I/298–9; Cambacérès, *Mémoires*, I/711–12; Las Cases, 1983, II/627; Beauharnais, I/91

22. CG, IV/646; Murat, III/90

23. Lentz, GC, 550

24. Ibid., 557

25. Waresquiel, 324; Pasquier, I/200; Barante, I/118, attributes the line to Boulay de la Meurthe

26. Quoted by Waresquiel, 334; Tulard, *Fouché*, 199

27. Claire de Rémusat, *Mémoires*, I/345–6

28. Jourdan, *Mythes*, 25

29. Lentz, GC, 521

30. Thibaudeau, 234; Ernouf, 228; Méneval, I/99

31. Boudon, *Histoire*, 146; Lentz, GC, 562

32. Lentz, GC, 562

33. Roederer, III/461; Cambacérès, *Mémoires*, I/720; Thibaudeau, 462

34. Lentz, NHPE, I/25

35. Miot de Melito, II/194

36. Lentz, GC, 573

CHAPTER 27:
NAPOLEON I

1. *NA*, Jackson Papers, FO 353/18, p. 15; Bailleu, I/273; CG, IV/769; Cambacérès, *Mémoires*, I/756

2. Boudon, *Histoire*, 239

3. Vigo-Roussillon, 133; Rapp, 5, 12–13; Durand, 49

4. Pelleport, I/200; Davout, I/79; Murat, III/90; see also Marmont, II/226

5. On the suicide/murder issue, see J-F Chiappe, *Georges Cadoudal et la liberté*, 1970; E. Erlannig, *La résistance bretonne á Napoléon Bonaparte*, 1980; B. Saugier, *Pichegru. De la gloire de la Hollande á la prison du Temple*, 1995; Lentz, GC, 554

6. Quoted in Boudon, *Histoire*, 238

7. Miot de Melito, II/166

8. Bouillé, 487–95, 531; Cambacérès, *Mémoires*, II/10

9. Jourdan, *Napoléon*, 27–31

10. Ségur, *Un aide de camp*, 68, 93, 75, 103

11. Morrissey, 2, 140–1; Burney, 273

12. McMahon, 122–3; Las Cases, 1983, I/568

13. Waresquiel, 306

14. Thiard, 40

15. Boudon, *Histoire*, 153

16. Napoleon, *Vues Politiques*, 58; Lentz, GC, 585; Lentz, NHPE, I/57–9; see also Tulard, *Sacre*, xix

17. See Lentz, NHPE, I/74; Tulard, *Sacre*, xix; Jourdan, *Napoléon*, 190

18. Lentz, GC, 416–18, 421ff.

19. CG, IV/775

20. Ibid., 774, 780; Ségur, *Un aide de camp*, 104

21. Pouget, 64–5

22. CG, IV/794

23. Ibid., CG, V/583–4; Las Cases, 1983, I/411–13; Cambacérès, *Mémoires*, I/564–5; Bausset, I/49–50; Savary, II/10–11; Mollien, I/404; Claire de Rémusat, *Lettres*, I/112, 139–40; Miot de Melito, II/128, 214; Bertrand, *Lettres*, 29ff.; Pouget, 64; Bailleu, I/59–60; Méneval, I/411–14; Campbell, 228–30; Rose, 114ff., 129–31, 145ff.

24. Marmont, II/226

25. Bailly, 589; Miot de Melito, II/241; see also Claire de Rémusat, *Mémoires*, I/245; Fouché, 1957, 156

26. CG, IV/828, 837

27. Ibid., 856–7, 886; Méneval, I/379

28. Masson, *Napoléon et sa Famille*, II/344, 363; Bailleu, II/301

29. Masson, *Napoléon et sa Famille*, II/354; Hortense, I/229; Masson, *Napoléon et sa Famille*, II/398

30. Masson, *Napoléon et sa Famille*, II/397–9, 400–1, 448–9, 451–2, 454–5; Miot de Melito, II/235–7; Hortense, I/165, 397–9

31. Masson, *Napoléon et sa Famille*, III/94–5

32. Ibid., II/451–2

33. Roederer, III/511; Hortense, II/58–9, 88–9; Chevallier & Pincemaille, 282

34. Fontaine, II/87; Charles de Rémusat, 50; see also Tulard, *Sacre*

35. Claire de Rémusat, *Mémoires*, II/71

36. Ibid., 71–2; Boulart, 124; Bailly, 591

37. Frénilly, 296–7; Miot de Melito, II/245; see also Lentz, NHPE, I/94

38. Barrès, 14

CHAPTER 28:
AUSTERLITZ

1. CG, V/21
2. Ibid., 20–1
3. Masson, *Napoléon et sa Famille*, II/17
4. Claire de Rémusat, *Lettres*, I/65–6; Fain, *Mémoires*, 230
5. CG, V/274
6. Bigarré, 155–6; Avrillon, I/186
7. CG, V/22
8. Boudon, *Le roi*, 109
9. Skowronek, 94; see also Cambacérès, *Mémoires*, II/39
10. CG, V/197–208, 343, 459–62, 400, 415, 570; Pelet de la Lozère, 195
11. Miot de Melito, II/259; CG, V/530, 565–7
12. CG, V/601, 607, 618
13. Bigarré, 162; Raymond de Montesquiou, 32–4, 103
14. Bausset, I/87; Barrès, 51; CG, V/797; Raza, 227–8
15. CG, V/808
16. Comeau de Charry, 205, 207; Raymond de Montesquiou, 69
17. Comeau de Charry, 208, 219; Pouget, 85
18. CG, V/850
19. Ibid., 837
20. Joseph, *Mémoires*, I/314, 291, 311, 317, 304; see also Cambacérès, *Lettres*, I/287ff., 308; Cambacérès, *Mémoires*, II/51; Claire de Rémusat, *Lettres*, I/384, 394
21. Ségur, *Un aide de camp*, 157
22. CG, V/866–7; Ségur, *Un aide de camp*, 157–60; Savary, II/174–98
23. CG, V/869
24. Malye, 24; Ségur, *Un aide de camp*, 165–7; Bulletins, 205–6; Barrès,

55; Fantin des Odoards, 71; Marbot, I/258–9
25. Barrès, 55–6; Lejeune, I/35–6
26. Lentz, NHPE, I/188
27. CG, V/876; Lentz, NHPE, I/189; Tulard, *Napoléon ou le mythe*, 185
28. Lentz, NHPE, I/192–3
29. CG, V/873–4; Lentz, NHPE, I/193; Ségur, *Un aide de camp*, 178
30. Méneval, I/452–7; Savary, I/320–3; CG, V/875; Hartley, 74
31. Waresquiel, 351; Dumonceau, I/145–7; Ligne, II/114
32. Archives Caulaincourt, AN, 95 AP 34, annexe no 2 (henceforth Annexe 2)
33. Cambacérès, *Lettres*, I/319; Claire de Rémusat, *Lettres*, I/384–94

CHAPTER 29:
EMPEROR OF THE WEST

1. Branda, *Le Prix*, 259–80; Joseph, *Mémoires*, I/314, 219, 311
2. Quoted in Lentz, NHPE, I/199
3. Branda, *Le Prix*, 279–80
4. Pelet de la Lozère, 236; Molé, I/59–60; Fain, *Mémoires*, 92–3
5. Fain, *Mémoires*, 114; Branda, *Secrets*, 92–4, 97
6. Chaptal, 337; Lavalette, 256; Mollien, II/150
7. Pelet de la Lozère, 7; Molé, I/55
8. Lentz, NHPE, I/94; Pelet de la Lozère, 155, 162–3, 166, 170; Molé, I/55; Bergeron, 46
9. Pelet de la Lozère, 187, 213–18; Molé, I/96–7
10. Las Cases, 1983, I/408
11. Fain, *Mémoires*, 3, 6–7
12. Ibid., 10–11

13. Ibid., 41–55
14. Ibid., 39–40
15. Ibid., 62–3, 109; Bausset, I/3
16. Fain, *Mémoires*, 202, 180
17. Avrillon, I/121–3, 196–8, 204–5, 375–6; Hortense, I/202, 207–8, 209–11; Fain, *Mémoires*, 307; Rével; Claire de Rémusat, *Mémoires*, III/333; Masson, *Napoléon et les Femmes*, 166–70
18. Méneval, I/424
19. Lentz, NHPE, I/232
20. Cambacérès, *Mémoires*, II/89
21. Las Cases, 1983, I/583
22. Molé, I/60; see also Lucien's conversation in Masséna, V/146
23. Fouché, 155
24. Barante, I/274–5; Masson, *Napoléon et sa Famille*, VI/36
25. Cambacérès, *Mémoires*, II/93; Bausset, I/14, 68; Fain, *Mémoires*, 293–4; Avrillon, I/251
26. Lentz, NHPE, III/423

CHAPTER 30:
MASTER OF EUROPE

1. Bailleu, I/505, 561; CG, VI/724
2. Annexe 2; CG, VI/826–8
3. CG, VI/826–8; Annexe 2
4. Annexe 2
5. CG, VI/823–4
6. Bodinier, 347–9; Lentz, NHPE, I/247–55
7. CG, VI/1032; Boulart, 138; Coignet, 127; Savary, II/310
8. Napoleon, *Mémoires*, III/281–2; Savary, II/292; Raza, 175–6
9. Annexe 2; Savary, II/300
10. Metternich, *Mémoires*, I/54
11. CG, VI/190
12. Ibid., 909, 924, 1078; Byrne, II/40; Tulard & Garros, 317
13. Murat, IV/483, 488
14. Ibid., V/64–5; CG, VI/1213; Potocka, 102
15. Barrès, 79; Raymond de Montesquiou, 163; Rumigny, 35–6; Berthézène, I/118
16. Annexe 2; Raymond de Montesquiou, 168
17. Potocka, 122; Savary, III/26; Boulart, 147
18. Potocka, 120; Kicka, 98
19. CG, VII/27, 46, 52, 63–4, 97, 102
20. Ibid., 105, 111; see also Trembicka, II/38
21. CG, VII/116, 118–19, 126, 127, 129–30, 132–3, passim; Sutherland, 108
22. Rapp, 106; Waresquiel, 365; Comeau de Charry, 281
23. Coignet, 143, 136; Wołowski; see also Berthézène, I/123ff.
24. CG, VII/176, 191; Bodinier, 349–50; Lentz, NHPE, I/275; Raymond de Montesquiou, 464; Rumigny, 44
25. CG, VII/472
26. Potocka, 146–9
27. Sutherland, 126–8; CG, VII/531; Wairy, I/417
28. Bodinier, 349–50; Rothenberg, 48; Lejeune, I/81
29. Hartley, 76
30. CG, VII/916; Coignet, 148; Rumigny, 48; Masson, *Napoléon et sa Famille*, IV/93–4
31. Lentz, NHPE, I/306; see also Raza, 151; Radziwiłł, 255, 268–86

CHAPTER 31:
THE SUN EMPEROR

1. Claire de Rémusat, *Lettres*, II/88, 105–6; Metternich, *Mémoires*, I/57

2. Driault, *Tilsit*, 241, 209; Lentz, NHPE, I/348; Bergeron, 85; Fouché, 1957, 160

3. Pontécoulant, III/165–6; Claire de Rémusat, *Mémoires*, III/218–221

4. Crouzet, I/69

5. Fouché, 1957, 160

6. CG, VI/113–14; Consalvi, 65–7; Pelet de la Lozère, 205–8

7. Consalvi, 672–4

8. Masson, *Napoléon et sa Famille*, IV/46, V/60–5; Haegele, 300–3

9. Fontaine, I/187; CG, VIII/120

10. Englund, 339; Dwyer, *Citizen Emperor*, 275

11. CG, VIII/36

12. See Talleyrand, *Mémoires*, 97ff.; Waresquiel, 378–83; Pasquier, I/329, 351; Beugnot, I/346; Cambacérès, *Mémoires*, II/189

13. Savary, II/250–7; CG, VIII/305–6, 314, 326, 333

14. Chłapowski, 66; Avrillon, I/363

15. CG, VIII/402, 423; Metternich, *Mémoires*, II/245; Broglie, 59; see also Bausset, I/217–19; Avrillon, II/2

16. Ernouf, 249; CG, VIII/448

17. Dwyer, *Citizen Emperor*, 272; Fraser, *Cursed War*, 487

18. Garros, 296; Mathieu Dumas, III/316; CG, VIII/470, 487, 489

19. Brandt, 11; Vandal, *Napoléon et Alexandre*, I/365; Fain, *Mémoires*, 70–3; Avrillon, I/372; Josephine, 225

20. Joseph, *Mémoires*, IV/336; Lentz, NHPE, I/404; Masson, *Napoléon et sa Famille*, IV/245–6; Haegele, 342

21. Haegele, 203–80; Bigarré, 201; Joseph, *Mémoires*, III/324

22. Joseph, *Mémoires*, IV/343, 366–7, 375

23. Ibid., 382–3, 366–98

24. CG, VIII/940–1

25. Joseph, *Mémoires*, IV/412–13, 420–3

26. Mathieu Dumas, III/321–2

CHAPTER 32:
THE EMPEROR OF THE EAST

1. Metternich, *Mémoires*, II/194–9, 207–14

2. Beugnot, I/388

3. Driault, *Tilsit*, 291

4. Lentz, NHPE, I/435–6

5. Fouché, 1957, 156–7; CG, VII/1337–8; Chevallier & Pincemaille, 333–5; Josephine, 219–220, 217; see also Metternich, *Mémoires*, II/140ff.

6. Cambacérès, *Mémoires*, II/231

7. Talleyrand, *Mémoires*, 152–3, 168–70

8. Alexander I, 20

9. Müffling, 23–5; Lentz, NHPE, I/416

10. Bausset, II/313, 316; Talleyrand, *Mémoires*, 161, 170, 183; Constant Wairy's account, II/9–10, of the bad dream should be treated with scepticism

11. Müffling, 21–2; Caulaincourt, I/258, 270, 273

12. Bausset, II/319–20, 321; Talleyrand, *Mémoires*, 178–82; CG, VIII/1126

13. Bausset, I/325

14. Branda, *Secrets*, 153–7; Savary, V/59–67; Masson, *Napoléon et sa Famille*, IV, 327; Beugnot, I/344–5; Chevallier & Pincemaille, 274; Boulart, 181

15. Crouzet, I/393; Caulaincourt, I/274; Napoleon's suggestion (Bertrand, *Cahiers 1818–1819*) can be dismissed, as can Talleyrand's convoluted account in *Mémoires*, 183

16. Dwyer, *Citizen Emperor*, 284; Metternich, *Mémoires*, II/248

17. Metternich, *Mémoires*, II/247–9

18. CG, VIII/1130, 1131–2; Savary, IV/6

19. Chaptal, 216–17; Claire Rémusat, *Mémoires*, II/271; Ségur, *Histoire*, IV/87, 79; Beugnot, I/460; Rapp, 4; Mollien, 325; Choiseul-Gouffier, 94

20. Chaptal, 216–17; see also Masséna, V/146; Mollien, I/40, 316–17; Ségur, *Histoire*, IV/78

21. See Savary, IV/47

22. Garros, 304; Bigarré, 229; Miot de Melito, II/18–19

23. Ségur, *Un aide de camp*, 257

24. Joseph, *Mémoires*, V/265–6, 281; also Miot de Melito, II/24

25. CG, VIII/1352, 1374–6, 1306, 1314; Wairy, II/22; Branda, *Le Prix*, 57

26. CG, VIII/1359–60

27. Ibid., 1377; Bodinier, 286; see also Petiteau, 49

28. Cambacérès, *Lettres*, II/604; *Le Moniteur*, 15 December, 1808, quoted in Lentz, NHPE, I/427

29. Pasquier, I/353–4

30. Cambacérès, *Mémoires*, II/250; Waresquiel, 398; Tulard, *Fouché*,

222–6; Masson, *Napoléon et sa Famille*, IV/393

31. Mathieu Dumas, III/339; Garros, 310; Malye, 65–6; Lentz, NHPE, I/422–3; CG, VIII/1438

32. Waresquiel, 400

33. Anatole de Montesquiou, 155; Pasquier, I/358; Waresquiel, 400–1, 402ff.; Lentz, NHPE, I/434; Hortense, II/30

34. Langsam, 32, 64

35. Ibid., 43–4; Bodinier, 252–3

36. Wołowski; Comeau de Charry, 291; Bausset, I/88

37. Las Cases, 1983, II/142; Lentz, NHPE, I/445; Lejeune, I/302; Cambacérès, *Lettres*, II/659

38. The figures given here, as elsewhere, are approximate. See Bodinier, 352–3; Lentz, NHPE, I/463

39. Anatole de Montesquiou, 168; Savary, IV/143; Marbot, II/201–12; Lejeune, I/357; Fouché, 1957, 168; Berthézène, I/235–6; Cadet de Gassicourt, 126–7; Chłapowski, 162

CHAPTER 33: THE COST OF POWER

1. Costa de Beauregard, 336; Chłapowski, 183–4

2. CG, IX/833

3. Bodinier, 353; there is much disagreement on the number of casualties and prisoners; Bulletins, 472–4; Garros, 326; Savary, IV/185; Chłapowski, 133, 193, etc.

4. Marmont, III/243

5. CG, VII/1321

6. Boudon, *Le roi*, 198–202

7. Ibid., 145

8. Potocka, 319; Masson, *Napoléon et sa Famille*, IV/304–5

9. Beugnot, I/371–2, 337

10. Rapp, 143

11. Tulard, *Napoléon ou le mythe*, 197; Grunewald, 139–41; Comeau de Charry, 318–19

12. Savary, IV/231; Joseph, *Mémoires*, VI/259, 274, 381–9, 59–73

13. Cambacérès, *Mémoires*, II/268–72; Cambacérès, *Lettres*, II/685–7

14. CG, V/927; Masson, *Napoléon et sa Famille*, VII/29

15. CG, IX/599

16. Ibid., 885; quoted by Lentz, NHPE, I/493; Fouché, 1957, 154, 169; Boigne, I/291

17. Berthézène, I/264; Macdonald, 152–9; Marbot, II/272–3; Boulart, 227

18. Pouget, 151–2

19. Abrantès, VII/93; Fantin des Odoards, 143

20. Broglie, I/73–4; Marmont, III/337; Berthézène, I/239–40

21. Mathieu Dumas, III/363; Cambacérès, *Lettres*, II/749

22. Cadet de Gassicourt, 108–9; Załuski, 176

23. CG, IX/1083, 1148, 1254, 1363, 1366; Branda, *Le Prix*, 57

24. Rapp, 125–9; see also Mathieu Dumas, III/384–5, and Savary, IV/223–4

25. Cambacérès, *Lettres*, II/718

26. Tulard, *Fouché*, 235–46; Cambacérès, *Mémoires*, II/279–87

27. Claire de Rémusat, *Mémoires*, II/265; Girardin, II/339; Branda, *Secrets*, 82–90

28. Chevallier & Pincemaille, 338–9; Bausset, II/368ff.; see also Wairy, I/197–9

29. Lentz, NHPE, I/496–7

30. Wairy, II/100–4; Hortense, II/42, 44–5

31. Lentz, NHPE, I/497–8; see also Claire de Rémusat, *Mémoires*, III/279–314

32. Cambacérès, *Mémoires*, II/315; Lentz, NHPE, I/499

33. CG, IX/1506, 1510, 1421, 1522, 1532, 1535

34. Chevallier & Pincemaille, 347, 343; Avrillon, I/166

CHAPTER 34: APOTHEOSIS

1. Ernouf, 272–3; Talleyrand, *Mémoires*, 195–7; Cambacérès, *Mémoires*, II/326–7; Lentz, NHPE, I/502, 506; Metternich, *Mémoires*, II/312

2. Ligne, II/222; Metternich, *Mémoires*, I/100; Beugnot, I/428

3. Savary, IV/317–18; Coignet, 187; Parquin, 176–7; Beugnot, I/423–4

4. Hortense, II/62; Garros, 341; Pontécoulant, III/123; Lejeune, II/30–1

5. Masson, *Marie-Louise*, 82–4; Dwyer, *Citizen Emperor*, 331–4

6. Pontécoulant, III/124; Dwyer, *Citizen Emperor*, 334

7. Wairy, II/125–6; Boudon, *Histoire*, 314; Clary, 48

8. Lejeune, I/32; Clary, 83

9. Boigne, I/274; Pasquier, I/381; Pontécoulant, III/129–30; Masson, *Marie-Louise*, 112–19

10. Consalvi, 211, 218, 238, 242, 246–7

11. Wairy, II/132–3; Thibaudeau, 278; Coignet, 191

12. Bertrand, *Cahiers, 1818–1819*, 18, 100, 263, 408, 411; Claire de Rémusat, *Mémoires*, II/336

13. Jérôme, IV/402

14. Ernouf, 282, also: Fouché, 1957, 173, 181–3; Savary, IV/320–40; Pasquier, I/390–404; Cambacérès, *Mémoires*, II/340; Boudon, *Histoire*, 310; Lentz, NHPE, I/512; Garros, 343; Jérôme, IV/401

15. Potocka, 200; Chastenay, 421; Masson, *Marie-Louise*, 233

16. Potocka, 215–18

17. Ibid., 281

18. Jourdan, *Louis*, 11–12, 18, 20, 31ff., 81ff.

19. Savary, IV/346; Jourdan, *Louis*, 150; CG, X/422

20. Savary, IV/353; Jourdan, *Louis*, 22

21. Lejeune, II/39, 33–4; see also Metternich, *Mémoires*, I/301–7

22. Dwyer, *Citizen Emperor*, 336; Lejeune, I/252–3; Marmont, V/2–3

23. Metternich, *Mémoires*, I/287, 286; Lentz, NHPE, I/522–3; Boigne, I/275

24. Chastenay, 420–1; Hortense, II/113–14, 116; Tulard, *Dictionnaire Napoléon*, I/353

25. Fontaine, I/219, 249–50, 275; see also Branda, *Secrets*, 105, and *Le Prix*, 44–8

26. Thibaudeau, 278

27. Savary, IV/355; Lentz, NHPE, I/516; Fouché, 1957, 298; Tulard, *Fouché*, 255

28. Savary, IV/311, 406; Hortense, II/117

29. Savary, IV/314, V/99; Lentz, NHPE, I/520; Pasquier, I/517; Hauterive, *Napoléon et sa Police*, 43

30. Jérôme, IV/410; Metternich, *Mémoires*, I/279; Chastenay, 433; Ségur, *Un aide de camp*, 280; Sutherland, 197–8; Josephine, 274; Hortense, II/116; Chaptal, 340

31. Metternich, *Mémoires*, I/283–4

32. Canova, 418; Lentz, NHPE, II/125

33. Lentz, NHPE, I/529; Marmont, III/340

CHAPTER 35: APOGEE

1. Las Cases, 1983, I/619

2. Metternich, *Mémoires*, I/286; Masson, *Marie-Louise*, 208–9

3. Metternich, *Mémoires*, I/297; Ségur, *Histoire*, III/476; Kemble, 165, 170

4. Vandal, *Napoléon et Alexandre*, II/318

5. Méneval, II/436; Hortense, II/127; Savary, V/146–9; Raza, 202–6; Castellane I/83; Kemble, 182–4

6. Boigne, I/291–2; Lentz, NHPE, II/13–14; Goethe, "Karlsbader Stanzen"

7. Hortense, II/125–8, 97; Wairy, II/154–5; Savary, V/147–9; Méneval, II/438; Avrillon, II/275, 307–8; Josephine, 267; Chevallier & Pincemaille, 348–51; Mollien, III/76

8. Driault, *Grand Empire*, 323

9. Ibid., 126; Miot de Melito, III/187

10. Branda & Lentz, 187; Bodinier, 385

11. Lentz, NHPE, II/85; Branda, *Le Prix*, 307–8, 365, 301–3, 308–11

12. Metternich, *Mémoires*, II/328; Savary, IV/318–19

13. Bigarré, 315; Haegele, 399; for a contrary view: Marbot, II/482–3

14. Haegele, 420; Joseph, *Mémoires*, VII/306, 488ff., VIII/42–272

15. Branda, *Secrets*, 153–7

16. Metternich, *Mémoires*, II/329

17. CG, VII/924

18. Comeau de Charry, 281; Rapp, 106; Broglie, I/177–9; Cambacérès, *Mémoires*, II/400

19. Napoleon, *Correspondance*, XX/149–54

20. Ibid., 159

21. Zamoyski, *1812*, 111

22. Kartsov & Voenskii, 50–1

23. Fain, *Manuscrit de 1812*, I/3; Palmer, 199

24. Zamoyski, *1812*, 70–1; Bignon, 46ff.; Metternich, *Mémoires*, II/407

25. Metternich, *Mémoires*, II/412–13; Ernouf, 319

26. Zamoyski, *1812*, 72

27. Caulaincourt, I/281–316

28. Zamoyski, *1812*, 75–6

29. Ibid., 76–7

30. Chastenay, 471; Branda, *Secrets*, 184; Beugnot, I/480–5; Pasquier, I/430–1; Lignereux, 142; Heine, 114

31. Metternich, *Mémoires*, II/422

CHAPTER 36:
BLINDING POWER

1. Napoleon, *Correspondance*, XXIII/191

2. Villemain, I/155–67; Zamoyski, *1812*, 106; Ségur, *Histoire*, IV/74

3. Bodinier, 309–12; Zamoyski, *1812*, 85, 88; Begos, 175

4. Zamoyski, *1812*, 88–9

5. Berthézène, I/328

6. Baudus, I/336; Fain, *Manuscrit de 1812*, I/46; Ségur, *Histoire*, III/65–9, 447–8, IV/125; Laugier, 9; Dumonceau, II/17, 48; Davout, III/155; Fantin des Odoards, 303

7. Jérôme, V/247; see also Zamoyski, *1812*, 83–4

8. Napoleon, *Correspondance*, XXIII/388

9. Fontaine, I/316

10. Pasquier, I/525

11. Fain, *Manuscrit de 1812*, I/61

12. Castellane, I/93

13. Beauharnais, VII/340; Savary, V/226; Comeau de Charry, 439; Lejeune, II/174

14. Méneval, III/25, 109; Caulaincourt, I/315

15. Fain, *Manuscrit de 1812*, I/68

16. Metternich, *Mémoires*, I/122; Cambacérès, *Mémoires*, II/395

17. Fain, *Manuscrit de 1812*, I/75; Pradt, 56–7; Savary, V/226

18. Villemain, I/163, 165–6; Chłapowski, 235

19. Zamoyski, *1812*, 132–3

20. Caulaincourt, I/342; Zamoyski, *1812*, 133–4

21. Zamoyski, *1812*, 132–7

22. Ibid., 117

23. Lejeune, I/172

24. Zamoyski, *1812*, 142–3

25. Bulletins, 487–8

CHAPTER 37:
THE RUBICON

1. Caulaincourt, I/344

2. Zamoyski, *1812*, 147; Bulletins, 488–9

3. Lejeune, II/175

4. Planat de la Faye, *Vie*, 71

5. Zamoyski, *1812*, 156–7

6. Anatole de Montesquiou, 208

7. Caulaincourt, I/354

8. Dubrovin, 20–5; CG, XII/787–9

9. Zamoyski, *1812*, 160; Bulletins, 501–3

10. Napoleon, *Correspondance*, XXIV/61

11. Zamoyski, *1812*, 161–4

12. Ibid., 166–8

13. Ibid., 168

14. CG, XII/879, 899

15. Ibid., 923–4

16. Zamoyski, *1812*, 190–2

17. Méneval, III/43; Napoleon, *Correspondance*, XXIV/128, 133; Fain, *Manuscrit de 1812*, I/289, 306; Mathieu Dumas, III/429; Castellane, I/126–7; La Flise, LXXI/465; Bourgoing, 98–100

18. Zamoyski, *1812*, 194–5; Dedem van de Gelder, 295; Caulaincourt, I/379, 407

19. Caulaincourt, I/382; Villemain, I/203–4, 208; also Zamoyski, *1812*, 196

20. Załuski, 241; Brandt, 261, 289; Chevalier, 189; Fain, *Manuscrit de 1812*, I/323

21. Fain, *Manuscrit de 1812*, I/394; Caulaincourt, I/393

22. Caulaincourt, I/406

23. Rapp, 167; Denniée, 62; Lejeune, II/199; Zamoyski, *1812*, 229

24. Bourgoing, 100; Brandt, 252–3

25. Pion des Loches, 287; Chevalier, 190

26. Caulaincourt, I/411

27. Sołtyk, 198–9; Roguet, III/474

28. Zamoyski, *1812*, 258–9

29. Bausset, II/84; Brandt, 272; CG, XII/1080

30. Rapp, 173–5

31. Ibid., 176; Thirion, 180; Vossler, 60–1; Holzhausen, 105

32. Zamoyski, *1812*, 271–2; Lejeune, II/217

33. Dedem de Gelder, 240; Zamoyski, *1812*, 287–8

34. Anatole de Montesquiou, 226–7; Sanguszko, 93; Thirion, 201

CHAPTER 38:
NEMESIS

1. Bourgogne, 13

2. Fain, *Manuscrit de 1812*, I/94–7; Rapp, 184

3. Ségur, *Histoire*, V/75

4. Caulaincourt, II/49

5. Zamoyski, *1812*, 349–50

6. Caulaincourt, II/23

7. Zamoyski, *1812*, 338–9

8. Ibid., 339

9. Belliard, I/112

10. Caulaincourt, II/26, 42, 56, 65

11. Fain, *Manuscrit de 1812*, I/151–2

12. Zamoyski, *1812*, 353–4

13. Ibid., 354–5

14. Ibid., 355; Rapp, 192–3

15. See Zamoyski, *1812*, 364–8

16. Ibid., 370–5, 377

17. Denniée, 118, 114–15; Volkonskii, 199–203; Caulaincourt, II/104–5

18. Zamoyski, *1812*, 379–81, 383–4

19. Ibid., 409

20. Pastoret, 470–1

21. Caulaincourt, II/141; Saint-Denis, 54; Méneval, II/93–4, writes that this was at Orsha

22. Bourgogne, 116; Roguet, III/518
23. Zamoyski, *1812*, 425
24. Ibid., 455–6, 378; Bertin, 251–2; Anatole de Montesquiou, 254–5, 267
25. Zamoyski, *1812*, 457
26. Caulaincourt, II/168, 173; also Zamoyski, *1812*, 459–60
27. Rapp, 213; Zamoyski, *1812*, 461ff.
28. Zamoyski, *1812*, 491–3; Bulletins, 556
29. Ernouf, 461–2
30. Caulaincourt, II/230ff.
31. Ibid., 263; Pradt, 207–18
32. Potocka, 331–4; Niemcewicz, 383; Koźmian, III/311
33. Caulaincourt, II/315
34. Zamoyski, *1812*, 522–3

CHAPTER 39: HOLLOW VICTORIES

1. Anatole de Montesquiou, 296–7
2. CG, XII/1305
3. Driault, *Napoléon et l'Europe*, 59
4. Masson, *Napoléon et sa Famille*, VII/342–3; CG, XII/1305; Caulaincourt, II/389–90, 393–4
5. Napoleon, *Correspondance*, XXIV/369; for the losses, see Zamoyski, *1812*, 536–40 and notes
6. Molé, I/155
7. Hortense, II/152; Mollien, III/169–70; GS, HA Ministerium, 10 February 1813; see also Collot, 50–4
8. Tulard, *Fiévée*, 154; Barante, I/371
9. Garros, 402
10. Lentz, NHPE, II/339; for Malet affair, see Boudon, *Histoire*, 366ff.; Savary, VI/2–35; Pasquier, II/12–34; Cambacérès, *Lettres*, II/914; Cambacérès, *Mémoires*, II/434; Molé, I/118–25; Price, 29–31

11. Fain, *Manuscrit de 1813*, I/129; see Lavalette, 328, for his annoyance at not being left the chance of reprieving Malet
12. Cambacérès, *Mémoires*, II429; Fain, *Manuscrit de 1813*, I/38
13. Caulaincourt, II/315; Molé, I/129, 131; Raumer, 23–4; Mollien, III/293–5
14. Lentz, NHPE, II/399, 403
15. Masson, *Napoléon et sa Famille*, VII/418, 448, 452, VI/74
16. Marmont, V/5; Durand, 144–5; Tulard, *Fiévée*, 150–1; Boussingault, I/53–5; Molé, I/144; Price, 91; Napoleon, *Correspondance*, XXIV/380–1
17. Haegele, 469–70; Lentz, NHPE, II/400
18. Hardenberg, XII/17, 13–15; Fain, *Manuscrit de 1813*, I/210, 231–7
19. Fain, *Manuscrit de 1813*, I/238–41, 296–9, 301–3, 306–7; Abrantès, XI/90–1; Castellane, I/222; Broglie, I/214, 218, 220
20. Shishkov, I/167; Zorin, 251, 264
21. Angeberg, I/5–7
22. Kraehe, I/43
23. Gentz, *Dépèches*, I/8–9
24. Ibid., I/13; Oncken, I/416–20; Buckland, 459ff., 491ff.; Fain, *Manuscrit de 1813*, I/296–9
25. Napoleon, *Correspondance*, XXIV/521; Fain, *Manuscrit de 1813*, I/222; Lentz, NHPE, II/358–60
26. Masson, *Napoléon et sa Famille*, VII/344
27. Napoleon, *Correspondance*, XXIV/196–7; Driault, *Napoléon et l'Europe*, 76

28. Fain, *Manuscrit de 1813*, I/247–75; Driault, *Napoléon et l'Europe*, 76; Oncken, I/439; Méneval, III/129

29. Oncken, II/624; CG, XIII/860

30. Wojciechowski, 81; Bertrand, *Lettres*, 190; Pelleport, II/65; Chłapowski, 310; Mallardi, 404

31. Beauharnais, IX/94; Wojciechowski, 82; Mathieu Dumas, III/499; Barrès, 158

32. Zamoyski, *Rites*, 52–3; Marmont, V/25

33. Oncken, II/673–8

34. Angeberg, I/13; Metternich, *Mémoires*, I/250; Driault, *Napoléon et l'Europe*, 91; Ernouf, 494, 533–4, 539; Fain, *Manuscrit de 1813*, I/390

35. Price, 66; Gross, 88

36. Fain, *Manuscrit de 1813*, I/390; Price, 70; Chłapowski, 348

37. Chłapowski, 324–5

38. Zamoyski, *Rites*, 61–2

39. Fouché, 1945, II/388–9

40. Fain, *Manuscrit de 1813*, I/426–7; Chłapowski, 341; Planat de la Faye, 43

41. Zamoyski, *Rites*, 63

CHAPTER 40:
LAST CHANCE

1. Cambacérès, *Lettres*, II/922, 967, 973, 994; Fain, *Manuscrit de 1813*, I/430; Price, 91–4; Belliard, I/125, 130

2. Cambacérès, *Mémoires*, II/907, 938, 971–2; Fain, *Manuscrit de 1813*, II/66–7; Fouché, 1824, II/196–7, 1945, II/404; Potocka, 350

3. Metternich, *Mémoires*, I/147–53, II/461–2; Nesselrode, V/108–15; Fain, *Manuscrit de 1813*, II/36–44; Price, 83

4. SUA, 12, 33/9

5. Angeberg, I/18–19

6. Fain, *Manuscrit de 1813*, II/79–80

7. Nesselrode, I/99–100; Humboldt, IV/52, 76; Hardenberg, XII/207; Price, 99–101

8. Price, 103–4

9. Fleury, 317; Boulart, 287; Skałkowski, 136; Marbot, III/257

10. SUA, 12, 33/21; Humboldt, IV/92

11. PRONI, 74, 72; Angeberg, I/74; SUA, 12, 33/22; BL Aberdeen, 161–3; Webster, 157; see also Price 103–9

12. These figures are approximate, as calculations vary wildly; on the subject of Russia's mobilisation, see Lieven

13. Beugnot, II/4–6; Beauharnais, IX/108, 117

14. See Nesselrode, I/103

15. Garros, 424

16. Hardenberg, XII/180

17. Lavalette, 278; Faucheur, 225; Mathieu Dumas, III/524

18. Marmont, V/255–6; Boulart, 249; Mathieu Dumas, III/524; Lentz, NHPE, II/443, 459; Szymanowski, 101–3

19. Macdonald, 224

20. Lentz, NHPE, II/467

21. Macdonald, 227; Pasquier, II/96–7; Dumonceau, II/387; Barrès, 194

22. Ginisty, 11–12; Macdonald, 232; Ségur, *Histoire*, VI/93; Sułkowski, *Listy*, 417–22

23. Lentz, NHPE, II/469–70; Masson, *Marie-Louise*, 509

24. Beugnot, II/38

25. Beauharnais, IX/299ff., 384–5, 295

26. Lentz, NHPE, II/516; Masson, *Napoléon et sa Famille*, VIII/251–6

27. Cambacérès, *Mémoires*, II/491, 495; Cambacérès, *Lettres*, II/1099–112; Lentz, NHPE, II/498–9, 503; Bodinier, 307, 320, 329

28. Pasquier, II/99; Bausset, V/256–7; Waresquiel, 422; also Cambacérès, *Mémoires*, II/507; Lentz, NHPE, II/471

29. Beugnot, II/54; Pasquier, II/100; Molé, I/174–6; Cambacérès, *Mémoires*, II/507

30. Lavalette, 279–80; Marmont, VI/7–8

31. Josephine, 359–60; Beugnot, II/78–80

32. Pasquier, II/110

CHAPTER 41: THE WOUNDED LION

1. Zamoyski, *Rites*, 125–8; Price, 154–61

2. Angeberg, I/77–8; Price, 161–9

3. Molé, I/139–40; Lentz, NHPE, II/511–12

4. Masson, *Napoléon et sa Famille*, IX/132, 84, 36ff., 76–7, 139, 150, 166–7, 175ff., 200, 259; Tulard, *Fouché*, 291–2; Madelin, *Fouché*, 295; Lentz, NHPE, II/491, 487–8; Beauharnais, IX/284–5, 295, 299ff.; Josephine, 361–2

5. Pasquier, II/143; Lavalette, 282; Pontécoulant, III/187; Hortense, II/174, 177

6. Fain, *Manuscrit de 1814*, 72–5; Vionnet de Maringoné, 105

7. Ernouf, 623; Garros, 439; Caulaincourt, III/15–16; Montbas, 805–6; Fain, *Manuscrit de 1814*, 75–8,

284–5; Napoleon, *Correspondance*, XXVII/223–4

8. Benckendorff, 349; FO 92, 3; Metternich, *Mémoires*, I/190; Méneval, III/213–15; Bertrand, *Lettres*, 375–94; Dumonceau, III/18, 29–30; Müffling, 469–71; Bodinier, 300; Ligneureux, 306–7; where the enemy had not been seen, the attitude was very different—see Lignereux, 310; Fontaine, I/385–6; Hauterive, 354; Price, 205–11

9. Joseph, *Mémoires*, X/63–149, 48

10. Ibid., 161; Ségur, *Histoire*, VI/248–9

11. Molé, I/286

12. Ségur, *Histoire*, VI/293–4

13. Grabowski, 179–83; Joseph, *Mémoires*, X/198

14. Cambacérès, *Lettres*, II/1131

15. Boulart, 319–20; Desmarest, 268

16. Joseph, *Mémoires*, X/31–3; Miot de Melito, II/353; Savary, VI/363–79; VII/3

17. Combe, 275–6; Pontécoulant, III/259–61; Béranger, 141; Savary, VII/12; Marmont, VI/240–9; Lavalette, 290

18. Belliard, I/171–2; Lentz, *Vingt Jours*, 31–2

19. Lentz, *Vingt Jours*, 41–4

20. Caulaincourt, III/167

21. Lentz, *Vingt Jours*, 57–69; Ségur, *Histoire*, VII/153

22. Marmont, VI/257–70; Belliard, I/180–6; Macdonald, 279, 286; Ségur, *Histoire*, VII/163–78; Caulaincourt, I/161–6; Lentz, *Vingt Jours*, 70–2, 107;

the most coherent account is in Price, 234–8

23. Lentz, *Vingt Jours*, 79ff.; Caulaincourt, III/233ff.; Masson, *Marie-Louise*, 568–82

24. Lentz, *Vingt Jours*, 220–1; Grabowski, 214–15; Szymanowski, 111–13; Boulart, 323

CHAPTER 42:
REJECTION

1. Lentz, *Vingt Jours*, 217
2. cf. Caulaincourt, I/314
3. Lentz, *Vingt Jours*, 135–9
4. Ibid., 131–2
5. Chevallier & Laot, ed., 303
6. Caulaincourt, III/343, 357–73; Ségur, *Histoire*, VII/196–200; Saint-Denis, 55–8; Fain, *Manuscrit de 1814*, 255–8; Belly de Bussy, 237; Lentz, *Vingt Jours*, 159–68
7. Caulaincourt, III/366; Macdonald, 299
8. Chevallier & Laot, 303–4; Sutherland, 255–8
9. Tulard & Garros, 549
10. Masson, *Marie-Louise*, 541; Price, 241; Pasquier, II/237–8; Anatole de Montesquiou, 305–6
11. Masson, *Marie-Louise*, 573–5; Price, 242–3
12. Masson, *Marie-Louise*, 580; Anatole de Montesquiou, 334–5; Dwyer, *Citizen Emperor*, 492; Lentz, *Vingt Jours*, 186–9
13. Chevallier & Laot, ed., 303–4
14. Campbell, 157
15. Ibid., 157, 160, 171–2, 182; Schouvaloff; Dwyer, *Citizen Emperor*, 493

16. Lentz, *Vingt Jours*, 202–3; Coignet, 331; Campbell, 185; Fain, *Manuscrit de 1814*, 398ff.
17. Lentz, *Vingt Jours*, 170
18. Campbell, 190
19. Ibid., 198–201; Peyrusse, *Mémorial*, 295–6; Schouvaloff, 809–29; Saint-Denis, 59; Lentz, NHPE, IV/158–65; Price, 244–8; Dwyer, *Citizen Emperor*, 493–8
20. Branda, *Le Prix*, 62–3; Lentz, NHPE, IV/205–10
21. Méneval, III/341, 375–6, 384; Lentz, NHPE, IV/168–72; see also Anatole de Montesquiou, 350
22. Jérôme, *Mémoires*, VI/474; Peyrusse, *Lettres*, 232; Saint-Denis, 60ff.; Pons de l'Hérault, 140, 191
23. Sutherland, 266–81; Saint-Denis, 78–80; Pons de l'Hérault, 211–14
24. Lentz, NHPE, IV/270–8; Branda, *l'Ile*, 58–64
25. Pons de l'Herault, 160–7; Brun de Villeret, 191–2; Campbell, 109, 156, 305; Dwyer, *Citizen Emperor*, 352–3; Masson, *Napoléon et sa Famille*, X/216–18
26. Campbell, 108, 318, 305, 352–3; Pons de l'Hérault, 371; Rose, 178; Lucien, III/459; Lentz, NHPE, IV/280–3; Lentz, *Vingt Jours*, 146
27. Pons de l'Hérault, 14, 128; Campbell, 242
28. Pons de l'Hérault, 383–4

CHAPTER 43:
THE OUTLAW

1. Macdonald, 343, 411–12; Saint-Denis, 90

2. Lentz, NHPE, IV/291; Saint-Denis, 90

3. Lentz, NHPE, IV/294–5; Peyrusse, *Mémorial*, 286–7

4. Miot de Melito, III/378–9; Ernouf, 645; Lavalette, 331–3

5. Pasquier, III/125; Barante, II/24; Macdonald, 287–8

6. Savary, VII/373; Lavalette, 333

7. Miot de Melito, III/381; Lavalette, 338–40; Mollien, III/419

8. Lucien, III/463; Miot de Melito, III/395

9. Hortense, III/1; Jal, 297–8; Lucien, III/263; Avrillon, II/381–4

10. Constant, *Journal*, 351, 349, 353; Constant, *Cent Jours*, 211, 209, 227

11. Lentz, NHPE, IV/393–7

12. Ibid., 400–2; Jal, 287–8, 283–5; see also Lavalette, 347, and Miot de Melito, III/400–1

13. Zamoyski, *Rites*, 460

14. Ibid., 461

15. Ibid., 447–8

16. Lucien, III/230

17. Madelin, 318–19, 330–1, 242–3; Fouché, 1945, 473, 478–9, 483–6; Fleury de Chaboulon, III/289, suggests Montrond's mission meant to bring Talleyrand over to Napoleon's side (see also Mollien, III/432; Waresquiel, 493–4; also Savary, VIII/31ff.); Méneval, III/445–6, claims Francis would have backed a regency if Napoleon had agreed to reside privately in Habsburg dominions; see also Lavalette, 342–5; Chaptal, 314–15; Tulard, *Fouché*, 326–9; Lucien, III/296, believes Napoleon was prepared to step down; the clearest account is in Price, 251–9

18. Pontécoulant, III/328; see also Rapp, 294–5, for his unwillingness to fight; Constant, *Cent Jours*, 211

19. Bodinier, 302; Miot de Melito, III/398

20. Ernouf, 657

21. Constant, *Cent Jours*, 209; Miot de Melito, III/395

22. Rumigny, 91; Constant, *Journal Intime*, 354; Miot de Melito, III/395

23. Hortense, III/14; Lavalette, 349

24. Bodinier, 366–9; Fantin des Odoards, 427

25. Rumigny, 102

26. Bulletins, 607–13; Lentz, NHPE, IV/507; see also Napoleon, *Mémoires*, IV/124–5

27. Bertaud, *Abdication*, 25, 27; Lavalette, 350

28. Bertaud, *Abdication*, 27, 48, 28, 319 (note 19)

29. Ibid., 49, 27; Constant, *Cent Jours*, 284

30. Bertaud, *Abdication*, 122

31. Lucien, III/347; Bertaud, *Abdication*, 159, 158, 160, 170; Fouché, 1945, 493–8; Lentz, NHPE, IV/515–16

32. Bertaud, *Abdication*, 194–5

33. Branda, *Secrets*, 29; Lentz, NHPE, IV/526 (note); Constant, *Journal Intime*, 355; Constant, *Cent Jours*, 287

34. Hortense, III/32–3

35. Planat de la Faye, 215; Rumigny, 112–13; Macdonald, 393; Savary, VIII/183

36. Savary, VIII/166–7

37. Lentz, NHPE, IV/527; Garros, 473; Bonneau, 420–3

38. Bertaud, *Abdication*, 302

39. Ibid.

CHAPTER 44:
A CROWN OF THORNS

1. Tulard & Garros, 592–3
2. Ibid., 593–4; Benhamou, 18–19
3. Zamoyski, *Rites*, 497
4. Saint-Denis, 136–8; Warden, Cockburn, etc.
5. Tulard, *Sainte-Hélène*, 11; Montchenu, 49
6. *Letters from the Cape*, 81
7. Abell, 20–1, 30–1, 39, 208, 72–3, 77
8. Las Cases, 1983, I/205–7
9. Ibid., 207–9
10. Planat de la Faye, 241; Martineau, 42
11. Zamoyski, *Phantom Terror*, 133
12. Cockburn, 7
13. Ibid., 25, 45, 76–7; *Letters from the Cape*, 12; Benhamou, 37
14. Aubry, I/199
15. Malcolm, 24–6
16. Aubry, I/203, 296, 219, II/79
17. Ibid., I/217–18
18. Fraser, *Venus*, 232
19. Aubry, I/220–3
20. Ibid., 215–16, II/74–7; *Letters from the Cape*, 202; see also Zamoyski, *Phantom Terror*, 129–35; and Hazareesingh for a wonderfully exhaustive study of the subject
21. Branda, *Le Prix*, 75–6; Benhamou, 77; Aubry, I/224
22. Martineau, 71–3; Aubry, I/225–9; Malcolm, 41, 44, 58, 62, 64
23. Branda, *Le Prix*, 78
24. Saint-Denis, 168–9
25. Malcolm, 44, 152
26. Aubry, I/245–6
27. Roberts, *Napoleon*, 788; Abell, 57; Aubry, II/159
28. Aubry, II/133
29. Ibid., 137–8
30. Jérôme, *Mémoires*, VI/298–9
31. Branda, *Secrets*, 246–51
32. Roberts, *Napoleon*, 798
33. Aubry, II/221
34. Molé, *Souvenirs de jeunesse*, 132
35. For an exhaustive treatment of the Testament, see Branda, *Le Prix*, 85–94
36. Heine, 115

Bibliography

ARCHIVES

Archives Nationales, Paris (AN)
Papiers Flahaut, Archives Nationales, 565 AP, carton 18–19, dossier 4
Archives Caulaincourt, 95 AP 34

British Library, London (BL)
Dropmore Papers, Add. 58891—Gentz to Lord Carysfort
Aberdeen Papers, XXXvII, Add. 43075

National Archives, Kew (NA)
Jackson Papers, FO 353/18, p. 15; CG, IV/769

Státní Ústřední Archiv, Prague (SUA)
Rodinný Archiv Metternišský I; Acta Clementina, 1, 3, 5, 14a

Landesarchiv, Berlin (LB)
Rep. 241, acc. 3932, Nr. 1: *Erinnerungen des preußischen Kammerdieners Tamanti an den Aufenthalt von Kaiser Napoleon in Potsdam und Berlin (1806)*

Geheimes Staatsarchiv, Berlin (GS)
Hatzfeld's reports III. HA Ministerium der Auswärtigen Angelegenheiten I, Nr 4955
Gentz to Lucchesini, PK, 27 B1 10–1v

Universitäts- un Statsbibliothek Köln (USK)
VI. HA Familienarchive und Nachlasse Nl Girolamo Marchese Lucchesini, Nr, 27, Bl 10–11v

Biblioteka Uniwersytetu Adama Mickiewicza, Poznań (BUAM)
Ms. 44/II. Pamiętnik Stanisława Zamoyskiego

Public Record Office of Northern Ireland, Belfast (PRONI)
Castlereagh Papers, D.3030/P

PRINTED SOURCES

Abell, Lucia Elizabeth, *Recollections of Napoleon at Saint Helena*, London 1844
Abrantès, Laure Junot, duchesse d', *Mémoires de Mme la duchesse d'Abrantès, etc.*, 12 vols., Paris 1835

———— *Le Roman Inconnu de la duchesse d'Abrantès*, ed. Robert Chantemesse, Paris 1927

Alexander I, Emperor of Russia, *Correspondance de l'Empereur Alexandre Ier avec sa soeur la Grande Duchesse Catherine*, Petersburg 1910

Andigné, Louis Marie Auguste Fortuné, comte d', *Mémoires du Général d'Andigné*, 2 vols., Paris 1900

Angeberg, Comte d' (Leonard Chodźko), *Le Congrès de Vienne et les Traités de 1815: précédé et suivi des actes diplomatiques qui s'y rattachent*, ed. M. Capefigue, 2 vols., Paris 1864

Antommarchi, Francesco, *Mémoires du Docteur F. Antommarchi, ou les derniers moments de Napoléon*, 2 vols., Paris 1825

Arnault, Antoine-Vincent, *Souvenirs d'un séxagenaire*, Paris 2003

Arnold, Theodor Ferdinand Kajetan, *Erfurt in sienem höchsten Glanze während der Monate September und Oktober 1808*, Erfurt 1808

Arnott, A., *An Account of the last illness, decease, and post mortem appearances of Napoléon Bonaparte, etc.*, London 1822

Artaud de Montor, Alexis-François, *Histoire de la vie et des travaux politiques du comte d'Hauterive, comprenant une partie des actes de la diplomatie francaise*, Paris 1839

Aubry, Joseph Thomas, *Souvenir du 12e Chasseurs*, Paris 1899

Avallon, Cousin d', *Bonapartiana, ou recueil des Réponses ingénieuses ou sublimes, Actions heroïques et Faits mémorables de Bonaparte*, Paris 1801

Avrillon, Mlle, *Mémoires*, 2 vols., Paris 1896

Bailleu, Paul, ed., *Preussen und Frankreich von 1795 bis 1807: Diplomatische Corrrespondenzen*, 2 vols., Leipzig 1881–87

Bailly, François-Joseph, *Souvenirs et anecdotes de Joseph Bailly*, in *Revue des Etudes Historiques*, 1904, pp. 585–602

Balcombe, Lucia Elizabeth, *La Petite Fiancée de Napoléon, Souvenirs de Betsy Balcombe à Sainte-Hélène (1815–1818)*, ed. Jacques Macé, Paris 2005

Bangofsky, Georges, *Les étapes de G. Bangofsky, officier lorrain: Fragments de son journal de campagne (1797–1815)*, Paris 1905

Barante, Amable Guilleaume Baron de, *Souvenirs du Baron de Barante*, Vols. I & II, Paris 1890–92

Barère, Bertrand, *Mémoires*, Vol. III, Paris 1843

Barral, P. A, vicomte de, *Souvenirs de guerre et de captivité d'un Page de Napoléon (1812–1815)*, Paris n.d.

Barras, Paul Jean-François Nicolas, vicomte de, *Mémoires de Barras, membre du Directoire*, ed. Georges Duruy, 4 vols., Paris 1895–96

Barrès, Jean-Baptistse, *Souvenirs d'un officier de la Grande Armée*, Paris 1923

Bartel, Paul, *La jeunesse inédite de Napoléon, d'après de nombreux documents*, Paris 1954

Bast, L. Amédée de, *Mémoires d'un vieil avocat, écrits par lui-même*, 3 vols., Paris 1847

Baudus, Lieutenant-Colonel K. de, *Études sur Napoléon*, 2 vols., Paris 1841

Bausset, Louis-François-Joseph, baron de, *Mémoires*, 4 vols., Paris 1827–29

Beauharnais, Eugène de, *Mémoires et correspondance politique et militaire du Prince Eugène, annotés et mis en ordre par A. Du Casse*, 10 vols., Paris 1858–60

Beauvollier, Pierre-Louis, comte de, *Mémoires sur l'expédition de Russie*, in *Mémoires secrets et inédits pour servir à l'histoire contemporaine*, 2 vols., Paris 1825

Begos, Louis, *Souvenirs des Campagnes du Lieutenant-colonel Louis Begos*, in *Soldats Suisses au Service Étranger*, Geneva 1909

Belliard, Auguste, *Mémoires du Comte Belliard*, 2 vols., Paris 1842

Bellot de Kergorre, Alexandre, *Un Commissaire des Guerres sous le premier Empire*, Paris 1899

Belly de Bussy, David-Victor, *Belly de Bussy*, in *Les Carnets de la Sabretache*, 1914, pp. 234–9

Benckendorff, Alexander, *Zapiski Benkendorfa*, Moscow 2001

Bennigsen, Count Lev, *Mémoires du Général Bennigsen*, 3 vols., Paris 1907–08

Béranger, P. J. de, *Ma Biographie*, Paris 1857

Bernoyer, François, *Avec Bonaparte en Égypte et en Syrie 1798–1900, 19 lettres inédites*, Laval 1981

Berry, Mary, *Extracts from the Journals and Correspondence of Miss Berry*, 3 vols., London 1866

Berthézène, General Baron Pierre, *Souvenirs Militaires de la République et de l'Empire*, 2 vols., Paris 1855

Berthier, Louis Alexandre, prince de Neuchâtel, *Relation des campagnes du général Bonaparte en Égypte et en Syrie*, Paris 1800

———, Gainot, Bernard, & Ciotti, Bruno, *Marengo: 14 juin 1800*, Clermont-Ferrand 2010

Bertin, Georges, *La Campagne de 1812 d'après des témoins oculaires*, Paris 1894

Bertrand, Capitaine, *Mémoires du Capitaine Bertrand*, Angers 1909

Bertrand, Henri-Gratien, Maréchal comte, *Campagnes d'Égypte et de Syrie 1798–1799*, 2 vols., Paris 1847

——— *Cahiers de Sainte Hélène*, 3 vols., Paris 1949–59

——— *Lettres à Fanny 1808–1815*, Paris 1979

Besancenet, Alfred de, ed., *Le Portefeuille d'un général de la République*, Paris 1877

Beugnot, Jacques Claude Comte, *Mémoires du Comte Beugnot, Ancien Ministre, (1783–1815)*, 2 vols., Paris 1868

Beyle, Henri (Stendhal), *Vie de Napoléon: Fragments*, Paris 1925

——— *Mémoires sur Napoléon*, Paris 1929

——— *Selected Journalism from the English Reviews*, London 2010

Białkowski, Antoni, *Pamiętniki starego żołnierza (1806–1814)*, Warsaw 1903

Bielecki, R., & Tyszka, A., *Dał nam przykład Bonaparte. Wspomnienia i relacje żołnierzy polskich 1796–1815*, 2 vols., Kraków 1984

Bigarré, Auguste, *Mémoires du général Bigarré, Aide de Camp du Roi Joseph, 1775–1813*, Paris 1893

Bignon, Édouard, baron, *Souvenirs d'un Diplomate*, Paris 1864

Blanqui, Adolphe, *Souvenirs d'un lycéen de 1814*, in *Revue de Paris*, 15 April 1916, pp. 847–65: 1 May 1916, pp. 103–15

Blocqueville, Marie-Adelaide Marquise de, *Le Maréchal Davout, Prince d'Eckmuhl, raconté par les siens et par lui-même*, 4 vols., Paris 1880

Boigne, Adèle comtesse de, *Récits d'une tante: Mémoires de la comtesse de Boigne, née d'Osmond*, 4 vols., Paris 1908

Bombelles, Marc-Marie marquis de, *Journal*, vol. V, Geneva 2002

Bonaparte, Lucien, *Lucien Bonaparte et ses Mémoires 1775–1840*, ed. Th. Jung, 3 vols., Paris 1882–83

Bonnau, *L'embarquement de l'Empereur à Rochefort: Relation de Bonnau, agent comptable à bord de l'Epervier*, in *Revue retrospective*, 1895, Tome II, pp. 420–3

Boswell, James, *The Journal of a Tour to Corsica; and Memoirs of Pascal Paoli*, London 1951

Bouillé, Louis-Joseph-Amour Marquis de, *Souvenirs et fragments pour servir aux mémoires de ma vie et de mon temps*, 3 vols., Paris 1906–11

Boulart, Jean François, *Mémoires Militaires du Général baron Boulart sur les guerres de la République et de l'Empire*, Paris n.d.

Bourgeois, René, *Tableau de la campagne de Moscou en 1812*, Paris 1814

Bourgogne, Adrien, *Mémoires du Sergent Bourgogne (1812–1813)*, Paris 1901

Bourgoing, Paul Charles Amable Baron de, *Souvenirs d'histoire contemporaine*, Paris 1864

Bourrienne, Louis Antoine, *Mémoires de M. de Bourienne Ministre d'État sur Napoleon*, 10 vols., Paris 1829

——— *Mémoires de M. de Bourienne Ministre d'État sur Napoleon*, 10 vols., Paris 1831

Boussingault, Jean-Baptiste, *Mémoires de J.B. Boussingault*, 5 vols., Paris 1892–1900

Brandt, Heinrich von, *Souvenirs d'un Officier Polonais: Scènes de la vie militaire en Espagne et en Russie (1808–1812)*, Paris 1877

Broekere, Stanisław, *Pamiętniki z wojny hiszpańskiej 1808–1814*, Gdynia 2004

Broglie, Achille-Charles-Léonce duc de, *Souvenirs du feu duc de Broglie*, Vol. I, Paris 1886

Browning, Oscar, ed., *England and Napoleon in 1803; being the despatches of Lord Whitworth and others, etc.*, London 1887

Brun de Villeret, Louis, Général baron, *Les Cahiers du Général Brun*, Paris 1953

Burney, Fanny, *Fanny Burney's Diary: A Selection from the Diary and Letters*, ed. John Wain, London 1961

Byrne, Miles, *Memoirs of Miles Byrne, Chef de bataillon in the service of France*, 3 vols., Paris 1863

Cadet de Gassicourt, *Voyage en Autriche, en Moravie et en Bavière fait à la suite de l'armée française pendant la campagne de 1809*, Paris 1818

Calosso, Colonel, *Mémoires d'un vieux soldat*, Turin 1857

Cambacérès, Jean-Jacques de, *Lettres inédites à Napoléon 1802–1814*, 2 vols., Paris 1973

——— *Mémoires inédits*, 2 vols., Paris 1999

Campbell, Major-General Sir Neil, *Napoleon at Fontainebleau and Elba, being a Journal of Occurrences in 1814–1815*, London 1869

Canova, Antonio, *Scritti*, Rome 2007

Carnot, Lazare Nicolas, *Mémoires historiques et militaires*, Paris 1824

Carr, Sir John, *The Stranger in France; or, a Tour from Devonshire to Paris*, London 1807

Carrington, Dorothy, *Portrait de Charles Bonaparte d'après ses écrits de jeunesse et ses memoires*, Ajaccio 2002

Castanié, François, *Les Indiscrétions d'un Préfet de Police de Napoléon*, Paris n.d.

Castellane, Boniface de, *Journal du Maréchal de Castellane 1804–1862*, Vol. I, Paris 1895

Caulaincourt, Armand Augustin Louis, Duc de Vicence, *Mémoires*, 3 vols., Paris 1933

Chailly, A., *Le Boursier de l'Empereur: Document sur la vie intime de Napoléon*, Paris 1857

Champagny, Jean-Baptiste, duc de Cadore, *Souvenirs de M de Champagny, duc de Cadore*, Paris 1846

Chaptal, Jean-Antoine, *Mes Souvenirs sur Napoléon*, Paris 1893

Chastenay, Victorine de, *Mémoires 1771–1815*, Paris 1987

Chevalier, Jean-Michel, *Souvenirs des guerres napoléoniennes*, Paris 1970

Chevallier, Bernard, & Laot, Jean-Michel, ed., *Napoléon & Joséphine: Correspondance, lettres intimes*, Paris 2012

Chłapowski, Dezydery, *Mémoires sur les guerres de Napoléon 1806–1813*, Paris 1908

Chłopicki, Jan, *Pamiętnik Jana Chłopickiego, porucz. 7 pułku Ułanów wojsk francuskich, z czasów kampanij Napoleona*, Wilno 1849

Choderlos de Laclos, Étienne, *Le fils de Laclos: Carnets de marche du commandant Choderlos de Ladclos (an XIV–1814)*, Lausanne 1912

Choiseul-Gouffier, Comtesse de, *Reminiscences sur l'empereur Alexandre Ier et sur l'empereur Napoleon Ier*, Paris 1862

Clary-et-Aldringhen, Charles, *Souvenirs: Trois mois à Paris lors du mariage de l'Empereur Napoléon 1er et de l'archiduchesse Marie-Louise*, Paris 1914

Cockburn, Rear-Admiral Sir George, *Extract from a Diary etc.*, London 1888

Coignet, Jean-Roch, *Les Cahiers du Capitaine Coignet*, Paris 1968

Colbert, Auguste, *Traditions et Souvenirs, ou Mémoires touchant le temps et la vie du général Auguste Colbert*, 5 vols., Paris 1863–73

Collot, Jean-Pierre, *Les Souvenirs du Receveur Général Collot*, ed. Clarisse Bader, Lyon 1897

Combe, Julien, *Mémoires du Colonel Combe sur les campagnes de Russie 1812, de Saxe 1813 et de France 1814 et 1815*, Paris 1853

Comeau de Charry, Sébastien-Joseph de, *Souvenirs des guerres d'Allemagne pendant la Révolution et l'Empire*, Paris 1900

Consalvi, Ercole, *Mémoires du Cardinal Consalvi*, ed. J Crétineau-Joly, Paris 1895

Constant, Benjamin, *Journal Intime*, Monaco 1945

———— *Lettres à Bernadotte: Sources et origine de l'Ésprit de conquête et de l'usurpation*, ed. Bengt Hasselrot, Geneva 1952

———— *Mémoires sur les Cent-Jours*, Tübingen 1993

Copies of Original Letters from the Army of General Bonaparte in Egypt, intercepted by the Fleet, Dublin 1799

Cornwallis, Charles, *The Correspondence of Charles, First Marquess Cornwallis*, Vol. III, London 1859

Costa de Beauregard, Marquis Henry de, *Un Homme d'autrefois: Souvenirs recueillis par son arrière-petit-fils*, Paris 1891

Coston, François-Gilbert baron de, *Biographie des premières années de Napoléon Bonaparte*, 2 vols., Paris 1840

Cuneo d'Ornano, François, *Napoléon au Golfe Juan*, Paris 1830

Daleki, J., *Wspomnienia mojego ojca żołnierza dziewiątego pułku Księstwa Warszawskiego*, Poznań 1864

Damas, Roger, comte de, *Mémoires du comte Roger de Damas*, Paris 1912

Davout, Louis-Nicolas, Prince d'Eckmühl, *Correspondance du Maréchal Davout, prince d'Eckmühl*, 4 vols., Paris 1885

Decaen, Charles-Mathieu, *Mémoires et journaux du Général Decaen*, 2 vols., Paris 1910–11

Dedem van der Gelder, Baron Antoine-Baudouin Gisbert van, *Mémoires du Genéral Baron de Dedem de Gelder, 1774–1825*, Paris 1900

Deifel, Joseph, *Mit Napoleon nach Russland: Tagebuch des Infanteristen Joseph Deifel*, Regensburg 2012

Denniée, P. P., *Itinéraire de l'Empereur Napoléon pendant la campagne de 1812*, Paris 1842

Denon, Dominique Vivant, *Voyage dans la Basse Égypte pendant les campagnes du général Bonaparte*, Paris 1998

Des Genettes, René, *Histoire médicale de l'armée d'Orient*, Paris 1802

————— *Souvenirs de la fin du XVIIIe siècle et du commencement du XIXe*, 2 vols., Paris 1835–36

————— *Souvenirs d'un médecin de l'expédition d'Égypte*, Paris 1893

Desmarest, Pierre-Marie, *Quinze Ans de Haute Police sous le Consulat et l'Empire*, Paris 1900

Divov, Elizaveta Petrovna, *Journal et Souvenirs de Madame de Divoff*, Paris 1929

Documents Particuliers en forme de lettres sur Napoléon Bonaparte, etc., Paris 1819

Douglas, Sylvester, *The Diaries of Sylvester Douglas (Lord Glenbervie)*, ed. Francis Bickley, 2 vols., London 1928

Dubrovin, N., ed., *Otechestvennaya voina v pismakh sovremennikov*, in *Zapiski Imperatorskoi Akademii Nauk*, Vol. XLIII, St Petersburg 1882

Ducrest, Georgette, *Mémoires sur l'Impératrice Joséphine, ses contemporains, la cour de Navarre et de la Malmaison*, Paris 2004

Dumas, comte Mathieu, *Souvenirs du lieutenant général comte Mathieu Dumas de 1770 à 1836*, 3 vols., Paris 1839

Dumonceau, François, *Mémoires du General Comte François Dumonceau*, 3 vols., Brussels 1960

Dumont Romain, J. Ps., *Détail exact de tout ce qui s'est passé dans l'intérieur du Directoire et de l'évènement qui y est arrive: Singularité sur Buonaparte*, Paris n.d.

Durand, la générale, *Mémoires sur Napoléon et Marie-Louise 1810–1814*, Paris 1886

Durand, Jean-Baptiste Alexis, *Napoléon à Fontainebleau: choix d'épisodes*, Fontainebleau 1850

Ebrington, H. F. Fortescue, viscount, *Memorandum of Two Conversations between the Emperor Napoleon and Viscount Ebrington, at Porto Ferrajo, on the 6th and 8th of December, 1814*, London 1823

Edgeworth, Maria, *Maria Edgeworth in France and Switzerland*, ed. Christina Colvin, Oxford 1979

Elbée, François-Henri d', *Mémoires du général d'Elbée*, in *Carnets de la Sabretache*, 1935, pp. 357–81, 453–84: 1936, pp. 21–30, 114–27, 179–204, 280–92, 368–86, 491–504

Ernouf, baron, *Maret, duc de Bassano*, Paris 1884

Fain, Agathon Jean François, *Manuscrit de Mil Huit Cent Treize*, 2 vols., Paris 1824

————— *Manuscrit de Mil Huit Cent Quatorze*, Paris 1825

————— *Manuscrit de Mil Huit Cent Douze*, 2 vols., Paris 1827

————— *Mémoires du Baron Fain*, Paris 1908

Fantin des Odoards, Général Louis Florimond, *Journal du Général Fantin des Odoards: Étapes d'un Officier de la Grande Armée*, Paris 1895

Farington, Joseph, *The Diary of Joseph Farington*, ed. Kenneth Garlick & Angus Macintyre, Vol. V, New Haven 1979

Faucheur, Narcisse, *Souvenirs de campagnes du Sergent Faucheur, fourrier dans la Grande Armée*, Paris 2004

Fiszerowa, Wirydianna, *Dzieje moje własne i osób postronnych*, London 1975

Fleury, M., *Mémoires de Fleury de la Comédie Française*, 6 vols., Brussels 1838

Fleury de Chaboulon, P. A., *Mémoires de Fleury de Chaboulon, ex-secrétaire de l'empereur Napoléon et de son cabinet, etc., Avec annotation manuscrites de Napoléon Ier*, 3 vols., Paris 1901

Fontaine, Pierre-François-Léonard, *Les Maisons du Premier Consul*, Paris 1911

——— *Journal, 1799–1853*, 2 vols., Paris 1987

Fouché, Joseph, *Mémoires de Joseph Fouché, duc d'Otrante*, 2 vols., Paris 1824

——— *Mémoires*, Paris 1945

——— *Mémoires de Joseph Fouché, duc d'Otrante, Ministre de la Police Générale*, Paris 1957

Fourès, Lieutenant, *Trois lettres du lieutenant Fourès, le mari de Bellilotte*, in *Revue des Études Napoléoniennes*, Vol. XLI, 1935, pp. 163–7

François, Charles, *Journal du Capitaine François (dit le dromadaire d'Égypte) 1792–1830*, 2 vols., Paris 1904

Frémeaux, Paul, *With Napoleon at St Helena; being the Memoirs of Dr John Stokoe, naval surgeon*, Lane 1902

Frénilly, François-Auguste de, *Souvenirs du Baron de Frénilly*, Paris 1908

Gajewski, Franciszek, *Pamiętniki Franciszka z Błociszewa Gajewskiego, pułkownika wojsk polskich 1802–1831*, 2 vols., Poznań 1913

Garnier, Jacques, ed., *Les bulletins de la Grande Armée*, Paris 2013

Garros, Louis, *Quel roman que ma vie! Itinéraire de Napoléon Bonaparte, 1769–1821*, Paris 1947

Gazo, Jean, *Mémoires sur l'expédition de Russie*, in *Mémoires secrets et inédits pour servir à l'histoire contemporaine*, 2 vols., Paris 1825

Gentz, Friedrich von, *Briefwechsel zwischen Gentz und Johannes von Müller*, Mannheim 1840

——— *Dépêches inédites aux Hospodars de Valachie*, Vol. I, Paris 1876

Geoffroy Saint-Hilaire, Étienne, *L'Expédition d'Égypte 1798–1802*, Paris 2012

George, Marguerite-Joséphine Wemmer, aka Mlle, *Mémoires inédits de Mademoiselle George*, Paris 1908

Ginisty, Paul, ed., *Mémoires d'Anonymes et d'Inconnus (1814–1850)*, Paris 1907

Girard, Étienne-François, *Les Cahiers du Colonel Girard 1766–1846*, Paris 1951

Girardin, Stanislas-Cécile comte de, *Mémoires de S. Girardin*, 2 vols., Paris 1834

Girod de l'Ain, Gabriel, *Désirée Clary d'après sa correspondance inédite avec Bonaparte, Bernadotte et sa famille*, Paris 1959

Goethe, Johann Wolfgang, *Sämtliche Werke: Briefe, tagebücher un gespräche*, Vol. XVII, Frankfurt 1994

Gohier, Louis-Jérôme, *Mémoires*, Paris 1824

Gourgaud, Général baron Gaspard, *Journal de Sainte-Hélène 1815–1818*, 2 vols., Paris 1944

Grabowski, Józef, *Pamiętniki Wojskowe Józefa Grabowskiego, oficera sztabu cesarza Napoleona I*, Warsaw 1905

Greathead, Bertie, *An Englishman in Paris: 1803: The Journal of Bertie Greathead*, London 1953

Griois, Lubin, *Mémoires du General Griois, 1792–1822*, 2 vols., Paris 1909

Gross, Johann Carl, *Erinnerungen aus den Kriegsjahren*, Leipzig 1850

Grouchy, Emmanuel comte de, *Mémoires du Maréchal de Grouchy*, 5 vols., Paris 1873–74

Grüber, Carl-Johann Ritter von, *Souvenirs du Chevalier de Grüber*, Paris 1909

Guitard, Joseph-Esprit-Florentin, *Souvenirs militaires du Premier Empire*, Paris 1934

Guitry, Paul Georges, *L'Armée de Bonaparte en Égypte 1798–1799*, Paris 1898

Hardenberg, Prince, *Mémoires tirés des papiers d'un homme d'état*, 13 vols., Paris 1828–38

Hautpoul, Armand d', *Souvenirs sur la Révolution, l'Empire et la Restauration*, Paris 1904

Hegel, Georg Wilhelm Friedrich, *Gesammelte Werke*, Hamburg 1968

—— *Werke: Auf der Grundlage der Werke von 1832–1845 neu edierte Ausgabe*, 20 vols., Frankfurt am Main 1986

—— & Knebel, Karl Ludwig von, *Briefe von und an Hegel*, Vol. I, Hamburg 1969

Heiberg, Peter-Andréas, *Souvenirs d'un Danois au service de la France*, in *Revue des Études napoléoniennes*, 1919, Tome I, pp. 195–217, 283–306

Heine, Heinrich, *Ideas: The Book of Le Grand*, in *The Harz Journey and Selected Prose*, trans. Ritchie Robertson, London 1993

Holland, Elizabeth Lady, *The Journal of Elizabeth Lady Holland*, 2 vols., London 1908

Hortense de Beauharnais, Queen of Holland, *Mémoires de la Reine Hortense*, 3 vols., Paris 1927

Humboldt, Wilhelm von, *Wilhelm und Caroline von Humboldt in ihren Briefen*, Vols IV & V, 1910–12

Hyde de Neuville, Jean-Guillaume, baron, *Mémoires et souvenirs du baron Hyde de Neuville*, 3 vols., Paris 1888

Jackson, B., *Notes of a staff-officer*, London 1903

Jal, Auguste, *Souvenirs d'un homme de lettres*, Paris 1877

Jérôme Bonaparte, King of Westphalia, *Mémoires et correspondance du Roi Jérôme et de la Reine Catherine*, 7 vols., Paris 1861–66

Joachim Murat, King of Naples, *Lettres et documents pour server à l'histoire de Joachim Murat 1767–1815*, 8 vols., Paris 1908–14

Johannes von Müller an seinen Bruder, 25 November 1806, in Johannes von Müller, *sämmtliche Werke*, Vol. VII, Tübingen 1812

Jomard, Edmé-François, *Souvenirs sur Gaspard Monge et ses rapports avec Napoléon*, Paris 1853

Joseph Bonaparte, King of Spain, *Mémoires et Correspondance politique et militaire du Roi Joseph*, ed. A. Du Casse, 10 vols., Paris 1854–55

——— *Lettres inédites ou éparses de Joseph Bonaparte à Naples (1806–1808)*, Paris 1911

Josephine, Empress Consort of Napoleon I, *Correspondance, 1782–1814*, Paris 1996

Kicka, Natalia, *Pamiętniki*, Warsaw 1972

Koch, G. G., *Histoire Abrégée des Traités de Paix, etc.*, Vol. X, Paris 1818

Köster, Albert, ed., *Briefe von Goethes Mutter*, Leipzig 1917

Koźmian, Kajetan, *Pamiętniki*, Vol. II, Warsaw 1972

Lacorre, Alexandre, *Journal inédit d'un commis aux vivres pendant l'expédition d'Égypte*, Bordeaux 1852

Lafayette, Marie-Joseph Gilbert du Motier, marquis de, *Mémoires, correspondance et manuscrits du général La Fayette*, Vol. V, Paris 1838

La Flise, N. D. de, *Pokhod Velikoi Armii v Rossiiu v 1812 g; Zapiski de la Fliza*, in *Ruskaia Starina*, Vols. LXXI, LXXII, LXXIII, July 1891–March 1892

Lagneau, L. V., *Journal d'un Chirurgien de la Grande Armée 1803–1815*, Paris 1913

Lameth, Théodore de, *Mémoires*, Paris 1913

——— *Notes et souvenirs*, Paris 1914

Lareveillère-Lépaux, Louis Marie de, *Mémoires*, 2 vols., Paris 1895

Larrey, Dominique-Jean baron, *Mémoires de Chirurgie Militaire et Campagnes du Baron D. J. Larrey*, 4 vols., Paris 1817

——— *Mémoires et campagnes du baron Larrey*, 5 vols., Paris 1983

Larrey, baron, *Madame Mère (Napoleonis Mater)*, 2 vols., Paris 1892

Las Cases, Émmanuel, comte de, *Le Mémorial de Sainte-Hélène*, 4 vols., Paris 1905

——— *Le Mémorial de Sainte-Hélène*, ed. Marcel Dunan, 2 vols., Paris 1983

——— *Le Mémorial de Sainte-Hélène. Le Manuscrit Original Retrouvé*, ed. Thierry Lentz, Peter Hicks, François Houdecek, and Chantal Prévot, Paris 2017

Laugier, Césare de Bellecour de, *Récits de Césare de Laugier, officier de la garde du Prince Eugene*, trans. Henry Lionnet, Paris 1912

Lavalette, Antoine-Marie Chamans, comte de, *Mémoires et Souvenirs*, Paris 1994

Lee, H., *Life of the Emperor Napoleon*, London 1834

Lejeune, Louis François, *Souvenirs d'un officier de l'Empire*, 2 vols., Toulouse 1831

Letters from the Cape of Good Hope in reply to Mr Warden, London 1817

Letters from the Island of St Helena, exposing the unnecessary severity exercised towards Napoleon, London 1818

Ligne, Charles-Joseph prince de, *Fragments de l'Histoire de ma vie*, 2 vols., Paris 1928

Louis Bonaparte, King of Holland, *Documents Historiques et réflexions sur le gouvernement de la Hollande*, 3 vols., London 1820

Lubowiecki, Ignacy, *Pamiętniki*, Lublin 1997

Macdonald, Jacques-Étienne, *Souvenirs du Maréchal Macdonald, Duc de Tarente*, Paris 1892

Malcolm, Clementina, *A Diary of St. Helena: The Journal of Lady Malcolm (1816, 1817) containing the Conversations of Napoleon with Sir Pulteney Malcolm*, London 1929

Mallardi, Giuseppe, *Durante il Regno di Gioacchino Murat: Diario di un capitano dei lancieri*, Polignano 2017

Mallet du Pan, Jacques, *Correspondance inédite de Mallet du Pan avec la Cour de Vienne (1794–1798)*, 2 vols., Paris 1884

Maquin, *Le débarquement au golfe Juan: Rapport d'un douanier*, in *Revue retrospective*, XII, 1890, pp. 135–7

Marbot, Antoine-Marcelin Baron de, *Mémoires du General Baron de Marbot*, 3 vols., Paris 1891

Marchand, Louis, *Mémoires de Marchand, premier valet de chambre et executeur testamentaire de l'empereur*, ed. Jean Bourguignon, Paris 1955

Marmont, Auguste, duc de Raguse, *Mémoires du Maréchal Marmont, duc de Raguse de 1792 a 1841*, 9 vols., Paris 1857

Martin, P., *Histoire de l'expédtion française en Égypte*, 2 vols., Paris 1815

Masséna, André, Prince d'Essling, *Mémoires de Masséna*, 7 vols., Paris 1848–50

Masson, Frédéric, *Napoléon Inconnu: Papiers Inédits (1786–1793)*, 2 vols., Paris 1895

Maubreuil, Marie Armand de Guerry de, Marquis d'Orvault, *Adresse au Congrès, à toutes les puissances de l'Europe*, London 1819

Méneval, Claude-François de, *Napoléon et Marie-Louise: Souvenirs Historiques*, Brussels 1843

———— *Mémoires pour servir à l'histoire de Napoléon Ier depuis 1802 jusqu'à 1815*, 3 vols., Paris 1893–94

Metternich, Prince Clemens Wenzel Lothar von, *Mémoires, Documents et Écrits divers laissés par le Prince de Metternich*, ed. A. de Klinkowstroem, Vols. I & II, Paris 1880

———— *Clemens Metternich-Wilhelmina von Sagan: ein briefwechsel 1813–1815*, Graz 1966

Millet, Pierre, *Le Chasseur Millet: Souvenirs de la campagne d'Égypte (1798–1801)*, Paris 1903

Miot, J., *Mémoires pour servir à l'histoire des expéditions en Égypte et en Syrie*, Paris 1814

Miot de Melito, André-François, *Mémoires du comte Miot de Melito, ancien ministre, ambassadeur, conseiller d'État et membre de l'Institut (1788–1815)*, 3 vols., Paris 1858

Moiret, Joseph-Marie, *Mémoires sur l'expédition d'Égypte*, Paris 1983

Molé, Mathieu-Louis comte, *Le Comte Molé: Sa vie, ses mémoires*, Vol. I, Paris 1922

———— *Souvenirs de Jeunesse (1793–1803)*, Paris 1991

Mollien, François-Nicolas comte, *Mémoires d'un ministre du Trésor public 1780–1815*, 3 vols., Paris 1898

Montalivet, Marthe-Camille Bachasson, comte de, *Fragments et souvenirs*, 2 vols., Paris 1899

Montchenu, marquis de, *La Captivité de Sainte-Hélène d'après les rapports inédits du marquis de Montchenu*, Paris 1894

Montesquiou, comte Anatole de, *Souvenirs sur la Révolution, l'Empire, la Restauration et le règne de Louis-Philippe*, Paris 1961

Montesquiou, Raymond-Émery, duc de Fezensac, *Souvenirs Militaires de 1804 à 1814*, Paris 1870

———— *Journal de la campagne de Russie en 1812*, Paris 2012

Montet, Alexandrine, baronne du, *Souvenirs de la Baronne du Montet, 1785–1866*, Paris 1914

Montholon, Albine, comtesse de, *Souvenirs de Sainte-Hélène*, Paris 1901

Montholon, Charles, comte de, *Histoire de la Captivité de Ste-Hélène*, 2 vols., Brussels 1846

Mounier, Claude-Philibert-Édouard, *Souvenirs intimes et notes du baron Mounier, secrétaire de Napoléon 1er, pair de France*, Paris 1896

Müffling, Baron Carl von, *The Memoirs of Baron von Müffling, a Prussian Officer in the Napoleonic Wars*, London 1997

Müller, Friedrich von, *Erinnerungen aus den Kriegszeiten 1806–1813*, Hamburg 1906

Muralt, Konrad von, *Hans von Reichard Bürgemeister des eidgenössischen Stades Zürich und Landamann der Schweiz*, Zürich 1839

Napoleon I, Emperor of the French, *Correspondance de Napoléon Ier*, 32 vols., Paris 1858–70

———— *Vues politiques*, ed. Adrien Dansette, Paris 1939

———— *Oeuvres littéraires et écrits militaires*, ed Jean Tulard, 3 vols., Paris 1967–69

———— *Napoléon à Sainte-Hélène: Textes préfacés, commentés et choisis par Jean Tulard*, Paris 1981

———— *Correspondance Générale*, 13 vols., Paris 2004–17

———— *Mémoires de Napoléon: La campagne d'Égypte (1798–1801)*, ed. Thierry Lentz, Paris 2011

———— *Les Bulletins de la Grande Armée*, ed. Jacques Garnier, Paris 2013

———— *Mémoires pour servir à l'histoire de France sous le Règne de Napoléon écrits à Sainte-Hélène, etc.*, ed. Désiré Lacroix, 5 vols., Paris n.d.

Napoléon à Waterloo, ou Précis de la Campagne de 1815, Avec des Documents nouveaux et des Pièces inédites, par un Ancien Officier de la Garde Imperiale, Paris 1866

Napoleon i Polacy, epizod z nieogłoszonych pamiętników, in *Czas*, 1874, pp. 161ff.

Nasica, Toussaint, *Mémoires sur l'enfance et la jeunesse de Napoléon*, Paris 1852

Nesselrode, A. de, ed., *Lettres et Papiers du Chancelier Comte de Nesselrode 1760–1850*, Vol. I, Paris n.d.

Niello-Sargy, Jean-Gabriel, *Mémoires sur l'expédition d'Égypte*, in *Mémoires secrets et inédits pour servir a l'histoire contemporaine*, 2 vols., Paris 1825

Niemcewicz, Julian Ursyn, *Pamiętniki Czasów Moich*, Paris 1848

Noel, J. N. A., *Souvenirs Militaires d'un Officier du Premier Empire*, Paris 1895

Notice sur le Dix-Huit Brumaire, par un témoin qui peut dire Quod vidi testor, Paris 1814

Oncken, Wilhelm, *Österreich und Preussen im Befreiungskriege*, 2 vols., Berlin 1876–79

Ouvrard, G.-J., *Mémoires de G.-J. Ouvrard*, 3 vols., Paris 1827

Pacca, Cardinal Bartolomeo, *Memorie Storiche del Ministero, de Due Viaggi in Francia, et della prigionia nel Forte de S. Carlo in Fenestrelle*, 2 vols., Orvieto 1843

Parquin, Denis-Charles, *Souvenirs du commandant Parquin*, Paris 1979

Pasquier, Étienne Denis, *Mémoires du Chancelier Pasquier*, 3 vols., Paris 1893

Pastoret, Amédée de, *De Vitebsk à la Bérézina*, in *La Revue de Paris*, 9e année, Tome II, 1902

Pelet de la Lozère, Privat-Joseph, *Opinions de Napoléon sur divers sujets de politique et d'administration, receuillis par un membre de son conseil d'État et récit de quelques évenements de l'époque*, Paris 1833

Pelleport, Pierre Vicomte de, *Souvenirs Militaires et Intimes du Général Vte de Pelleport*, 2 vols., Paris 1857

Pelletreau, Gédéon-Henri, *L'embarquement de l'Empereur à Rochefort*, in *La Nouvelle Revue Retrospective*, 1895, Tome II

Peyrusse, Guillaume Baron, *Mémorial et archives 1809–1815*, Paris 1869

———— *Lettres Inédites du Baron Guillaume Peyrusse écrites a son frère André pendant les campagnes de l'Empire*, Paris 1894

Pion des Loches, Antoine, *Mes campagnes (1792–1815)*, Paris 1889

Planat de la Faye, Nicolas Louis, *Rome et Sainte-Hélène de 1815 a 1821*, Paris 1862

——— *Vie de Planat de la Faye*, Paris 1895

Plumptre, Anne, *A Narrative of Three Years' Residence in France, etc.*, 3 vols., London 1810

Pons de l'Hérault, André, *Souvenirs et anecdotes de l'Île d'Elbe*, Paris 1897

Pontécoulant, Louis Gustave comte de, *Souvenirs historiques et parlementaires du comte de Pontécoulant*, 4 vols., Paris 1861–65

Potocka, Anna, *Mémoires de la Ctesse Potocka (1794–1820)*, Paris 1897

Pouget, Général Baron, *Souvenirs de Guerre*, Paris 1895

Poupé, Edmond, ed., *Lettres de Barras & de Fréron en mission dans le Midi*, Draguignan 1910

Pradt, Dominique Dufour de, *Histoire de l'ambassade dans le Grand Duché de Varsovie en 1812*, Paris 1816

Radozhitskii, I. T., *Pokhodnia Zapiski artillerista s 1812 goda*, Vol. I, Moscow 1835

Radziwiłł, Louise de Prusse, princesse Antoine, *Quarante-cinq années de ma vie (1770 à 1815)*, Paris 1911

Rapp, Jean, *Mémoires du Général Rapp, Aide de Camp de Napoléon*, London 1823

Raumer, Georg Wilhelm von, *Preußens Lage, vor dem Ausbruch des Kriegs gegen Napoleon im Jahre 1813*, in *Berliner Taschenbuch*, Berlin 1849

Raza, Roustam, *Souvenirs de Roustam Mamelouck de Napoléon Ier*, Paris 1911

Réal, Pierre-François, *Indiscrétions. 1798–1830: Souvenirs anecdotiques et politiques tirés du portefeuille d'un fonctionnaire de l'Empire*, 2 vols., Paris 1835

Recueil complet des discours prononcés par le citoyen Barras, président du Directoire, par le général Bonaparte, par les ministres des Relations extérieures et de la Guerre, et par le général Joubert et le chef de brigade Andréossy, à l'audience solennelle donnée par le Directoire, le 20 frimaire an VI, pour la ratification du traité de paix conclu à Campo-Formio par le général Bonaparte, et la présentation du drapeau de l'armée d'Italie; accompagné de la description fidèle de cette fête et des hymnes qui y ont été chantés, Paris [1797]

Reichardt, Johann Friedrich, *Vertraute Briefe aus Paris Geschrieben in den jahren 1802 un 1803*, Hamburg 1804

Reinhard, Marcel, *Avec Bonaparte en Italie: D'après les lettres inédites de son aide de camp Joseph Sulkowski*, Paris 1946

Remacle, comte L., *Bonaparte et les Bourbons: Relations secrètes des agents de Louis XVIII à Paris sous le Consulat*, Paris 1899

Rémusat, Charles de, *Mémoires de ma vie*, Vol. I, Paris 1958

Rémusat, Claire Elisabeth comtesse de, *Mémoires de Madame de Rémusat 1802–1808*, 3 vols., Paris 1880

——— *Lettres*, 2 vols, Paris 1881

Revel, Jean-François, *Souvenirs*, in *Nouvelle Revue Rétrospective, 1er janvier & 1er février* 1903, pp. 1–24, 73–91

Ricard, Joseph de, *Autour des Bonaparte: Fragments de mémoires*, Paris 1891

Rochechouart, Léon Comte de, *Souvenirs sur la Révolution, l'Empire et la Réstauration*, Paris 1889

Roederer, Pierre-Louis, *Oeuvres du comte P.L. Roederer*, 8 vols., Paris 1853–59

Roguet, Christophe Michel, *Mémoires Militaires*, 4 vols., Paris 1862–65

Rousseau, Jean-Jacques, *Du Contrat Social*, in *Oeuvres complètes*, Vol. V, Paris 1832

Routier, L. M., *Récits d'un soldat de la République et de l'Empire*, Paris 1899

Rumigny, general comte Théodore de, *Souvenirs du général comte de Rumigny, aide de camp du roi Louis-Philippe (1789–1860)*, Paris 1921

Saint-Denis, Louis Étienne, *Souvenirs du Mameluck Ali sur l'Empereur Napoléon*, Paris 1926

Saint-Elme, Ida, *Souvenirs d'une courtisane de la Grande Armée*, Paris 2004

Sanguszko, Eustachy, *Pamiętnik 1786–1815*, Kraków 1876

Savary, Anne-Jean-Marie, duc de Rovigo, *Mémoires du duc de Rovigo, pour servir à l'histoire de l'Empereur Napoléon*, 8 vols., Paris 1828

Schouvaloff, Paul, *De Fontainebleau a Fréjus—Avril 1814*, in *Revue de Paris*, 15 avril 1897

Scott, Walter, *Scott on Waterloo*, London 2015

Ségur, Philippe-Paul, comte de, *Histoire et Mémoires*, 7 vols., Paris 1873

———— *Un Aide de Camp de Napoléon (1800–1815): Mémoires*, Simon, Paris n.d.

Senfft von Pilsach, Count, *Mémoires du comte de Senfft, ancien ministre de Saxe*, Leipzig 1863

Shishkov, A. S., *Zapiski, Mnenia i Perepiska Admirala A.S. Shishkova*, 2 vols., Berlin 1870

Shorter, Clement, ed., *Napoléon and His Fellow Travellers. Being a Reprint of Certain Narratives of the Voyages of the Dethroned Emperor on the Bellerophon and the Northumberland, etc.*, London 1908

Skałkowski, A. M., ed., *Fragmenty*, Poznań 1928

Sołtyk, Count Roman, *Napoléon en 1812, Mémoires Historiques et Militaires sur la Campagne de Russie*, Paris 1836

Some account of the early years of Buonaparte at the military school of Brienne and his conduct at the commencement of the French Revolution, by Mr. C.H. one of his school fellows, London 1797

Soult, Jean de Dieu, duc de Dalmatie, *Mémoires: Espagne et Portugal*, Paris 2013

Staël-Holstein, Anne-Louise-Germaine baronne de, *Considérations sur la Révolution française*, in *Oeuvres complètes*, Vol. XIII, Paris 1820

———— *de l'Influence des Passions sur le Bonheur des Individus et des Nations*, Paris 1845

———— *de la Littérature considérée dans ses rapports avec les Institutions Sociales*, Paris 1845

———— *Dix Années d'Exil*, La Renaissance du Livre, Paris n.d.

Sturmer, Baron Bartholmeus von, *Napoleon a Sainte-Hélène*, ed. Jacques St Cere & H. Schlitter, Paris n.d.

Sułkowski, Antoni, *Listy do żony z wojen napoleońskich*, Warsaw 1987

Sułkowski, Józef, see Reinhard

Suphan, Bernhard, *Napoleons Unterhaltungen mit Goethe und Wieland und Fr. v. Müllers Memoire darüber für Talleyrand*, in Goethe-Jahrbuch, Bd. 15 (1894)

Szymanowski, Józef, *Pamiętniki jenerała Józefa Szymanowskiego*, Lwów 1898

Talleyrand, Charles Maurice Prince de, *Lettres Inédites de Talleyrand à Napoléon*, Paris 1889

———— *Lettres de M. de Talleyrand à Madame de Staël*, in *Revue d'Histoire Diplomatique*, 1890, I/78

———— *Mémoires: L'époque napoléonienne*, ed. Jean Tulard, Paris 1996

Tarnowska, Urszula, *Król Hieronim w Warszawie w roku 1812*, in *Ruch literacki*, 1876, Tome II, pp. 54–5

Thiard, Marie-Théodose de, *Souvenirs diplomatiques et militaires du Général Thiard*, extrait de la Nouvelle Revue, Tome III, vingt-et-unième année, 1900

Thibaudeau, Antoine-Clair, *Mémoires de A.-C. Thibaudeau 1799–1815*, Paris 1913

Thirion, Auguste, *Souvenirs Militaires*, Paris 1892

Trembicka, Françoise, *Mémoires d'une Polonaise pour servir à l'histoire de la Pologne, depuis 1764 jusqu'à 1830*, 2 vols., Paris 1841

Truchsess-Waldburg, baron, *Nouvelle relation de l'itinéraire de Napoléon de Fontainebleau à l'ile d'Elbe…*, Paris 1815

Tulard, Jean, ed., *Napoléon à Sainte-Hélène*, Paris 1881

———— *Procès-verbal de la cérémonie du Sacre et du couronnement de Napoléon*, Paris 1993

———— & Garros, Louis, *Itinéraire de Napoléon au jour de jour 1769–1821*, Paris 1992

Versini, Xavier, *M. de Buonaparte, ou le livre inachevé*, Paris 1977

Victor, Claude Perrin, duc de Bellune, *Extraits des Mémoires Inédits de feu Claude-Victor Perrin, duc de Bellune*, Paris 1846

Vigo-Roussillon, François, *Journal de Campagne (1793–1837)*, Chaintraux 2013

Villemain, Abel François, *Souvenirs contemporains d'histoire et de littérature*, Vol. I, Paris 1854

Villiers du Terrage, Édouard de, *Journal et Souvenirs sur l'Expédition d'Égypte 1798–1801)*, Paris 1899

Vionnet de Maringoné, Louis Joseph, *Campagne de Russie et de Saxe*, Paris 1899

Volkonskii, S. G., *Zapiski*, St Petersburg 1902

Voss, Sophie Marie Gräfin von, *Neunundsechzig Jahre am Preussischen Hofe*, Leipzig 1887

Vossler, H. A., *With Napoleon in Russia 1812: The Diary of Lt. H.A. Vossler, a soldier of the Grand Army*, trans. Walter Wallich, London 1969

Wairy, Louis Constant, *Mémoires de Constant, premier valet de chambre de l'empereur sur la vie privee de Napoleon, sa famille et sa cour*, 2 vols., Paris 1967

Warden, William, *Letters written on board His Majesty's Ship the Northumberland and at Saint Helena, etc.*, London n.d.

Wellington, Arthur Wellesley, Duke of, *Supplementary Despatches, Correspondence, and Memoranda*, Vol. IX, London 1864

Westmorland, John Fane, Earl of, *Memoirs of the Great European Congresses of Vienna-Paris, 1814–1815—Aix-la-Chapelle, 1818—Troppau, 1820—and Laybach, 1820–1821*, London 1860

Williams, Helen Maria, *A Narrative of the Events which have taken place in France, from the Landing of Napoleon Bonaparte on the 1st of March, 1815*, London 1815

Wojciechowski, Kajetan, *Pamiętniki Moje w Hiszpanii*, Warsaw 1978

Wołowski, Aleksy, *Główna kwatera Napoleona*, in *Rozmaitości lwowskie*, 1835, 29 & 30

Wybicki, Józef, *Pamiętniki*, Warsaw 1927

Załuski, Józef, *Wspomnienia*, Krakow 1976

STUDIES

Adams, Michael, *Napoleon and Russia*, London 2006

Alger, John Goldworth, *Napoleon's British Visitors and Captives 1801–1815*, London 1904

Amini, Iradj, *Napoleon and Persia: Franco-Persian Relations under the First Empire*, London 1999

Aubry, Octave, *Sainte-Hélène*, 2 vols., Paris 1935

Bahr, E., & Saine, T., eds., *The Internalized Revolution: German Reactions to the French Revolution, 1789–1989*, New York 1992

Barbero, Alessandro, *Waterloo*, Paris 2005

Benhamou, Albert, *L'Autre Sainte-Hélène: La captivité, la maladie, la mort et les médecins autour de Napoléon*, Hemel Hempstead 2010

Béraud, Stéphane, *Bonaparte en Italie: naissance d'un stratège (1796–1797)*, Paris 2008

——— *La révolution militaire napoléonienne*, 2 vols., Paris 2007–13

Bergeron, Louis, *L'Épisode napoléonien: I. Aspects intérieurs 1799–1815*, Paris 1972

Bertaud, Jean-Paul, *Le duc d'Enghien*, Paris 2001

———— *L'Abdication: 21–23 juin 1815*, Paris 2011

————, Forrest, Alain, & Jourdan, Annie, *Napoléon, le monde et les Anglais: Guerre des mots et des images*, Paris 2004

Bien, David, *The Army in the French Enlightenment: Reform, Reaction and Revolution*, in *Past & Present*, No. 85 (Nov. 1979), pp. 68–98

Blaufarb, Rafe, *The French Army 1750–1820: Careers, Talent, Merit*, Manchester 2002

Blin, Arnaud, *Iéna*, Paris 2003

———— *Wagram*, Paris 2010

Bodinier, Gilbert, *La Révolution et l'armée; Les campagnes de la Révolution; Du soldat républicain à l'officier impérial: Convergences et divergences entre l'armée et la société; L'armée impériale; Les guerres de l'Empire*, in Jean Delmas, ed., *Histoire Militaire de la France: 2—De 1715 à 1871*, Paris 1992

Bonnet, J. C., *L'Empire des Muses*, Paris 2004

Boudon, Jacques-Olivier, *Histoire du Consulat et de l'Empire*, 2003

———— *Le roi Jérôme, frère prodigue de Napoléon*, Paris 2008

———— *Napoléon et la campagne de France*, Paris 2014

Bourdon, Jean, *Napoléon au Conseil d'État*, Nancy 1963

Bouvier, Félix, *Bonaparte en Italie 1796*, Paris 1899

Branda, Pierre, *Le Prix de la Gloire: Napoléon et l'Argent*, Paris 2007

———— *Napoléon et ses hommes: La Maison de l'Empereur (1804–1815)*, Paris 2011

———— *L'Île d'Elbe et le retour de Napoléon 1814–1815*, Paris 2014

———— *Les secrets de Napoléon*, Paris 2014

———— & Lentz, Thierry, *Napoléon, l'esclavage et les colonies*, Paris 2006

Brauer, Kinley, & Wright, William E., *Austria in the Age of the French Revolution 1789–1815*, Minneapolis 1990

Brégeon, Jean-Joël, *L'Égypte de Bonaparte*, Paris 2006

———— *Napoléon et la guerre d'Espagne*, Paris 2006

Broers, Michael, *The Napoleonic Empire in Italy, 1796–1814: Cultural Imperialism in a European Context*, London 2005

———— *Napoleon's Other War: Bandits, Rebels and Their Pursuers in the Age of Revolutions*, Oxford 2010

———— *Napoleon: Soldier of Destiny*, London 2014

———— *Europe under Napoleon*, London 2015

Brown, Howard G., & Miller, Judith A., *Taking Liberties*, Manchester 2002

Bruce, Evangeline, *Napoleon and Josephine: An Improbable Marriage*, London 1995

Buckland, C. S. B., *Metternich and the British Government from 1809–1813*, London 1932

———— *Friedrich von Gentz' relations with the British Government*, London 1933

Carrington, Dorothy, *Napoleon and His Parents*, New York 1990

———— *Portrait de Charles Bonaparte: D'après ses écrits de jeunesse et ses mémoires*, Ajaccio 2012

Casanova, Antoine, *Napoléon et la pensée de son temps*, Paris 2008

Castle, Ian, *Austerlitz: Napoleon and the Eagles of Europe*, Barnsley 2005

Chaline, Nadine-Josette, *La paix d'Amiens*, Amiens 2005

Chandler, David, *Austerlitz 1805*, London 1990

Chanteranne, David, *Le Sacre de Napoléon*, Paris 2004

Chappey, Jean-Luc, & Gainot, Bernard, *Atlas de l'Empire Napoléonien 1799–1815: Ambitions et limites d'une nouvelle civilisation européenne*, Paris 2008

Chardigny, Louis, *L'Homme Napoléon*, Paris 2010

Charles-Roux, Charles, *Les Origines de l'expédition d'Égypte*, Paris 1910

Chatel de Brancion, Laurence, *Le Sacre de Napoléon: Le rêve de changer le monde*, Paris 2004

Chevallier, Bernard, & Pincemaille, Christophe, *L'impératrice Joséphine*, Paris 1988

Chuquet, Artur, *La Jeunesse de Napoléon*, 3 vols., Paris 1897

Clayton, Tim, *Waterloo: Four Days That Changed Europe's Destiny*, London 2014

Colson, Bruno, *Leipzig: la bataille des Nations (16–19 octobre 1813)*, Paris 2013

Coston, baron de, *Premières années de Napoléon*, Paris 1840

Crouzet, François, *L'Économie britannique et le blocus continental (1806–1813)*, 2 vols., Paris 1958

Cyr, Pascal, *Waterloo: origines et enjeux*, Paris 2011

Dard, Émile, *Napoléon et Talleyrand*, Paris 1935

Defranceschi, Jean, *La Jeunesse de Napoléon: Les dessous de l'histoire*, Paris 2001

De Jaeghere, Michel, & Graselli, Jérome, *Atlas Napoléon*, Paris 2001

Derrécagaix, Général, *Le Lieutenant-général comte Belliard*, Paris 1908

Driault, Édouard, *La politique extérieure du Premier Consul (1800–1803)*, Paris 1910

———— *Tilsit: France et Russie sous le Premier Empire*, Paris 1917

———— *Le Grand Empire*, Paris 1924

———— *Napoléon et l'Europe: La chute de l'Empire. La Légende de Napoléon*, Paris 1927

Dufraisse, Roger, & Kerautret, Michel, *La France napoléonienne: Aspects extérieurs 1799–1815*, Paris 1999

Durey, Michael, *William Wickham, Master Spy*, London 2009

Dwyer, Philip, *Napoleon: The Path to Power 1769–1799*, London 2007

———— *Citizen Emperor: Napoleon in Power 1799–1815*, London 2013

Englund, Stephen, *Napoleon: A Political Life*, New York 2004

Ernouf, Alfred Auguste, *Maret duc de Bassano*, Paris 1878

Esdaile, Charles J., *The Wars of Napoleon*, London 1995

Espitalier, Albert, *Vers Brumaire: Bonaparte à Paris, 5 décembre 1797–4 Mai 1798*, Paris 1913

Forrest, Alan, *Conscripts and Deserters: The Army and French Society during the Revolution and Empire*, Oxford 1989

——— *Napoleon's Men: The Soldiers of the Revolution and Empire*, London 2002

——— *Napoleon: Life, Legacy, and Image. A Biography*, London 2011

Fraser, Flora, *Venus of Empire: The Life of Pauline Bonaparte*, London 2009

Fraser, Ronald, *Napoleon's Cursed War: Popular Resistance in the Spanish Peninsular War*, London 2008

Fugier, André, *Napoléon et l'Italie*, Paris 1947

Garnier, Jacques, *Austerlitz: 2 décembre 1805*, Paris 2005

——— *Friedland, 14 juin 1807: Une victoire pour la paix*, Paris 2010

Godechot, Jacques, *Les institutions de la France sous la Révolution et l'Empire*, Paris 1998

Goetz, Robert, *1805: Austerlitz*, London 2005

Grainger, John D., *The Amiens Truce: Britain and Bonaparte, 1801–1803*, Woodbridge 2004

Graziani, Antoine-Marie, *La Corse Génoise: Economie, société, culture*, Ajaccio 1997

Gries, Thomas E., ed, *Atlas for the Wars of Napoleon*, West Point Military History Series, Wayne, NJ 1986

Grot, Zdzisław, *Dezydery Chłapowski 1788–1879*, Warsaw 1983

Grunewald, Constantin de, *Baron Stein, Enemy of Napoleon*, London 1936

Gruyer, Paul, *Napoléon roi de l'Île d'Elbe*, Paris 1906

Gueniffey, Patrice, *Le dix-huit brumaire: l'épilogue de la Révolution française, 9–10 novembre 1799*, Paris 2008

——— *Bonaparte*, Paris 2013

Guery, Alain, *Les comptes de la mort*, in *Histoire et Mesure*, Vol. VI, no. 3–4, 289–312, Paris 1991

Haegele, Vincent, *Napoléon et Joseph Bonaparte: Le Pouvoir et l'Ambition*, Paris 2010

Hampson, Norman, *A Social History of the French Revolution*, London 1966

Hanley, Wayne, *The Genesis of Napoleonic Propaganda 1796–1799*, New York 2005

Hartley, Janet M., *Alexander I*, London 1994

Hauterive, Ernest d', *Mouchards et Policiers*, Paris 1936

——— *Napoléon et sa Police*, Paris 1943

Hazareesingh, Sudir, *The Legend of Napoleon*, London 2004

Healey, F. G., *Rousseau et Napoléon*, Geneva 1957

——— *The Literary Culture of Napoleon*, Geneva 1959

Helfert, Joseph Alexander freiherr von, *Napoleon I: Fahrt von Fontainebleau nach Elba. April-Mai 1814. Mit Benutzung der amtlichen Reiseberichte des kaiserlichen österreichischen Commissars General Koller, hrsg. von Joseph Alexander Freiherr von Helfert*, Vienna 1874

Hippler, Thomas, *Citizens, Soldiers and National Armies: Military Service in France and Germany, 1789–1830*, London 2008

Hofschröer, Peter, *Wellington's Smallest Victory: The Duke, the Model-Maker and the Secret of Waterloo*, London 2004

Holzhausen, Paul, *Les Allemands en Russie avec la Grande Armée en 1812*, trans. Commandant Minard, Paris 1914

Jomard, Edmé-François, *Souvenirs sur Gaspard Monge et ses rapports avec Napoléon*, Paris 1853

Jomini, A. H. de, *Vie politique et militaire de Napoléon, racontée par lui-même, au tribunal de César, d'Alexandre et de Frédéric*, 2 vols., Brussels 1842

Jourdan, Annie, *Napoléon: Héros, Imperator, Mécène*, Paris 1998

——— *Mythes et légendes de Napoléon: Un destin d'exception entre rêve et réalité...*, Toulouse 2004

Jourdan, Annie, ed., *Louis Bonaparte: Roi de Hollande*, Paris 2010

Kartsov, Yu, & Voenskii, K., *Prichiny Voiny 1812 goda*. St Petersburg 1911

Keegan, John, *The Face of Battle*, New York 1976

Kemble, J., *Napoleon Immortal: The Medical History and Private Life of Napoleon Bonaparte*, London 1959

Knight, Roger, *Britain against Napoleon: The Organization of Victory 1793–1815*, London 2013

Kraehe, Enno, *Metternich's German Policy*, 2 vols., Princeton 1963–83

Langsam, W. S., *The Napoleonic Wars & German Nationalism in Austria*, Columbia 1930

Latreille, C., *Le Catéchisme Imperial de 1806*, Lyon 1935

Launay, Louis de, *Un Grand Français: Monge, Fondatuer de l'École Polytechinique*, Paris n.d.

Laurens, Henry, *L'expédition d'Égypte 1798–1801*, Paris 1997

Lefèbvre, Georges, *Napoléon*, Paris 1953

Leggiere, Michael V., *The Fall of Napoleon: The Allied Invasion of France*, Cambridge 2007

——— *Napoleon and the Struggle for Germany: The Franco-Prussian War of 1813*, 2 vols., Cambridge 2015

Le Nabour, Eric, *Napoléon et sa famille: Une destinée collective*, Paris 2012

Lentz, Thierry, *Le Grand Consulat 1799–1804*, Paris 1999

——— *Le 18 brumaire: Les coups d'état de Napoléon Bonaparte (novembre-décembre 1799*, Paris 2010

——— *Nouvelle Histoire du Premier Empire*, 4 vols., Paris 2010

——— *Les vingt jours de Fontainebleau: La première abdication de Napoléon 31 mars–20 avril 1814*, Paris 2014

Lescure, A. de, *Le château de la Malmaison*, Paris 1867

Lieven, Dominic, *Russia against Napoleon: The Battle for Europe 1807 to 1814*, London 2009

Lignereux, Aurélien, *L'Empire des Français 1799–1815*, Paris 2012

Madelin, Louis, *Fouché 1759–1820*, Paris 1979

Malye, François, *Napoléon et la folie espagnole*, Paris 2007

Manceron, Claude, *Austerlitz: The Story of a Battle*, trans. George Unwin, London 1966

Mansel, Philip, *The Eagle in Splendour: Inside the Court of Napoleon*, London 2015

Marcaggi, J. B., *Une Genèse*, Ajaccio 1895

Marquis, Hugues, *Agents de l'ennemi: les espions à la solde de l'Angleterre dans une France en révolution*, Paris 2014

Martin, Andy, *Napoleon the Novelist*, Cambridge 2000

Martineau, Gilbert, *La Vie Quotidienne à Sainte-Hélène au temps de Napoléon*, Paris 1966

Masson, Frédéric, *Napoléon et les Femmes*, Paris 1894

——— *Napoléon et sa Famille*, 12 vols., Paris 1897–1919

——— *L'impératrice Marie-Louise*, Paris 1902

——— *Joséphine impératrice et reine*, Paris 1910

——— *Napoléon dans sa jeunesse, 1769–1793*, Paris 1911

Masson, Philippe, *La marine sous la Révolution et l'Empire*, in Jean Delmas, ed., *Histoire Militaire de la France: 2—De 1715 à 1871*, Paris 1992

Mathew, Nicholas, *Political Beethoven*, Cambridge 2013

McMahon, Darrin M., *Divine Fury: A History of Genius*, New York 2013

Montbas, vicomte de, *Caualaincourt à Châtillon*, in *La Revue de Paris*, June & July 1928

Morrissey, Robert, *The Economy of Glory: From Ancien Régime to the Fall of Napoleon*, Chicago 2014

Muir, Rory, *Britain and the Defeat of Napoleon 1807–1815*, London 1996

——— *Tactics and the Experience of Battle in the Age of Napoleon*, Yale 1998

——— *Wellington: Waterloo and the Fortunes of Peace, 1814–1852*, London 2015

Napoléon, Charles, *Bonaparte et Paoli, aux origines de la question corse*, Paris 2008

Naulet, Frédéric, *Eylau, 8 février 1807*, Paris 2007

Pachoński, J., *Władysław Jabłonowski*, in *Polski Słownik Biograficzny*, Vol. X, Warsaw 1964

Palmer, Alan, *Alexander I: The Tsar of War and Peace*, London 1974

Paoli, François, *La Jeunesse de Napoléon*, Paris 2005

Parsons, Timothy, *The Rule of Empires; Those Who Built Them, Those Who Endured Them, and Why They Always Fail*, Oxford 2010

Petiteau, Natalie, *Guerriers du Premier Empire: Expériences et mémoires*, Paris 2011

Pigeard, Alain, *Arcole: un pont vers la legende (15–17 novembre 1796)*, Paris 2009

Price, Munro, *Napoleon: The End of Glory*, Oxford 2014

Ramm, Agatha, *Germany 1789–1919: A Political History*, London 1967

Reiss, Tom, *The Black Count: Napoleon's Rival and the Real Count of Monte Cristo—General Alexandre Dumas*, London 2013

Rey, Marie-Pierre, *Alexandre Ier*, Paris 2009

Richardson, Frank, M.D., *Napoleon: Bisexual Emperor*, London 1972

Roberts, Andrew, *Waterloo*, London 2005

—— *Napoleon the Great*, London 2014

Rodger, Alexander, *The War of the Second Coalition 1798–1801*, Oxford 1964

Rodger, N. A. M., *The Command of the Ocean*, London 2004

Rolin, Vincent, *Rivoli, 14–15 janvier 1797: La conquête de l'Italie*, Paris 2001

Rose, J. Holland, *Pitt and Napoleon: Essays and Letters*, London 1912

Rothenberg, Gunther E., *The Art of Warfare in the Age of Napoleon*, London 1977

—— *Atlas des guerres Napoléoniennes*, Paris 2000

—— *The Emperor's Last Victory: Napoleon and the Battle of Wagram*, London 2004

Saada, Leila, *Les interventions de Napoléon au Conseil d'État sur les questions familiales*, in *Naopoleonica*, No. 14, 2012

Sale, Nigel, *The Lie at the Heart of Waterloo*, Stroud 2014

Salvatorelli, Luigi, *Leggenda e realta di Napoleone*, Rome 1960

Schroeder, Paul W., *The Transformation of European Politics, 1763–1848*, Oxford 1994

Schuermans, Albert, *Itinéraire Général de Napoléon Ier*, Paris n.d.

Schwarzfuchs, Simon, *Napoleon, the Jews and the Grand Sanhedrin*, London 1979

Sédouy, Jacques-Alain, *Chateaubriand: Un diplomate insolite*, Paris 1992

Simiot, Bernard, *De quoi vivait Bonaparte?*, Paris 1992

Skowronek, Jerzy, *Antynapoleońskie koncepcje Czartoryskiego*, Warsaw 1969

Sokolov, Oleg, *Austerlitz: Napoléon, l'Europe et la Russie*, Saint-Germain-en-Laye 2006

Sparrow, Elizabeth, *The Alien Office*, in *Historical Journal*, 33, 1990

Strathern, Paul, *Napoleon in Egypt*, London 2007

Sutherland, Christine, *Marie Walewska: Le Grand Amour de Napoléon*, Paris 1979

Tombs, Robert, *The English and Their History*, London 2014

Tulard, Jean, *Joseph Fiévée, conseiller secret de Napoléon*, Paris 1985

—— *Joseph Fouché*, Paris 1998

—— *Le 18 brumaire: commment terminer une révolution*, Paris 1999

—— *Dictionnaire Napoléon*, 2 vols., Paris 1999

BIBLIOGRAPHY

———— *Napoléon et la noblesse de'Empire*, Paris 2003

———— *Napoléon ou le mythe du sauveur*, Paris 2011

———— *Napoléon, chef de guerre*, Paris 2012

————, Fayard, Jean-François, & Fierro, Alfred, *Histoire et Dictionnaire de la Révolution Française 1789–1799*, Paris 1998

Uffindell, Andrew, *The Eagle's Last Triumph: Napoleon's Victory at Ligny, June 1815*, London 2006

Uglow, Jenny, *In These Times: Living in Britain through Napoleon's Wars, 1793–1815*, London 2014

Vandal, Albert, *Napoléon et Alexandre 1er: L'Alliance Russe sous le Premier Empire*, 3 vols., Paris 1891

———— *L'Avènement de Bonaparte*, 2 vols., Paris 1903

Vergé-Franceschi, Michel, *Paoli: Un Corse des Lumières*, Paris 2005

———— *Napoléon: Une enfance corse*, Paris 2014

Waresquiel, Émmanuel de, *Talleyrand: Le prince immobile*, Paris 2003

Webster, C. K., *The Foreign Polisy of Castlereagh 1812–1815*, London 1931

Welschinger, *Le divorce de Napoléon*, Paris 1889

Woolf, Stuart, *Napoleon's Integration of Europe*, London 1991

Zamoyski, Adam, *1812: Napoleon's Fatal March on Moscow*, London 2004

———— *Rites of Peace: The Fall of Napoleon and the Congress of Vienna*, London 2007

———— *Phantom Terror: The Threat of Revolution and the Repression of Liberty 1789–1848*, London 2015

Zorin, Andrei, *Kormia Dvuglavovo Orla*, Moscow 2004

Illustration Credits

Napoleon's mother Letizia Bonaparte in 1800, by Jean-Baptiste Greuze. *(Granger Historical Picture Archive/Alamy Stock Photo)*

Two sketches of Bonaparte by Jacques-Louis David. *(Sketches of Napoleon Bonaparte, 1797 (pencil), David, Jacques-Louis (1748–1825)/Musée d'Art et d'Histoire, Palais Massena, Nice, France/Bridgeman Images)*

Bonaparte during the Italian campaign of 1796, by Giuseppe Longhi. *(Paul Fearn/Alamy Stock Photo)*

Bonaparte leading his troops across the bridge at Arcole, by Antoine-Jean Gros. *(Photo by Universal History Archive/Getty Images)*

Bonaparte in 1797, by Francesco Cossia. *(Photo by Fine Art Images/Heritage Images/Getty Images)*

Josephine Bonaparte in 1797, by Andrea Appiani. *(ART Collection/Alamy Stock Photo)*

Auguste Marmont, by Georges Rouget. *(Wikimedia Commons)*

Andoche Junot, by David. *(© President and Fellows of Harvard College)*

Joachim Murat. *(ART Collection/Alamy Stock Photo)*

Josephine's son Eugène de Beauharnais, by Gros. *(Hirarchivum Press/Alamy Stock Photo)*

Napoleon's younger sister Pauline, by Jean Jacques Thérésa de Lusse. *(flickr/lost gallery/Pauline Bonaparte, Princess Borghese/De Lusse/CC by 2.0)*

Bonaparte visiting plague victims at Jaffa during his Syrian campaign, by Gros. *(Photo by Archiv Gerstenberg/ullstein bild via Getty Images)*

Joseph Bonaparte. *(Photo by Stefano Bianchetti/CORBIS/Corbis via Getty Images)*

Jean-Baptiste Bernadotte, by Nicolas Joseph Jouy. *(Heritage Image Partnership Ltd/Alamy Stock Photo)*

Napoleon's younger brother Lucien, by François-Xavier Fabre, c.1808. *(ART Collection/Alamy Stock Photo)*

Bonaparte in 1800, by Louis Léopold Boilly. *(Napoleon Bonaparte (1769–1821) Premier Consul (oil on canvas), Boilly, Louis Léopold (1761–1845)/Private Collection/Archives Charmet/Bridgeman Images)*

The house in the rue de la Victoire. *(Photo 12/Alamy Stock Photo)*

The Tuileries, c.1860. *(Photo by LL/Roger Viollet/Getty Images)*

ILLUSTRATION CREDITS

Jean-Jacques-Régis Cambacérès, by Greuze, 1805. *(Cambacérès/Photo © CCI/ Bridgeman Images)*

Charles-Maurice de Talleyrand in 1804, by David. *(Photo Josse/Leemage/Corbis via Getty Images)*

Joseph Fouché. *(Portrait of Joseph Fouché (1759–1820) Duke of Otranto, 1813 (oil on canvas), French School, (19th century)/Château de Versailles, France/Bridgeman Images)*

Josephine's daughter Hortense de Beauharnais, by François Gérard. *(Paul Fearn/Alamy Stock Photo)*

The Château of Malmaison, by Henri Courvoisier-Voisin. *(Photo Josse/Leemage/ Corbis via Getty Images)*

Napoleon's younger brother Louis in 1809, by Charles Howard Hodges. *(Photo by Fine Art Images/Heritage Images/Getty Images)*

Napoleon crossing the Alps in 1802, by David. *(Photo by GraphicaArtis/Getty Images)*

The Emperor Napoleon I in 1805, by David. *(Photo Josse/Leemage/Corbis via Getty Images)*

A fragment of David's painting of the coronation, showing Joseph, Louis, Napoleon's three sisters, Hortense and her son Napoléon-Charles. *(Photo Josse/Leemage/Corbis via Getty Images)*

Napoleon's youngest brother Jérôme, 1805. *(Courtesy of the Maryland Historical Society, xx.5.52)*

Napoleon at Eylau, by Gros *(Photo by Universal History Archive/Getty Images)*

Marshal Jean Lannes, by Gérard. *(Photo by Fine Art Images/Heritage Images/ Getty Images)*

General Armand de Caulaincourt, sketched in 1805 by David. *(Portrait of Armand Augustin Louis. Marquis de Caulaincourt (1772–1827) (pencil on paper) (b/w photo), David, Jacques Louis (1748–1825)/Musée des Beaux-Arts, Besancon, France/Bridgeman Images)*

General Géraud-Christophe Duroc, by Anne-Louis Girodet-Trioson. *(Portrait of Duroc, Grand Marshal of the Palace (oil on canvas), Girodet de Roucy-Trioson, Anne Louis (1767–1824)/Musée Bonnat, Bayonne, France/Bridgeman Images)*

Napoleon I in 1806, by Jean-Auguste-Dominique Ingres. *(Photo Josse/Leemage/ Corbis via Getty Images)*

View of the proposed palace for the King of Rome, by Pierre-François Fontaine. *(From Projets d'architecture, plan number 32, France, 19th century/De Agostini Picture Library/Bridgeman Images)*

Napoleon *en famille*, by Alexandre Menjaud. *(Napoleon I (1769–1821), Marie Louise (1791–1847) and the King of Rome (1811–73) 1812 (oil on canvas), Menjaud, Alexandre (1773–1832)/Château de Versailles, France/Bridgeman Images)*

Napoleon in early 1812, by David. *(Photo by Ann Ronan Pictures/Print Collector/ Getty Images)*

Napoleon on the bridge of HMS *Bellerophon*, by Charles Lock Eastlake, 1815. *(Granger Historical Picture Archive/Alamy Stock Photo)*

The house at Longwood on St Helena, where Napoleon spent his last years. *(Photo by The Print Collector/Getty Images)*

Napoleon on St Helena, 1820. *(Paul Fearn/Alamy Stock Photo)*

Index

Maximilian (King of Bavaria), 485, 594,
    596, 654
Méhul, Étienne, 6, 181
Melas, Michael von, 280, 282–283, 284–285,
    286
Melzi d'Eril, Francesco, 168, 317, 319, 320,
    351, 384
Mémorial de Sainte-Hélène (Las Cases), 669
Ménard, Claude-François, 313
Méneval, Claude-François, 331, 355, 357,
    384, 397, 408, 427, 528, 568, 625
Menou, Jaques, 98, 310
Le Mercure (journal), 254
Meszaros, Johann, 139
metric system, 127, 268
Metternich, Klemens von, xiii, 419, 442,
    498, 501–503, 620
    affair with Napoleon's sister Caroline,
        451, 593
    announcing alliance with Russia, 586–587
    German campaign and, 572, 573–574,
        575, 578
    Napoleon's return after escape from Elba
        and, 637
    negotiating terms for Napoleon, 616
    peace negotiations with France and, 586,
        587
    peace proposals, 583–584, 598, 599, 600
    on relations between Russia and France,
        511, 515, 520
    spies on Elba, 627
    Talleyrand and, 457–458, 490
    Treaty of Vienna and, 485
Milan
    Josephine in, 136–137, 151–152
    Napoleon in, 129–130, 143, 385
    Napoleon taking, 282–283
ministers, Napoleon's, 252–253
Miollis, Sextius Alexandre François, 480
Miot de Melito, André François, 159, 160–161,
    168, 171, 366, 375, 507, 632, 633, 640
Mirabeau, comte de (Honoré Gabriel
    Riqueti), 47

mission civilisatrice, 164
Moiret, Joseph-Marie, 192, 203
Molé, Mathieu, 216, 257, 265, 269, 296,
    568, 599–600, 605, 632, 669
Mollien, Nicolas François, 257, 293, 401,
    402, 459, 506, 521, 568, 632, 633
Mombello, 158–159
Moncey, Bon-Adrian Jeannot de, 282, 443,
    607, 610, 615
Monck, General George, 245, 300
monetary crisis, Napoleon and, 273–275
Monge, Gaspard, 132, 176, 180, 181, 183, 213
Le Moniteur (newspaper), 263, 350, 462,
    480, 604
Monroe, James, 348
Montagnards, 67, 69
Montalivet, Jean-Pierre Bachasson de, 51
Montansier, Madame de, 102
Montchenu, marquis de, 666
Montesquiou, Anatole de, 559, 620
Montholon, Albine de, 655, 656, 662, 663,
    664, 667
Montholon, Charles Tristan, 647, 662, 665,
    666, 669
Montholon, Josephine, 664
Monts, Raymond de, 28
Moore, John, 460, 461–462
Morand, Charles Antoine, 182
Moreau, Jean-Victor
    Army of the Rhine and, 107, 132–133, 155,
        279, 280
    coup against Directors and, 231
    death of, 589
    as dissident, 288, 326, 327
    plot to restore Bourbons and, 163, 353–354
    popularity of, 224, 227–228, 292
    trial and sentence of, 365–366
    victory over Austrians at Hohenlinden,
        302–303
Moreau le Jeune, Jean-Michel, 132
Morkov, Arkadyi, 348
Mortier, Édouard, 349, 420, 548, 554–555,
    606, 607

INDEX

Courtesy of the author

ADAM ZAMOYSKI is the author of numerous books about Polish and European history and has written for publications including the *Times* (London), the *Times Literary Supplement,* and the *Guardian.* He lives in London and Poland.